He's Behind You!
Eleven gay pantomimes

by

Jon Bradfield & Martin Hooper

The complete scripts as originally performed at Above The Stag Theatre.

Grosvenor House
Publishing Limited

This book is published by
Grosvenor House Publishing Ltd
Link House
140 The Broadway, Tolworth, Surrey, KT6 7HT.
www.grosvenorhousepublishing.co.uk

A CIP record for this book
is available from the British Library

ISBN 978-1-83975-232-2

Praise for the pantomimes in this book:

"It's often said that panto is a uniquely British institution. A bizarre hybrid of music hall, camp, zeitgeist and spectacle. In Jon and Martin's hands you can add screamingly funny, utterly filthy and unexpectedly moving. The Stag Pantos have, in a short time, become a genuine institution and a highlight of loyal audiences' Christmases. Literate, clever and oddly beautiful little gems - they really are, in a crowded field, "the fairest of them all". "
Mark Gatiss

"Despite being savagely funny, very adult and very queer, Jon and Martin's pantomimes have huge heart. I haven't missed one for years. They are literally my favourite thing about Christmas"
Matthew Todd, former editor of Attitude Magazine and author of *Straight Jacket*

"Panto dream team Jon Bradfield and Martin Hooper"
Time Out

"Bradfield and Hooper are masters of their craft"
Richard Unwin, Gay Times

"The Above The Stag pantos are fast approaching legendary status. Bradfield and Hooper's reliable formula fuses traditional pantomime characters and situations with modern club culture and social satire."
Paul Vale, The Stage

"Above The Stag's boutique gay pantos seem to get better every year"
Howard Loxton, British Theatre Guide

"Above The Stag pantomimes have developed a cult following, blossoming into a staple 'must-see' for the theatrically adventurous and LGBT+ friendly, regularly selling out."
The Resident

"The annual panto at Above The Stag is really in a league of its own"
Dave Cross, Boyz Magazine

"We are now in a world where adult pantos are everywhere and it has become common place to go on a search for Dick and his little pussy, but London's only dedicated LGBTQ theatre continues to lead the way"
LGBTQ Arts

"The hottest panto in town"
Theatre Weekly

"Lines that will have mulled wine snorting from your nose"
QX Magazine

"I loved this very naughty, very adult pantomime"
Graham Norton on *Pinocchio: No Strings Attached*

As well as the pantomimes in this book, Jon Bradfield and Martin Hooper have written two musicals, *He Shoots! He Scores!* and *Get 'Em Off!*; and a play, *A Hard Rain*, produced at Above The Stag Theatre in London and separately at Theater for the New City in New York. It is published by Nick Hern Books.

Jon wrote "Missing Alice", an acclaimed a standalone episode of BBC4 and the Old Vic Theatre's *Queers* series. He was the lead writer on *Cinderella: A Drag Pantomime* at Trafalgar Studios in the West End, which in 2020 was voted Best Studio 1 Show of the Decade in a public poll. His play *Animal* was shortlisted for the 2020 Papatango Prize.

Contents

Performing Rights

Applications for performance, including readings and excerpts, by amateurs and professionals throughout the world should be addressed in the first instance to Alec Drysdale at Independent Talent, 40 Whitfield St, Bloomsbury, London W1T 2RH. 020 7636 6565. www.independenttalent.com

Foreword

By Paul Vale

Matthew Baldwin as Nanny Fanny in *Snow White: Rotten to the Core*. Photo by PBGstudios.

Pick up any book about British theatre and you will probably find that pantomime is relegated to a few paragraphs, shoe-horned between Music Hall and Variety. In truth, the evolution of pantomime in the UK is as relevant a touchstone to public mood and mores as Coward, Pinter or Orton. From its earliest days there was slapstick, magic, popular music and instantly recognisable stock characters. Theatre archivists may bang on about its roots in Italy's Commedia dell'arte, but pantomime as we recognise it today was fuelled by the music hall, burlesque stages and comic operas of the Victorian Age. Pantomime is a patchwork entertainment with an egalitarian appeal.

Yet for all the traditions associated with pantomime its continued survival, like all live entertainment, depends on its ability to move with times. A good pantomime entertains but a great pantomime knows its audience, nurtures their appreciation and sings out to them in their own language. It's no co-incidence that audience participation has become a defining characteristic of the genre.

Today pantomime is still hugely popular and plays a vital role in the ecology of the theatre industry. It can command good houses and plenty of advance sales, providing employment at every level from Front of House to the performers. And it is often a child's first experience of live theatre, so it can also be perceived as a recruitment drive for future audiences.

Jon Bradfield and Martin Hooper's first pantomime collaboration was *Dick Whittington*, cheekily subtitled *Another Dick in City Hall*. Presented in 2009 in a room above The Stag, a gay pub in Victoria, it was an immediate success. What it may have lacked in spectacle it more than made up for in humour and the writers intuitively knew their audience. Boris Johnson, the then Lord Mayor of London, may have been an easy target but this pantomime was clever. For once, queer characters weren't the punchline, they were the plot and audiences loved it.

Producer Peter Bull founded the venue Above The Stag the previous year, aimed at mounting plays, musicals and cabaret with a predominantly gay theme. Remarkably, this was the only venue of its kind in the UK and gradually a dedicated audience began to form. Opening nights at Above The Stag were celebratory, none more so than those for its seasonal pantomime. Bull encouraged a family atmosphere and soon regular names began to appear in the programme. Matthew Baldwin, popped up for the first time as the Sheriff of Nottingham in 2010s *Robin Hood - Queen of Thieves*. Designer David Shields raised the bar with *Sleeping Beauty - One Little Prick* the following year, which also marked the first appearance of Andrew Beckett, the venue's current artistic director.

In a city thirsty for off-beat entertainment during the festive season, 'boutique' pantomimes were becoming commonplace among London's fringe venues. Adult pantomimes were not a new idea but all too often, it was difficult to hit the right tone. The Above The Stag pantomimes were delivering slick production values, plenty of bawdy, queer humour and a healthy respect for pantomime's traditions. But they were also shamelessly romantic and filled with warmth, somehow managing to champion gay and LGBT+ lifestyles, while at the same time lampooning them mercilessly.

Bradfield and Hooper and the rapidly expanding team worked at their formula but in 2012 The Stag pub closed for redevelopment and the future of the whole company seemed in jeopardy. Despite being homeless, Bull insisted that the pantomime go ahead and *Get Aladdin!* opened at the Landor Theatre in Clapham to a sell-out season.

By the following year there was a new venue in Miles Street in Vauxhall, an area that had practically taken over as the centre of London's gay community following the encroaching gentrification of Soho. The Above The Stag name and brand remained however and *Jack Off The Beanstalk* sold-out in 2013. The team was in its stride, with runs extended and a wider audience wanting in on the action. By 2017, *Snow White: Rotten to the Core* was to be the final show at Miles Street, with plans afoot to open a brand-new venue within two large, linked railway arches right in the heart of Vauxhall on Albert Embankment.

This new venue opened in June 2018 with a revival of Jonathan Harvey's *Beautiful Thing*, but the tickets were already practically sold out for *Mother Goose Cracks One Out!* at the end of the year. A decade earlier *Dick*

Whittington - Another Dick In City Hall ran for three weeks in a 57 seat room above a pub. In 2019 *Pinocchio - No Strings Attached* played 57 performances in a 100 seat, specially developed venue.

The success of the Above The Stag Theatre has run parallel to the success of Bradfield and Hooper's pantomimes. They have become a tradition in their own right and represent an important cultural date, not just on the LGBT+ calendar but in the theatregoer's roster of Christmas shows. Hopefully this volume will offer some kind of perspective on queer life in London over the last decade, the highlights and the slightly less salubrious elements - no judgement.

For my own part, as that rare theatre critic who adores pantomime, I feel fortunate to have witnessed how Bradfield and Hooper's work has developed from the outset. I am consistently amazed by the attention to detail and how they manage to keep the material fresh and exciting. In a genre where new writing is consistently side-lined in favour of traditional routines and star turns, Bradfield and Hooper are a writing team that deserve to be top-of-the-bill.

Paul Vale has been a theatre critic and features writer for The Stage since 1998.

Introduction and Thank You

Briony Rawle as Marina and Ellen Butler as Miranda in *Treasure Island: The Curse of the Pearl Necklace*. Photo by Derek Drescher

If theatre is ephemeral, pantomimes are doubly so. They're very "live" experiences. Topical gags pin them to the year of their performance, and a panto is nothing without its audience, which becomes both a character and kind of Greek chorus. But pantos are plays, too, and each of the scripts in this book tells an ancient story, bent to reflect the concerns and manners of its time and its audience (this is true of many plays, if less overtly). Whether you're encountering our comedies for the first time or reading to reminisce, we hope this book raises a chuckle.

For readers not brought up in the UK: the British pantomime has little to do with mime. Pantomimes are theatrical comedies based on fairy tales, legends and adventure stories. If Disney would turn it into a film, the Brits will turn it into a pantomime. Pantos feature songs, rhyming verse, direct address, local and timely references, ritualised audience interaction and cross-gendered performances, nowadays most notably in the role of the "dame", a matronly but sexually alert woman played by a man. Every town puts on a pantomime around Christmas, and though there's nothing inherently Christmassy about them, what better way to spend a cold winter night than huddled together, telling stories, making believe.

Adult pantomimes are like regular pantomimes, but with jokes about fisting.

Well, that's part of it. Writing for adults also lets us flesh out these stories with slightly more nuanced relationships. And for two writers who grew up at a time when gay representation was almost non-existent it's been a particular joy to put queer characters front and centre in the stories we all grew up with.

We were both members of the gay and lesbian rubbing club (as it was described then) the London Frontrunners, when someone suggested that the club should present a pantomime as the entertainment for its Christmas party. We didn't know each other well but were both arrogant enough to put ourselves forward to write what was to be a running-themed take on Cinderella, in which the handsome prince was replaced by a champion athlete and the ball became a race – think *Starlight Express* without the skates, tunes or technology.

After three years of running club pantos it occurred to us that if we could put all that effort into writing shows for a single performance, perhaps we could be writing them for proper theatre runs – if we could find someone who'd let us. (We'd also come to think it was unfair to keep foisting our increasingly long scripts on a crowd who were, rightly, there to drink, dance and snog.) Thank you to the club and its members, especially those who performed in those early shows of ours, and to Gary Wright who patiently directed us, teaching us much in the process. Thanks too to Nick Borsing, whose idea to put on a panto in the first place is why this book exists.

We sent a couple of scripts to Peter Bull, an itinerant producer and director of gay-themed theatre. He took us for lunch in Soho which felt very grown-up and exciting, as did the fact that he'd just arrived back from LA and was about to jet off to New York. What kind of globetrotting hotshot was this? (As we later found out, one who also worked as cabin crew for British Airways.) Peter was tired of being a theatrical nomad and had decided to set up his own theatre. He didn't, in his own words, "get" pantomime; but he saw something in our writing and understood that a new British theatre should have its own panto. Thank you to Peter for the leap of faith, and for the many subsequent commissions.

A big curtsey, too, to Andrew Beckett who directed the eight most recent pantomimes in this book, and with whom we've enjoyed an increasingly rewarding creative relationship. The invention and wit he's brought to these shows are a huge part of their success, and he's a skilled and kind team leader too. He and the many wonderful actors and creative team members listed throughout this book have had a profound influence on these scripts. Thanks to them all, and to the whole Above The Stag team, past and present.

We never have "final" versions of our panto scripts. We make a lot of changes in rehearsal and in previews, and once a show is over it never seems quite worth sitting down at a computer to make a definitive version. But we were keen that the scripts in this book reflected the shows as performed, which wouldn't have been possible without the loan of annotated scripts and the occasional archive recording. Thank you to the actors and other excellent people who have helped us with this including Matthew Baldwin, Chris Barley, Mandy Dassa, Mansel David, Ian Hallard, Chris Lane, Lucas Livesey, Michael Lowe, Tom McGregor, David Moss, Jamie Platt, Briony Rawle and Rebecca Travers. To photographers Alan Day, Derek Drescher, Thomas Jewett and Gaz Sherwood for allowing us to use their beautiful pictures. And to Paul Vale for his kind and thoughtful foreword.

Jon Bradfield & Martin Hooper

Pinocchio: No Strings Attached!

Shane Barragan as Pedro, Oli Dickson as Joe, Jared Thompson as Pinocchio and Matthew Baldwin as Geppetta in *Pinocchio: No Strings Attached*. Photo by PBGstudios.

Pinocchio: No Strings Attached!

As soon as we announced we were writing a gay, adult version of Pinocchio, people made the obvious (and correct!) assumption that it wouldn't be the boy's nose that would grow when he lied. But the story's other appeal was the opportunity to bring a young man to life, fully formed, who was gay but who had no awareness that this was not the norm, or something that might be stigmatised.

The Adventures of Pinocchio was published in 1883, collating Carlo Collodi's serialised magazine stories about a wayward puppet. Pinocchio has become one of the most reimagined characters in children's literature, most notably in the gorgeous 1940 Disney film, which made Pinocchio far less brattish that Collodi's creation. There have been several theatrical productions, including a major staging at London's National Theatre in 2017.

Most pantomimes and fairytales have their "landmark" moments – those memorable, often visual motifs or events that pin a story in place. Think of the magic mirror in Snow White, the flying carpet in Aladdin or Cinderella's transformation. The fun of adapting such familiar stories for an adult audience is that you can either honour these moments literally, or play with expectations: our Cinders rides to the ball in a phallic coach made from a courgette, while our Snow White takes refuge in a little cottage inhabited not by dwarves but "bears". Pinocchio is packed with these landmark moments, such as the puppet coming to life, his growing nose, the naughty boys' turning into donkeys in Toyland, and Geppetto being swallowed by a whale - or giant shark as in the book. But perhaps because the stories were originally serialised, they feel a bit one-thing-after-another and it was a challenge not to make our show feel episodic. (Mother Goose, which we'd tackled the previous year, is the opposite – it has hardly any well-known moments but has a brilliant story arc.)

Pinocchio lacks strong female characters and we needed a dame, so here the puppet-maker Geppetto becomes Geppetta, who is more integral to the story and has a character journey of her own. As in Collodi's original we violently dispense with the cricket almost as soon as he's appeared, giving our fairy a fuller role as Pinocchio's guide.

We liked the idea of retaining an Italian flavour, bringing a touch of sunshine to the London winter, so we set our version a bit further south on the Amalfi coast, in the "quaint little harbour town of Placenta". Jon and orchestrator Aaron Clingham nodded towards Italian opera and folk in the songs and arrangements.

In the real world: financier Jeffrey Epstein was convicted of sex trafficking offences leading to claims by Virginia Giuffre that she had been coerced into having sex with his friend Prince Andrew when she was 17; Tom Daley and his husband Dustin Lance Black now had a one-year-old son through surrogacy; and a general election fell slap-bang in the middle of this year's run when Boris Johnson's Conservatives won a majority with a promise to "get Brexit done", forcing Labour leader Jeremy Corbyn to resign.

Pinocchio: No Strings Attached!

By Jon Bradfield & Martin Hooper
Songs by Jon Bradfield
Inspired by the characters and stories of Carlo Collodi

Characters

Fatima, a fairy. Originally from Astoria, a country far away.
Figaro, a suave and evil fox. The villain.
Cornetta, an artist.
Chianti, a cat.
Geppetta, an artisan puppet maker and Cornetta's aunt. The dame.
Pedro, a middle-aged boatman.
Pinocchio, a puppet who comes to life.
Joe, a footballer from the West Midlands.
Rustic locals.

Pedro[1] speaks with a strong and expressive Italian accent, as if speaking English as a second language. The other Italian characters should speak in British accents - Geppetta and Cornetta would be some sort of luvvie-RP. Fatima[2] could be RP, or could have a foreign accent or even a well-spoken Welsh or Scottish. Joe has a Brummie or Black Country accent.

Pinocchio: No Strings Attached! **was first performed at Above The Stag Theatre on 19 November 2019 with the following cast and creative team:**

Fatima: Dami Olukoya; Figaro: Christopher Lane; Cornetta: Christy Bellis; Chianti: Briony Rawle; Geppetta: Matthew Baldwin; Pedro: Shane Barragan; Pinocchio: Jared Thompson; Joe: Oli Dickson

Director: Andrew Beckett; Musical Director, Arranger and Orchestrator: Aaron Clingham; Choreographer: Carole Todd; Set Designer: David Shields; Costume Designer: Jackie Orton; Wigs: Sue Michaels; Lighting Designer: Jamie Platt; Sound Designer: Nico Menghini; Casting Director: Harry Blumenau; Stage Management Team: Andy Hill, Toby Hillaby, Matthew Mortimer, James Prendergast; Scenic Artists: Fern Hawkins, Zoë Hurwitz, Gina Lee; Press & PR: Madeleine Bennett and Stella Reilly at PREMIER; Poster illustration: Matthew Harding; Production photography: Gaz at PBGstudios.com

---

[1] We realised some way into writing that Pedro is a Spanish name rather than Italian, but perhaps his parents had pretensions and wanted him to sound exotic...
[2] Dami Olukoya decided to play Fatima with a broad Caribbean accent, which worked a treat.

Scene 1: The seafront/harbour

A sweet little Italian coastal town built on a natural cove. Coloured houses and a church or three rise from the sea, stacked up in a quaint jumble. We can hear gentle waves; perhaps the clang of cables on boat-masts; a few gulls.

FATIMA, a fairy, appears.

FATIMA

Hello boys and girls! Ah just look at that sea,
And the sweet painted houses: white, blue and magenta,
We're just down the coast from Napoli
In the quaint little harbour town of Placenta

It isn't on the tourist trail
They only have twenty-two types of gelato,
And change happens slow here - time moves like a snail:
There's choir that still boasts at least one castrato.

The churches are teeming with second-rate art,
The market sells veg that Sorrento rejects,
An unlikely place for adventures to start
But adventures there'll be, and more I expect!

A coming of age tale, an epic, a farce,
Of a boy who must learn to be brave, kind and plucky
With magic and mayhem to rouse your fine hearts
And all kinds of love, from maternal to mucky

I hope you'll feel welcome, I know you've come far
I came here from far away too don't you know,
Now give me a cheer! And a boo! And an ahhh!
Please, enjoy the strange tale of Pinocchio!

Several RUSTIC LOCALS enter, with fishing rods, baskets of produce and so on, gossiping among themselves.

FATIMA
How perfect! Rustic locals!

RUSTIC LOCALS
Ciao Fatima!

FATIMA
Yes, ciao rustic locals.

A RUSTIC LOCAL hands a few coins to FATIMA.

RUSTIC LOCAL
Here you go Fatima, that's for the fortune telling you did for our Nico.

FATIMA
If you're sure.

RUSTIC LOCAL
Yeah, fair play, you were spot on. It *was* terminal.

FATIMA
Now, what say you help me show the boys and girls about town?

FATIMA waves her wand, and music starts.

SONG: WELCOME TO PLACENTA

Oh welcome to Placenta
You'll find us very friendly if we're left alone
Have you thought about Siena?
They say the food's terrific, or why not go to Rome

Our winding streets are charming
To wander at night
Put up a fight when you're mugged at knifepoint

Some say we have the plague here
Is it tuberculosis, it might just be halitosis
Don't let it put you off
Leave with a suntan and just a little cough

Our ivy-clad tavernas do bed and board
They don't win awards but you'll not stay long now will you?

Our churches squares and markets are of minor renown
So why not rent a Vespa to explore our little town
You'll find our drivers excellent they rarely mow you down
Our young men like their fashion, they dress fancy
But don't mistake our handsome sons for nancies

See Capri across the water
Sparkling in the sea there, perhaps you'd rather be there?
We're sure you'll be gone in an hour or two
Until then Placenta welcomes you!

FIGARO enters, a suave fox with a flashy blazer and an impressive tail. He carries a cane and looks like someone who probably wears a gun. He strikes fear into the Rustic Locals.

FIGARO
On your way, be about your businesses. Florenza, once again those zucchini you delivered yesterday were

suspiciously sticky, don't think you're getting paid. Alfredo, clean out your fishing boat, it stinks of piss, because I've had a piss in it. Subito!

The RUSTIC LOCALS exit.

FIGARO
And you, Fatima, what are you doing with your dirty feet on our traditional unspoilt Italian seafront?

FATIMA
Look closer signore, if you care to bother,
I don't touch the ground – I slightly hover
So don't pick on me, it isn't fair
I just wanted to take the air.

FIGARO
Is there nothing you people won't scrounge? And I've told you, we've no call for your backward mumbo jumbo magic here. We have the church. (To the audience) Hello fucknuts. I'm Figaro, and I'm the foxiest fucking fox in all of Campania. Gucci, Versace, I've got the whole range!

FATIMA
From where I'm standing I'm sure he's got mange.

FIGARO
I'm a pillar of the community, I put the "ah!" in patriarchy! Yes, I'm the beloved owner of Placenta Football Club, a thriving landlord, all round local bigwig and I've a face so handsome my own dear mother pictures it when she's struggling to bring herself off. (To Fatima) You see, dear Fatty, I'm marvellous.

FATIMA
I'm sure your shit stinks like the rest of us
In fact as a fox it's probably worse

FIGARO
That's true I'm afraid, it's rather a curse.

FIGARO catches the eye of a man in the front row. He likes what he sees.

FIGARO
Ciao young man. Welcome to Placenta. It's quite a warren, and I'm afraid I've shut down the Tourist Information office because frankly it's 2020, fucking google it, but I'd be glad to guide you into a favourite passage or two. What's your name? Ah, [name]. I'll name one of my churches after you! Saint [name]! It has a lovely ring to it. Do you have a lovely ring to you? (He

looks at the rest of the audience) Are you all like this...? Oh dear! This is Italy, the country of fashion! Never mind, I'm sure it all looked less insane on the Asos model. Well, lovely having you all, the station's that way, harbour's just there, the airport's in Naples, I believe you'll want the gates with higher numbers for the budget airlines, best of luck with the in-flight lottery. (To Fatima) You can fuck off too, there's no reason to stay; I think you'll find most of the men here are gay.

FATIMA
Gay? In a theatre? I'm shocked, did you ever?
The thing is, Figaro, I'm what's known as a lezza.

FIGARO
A lesbian! Well you won't find many lesbians here.

FATIMA
I'm sure *you've* turned a few women queer.

FIGARO
And several men, I assure you, dear.
Enough of your talk, enough of your whining
I'm off to prepare for my sexy new signing.

FATIMA
A footballer? I love football. I was in defence for our national women's B-team. Where does he play?

FIGARO
Until recently, somewhere called Walsall.

FATIMA
But in what position will you put him?

FIGARO
That's the spirit! Right I'm off to hassle my tenants. I'll start with the newcomers. A ridiculous puppet maker called Geppetta and her niece. Ciao, tramps!

FIGARO exits.

FATIMA
Geppetta! I heard that name in a dream!
No not one like that boys and girls, keep it clean,
Perhaps she needs help, or indeed just a friend,
I'll pay her a visit - I'm at a loose end.
Now because I'm only one quarter fairy
(I'm no Tinkerbell, I'm no Julian Clary)
My powers are weak, they're more dial-up than fibre,
I mustn't help myself, and I can't do harm neither
Be that as it may, on with the show -
Let's pay a visit to Geppetta's studio!

Scene 2: Geppetta's studio

A workshop full of marionettes and other puppets. There's a workbench where Geppetta makes her puppets – a puppet boy is on it, nearly finished. On the floor is an empty wine bottle on its side, and a wine glass, ditto. Part of the studio is given over to Cornetta's not-very-good paintings, and an easel supporting a work in progress, which we can't see. There is a door to the street with a large practical cat flap in it, and at least one entrance into Geppetta and Cornetta's living quarters behind the shop.

Lights up on Cornetta at her easel.

CORNETTA
Ciao boys and girls you scrummy things! My name's Cornetta. Welcome to my studio that I share with my auntie Geppetta. That's where she makes her puppets and this is where I do my paintings. You won't believe this but I haven't actually trained, no it's more an instinctive thing. *(She picks up the wine bottle and puts it on the workbench)*. Auntie, what are you like! We're actually rather new here in Placenta so I haven't many friends yet. (Aww!) Well quite, it's something of a bummer. Talking of bummers, will you be my chums? Don't worry, it's only for a couple of hours so it's not a big commitment. Will you be my chums? Thank you! Now listen, I know you Brits are excellent at languages so I'm going to teach you some Italian. Whenever I come on, why don't you say, *"Come stai Cornetta?"* That means "how's it going, Cornetta?" *Come stai Cornetta.* Can you say that? That's marvellous. I'll pop behind my easel and when I come out again you can give it a whirl.

She goes behind her easel and returns, cupping her ear. The audience shout, "Come stai Cornetta?)

Abbastanza bene, grazie! E tu? (waits for response, which is unlikely to come) Glad to hear it! But now that we're chums you should meet my cat. Chianti! Chianti! (beat) You're going to have to help me call her. Can you do that? One two three.... Chianti!!

Chianti clambers awkwardly through the cat flap.

CORNETTA
Chianti! Who's a good girl?

CHIANTI
I was coming *anyway*. I didn't even hear you. I've got my headphones in. Fuck. Wait there.

CORNETTA
What's the matter?

CHIANTI
Nothing, chill out. I got you something. *(As she goes)* I hope you like it.

CHIANTI goes back out using the main door like a human and immediately returns clambering back through the cat flap. She has a dead and bloody pigeon in her mouth. She holds it out to Cornetta.

CORNETTA
Oh good lord.

CHIANTI
Do you like it?

CORNETTA
(Trying to sound pleased) I'll get the dustpan and brush.

CORNETTA does, and proceeds to scoop the pigeon up.

CHIANTI
I knew you'd like it! You always get the dustpan and brush when you like it. So you can put it with all the other ones.

CHIANTI stares at someone on the front row for a while, and scratches her ear.

CHIANTI
What's your name? ... (She laughs at the name) Yeah, no I'm going to go and sit on this one.

CHIANTI goes and sits on the knee of a man further along the row.

CORNETTA
You don't mind do you sir? Are you alright there Chianti?

CHIANTI
Yes thank you. You know that thing when men get like a hard sausage in their trousers? He's got that.

CORNETTA
I'm so sorry sir.

CHIANTI
But smaller.

CHIANTI gets up and makes to exit.

CORNETTA
Where are you going now!

CHIANTI
Can you not always check on me please.

CHIANTI makes herself comfortable in a corner and naps.

CORNETTA
Oh but boys and girls, you should meet my auntie Geppetta! Auntie! Auntie! Are you coming?

GEPPETTA
Absolutely not.

CORNETTA
We have visitors. They want to meet you don't you!

(Yes!)

GEPPETTA
I do not want to see another local as long as I live.

CORNETTA
They're not locals. They're from London.

GEPPETTA
Well that changes everything.

A spotlight hits the stage. Music begins. GEPPETTA steps into the spotlight.

GEPPETTA (singing)
Oh! bloody hell, Placenta
Where everyone is dreadful, and has a dreadful time,
Oh! Let's have an adventure,
If you play your cards right I'll take you back to mine.

CORNETTA is by now behind her easel, painting. Every now and then she stares at someone in the audience before returning to her work.

GEPPETTA
Ciao bambinos and bambinas! ("Ciao!") Yes I understand there's a language barrier over which we have to clamber, but I think we can do a *little* better than that, after all we are one big happy European family![3] Ciao boys and girls! ("Ciao!") Ah, Londoners! I'm ever so fond of your British culture. Do you know your pantomimes can be traced very vaguely back to Italian *commedia dell'arte*. Just as your pizzas and pasta dishes can be traced very vaguely back to Italian cooking. Welcome to my little studio, my little atelier

in the back streets of Placenta. Our newly adopted hometown. It's quaint, it's quiet, a world away from the hustle and bustle of Rome. I can't bear it - I saw more signs of life in Pompeii. Have you been,? Lifeless bodies in all positions. My friend Antonio said it calls to mind one of his Easter weekend get-togethers. He's very handsome, Father Antonio. Sadly the only thing he ever asked *me* to spread was the word of the Lord.

She sees the wine bottle and picks it up, peering it at, disappointed that it's empty.

Now, Cornetta darling, for goodness sake, you haven't told the boys and girls that we are in fact fugitives from Rome, on the run from the law, have you, in spite of the sexual allure such a disclosure would undoubtedly lend us?

CORNETTA
Of course not.

GEPPETTA
Good girl.

CORNETTA
You have.

GEPPETTA
Dammit! Well it's true darlings. Cornetta and I maintained a little stall near the Vatican. Paintings and puppets. I used to do a Jesus puppet, he was terribly popular. There were little holes in his hands for the strings to go through, so he was very accurate, and if you pulled the strings he did this. (*She spreads her arms as though being crucified.*)

CORNETTA
Anyway, one day I was taking my lunch break when Auntie sold one of my paintings for three million euros! You see, it turns out, I'm so good I'd accidentally painted an exact replica of a piece of modern art from the Pope's own private collection!

GEPPETTA
Imagine, if you will, the apocryphal monkey with the typewriter who one day churns out the works of William Shakespeare, except this monkey's illiterate and has been allowed to play in the painting corner instead. Well now! Here's the twist. It so transpired that that very same week, the Pope's own painting had gone missing! Naturally, the Vatican police put *due* and *due* together and made *cinque*.

---

[3] Boris Johnson had just won the general election and we were in the middle of "get Brexit done" fever.

CORNETTA
They placed us on a wanted list for grand art theft! We had to get out of Rome, and pronto. And after an epic journey by train, bus...

GEPPETTA
Tractor

CORNETTA
Fishing boat

GEPPETTA
Tuk-tuk

CORNETTA
...we arrived in Placenta, and have been keeping things on the down-low ever since.

GEPPETTA
I think you missed a bit.

CORNETTA
I think that's everything.

GEPPETTA
The bit where you threw a suitcase containing THREE MILLION EUROS into the fucking sea.

CORNETTA
The boat sprung a leak boys and girls! We had to throw our luggage overboard just to stay afloat! I nearly died!

GEPPETTA
I should have finished the job off.

CORNETTA, at her easel, points to the audience member she's painting.

CORNETTA
Sorry sir, do mind sitting still?

GEPPETTA
Our one chance to have the kind of money that my lifestyle and character so evidently deserve. Dashed! So yes, here we are, somewhat broke. I've left behind my friends, my lovers, and an atrocious reputation that took years to cultivate. All gone! Still, perhaps it's time I calmed down now that I'm nudging at youth's upper end. *(She sees a young man)* I shouldn't mind nudging at this youth's upper end. Hello bambino, what's your name? Hello [name]. Aren't you handsome!

CORNETTA
He probably wants someone nearer his own age.

GEPPETTA
Cornetta could paint you, albeit without any success. (To someone else) That's a lovely watch sir - where did you win it? Oh but I have a lot of love to give, darlings. It's just so hard to meet people when we're keeping a low profile, and it's not as though there are esta-blishments in Placenta where I might encounter *my* class of gentleman.

CORNETTA
There's a police station down by the harbour.

GEPPETTA
I mean where's the art? Where's the music? The theatre? I've seen more culture on a swab. Yes sir, you know what I'm talking about. The last time you saw drama in the West End it was two bears fighting over the last of the PrEP in Dean Street[4]. Yes and to add to it all I've stopped drinking.

CORNETTA
Have you?

GEPPETTA
Not intentionally. I put my glass down fifteen minutes ago and can't think where I put it.

CORNETTA
It's alright for you, there are men everywhere. I'm the only lesbian in town.

GEPPETTA
Yes, but you have a cat.

A jingle-jangle as PEDRO enters the shop. Pedro is middle aged and expressive and has an Italian accent.

GEPPETTA
Ah, Pedro

PEDRO
Geppetta! My peach, my pineapple, my plum.

GEPPETTA
That's quite enough of the fruity language.

PEDRO
I stare at you every day through your window, you look so sad. I bring you something to put a smile on your face.

_____
[4] The popular and forward-thinking sexual health clinic at Dean Street in Soho has been pioneering in the trialling of the HIV prevention drug PrEP (Pre-exposure prophylaxis).

GEPPETTA
Is it some curtains?

PEDRO
No! A great pink salami for your pretty lips.

GEPPETTA
Now really!

CORNETTA
Don't be filthy Auntie he's talking about cured meat.

GEPPETTA
Dare I ask what it's been cured of?

PEDRO
When can I take you for a turn in my little boat?

GEPPETTA
Oh! In a year or two I expect.

PEDRO
Life is short!

GEPPETTA
Well quite, then let's not waste my time or yours.

PEDRO
It's no waste of my time. We have so few visitors these days, my boat is idle. That Signore Figaro has turned Placenta from a tourist magnet into a ghost town. Let us find what joy we can!

GEPPETTA
I'm a little busy Pedro

PEDRO
(Perfectly upbeat) As you wish! Same time tomorrow then?

GEPPETTA
I expect so!

PEDRO exits.

CORNETTA
You could at least have a go in his boat.

GEPPETTA
The man's barely been outside of the town his whole life; he wouldn't know subtlety if it slapped him round the face with its cock; and he dresses like a silly walk-on part in a tawdry theatrical presentation. What would the neighbours think?

CORNETTA
The neighbours think you're a stuck-up drunk. And they're right. If you made an effort you might get to like it here. You know, I think I could make a real go of things. They say the quality of the light is perfect for artists.

GEPPETTA peeks at the painting CORNETTA is working on, and frowns.

GEPPETTA
Perhaps it's something to do with your brushes then.

CORNETTA
I haven't finished it yet.

GEPPETTA
I know darling, I'm just trying to prevent any further damage.

CHIANTI has woken up.

CHIANTI
Oi! Her paintings are brilliant.

GEPPETTA
Alright Sister Wendy.

CHIANTI randomly gives Geppetta a long hug.

GEPPETTA
Ah that's better that's nice. What's this?

CHIANTI
Did you know that cats can tell when someone's got cancer?

GEPPETTA
Right...?

CHIANTI
Can I have squeezy pouchy food today?

CORNETTA
No baby it's expensive. You can have biscuity bits.

CHIANTI
I'm not being funny right but I brought you a pigeon. I hate it here. (To Geppetta) I hate you. Dragging me here, it's horrible. Rome was brilliant.

GEPPETTA
Let's not bicker. It's just cabin fever.

FIGARO enters from the street with a suitably menacing burst of music.

FIGARO
Friends! Romans! Cunts.

GEPPETTA
We're not from Rome! Are we boys and girls!

9

FIGARO
I didn't say you were. You were the third thing. Where are you from?

GEPPETTA
Oh we wouldn't want to bore you! Signore Fox! What a pleasant surprise.

FIGARO
Come off it. Act one, scene two, you're the penniless dame, I'm the mercenary but irresistible landlord, I think we all know what I'm here for.

GEPPETTA
Very well, but I warn you, I haven't clippered my shins since Thursday.

FIGARO
My rent. Now!

CORNETTA
Would you accept payment in kind.

FIGARO
If by payment in kind you mean a weekend away with Tom Holland and a bondage rig so elaborate it would make Ivan Massow blush then yes. If you mean a terrifying puppet and one of your degenerate scrawlings then absolutely not.

GEPPETTA
Give us till tomorrow darling! If only to give yourself the excuse to visit again you persistent little thing!

FIGARO
I warn you. If you haven't got the money by tomorrow, I'll take the cat instead! Ahahaha!

CORNETTA
You can't take Chianti!

FIGARO
Oh yes I can!

CORNETTA
Oh no you can't!

FIGARO
Oh yes I can!

FIGARO exits.

CORNETTA (and audience)
Oh no you can't!

FIGARO (off)
I can't hear you!

CORNETTA
He can't take Chianti!

GEPPETTA
Then we'd better hope our fortunes change. Now, go and give Chianti her worming tablets.

CHIANTI
Fuck off!

GEPPETTA
What am I saying, I mean, her "peanut M&Ms"

CHIANTI
Aw yeah!

CORNETTA and CHIANTI exit into the house as FATIMA enters from the street.

GEPPETTA
Visitor number three - I feel like Scrooge! Remember boys and girls, trust nobody. She could be from the Vatican Secret Police! Ciao signora, welcome to our studio. The finest Italian marionettes. The perfect souvenir.

FATIMA
Thank you, but I live here. Five years now. You're from Rome?

GEPPETTA
Rome! You've been misled by my sophistication, cosmopolitan taste and hard-to-place musk. We're from Placenta!

FATIMA
Since birth?

GEPPETTA
Just a little after birth. Rome! I've never even heard of it!

FATIMA
The forum? The colosseum? The pantheon?

GEPPETTA
Darling I'm hardly in the market for a gay sauna.

FATIMA
Well I just popped by to extend the hand of friendship.

GEPPETTA
(To the audience) It's a trap!

FATIMA
Sorry?

10

GEPPETTA
I said... shut your trap! But goodness, how rude - forgive my brusque, big city, Roman ways. (realises) Dammit!!

FATIMA
You seem a little paranoid.

GEPPETTA
Why, what have you heard? No it's my artistic temperament. We creatives are highly volatile. It's all the insecurity and sexual harassment.

FATIMA
That's terrible.

GEPPETTA
Well I try not to make a habit of it. Please don't tell anyone where we're from. We had to flee.

FATIMA
Oh but so did I! I left so much behind.

GEPPETTA
So much!

FATIMA
My nearest and dearest.

GEPPETTA
My closest and mostest.

FATIMA
Just to escape.

GEPPETTA
Fugitives!

FATIMA
From war, persecution and death.

GEPPETTA
Alright it's not a competition. (beat) I left behind a very rich and fulfilling life. Dinner party after glorious dinner party that I fully intended to get around to hosting.

FATIMA
Yes I had all that. In Astoria.

GEPPETTA
Astoria!

FATIMA
You've heard of my country?

GEPPETTA
Of course! I signed a petition. I almost donated.

FATIMA
I had a social life. Culture. Music, dancing, dining. Did you have a special someone?

GEPPETTA
Oh yes, oodles.

FATIMA
I had one. I don't know where she is now.

GEPPETTA gives her a squeeze.

FATIMA
Thank you.

A cuckoo clock chimes six.

GEPPETTA
Good heavens!

FATIMA
Where does the time go?

GEPPETTA
No it's not that - we don't have a cuckoo clock. Well, time to close up.

FATIMA
Before I go, may I do something for you? I can't promise it'll work.

GEPPETTA
I'm ticklish, I warn you. I'm liable to kick. I once took a chiropodist's jaw clean off.

FATIMA
The first star that you see tonight
Make a wish by its silvery light
And though this might sound very strange
Perhaps you'll find your fortunes change.

GEPPETTA looks at Fatima and has a thought.

GEPPETTA
Yes... Did I mention that we also sell scented candles and homeopathy starter kits and a range of Native American dreamcatchers handmade in Bangladesh?

She grabs a candle off a shelf and holds it to Fatima, who sniffs it.

FATIMA
That's not scented.

Geppetta rubs it under her armpit and holds it out again.

GEPPETTA
Try it now.

11

FATIMA
I'm not a fool. I'm not naïve.
It's up to you whether you believe.
Buona notte.

GEPPETTA
Buona notte.

FATIMA exits. Over the next line GEPPETTA locks the door and finds a bottle of something and takes it with her to her workbench. She starts working on her puppet.

GEPPETTA
Wish upon a star! What nonsense. Well boys and girls, I have a young man to finish off. (She holds up her puppet). If only I had a real man again I'd be happy.

SONG: ONE MORE ROMANCE

Men who've adored me, men who have bored me, men who came
From every nation; Men in stations, men on trains;
Men who were older, men who were soldiers, great men of fame
Men with beautiful brothers I took for lovers, shame on me!

Men who were brainy, men who were vain, men in the arts,
Men who were cute and men who were brutes who lit their farts
Men who were loyal - one who was royal broke my heart
Men with suffering mothers, and all the others, lost to me

Viva amore! Viva romanza!
Dear wooden puppet how I wish you were the answer.

Men who wore flares, or came in pairs and threes and fours
Men with great abs who gave me crabs and men who snored
Men who were dense and earned not a cent but won awards
Men who thought me too rude then painted me nude to remember me.

Viva amore! Viva romanza!
Dear wooden puppet how I wish you were the answer.

Men who have taught me, men who fought me and men who cried
Men who were quiet, men on diets and men who died!
Men with spare tyres, men in choirs and men of means
Men who were mainly queens
Men who were in their teens

Give me someone to hold and keep off the cold in winter
Someone who's kind and brings me wine - a vintner!
What use is a puppet? I want someone up it, and not get splinters,
Someone I can look after, share my laughter, and my bed

Give me one more affair, one more chance!
One more man to care for me, just one more romance!

By the time the song finishes it is night. The light has faded until there is just the glow of Geppetta's lamp or candle on her workbench.

GEPPETTA
How quickly night falls. (beat) Wish upon a star, what nonsense! (She peers outside) I can't see a single star.

A star appears, perhaps lowered down on a string. The audience responds.

GEPPETTA
What? Oh - you think *I'm* a star, that is kind and perceptive of you. (She notices the star) Oh! Look at that! A star! Like in... Bethlehem!

She looks up to heaven, and puts her hands to her stomach as if cradling a pregnancy.

I'll make a wish. Should I kneel do you think?

She pulls a little rug into the centre of the stage and kneels on it.

This is from Jakarta. It isn't a prayer rug *per se* I but have lain on it a few times shouting "thank you god!" Right, settle down.

She makes a wish and gets up.

What silliness. Well I think it's time for my beauty sleep boys and girls. All alone. Buona notte!

She turns out the light and leaves us in darkness. A clock ticks. After a while, we hear a guitar or mandolin and PEDRO (off) sings a ballad loudly and terribly. GEPPETTA re-enters in her nightie, tentatively excited. She opens the door.

GEPPETTA
Pedro! Are you drunk?

PEDRO
Yes! Drunk and free! Geppetta! I had a dream, a dream that you are sad and lonely. I thought I must come and cheer you up.

He starts playing again, this time crooning Cher's "Believe". Geppetta slaps him twice on the cheek.

GEPPETTA
(Like Cher in Moonstruck) Snap out of it!

PEDRO
We could make sweet music together. Me on my mandolin, you on my mouth organ.

GEPPETTA
I've fallen for that line too many times. Oh, shoot. I know what this is. You're my bloody wish come true.

PEDRO
I am? Magnifico! What a night, what a moon, what a woman. Come for a stroll.

GEPPETTA
Yes well the thing is you're not quite what I ordered.

PEDRO
Well if you're sure. Tomorrow then.

GEPPETTA
I expect so. Goodnight.

Once she's closed the door on him, a little smile passes across her face. Blackout.

Scene 3: Geppetta's studio

Darkness gives way to a soft dawn light. A cockerel greets the morning. The puppet has disappeared from Geppetta's workbench.

From behind the workbench, PINOCCHIO emerges. He levers himself into a standing position then immediately falls over – it sounds like the end of a game of Jenga. He gets up again and gets the hang of walking. He starts taking in his surroundings. He sees the audience and is startled, then curious. He sits on a stool, exactly replicating an audience member's posture.

PINOCCHIO
Hello goysy burls!

He frowns. That's not right. He knocks himself on the head and it sounds like a woodblock.

Hello boys and girls! I'm – oh but I don't know who I am! I know you're the boys and girls, everyone knows that, that's just how these things work, but... Do you know my name? ("Pinocchio") Pinocchio. Pin-o-cchi-o. Why do I get such a stupid name?

There is a buzzing noise, the sound of an insect. PINOCCHIO is startled. The sound stops.

PINOCCHIO
...Hello?

CRICKET (unseen)
Hello!

PINOCCHIO
Ahh! Who said that??

CRICKET
By jiggety silly billy, I'm right here!

PINOCCHIO
I can't see you.

CRICKET
That's because I'm very small. A chirrupy little cricket, no less and no more! I'm right here on your shoulder!

PINOCCHIO sees the cricket, freaks out, flicks it off his shoulder, then stamps on it. There's a big squishy crunchy noise.

PINOCCHIO
Oh that is sad, I've got him all over my shoe.

There's a knocking at the door. PINOCCHIO reacts in terror, as though he's being shot at. He dives for cover, grabbing a knife off the workbench.

PINOCCHIO
What's that noise boys and girls? The door? How do I make it stop?

They tell him to answer it. He does, FATIMA enters. She looks at Pinocchio

FATIMA
It worked it worked! I've gone to town
I'm like David Blane, I'm Derren Brown,
From lifeless wood I've created life!
Oh Jesus Christ he's got a knife!

FATIMA takes the knife from him gently but firmly and puts it aside.

FATIMA
Hello, I'm Fatima. I won't hurt you. What's wrong Pinocchio? (She looks at the audience) Did one of them touch you?

PINOCCHIO
I don't like my name.

FATIMA
Well you can't change it, it'll fuck up all the hashtags. Well now, this must seem very strange.

PINOCCHIO
I don't really have a frame of reference, so...

FATIMA
But here I am to help and guide you!

PINOCCHIO
I'm fine, honestly.

FATIMA
Keep you on the straight and narrow.

PINOCCHIO
Boring!

FATIMA
Right young man.

FATIMA fishes a stethoscope from a pocket and holds it to Pinocchio's chest.

PINOCCHIO
It's cold!

FATIMA
Excellent, your temperature sensors are working. (She listens through the stethoscope)
No rot, no woodworm, no woodlice; Now what comes next? Ah yes, advice!

PINOCCHIO
Advice?

FATIMA
Look both ways before crossing the road. Don't run with scissors. Return your clothes to Asos within three days or you'll never get round to it. Neither a borrower nor a lender be.

PINOCCHIO
I'd better write these down! Can I borrow a pen?

FATIMA
Of course, very wise.

PINOCCHIO
Ha! But you just said not to borrow or lend. Why should I listen to you?

FATIMA
Do as I say, don't do as I do.
And most important of all – don't sigh -
You must never tell a lie.

PINOCCHIO
Why?

FATIMA
And another thing. Should you ever get into trouble, just give a little whistle and I'll be right there.

PINOCCHIO
A little whistle?

FATIMA
A little like this.

FATIMA whistles. PINCCHIO tries to whistle. He can't.

FATIMA
Oh dear. We'll soon have that in working order.

She takes out her wand.

FATIMA
Now, try again.

FATIMA whistles. She waves her wand at PINOCCHIO, who tries to whistle, but farts loudly instead.

FATIMA
This wand's not been right since it fell in the loo.
Change of plan – if in trouble, just fart, that'll do,
Well good luck and goodbye, be good, have a blast
Oh my, boys and girls – they grow up so fast!

FATIMA exits, closing the door behind her. Footsteps approaching: PINOCCHIO hides. CORNETTA enters.

CORNETTA
Ciao boys and girls!

She raises a hand to her ear to encourage the audience to greet her. "Come stai Cornetta?"

CORNETTA
Sono un po' stanco. Morning boys and girls, you're up early!

GEPPETTA enters in a long floaty dressing gown with a bold pattern and her hair in curlers. She's half asleep. She has a bottle of prosecco and a glass and pours herself a drink.

GEPPETTA
I've had the strangest dream. (She looks at her workbench) It's gone! The puppet! This can only mean one thing! We must have...

CORNETTA
An intruder!

GEPPETTA
I know the fucking line! I'm pausing. Drama darling, drama. Eight bloody dots, that one.

GEPPETTA
Boys and girls, you will let us know if you see anybody won't you?

Pinocchio peers from behind the workbench. The audience shout, "behind you!"

GEPPETTA
What's that? Behind us?

GEPPETTA and CORNETTA
Well! We'd better have a look then, hadn't we!

By the time they have turned round, Pinocchio is nowhere to be seen. Geppetta tells them off.

GEPPETTA
Darlings I don't think that's very funny. There's a very vulnerable young woman here, and her niece, all alone with an intruder.

At this, Geppetta undoes a button. Pinocchio peers out over the workbench again. "He's behind you!"

GEPPETTA
What?? Behind us??

GEPPETTA and CORNETTA
Well! We'd better have a look then, hadn't we!

They look behind the workbench and scream. Pinocchio stands and screams too. They all scream.

CORNETTA
It's your puppet! It's alive!

GEPPETTA
Most wonderful!

CORNETTA
Kill it!

GEPPETTA
Yes! What?

CORNETTA
You've made a monster!

GEPPETTA
A *creature*! My wish came true! Hello young man.

PINOCCHIO
Mama!

GEPPETTA
Yes! No! What? (aside) That's not how this was meant to go. And yet, what are these maternal feelings? I shall go along with it for now and should he develop Oedipal tendencies we'll cross that bridge as and when. (To Pinocchio) Ah, my son! I'm your mama Geppetta!

PINOCCHIO
I'm Pinocchio.

CORNETTA
Ha! What kind of name is that!

PINOCCHIO
It's the best name.

GEPPETTA
(To Cornetta) Say hello to your cousin.

CORNETTA
He's not my cousin, he's a straight-to-Netflix horror film.

GEPPETTA
Welcome home Pinocchio. Oh, at last someone deserving of my familial affection.

CORNETTA
He can't stay here. He'll murder us in our sleep. Anyway, we only have two bedrooms.

GEPPETTA
We'll put a camp bed in the kitchen. (Still to Cornetta) You'll be perfectly comfortable in there.

A knock at the door.

PINOCCHIO
I'll get it Mama!

GEPETTA
How clever he is!

CORNETTA
Wait! Should we let people see him?

GEPPETTA
No! Right. Pinocchio darling, lie down for mummy and stay very, very still.

PINOCCHIO
Why?

GEPPETTA
It's a little game.

PINOCCHIO
What do I win.

CORNETTA
My entire life, apparently.

PINOCCHIO lies down on the workbench like a lifeless puppet. GEPPETTA opens the door to an attractive young man in expensive smart-casual wear. He has a strong west midlands accent.

JOE
How do. Am yow all right?

They just stare at him. Geppetta is rather entranced.

JOE
Hello?

GEPPETTA
Terribly sorry, we only speak Italian.

JOE
Ow! Sorry. *Ciao.*

GEPPETTA
Well, come in.

GEPPETTA takes Joe's hand and kisses his cheeks.

JOE
I can never remember how many it is.

GEPPETTA
Just keep going I'll tell you when to stop.

JOE extracts himself after a fair number of kisses.

CORNETTA
We're actually not open yet.

GEPPETTA
(Too excited) Nonsense! I mean, stay, have a coffee.

JOE
Have you got proper stuff?

GEPPETTA
Darling you're in Italy.

JOE
Bostin'. I'll take a Maxwell House then, ta.

GEPPETTA
How I adore an English accent! (aside) Though perhaps not that one.

JOE
I expect you know who I am.

GEPPETTA
I might ask you to fill me in.

JOE
I've come to play football.

GEPPETTA
Ah... Yes, I'm afraid you see this is an arts and crafts studio.

JOE
(Holds out a hand) It's Joe? Joe Fish?

GEPPETTA
Or as we would say in Italian, Joe Pesce.

JOE
I've done a bit of telly and all. Celebrity Crimewatch; I'm Famous Where's Me Pudding; What Do You Think You're Like? But I've really set me sights on Strictly.

CORNETTA
Strictly?

GEPPETTA
Some sort of late night BDSM programming I shouldn't wonder!

CHIANTI enters through the cat flap. Perhaps she's wearing a garland of plastic flowers.

CORNETTA
Chianti!

CHIANTI
Oh my god babes I have had the most insane night.

JOE
You've got a lovely little pussy!

GEPPETTA
And it's practically purring.

CORNETTA
He said little. Yours is like La Scala.

CHIANTI lies on her back and looks inviting.

JOE
Do yow want me to rub your tummy? Do you want me to rub your tummy?

JOE gives her a good rub. CHIANTI purrs.

CORNETTA
She likes you.

CHIANTI
Oh my god he touched my fanny!

JOE
I didn't!

CHIANTI
Are his hands clean? I hate when I get an infection down there. It tastes horrible.

JOE inspects the marionets hanging on the wall.

JOE
Are these muppets?

GEPPETTA
They're puppets.

JOE
Where do I put me hand?

GEPPETTA
Come upstairs and I'll show you. (Fishing) The perfect gift for your... children?

JOE
I don't have any children.

GEPPETTA
(pointed) Well if you need any help...

JOE
I want to commission a portrait. (To Cornetta) Are you the artistic one?

GEPPETTA
Artistic? She's barely on the spectrum.

JOE
I can try elsewhere.

GEPPETTA
Wait!! I'm joking. Cornetta is your woman!

JOE
I want to present it to the team to hang in the stadium on me first day.

GEPPETTA
Cornetta! At easel! Joe, take your shirt off.

JOE
Is that necessary?

GEPPETTA
The foundation of a good portrait is a firm grasp of anatomy. A *very* firm grasp.

She helps JOE takes his shirt off. PINOCCHIO is rather dazzled.

PINOCCHIO
Fuck me!

JOE
It spoke! Your puppet spoke!

GEPPETTA
A talking puppet?! Unthinkable. It was probably the cat.

FIGARO enters

FIGARO
Ahahahahaha! I see you've met my new star signing.

CORNETTA
We're in the middle of a sitting.

FIGARO
He can have a sitting on my big fat tongue. (He runs a finger down Joe's torso) I see you've met my new star signing. I saw this young man on a Panini football sticker and knew at once I must have him. Though the only thing I hope to peel from *his* back is my own dried nut-butter.

JOE
Are you Mr Fox?

FIGARO
The very same! Join me at my mansion for a little drink, and a spot of keepie-uppie in the steam room.

JOE
You play football in the steam room?

FIGARO
Who said anything about football?

JOE
I er... I want to check out me accommodation.

FIGARO
Indeed! You're staying with me you lucky thing. (To Geppetta) Right, have you got it?

GEPPETTA
Well I did have it, but it seems to have cleared up.

FIGARO
Nobody could say I'm not a generous man. Heaven knows, those donations to Leave UK put a dent in my balance. But I won't be taken for a fool. Geppetta, my rent.

GEPPETTA
I don't have it.

CORNETTA
We will when he's paid for the painting!

FIGARO
Too late! The cat comes with me.

CORNETTA
No!

CHIANTI
Don't I get a say?

CORNETTA
Of course you get a say!

CHIANTI
(To Figaro) Come on let's get out of here.

CORNETTA
You don't want to leave me do you?

CHIANTI
Have you seen his fucking house?

FIGARO
Come along. Ciao! Ahahaha!

JOE, CHIANTI and FIGARO exit. PINOCCHIO gets up and goes to follow them.

GEPPETTA
No darling, you stay here.

PINOCCHIO
But I want to see the world and have adventures.

CORNETTA
I don't believe this.

GEPPETTA
So much to think about. I must plan for your education.

CORNETTA
Yes. Send him to boarding school.

GEPPETTA
I'll home educate him. He can't go to school with little boys and girls!

CORNETTA
We could try the adult learning centre.

GEPPETTA
People in Slayer t-shirts with B.O. learning to rewire a plug and doing collages of the children they're no longer allowed access to? Unthinkable darling.

CORNETTA
You don't want him thinking of you as a boring old teacher do you?

GEPPETTA
Very well. Of course his real education will be down to me. The arts, you know. (To Pinocchio) And we must find you a piano teacher. A good one!

CORNETTA
We don't have a piano.

GEPPETTA
A *very* good one. Now listen darling, this is important. Should anyone ask, Cornetta and I are not from Rome. Got that?

PINOCCHIO
I'm not allowed to tell lies.

CORNETTA
Sometimes it's ok to lie. Like if someone asks if you like their new hat, or if you're Boris Johnson.

GEPPETTA
Or if a friend asks you to. Now, let's get you ready. What a safe, stable and happy life you'll lead!

Scene 4: The seafront/harbour

There should now be an old, faded and torn billboard or large poster advertising Anarchy Park. PINOCCHIO enters.

PINOCCHIO
Hello boys and girls. I've just done my first morning at school. I've been learning things. What I mainly learnt was that school is really shit. Everyone teased me. Nobody sat next to me. And everyone calls me woody which they find very funny for some reason.

PINOCCHIO notices the poster for Anarchy Park.

PINOCCHIO
Anarchy Park... That looks more fun than school! I want to go there. Will you come with me?

FIGARO and CHIANTI enter. FIGARO strides along, CHIANTI is behind loaded down with bags.

FIGARO
Hi diddle-de-dee, I think my cat's got fleas! Hurry up Chianti. We don't have all day. Well well, what have we here?

PINOCCHIO
I'm Pinocchio.

FIGARO
Enchanted to meet you.

CHIANTI
You've got to say it back idiot.

PINOCCHIO
I can't. I don't know if it's true and I don't want to lie.

CHIANTI
Shall we deck him. Go on, you deck him and I'll stand here and laugh.

FIGARO
That's alright Chianti. You've really taken to this sidekick thing haven't you.

FIGARO shakes PINOCCHIO's hand. Then knocks on his head – it sounds like a woodblock.

FIGARO
Interesting.

CHIANTI goes over to PINOCCHIO and starts scratching at his front leg. FIGARO kicks her.

FIGARO
Chianti, the boy is not a scratching post. He's (he whispers) a puppet. A puppet! But wait! He can tell me where that bohemian buffoon Geppetta has appeared from, if you really can't tell me.

CHIANTI
I told you, cats only have two months memory. We got less storage than your mum's smartphone.

FIGARO
(To Pinocchio) Dear Pinot Grigio, I expect you're acquainted with Placenta's finest puppet maker, Geppetta.

PINOCCHIO
Mama!

FIGARO
Quite the mystery, those two. Nobody knows where they've sprung from. Can you tell me?

PINOCCHIO
What should I do boys and girls? Should I lie?

FIGARO
Don't talk to *them* dear, this isn't Fleabag. Do you know where they're from?

CHIANTI
I doubt he'd know sir, a blockhead like him.

FIGARO
Let him speak!

PINOCCHIO
No! No I don't.

PINOCCHIO squeals slightly as if in pain.

PINOCCHIO
What's happening?!

He clutches his stomach he runs off. He screams offstage.

FIGARO
Where the hell has he gone?

PINOCCHIO re-enters... he has a very long nose.

FIGARO
Interesting. As I was saying, are you sure you don't know where they're from?

PINOCCHIO
Yes! I'm sure.

PINOCCHIO squeals again and runs off.

FIGARO
There's no need to be embarrassed.

PINOCCHIO enters – he now has a normal nose but enormous ears.

FIGARO
Remarkable.

PINOCCHIO
Ow!

FIGARO
What?

PINOCCHIO
You're really loud!

FIGARO
As I was saying, Geppetta and Cornetta... They wouldn't be from, oh I don't know, Rome?

PINOCCHIO
Boys and girls what should I do? Do I really have to lie? (They answer) No, no they're not from Rome.

PINOCCHIO runs off again

FIGARO
Well I'm very sorry boys and girls he must have forgotten a prop or something.

A very long penis starts to protrude from the wings. It is wooden, and very long, but in all other ways it is unmistakably a penis. Eventually, Pinocchio emerges, on the end of it. Fatima appears.

FATIMA
Well boys and girls. It's £28 a ticket this year, we had to meet your expectations.

Fatima exits. FIGARO starts laughing at Pinocchio. CHIANTI joins him and starts laughing too. PINOCCHIO runs off.

FIGARO
Come back! I'm sorry. We weren't laughing at you. We were laughing... because we're happy to have met such a remarkable young man.

PINOCCHIO enters, minus the penis. He looks unsure.

FIGARO
That's it, chin up! Why the long penis? *Face*, face.

PINOCCHIO looks at the advertisement for Anarchy Park again.

PINOCCHIO
I want to go here. It looks amazing.

FIGARO
You wouldn't like it at Anarchy Park. No it would be a very bad idea for a young lad to go to such a place.

PINOCCHIO
Why?

CHIANTI
It's right on the cliffs. It's dangerous.

FIGARO
Nonsense! No no it's – well, there's nobody to keep an eye on you, or tell you what to do! You could get up to anything you like – can you imagine!

PINOCCHIO
So nobody would make me go to school?

FIGARO
Exactly! No school! Nobody laughing at you.

CHIANTI laughs at Pinocchio.

FIGARO
Nobody shoving you.

CHIANTI shoves him.

FIGARO
Nobody stealing your pocket money.

CHIANTI steals money from Pinocchio's pocket.

FIGARO
Oh yes, it's a hard time at school when you're different.

PINOCCHIO
Because I'm a puppet?

FIGARO
Well, there's that... I wonder, have you considered a career in showbusiness?

PINOCCHIO
I want to have fun and adventures and see the world.

FIGARO
Then showbusiness it is! There's no business like it! After all, do you want to be different – or do you want to be *special*?

21

PINOCCHIO
Special!? What do you think boys and girls – should I go with these nice people?

SONG: SPECIAL

FIGARO
When the moon shines in the piazza
Imagine your name up in lights
You're a star! You're an actor!
All you need is some training and three pairs of tights

Normal people can be quite the devil,
They're not cruel they just don't understand,
You're not different - You are special!
And there's no need to weep
When you've like-minded people,
Enough with these sheep!
Did you know you can sleep with your fans?

FIGARO & CHIANTI
Be an actor, be a star!
Work for two hours a day in some scandalous play
Then get drunk with McKellen and lovely Dame Helen
You trooper!
You'll be feted from afar
And forever pursued for opinions and nudes, oh it's super-duper!

FIGARO
You'll recite from The Bard and Goldoni
Explore the great human truths!
Learn to sword fight, ride a pony
Take advantage of sweet and delicious ambitious youths

FIGARO, CHIANTI, PINOCCHIO
Let's be special, let's have fun
Let's be Hollywood stars, drive luxury cars
Play a king, play a cat, sing and dance and all that
Be a trooper
You'll be feted from afar
And give great interviews and be horribly rude, It's super-duper!

FIGARO & CHIANTI
When you're famous be sure to remember
As you hobnob in Cannes or L.A.
Your friends who first called you special,
Yes you're special

FIGARO (aside)
and probably gay

FIGARO, CHIANTI, PINOCCHIO
Yes you're special say hip hip hooray!

By the end of the song we have transitioned into the next scene – they are now in Figaro's mansion.

PINOCCHIO: NO STRINGS ATTACHED!

Scene 5: Figaro's mansion

Chianti exits and they find themselves in a great hall in Figaro's large house. Marble, gold, fine furniture. The bottom of a grand staircase leads into the wings. There's an enormous portrait of Figaro.

FIGARO
Welcome Pistachio, welcome to your digs!

PINOCCHIO
What's digs?

FIGARO
You'll soon get your mouth around an actor's lingo. We sleep in digs, we dress in frocks, and we dine out whenever invited by someone with arts council subsidy.

PINOCCHIO
It's so beautiful! You must be very successful.

FIGARO
One day you'll have a place like this of your own! Such an exciting world you've entered, all our customs and rules and sayings. "Break a leg", "Your round, old chum", and the most important of all: "What happens on tour stays on tour."

PINOCCHIO
What stays on tour?

FIGARO
Second-rate thrillers and Joe McElderry.

PINOCCHIO
Ok. Well I'm going to go exploring, what time is dinner?

FIGARO
Exploring? Everything you could possibly need is here. No, you must never go outside the walls of the mansion alone. Anything could happen to you. You are very... precious.

PINOCCHIO
Special!

FIGARO
That's it!

CHIANTI enters, carrying a bloody pigeon. She presents it.

CHIANTI
I got you something. I hope you like it!

FIGARO
Holy shit!

PINOCCHIO
Shitty hole!

FIGARO
Get that disgusting thing out of here at once! What were you thinking!?

CHIANTI
I don't know...

CHIANTI starts to exit sadly.

FIGARO
Wait! Take the boy. Show him to his room.

CHIANTI and PINOCCHIO exit as the doorbell chimes.

FIGARO
And answer that while you're at it.

PEDRO enters.

PEDRO
Signore Figaro! You wanted to see me?

FIGARO
Well that's overstating it. Do you know why you're here?

PEDRO
Yes! To live, to work, to love!

FIGARO
No, you fool. *Here.* I have something to give you.

PEDRO
Signore Fox!

FIGARO
(Pulling out a piece of paper). An eviction notice.

PEDRO
An evic- Mr Fox! I live in my little house many years, my papa before me.

FIGARO
Was there something else?

PEDRO
Prego Mr Fox!

FIGARO
Look I'm sorry but evicting tenants really is a most upsetting business, you insensitive scrote, and I need some time to myself.

23

PEDRO
Oh... of course. It is what it is! I will sleep in my little boat.

FIGARO
Boat? Ah, no. Repossessed I'm afraid. In lieu of rent. Two bailiffs nipped down to the harbour not two hours ago. One of them was to *die* for! Right, piss off.

PEDRO nods, sadly, and exits.

FIGARO
Ooh I've got quite the lob-on after that. (to the audience) Anyone...?

JOE enters. FIGARO is immediately full of nervous energy and adjusts his hardon.

FIGARO
Joe! Dear Joe. Is everything to your liking? Can I do anything to make you more comfortable?

JOE
Like what?

FIGARO
Loosen your clothing?

JOE
It's a bostin' place you got here.

FIGARO
Isn't it! The marble comes from the very quarry that Michelangelo liked to go cruising in.

JOE
Cruising?

FIGARO
Imagine a cross between Grindr and Pokemon Go.

JOE
So er, you must be a big football fan then?

FIGARO
Had you known me back in the day, you'd frequently have seen me wearing a Barcelona top out. Though I couldn't tell you his name.

JOE picks up a painting that is leaning against the wall. We can't see what it is. FIGARO slightly panics.

FIGARO
Yes er leave that! I er, I'm something of an art collector. That's a recent acquisition.

JOE
Just like me! What is it?

FIGARO
It's actually a bottom.

JOE
Just like me! So when do I meet the other players?

FIGARO
Your first match is on Sunday after mass.

JOE
(Appalled) Sunday? Is Placenta a Sunday league club??

FIGARO
Not for long! Now, limber up, then join me in the drawing to practice heading.

JOE
You play football in the drawing room?

FIGARO
Who said anything about football. Ciao.

FIGARO exits. JOE starts doing some lunges and stretches. PINOCCHIO enters and stares.

PINOCCHIO
Shitty hole!

JOE
Alright? Wait – I seen you before.

PINOCCHIO
I'm Mr Figaro's new star!

JOE
I don't think so. I'm Mr Figaro's new star. You ain't no footballer.

PINOCCHIO
I'm an actor. You're not an actor.

JOE
I've done pantomime.

PINOCCHIO
That doesn't count!

JOE
Do you even know what pantomime is?

PINOCCHIO
No! It was just a cheap joke with no basis in character, story or circumstance!

JOE
Well, that is the beauty of pantomime.

PINOCCHIO
Anyway, an actor's better than a boring footballer.

JOE
A sportsman's better than a poncy actor. You'll never be his favourite.

PINOCCHIO
Will.

JOE
Won't.

PINOCCHIO
Will.

JOE
Won't.

JOE shoves PINOCCHIO, who shoves him back. They get into a proper fight and are soon writhing and scrapping on the floor. Until – of course – they lock eyes, fall for each other and kiss. It's hot and intense. From off, we hear Figaro.

FIGARO (off)
Joe!

JOE pulls away from Pinocchio in panic and looks about him, terrified.

JOE
We can't do this.

PINOCCHIO
Why? That was amazing.

JOE
You get used to being cautious in case you get seen.

PINOCCHIO
I was only kissing you.

JOE
Yeah I know, it's silly.

PINOCCHIO
It's not like I was going to fist you and then piss in the hole or anything. We're only in act one.

The stand-off ends. They start kissing again.

PINOCCHIO
I can't believe we were arguing and then it turned out we actually fancied each other! How mad is that!

They kiss again. FIGARO enters.

FIGARO
Traitors! Scoundrels! (beat) Chianti!

CHIANTI enters, pushing a large cage on wheels. (Or the cage can always have been there with a cloth over it and Chianti pulls the cloth off.) Figaro grabs Pinocchio, puts him in the cage and locks it.

FIGARO
That's where you'll live now you little slut!

PINOCCHIO
But I want to be an actor.

FIGARO
Yes! And now you're in *La Cage* hahaha!

JOE
We weren't doing anything.

PINOCCHIO
We were only kissing.

FIGARO
Kissing! What if people saw!

JOE
Pinocchio's right. Why should I hide who I am? From now on I'm going to be an openly gay footballer.

FIGARO
Oh no he isn't!

(Oh yes he is!)

JOE
Why not?

FIGARO
We're sponsored by the Vatican! (Melodramatic, but to himself) And think of all the other men who'll want a piece of you!

JOE
A star as big as me could really change things.

FIGARO
I'm not having some poofter on my football team. Check your contract. Ahahahaha! Right. I'm off to choose the subs for Sunday. And no, I didn't say anything about football.

FIGARO exits. JOE tries to unlock the cage.

JOE
I can't open it.

PINOCCHIO
Ok. I'll call Fatima.

JOE
Who?

PINOCCHIO
A fairy.

JOE
Is he discreet?

PINOCCHIO
Wait there.

PINOCCHIO farts. JOE bursts out laughing at him.

PINOCCHIO
What's funny?

JOE
You farted!

FATIMA enters. JOE panics and exits in haste.

PINOCCHIO
Come back!

FATIMA
How are things, no-strings? Why aren't you at school?

PINOCCHIO
Because I'm special, duh. I'm going to be on stage.

FATIMA
You can't be that special, locked in a cage. Let's get you out of there.

She waves her wand and the door swings open.

FATIMA
Now, tell me what's going on.

PINOCCHIO
I did kissing on a man called Joe, and it was brilliant, but then he got really weird about it, and then I got locked in there so I farted like you told me and he didn't like that at all. (beat) Why did he get weird about kissing?

FATIMA
Perhaps he's not out.

PINOCCHIO
Out of what?

FATIMA
Out as gay.

PINOCCHIO
What's gay?

FATIMA
Oh boy. You don't know. Where to begin.

PINOCCHIO
Begin at the beginning.

FATIMA
Alright. Once upon a time, God made a man called Adam and a man called Steve. And, well, look now: some men are attracted to women. And some men are attracted to men. And we call those men "gay".

PINOCCHIO
Ok. But why didn't Joe want me to tell you?

FATIMA
Because gay people are a minority, and minorities are often the victims of abuse or discrimination, and to some people being gay is a weakness, and when you consider that in particular male sports teams often come to symbolise the strength and pride of their community-

PINOCCHIO
Stop it!

FATIMA
Sorry.

PINOCCHIO
I'm not special at all! I'm a freak. I don't want to be gay! I'm already different! Shitty hole, *this* is the kind of thing they should teach people about in schools.

FATIMA
Yes well we'll get onto that another time. Now young man, talking of school-

PINOCCHIO
I'm not going to school.

FATIMA
Then let's get you home.

PINOCCHIO
I'm not going home! Cornetta doesn't want me there. I'm not doing anything you or anyone else tells me! I can't believe you made me have to fart just to talk to you and I can't believe you made me gay! I'm getting out of here.

PINOCCHIO runs off.

FATIMA
Pinocchio!

FATIMA runs off after him. FIGARO and CHIANTI enter. They see the empty cage.

FIGARO
Theft! Kidnap!

CHIANTI
Shall we send out a search party?

FIGARO
Oh no. There's no need for that. I know exactly where he'll be. Ahahaha! Ahahahahaha!

He encourages Chianti to laugh but she just stands there.

FIGARO
Look, do you want to be a sidekick or not?

CHIANTI
What? Yeah man. Read minds and talk to the dead and see into the future...!

FIGARO
Side. Kick.

CHIANTI
Ohhhh... No, yeah, I do.

FIGARO laughs manically again. Chianti joins in, goes into a coughing fit, and coughs up a furball.

Scene 6: The seafront/harbour

CORNETTA and GEPPETTA enter.

CORNETTA
Ciao boys and girls!

"Come stai Cornetta?"

CORNETTA
Tutto a posto, grazie!

GEPPETTA
Hello darlings! Do you know what I was just saying? Yes, I was just saying, I haven't been on in ages.

CORNETTA
Well I shouldn't think you're pregnant.

GEPPETTA
The chance would be a fine thing. And just for today, [name] that chance is yours. You look a little pale darling, I think you're low in sugar. I know what you need. A sweetie!

GEPPETTA digs in her handbag and pulls out a handful of sweets. She gives one to her boy.

CORNETTA
Aren't you forgetting something?

GEPPETTA
A line or two I imagine. Some bon motte that was briefly topical in August when it was written ... (realises) Oh! How rude, there you go darling.

GEPPETTA offers Cornetta a sweet.

CORNETTA
Auntie! Boys and girls who'd like a sweet?

They throw sweets out to the audience.

GEPPETTA
Now bambinos and bambinas you will forgive us, but we must continue to look for Pinocchio. He hasn't returned from school and I'm a little worried.

CORNETTA
He'll be fine.

GEPPETTA
Fine! This is all your fault. You made him feel most unwelcome.

PEDRO enters, with a shabby rucksack and sleeping bag and a few other pieces from his home.

GEPPETTA
Oh goodness it's Pedro.

PEDRO sees the women and stops, a little ashamed and sad.

GEPPETTA
Any minute now he'll rush towards me, the tedious bumpkin, pestering me to come in his boat.

He doesn't.

CORNETTA
I think he's finally gone off you.

GEPETTA
Gone off me! Well – well – good! I'd be glad if he had. If I could even remember who we were talking about. Which I can't... Do you think it's this dress.

CORNETTA
I'm sure he's got nothing against cheap dye and polyester.

GEPETTA
Or is it my hair?

CORNETTA
I'm sure he's got nothing against cheap dye and polyester. Pedro!

PEDRO
Oh, er, beautiful ladies... Excuse me.

GEPPETTA
Wait! Is everything alright?

PEDRO
I have just had some sad news. Excuse me.

CORNETTA
What's happened? Where've you been?

PEDRO
Oh nowhere. Just to Signore Fox's mansion.

GEPPETTA
Well, how do you like that. He gets invited up to the big house, and here I am, I who have jostled fondue forks with the cream of society.

28

PEDRO

Oh but Geppetta! I see Signore Fox has one of your magical puppets! It is so lifelike I thought it walked all by itself. You are a genius. Excuse me.

PEDRO exits.

GEPPETTA

Pinocchio, up at the big house!? But of course. I expect Figaro has seen in Pinocchio some fine, inherent, noble quality and has taken him under his wing for a little private tuition, measure him up for a suit or three, set him up with a trust fund that it will be my duty to administer with imagination and panache. Yes, that'll be it. Goodbye boys and girls!

They go.

Scene 7: Anarchy Park

An ominous rumble of thunder. A flash of lightning. We're in an eerie, rundown old fairground. There's an entrance to a Hall of Mirrors; another to a "Tunnel of Love". There is a ghost train, a stall or two. Perhaps a big old sign saying Anarchy Park, its once-illuminated letters blinking and fizzing intermittently. To the side, marked with a warning sign, is a drop - the edge of a cliff. From out of the mist stumbles Pinocchio, a bit drunk, holding a drink in a cardboard cup.

PINOCCHIO
Hello goys and birls! I said hello goys and birls! (re the drink) This is deciduous. It's a vodka flush slushie. Plush fluffy. Slush puppy. (He gives what he thinks is a gracious bow of welcome) This place is brilliant. I can do anything I want! Don't have to go to school. Nobody bullies me. And I'm not different to anybody else because there isn't anybody else!

He sees something on the floor and picks it up: a little transparent plastic "baggy" with a pill in it.

A sweetie!

He eats it, grimacing at the taste.

A black-out.

ANNOUNCER (V/O)
Forty five minutes later.

Lights back up on Pinocchio, techno music blaring loudly. He's dancing ferociously, his top off or open.

PINOCCHIO
Oh man I feel so good I want this scene to last forever. *(To someone in the audience)* Can I touch your hair it looks dead soft

JOE enters, a take-out coffee in his hand.

JOE
Pinocchio!

PINOCCHIO
Joe! (He staggers towards him). This is beautiful! You're beautiful. Dance with me.

JOE tries to but is soon quite put off.

JOE
What have you taken?

PINOCCHIO
Lovely things! I love you.

PINOCCHIO falls over. JOE crouches and gives him his coffee.

JOE
Drink this.

PINOCCHIO
Yay!

He drinks it all and sobers up. Music stops, lighting calms down.

PINOCCHIO
Boo. What are you doing here?

JOE
I've run away from that wanker. I'm going to find a football team where I can be myself. But first I wanted to find you. Come on, let's go. I'll help you.

PINOCCHIO
No.

JOE
I can carry you if you like. When I came fourth on Skating on Telly I had to do three laps with Kate Hoey on me shoulders. Come on.

PINOCCHIO
I'm staying here.

JOE
Oh. Alright. Well. I guess we can hang out here.

JOE puts an arm round PINOCCHIO who shrugs him off.

JOE
You do know that I've got my own calendar like? 2016 it was. (beat) You were all over me a minute ago.

PINOCCHIO
(re the coffee) That was before you gave me this.

JOE
I haven't felt this rejected since I got voted off Lorraine's Bathroom Nightmares.

PINOCCHIO
You're so boring. Leave me alone.

JOE
I've been searching all week for you! Alright, let's... have fun. (he laughs) You're such a hot mess.

JOE approaches him.

PINOCCHIO
And I'm not gay, alright.

JOE
Oh yes you are! You're so gay you could go on the Bake-Off. You're so gay you could write for Doctor Who.

PINOCCHIO
I'm not gay!

PINOCCHIO's penis starts to grow.

JOE
Then what's that about.

PINOCCHIO
I'm thinking about a sexy lady.

The penis is now enormous.

JOE
Shit. That ain't right! That ain't right at all! I'll go and get help.

JOE exits. THE penis retracts. FIGARO enters disguised as a Fortune Teller. He has clearly been watching from a hiding place.

FIGARO
Fortunes! Fortunes! - It's me in a cunning disguise! Interesting, the boy's penis grows when he lies... But wait! Last time that happened he was talking about Geppetta and Cornetta. They *are* from Rome! (To Pinocchio) Young man. Let me tell your fortune and show you what lies ahead.

PINOCCHIO
I could just read the script.

FIGARO
(Bitter) I wish I had.

PINOCCHIO
Can you tell me if I'm going to be gay or straight?

FIGARO finds this hilarious. Then stops laughing.

FIGARO
I mean, er, yes, yes, everything. Right, the best place to do it is in the hall of mirrors! It's all the glass you see, it helps me look into the future.

FIGARO points the way.

PINOCCHIO
What do you think boys and girls?

No!!!

PINOCCHIO
I want to stay out here.

FIGARO produces a Cadburys Crème Egg as if by magic.

FIGARO
But heavens to Betsy and holy shit! It's a Cadbury's Crème Egg! Goodness they appear earlier each year don't they, and yet still there are those who insist climate change is a myth. Go on, try it.

FIGARO lobs the egg into the hall of mirrors. PINOCCHIO runs after it.

PINOCCHIO (off)
Oh wow! These mirrors make me look such a funny shape.

FIGARO
Yes! TK Maxx were having a re-furb.

PINOCCHIO (off)
This one makes me look tall! This one makes me look tiny! (laughing) This one's brilliant! I look like a donkey!

FIGARO
A donkey?

PINOCCHIO
Yeah, a stupid donkey!

PINOCCHIO emerges – he is a donkey, with big donkey ears, a donkey tail and donkey hooves.

PINOCCHIO
Aren't you coming in? You didn't tell my fortune.

FIGARO
Because it's all so clear young Pomegranate. Feel your arse and your head.

PINOCCHIO does, he screams.

FIGARO
Your future is as a donkey. My donkey! I don't think you'll be seducing any more of my footballers looking like that!

He puts a tether around PINOCCHIOs neck so he is tethered up. FIGARO exits laughing.

PINOCCHIO
What am I going to do now? (He brays, which scares him) Fatima! I'll call Fatima!

He strains to fart – but the sound that follows is a big wet squelch. He's shat himself.

PINOCCHIO
Oh god! That wasn't a fart! (He brays again)

JOE (off)
Pinocchio!

PINOCCHIO
Oh fuck though.

JOE
Pinocchio!

PINOCCHIO
Oh but Jesus.

He starts wafting a terrible smell away from him and absentmindedly puts his hand to his head – which reminds him of his donkey ears. He screams. He tries to put his cap on to cover the ears but it won't fit. In frustration he throws the cap over the cliff edge. As JOE enters, PINOCCHIO hides behind something. JOE is holding a hot dog. He sniffs it, disgusted.

JOE
I told you this stuff is junk, it smells gross. It's worse than when I did Celebrity Colonics. (He smells it again) I don't think it is the hot dog. Pinocchio?

PINOCCHIO (off)
Go away!

JOE
Pinocchio?

PINOCCHIO (off)
Run! This place is dangerous!

JOE
I can't hear anything over the sound of that noisy donkey. Shut up donkey! (he discovers Pinocchio) Oh my god that is the most minging, smelly donkey I've ever seen. Poor thing!

FIGARO enters.

FIGARO
Ahahahahaha! Joe, Joe, Josephine, stupid little Brummie queen.

JOE
Where's Pinocchio?

FIGARO points over the cliff. JOE looks down.

JOE
His hat! You've thrown him off the cliff!

FIGARO
As if I would! That petulant puppet is worth far too much to me. You however are worth nothing. Except as a source of excellent ideas.

JOE
Oh yeah, like what?

FIGARO
Pushing people off cliffs!

He pushes JOE over the cliff edge. He looks at his watch. He removes a hip flask from a pocket and takes a swig then returns the flask. He looks at his watch again. Eventually there's a big splash. FIGARO laughs.

FIGARO
Thought you'd escape me, did you, you wooden topped twat! You signed a ten-year contract and you will see out every minute of it - as a donkey! A dancing puppet donkey! You will never get away from me. Never!

He gives an evil laugh and exits. PINOCCHIO starts to neigh sadly.

In another place, FATIMA appears.

FATIMA
A donkey, a donkey! not even a mule,
Well that's what happens to boys who skip school,
It's harsh I concede – I hope things get better
As long as his farts don't get any wetter,
So what's to become? We need resolutions
But first get a drink and perform your ablutions
And mingle and flirt and swap notes on the plot,
And we'll see you back here, you beautiful lot!

INTERVAL

32

Dami Olukoya as Fatima in *Pinocchio: No Strings Attached*. Photo by PBGstudios.

Christy Bellis as Cornetta, Matthew Baldwin as Geppetta and Shane Barragan as Pedro in *Pinocchio: No Strings Attached*. Photo by PBGstudios.

Scene 8: Anarchy Park

FATIMA

Welcome back boys and girls, settle down, engage brains,
And try to ignore those pesky trains,
There's a rumour in town, passed from husband to wife,
That at Anarchy Park there've been strange signs of life,
Is it gypsies? Or something to do with the mayor?
Or is it the ghosts that are said to live there?
It might make fun day out at any rate!
So Cornetta decided to investigate...

She exits. Curtain out on Anarchy Park. It is still really dark and eerie. CORNETTA enters.

CORNETTA

Ciao boys and girls! ("Come stai Cornetta?") Not bad at all thank you. This is fantastic! (She takes a photo with her phone) If there's one thing Instagram likes more than a twink's new fade it's an abandoned amusement park. Auntie!

GEPPETTA enters.

GEPPETTA

I'm not staying another minute in this shithole! (To the audience) Oh, Bambinos and bambinas! Are we well? Are we quorate? Sometimes a few stragglers go missing in the Pleasure Gardens and we have to send a sheepdog out. With wet wipes. Do you know, I've spent the last twenty minutes timing myself while I ran as fast as I could between the bar and the loos. That's right – I've been interval training! Cornetta, please can we go, this place is long past its best.

CHIANTI enters

CHIANTI

A bit like some of its visitors.

CORNETTA

Chianti! Baby! Are you alright? What are you doing here?

CHIANTI

I'm always up here. This is where my cool friends hang out. We chase rats. We do dogs fights. Sing a madrigal if we got the numbers. I have got other friends you know. This wasn't even the only panto I got offered this year. I got offered Dick in Hackney.

GEPPETTA

I'd have taken Dick in Hackney. Now come on, we've seen enough. Let's all go home.

CHIANTI

Oh. Oh I see. Right...

CHIANTI "subtly" pulls on a big lever. Lights start to sparkle, things become bright, music from a fairground organ crescendos and accelerates. The park has come to life! It's like some kind of spirit has possessed Geppetta.

CORNETTA

It is open after all!

GEPPETTA

I feel... I feel... I think the word is jolly. Yes! I'm feeling jolly. What's going on?

The music settles into the accompaniment for a song. It sounds like a fairground organ and should be performed a bit music-hall.

SONG: FUNTIME AT THE FAIR

GEPPETTA

When I was a teenage girl the funfair came
I met a handsome gypsy - I forget his name
He took me on the waltzers, he took me on the wheel
He took me up the log chute oh you should have heard me squeal!

GEPPETTA, CORNETTA, CHIANTI

So hold on tight, we're letting go
Live your life like a travelling show
Oh buckle up and feel the air
Win me a goldfish win me a teddy bear

GEPPETTA

I'm rather getting into it now!

CORNETTA

See! I knew you would.

CORNETTA

When I was a teenage girl the funfair came
I met a gypsy girl I don't recall her name
She took me on the coaster to see from high above
She took my hand and led me up her tunnel of love

GEPPETTA, CORNETTA, CHIANTI

So hold on tight, put your purse in your bra
Whiz through life like a dodgem car
Oh buckle up and feel the air
Win me a goldfish win me a teddy bear

GEPPETTA

Do you know boys and girls my favourite was always the games and side-shows. A fellow once beckoned me over to have a go on his hook-a-duck stall. Hooker duck I said, whatever next?! And I think the correct term is sex worker.

> GEPPETTA, CORNETTA, CHIANTI
> And though it's rather terribly frightening
> With noises in the dark and it's a fiver for a ride
> We love the colourful flattering lighting
> Perhaps we'll get a fingering by the helter-skelter slide
> We'll go down with pride!

> CHIANTI
> When I was a kitten and the funfare came
> I met a skanky tomcat I forget his name
> We played the catch-the-rat game, we lived the fucking dream
> Oh yeah because that night I was the cat that got the cream

> GEPPETTA, CORNETTA, CHIANTI
> Oh hold on tight and come with us
> Spin through life like the octopus
> Oh buckle up and feel the air
> Win me a goldfish win me a teddy bear

GEPPETTA

Another chap had a stall where you could knock tin cans over to win a prize. He said give me a euro and I'll give you two balls. I said, that sounds promising, what do I get for a fiver?

> BOTH
> So hold on tight, we're letting go
> Live your life like a travelling show
> Oh buckle up and feel the air
> Win me a goldfish, win me a teddy,
> Win me a goldfish, win me a teddy bear!

GEPPETTA

Didn't I tell you this would be fun?

CORNETTA

Look, there's candyfloss!

GEPPETTA

Candyfloss!

CORNETTA

Shall I get two?

GEPPETTA

Just one, Cornetta. Give it to me.

CORNETTA exits.

GEPPETTA

A tunnel of love! Or as my mother called it, the subway of shame. Yes, she was quite the fan. Now who might enjoy a little dip into the tunnel of love with me?

She approaches an audience member she spoke to earlier.

GEPPETTA

Hello [name]. I note that the gleeful enthusiasm on your friend's face is not quite reflected in your own expression. Never mind, this is not the time for inexperience. I shall go in alone.

She walks over to the Tunnel of Love and looks back at them.

GEPPETTA

Yes! Into the Tunnel of Love I go, all on my own.

She pauses just before she is about to go in.

GEPPETTA

There's a rather stagnant smell boys and girls...

She exits into the tunnel of love. She runs out again screaming. PEDRO follows, his trousers are around his ankles and he holds a porn magazine. He has just managed to pull up his underpants.

PEDRO

Sweet signora a thousand apologies!

GEPPETTA

Pedro! What a surprise.

PEDRO

Yes! I did not expect to come across you.

GEPPETTA

(Wiping her dress) Oh lord, did you?

CORNETTA enters

CORNETTA

Pedro what are you doing here?

PEDRO

Since Figaro evicted me I have been sleeping here, dreaming of you sweet Geppetta.

GEPPETTA

But not washing here from the smell of it.

PEDRO
Forgive me, I stink.

CORNETTA
What about the rats?

PEDRO
They do not seem to mind.

GEPPETTA
Well for goodness sake pull your trousers up. Heaven knows I shan't forget what I just saw in a hurry. It's no wonder you've barely travelled. The size of the thing, I expect the airlines charge you extra just to bring it on board.

PEDRO
There is no shame in carnal pleasure. I am how you say, sex positive.

GEPPETTA
I'm a woman of the world Pedro but I've yet to meet anyone identifying as sex positive who wouldn't be better described as a common flasher. (to the audience) Oh yes, I've seen your tweets. (To pedro) Are you... alright?

PEDRO
It is... an adventure! Of course, if somebody kind had a little space for just a few nights, even a camp bed on a kitchen floor, it would be a dream come true...

GEPPETTA
Yes I expect it would. Such a shame.

CORNETTA
Let's go on the ghost train!

PEDRO
We could-

GEPPETTA
Absolutely not.

CORNETTA
Oh come on. You two are so boring.

She gets in the little car and it glides off into the ghost train. Spooky sounds. CORNETTA screams then runs out of the ghost train on foot, stopping just before she reaches the cliff edge. The car returns to its station, empty.

PEDRO
Mama mia. Anyone would think there are real ghosts in there!

Pedro gets in the car and slides into the ghost train. He runs out screaming, stopping just before the cliff edge. The car returns, empty.

GEPPETTA
For goodness sake darlings! Ghosts do not exist. It's perfectly safe. Look. (She gets in the car) Ooh the seat's nice and warm. And wet.

GEPPETTA glides into the ghost train. There is screaming – and a ghost runs out, terrified. He stops at the cliff and looks back at the ghost train, from which Geppetta is emerging. He decides the cliff is the better option and jumps off. We hear a big splash.

FIGARO enters with PINOCCHIO on his tether. PINOCCHIO is still a donkey.

FIGARO
Ahahaha! Welcome, welcome, are we having fun? Who'd like to ride this dumb animal?

GEPPETTA
Don't ask the boys and girls for heaven's sake we'll be here all day and we don't have that sort of license.

PINOCCHIO
Mama!

PEDRO
Sweet signora, I buy you a ride.

GEPPETTA
On that mangey mule?

PINNOCCHIO
Mama it's me, Pinocchio.

GEPPETTA
Yes yes, hee-haw, hee-haw.

PINOCCHIO
No listen! It's me!

GEPPETTA
What a noisy donkey!

PINOCCHIO
Mama!!!

GEPPETTA
Yes yes, "Hee-haw!" Shut up you noisy thing. Signore Figaro, how is darling Pinocchio?

PINOCCHIO
I've been fucking better.

FIGARO
Oh! But haven't you heard? Oh it's heart-breaking! Our little wooden friend is no more. You see he walked rather too close to the cliff edge, just there, and... well.

PINOCCHIO
It's not true mama!

FIGARO
Splash!

PEDRO, GEPPETTA and CORNETTA look over the cliff

PEDRO
Look! His little yellow hat! Bobbing in the waves by itself.

CORNETTA
Oh my god. What if he jumped. This is all my fault.

GEPPETTA
My boy! Lost to me! Come at once. We must go and grieve in something chic and mysterious.

GEPPETTA, CORNETTA and PEDRO exit

PINOCCHIO
No!

FIGARO
Ha, ha, now they will never come looking for you! Not least because they'll soon be in jail. (He pulls out a phone and calls). Hello, Vatican Secret Police? Yes, it's me. It turns out we *do* have a couple of romans in town. I'll leave it to you! (He hangs up) Now, back to the mansion to rehearse for your adult puppet show. Punch-fuck and Judy. Ahahahahaha!

Scene 9: The seafront/harbour

There is a huge wanted poster up with a picture of CORNETTA and GEPETTA on it. PEDRO CORNETTA and GEPETTA trudge on. GEPPETTA looks at it and screams a howl of fear and rage.

CORNETTA
Oh god!

GEPPETTA
It's a disaster! Of all the pictures they could have used! I, who modelled for so many of our nation's greatest artists.

CORNETTA
Yes you had a good Renaissance didn't you. Let's take it down and get back to the studio.

PEDRO enters

PEDRO
Geppetta! My diamond, my ruby, my sapphire.

GEPPETTA
That's got a ring to it.

PEDRO
Your studio, it is more beautiful than ever.

GEPPETTA
Our studio?

PEDRO
Pictures of your radiant face all over it. (Sees the wanted poster) Yes, just like that one.

GEPPETTA
Oh shoot! The police are closing in on us, my week-old adult son is drowned and there are posters of my crow's feet all over town!

PEDRO
Do you know what I do in times of trouble?

GEPPETTA
Yes. You lie in wait in the Tunnel of Muck with your willy in your hand.

PEDRO
I sing a special song.

CORNETTA
A song! What is it?

PEDRO
It's a setting of words to a melody but that is not important right now. I sing for you a simple heartfelt song of our region.

PEDRO sings

SONGSHEET SONG

Orecchiette Sacchettoni Rigatoni e Linguine
Fusilli Fettucine Macaroni Fregula
Pappardelle Pizzoccheri Cannelloni Tortellini
Tagliatelle Ravioli Gnocchi Penne Lasagna

CORNETTA
I feel better already. Why don't we join in aunty?

GEPPETTA
Absolutely not, what a racket.

CORNETTA
Come on.

GEPPETA
Very well darling, but on one condition.

CORNETTA
A condition? What is it?

GEPPETTA
It's a criterion to be fulfilled by one party to secure the other's participation in a deal, but that's not important right now. I shall join in if the boys and girls sing along with us too.

A large "menu" is brought on displaying the words to the song. They lead the audience in a few rounds of it, getting faster and faster. When it's finished they get the audience to give themselves a round of applause.

FATIMA enters.

FATIMA
Fortune telling! Palm readings! Close up magic!

GEPPETTA
Fatima darling! All is woe!

FATIMA
What's wrong? (Sees Cornetta) Oh. Hello.

CORNETTA
Hi! Cornetta.

GEPPETTA
Have you two not met?

FATIMA
I don't think so?

GEPPETTA
Oh! Well! This is perfect. You can be... friends.

CORNETTA
We're in in the middle of a crisis.

GEPPETTA
That's ridiculous, you've only just met.

CORNETTA
Something terrible happened at the cliff!

FATIMA
At the cliff! What is it?

CORNETTA
It's a vertiginous rock face formed by erosion, but that's not important right now.

GEPPETTA
Pinocchio is drown-ed!

FATIMA
Drowned?

GEPPETTA
Drown-ed! Don't correct me in your second language.

FATIMA
Italian's my fourth language. Let me get this straight. The puppet has drowned.

GEPPETTA, CORNETTA, PEDRO
Yes!

FATIMA
The wooden puppet, that is made of wood, that floats because wood floats, has drowned?

GEPPETTA
This is no time to be cryptic!

CORNETTA
She's right! He won't have drowned. He'll have floated off somewhere.

FATIMA
Gold star for you! Geppetta I must question your parenting skills. You've only had Pinocchio a week. Has he even had his MMR?

GEPPETTA
Oh, well, look, it's all very easy for you to judge isn't it, you Absent Fairy. All you did was pop round one night, wave your wand a few times, teach the boy to fart and then vanish from his life, occasionally rocking up out of nowhere like the big I-Am and you think that gives you license to lecture me?

CORNETTA
Can you help us find him?

FATIMA
Not unless he breaks wind, and if the boy isn't eating-

CORNETTA
Can't you use magic?

FATIMA
He's made of wood.

GEPPETTA & CORNETTA
Yes?

FATIMA
And there are lots of trees in this region.

GEPPETTA & CORNETTA
Yes?

FATIMA
It's hard to tell the wood from the trees.

GEPPETTA
Then I shall search for him! Somehow obtain the use of a boat and search the ocean until I find his little bobbing body.

PEDRO
Well, forgive me but I am very tired, I have slept in a tunnel for two weeks. I must go and lie down in my tiny boat.

GEPPETTA
I thought you'd lost your tiny boat.

PEDRO
I have lost my *little* boat. There is just enough room in my *tiny* boat to lie down. This will be my humble home. After all, there is nowhere else for me to sleep...

GEPPETTA
But – did you hear what I just said?

PEDRO
Geppetta you are many things but you are not a sailor. You would not be safe at sea without me but as it is a very tiny boat and as you do not enjoy my company you would not be happy in so proximate a situation.

GEPPETTA
Alright, very nicely done. (pause) Pedro, I would be... delighted if you might accompany me in your tiny boat on a quest to find Pinocchio.

PEDRO
A great honour!

CORNETTA
What about Free Fanny?

GEPPETTA
Free Fanny?

FATIMA
Free Fanny! A monstrous whale said to inhabit these waters.

GEPPETTA
Oh, Pedro, she'll swallow me whole! And possibly the rest of me!

PEDRO
She is a myth, an old wives' tale! Like the abominable snowman, or the Loch Ness Monster, or three hundred and fifty million pounds per week for the NHS[5]. Yes, when I was young my papa told me, there's no such thing as Free Fanny. Geppetta, my queen. The sea is calling. Goodbye boys and girls!

PEDRO and GEPPETTA exit.

CORNETTA
Oh Lord, what do I do! I know – I'll don a disguise in case someone recognises me.

_____

[5] The controversial promise painted on a bus by the official Leave campaign during the 2016 EU referendum.

FATIMA
Disguises I can do, just come with me,
I know exactly what you shall be!

CORNETTA
Thank you. So are you... new round here?

FATIMA
Not very.

CORNETTA
Right. (beat) So er... where do you er like to go out?

FATIMA
Oh. Well. Here and there. (beat) I mean... have you heard of the er... the Muff Bar?

CORNETTA
The muff bar?

FATIMA
It's a bit pokey and out of the way.

CORNETTA
Right. I'll check it out. Is it good?

FATIMA
Well - it depends on what you're into. And there's an Australian-themed café I quite like. That's called, um, Sheilas? And there's, well, the Dungaree Downlow but that's just every second Thursday.

CORNETTA
Great! Great... I do like your outfit.

FATIMA
(Awkward) Yes, I mean, thank you... It's what I've always worn,
Now spit spot Cornetta, let's get you transformed.

They exit.

Scene 10: Figaro's mansion

Pinocchio is back in his cage. He still has his tail and donkey ears. CHIANTI is on the stairs, licking her fur to clean it. Pinocchio sings.

SONG: STRINGS

How do you live a life that's good
When you can't tell a lie and you're made of wood
And people pull your strings even though you're stringless?
Days into this life all I want now is nothingness

Put me away high on a shelf
Don't want adventures, fun or wealth
I'll only fart and shit myself
Don't want to spread my wings
I wish that I had strings

Don't teach me words that I can't speak
But me on show like I'm a freak
Use me until I fucking squeak
And tell me I'm nothing
I'd rather be on strings

I got no strings to hold me up
So tie me down and wreck me
Just take control,
Sand me down and drill my hole
Shut me down with no regretting
To factory settings

Don't teach me rules then change the game
Don't say I'm special, call me names
Don't make love a love that shames
There'll be no carefree flings
Just want to be on strings
I wish that I had strings.

PINOCCHIO

Oh boys and girls. If only I hadn't pushed Joe away. If only I hadn't pretended to be straight. None of this would have happened. I'd love to be off being gay with Joe right now.

FIGARO enters.

FIGARO

How it warms my heart to have you back, the family together again! And rehearsals for my erotic puppet show are going so well, we'll be touring in no time.

PINOCCHIO

Let me out of here!

FIGARO

Stop that infernal neighing. Chianti! You're supposed to be guarding our little friend. Stop preening.

CHIANTI

I'm a fucking cat! You might as well try and stop a fox from scrounging in dustbins.

FIGARO

How dare you!

CHIANTI

I've seen you. At night. Snaffle snaffle.

FIGARO

(Confessional) I can't help it! No matter how much I civilise myself, chicken just doesn't taste right without a coating of cake crumbs and toenails. Anyway, stop it and stand guard.

CHIANTI

I want to look nice. There's a this well fit tabby keeps looking at me from the house across the street. We make eye contact from balcony to balcony. It's like Romeo and Juliet.

FIGARO

That's absurd! There's only one balcony in Romeo and Juliet. You're thinking of Private Lives... I thought you'd been spayed?

CHIANTI

I still like a cuddle.

FIGARO

You'll stop seeing him! Now, stay here and keep your eyes on the prize. If anything happens to him I'll track you down, have your fur for a pair of thermal pants and take a chainsaw to him until he's nothing but sawdust.

FIGARO exits

PINOCCHIO

Shitty hole. She should be allowed to see who she wants.

CHIANTI

I should! (beat) I thought it'd be great living here.

PINOCCHIO

Me too. (Realising) You understood me!

CHIANTI
Yeah?

PINOCCHIO
You can speak donkey!

CHIANTI
Evidently. Donkey, hedgehog... What's the thing with a bill like a duck.

PINOCCHIO
A duck-billed platypus.

CHIANTI
What?! No. A goose.

PINOCCHIO
What was it like living with Geppetta and Cornetta?

CHIANTI
Ha! Those losers! They dragged my sorry arse hundreds of miles from my home and my friends to come to this backwater. Insisted on getting me here, even though they couldn't carry much else and had to throw all their luggage in the sea.

PINOCCHIO
That's quite nice of them if you think about it.

CHIANTI
Oh. Well yeah, I suppose. *But*, they always gave me boring cheap shitty biscuity bits for dinner, *every* day...

PINOCCHIO
They gave you dinner every day?

CHIANTI
Yeah. Even when they couldn't really afford to eat anything themselves... so I guess that *sounds* quite nice too. *But*, I never had my own room to sleep in like I do here, so I had to snuggle up on Cornetta's bed... Oh god I miss her! I ain't staying here one more minute!

PINOCCHIO
Wait! Can you do something?

CHIANTI
If it takes less than one minute.

PINOCCHIO
Let me out?

CHIANTI
You heard what he said! He'll have my fur for pants! And you signed a contract. Modern capitalist societies only function because of the sanctity of contract law.

PINOCCHIO
But if you don't let me out we won't be able to do the scene where I'm in swimwear.

CHIANTI
Boys and girls, shall I let him out? (yes!) Alright!

She lets him out.

FIGARO (off)
Pain au chocolat! It's time for rehearsals!

CHIANTI
This way!

She grabs his hand and pulls him to the front of the stage.

PINOCCHIO
This way??

CHIANTI
And quick. Pull that curtain.

PINOCCHIO goes to where the front cloth hangs at the side of the stage.

PINOCCHIO
This one?

CHIANTI
That's it!

PINOCCHIO pulls the curtain across, the mansion disappearing from view. We are now back at the seafront.

Scene 11: The seafront/harbour

Continuing from the previous scene, PINOCCHIO and CHIANTI have escaped to the seafront.

PINOCCHIO
What do we do now?

CORNETTA enters dressed as a Cardinal, with a fake beard.

CORNETTA
(Quietly) Ciao boys and girls! ("Come stai Cornetta!") Sshh! I'm in disguise!

She bumps into CHIANTI.

CHIANTI
Sorry your holiness.

CORNETTA
Ave... Maria Callas... Gloria Estefan... Angelus... Lansbury... Oh! (stage whisper) Chianti it's me!

CHIANTI
What the fuck is wrong with you?

CORNETTA
I'm in disguise. The police clearly think we're in Placenta. I can't even go back to the studio, I've been sleeping rough. Why are you walking around with a stupid donkey?

CHIANTI
It was good enough for Jesus. Look. It's Pinocchio. Figaro turned him into a donkey.

CORNETTA
Of all the things I thought Figaro was going to do to you that wasn't even in the top ten. Oh bollocks! Geppetta and Pedro have gone off to sea to look for him. They've been gone a week. (To Chianti) Still I don't suppose you care now that you live at the mansion.

CHIANTI
No. I've quit. I'm not going back.

CORNETTA
I suppose you think you'll just start hanging out with me again like nothing happened.

CHIANTI
I suppose you think I'd want to.

A moment. CORNETTA gives CHIANTI's ears a tickle. She purrs.

CORNETTA
Well we can't go back to our studio. I'm a wanted woman.

CHIANTI
Things *have* changed. Let's go and see Cats!

CORNETTA
The film?

CHIANTI
Yeah. Have you seen the trailer? It looks fucking brilliant. They look exactly like cats. I actually can't believe how well they've caught us.

CORNETTA
You don't mind that they've got Judi Dench taking a cat role?

CHIANTI
It's called acting. It's what actors do. Cats can't act. We're not like lions.

CORNETTA
Can lions act?

CHIANTI
Oh my god. The Lion King Live Action Remake. We saw it together. Come on.

CORNETTA
No, look, we need to find Auntie and we need to get Pinoc' fixed.

CHIANTI
I suppose. You'd better call that fairy.

CORNETTA
I... don't have her number.

CHIANTI
I'm talking to Pinocchio. (She thinks, then:) *Don't* you?

CORNETTA
No.

CHIANTI
Oh. I just assumed.

CORNETTA
I've met her once.

CHIANTI
Alright. Don't pop a cyst. Pinocchio do your thing.

PINOCCHIO
Last time I tried I... I made a bit of a mess of it.

43

CHIANTI
Try!

PINOCCHIO grimaces trying to fart, a tiny little sound comes out.

CORNETTA
That's no good! Chianti, we'll have to help him. One, two, three.

They all fart, it is still not loud enough.

CHIANTI
That's still not loud enough. Boys and girls, after three, we need you all to make a big farting noise. One, two, three!

They do. PINOCCHIO, CORNETTA and CHIANTI cough and hold their noses. CHIANTI walks over to an audience member.

CHIANTI
I actually said just make a farting *noise* mate.

FATIMA enters. She has a handbag.

CORNETTA
(A bit too enthusiastic) Fatima!! (Calmer) I mean, yeah, hi.

FATIMA
Pinocchio!

CORNETTA
Yes, there's that. And we need to find Geppetta and Pedro.

FATIMA
Right. (She takes a hefty crystal ball from her handbag bag) Wondered why that was so heavy. (She puts the ball aside without even looking at it) That's better. Now...

FATIMA waves her arms and casts some kind of spell. She looks into the distance.

FATIMA
Oh my. How unusual!

CORNETTA
I know! Three women and a fully dressed man on stage at Above The Stag.

FATIMA
No listen. They've been swallowed by a whale!

CORNETTA
Free Fanny!

CHIANTI
You said that out loud.

CORNETTA
Can you *do* something?

FATIMA
My magic can't reach them.

CHIANTI
That's useless!

FATIMA
But I can sort this one out.

FATIMA casts a spell and turns Pinocchio back into a boy puppet.

CORNETTA
That was very impressive.

PINOCCHIO
It's not impressive. She just turned me back to what I was before.

FATIMA
You're very fractious. Don't shout at me young man. It's not easy, you know. I can use just enough magic to add a bit of sparkle to the story but not so much that I can simply save the day at click of my fingers and destroy all sense of drama or danger. You're going to have to rescue them.

PINOCCHIO
Fuck's sake.

CORNETTA
You said you wanted adventures.

PINOCCHIO
I meant... you know. Interrailing, or chemsex, or an escape room or something. Not swimming for miles.

CORNETTA
For god's sake she's risked her life for you.

PINOCCHIO
Alright. I'll do it! Which way do I swim?

CHIANTI
Do butterfly. It's the gay one.

FATIMA
Come on - The ocean's calm, the weather's pleasant, So off you go –no time like the present.

PINOCCHIO
Wish me luck boys and girls.

He exits. We hear a splash.

FATIMA
Well. I'll be off.

CORNETTA
Yes, of course. (beat) Wait. Do you want to... get a coffee sometime? Or, I dunno. Watch some telly?

FATIMA
Some telly? You're homeless, and I live in a magical realm.

CORNETTA
(Embarrassed) Of course.

FATIMA
That reminds me I must water the plants. (she casts a little spell) All done. Buongiorno.

FATIMA begins to exit. CHIANTI stares at Cornetta, amused.

CORNETTA
Shut up.

CORNETTA & CHIANTI exit.

FATIMA
Be brave Pinocchio! Be brave!

Scene 12: Inside the whale

A cavernous and biological space. Sounds of drips and gurgles. There are a lot of different objects about that the whale has swallowed, such as plastic debris. There are also the remains of dead fish. PEDRO is picking seaweed from GEPPETTAS hair.

GEPPETTA

Well as you can see boys and girls we're having a whale of a time. Who would have thought it would come to this. Trapped in the belly of a whale for eternity with a fool.

PEDRO

Ah Geppetta, how do you stay so young and beautiful?

GEPPETTA

Believe you me, there's more filler in here than a mid-season episode of Drag Race.

PEDRO goes rummaging among the debris.

PEDRO

We will be out in no time. And then beautiful Geppetta we will live our lives anew as only one who has faced death can do. You will emerge with a burning desire to do the things you have always wanted to do.

GEPPETTA

I tell you what, if we do escape I'm getting out of Placenta, moving to somewhere more stimulating and finding a nice gentleman. Or a gentleman. Or a man.

PEDRO

Always she is running away! Sometimes, we have to begin with what's inside us.

GEPPETTA

(Points at someone in the audiece) There's a young man there who's just remembered he hasn't douched. Oh I don't know. I suppose I might do a course. Some years ago I spent 12 weeks learning Welsh. Not the language, just the accent but it was nice to exercise the grey matter. How will we get out?

PEDRO finds a little blister pack of tablets.

PEDRO

With these! Look. Constipation relief tablets. If we scatter these about us, Free Fanny will have a great movement and we will be flushed into the shimmering sea! Ah, no. It is empty. (He finds a prosecco bottle and hands it to her) Look! It must have fallen from a yacht.

GEPPETTA

Rude not to.

JOE enters. He is dancing a tango badly and has an old cassette recorder in his hand. His clothes have shrunk. He sees the newcomers.

JOE

Gordon Bennet!

GEPPETTA

Joe! What on earth! I thought you'd gone back to Ballsall! Thank heavens you're just in time.

JOE

In time for what?

GEPPETTA

We need to populate this place! What are you doing here?

JOE

Figaro pushed me in the sea. Then before I knew it a great whale swallowed me.

GEPPETTA

And who wouldn't.

PEDRO

Well! It is not the first time I bet that you have been deep in the gut of some magnificent specimen, eh! Is a great shame, you know, you come to Placenta at such a time. Is not what it was. We had a fabulous gay club: XXS.

JOE

Did it get shut down?

PEDRO

It fell victim to its own door policy. No lesbians. No bisexuals. No trans. No gays... But one day Placenta will rise from the ashes like Joaquin Phoenix. Back on the map like your English Margate! Is not so different - we have the sea, the vintage amusement park, the xenophobic nationalism.

GEPPETTA

Dammit, Thanet!

JOE

We're going to die here ain't we.

GEPPETTA

My life's flashing before my eyes. Not even flashing. Barely a flicker.

JOE
There must have been highlights?

GEPPETTA
Oh yes, highlights, and at least one terrible perm. I did once have a terrific threesome with a pair of accountants. Taught me a lot about double entry. No you're quite right Pedro I should have let you show me more of Placenta. There must be the odd diversion.

PEDRO
Yes! I take you to the wax museum!

GEPPETTA
A wax museum, how hilarious, who have they got?

JOE
Maybe I'm in it!

GEPPETTA
No darling, famous people. Grace Kelly, Fred Astaire, Ginger Spice, maybe Cher.

PEDRO
No, it is a wax museum. A room full of candles and a beehive. And there is our music society.

GEPPETTA
Really?

PEDRO
Next week, is a concert of Norwegian piano music.

GEPPETTA
Well it's all Grieg to me.

PEDRO
(To Joe) But what is this you are doing when you come in, it looks like the tango.

JOE
That's right. Thought I'd make use of the time like, so I'm practising in case I get on Strictly.

PEDRO
But where is your passion? Your romance! Your grace!

CORNETTA pops on, dressed as the cardinal.

CORNETTA
Yes? Oh! Sorry.

She exits.

PEDRO
I am Placenta Latin American dance champion twelve years in a row.

GEPPETTA
Good heavens!

PEDRO
I show you how it is done. Signorina, will you dance with me.

GEPPETTA
Absolutely not, it's slippery and I haven't drunk enough.

JOE
Oh go on. Have a twirl.

GEPPETTA
I'll take a finger. Oh very well darlings. Pedro, do your worst.

Pedro
The tango is all about passion, lust and longing. To begin, you take your fine woman firmly like so.

He takes GEPPETTA in a hold.

PEDRO
If only we had some music.

JOE
But we have! Look, it's a cassette player like our great great grandparents would have had. It was lying about in here.

Joe switches the cassette on, music plays.

PEDRO
And so we will demonstrate.

PEDRO and GEPPETTA tango.

PEDRO
All the time you must look into your partners eyes.

And the tango turns into a...

SONG: TWO TO TANGO

PEDRO
In a bar of ill repute where Uruguay meets Argentina
A sailor slammed his Malbec on the table
He swaggered as he staggered to the sweetest signorina
She said you're drunk, he said you're right! Let's dance while I'm still able

With loose-limbed ease he taught her to go
Slow, slow, quick-quick slow
And soon she knew she'd not regret it

GEPPETTA
Oh she said, I think I get it!

BOTH
It's not just a dance, it's a connection
Oh! She said, is that your erection poking me, provoking me?
As he blushed, she said oh I'm not complaining
Why am I wet it's not even raining
Hold me, I'll hold you too,
In this moment, I love you.

GEPPETTA
If we ever reach dry land give us a wave as we pass by
We'll dance our dance from Roma to Milano
But if we're stuck forever in this whale until we die
At least I'm here with quite the man, oh baby it takes two to tango

Lead the way with grace and pride
We go Step, step, drag and slide
What is this feeling, quite unplanned?
I'm just starting to understand

BOTH
It's not just a dance, it's a connection
Oh! She said, is that your erection poking me, provoking me?
As their feet found the beat, their hearts were skipping
Jesus she said, I'm fucking dripping
Hold me, I'll hold you too,
In this moment, I love you, I love you, I love you!

GEPPETTA
(Aside) Bambinos and bambinas, I think I've just experienced what the little pop gays refer to as "all the feels". (To the chaps) Oh but what does any of it matter, we are doomed!

JOE
You know what I do when things look bleak? I sing.

GEPPETTA
No! We tried that. Ended up in a fucking whale. No this is it. No one is going to rescue us are they boys and girls.

PINOCCHIO enters, he wears tiny speedos that match the shorts he has worn previously.

PEDRO, JOE and GEPPETTA
Pinocchio!

PINOCCHIO
That's my stupid name! This is brilliant!

GEPPETTA
It is?

PINOCCHIO
I found my hat!

He retrieves it from somewhere among the debris.

GEPPETTA
Look at you there! I'm reminded of the time I was nearly selected to be surrogate mother for Tom Daley. Oh yes, I made it to the final round. I told them I was perfectly comfortable with a turkey baster, but they took a look up me and said it would probably take a water cannon. Tom was very sweet about it. He said he was just the same.

JOE
But – but now you're stuck here too. I've tried climbing out but I keep slipping. Everything's so slimy.

PEDRO
Perhaps it is a sperm whale.

JOE
We need a big wooden pole or something like that to hold on.

A "ping" sound as all four of them have the same, obvious thought.

PINOCCHIO
That's it! Ask me a question.

PEDRO
What is the capital of Italy.

PINOCCHIO
Nairobi!

PINOCCHIOs penis starts to grow.

JOE
Who won the FA Cup last year?

PINOCCHIO
The Cock Destroyers!

GEPPETTA
Am I Prince Andrew's type?

PINOCCHIO
No, you're far too young for him!

The penis continues to grow.

GEPPETTA
Have I been a good mother to you?

PINOCCHIO
You'd win awards!

GEPPETTA
This will take ages. We need some help. Boys and girls, can anyone ask Pinocchio a question?

They do. Pinocchio lies. The penis is enormous and fills the stage.

PINOCCHIO
Ok everyone, grab hold of my shaft. Hold tight, stay steady, and away we go!

Scene 13: The seafront/harbour

Figaro is making a speech. A crowd can be heard responding wildly.

FIGARO

Oh yes, dear Placentians! Our town is not what it was! Enemies of the people live among us! Disgusting English immigrants like Joe, who would turn our great, masculine, family-friendly sport of football into an episode of RuPaul's drag race!

JOE enters covered in seaweed. He has the cassette recorder with him. He sees what's going on and hides in a corner.

Debauched so-called artists like Cornetta, twisting the way we see the world! Lazy layabouts like Pedro dragging down our economy.

Pedro enters covered in seaweed and holding a suitcase covered in barnacles and limpets. He sees what's going on and joins Joe in the corner.

Dangerous interlopers like Fatima, practising magic under our noses! Liberal Roman elites like Geppetta, who makes puppets that mock our very religion, and who looks down on us even though she is nothing but a common criminal!

Geppetta enters covered in seaweed. She sees what's going on and joins the men.

And worst of all – Pinocchio! The walking dead. Wood, come to life to commit who knows what atrocities!

Pinocchio enters covered in seaweed. He waves to the others and indicates to the other side of the stage and, ducking down, they all cross the stage right in front of FIGARO who doesn't notice them. They exit the other side.

Be on the lookout for these rogues! Do your duty. Love your town. Bring them all to me. Ahahahaha!

Scene 14: A church

A traditional old church, dilapidated and creaky. Coloured light falls from the windows. A giant crucifix looms over us. CORNETTA, still dressed as a Cardinal, is sketching. CHIANTI is looking bored.

CORNETTA
Ciao boys and girls. (*"Come stai Cornetta"*) And also with you.

CHIANTI brattishly knocks the sketch book out of her hand.

CORNETTA
Chianti! Stop it.

CHIANTI
I'm bored. Why do we have to stay here?

The door rattles. Someone trying to get in.

CORNETTA
There's someone coming.

They both hide. GEPPETTA, PEDRO. JOE and PINOCCHIO enter. They are still covered in seaweed. JOE has the little cassette recorder with him. PEDRO still has the suitcase.

PEDRO
(whispering) We will be safe here. No one will think of looking for us in a church.

CORNETTA and CHIANTI come out of hiding.

PEDRO and GEPPETTA
(whispering) Your holiness.

CORNETTA
(whispering) Aunty it's me.

GEPPETTA
(whispering) Cornetta! Why are we whispering?

CORNETTA
(whispering) What did you say?

GEPPETTA
(whispering) Why are we- (Normal) Why are we whispering? Oh but don't you look nice in your little hijab darling, it reminds me of my travels in Japan.

CORNETTA
You made it back!

PINOCCHIO
Me and Joe built a raft from stuff in the sea.

PEDRO
Thanks be to God for single-use plastics.

GEPPETTA
Take that, Greta Thunberg! There's a girl who'll be dead at 27 from a crack habit.

CHIANTI hisses and raises her claws at GEPPETTA. They hear FIGARO singing Mozart's Queen of the Night aria.

PINOCCHIO
It's Figaro!

GEPPETTA
Magic Flute I think.

PINOCCHIO
No, it's *Figaro*.

They all hide. FIGARO enters.

FIGARO
Ahahahahaha! Welcome to the church of Saint [name of audience member]. While my angry minions search for those rogues, I'm here to meet a mysterious cardinal who helped me acquire something rather special.

GEPPETTA, JOE, CORNETTA, PINOCCHIO, PEDRO, CHIANTI
A cardinal!

FIGARO
I have a little transaction to complete. A little money to hand over.

GEPPETTA, JOE, CORNETTA, PINOCCHIO, PEDRO, CHIANTI
Money!

GEPPETTA pushes CORNETTA out.

GEPPETTA
You're a cardinal and he's going to give you money!

FIGARO
Cardinal! There you are! You're early.

CORNETTA
Blessed are the... punctual.

FIGARO
Now, Cardinal, have you met the boys and girls? Don't get excited it is merely a saying. These are all of age, some of them excessively so. Occasionally there's a dead one left when lights come up and we have to

smuggle them into Chariots the back way then make an anonymous phone call to the police. (Aside) There's something suspicious about this cardinal. I don't know what it is but there's something not quite right about her. (To Cornetta, suspicious) How long have you been in the Church?

CORNETTA
Ooh, quarter of an hour?

FIGARO
Aha, very droll. Tell me, what is Jesus' favourite animal?

CHIANTI
A cat.

CORNETTA
(To Chianti) Shut up! (To Figaro) He doesn't have a favourite animal. He made all the animals as part of his creation.

FIGARO
Ah. Then what of those creatures that were bred only recently by man?

CORNETTA
That's half the back row.

FIGARO
Like dogs, for example. What about a cockerpoo?

CORNETTA
Neither, thank you. Now signore, how about this money.

FIGARO
Such haste. But alright. I thank you for your involvement in my little venture. The pope's buttocks arrived in perfect condition.

CORNETTA
The pope's buttocks?

FIGARO
Yes! It will look fabulous over my headboard.

PINOCCHIO, GEPPETTA, PEDRO, CHIANTI
The painting!

FIGARO
Ah, to finally get my hands on the pope's buttocks! No need to be coy. Quite the thing, smuggling a painting from the Vatican.

CORNETTA
Well you know what they say. If anyone can, the Vatican.

FIGARO
Do they say that?

CORNETTA
They should, it's fucking brilliant.

FIGARO
Fair's fair. I'll give you what I owe.

He gets a brown paper bag out of his larger bag.

FIGARO
Here we are..

He goes to hand CORNETTA the bag but pulls it back and pulls a gun out.

FIGARO
Ha! Pay you? As if! You know too much. What if you blurted it out in confession? Oh no. I'm going to kill you.

He points the gun at CORNETTA. PINOCCHIO and PEDRO come out of hiding.

PEDRO and PINOCCHIO
Oh no you won't.

FIGARO
Piccolo! Oh yes, I will.

PEDRO and PINOCCHIO wrestle the gun from FIGARO. Eventually they succeed. With him held, CORNETTA punches him in the face before helping to hold him. As PEDRO and CORNETTA hold FIGARO, PINOCCHIO takes the gun and points it at him.

PINOCCHIO
Don't move. You stole the Pope's painting. We have it on tape!

FIGARO
What? No you don't.

JOE has the cassette recorder in his hand and presses play. We hear Figaro's voice. "Smuggling a painting out of the Vatican..."

JOE
What should we do with him now?

PINOCCHIO
What do you think boys and girls? Into the sea?

As the audience are agreeing, FIGARO lunges and pushes the crucifix. It starts to fall very slowly. JOE is directly in its path.

GEPPETTA, CORNETTA, PEDRO, CHIANTO
Joe!!!

PINOCCHIO turns and sees. He pushes JOE out of the way just in time – and the crucifix falls on Pinocchio, knocking him to the ground and crushing him.

EVERYONE
Jesus Christ!

As they stare at PINOCCHIO...

FIGARO
Sayonara, lowlifes.

FIGARO exits. PEDRO grabs the gun from where it has fallen beside PINOCCHIO and brandishes it proudly.

PEDRO
Not so fast you egregious shitwagon!

PEDRO runs out in chase of FIGARO. We hear five loud shots. Then silence. Then a sixth shot.

GEPPETTA
And that's six. Always count the shots darlings.

There is now a loud splash. GEPPETTA turns her attention to PINOCCHIO.

GEPPETTA
My son!

JOE
Pinocchio!

CORNETTA
He'll be alright won't he? I mean he's just made of wood right? Right Pinoc'?

CORNETTA gives him a little shake.

CORNETTA
Oh my god. He's come to pieces.

She lifts up a wooden arm, detached. CHIANTI starts playing with something.

CORNETTA
Chianti! Put his penis back!

CHIANTI continues to play with the little wooden, non-erect penis. It rolls under a seat in the front row.

CORNETTA
Excuse me darling can you just grab that penis for me. No, the prop.

She takes the penis and hands it to JOE who sadly strokes it. FATIMA enters.

FATIMA
What a glorious day! But deary me
What on earth is the matter now? Oh – I see.

GEPPETTA
Is that all you can say?

FATIMA
You think that's where the story ended?
Fear not! Least said, soonest mended.
Pinocchio, you've been brave, kind and true
Now be alive – and be human, too.

She waves her wand. There is a flash of light and PINOCCHIO rises. He feels his body in wonder and delight. Then his hand reaches his crotch and he looks panicked. FATIMA takes the penis from JOE, puts it in PINOCCHIO's shorts and waves her wand again.

JOE hugs and kisses PINOCCHIO.

JOE
You feel soft! You feel warm!

PINOCCHIO
What, like poo?

JOE
No. Like a... human. Like a man. Like a sexy gorgeous human man!

GEPPETTA has picked up CORNETTA's sketchbook and looks at what she's drawn.

GEPPETTA
What a lovely sketch.

CORNETTA takes the book from her.

CORNETTA
Oh, it's... just a doodle.

GEPPETTA
It's excellent.

CORNETTA
Thanks. (beat) Do you know that's the first time you've said anything nice about my art since we've been in Placenta.

GEPPETTA
Well, there you go. You're improving!

CORNETTA
I suppose you'll be wanting to get back to Rome. Set up our stall.

GEPPETTA
Drop my knickers in another hall... Yes, I can barely afford the train but I suppose there's nothing keeping me here.

PEDRO enters with the gun. GEPPETTA runs to him.

GEPPETTA
Pedro!

PEDRO
I have not seen one of these rare seven-bullet revolvers in many years! And yet it was completely empty! Oh, but did you hear the little kiddies playing with firecrackers outside! They gave Figaro such a great fright he fell into the harbour and immediately, splat, he is hit by a speedboat.

Everyone cheers.

GEPPETTA
Oh you wonderful man.

PEDRO
Yes yes but now, before we were interrupted by that nincomshit, I was going to give you something.

PEDRO fetches the suitcase he was carrying when he first entered the church.

PEDRO
I saw it bobbing in the sea on the way back. It has a beautiful gold G on it. Pedro, I say to myself, Geppetta will love this.

GEPPETTA
How funny, it's just like my old monogrammed suitcase that we stowed the three million euros in.

CORNETTA
Open it!

CORNETTA and GEPPETTA try to open the case, but can't. JOE steps up and forces it open. It's full of money. Everybody cheers.

GEPPETTA
We're rich! Pedro Thank you. What better way to start spending it than on a wedding.

JOE
I haven't asked him yet!

GEPPETTA
Not yours darling. Mine.

PEDRO
You're getting married?

GEPPETTA
That's rather up to you. Sometimes one fails to see that we have something rather special right in front of us.

PEDRO
I say this all along, your bosom is magnifico.

GEPPETTA
Well, thank you, but, or indeed *therefore*: will you marry me?

PEDRO
Marry you! My dream! (Then, sadly) But one man is not enough for you.

GEPPETTA
Don't worry about that darling, I've had plenty.

PEDRO
Then there plenty of happy, lucky men in this world. But none is so happy and lucky as Pedro. Yes, yes I will marry you!

They kiss.

GEPPETTA
But listen, I'm rather old fashioned. I like to try before I buy. Pedro, take me to the nearest hotel! Goodbye boys and girls. See you at our wedding!

GEPPETTA and Pedro exit.

CHIANTI
Must be fucking desperate.

CORNETTA
Pedro's actually very sweet.

CHIANTI
Exactly. He must be fucking desperate.

CORNETTA
I suppose you want to get back to Rome?

CHIANTI
That was before I clapped eyes on Petruchio.

CORNETTA
Petruchio?

CHIANTI
My hunky tom-cat.

CORNETTA
You've got a boyfriend! Can I see?

CHIANTI
Alright come on but keep your distance. I don't want to put him off.

CORNETTA
Ciao boys and girls!

CORNETTA and CHIANTI exit

JOE
I guess it's just us left then.

FATIMA
Don't mind me.

PINOCCHIO
I guess we'd better start planning our wedding.

JOE
Is that what you want?

PINOCCHIO
I don't know. It's what the hero does at the end of a pantomime isn't it? I've lived my whole life in a pantomime. I don't know anything else.

JOE
Yeah but what happens when it ends? What happens when it's just us? When the boys and girls have moved on from this show to... Ibsen in German at the Barbican or something.

PINOCCHIO
I want to see the world. But I want to see it with you.

JOE
Where do you want to go first?

PINOCCHIO
I don't know. I don't know anything about anywhere.

JOE
We could start with Walsall.

PINOCCHIO
Absolutely not Walsall. What about India? That sounds appropriate.

JOE
Why?

PINOCCHIO
Cos I'm really "India".

They kiss.

JOE
You best come and get into me then.

They run off. Fatima steps forward to wrap things up. Music starts to play.

FATIMA
And that's where we'll leave it, when everyone's winning,
For us it's an ending, for them a beginning:
New friends, new lovers, all shiny and strange...

CORNETTA enters unseen by FATIMA. She's awkward about disturbing Fatima's rhymes.

CORNETTA
Sorry – sorry. I left my sketchbook here. I'll just...

The music stops.

CORNETTA
Look, are you bloody gay or not?

FATIMA
...yes?

CORNETTA
Right. *Thank* you. So do you want to do something about it?

FATIMA
Because I'm the first lesbian you've seen?

CORNETTA
No! Well... no. Because you're nice. (beat) I did think I was the only lesbian in town.

FATIMA
There are at least 45 registered lesbians in Placenta.

CORNETTA
Are you joking?

FATIMA
We don't make a song and dance, do we. Not like *them*. (Then, slightly warmer) Look, I've got my book group tonight. Do you want to come?

CORNETTA
Yeah!

HE'S BEHIND YOU: ELEVEN GAY PANTOMIMES

FATIMA
Then afterwards we usually all pile into the Muff.

CORNETTA
I'm sorry?

FATIMA
The Muff Bar. For a drink.

CORNETTA
Oh! Great.

FATIMA
I'll introduce you to my friends. You can... sleep with them and so on.

CORNETTA
Amazing!

FATIMA
Alright, just - bring a salad.

CORNETTA
I'll bring two!

FATIMA
Nobody likes a show-off. I'll meet you in the square at eight. Now listen, if you want to be a good lesbian, you can engage in a little stage management. Pull the front-cloth in.

CORNETTA
Right-o! Ciao boys and girls!

CORNETTA pulls the curtain in and exits. FATIMA steps forward.

FATIMA
And that's where we'll leave it, when everyone's winning,
For us it's an ending, for them a beginning:
New friends, new lovers, all shiny and strange,
Adventures to plan, a wedding to arrange.

They move into Figaro's big house in Placenta,
They live in one wing, the rest's an arts centre
With paintings and puppet shows - some of them gay,
And a gift shop and even a cat café.

A real boy - a real human! - but what does that mean?
Pain, frustration, hard work; relationships, dreams,
All in one human lifespan - I don't think he'll waste it,
That kid'll grab life by the labia and face it.

So take one last look at that sweet southern sky,
And with love, and kind wishes, safe home now - bye bye.

At the curtain call, Geppetta should be in a wedding dress.

THE END

Mother Goose Cracks One Out!

Scott Dale as Dandelion/Thor in *Mother Goose Cracks One Out!* Photo by PBGstudios.

Mother Goose Cracks One Out!

Although Mother Goose was popular in the seventies and eighties it is performed less often these days, and it's not a show either of us was familiar with. Unlike most pantomime stories, it doesn't exist outside of pantomime - the figure of "Mother Goose" pops up in earlier fairy tales but the story as we know it dates from a 1902 panto created as a star vehicle for the comedian Dan Leno.

Aside from a couple of less-than-inspiring scripts we found online we didn't have much source material to draw on. Luckily, a Fairy Godmother came to our aid in the form of the lovely Su Pollard, who was able to get hold of a script by Bill Roberton, which had belonged to the late John Inman who had made the part his own. It gave us a shape, as well as the idea for putting Mother Goose on trial at the end. (We only stole one line from it, promise – a gag about the golden egg-laying goose having eating "24 carats".)

Mother Goose Cracks One Out! is one of our favourite scripts and perhaps our best-received show, and we came to love the story – a simple Faustian tale of temptation, corruption and ultimate redemption. Almost every pantomime features a dame, but Mother Goose is the only one to build the story around her, and it was a delight and privilege to have our brilliant frequent collaborator Matthew Baldwin in the role.

2018 was the year of the Salisbury spy poisonings. In October the Supreme Court judged that Ashers Bakery in Belfast had not discriminated against Gareth Lee by refusing to ice a cake with the words "Support Gay Marriage" on the grounds that they would have refused any customer such a request. The second season of the rebooted *Queer Eye* aired, and the gay-themed film *Call Me by Your Name* had been a home-streaming hit having been released in October the previous year.

Mother Goose Cracks One Out!

By Jon Bradfield and Martin Hooper
Songs by Jon Bradfield

Characters

Thor, a good fairy.
Mephista, an evil witch. She always has her cat with her.
Mother Goose, a middle aged woman.
Tommy Goose, her son. An amiable lad-next-door type.
Amos Cleghorn, the town squire and mill owner.
Chester Cleghorn, Amos' very camp son.
Dora Cleghorn, the Mayor of Rugburn.
Priscilla, a human-sized goose. Scottish.
Townspeople, to be played by members of the company.

Mother Goose, Tommy, Amos and Chester all have North West accents. Dora too, albeit more RP. There is a brief appearance by a non-speaking bodyguard in scene 6, to be played by the actress playing Mephista. Although the fairy's real name is Dandelion, he's usually called Thor in the show so we've called him that in the script.

At a couple of points it says "badum-tsh" after a corny joke, suggesting the use of a drum-and-cymbal sound effect.

Mother Goose Cracks One Out! **was first performed at Above The Stag Theatre on 27 November 2018 with the following cast and creative team:**

Thor: Scott Dale; Mephista: Briony Rawle; Tommy Goose: Liam Woodlands-Mooney; Mother Goose: Matthew Baldwin; Chester Cleghorn: Christian Andrews; Amos Cleghorn: Christopher Lane; Priscilla: Laura Blair; Dora Cleghorn: Ellen Butler

Director: Andrew Becket; Musical Director & Orchestrator: Aaron Clingham; Vocal arrangements: Jon Bradfield & Aaron Clingham; Choreographer: Carole Todd; Assistant Choreographer: William Spencer; Designer: David Shields; Costume Designers: Robert Draper & Sandy Lloyd; Lighting Designer: Jamie Platt; Sound Designer: Nico Menghini; Casting Director: Harry Blumenau for Debbie O'Brien Casting; Casting Associate: Shaun McCourt for Debbie O'Brien Casting; Stage Manager: Andy Hill; Production Assistant: Lucas Livesey; Poster illustration: Matthew Harding; Production photography: Gaz at PBGstudios.com; Producer: Peter Bull for Above the Stag

Thanks to Toby Joyce, Gina Rose Lee, Su Pollard and Stephanie Willson.

Scene 1: A road on the outskirts of town

A male fairy enters.

THOR
There's a quaint little town it's built on three hills
With wet cobbled streets and chimneys and mills
It lies on the edge of the north west conurbation
A very minor jewel in the nation

There's a colliery band, though the mine's been dismantled
They practice for gigs but they tend to get cancelled
The youths don't have much to do but get stoned
And even the bunting is sepia-toned

The high street's all pound shops, it's on its last legs
Fine dining round here is a steak bake from Gregg's
There's no indoor crazy golf, as far as I know
They think gentrification's what trans men undergo

But it's home to our heroine Mother Goose, oh she's poor,
With a big kind heart, and feet firm on the floor
She's no Snow White or Cinders, of that there's no doubt
When Disney came calling she must have been out

And me, I'm a fairy, you'll all get to know me
My name is Dandelion - make a wish sir and blow me
I'm here to protect Mother Goose's soul
And hopefully find me some northern hole

But enough boys and girls! we've a panto to do
Can I get a cheer? And an ah? And a boo?
You've done this before boys and girls I deduce,
Now sit back and enjoy our tale of mother goose!

Thank you boys and girls, and welcome to Above The Stag Theatre's first ever 100 percent totally child-friendly pantomime! (boooo!) I know, but one of our regular and most generous supporters is an avid paedophile and he asked very nicely. We did suggest a nativity play with a real infant Jesus, but he said that babies in live theatre are quite hard to pull off.

MEPHISTA (off)
Hahahahahaha!

A crashing sound and she curses. She enters with a broomstick that's broken in two. She is a witch.

MEPHISTA
Hahahaha!

THOR
Oh look! A lovely cheerful lady having a good old chuckle.

MEPHISTA
I'm not cheerful I'm misanthropic.

THOR
Nice to meet you Miss Anthropic.

MEPHISTA
It means I hate people.

THOR
Oh but I'm not people, I'm a fairy!

MEPHISTA
A fairy? I see, What's your name?
Go on tell me so I can learn it,
I bet it's really shit and lame,
What is it. Daffodil, Lettuce or Turnip?

THOR
It's nothing like that. What do you take me for?
It's actually very butch. My name is er... Thor!

MEPHISTA
Thora. Ok.

THOR
Thor.

MEPHISTA
Yeah I heard you first time Thora.

THOR
What if it was Thora? There's surely no shame,
In having a slightly feminine name.

MEPHISTA
Where do you think you are, Hackney fucking Wick?
You'll get beat up round here.

THOR
By who?

MEPHISTA
By me with me stick. My name's Mephista. What are you doing?

THOR
I'm looking for the generic northern town of Rugburn.
I've never been to a human town before.

MEPHISTA
It's over there. I got a guidebook, you can have it,
I don't want it no more.

She hands it over.

THOR
Thanks! Why is it sticky?

MEPHISTA
My cat did a vomit on it. That's why I don't want it no more. Don't get into a flap. (She finds a woman in the audience) Hello miss. I wouldn't mind getting into your flaps.

THOR
Ew!

MEPHISTA
Oh yeah, I forget gay men are scared of vaginas. And that's before they've seen mine.

THOR reads from the guidebook.

THOR
"Rugburn is famous for its mills. Woollen mills, cotton mills, flour mills; Heather Mills visited in 2005." Is there a gay bar? I've never been to a gay bar.

MEPHISTA
There used to be, but someone wrote to the council and complained about the smell of fisting so it got shut down. I can't think who'd have written a thing like that with her special witchy pen that she got for free at a witch conference in 2014. It didn't even smell like fisting it smelled quite nice.

THOR
Why don't you like people?

MEPHISTA
Cos they're all selfish dickheads.

THOR
I bet the boys and girls aren't.

MEPHISTA
Oh yes they are.

THOR
Oh no they're not.

MEPHISTA (pointing at audience members)
This one clicks attending on Facebook events he's got no intention of going to, resulting not only in disappointment but also over-catering which is one of the leading causes of climate change. And this one promised a sexual health worker he was going to talk to everyone he'd slept with in the past two months, but he only texted the one that he didn't really fancy.

THOR
I bet he gives to charity.

MEPHISTA
Oh yeah! Three quid a month to Save the Rabbits cos a cute boy signed him up in the street. But when the call centre phoned and asked him to increase his donation to a fiver, cos there'd been a horrific rabbit accident in Preston, he said no he couldn't possibly afford it. The very next day he spent 70 quid on three pairs of complicated boxer-briefs.

THOR
There must be some good people?

MEPHISTA
Anyone can be corrupted. Tell you what, we'll we have a bet.

THOR
A bet! You're on.

MEPHISTA
There is a kind and humble woman called Mother Goose.

THOR
She was in my poem!

MEPHISTA
I bet I can turn her into a monster.

MEPHISTA offers a hand. THOR shakes it. He gets a violent noisy electric shock.

THOR
Ow! That hurt!

MEPHISTA
Quite good isn't it. Anyway, I will cast a spell to bring temptation into Mother Goose's life and she won't be able to resist. All I got to do is get her to show me some kindness, and the magic will be unleashed.

THOR
Why don't you just unleash it now?

MEPHISTA
I don't make the fucking rules, I ain't got a computer. Right I've done all my lines so I'm going to go now. Bye.

THOR
Um. Bye...

MEPHISTA points at one more audience member.

MEPHISTA
This one didn't visit his mate in hospital cos he was too busy doing chemsex with a Nazi.

She holds her broomstick together, revs it and goes off at a lick.

THOR
Oh no boys and girls! It's my very first mission
And because I'm on probation

I can't use magic until at least the intermission
So I'll need my imagination,
You'll see though, I'll manage! By the end of the show
There'll be weddings and smiles and riches all round
But now boys and girls, get set, off you go,
To Mother Goose's salon in town!

Exit.

Scene 2: Mother Goose's beauty parlour

Mother Goose's hair salon and beauty parlour. Cheap and cheerful with a few pretensions that don't quite work. There's a traditional barber's chair. TOMMY enters.

TOMMY

Hello boys and girls! My name's Tommy – that's pantomime for Thomas. I work here at my mum's unisex hair salon and beauty parlour. We straighten ladies' hair. We make gents' hair gayer. (To a man in the audience) We're even offer follicle rejuvenation sir. Thing is I've only got me mam for a colleague and she's the boss too, so will you lot keep me company? Tell you what, whenever I come on, I'll shout "Alright team!" and you can reply "Alright our kid Tommy!" Can you do that? Let's give it a shot.

TOMMY exits and enters.

Alright team! (Alright our kid Tommy). That were mint! Now I'd best get on. I work ever such long hours and I'm still very poor. (ahh) No I'm harder working and poorer than that! You see, me mum's a terrible businesswoman. She's no clue wi' brass and she's kind to a fault so she keeps giving away free haircuts to the poor.

There's a ring at the door.

TOMMY

I wonder who that is! Will I go and see?

He goes to answer the door. TOWNSPEOPLE appear. As many as possible. One has a charity collection tin.

TOWNSPERSON 1

Morning Tommy.

TOMMY

Morning townspeople. We're not open yet.

TOWNSPERSON 2

We're here to see Mother Goose. I'm collecting.

TOMMY

I was just telling the boys and girls about her. We're not sure why she's called Mother Goose but happen a plot point will soon come along to make sense of it.

SONG: HAVE YOU MET MOTHER GOOSE

Have you met Mother Goose?
Her life is a mess
But she's the kindest and best that we know
Have you met Mother Goose?
With a hug and a smile
She'll go the whole mile
She's poor but she always seems footloose
How we love Mother Goose

She brought me soup when I had the pox
She lent me a tampon, the last in the box
We trust her so much we'd give her our proxy vote
So we won't hear a word of abuse
About Mother Goose

Have you met Mother Goose? Have you met Mother Goose?
You must know Mother Goose! You should meet her!

Have you met Mother Goose?
She's the heart of the town
And there's never a frown on her face
Have you met Mother Goose?
She's hopeless with money
But she makes the place sunny
She drinks orange squash but she'll offer you juice
How we love Mother Goose

She helped me solve my Rubik's Cube
She gave me a Rolo, the last in the tube
She gave me some hair wax when I'd run out of lubricant
Now we bet you all want to seduce Mother Goose

And is it just me? I'm sure it can't be,
It's just that you see
She slightly irritating, I'm only saying
It's a price worth paying...

If there were a fight she'd fix a truce
She's like Mother Theresa without the dodgy views
Her Christmas tree is plastic but she'd like a spruce
How we love Mother, you should meet Mother,
You're gonna love Mother Goose!

MOTHER GOOSE enters as the song ends.

MOTHER GOOSE
Hello boys and girls! Oh dear I did so hope we might be friends. We'll try that one more time shall we. Hello boys and girls! What a treat! And don't you smell nice. Very fruity. It's like that special edition Mulled Wine body spray I got you from the 99p shop.

TOMMY
You said it was from the pound shop.

MOTHER GOOSE
I know, I was embarrassed. (She greets the audience) Hello sir, are you well? Hello madame, welcome. Hello sir how's your mother, has she forgiven you? But where are my manners! Who would like a sweetie!

She starts throwing sweets out.

TOMMY
Mum! You can't be giving stuff away all the time.

MOTHER GOOSE
Oh yes she can! Have you met my fabulous gay son Tommy? He's very sensible, I'm ever so proud of him.

TOWNSPERSON 2 rattles a tin.

TOWNSPERSON 2
Morning Mother Goose

MOTHER GOOSE
Morning townsperson, what beautiful singing! What are you collecting for?

TOWNSPERSON 2
I'm just saving for a rainy day.

MOTHER GOOSE
Very wise! Tommy, fetch her a cagoule! I'm joking. Here's five pounds.

TOWNSPEOPLE
Thank you Mother Goose!

The TOWNSPEOPLE scuttle off. Tommy locks the door behind them.

MOTHER GOOSE
Good boy Tommy but it's time to open up! Do you think you could open up for me?

TOMMY
I'll give it a go. (He coughs) Sometimes I feel so ever so insecure. I'm proud to be gay but I also don't want it to define me and I worry about how it might limit my social and professional life choices if I box myself in to expected behavioural norms... Right I feel better now. Oh look at the time, I'd better unlock the door!

MOTHER GOOSE
And leave it open. We can whack the heating up.

TOMMY
We've no money!

MOTHER GOOSE
Such glorious weather!

TOMMY
It's thick cloud mum.

MOTHER GOOSE
I didn't say *where*. Cheer up, you. Turn that smile dial up to eleven. We've a roof over our heads, scran in our bellies and a day of human interactions ahead of us! That is the rewarding thing about running such an establishment. Everyone leaves with a little more self-worth than when they came in. Sort of the opposite of Chariots[6].

Yes! Welcome to my little salon. Or salon, as the jingles used to have it. No but you see I'm very proud and excited boys and girls. Do you know why I'm very proud and excited? Then I'll have to tell you! I have just completed the final session of my waxing course! Very expensive it was. You could say it was a rip-off! Now, the thing is it was an online course - ever so good, 12 webinars - but I need to get some real-world practice in.

She approaches a man in the audience.

Hello sir. Might I prepare a hot little strip for you? Would you like that? What's your name sir. Hello [name]. Tommy, put [name] in the appointment book. Would you say you were particularly hairy? Do you know, I had a brief romantic entanglement with a gentleman so hirsute I've no idea to this day what age or ethnicity he was.

TOMMY
Mum!

MOTHER GOOSE
Tommy's appalled. Of course I understand most of you wouldn't dream of meeting a gentleman without first

---

[6] Chariots is a gay sauna.

knowing his age or ethnicity, not to mention his height, size of appendage, tone of voice and whether he voted leave or remain. I'm a little more old-fashioned. As my dear father used to advise, keep your mind and thighs open and enlightenment awaits. That was before he ran off to London. I can't be more specific. Somewhere south. Cauliflower. No not cauliflower. Brockley. Now if I'm going to be cutting hair all day I should warm up with a practice run!

She takes another audience member's hand and hauls him on stage.

Come with Mother Goose sir. What's your name? Boys and girls, say "hello [name]". Aren't you handsome [name] I shall take a photo of you after we've finished to put in my window. Take a seat, that's it. Now some gentlemen find the proximity of a woman hairdresser pushing up against them very stimulating so we'll give you a cape in order to hide your embarrassment or fumblings. *(She puts a cape on him)* You use very good hair dye sir it's only the streaks on your scalp give it away. Good and thick isn't it. Good for grasping onto. Tommy?

TOMMY hands her a water spray bottle.

Soon soften it up. *(She sprays him)*. Tommy?

TOMMY hands her some scissors.

Good boy! Any holiday plans [name]?

She cuts away furiously behind him and – from a hidden pocket in the back of the chair or in her overall – throws large chunks of hair clippings onto the cape.

You've a little trouble with dandruff [name].

She throws some white confetti onto the cape too.

All done! Mirror, Tommy.

Tommy hands her a mirror which has Boris Johnson's face, resplendent with messy hair, covering the glass. She shows it to the volunteer. Then reveals the mirror to the audience.

How's that sir? Happy? Give [name] a big round of applause boys and girls!

He returns to his seat.

Oh but Tommy, how lucky we are!

TOMMY
I don't even want to work in a salon.

MOTHER GOOSE
But it's the perfect job for a handsome young gay.

TOMMY
I want to make my own way in the world. I tell you what, I'd love to go work in the mill.

MOTHER GOOSE
But why?! When you have a job here and you can work with your old mum for ever and ever and ever and ever. I know why Tommy wants to work in that mill. It's because his boyfriend Chester works there. In fact, Chester is the owner's son! The squire's son no less! Just imagine, my Tommy and Chester the squire's son having Rugburn's first gay wedding.

TOMMY
I wouldn't go buying a hat just yet.

MOTHER GOOSE
Buy a hat! I'll wear me bobbly one. Do you know what I'd do if I was a woman of wealth and relative influence?

TOMMY
What's that mum.

MOTHER GOOSE
I'd instigate Rugburn's first gay pride. Because I am right proud of you Tommy, and the contribution you've made to my salon, to our community, and to this pantomime thus far.

TOMMY
Oh. Thanks mum.

CHESTER enters. He's a young man more obviously gay than Tommy.

MOTHER GOOSE
Chester!

CHESTER
Mother G!

MOTHER GOOSE
Gurfriend!

CHESTER
Gurlfriend!

CHESTER and MOTHER G do three well-rehearsed enthusiastic air kisses.

CHESTER
Oh my God though I like literally died on the way here.

MOTHER GOOSE
That's very sad to hear Chester, now say hello to the boys and girls. Some of them are gays.

CHESTER
Oh.

TOMMY
It's not like you to be shy.

CHESTER
It's just that they'll be proper snatched London gays from London.

MOTHER GOOSE
Yes but these ones are neither unkind nor aggressively successful.

CHESTER
Alright sound. Hiya boys and girls!

TOMMY
That's an outfit.

CHESTER
Thanks. Primark, women's floor ages 9 to 13. I think it's good to have something about you that makes it obvious you're gay. You never know who might be looking. That's literally the reason I got myself a boyfriend. Only joking handsome. (Kisses TOMMY) I love you.

TOMMY
(A bit embarrassed) I love you too.

CHESTER
Will you love me for ever and ever?

TOMMY
I expect so, unless something happens to Meghan Markle.

MOTHER GOOSE
But Chester you're just in time! I need someone to practise my waxing on. I've done what I can on myself but there's parts I can't get a good angle on.

CHESTER
Will it hurt?

MOTHER GOOSE
Just a smidge.

CHESTER
That's alright I got some poppers somewhere.

MOTHER GOOSE
I'll attempt what we professionals call a crack.

CHESTER
What?!

TOMMY
Oh go on.

CHESTER
I'm not even all that hairy.

TOMMY
Well...

CHESTER
You should have said if you wanted me to wax my ass.

TOMMY
It's not a big deal.

CHESTER
I'll leave it then.

TOMMY
No! You might as well as it's on offer.

CHESTER
I'll be like a teenager down there.

TOMMY
Yeah!

MOTHER GOOSE
You are kind Chester. When I attempted this on myself, I thought I'd ripped my sphincter off. Turned out to be an undigested Cheerio. Chew your food boys and girls.

CHESTER
No! I'll leave it... Me mum says hi Mother G. Here Tommy did you hear what mum's been saying?

TOMMY
Chester's mum's the mayor of Rugburn.

MOTHER GOOSE
She was always very determined. Even at school. I certainly wouldn't say pushy. Or mercenary, or ruthless or owt like that. Give her my regards.

CHESTER
Yeah anyway she says she's going to organise Rugburn's first gay pride event.

MOTHER GOOSE
Oh is she now! Well I dare say that's very showy of her. Of course she has the money and the connections. No that's a lovely, I hope it won't rain.

CHESTER
I'll need to make sure dad's out of town. I can't tell him I'm gay.

MOTHER GOOSE
I think he probably knows. Nobody heterosexual keeps a list of his top ten favourite Liz McDonald outfits stuck to the fridge.

TOMMY
Mum you can't just tell who's gay and who isn't. Gay people's as varied as straight people.

MOTHER GOOSE
Now Tommy I've seen the pictures in your gay magazines and I know that's not true.

CHESTER
It'd literally break his heart and he's under a lot of stress at the moment. Talking of dad, I meant to warn you. He's on the towpath.

MOTHER GOOSE
What's he doing there?

CHESTER
No not towpath lol. War path. I don't actually know what a war path is. The towpath's where you go if you want to give a blowy for twenty quid. Anyway, me father's after your rent money.

MOTHER GOOSE
I'll talk to him.

TOMMY
Flirt with him!

MOTHER GOOSE
I do not flirt with him! Good heavens Tommy it's been years enough since anything like that-

SQUIRE AMOS CLEGHORN enters. MOTHER GOOSE tarts her hair up a bit.

AMOS
There you are Mother Goose!

MOTHER GOOSE
Oh ha ha ha, where did you think I'd be, lazing by a pool in nothing but my bikini? I suppose you're here for me period.

AMOS
I'm here for your rent.

MOTHER
That's it. Every month and a bloody pain! (ba-dum tsh)

AMOS
A nice girl shouldn't talk like that.

MOTHER GOOSE
You're right Amos I'll try it again. (Posher voice) Every month and a bloody pain.

AMOS
Hello Chester, son!

CHESTER (quite butch)
Er yeah how-do dad.

AMOS
Getting a haircut eh? Impress the ladies? That's it. Short up top, long where it counts. Heh heh. Morning gay Tommy.

TOMMY
How do Squire Cleghorn.

AMOS
Heh heh heh his little gay voice eh! What's it like. Now listen Mother Goose. I've been very lenient.

MOTHER GOOSE
(Getting a bit handsy) Amos Clegg, Squire of our town, can I get you a brew you look agitated.

AMOS
I am agitated! I've lost Ramsbottom.

MOTHER GOOSE
Your little racing dog!

AMOS
Bugger slipped the leash as I was walking over. He must be somewhere. I don't suppose you've seen me whippet out?

MOTHER GOOSE
Well I have, Amos, as you know, many years ago. Don't need to raise it now so to speak! After all, you decided the head girl was a more suitable marriage prospect for a young man of your standing than the likes of me, and I'm sure that was for the best even if she did turn out a lesbian in the end. Sorry for calling your mum a lesbian Chester.

AMOS
How differently things might have turned out...

CHESTER
If they had, I wouldn't have been born!

MOTHER GOOSE
You're quite right Chester and then our Tommy wouldn't have had such a nice-

TOMMY
-such a nice heterosexual friend to call his own. Squire Cleghorn, if Ramsbottom doesn't show up soon I'll go look for him.

AMOS
That's very kind gay Tommy. Take Chester with you, for protection you know.

TOMMY
You what?

AMOS (bonding)
Here gay Tommy, me and Chester saw that Gary Norton show on telly last night.

TOMMY
Graham Norton.

AMOS
Pardon me for not knowing the lingo! No, hand on heart, he's very good I'll give you that. Who did he have on the couch Chester. Big-built in a nice way.

CHESTER
Chris Hemsworth, oh my god we stan.

AMOS
No no, curvy minx who does the politics. Swarthy.

TOMMY
Diane Abbott?

AMOS
That's it. Saucy. She could sit on my front bench any day.

MOTHER GOOSE
Well I think we've all learnt something there, now I suggest we make the best of the day. Lovely seeing you.

AMOS
I'm sorry Mother Goose but thing is, times is hard up at the mill, times is hard. We're this close to closing.

MOTHER GOOSE
How close.

AMOS
Very close.

MOTHER GOOSE stands very close to Amos

MOTHER GOOSE
This close?

AMOS
Even closer.

She gets closer still. AMOS is a bit bewitched by her.

MOTHER GOOSE
As close as this...?

AMOS (snapping out of it)
Like I say I'm sorry but I need your rent. Even just the last month's worth.

MOTHER GOOSE
Amos, is this about money?

AMOS
Yes!

MOTHER GOOSE
Yes the thing is, I'm just not very interested in things like money.

AMOS
Well I am and so are the people whose livelihoods depend on me. One month's rent, now, or you'll have to leave.

MOTHER GOOSE
But I've only just done me online waxing course. Six hundred quid that cost me.

AMOS
Six hundred pounds!

MOTHER GOOSE
An investment! You've got to inseminate to procreate. I'll turn things around, you'll see. Besides I don't know how to do anything else!

AMOS
I'm sure you can turn your hand anything you set your mind to. Like that actress. Versatile. You know who I mean, the saucy one. Muriel something. Stripe. Myrtle Stripe.

CHESTER
Meryl Streep.

AMOS
Aye. Saucy one. Bet you like her don't you Chester. Who's that lass you got on your wall. Chanteuse of sorts. Saucy one... Fern Britten.

CHESTER
Britney Spears.

AMOS
Britney Spice. Saucy. I got you a calendar of her didn't I. Just a knock-off one. Cos that's what he uses it for, knocking one off! Heh heh. He's got it pinned up next to his British male diving calendar. Sporty. Right. I'm off to the mill. I'll be back at lunchtime and you'll have that money or you're out.

MOTHER GOOSE
I'm closed at lunch.

AMOS
What time do you close.

MOTHER GOOSE
...What time do you have lunch?

AMOS
Just be here.

MOTHER GOOSE
What a treat! Where are you taking me.

AMOS
I suppose we could go for a meal. Not a... date of course.

MOTHER GOOSE
Of course not!

AMOS
Nothing like that. Just... for old times.

MOTHER GOOSE
Oh Amos...!

AMOS
Sunday?

MOTHER GOOSE
Are you insane? That's my day off. I spend it volunteering at the old folks home doing their hair for them they'd miss me terribly.

AMOS
Dinner then - Tuesday.

MOTHER GOOSE
I lead the Girl Guides.

AMOS
Wednesday.

MOTHER GOOSE
Brownies.

AMOS
Thursday.

MOTHER GOOSE
Flapjacks. Don't *pressure* me Amos!

AMOS
Rent it is then!

MOTHER GOOSE drops to her knees.

MOTHER GOOSE
Amos!! Please!! You'd not turf me out on the cobbles!?

AMOS
Good day.

AMOS leaves. MOTHER GOOSE stays in despair for a second then relaxes.

MOTHER GOOSE
That was quite good today I thought. Lots of energy in the room.

CHESTER
I think he's serious this time.

TOMMY
Mum. Listen. We have to make money today. No free haircuts. No gossiping with people not interested in buying. Once we've found Ramsbottom I'll hand out some flyers, see if we can drum up some customers.

MOTHER GOOSE
Yes my love. Turn up the gay a bit it's good for business. Oh Tommy what are we going to do.

There is a whooshing sound, a screech, a crash. We hear MEPHISTA say "Fuck's sake". She enters. Her broomstick is mended badly with some tape.

MEPHISTA
Hahahahaha!! *(booo)* They are so obsessed with me.

TOMMY
Get out Mephista.

69

MOTHER GOOSE
I don't know what's got into him, welcome m'love.

TOMMY
She's horrible.

MEPHISTA
Oh no I'm not!

MOTHER GOOSE
What a thing to say!

TOMMY
You just can't say anything negative can you! Sometimes the weather's shit. Sometimes people are horrible. It doesn't make you a better person just cos you can't say it.

MOTHER GOOSE
I expect she had a difficult childhood.

TOMMY
Come on Chester. And mum, remember. We're a business. Not a charity.

They go.

MOTHER GOOSE
Little trim, straighten you out, spot of colour?

MEPHISTA
Things are a bit tight.

MOTHER GOOSE
Well you'll want a doctor for that or some sort of gynaecological osteopath, but a nice little trim up top should take your mind off. Have a perch.

MEPHISTA
I'm ever so poor.

MOTHER GOOSE
That's all right I'll take fifty percent off.

MEPHISTA
You said a little trim! No I'll leave it. Even though I'd love a nice haircut I don't deserve one...

MOTHER GOOSE
It's on the house. *(She removes Mephista's hat)* Oh goodness.

MEPHISTA
I know, I got nits.

MOTHER GOOSE
You've got woodlice.

MEPHISTA
Well hurry up they'll get chilly.

MOTHER GOOSE picks up some scissors.

MOTHER GOOSE
Hold tight!

She snips frantically and loudly like Edward Scissorhands doing a hedge. After a very short time she stops and steps back. MEPHISTA now has a very smart black bob.

MOTHER GOOSE
Ta-dah.

She picks up a mirror and holds it behind Mephista's head at various angles to show her.

MEPHISTA
What the fuck are you doing.

Mephista snatches the mirror.

MEPHISTA
Oh I quite like that. No I do it's very... What would you call it.

MOTHER GOOSE
Well I suppose it's a bob.

MEPHISTA
Bob. Yeah, no. I'm going to call it Susan. Bye bye. (She pats her hair) Come on Susan. *(She goes to leave.)* But wait! I almost forgot!

MOTHER GOOSE
Yes?

MEPHISTA
You fucking stole my fucking hat.

MOTHER GOOSE
Sorry. Here you go.

MEPHISTA
But wait! I almost forgot! *(She clears her throat then speaks as if reading monotonously from a script)* You have shown to me much kindness Mother Goose. Because you have given all that you have, you will be rewarded in due course.

MOTHER GOOSE
How exciting! You don't know how and when by any chance?

MEPHISTA
No that's all I got. Anyway thanks.

70

She offers a hand to Mother Goose who shakes it. She gets a massive comedy electric shock.

MOTHER GOOSE
Oh, GOD! Ow.

MEPHISTA
Yeah sorry. Difficult childhood. Seeya bye.

MEPHISTA leaves.

MOTHER GOOSE
Rewarded! In due course! But what could it be?

TOMMY enters

TOMMY
Alright team! You won't believe this mum!

MOTHER GOOSE
You've found the world's smallest goose!

TOMMY
No. The opposite.

MOTHER GOOSE
You've lost the world's smallest goose!

TOMMY
Wait there.

TOMMY runs out.

MOTHER GOOSE
Don't be too hard on yourself! It's easily done if it's as small you say it is.

TOMMY enters leading PRISCILLA after him. She has a little sign round her neck.

MOTHER GOOSE
The world's biggest goose!

TOMMY
Look. It says "please look after this goose"

MOTHER GOOSE
The poor thing! Come on in. Come on. Do you think she has a name?

PRISCILLA
Aye it's Priscilla.

TOMMY
She can talk!

MOTHER GOOSE
Hello Priscilla, my name is Mother...

As she realises, MOTHER GOOSE squeals in delighted shock

MOTHER GOOSE
But my name's Mother Goose! Priscilla, this is fate! You and I are going to get along famously.

TOMMY
She can't stay here. It's unhygienic.

PRISCILLA
Then do some cleaning you pair of tramps.

MOTHER GOOSE gives PRISCILLA a stroke.

MOTHER GOOSE
Such soft feathers.

PRISCILLA
What are you doing?

MOTHER GOOSE
I'm feeling a little down! (Ba-dum tsh) Ha. Boys and girls we can let Priscilla stay here can't we?

PRISCILLA
What is this place?

TOMMY
It's a beauty salon. People have their hair and nails done.

PRISCILLA
You pluck them?! Help!

MOTHER GOOSE
We won't pluck you.

TOMMY
We could... at Christmas?

MOTHER GOOSE
Tommy Goose!

PRISCILLA
What are all these humans doing.

TOMMY
They're watching a pantomime. That's-

PRISCILLA
I know what a pantomime is I did Barnstaple in 2009. Aren't they a bit old for a panto?

MOTHER GOOSE
Ah well now a lot of them are homosexual so they don't grow up in the usual sense.

71

PRISCILLA
Ah shite!

MOTHER GOOSE
Are you homophobic love?

PRISCILLA
Not yet. No, there's something happening in my lower regions.

TOMMY
She can't crap in here!

PRISCILLA
Christ on a hoverboard.

MOTHER GOOSE
Does she need winding (to rhyme with wine)?

PRISCILLA
Winding?

TOMMY
Winding! (To rhyme with win)

MOTHER GOOSE
Ohhh that makes a lot more sense.

There is a loud rumble from PRISCILLA's bowels. With a terrible moan she lays an enormous gold egg.

MOTHER GOOSE
It's an Easter egg! Ha ha, bring it here and get that foil off our Tommy.

TOMMY goes to lift it.

TOMMY
It's really heavy.

MOTHER GOOSE
Oh goodie, it'll be a proper thick one like they do in Marks's. There'll be enough for the whole town!

TOMMY
I don't think it's foil... Mum I think it's gold.

MOTHER GOOSE
Don't say that, I was looking forward to a nice bit of choccy. One way to find out.

She gives the egg a kick. It makes a sound like a great bell being struck.

MOTHER GOOSE
There, typical. It's hollow.

TOMMY
Mum, don't you get it? It's gold. We're rich!

PRISCILLA
You're rich? It's my egg.

MOTHER GOOSE
Did you eat something funny?

PRISCILLA
Aye. Twenty-four fucking carrots.

TOMMY
Mum we can pay our rent – probably ten times over! You can retire, and I can learn a trade! Get my own place with Chester!

MOTHER GOOSE
Move out?! We can all live together!

PRISCILLA
I feel sick.

TOMMY
Maybe you need to do another egg?

PRISCILLA
I just shat a metal object out of me like a pervert in A&E, I'm freaking out here.

MOTHER GOOSE
Can you do a chocolate one next?

PRISCILLA
Only in the most disgusting sense. I need a vet!

MOTHER GOOSE
You shall have your own personal vet! And a room of your own! That horrible nice lady was right - my kindness has been rewarded and you are my reward! Oh boys and girls, only good can come from this!

BLACKOUT

Scene 3: A road on the outskirts of town

MEPHISTA has a large book of spells, and a newt. She puts the book down and pokes the newt in the eye.

MEPHISTA
Hello nobs and twats. (Booo!) Yeah keep doing that it goes right to me clit. Why does every magic potion need a newt's eye? They're a bitch to get out... Shit I've squished it. *(Picking up the book)* What else do I need? A clammy shrivelled penis, untouched for many a year. Where am I going to find a clammy shrivelled penis untouched for many a year?

She looks at the audience and walks over to someone in the front row.

MEPHISTA
Sir.

THOR enters

THOR
Mephista! My sister from another mister.

MEPHISTA
If you say that again I'll cut you.

THOR
Your negativity won't get me down. I am having such a buzz in Rugburn town! I got a phone. I got Grindr, I completed Grindr, I got Hornet which is the same guys but claiming to be younger. I got shouted at by a lady in a public toilet. I learnt the signs for male and female toilets. Oh and the food! Chips and gravy. Tripe. And something called dripping.

MEPHISTA
I like dripping. *(Indicates the woman she fancies)* So does she, she's doing it now cos of her feelings about me. What's your name nice lady? Hello. Just so you know, when you and me have a baby, we're just adopting. I don't want to be bothering some gayboy for his semen. If I wanted gay semen I'd run a cloth around the urinals here. Though I think the members get first dibs... (To THOR) So, you're not exactly paying attention to the Mother Goose thing.

THOR
Well, we all know she's good! Just after we made our bet, that old lady Mrs Protheroe was crossing the road when the bottom fell out of her bag-for-life and her groceries went everywhere.

MEPHISTA
What a shame for the stupid old bat,
I cannot think what could have caused that

THOR
The one who did the rhyme did the crime!

MEPHISTA
Oh no you got me. At this rate I am never going to get an MBE for services to the community.

THOR
Well anyway, Mother Goose rushed out her beauty parlour, leapt into the road, stopped the traffic and saved Mrs Protheroe and her groceries!

MEPHISTA
You ain't seen her since?

THOR
I lost two weeks to crystal meth and I had to finish watching Queer Eye. Why, what's happened?

MEPHISTA
She's moved to a massive warehouse conversion
The glassware's Venetian, the carpets are Persian,
And everything's gold from the lamps to the lav,
As warehouses go it's fit for a chav
And she's starting to change, the seeds have been sown,
She's going to get mean – she'll end up alone!

THOR
If she changes a bit it'll only be fleeting
And you can't meddle Mephista! That's cheating!
But still boys and girls, something needs to be done
I'll befriend Mother Goose - and her handsome son!

MEPHISTA
Oh yeah? Check your instructions, you'll see they instruct
That those in your care are not to be fucked
So keep it in your pants, or at least use your hand,
Or you'll be sent back to fairy land!

THOR
Aw!

MEPHISTA
But I haven't got time for titty-tattle I need to get more bits for me potion, I'm going to have to go to the fucking wholefoods. They don't like me there. Bye.

She picks up her cat and gets on her broomstick and jets off.

THOR
If this was a proper fairy tale
It would probably be foretold

That a magical swan picks me up and sets sail
For the wonderful warehouse of gold
But for me it's the bus if it's not on diversion,
I'll see you at the Golden Warehouse Conversion!

Scene 4: The golden warehouse conversion

Everything is very bling. MOTHER GOOSE sings, with TOMMY and PRISCILLA on backing vocals.

SONG: RICH

Think of all the years, the tiny flat above the shop
Working till I dropped, too tired for dreams
Empty little cupboards, I've not had nowt to hoard
But now I've been rewarded, so it seems…

Who'd have thought I'd see this day!
I'll probably give most away
I don't need much, pay off my debts
I don't need a lot to live
I won't get posh, don't like polenta
I'll fund a nice community centre
And if they name it after me
That's their prerogative

But then I say, it might be nice
To holiday just once or twice
A month, and buy a little place
in Cos or Corfu

We're gonna be rich, rich, rolling in it
Dripping in diamonds and loaded and shit
Filthy dirty wealthy having a ball
But it won't change me at all!

I'm hardly Kim Kardashian
I'm barely into fash-i-on
I'll keep the friends I've always had
I won't be a stuck up cow

I've never put on airs and graces
Worn a posh hat to the races
It's not me it's not my style
And it's not gonna change me now

But then again it's kinda sweet
To live upon a better street
And walk past Asda on my way to
Waitrose instead

We're gonna be rich, rich, rolling in cash
Dripping in diamonds and ever so flash
Stinking reeking wealthy walking tall
But it won't change me at all

I've always been one of life's survivors
Now I can wipe my bum with fivers
I can be rich and I can be nice
Like JK Rowling or Bill Gates and his wife

Rich benevolent rich benevolent
Bitch irrelevant bitch irrelevant bitch
I mean rich
But it won't change me at all!

MOTHER GOOSE
Boys and girls! Welcome to my golden warehouse conversion. We've got all the mad cons. A rain shower. A jacuzzi bath. A toilet. Is that the word?

TOMMY
Is what the word?

MOTHER
Toilet. What do our class of people call it? Loo? Lavatoire? WC?

TOMMY
Why don't we ask the boys and girls?

MOTHER
Clever boy! Hello young man, what do *you* call the smallest room? (Get answer) Tommy write that down so as to remind us never to call it that.

The doorbell rings. TOMMY opens the door. CHESTER enters and looks at the place.

CHESTER
OMG Mother G! My wig is snatched! Usually you only get to see inside homes like this if you go on Grindr in Didsbury.

MOTHER GOOSE
Chester love! Come in! Shoes.

CHESTER
Shoes?

MOTHER GOOSE
This rug's come all the way from the Trafford Centre I don't want it mucking.

TOMMY
Mum-

CHESTER
I don't mind.

75

TOMMY
It's just it's going to slow everything up if people have to take their shoes off every time they come on.

CHESTER
Oh yeah. I'm not good at laces.

MOTHER GOOSE
I'm only giving the King Lear of female roles here but no no, you worry about the supporting cast and their footwear.

TOMMY
Do you want a beer?

CHESTER
Ooh butch! But actually babe I haven't come to see you. Thing is Mother G yeah, can we have that rent you owe us?

MOTHER
You must be a bit muddled lovey. I own this place outright. I shouldn't have said that, I can hear millennials grinding their teeth in the back row.

CHESTER
But you owe six months from the old place.

MOTHER GOOSE
Oh Chester, there's more to life than money.

CHESTER
That's easy for you to say. You're more loaded than a Stockwell bottom on a bank holiday Monday.

MOTHER GOOSE
Tell you what, why don't you and our Tommy take this, get a taxi to Manchester and have a nice night out on Canal Street.

MOTHER GOOSE thrusts two fifty-pound notes at him.

CHESTER
A hundred pounds! Thanks Mother G.

TOMMY
I don't want to go to Manchester. I hate all that scene stuff.

CHESTER
Come on it'll be a laugh. There's some right bops out at the moment.

PRISCILLA
I'll come.

MOTHER GOOSE
No love, Canal Street's all gay bars and nightclubs, it's for dancing and such.

PRISCILLA
I like dancing.

CHESTER
Do yer Priscilla?

Music plays. Something urban. PRISCILLA dances splendidly and enthusiastically.

MOTHER GOOSE
No love.

PRISCILLA
I'm so bored!

MOTHER GOOSE
You're just very precious to us. We don't want you getting goose-napped.

CHESTER
Come on Tommy. I got pills.

PRISCILLA
I want a pill.

MOTHER GOOSE
No!

PRISCILLA
Just a half!

MOTHER GOOSE
No!! *To TOMMY)* Hold on love, I just remembered. I got you this!

She picks up an expensive looking carrier bag and takes out a very small tight fitting, cropped, bright pink and shiny t-shirt. It might have "Miss Vanjie" written on it. TOMMY takes trying to look grateful. MOTHER GOOSE holds it up onto his body.

CHESTER
Yass queen.

MOTHER GOOSE
Put it on then.

TOMMY
I can't wear this can I boys and girls?

Yes!

MOTHER GOOSE
Aren't you good. Have a Ferrero Rocher.

She hands an audience member a Ferrero Rocher. Tommy takes off his shirt and puts the t-shirt on.

MOTHER GOOSE
I bought you these and all.

She hands him a tiny pair of gold shorts.

CHESTER
Where'd you get them?

MOTHER GOOSE
Well, after I bought the t-shirt I started getting all sorts of Facebook advertisements. I've got you a pair of underpants somewhere that look like a satsuma net. Put them shorts on then.

TOMMY
I dunno.

CHESTER
FML babe put them on.

TOMMY starts to take his trousers off.

MOTHER GOOSE
Chester. By the way. As it happens. You don't have your mother's number?

CHESTER
I thought you didn't like her.

MOTHER GOOSE
Not like her! Not like our Mayor! My old bestie from school! Us ladies of the higher echelons of the Court of King Caractacus like to lunch together. I'm going to invite her for a bite of Viennetta.

CHESTER
Fair enough!

CHESTER pings her his mum's number. TOMMY now has the shorts on. He looks uncomfortable.

MOTHER GOOSE
There now. See you later boys!

TOMMY and CHESTER start to exit but TOMMY stops.

TOMMY
No, I'm not going. Sorry Chester.

CHESTER
What?

TOMMY
It's not right us flashing the cash, we never earned a penny of it. Besides, don't you think there's something very suss about all this?

MOTHER GOOSE
It's karma. Our reward for being nice people. It's our true destiny.

TOMMY
Life doesn't work like that. Come on, a magic *goose* turns up at the salon of someone called Mother *Goose*?

CHESTER
I'm called Chester and I once got fisted by a guy *from* Chester, I didn't get all weird about it. Babes, it's a night out. You deserve it. If you can't love yourself how in hell you gonna love somebody else?

TOMMY
It's not my thing.

CHESTER
Some gay you are.

TOMMY
Well at least I'm out!

CHESTER
Well at least I'm out to myself!

MOTHER GOOSE
Ooh Chester very good.

CHESTER
IKR

TOMMY
Well I'm sorry I'm not good enough for you.

CHESTER
Well I'm sorry I'm not boring enough for you.

He starts to leave. MOTHER GOOSE coughs.

MOTHER GOOSE
If you're not going into Manchester you won't be needing that hundred love will you.

CHESTER hands her the money back and leaves.

TOMMY
I'm going to my room.

He exits.

MOTHER GOOSE
Well how do you like that Priscilla? (She starts to pick up TOMMY's clothes) I don't expect many women of my wealth and standing go about picking up clothes off the floor themselves, eh?

PRISCILLA
How do you think I feel? I'm goose royalty.

MOTHER GOOSE
"Priscilla, queen of..." It doesn't quite roll off the tongue. Now, it must be eggy-weg time!

PRISCILLA
If I do another egg today I'll prolapse.

MOTHER GOOSE
You're a bird. It's what you're for! At least until it's time to eat you!

They both gasp.

MOTHER GOOSE
Boys and girls that was uncharacteristic of me, but rather than give thought to such a change in my behaviour I'll squish it down into the recesses of my er...

PRISCILLA
Memory.

MOTHER GOOSE
That's it. I'm sorry Priscilla. Do you know what I need?

PRISCILLA
Aye but pity the man given the task.

MOTHER GOOSE
A butler! But where would I find one. *(to the man she spoke with earlier)* Young man, would you fancy entering my service?

The doorbell chimes. MOTHER GOOSE looks to the audience or someone to answer it. No one does.

MOTHER GOOSE
I'll get it shall I.

She answers it. THOR enters, dressed as a butler.

MOTHER GOOSE
Good morrow young man. Can you tell me where I might find a butler?

THOR
A butler? But I'm a butler!

MOTHER GOOSE
Alexa must have been listening!

THOR
My name's Thor. Like the god.

MOTHER GOOSE
Like a god!! Shoes.

THOR
Are we doing that?

MOTHER GOOSE
Apparently not.

THOR (twirling)
Oh it's the goose!

He gives PRISCILLA a stroke. She likes it.

MOTHER GOOSE
Careful with that! I mean, with *her*. Right, I'll do your job interview. First question - what is the correct way to address a very fine and special lady?

THOR
"Hello Mother Goose"?

MOTHER GOOSE is tickled pink by this and feels very flirted with.

MOTHER GOOSE
Aha aha ahahahahaha! Why don't we try some more *personal* questions. What sort of things do you say while making love?

THOR
I'm sorry?

MOTHER GOOSE
No that won't do at all.

THOR
I'm just not that way inclined.

MOTHER GOOSE
Even worse.

THOR
Perhaps I shouldn't have come.

MOTHER GOOSE
That depends on where!

THOR
I think I've made a mistake.

MOTHER GOOSE
It's no mistake! I *wanted* you up the back way!

THOR
What?

MOTHER GOOSE
What?

THOR
Are you alright?

MOTHER GOOSE
I don't know.

THOR
Look at this place! You'll have men flocking to you like seagulls to chips.

MOTHER GOOSE
I'm more than my money!

THOR
Of course you are!

MOTHER GOOSE
When can you begin?

THOR
Right away.

MOTHER GOOSE
You won't leave me?

THOR
Of course not. What shall I start with?

MOTHER GOOSE
How about the scene change. Bye bye boys and girls!

Scene 5: The goods yard of the mill

It is very run down. Bags of flour, an old cartwheel, a couple of tyres. A rope and pulley for raising things up to an overhead warehouse. A couple of sacks of wheat are suspended from it. CHESTER is sat among the flour bags playing a game on his phone. He looks up.

CHESTER

Hey boys and girls! This is our old mill, like you see in northern episodes of Who Do You Think You Are.

AMOS (Off)

Ramsbottom! Heel! Heel!

AMOS enters dragging Ramsbottom the dog with him and carrying a huge stack of envelopes and papers. Ramsbottom is an awkward old thing, a stuffed dog mounted on wheels.

AMOS

Oh dear oh dear.

CHESTER

What's up our dad the squire?

AMOS

Bills! Invoices! A GDPR fine! Things are bleak...[7]

DORA enters. Smartly dressed and wearing her mayoral chain.

DORA

Now listen I can't stop. Chester!

CHESTER

Hiya mum.

AMOS

If it isn't my former wife Dora, local businesswoman and our lady mayoress.

DORA

Lady Mayoress? I'm the mayor!

AMOS

Oh you've had a promotion have you? You might have said you were coming this early.

DORA

Funny, I used to say that to you. (Takes out her phone) Sorry, must take this. (Into phone) Yes? Yes. (Hangs up) Chester darling, a little something. (She hands him some tickets)

CHESTER

Kylie tickets oh my god WIG![8] (butching up) I mean er right yeah thanks sound.

AMOS

Kylie eh! Saucy. I expect you like her too Dora now that you're a lesbian.

DORA

Do *you* fancy every woman you see?

AMOS

Yes.

DORA's phone rings.

DORA

Must take this. (Into phone) I'll be there right away.

Dora exits. After about five seconds she comes back on, no longer on the phone.

DORA

Crisis averted. Well now, good to see the old place is as it was. So nice that in this ever-changing world some things are still the same as they were twenty years ago. No that's unfair, it's dustier.

AMOS

There's nowt wrong with tradition Dora, I say there's nowt wrong with tradition.

DORA

Embrace change, Amos! Embrace diversity. A flour mill in this day and age and one that only makes plain white flour!

AMOS

It's been good enough for folk for the last seventy years.

DORA

Old and white is out, haven't you heard? But then you never were one for variety were you. Downstairs or up.

---

[7] The European Union's General Data Protection Regulation came into force in May 2018, with many organisations scrambling to make sure they were compliant in their use of personal data.

[8] To be so "shook" that one's wig has flown off.

CHESTER
How's business Mum? Still plenty of dogs need grooming?

DORA
He's asking after my grooming business boys and girls. It's doing rather well as it happens. Yes, Dora's "Doggie Style" is in high demand in all the better households. That mutt of yours could use a good brushing.

AMOS
Ramsbottom might sniff the odd arsehole but he's not a poofter.

DORA
Now listen I'm in a rush. I'm seeing a dentist at five, a doctor at six and a masseuse at eight.

CHESTER
What's wrong?

DORA
Ah, no, by seeing I mean dating. It's just more efficient to line them up of an evening and get it out of the way. Amos, you'll have heard about Rugburn's very first Pride.

CHESTER
It's a... parade dad. A carnival!

AMOS
Tits and feathers eh? No wonder he's excited.

DORA
Think what a good business opportunity it could be.

CHESTER
We could have a float!

AMOS
Always thinking of the business! He was listening to a "playlist" of Eurovision songs the other day so he'd have something to talk about when we start selling flour in Europe.

DORA
I'll put you down for a float. Two hundred deposit and the other eight a week before.

AMOS
A thousand pounds? What's the float made of? Bitcoins?

DORA
Always so tight!

AMOS
I bloody am well not.

DORA
You bloody am well are!

AMOS
Don't be arguing in front of the boy he doesn't like.

CHESTER
No I fucking don't!

DORA & AMOS
Mind your fucking tongue!

DORA
Anyway, that's me. I'm lunching with Mother Goose of all people! She'll be busy with a tin opener no doubt. Bye Chester love.

DORA exits

AMOS (Not very convincing)
Your mother's a very... sensitive soul Chester. She's still getting over me in her way. That's why she can seem a bit tough on me at times...

CHESTER
You know I love you dad, yeah?

AMOS
Lunch with Mother Goose though! Mother Goose'll spend a pretty penny on that.

CHESTER
Yeah, well they're rich now aren't they. They've got that goose that lays golden eggs.

AMOS
A real goose or a metaphorical goose?

CHESTER
It's got nowt to do with the weather dad!

AMOS
Then that's the answer lad, that's the answer! We'll get that goose.

CHESTER
Steal her?

AMOS
Reclaim our debt!

A whooshing sound and a crash. MEPHISTA enters with her CAT

MEPHISTA
Hahahahaha!

AMOS
It's that weird old coot.

MEPHISTA
My friends call me Mephista.

AMOS
What friends!

MEPHISTA
Shirley Bassey. Nick Jonas. I'm not gonna list them. Martin Bashir. Anyway. What do you want?

AMOS
What do I want? You came here.

MEPHISTA
Oh yeah. If I do a sneeze in the flour will I spoil it?

AMOS
Yes.

MEPHISTA
I'll see what I can muster up.

Her cat hisses at RAMSBOTTOM. RAMSBOTTOM growls. MEPHISTA goes to kick RAMSBOTTOM

AMOS
I'd thank you to keep your cat away from my Ramsbottom.

MEPHISTA
My cat ain't interested in that scally wanker.

MEPHISTA clicks her fingers and the bags of flour hanging from the pulley descend and land on AMOS' head.

AMOS
Jeepers! What could have made that fall? I tethered it myself.

MEPHISTA cackles

MEPHISTA
Anyway I've come to help you.

AMOS
You want to invest in the factory?

MEPHISTA
I'd rather sixty-nine the cat again. Turns out, cats have got very rough tongues. No, I understand you're acquainted with Mother Goose. That means you know

who she is you thick fuck. You know she has that goose that lays golden eggs.

CHESTER
Well she deserves some good luck. She's worked hard all her life.

MEPHISTA to audience
(Aside) Drat, they still like her. (To Chester) And do you know what Tommy got up to last night?

CHESTER
He stayed in.

MEPHISTA
He stayed in... a hotel in Manchester.

CHESTER
Oh no he didn't.

MEPHITSTA
Oh yes he did.

CHESTER
Who with?

MEPHISTA looks at the audience and points to someone

MEPHISTA
Him. Tommy was with him.

CHESTER
What? Yeah right mr lady.

MEPHISTA
I mean I'm not saying he's proud of it. Perhaps this will convince you?

She takes out a dirty looking crystal ball. They lean in to look at it.

CHESTER
I can't see owt.

MEPHISTA
Yeah it's dirty. Fucks sake. (She holds the ball to an audience member) Spit on it. (They spit) I can tell you're not used to spitting. (She rubs the ball clean on another audience member.) Now.

She holds it right in front of the audience member.

MEPHISTA
The one you see inside the glass
Did spend the night in Tommy's ass

The CHESTER looks into the ball, then points at the audience member behind it.

CHESTER
Oh my god! It's you!

AMOS
Is he not just seeing his face through the-

MEPHISTA
Shut it Penn and Teller.

CHESTER
You dirty bastard!

AMOS
Chester Cleghorn I'm ashamed of you I am! You heard your mother. Embrace difference lad, embrace it. Some bat for the other side. It's not their fault. And I don't suppose this young man wanted everyone else here to know he's a gay! You didn't think of that did you? (To audience member) I hope you don't feel out of place lad.

MEPHISTA
I'll be off then.

CHESTER
Thank you for letting me know

MEPHISTA
Oh mate it was a pleasure.

She offers a hand. CHESTER shakes it and gets a massive electric shock. MEPHISTA cackles and exits

CHESTER
I can't believe it.

AMOS
Now Chester, you knew your best mate gay Tommy was an airy fairy. What did you suppose he got up to eh? It's not just disco music. Tommy's the first poof we've had in this town, and I dare say it's like when they invented the telephone - it's a lonely affair until there's two of them.

CHESTER
So you're... ok with that?

AMOS
It's no skin off my knees. I'm comfortable enough in my own masculinity. I even took your mother up the servant's stairs on a couple of occasions if you catch my meaning. Just be grateful it's not you eh? My only son! Now two *birds* shagging... Have I shown you my pornos?

CHESTER
Dad, we got something more important to do.

AMOS
We have?

CHESTER
We're going to steal that goose!

Scene 6: The golden warehouse conversion

MOTHER GOOSE sips champagne and has a packet of biscuits. Her dress isn't quite zipped up properly. THOR is doing housework. PRISCILLA sits looking bored.

MOTHER GOOSE
There you are boys and girls, do excuse me I'm not fully zipped. Thor, do the honours?

THOR
It's tight! It's all this rich food.

MOTHER GOOSE
I'm not big, it's the dresses that got small. Now chop, chop. The Mayor will be here any minute.

The doorbell chimes.

MOTHER GOOSE
Thor. The door!

THOR opens the door. DORA enters.

DORA
Old Mother Goose!

MOTHER GOOSE
Just Mother Goose is fine, no need to be formal. (aside) Or a cunt. Thor what have we learned about visitors?

THOR escorts DORA back to the door.

DORA
What's happening?

THOR (grandly)
Mayor Dora Cleghorn!

MOTHER GOOSE
I'm teaching him to announce guests as they arrive. It's what those in our circles do.

DORA
I think that's mainly just balls.

MOTHER GOOSE
I agree! Total balls! Thor stop it at once.

THOR
It was a bit much when you made me introduce the Amazon man this morning.

DORA
Now, darling I can't stop long but how *are* you. (Reaching for her phone) Sorry I must take this.

MOTHER GOOSE
Take anything you like!

PRISCILLA
Take me!

MOTHER GOOSE
Thor, get Dora a canapé and a glass of shampoo.

DORA (hanging up)
You're an impressive bird alright.

MOTHER GOOSE
Thank you!

PRISCILLA
I'm a pedigree.

DORA
She talks!

MOTHER GOOSE
She copies the odd sound but it doesn't mean anything to her! Shut it Goosy!

DORA
She's enormous!

MOTHER GOOSE
Yes! I've had to order a bigger oven aha ha ha.

THOR returns with a bottle of champagne and a plate of liquorice allsorts.

THOR
Canape?

DORA takes a Liquorice Allsort and stares at it. MOTHER GOOSE nods encouragingly.

MOTHER GOOSE
Well this is nice! That's not me coming on to you what with you being a lesbian, I'm just saying. This is Thor. He keeps the place looking nice.

DORA
Did he do your interiors?

MOTHER GOOSE
Not yet! Aha ha ha! Now Dora! A little bird tells me you're organising our very first Pride event.

DORA
I say, I know it's an imposition but might you like to get involved?

MOTHER GOOSE
You read my mind!

84

DORA
And without a microscope!

MOTHER GOOSE
But what to wear!

DORA
To wear?

MOTHER GOOSE
On the leading float! A lady of my standing, supporting our fledgling Pride, opening the event?

DORA
Oh! I was thinking more that you might chip in or organise a cake sale. Pride is not an opportunity for self-promotion.

MOTHER GOOSE
Well that's fucking naïve. Who does get to go on the leading float?

DORA
It's for the LGBT community. So the gay men are going on it.

MOTHER GOOSE
They have the best parties already.

DORA
No, *we* do. We just don't flood the internet with pictures. I'm sure there'd be a walking space for an ally such as yourself.

MOTHER GOOSE
You can bend the rules for little me! We were thick as thieves at school.

DORA
And you have the O-level results to prove it. *(Reaching for phone)* Sorry, must take this.

MOTHER GOOSE snatches the phone.

MOTHER GOOSE
Mayor Dora. Do you know who I am?

DORA
(snatching it back) The former owner of an undesirable backstreet barbers.

MOTHER GOOSE
Undesirable! People fought over my slots!

DORA
Come off it love, you were hardly Andrew Collinge.

MOTHER GOOSE
I've got a gay son!

DORA
So have I! And he's gayer than yours!

MOTHER GOOSE
I dreamed of giving him a Pride parade!

DORA
But you didn't think to organise one or even volunteer. You just want the glamour.

MOTHER GOOSE
Well! I must say it looks corrupt. Our lesbian Mayor draining public time and funds for a pride event.

DORA
You think *that's* corrupt? I had to give one of our councillors public land for a private fucking tennis court just to swing this!

MOTHER GOOSE picks up a carton of popcorn and leans in, rapt.

DORA
Public life. It's a minefield. If half the stuff that goes on got out we'd be crucified. Even the innocent things. I mean I've been waiting for a replacement bank card all week so I've been running everything through my expense account to tide me over but it would look ever so dodgy printed in a newspaper. Especially with some of my outgoings! Fortunately we have excellent security. As I'm sure you do.

MOTHER GOOSE
Yes! What?

DORA
Well, place like this, your trinkets out for all to see.

MOTHER GOOSE checks that her breasts aren't hanging out.

MOTHER GOOSE
Oh I see!

TOMMY enters through the front door, THOR escorts him back.

THOR
Master Thomas Goose!

MOTHER GOOSE
Thor! We are not doing that!

TOMMY
Hiya team! How-do Dora.

MOTHER GOOSE
Tommy we were just saying, we need security.

TOMMY
I suppose. In the meantime why don't we ask the boys and girls to keep an eye on things. Boys and girls, if you see any intruders would you tell us?

THOR
And make sure you're really specific about where they are, such as just for example if they happen to be behind us.

MOTHER GOOSE
Clever boys. Thomas, join us.

CHESTER and AMOS sneak in from the back, maybe through a window. AMOS has RAMSBOTTOM the Whippet with him. All three wear balaclavas. CHESTER carries a sack.

MOTHER GOOSE
No, no, darlings we don't need to practice. We're trying to talk.

DORA
Where? Behind us? [etc]

CHESTER and AMOS head towards PRISCILLA who sees them and squeals. TOMMY looks around but AMOS and CHESTER move the opposite way so he does not see them.

TOMMY
Are you winding us up team?

MOTHER GOOSE
Thomas stop fussing.

DORA
The poor birdie sounds like she's in pain.

DORA runs over to PRISILLA who moves in the opposite direction. CHESTER is just about to put the sack over PRISCILLA and puts it over DORA instead. DORA screams and blows a whistle. An armed bodyguard rushes in and pushes AMOS and CHESTER away. DORA is released from the sack. The bodyguard exits. TOMMY pulls the balaclava off CHESTER. AMOS removes his.

DORA
Chester! What is the meaning of this! Have the Russians got to you?

MOTHER GOOSE
They're trying to take my goose!

DORA
But it's just a silly goose.

TOMMY
You burgled us?!

CHESTER
I didn't think you'd mind seeing as you already got burgled last night.

TOMMY
Eh?

CHESTER
Bum burgled.

TOMMY
I was here all night!

MOTHER GOOSE
None of this excuses your breaking into my golden warehouse conversion!

DORA
I need a drink.

THOR comes over with a bottle of champagne and glass, DORA takes the bottle and drinks from it. PRISCILLA is crying.

TOMMY
Priscilla!

PRISCILLA
It's just, I'm the victim here and nobody seems to be very interested.

MOTHER GOOSE
If she's egg-bound after this I'll be livid.

TOMMY
Get out!

CHESTER
I'm sorry.

TOMMY
Both of you. Out!

AMOS and CHESTER and leave

THOR (to Tommy)
That was very masterful.

TOMMY
Thanks Thor! I'm going to my room.

MOTHER GOOSE
You really do masturbate at the strangest moments.

THOR
If you need to talk or anything you know where I am.

TOMMY
Ok. Thanks.

THOR
Not at all. Anytime - day or night. (aside) Boys and girls what am I doing flirting with him! I need to keep my mind on the nob. Job

TOMMY exits. DORA prepares to leave.

DORA
Before I go, Mother Goose, a friendly word.

MOTHER GOOSE
Is it cuddle?

DORA
Money can buy you possessions. It can even buy you processions. It can buy you power, influence. It can take you to wonderful places. I've been around the world

MOTHER GOOSE (sings)
And I, I, I, I can't find my baby...

DORA
But it can make you mean, if you let it. And then all the money in world won't stop a certain ugliness come through, inside and out.

MOTHER GOOSE
People tell me I look half my age!

DORA
Jesus how old are you? Well, if that's what you care about, I'm sure a little nip and tuck will put a pause on the crow's feet. For a year or two. If you'd started ten years ago. Thor, would you pass me my coat. I have three dates to get to.

MOTHER GOOSE
I think you'd better leave Dora Cleghorn.

DORA
That's why I'm getting my coat!

THOR hands DORA her coat. She exits, taking the champagne with her.

MOTHER GOOSE
Three dates! Why don't I have a date. Am I unattractive?

THOR
Why worry about things you can't control.

MOTHER GOOSE
If only I were beautiful I'd be happy. And loved. Good heavens there's a woman just flown by on a broomstick.

We hear a crash. The doorbell chimes. THOR and MOTHER GOOSE look at each other.

MOTHER GOOSE
Thor. The door.

THOR opens the door. MEPHISTA enters.

MOTHER GOOSE
Yes hello I like your hair. Oh it's you.

THOR
Mephista!

MEPHISTA
Yeah that's my name, that you shout out every single time you orgasm. That your write in your own shit on the bathroom tiles every morning.

As she says this she crosses the room and exits the opposite side.

MOTHER GOOSE
Where's she gone?

MEPHISTA returns

MEPHISTA
Having a nosy. Wooden floors. I don't like wood in the bedroom I like a rug. Mother Goose, I am at your service.

THOR
She won't be tempted by anything you can offer.

MEPHISTA
No I'm sure she wouldn't be tempted by... Eternal Beauty!

MOTHER GOOSE
Eternal..! - what was it?

MEPHISTA
Beauty.

87

MOTHER GOOSE
I would look young and beautiful forever?

MEPHISTA
You'd make Jane Fonda look 80.

THOR
Jane Fonda is 80.

MEPHISTA (surprised)
Fuck off!

THOR
I know!

MEPHISTA
Fair play. (coughs) I can take you away to the lake of eternal beauty. When you emerge from the waters, you'll be like Helen of Troy! Cleopatra! Princess Diana!

MOTHER GOOSE
Dead?

MEPHISTA
Life's hard enough for us women. We don't even have pockets. (To her audience friend) And I like a woman's pocket [name]. Might as well play the system. What do you say?

THOR
No! If you do this, the next time you look in the mirror there'll be a different person looking back. This is the face of a kind, selfless, popular woman. Don't lose sight of her. In your heart you know it won't just be the outside that changes forever.

MEPHISTA
Typical man! Trying to control what a woman does with her body.

MOTHER GOOSE
Yes you're confusing me Thor! Give me some peace. Go and put a load in.

THOR
A what?

MOTHER GOOSE
Washing! Now.

THOR exits.

SONG: NO TURNING BACK[9]

MEPHISTA
Decades of kindness with nothing to show
Until you met me and your life turned to gold!
But where's the admiration, where's the respect?
The old pecking order needs to be pecked
You deserve it my girl!

This is the moment, there's no going back
Don't ask for atonement, go on the attack,
Who'd choose plain and humble? not me
When you can be hot, as hot as can be

MOTHER GOOSE
I remember a girl who thought she was content
Then I got a taste of what envy meant
But isn't all this enough of a miracle?
I'm not scared of change but this feels so physical

MEPHISTA
You deserve it my girl

BOTH
This is the moment the fork in the path
Do it your own way do it with a laugh
Who cares about personality
When you can be hot as hot as can be

Ditch the fear you need to dump this
You don't need a friend you need an accomplice
Be the brightest star in the firmament
You're not scared of change let's make it permanent

This is the moment turn away from the sun
Walk into darkness it's so much more fun
This is the moment the point of no return
Don't look over your shoulder my girl it's your turn!

MOTHER GOOSE walks to the Lake of Eternal Beauty.

INTERVAL

---

[9] Jon: I was thinking of songs like "Defying Gravity" from *Wicked* and "Past The Point of No Return" from *Phantom* as a model here. There's nothing inherently cliff-hangery about a lake of eternal beauty – why shouldn't the lass be allowed to get her tits done? – unless you can make it feel like it stands for something bigger; a real fork in the road.

Laura Blair as Priscilla, Matthew Baldwin as Mother Goose, Christian Andrews as Chester in *Mother Goose Cracks One Out!* Photo by PBGstudios.

Liam Woodlands-Mooney as Tommy, Ellen Butler as Dora, Laura Blair as Priscilla, Matthew Baldwin as Mother Goose, Christian Andrews as Chester, Christopher Lane as Amos and Briony Rawle as Mephista in *Mother Goose Cracks One Out!* Photo by PBGstudios.

Scene 7: The Lake of Eternal Beauty

Moonlight. Dry ice hugs the stage. A large clam shell fills the stage like the one in Botticelli's Venus. As the song – a brassy, jazzy number – begins, MOTHER GOOSE emerges from the shell, seaweed and crabs caught up in her hair.

SONG: BILLBOARDS BABY
Sung by Thor; and Mother Goose (italicised lines)

Mother Goose got invitations
Mother Goose was the talk of town
Mother Goose was in the papers
Don't look back no looking down

And of course the gays all loved her
A rags to riches girl with no discernible skills?

I'm the face of Aldi's own-brand wrinkle cream
I'm on billboards baby ain't that a scream?
Gonna tell my story, my biography
Bring Gemma Collins' ghostwriter to me

Mother Goose went on Loose Women
Mother Goose went on Question Time
Mother Goose went on Saturday Kitchen
Mother Goose got offered pantomime

You could call it stratospherical
How bloody dare you I'm in beautiful shape!

They know my face from Paisley to Plumstead
I divided the nation tweeting 'bout something
Donald Trump said
I'm the agony aunt for two magazines
I want Scarlet Johansen to play me on screen

So forget what you thought of her
The long and the short of her
From golden eggs to perfect legs
I'm getting laid and not with the dregs
Looks, wealth, got all I need
Life is looking rosy yes indeed!

Scene 8: The golden warehouse conversion

There is a large cage covered in a cloth. TOMMY enters, an open bottle of champagne in his hand. He swigs from it. He's not steady on his feet. His hair's a mess and he's a bit bedraggled and his clothes aren't clean - yellowy patches around his armpits and some food stains. There needs to be a small wastepaper bin on stage.

TOMMY
Hi team! Welcome back boys and girls! Will you forgive me for being a little bit drunk? Then I'll forgive you for being a little bit drunk! Thing is, for all this money I've got nothing to do and no purpose in life. I've taken to the bottle. I haven't showered in a week. I mean obviously I've given my bumhole a splash twice a day cos you never know what might crop up, but who's going to fancy me like this? Here, don't tell mum, but I applied for this really cool job as an apprentice blacksmith. In the interview, I had to fit a horseshoe. I totally nailed it! (badum-tsh)

TOMMY's phone rings. He answers.

TOMMY
Hello? - it's the blacksmith! - Oh... Oh right I see. Well, bye then. (Hangs up) I didn't get the job! No I'm more disappointed than that. He had really good arms and all. Apparently, my reference from my previous employer was terrible! But who was my previous employer boys and girls? You're right! It was mum! She's ruining everything!

PRISCILLA is heard from inside the cage.

PRISCILLA
Help!

TOMMY
Where did that come from boys and girls?

He takes the cloth off the cage.

TOMMY
Priscilla!

PRISCILLA
No it's Jemima fucking Puddleduck. The woman's locked me up! And thrown away the key!

TOMMY
Thrown away the key?!

PRISCILLA
Aye, in the little bin just there. Get it.

He goes to get the key. THOR enters

THOR
Good morning sir!

TOMMY
It's afternoon Thor.

THOR
I realise that sir, I was trying to make you feel better. Now, what is that smell?

TOMMY
I know, it's the pits.

THOR (going to sniff his armpits)
I thought so! Mmmm!

TOMMY
Don't I'm gross.

THOR
You just need shaking up a bit! I've seen Queer Eye: We'll dress you in layers, do the bare minimum to an avocado and I'll compare your every worry to my coming out story. Reaction shot! *(He pulls a camp face)* You'll be right as rain and twice as cute.

TOMMY
I'm a bit drunk. Maybe you should take me to bed?

THOR
You mean *put* you to bed?

TOMMY
No. Where's the fun in that?

They kiss.

THOR
No, I can't!

TOMMY
It's ok. I know no-one would fancy me right now.

THOR
Oh it's not that, believe me! Oh boys and girls. Gay sex is so new to me, I'm still in the binging phase. I'm sure that only lasts a few weeks! No, I've decided! Tommy, I am going to fuck you right in the bum.

TOMMY
You're kind of meant to ask first.

THOR
Ok! Boys and girls, shall I fuck Tommy right in the bum?

PRISCILLA
No! Wait!

TOMMY
Guys, if mum comes back please don't tell her what we're up to!

TOMMY leads THOR to his bedroom.

PRISCILLA
Come back you bastards!

MOTHER GOOSE enters with MEPHISTA

MOTHER GOOSE
Boys and girls! Fans and fannies! I'm brighter and tighter and cuter and astuter! My legs are longer, my arms are stronger, my tits are bouncier, my hips are flouncier. I've been to fashion shows, film premieres, charity auctions. Oh yes [name] I'm a very edible young woman now. Do I mean edible? No! I mean bangable!

The doorbell rings.

Well that's broken the romantic mood! Thor! Thor!

She answers the door herself. It is a TOWNSPERSON.

TOWNSPERSON
Mother Goose!

MOTHER GOOSE
Oh! Boys and girls it's Townsperson One.

TOWNSPERSON
No I'm Townsperson Two!

MOTHER GOOSE
Understudy night is it?

TOWNSPERSON
Mother Goose, can you sponsor me for my fun run?

MOTHER GOOSE
How clever to ask me in front of all the boys and girls. What's it in aid of?

TOWNSPERSON
It's for Fuck Cancer. I need to raise £500.

MOTHER GOOSE
£500?! Is that all it costs to fuck cancer? I shall give the entire amount!

We hear the sound of rapturous applause. MOTHER GOOSE bows and smiles.

MOTHER GOOSE
Tell me, are they a particularly effective charity? Or did mummy suffer perhaps?

TOWNSPERSON
No... it's just they had a place available in the fun run and it was sold out else.

MOTHER GOOSE
I see! Except... now that you've rightly if very pubicly reminded me of my philanthropic obligations, would it not be more ethical if I researched a number of charities, and gave £500 to the one that seems to do the most good?

TOWNSPERSON
I suppose...

MOTHER GOOSE
There we go! Good luck!

TOWNSPERSON
Wait! Have you done something to your hair? You look amazing.

MOTHER GOOSE
Oh thank you! *(She quickly writes a cheque)* Here's the money! Run along!

The TOWNSPERSON exits.

MOTHER GOOSE (chuckling to herself)
"Run along"! But that reminds me boys and girls will you excuse me while I pretend somewhat unconvincingly to make a phone call. (She dials) Hello – hello! - is that Kittens for Granddads? It's Mother Goose here. Nice to meet you Arthur. Now, I want to rationalise my charitable giving to make it more efficient.... It means I want to cancel my direct debit. Yes. I've decided to focus on gay charities. They invite me to the most wonderful dinners. Elton John, Tom Daley, Rupert Everett - yes I agree Arthur, he is very underrated. Goodbye.

There's a knock at the door.

MOTHER GOOSE
No bell. That's strange.

MEPHISTA kicks the door open and enters.

MEPHISTA
Hello wankers. Hello Mother Goose. Just doing a courtesy follow-up after your Lake of Eternal Beauty experience. Have you been yet? I mean, er, oh don't you look lovely!

MOTHER GOOSE
I know! But Mephista I've been thinking. I must do something meaningful with my life, what with my newfound status and influence. Then again: Melania.

MEPHISTA
What are your talents?

MOTHER GOOSE
I'm good with hair.

MEPHISTA
Well then, on balance,
You'd make a good... mayor!

MOTHER GOOSE
Mayor! We have a mayor.

MEPHISTA
She looks down on you.

MOTHER GOOSE
You're right! And who was sent a magic goose by God himself? Me! I'm the chosen one. What do I need in order to be mayor.

MEPHISTA
I don't know much about normal jobs.

MOTHER GOOSE
What *did* your school careers advisor say to you?

MEPHISTA
She said did you put bacon in my fax machine and I said no. But I had. What about policies?

MOTHER GOOSE
Very good! What do people like?

MEPHISTA
They quite like Dua Lipa. And free shit they love that.

MOTHER GOOSE
Free badges!

MEPHISTA
Aim a bit higher.

MOTHER GOOSE
Free hats! Oh this hopeless. Perhaps Tommy could help. Tommy! Have you seen him boys and girls? Are you sure?

MEPHISTA
He'll be in bed.

MOTHER GOOSE
At *this* hour?

MOTHER GOOSE marches off to the bedroom. She shrieks. She returns holding both THOR and TOMMY by the ear. They are partly undressed.

MOTHER GOOSE
You have betrayed me Thor! Out! Out of my golden warehouse conversion at once!

THOR
I was only trying to cheer him up.

TOMMY
A pity fuck!? That's nice!

MOTHER GOOSE
And you! Fratriciding with the servants!

TOMMY
You're just jealous.

MOTHER GOOSE
How dare you!

MOTHER GOOSE grabs THOR by the scruff of his neck. MEPHISTA opens the door (or holds back a curtain). MOTHER GOOSE chucks THOR out.

MEPHISTA
I'm going to go now because I'm not very interested in the next bit. I've had a busy fucking year what with Salisbury and everything. Bye.

MEPHISTA exits. The doorbell immediately rings. TOMMY answers it. It's AMOS and CHESTER

AMOS
Hullo gay Tommy.

MOTHER GOOSE
If it isn't Amos Cleghorn come to gawp.

AMOS
Mother Goose, I have come cap in hand I have, cap in hand. We're on the verge of collapse. I need a loan.

MOTHER GOOSE (sings)
"How can I get you a loan..."

CHESTER
Yeah can you give us one though?

AMOS
Mother Goose you're as beautiful as ever.

MOTHER GOOSE
As ever? I am *more* beautiful than ever! Amos if that's the amount of attention you pay to what's going on then I shall be glad to watch you go under!

AMOS
Are you being saucy?

MOTHER GOOSE
No!

AMOS
Then that's it! The Cleghorn flour-milling days are over.

TOMMY
Nobody wants that, Squire Cleghorn. How much do you need?

AMOS
Ten grand to start with.

TOMMY
Mother. Can I borrow ten thousand pounds please.

MOTHER GOOSE
Yes certainly you can one moment.

She pulls out her phone, presses it a lot of times, there is a sound like a slot machine paying out.

MOTHER GOOSE
There you go Thomas that's in your account now.

TOMMY pulls out his phone, presses it once, there is again a sound like a slot machine paying out.

TOMMY
There you go squire that's in your account now.

MOTHER GOOSE
You scheming little brat! That's it I'm going for my bath. Thor! Thor!!

TOMMY
You fired him!

MOTHER GOOSE slumps in a chair.

AMOS
You're a good lad gay Tommy. Though it doesn't solve our long-term problems.

TOMMY
No, but you'll work on a new strategy. You need to diversify. Segment your market, design specific products for each of them, and communicate to them the benefits they'll relate to the most. Posh mums with breadmakers - ready mixed flour with linseed and sunflower seeds. Health fanatics - wholemeal flour with all the ruffage. Spelt flour for people with allergies. Heritage grains for hipsters. And for the gay market - the zero carb flour!

AMOS
The zero carb flour! How does that work?

CHESTER
We already got something like that. It's twenty-five quid a bag but it's mega slimming.

TOMMY
Squire Cleghorn, let me come and work at your mill. I'll even do the first week for free as a trial. After all, why be wealthy if you can't benefit from an unpaid internship?

AMOS
Yes lad. I say yes. Tommy, Chester, after me.

AMOS exits

CHESTER
Yay babes! Together again!

TOMMY
This is strictly a working relationship.

CHESTER
I got my Pump jock on.

TOMMY
When did you get a Pump jock?

CHESTER
When someone left it at mine.

CHESTER exits

TOMMY
Whatever.

MOTHER GOOSE
Tommy!

TOMMY
Bye mum.

He exits

MOTHER GOOSE
Nooooo! It's not *right* boys and girls. But, as Whitney Houston inaccurately had it, it's ok. I'll make him proud of me. You'll see!

Scene 9: A road on the outskirts of town

THOR enters.

THOR
I barely managed half a thrust
And now I've gone and lost their trust
I've lost my purpose, I'm of zero use
Now how can I keep watch on Mother Goose?
A huge thunderclap. Darkness except for a spotlight on THOR.

THOR
A spotlight! (Sings) *Never know how much I love you, Never know how much I care...*

We hear the terrifying voice of the FAIRY QUEEN

FAIRY QUEEN (off)
Dandelion! You naughty fairy!

THOR
Fairy Queen!

FAIRY QUEEN (off)
Enough! You broke the rules! You had carnal relations with a mortal in your care without thought for your position!

THOR
There was only time for one position.

FAIRY QUEEN
You will return to fairy land – at once!

A puff of smoke. THOR vanishes.

Scene 10: The yard of the mill

It is decorated with rainbow bunting and balloons. TOMMY enters.

TOMMY
Hi team! Welcome to Pride! I can't believe it. Rugburn having its own Pride. Place is coming up in the world! Whatever will we get next. Immersive theatre! Cafes that sell street-food but indoors for fifteen quid a plate! Only, thing is, it'd be much more fun if things weren't really awkward between me and the only other two gays I actually know.

CHESTER enters. He wears little angel wings and a lot of glitter on him.

CHESTER
Hiya boys and girls!

TOMMY
You might have dressed up for the occasion.

CHESTER
Yeah well. I was too busy waxing my arse.

TOMMY
Oh... How's that then.

CHESTER
Tell you what, it makes my farts come out squeaky. I dunno why I said that.

TOMMY
What does your badge say?

CHESTER
Never kissed a Tory.

TOMMY
Why you wearing that?

CHESTER
Cos I haven't kissed one and I thought, if I wore this, one of them might try and be my first. So actually, it's actually very inclusive, actually. Why, do you mind?

TOMMY
Why would I mind? (Pointing at his outfit) Don't you think your old man's gonna put two and two together?

CHESTER
I don't care. I've decided. I am what I am and what I am is the most fabulous faggot in Rugburn.

TOMMY
Right well, will we do the Pride song then?

CHESTER
What Pride song?

TOMMY
The LGBTQIA song.

CHESTER
Yeah ok. I'm an LGBTQIA!

TOMMY
Do you even know what LGBTQIA stands for?

CHESTER
Yeah! Duh. Ladies who are gay... Gay... Bit gay...

TOMMY
I think we should do the song.

CHESTER
How will I know the words?

A song sheet unfurls.

TOMMY
There you go. Alright boys and girls I'm going to teach Chester the song, but I think he might want a bit of help ok? I'll sing it through.

He sings the song. It is to the tune of Heads Shoulders Knees and Toes.

LGBTQIA, QIA
LGBTQIA, QIA
It's the ABC of the rainbow family,
ABGILQT, LQT

Shall we have a try team? You ready Chester?

They sing.

That's dead good boys and girls! Now it's time to learn the actions. So watch carefully. Don't worry. You can do all these with the hand that's not holding your drink. Now, L – that's easy that's an L shape like this. G...

CHESTER
Do this like you're downing a shot of G[10].

TOMMY
B – flap your hand like a little buzzy B.

---

[10] G, or GHB, a liquid drug.

CHESTER
T – put your hand like this like you've got some dead good gossip and you're gone spill the Tea.

TOMMY
Q – hand down here like the little tail on the letter Q.

CHESTER
I... that's easy just point at your eye.

TOMMY
And A... cup your ear like you're bit deaf and can't hear and you're going "eh?"

They do this. And maybe split the audience into teams. When they're done, DORA enters. She has a garland of fake flowers round her neck instead of her chain.

DORA
Boys and girls! Now, I can't stop but welcome to Rugburn Pride! Am I the only lesbian?

MEPHISTA enters singing to the tune of Englishman in New York. She has a little rainbow bow on her hat but is otherwise dressed the same.

MEPHISTA
Oh-oh I'm a lesbian, I'm an evil lesbian
I'm a lesbian in in the North.

She blows the loudest plastic whistle in the world and cackles.

TOMMY
Are you really a lesbian?

MEPHISTA
Who are you, border control? Yes. I even had a girlfriend. But she was prejudiced.

DORA
Oh I'm sorry.

MEPHISTA
Yeah, against baddies. Also she wasn't into me peeing on her.

CHESTER
At least she gave it a go.

MEPHISTA
It's not my fault - I thought she was asleep. Also she kept saying she was straight so I released her in the end. Straight! Two days later there she was in fucking Homebase.

DORA
Homebase! I'd no idea. Right! It's time to begin the parade!

TOMMY
It's a march. It's not just some party.

DORA
Either way, I'll tell you the route. When the parade – march – is assembled, you'll take a left out of the yard and go straight up Lower Fanny Passage. Oh but how funny I said straight! Then take a right onto the high street, past the Church of St Justin of the Awkward Ecumenical Compromises and there in the town square-

CHESTER
Town square Tommy, that's you.

DORA
-you will see an outdoor stage, upon which the Pet Shop Boys, Years and Years and Camila Cabello have all performed when it was previously used at a number of premium festivals.

AMOS enters.

AMOS
Morning gay Tommy! Just what the town needs I say, just what the town needs. It's a fine day the day we show the world how proud we are to be Rugburnians.

HE looks at Chester

AMOS
Chester?

CHESTER
(Butch) Er yeah hi dad.

AMOS
Chester lad, I am proud of you too. I see what you're aiming at and while the Angel of the North's not even on this side of the country, still it warms my heart to see you embrace our northern heritage. (AMOS sees Dora's garland) Here this is saucy.

DORA
Get off! I can't find my mayoral chain anywhere. I can't think where it's got to.

A trumpet fanfare. PRISCILLA enters breathing heavily pulling a float. On the float is MOTHER GOOSE in a very over the top rainbow dress. She wears the mayoral chain and carries a whip.

PRISCILLA
Ooooch! The Loch Ness Monster would be lighter to pull than this lard laden clootie.

MOTHER GOOSE whips her.

MOTHER GOOSE
Halt!

TOMMY
Mum?

DORA
Is that my chain?

MOTHER GOOSE
What a lot of people have come to see me

TOMMY
We're here for Pride.

MEPHISTA
Let her fucking speak fag. I like a political speech.

AMOS
I don't know much about politics but I tabled a motion this morning!

MOTHER GOOSE
If those at the front might kneel before me so that everyone can see and admire me.

AMOS
This is my property! I'll kneel before no one.

MOTHER GOOSE
But will it be for much longer, Squire Cleghorn? Kneel!

They all kneel

MOTHER GOOSE
Gays! Lesbians! Bifocals. Trans...

TOMMY
Gender!

MOTHER GOOSE
Female, duh. Yes, to all who march under the little plus sign of inclusivity! Can I get a whoop-whoop? What an enormous honour it must be to have my support at our first Pride. You see, I want to help those less fortunate than myself.

TOMMY
Less fortunate?

MOTHER GOOSE
As we all know, the modern fight for queer civil rights began at the Stonewall Inn when Oscar Wilde threw a strop at a policeman. It ended at my former beauty salon here in Rugburn, a haven for society's waifs and gays. That is why I'm using this event to announce my candidacy for mayor!

DORA
I'm the mayor!

MOTHER GOOSE
We'll see about that! I have the first edition of the Rugburn Reporter. "Mayor Dora in secret deal to save millionaire's tennis court."

AMOS, TOMMY, MEPHISTA
Corruption!

MOTHER
That's not all! Mayor Dora used her expense account to pay for an escort!

AMOS
I thought she had a limo.

DORA
I have never paid for male escorts.

ALL
(Assured) Oh. (Scandalized) Oh!

DORA
It's perfectly simple! The chip in personal debit card cracked so I used my expenses account to purchase the company of a handful of respectable-

MEPHISTA
Boo!

DORA
I was going to pay it back!

CHESTER
Mum!

MEPHISTA
They knew you was a lesbo but they didn't think you did the actual sex.

DORA (phone)
Sorry must take this. Yes? (Hangs up) That was Councillor Skeggins. I've been summoned to the town hall! I'm ruined!

She starts to cry.

CHESTER
Oh mum!

DORA
Darling boy.

She goes to hug him. CHESTER screams.

CHESTER
You'll ruin my glitter!

DORA exits.

MOTHER GOOSE
Only I can be the leader you deserve! Only I can give you the protection and special status you require!

CHESTER
Will you make Geoff the Baker do proper gay wedding cakes and not just sarcastic ones?

MOTHER GOOSE
I'll do better than that! There will be special gay bakeries for the gays to use.

CHESTER
What about bisexuals?

MOTHER
They can start with the straight bakeries, then when they've finished coming out they can use the gay ones along with the gays, lesbians and the trans folk.

TOMMY
What about heterosexual trans people?

MOTHER GOOSE
Don't complicate things! Christ, does everyone want equality now?! But - that's just phase one! Phase two I will build you a place where you can be together!

CHESTER
A gay bar?

MOTHER GOOSE
Streets of your own where you can make pink gin and produce theatre and fashion safely away from a world that doesn't love you.

TOMMY
A ghetto?!

MOTHER GOOSE
It's what you want isn't it? After all, there's five perfectly good parks in Rugburn but as soon as the sun's out you all gather on the same little strip of lawn by the lido with your tiny speedos, and I know at least half of you don't even swim what with your hair. And while we're on the subject, on such days you might leave a pot or two of hummus on the shelves for the rest of us. But you see, the gays are such nice people there is no divide within their community. My own son, Thomas, heir to my fortune, was happy to fornicate with my servant.

CHESTER
You tramp!

AMOS
Hey our Chester. Gay Tommy's gay, get over it. He's been very brave coming to this Rugburn Pride event as the only gay, don't make him feel out of place.

TOMMY
For fuck sakes tell him Chester.

AMOS
Tell me what?

TOMMY
Your son is what's known as a friend of Dorothy.

AMOS
Her at butchers? Saucy.

MOTHER GOOSE
This world is not for you! It's a terrible state of affairs when young men like Chester here can't come out to their own fathers!

CHESTER
Dad, I-

MOTHER GOOSE
Silence! An icon is speaking!

AMOS
You're making an arse of yourself woman, you're making an arse of yourself.

PRISCILLA
You've lost your marbles.

MOTHER GOOSE
Just get laying Goosey.

She kicks PRISCILLA. TOMMY runs over and unties PRISCILLA.

TOMMY
You're free Priscilla! You're free to go if you want.

PRISCILLA
Aye too right I want! But first, I want to say goodbye to Mother Goose.

She headbutts MOTHER GOOSE and starts to run off.

MOTHER GOOSE
You're going nowhere!

MOTHER GOOSE chases her

TOMMY
Mum. Let her go.

TOMMY chases MOTHER GOOSE.

MEPHISTA
Stay out of it faggot!

MEPHISTA chases TOMMY

CHESTER
You keep away from Tommy!

CHESTER chases MEPHISTA. Eventually Mother Goose trips and all land in a heap except for PRISCILLA who runs off.

MOTHER GOOSE
Look what you've done Thomas Goose!

She picks herself up and exits after PRISCILLA calling for her. All look towards her exit, silently.

AMOS
I'll tell you one thing Chester. Mother goose is quite right I say, quite right. There *are* young men just like you, but who are gay, and can't come out to their fathers because of how disappointed they'll be. Think about that Chester. A little pity is what they need.

TOMMY
I just hope that now Priscilla's gone, Mum will go back to being her normal kind and humble self!

MOTHER GOOSE returns.

MOTHER GOOSE
No more gold! Ah well. Mustn't let it spoil the day! Who wants to pull my float?

ALL
No!

TOMMY
You ruined Pride!

MEPHISTA
Come on boys! It's Pride! It's no time for hating,
The sun's out there's guns out and the Vengaboys are waiting.

TOMMY
She's right. Let's not spoil the whole day. Let's march. With Pride!

MOTHER GOOSE
But what about me?

CHESTER, TOMMY and MEPHISTA exit. AMOS starts to follow.

MOTHER GOOSE
Amos can I march with you?

AMOS shakes his head

MOTHER GOOSE
But we're old friends

AMOS
Old. Aye maybe. Friends. Not anymore, I say, not anymore.

AMOS exits. MEPHISTA follows.

MOTHER GOOSE
Oh howl, howl, howl boys and girls. Everything's gone wrong! Everybody's left me! All is lost. I don't suppose you could find it in you to still love me? Can you do that boys and girls? Thank you. I'll walk home. Alone. At least the sun is shining.

MEPHISTA enters and clicks her fingers. The sound of thunder and then rain. MEPHISTA puts up an umbrella and exits. MOTHER GOOSE sighs and exits.

Scene 11: The golden warehouse conversion

It's a mess and unkempt. There are bills scattered across the table and cobwebs everywhere. There is a teacup on the table with a used tea bag beside it. MOTHER GOOSE enters, holding a mug, she picks up the used tea bag and squeezes it into the new mug she has then drops it in.

MOTHER GOOSE
Three months have passed, and this is what it has come to, recycling my tea bags. I can't tell you how pleased I am that we changed it to tea bags from tampons in rehearsal. Well, there's no VAT on teabags. I've no money now that Priscilla's gone. At least I've still got my looks, as Anne Boleyn once thought to herself very briefly.

MOTHER GOOSE goes up to an audience member she was speaking to earlier.

MOTHER GOOSE
Hello [name] is my beauty still enough for you now that I'm poor?

The doorbell rings. It is no longer a full chime but just half a chime. MOTHER GOOSE looks for someone to answer it, sighs and answers it. TOMMY enters.

MOTHER GOOSE
Our Tommy! You haven't to ring the bell chuck you've got a key. It's not just for sniffing your gay drugs you know!

TOMMY
I live at mill now Mum.

MOTHER GOOSE
So are you and Chester...?

TOMMY
You're having a laugh. No, I work there now, proper like.

MOTHER GOOSE
I had such hopes for you.

TOMMY
I never wanted to be a hairdresser.

MOTHER GOOSE
Yes, yes, I understand.

TOMMY
Do you?

MOTHER GOOSE
Yes! What about the airlines, they always want people. Or something in the theatre? You could take me to shows, do they still have Cats?

TOMMY
Sometimes but it's shit now.

MOTHER GOOSE
Well something else. Lulu's going into Follies[11].

TOMMY
I'm happy at mill. It's paying for my evening course. I'm learning to do walls.

MOTHER GOOSE
Interior design!

TOMMY
Brick laying.

MOTHER GOOSE
Stay for your tea eh? I've a couple of tins we can share.

TOMMY
Alright, I'll have a beer.

MOTHER GOOSE
No love. Pilchards.

TOMMY
No I just came for some bits from my room.

MOTHER GOOSE (very embarrassed)
...It's in the dishwasher.

TOMMY
What is?

MOTHER GOOSE
Your plastic willy thing.

TOMMY
Why?

MOTHER GOOSE
It got a bit... look never mind about that. How is Squire Amos? Does he speak of me?

TOMMY
He's great. The mill's making money again.

---

[11] She wasn't, but she had recently gone into *42nd Street*.

MOTHER GOOSE
So he's got brass has he?

TOMMY
Is that all you care about?

MOTHER GOOSE
They shun me in the town. After all I used to do for them.

TOMMY
I'll get my stuff then.

MOTHER GOOSE
I'll have to sell my body!

TOMMY
Good idea. Start with a kidney and take it from there. I'll get my stuff.

He exits to his room.

MOTHER GOOSE
Come home our Tommy. Please!

The doorbell chimes. MOTHER GOOSE looks around for someone to answer it then walks over and answers it. DORA runs in. She is wearing expensive looking running kit - along with her mayoral chain. She jogs on the spot during this. Perhaps with the occasional lunge or stretch.

DORA
I can't stop, just happened to be passing. (Looking at the place) Oh dear.

MOTHER GOOSE (pointing at the chain)
But - you're still the mayor?

DORA
Just a silly misunderstanding, soon cleared up. And I've got far too much dirt on them all.

MOTHER GOOSE
Can I get you a drink? I've some lovely fresh tap water.

DORA
Please don't. I'm training for Rugburn's first half marathon - I'm sponsoring it. I just wanted tell you about an opportunity. I've a part time vacancy in my Levenshulme shop. I don't know if you'd be interested.

MOTHER GOOSE
Well - I suppose grooming dogs can't be much different from grooming people!

DORA
Grooming? Goodness no! That takes years to master, along with a certain... inherent taste and an instinct for style. No, we need someone to sweep the dog hair, and mop up when one of the dogs gets nervous if you catch my drift.

MOTHER GOOSE
Right.

DORA
Oh! I said I'd hand you this.

DORA hands MOTHER GOOSE a letter.

MOTHER GOOSE
It's from the Council. (She opens it) A compulsory purchase order?! My golden warehouse conversion!

DORA
Afraid so! But it's all for the greater good. Don't worry, you'll get the market value. Seventy five.

MOTHER GOOSE
Is that all? Seventy-five grand?

DORA
Seventy-five pounds. Outrageous isn't it. Something to do with the effect of your reputation on the property. It's like when a house that's had a murder in it goes on the market but without the lurid fascination. Ridiculous I know!

TOMMY returns with a bag.

TOMMY
Aye up Mayor Dora.

DORA
Tommy please, we're friends. Just "Mayor" will do.

TOMMY
I'm off home. To t'mill.

MOTHER GOOSE
Tommy!

TOMMY
Ta ra.

TOMMY exits

DORA
So what do you say? Come and work for me?

DORA's phone rings.

102

DORA

Must take this. Yes? (Beat) Buckingham Palace? (beat) Yes I have heard of it. How can I assist? (to Mother Goose) It's one of the Queen's people. Perhaps they want to make me a dame!

MOTHER GOOSE

Listen chuck. There's only room for one dame in this pantomime!

DORA

Best take this in private. See you! (As she goes) "Dame Dora Cleghorn...!"

DORA exits

MOTHER GOOSE

If only things could go back to how they were. Who can possibly help me now?

The doorbell half chimes. MOTHER GOOSE looks for someone to open the door, realises there is no one and opens it. THOR enters, he holds a magic wand.

MOTHER GOOSE

Thor! You came back to me!

THOR

I can't leave the job half done.

MOTHER GOOSE

But I can't pay you.

THOR

Not that job! I was never a real butler. I'm here to give you a happy ending.

MOTHER GOOSE

Tell me more.

THOR

You have to apologise to Priscilla.

MOTHER GOOSE

I don't know where she is.

THOR

I do. She's gone... to Gooseland!

MOTHER GOOSE

Goose...! What was the second bit?

THOR

Gooseland. It's a magical place, just south of Rochdale.

MOTHER GOOSE

I've never heard of it.

THOR

It's where all those paedophiles were. Oh, you mean Gooseland! It's invisible to humans.

MOTHER GOOSE

Then how can you...? But what are we...? So how do I...?

THOR

Are you alright?

MOTHER GOOSE

No! There's a word missing from the end of each of my lines. So how do I get there?

THOR

By magic!

THOR holds his wand in front of her

MOTHER GOOSE

Anyone can glue a star to a stick chuck, that's not magi- Oh! Is it a real star?!

THOR

A flick of my wand and we'll be on our way to Gooseland! What do you say?

MOTHER GOOSE

Abracadabra!

Scene 12: A road on the outskirts of town

TOMMY enters.

Hey team. I tell you what. It's great working at the mill, but – well it's really hard having Chester about all the time. I mean he's an idiot, obviously - I don't want to get back with him... But I dunno, like when he's sat there having breakfast, eating his Lucky Charms, I can't take me eyes off him.

SONG: THE CRYING & WANKING SONG

TOMMY
I've been betrayed, But I'm afraid,
Of being alone or even worse with someone else who isn't him

CHESTER appears spot-lit in a different place.

CHESTER
We're different types, with different likes,
But we rubbed along ok and now I've thrown it in the bin

BOTH
I've been spending every evening with my curtains half drawn
All I see is his face while I'm searching endless porn

Did you ever see a sadder, lonelier, hornier guy?
I'm crying while I'm wanking and I wank till I cry
I'm in a sorry state I'm in a deep blue funk
As my tears fall on my chest and mingle with my spunk

TOMMY
There's other guys, They catch my eye,
I go on Grindr and get scared he'll see me from a blank profile

CHESTER
Still I go out, I try and put it about,
But the minute that we finish I just want to run a mile

BOTH
I've been spending every morning wondering what to do
It's not just my heart that's bruised - my dick is black and blue

Did you ever see a sadder, lonelier, hornier guy?
I'm crying while I'm wanking and I wank till I cry
I wish I had another hand cos both these wrists are shot
Then my cum lands on my face and mixes with my snot
Did you ever see a hotter, wetter, stupider mess
I take selfies in the mirror wearing boxers or less
I need validation but I don't want to go out
So I think about him, and crack one out.

CHESTER fades away after the song, leaving TOMMY alone. MEPHISTA enters, in disguise, carrying a basket.

MEPHISTA
Tissues! Tissues! - shut up I'm doing a disguise – Young man, I am but a poor old lady selling tissues. Might you have a use or even two uses for a packet of tissues?

TOMMY
Funny you should say that.

MEPHISTA gives him her basket.

MEPHISTA
Choose a packet deary.

As TOMMY rummages, MEPHISTA hits him over the head with a stick. He falls to the floor unconscious. MEPHISTA laughs.

BLACKOUT.

Scene 13: Gooseland

A dark, bleak and damp looking place. It was clearly some kind of wetlands nature reserve at some point. A sign saying Gooseland, and a statue of a goose with ivy starting to grow on it. MOTHER GOOSE enters.

MOTHER GOOSE
Boys and girls! I'm lost and confused and I don't know where I am – I feel like Britney at Brighton Pride[12]. Thor?!

No answer, just an echo.

So this is where Priscilla was born and bred. And she called my salon unhygienic! Oh where is she boys and girls, I need to make things right with her.

THOR enters with candyfloss.

MOTHER GOOSE (con't)
Where've you been?

THOR
Kiosk.

MOTHER GOOSE
Have you found her?

THOR
Who?

MOTHER GOOSE
Priscilla! Boys and girls, will you keep your eyes peeled and tell us if you see her?

PRISCILLA appears.

MOTHER GOOSE
What was that? Where? Behind us? Well, we'd better have a look then!

They do. She's gone. MOTHER GOOSE chastises the boys and girls. PRISCILLA appears again, in disguise.

MOTHER GOOSE
Where? Behind us? Well, we'd better have a look then!

Again she vanishes. Again chastises them – "wild goose chase" etc

MOTHER GOOSE
Where? Behind us? Well, we'd better have a look then!

---

[12] At her headline appearance at Brighton Pride in 2018, Britney Spears was heard asking a backing dancer "Where are we?" before shouting to the crowd "What's up Brighton Pride!".

PRISCILLA takes THOR's place. As MOTHER GOOSE continues to look, PRISCILLA pecks her bum.

MOTHER GOOSE
Thor! You mustn't pinch a lady from behind! You must seize her from the front.

THOR appears in front of her.

MOTHER GOOSE
Exactly!

PRISCILLA pecks her again. MOTHER GOOSE turns.

MOTHER GOOSE
Not now Priscilla, I'm embarking on foreplay with- Oh! Priscilla! How wonderful to see you.

PRISCILLA
The feeling is nae mutual hen.

MOTHER GOOSE
I have come to apologise for the way I treated you. I was a greedy, vain, beautiful woman. Come back and live with us.

PRISCILLA
I'm no' a slave!

MOTHER GOOSE
As a member of our family.

PRISCILLA
Aye, well it's not that simple.

MOTHER GOOSE
Of course it is! Come, we're going home.

MEPHISTA enters

MEPHISTA
Oh no you don't!

MOTHER GOOSE
Oh yes we do!

THOR
You've lost your bet Mephista! She's seen the error of her ways!

MEPHISTA
I don't want her back in the town, do-gooding, making all us normal evil people look bad. She's staying put. Cos if you don't, I'll kill your son.

TOMMY enters, his hands together.

MOTHER GOOSE
Our Tommy!

He tries to break free

TOMMY
She's been playing you this whole time!

MOTHER GOOSE
Thor! Do some magic.

MEPHISTA
Oh yeah Dandelion. Do some magic!

MOTHER GOOSE and TOMMY
Dandelion!

THOR waves his wand, there is a small flash of light. Maybe a bit of confetti.

MEPHISTA
That ain't a spell. This is a spell.

MEPHISTA clicks her fingers there is a bigger flash of light and the sound of thunder

THOR
This is a hate crime! He's gay.

TOMMY
Don't make it about my sexuality.

MEPHISTA casts another spell. From now on TOMMY is very, very camp.

MEPHISTA
Say that again?

TOMMY
Er bitch please if you cleaned your fugly ears out once in a blue moon you might have heard the first time. Oh my God what actually is this place? My skin is *crawling*.

MEPHISTA
Ahahahaha! Mother Goose, get next to him. Kneel down the pair of you.

TOMMY
Kneel? Girl I don't kneel unless there's a much bigger incentive than you in front of me. And even then not in *these* jeans.

THOR waves his wand

MEPHISTA
Your magic's useless against me.

THOR
But I can get help.

MEPHISTA
Who from, the boys and girls? You're having a laugh.

THOR waves his wand. Rambo music plays (or the Avengers movie theme). CHESTER bursts in wearing army fatigues. He looks and sound very macho and butch.

CHESTER
Get away from my man!

TOMMY
Oh my god she is serving military realness!

CHESTER throws himself towards TOMMY and MOTHER GOOSE but shouts as he can't reach him

MEPHISTA
You won't break through my force field. I'll send you back home!

CHESTER
Nothing is going to keep me from my boy!

He throws himself at TOMMY again, there is flash of light. He gets through and carries TOMMY away. MOTHER GOOSE coughs

MOTHER GOOSE
What about me?

CHESTER
Fuck's sake.

CHESTER puts TOMMY down, pushes through the forcefield, picks MOTHER GOOSE up, and rescues her too.

MEPHISTA
You think you're so smart! By the power of gayskull, one final spell to kill you all!

THOR
Tommy! Grab her! Mephista can't cast a spell if she can't click her fingers.

MOTHER GOOSE
I can't click my fingers. I *can* roll my tongue, can you roll your tongue?

They all try, including Mephista.

THOR
Tommy! Grab her.

TOMMY
She's filthy

MEPHISTA raises her arms about to cast a spell. TOMMY grabs her.

MEPHISTA
Get off!

MEPHISTA tries to get away. THOR raises his wand.

MEPHISTA
Alright Dandelion, watcha gonna do? Banish me? Marry me off to someone shit? That's what normally happens in pantomimes isn't it.

THOR
Oh no. I'm not sending you anywhere. You're staying here. Throw her in the swamp.

CHESTER and TOMMY pick up MEPHISTA and get ready to throw off stage.

MEPHISTA
I'll drown!

THOR
No it's a magic swamp. You'll just come back looking a bit different.

MOTHER GOOSE
Like the lake of eternal beauty?

THOR
No! We're in Gooseland.

MEPHISTA
I'll come back as a goose!

THOR
Bye.

TOMMY and CHESTER throw MEPHISTA. She screams.

TOMMY
Babes you saved our lives!

CHESTER
It were nothing like.

TOMMY
Soz for being an angry bitch.

CHESTER
Well I did try and take your goose. So I'm er, sorry too. Here, we've been partners for a while now yeah?

TOMMY

Partners?!

CHESTER (kneeling)
So er, what do you say to making it official?

TOMMY
Squeeaal!

He claps his hands in excitement. THOR hands CHESTER an engagement ring in a box.

CHESTER
Will you marry me Tommy?

TOMMY
Oh.

CHESTER
Doesn't matter. Forget I said it.

TOMMY
Aw babes no I'm totes emosh', it's just I thought you were gonna say like we could get a joint Grindr account or something. Course I'll marry you!

CHESTER
Which one's your ring finger.

TOMMY
I usually start with this one.

They embrace. MOTHER GOOSE's smile fades.

PRISCILLA
Look happy lassie.

MOTHER GOOSE
Oh I am. I waved placards for this. But he'll live at mill and forget about his mum and what about me? The shops gone. I've no friends any more. I'll have nowhere to live. And what's Amos going say about this?

THO
Let's find out.

AMOS enters with RAMSBOTTOM and DORA

DORA
Now, I can't stop.

TOMMY
Here she is! The squire's on fire!

AMOS
Heh heh there it is, his little camp voice. Bloomin' 'eck though, I were just taking Ramsbottom out for his evening shit and I bumped into Dora. We started

107

gassing and must have taken a wrong turn. It's grim here I say, it's grim here. Are we in Yorkshire?

CHESTER
How'd you get on with Council Mum?

DORA
I explained that it was just a silly misunderstanding. And I have resigned as Mayor.

ALL
Resigned as Mayor!

DORA
That's what I said. I'm moving to London. It seems Her Majesty the Queen has heard about Dora's Doggy Style and is rather keen to give it a go. I'm to be stylist to the Royal dorgis[13].

TOMMY
Oh my god *wig* Mrs C I am literally bald. But you will be here for our wedding?

AMOS
Who are you marrying gay Tommy?

CHESTER
Dad...

AMOS
I'm only asking son. (beat) Chester lad, can we have a little word. In private like?

CHESTER
Ok.

They take exactly one step away from the others.

MOTHER GOOSE
Where've they gone?

AMOS
I hope you don't me asking you this lad, I say I hope you don't mind me asking.

CHESTER
Go on.

AMOS
Are you er, are you...

CHESTER

_____
[13] We were shaken to learn that in 2018 Liz no longer owned any corgis, and had instead a quartet of dorgis: a corgi and dachshund cross.

What?

AMOS
Are you... you know, what gay Tommy is?

CHESTER
You mean am I gay?

AMOS
Alright don't overreact! It's just – it's the army gear, I've been reading up on gay people what with us employing gay Tommy and apparently some of them like a uniform and I leapt to a conclusion like a fool.

CHESTER
Dad – I am gay.

AMOS
I see...

CHESTER
Dad?

AMOS
It's just you could have told me lad, you could have told me!

CHESTER
You said you'd be disappointed.

AMOS
Perhaps I alluded to such a thing. It's only because I... love you. Well, Chester, I'm not disappointed. I'm proud. You know your mind better than I did at your age.

CHESTER
You ain't gonna do the fucking dad speech from *Call Me By Your Name* are you.

AMOS
Well now. Our Chester marrying gay Tommy! Let's go home and celebrate. Where do gays get married?

DORA
Instagram.

MOTHER GOOSE looks upset, DORA nudges AMOS

DORA
Go on Amos.

AMOS
What?

DORA
Who's the woman you've secretly loved for years?

AMOS
Oh, aye. Holly Willoughby. Smashing pair of-

DORA
Amos.

AMOS
Aye alright.

He walks towards Mother Goose

AMOS
It may be bleak here but at least there's one thing brightens this place up.

MOTHER GOOSE
And what's that?

AMOS points a finger at her. She looks at it.

MOTHER GOOSE
Amos if you're going to say pull my finger and then do a fart it had best be a good one.

AMOS
It's you lass! I'm going to ask you something I should have asked you years ago. Mother Goose will you marry me?

MOTHER GOOSE
Yes Amos Cleghorn, I'll marry you!

AMOS
And will you take my name and wotnot?

MOTHER GOOSE
Your wotnot certainly, we'll see about the name. Thor get us home.

THOR waves his wand, nothing happens.

PRISCILLA
It's not that easy I'm afraid. You treated me cruelly. So you have to face trail.

MOTHER GOOSE
I'm a changed woman. Redeemed! Like a... Nectar point!

PRISCILLA
We're in Gooseland. You have to live by our laws. If you're found not guilty you can leave, if you're guilty you'll spend the rest of your days here.

MOTHER GOOSE
You didn't mention a trial!

THOR
It's fine! I'll represent you.

MOTHER GOOSE
But who's going to try me?

PRISCILLA
The Queen of Gooseland.

MOTHER GOOSE
A Queen! It's a good job I studied all those photos of Theresa May curtsying[14]. *(She mimics this).* Who is the queen?

PRISCILLA
That would be me.

MOTHER GOOSE
Ah poo.

PRISCILLA
I fucking told you I was royalty. Scene four.

THOR
My client is waiting. If you have charges to bring, bring them.

PRISCILLA
Right. First, can you pass me that little black cap.

MOTHER GOOSE
You haven't even tried me yet!

AMOS
Whatever happens I'll be waiting for you

PRISCILLA
Now, I need a jury of impartial and independent peers.

TOMMY
Your majesty. The boys and girls could be your jury. Couldn't you boys and girls?

PRISCILLA
Alright. Now I have tae swear the bastards in.

MOTHER GOOSE
What does that mean?

PRISCILLA
I'm guessing each of them has to say a rude word. You can start mate.

She points to someone in the front row.

---

[14] A quick internet image search will reveal that it is not merely that we are unused to seeing curtsying much these days, but that Theresa May had a particularly... striking curtsy style.

DORA
We'll be here all night! No no they can do it together. Boys and girls, after three, I want you all to swear as loudly as you can! Any word will do. One. Two. Three!

PRISCILLA
Alright. Now I'll call the first witness. Priscilla the Goose. That's me. Priscilla, do you promise to tell the fucking truth? Yes I fucking do. Good, I fucking believe you. Now Priscilla, were you made into a slave and kept in a cage after having been tricked by an offer of hospitality from somebody? Aye, I was your honour, it was exactly as you objectively describe it. I see. And can you see the devious villain here? Aye I can. It was her. Mother Goose?! Aye. Thank you Priscilla. You have been exceptionally brave and very moving. (beat) Your go you weirdo.

THOR
I call as my witness the accused.

MOTHER GOOSE
Don't call me that! It sounds terrible.

THOR
Mother Goose. It has been said that you tricked Priscilla with an offer of hospitality. Did you expect her to arrive at your humble, honest, popular and respected beauty salon?

MOTHER GOOSE
Of course not she's a giant bloody goose!

THOR
And when you made your kind offer of hospitality, was that before or after Priscilla laid - *flaunted* even - a dirty golden egg on your spotless floor?

MOTHER GOOSE
I made the offer before Priscilla laid her... beautiful egg. Oh but boys and girls of the jury, I beg you to listen. I don't deny my wrongdoing. I was once a kind, poor, happy woman. Well perhaps I wasn't entirely happy, only I couldn't admit it. And then this... majestic Goose came along and I became greedy. I wanted more and more. I enjoyed the power and respect it gave me. I have lost those I care about, and what is worse I treated this poor goose terribly. Please, let me try again.

THOR
Boys and girls of the jury, we live in complex times. Things are not black and white.

MOTHER GOOSE
Objection! What about zebras.

THOR
My client lived her life as a beacon of kindness and self-sacrifice. It just happens that for the couple of hours you've been watching she's been a bit of a cock. To issue a life sentence on such grounds, we would lose not only our humanity! We would lose a good, kind woman forever.

PRISCILLA
Right. My turn. Mother Goose. All I know is, I suddenly woke up in the cobbled streets of Rugburn and you gave me a home. And I felt that maybe humans, and the human world, with its kindness and beauty, might be better than Gooseland after all. And then you treated me worse than I've ever been treated. And it was horrible. What do you say?

MOTHER GOOSE
Priscilla. I'm really sorry. I judged you on your rough ways and failed to see you as the creature deserving of love and kindness that you surely, truly are.

PRISCILLA
Thank you.

MOTHER GOOSE
Thank you.

PRISCILLA
Boys and girls of the jury. If you reach for the electronic voting buttons under your seat – no I'm fucking joking! Can we let her go? Then I say we get out of this shithole!

MOTHER GOOSE
Dandelion, can you cast a spell to get us back to Rugburn?

THOR
Of course!

MOTHER GOOSE
Also you might want to sort the boys out.

THOR waves his wand

CHESTER (camp again)
Oh my god that was dead weird it was like I had Chris Pratt, Chris Hemsworth and Chris Evans inside me. And not a good way. Now babes we've got to put a wedding playlist together. We'll split it fifty fifty. Fifty percent Britney fifty percent Ariana. We'll have a horse drawn carriage, white horses, white suits.

TOMMY (still camp)
White?! You know white drains my skin!

MOTHER GOOSE looks at THOR

THOR
I didn't do his spell so I can't change him back.

DORA
There is one other thing. Following my resignation we're without a Mayor. Mother Goose are you still interested?

MOTHER GOOSE
Me?! No love. Christ can you imagine? Place'd go to pieces!

Everyone agrees with this.

DORA
Then who can be the new Mayor of Rugburn?

MOTHER GOOSE takes the chain from DORA and walks over to her favourite audience member.

MOTHER GOOSE
[Name] I know that you must be disappointed that I've been stolen from you by another man but as a consolation would you do us the great honour of being the new Mayor of Rugburn.

She puts the chain around his neck.

TOMMY
Oh my god can we go please?

MOTHER GOOSE
Send us back then Dandelion! We've a wedding to plan. Tara boys and girls!

THOR waves them away until only he is left on stage.

THOR
And so boys and girls, it came to pass,
That Mother Goose married her true love at last,
And Rugburn witnessed a wedding like no other,
A father, his son, the son's chap, and his mother.

They didn't trust the baker to do the gay cake,
The boys made it themselves – like gays should for fuck's sake,
And rainbow bunting was hung in the square,
And it looked so pretty they've kept it there.

Tommy and Chester moved to Salford Quays
Where Tommy builds sets for the BBC
But what's really got Mother Goose's blessing
Is that Chester's doing a course in hairdressing.

Mother Goose settled in at Amos's mill,
They're both shit with money but the sex is a thrill...
(Less certain) But - what's our tale's moral? Is it just: know your place?
Or if lost geese turn up, close the door in their face?

Well fuck it my loves, that's not our concern
You came for the smut, you're not here to learn,
So we thank you for helping our goose to fly,
With our love, and fond memories, sweet friends – goodbye.

THE END.

Snow White: Rotten to the Core

Kris Marc-Joseph as Grizzly Bear, Shaun Mendum as Snow White and Michael Robert-Lowe as Honey Bear in *Snow White: Rotten to the Core*. Photo by PBGstudios.

Snow White: Rotten to the Core

In 2017, Donald Trump was sworn in as US President and announced a visit to the UK, which was subsequently put on hold, possibly out of fear of large-scale protests. Theresa May remained Prime Minister – just – having called a general election to bolster her leadership in which the Conservatives actually lost their small majority, causing them to form a minority government with support of the homophobic Democratic Unionist Party of Northern Ireland. Following allegations of sexual assault, film producer Harvey Weinstein was dismissed from his company and expelled from the Academy of Motion Picture Arts and Sciences.

We knew our audience would be familiar with the 1937 Disney film *Snow White and the Seven Dwarves*, and we wanted to honour that story and the original 19th Century German fairy tale while also toying with people's expectations. For years we'd spoken about writing a version of Snow White, knowing that we would not be able to afford a cast large enough (or perhaps small enough) to include seven dwarves. Peter Bull had often suggested we tackle Goldilocks and the Three Bears as a pantomime, which we'd resisted; but that suggested a nice alternative to dwarves, and a great opportunity to celebrate the larger, hairier gay man. Coincidentally, at around the same time as we went into rehearsal, Rowse Honey launched a series of online adverts featuring three "bears" – chunky, bearded gay housemates sharing a wooden cottage in the woods.

Jon: "The first piece of theatre I saw was an elaborate puppet show of Snow White at the Grand Theatre in Wolverhampton. The second was the same story in the same venue, this time as a pantomime starring Dana, the Irish Eurovision winner who went on to become an Irish politician and presidential candidate and who campaigned vigorously against the introduction of same-sex marriage. I can only wonder what horrors she experienced at the hands of homosexuals, during her time in pop and theatre, to turn her so against us."

Snow White: Rotten to the Core

By Jon Bradfield and Martin Hooper
Songs by Jon Bradfield

Characters

Fairy, 30, a bit hippyish.
Queen Babs, the (male) queen of Lumley-by-Gosh.
The Prince, a young man.
Taleesha, a palace servant.
Mirror, a magic mirror.
Snow White, a young man.
Nanny Fanny, the dame, Snow White's nanny.
Honey Bear, a plump and hairy gay man.
Grizzly Bear, a plump and hairy gay man.
Town Crier
Dilwyn, a Welsh hiker.
Citizens, to be played by members of the company.

The mirror, the town crier and Dilwyn are to be played by the same actor.

Snow White: Rotten to the Core was first performed at Above The Stag Theatre on 30 November 2017 with the following cast and creative team:

Fairy: Ellen Butler; Queen Babs: Christopher Lane; Prince: Scott Howlett; Taleesha: Briony Rawle; The Mirror/Dilwyn/ Town Crier: Andrew Truluck; Snow White: Shaun Mendum; Nanny Fanny: Matthew Baldwin; Honey Bear: Michael Robert-Lowe; Grizzly Bear: Kris Marc-Joseph

Director: Andrew Beckett; Designer: David Shields; Lighting Designer: Jamie Platt; Musical Director: Aaron Clingham; Choreographer: Liam Burke; Costume Designer: Sandy Lloyd; Sound Designer: Andy Hill; Production photography: PBG Studios; Produced by: Peter Bull for Above the Stag

Prologue: The forest

A FAIRY enters. She's quite scruffy, with twigs in her hair.

Welcome boys and girls! I'll be brief but thorough,
You're in the former London borough
Of Lumley-by-Gosh, on the Central Line -
Though the trains haven't stopped here for a very long time.

It's now a rogue state, by which I mean
It's ruled by a vile and vain old queen,
Who's run the old borough into the ground -
It's now three thousand Goshes to one British pound.

The old council houses are still owned by the state
But the queen charges rent at a crippling rate
To pay for his shoes and for each nip and tuck,
And the hot foreign boys that he ships in to fuck.

The smog glows brown as the day is dawning,
And everything's grey as an Aberdeen morning,
To keep people out, a great wall surrounds it
They say there's a tunnel but I've never found it.

And from my clearing in these old woods,
What's clear is we need a new leader who's good.
There is one young man... but he's only a slave,
And in danger – so watch out, you might need to save him!

Now get this, right: I'm a fairy! I see you're impressed
But lately somehow I've got a bit stressed:
Helping heroes and lovers to get problems solved
Has taken its toll, see I get too involved.

But let us begin! Are you ready my dears?
Can I hear you say boo? And an ahh? And some cheers?
There'll be magic and romance, and tantrums, and tights,
Welcome boys and girls to our panto, Snow White!

BABS enters

BABS
On your knees! It is I, Queen Babs! Fair ruler of this perfect land.

FAIRY
Booo!

BABS
On the booze already are we?

FAIRY
What brings you to this notorious part of the forest?

BABS (feigning ignorance)
Oh...! Notorious is it? I have been for my majestic morning run, gracing the world with my beautiful visage.

FAIRY
That must be like a face but more slappable.

BABS
I could have you killed.

FAIRY
I could turn you into a trifle.

BABS
I've turned into a secluded lay-by on occasion... (He does some stretches) The efforts I go to! The exercise and rituals and treatments just to stop the horrors of ageing! This morning I spent half an hour massaging a 16 year old's piss into my crows' feet.

FAIRY
What does that do?

BABS
Nothing. It just takes my mind off the horrors of ageing. And next I've two hours in the gym to come. Though I may manage that quicker with a little help... (To a man in the audience) Hello there. Do you go to the gym? [If no: "No, obviously, it wasn't a serious question". If yes: "Yes.... you can clog me up with your protein shake any time"] Still, at least it's not leg day! Do you know why that's funny? That's right. Because it's never leg day!

FAIRY
I prefer yoga.

BABS
Yes, I can just imagine you downward dogging in a circle of cheap scented candles and vodka miniatures. Who are you?

FAIRY
I believe from our respective entrances
And the vile green light in which you stand
That I am supposed to be your nemesis
And see you banished from this sorry land.

BABS
It's not a democracy you silly trout
I can't just be impeached.

And leave my entrance out of it
It's still sensitive from the bleach.

FAIRY
Well fear not, love, it's your lucky day
Perhaps it's wisdom, perhaps I'm older
But the problems of this sorry state
Are too big for this little fairy to shoulder

BABS
Then good riddance. I must prepare myself for this evening's beauty pageant.

FAIRY
I went to one of your pageants once. It was less Paris is Burning, more Southend is Sinking.

BABS
The fairest youths in the borough parade for my judges to decide which of them comes closest to my own, unscalable heights of beauty. The winner receives a night with me he'll remember as long as he lives!

FAIRY
As long as he lives?

BABS
Yes - you see, I have him put to death before breakfast. Well one hates to waste good food. Goodbye.

FAIRY
I can take you as far as the town square.

BABS
By what means?

FAIRY
By a flick of my wand.

BABS
I'd rather a flick of his. (To the audience) Why, you must all come to my pageant! Especially if you look anything like my young friend (his chosen boy) – oh, oh dear no. Christ it's like an EDL march. Were the tickets cheaper this year or something?

FAIRY
Boooo!

BABS
Hahaha!
BABS exits.

FAIRY
Now come with me to our proud town square
A scene of great markets, and hangings, and fairs,
Where basics and extras just hang out and stare
But a panto ain't a pantomime without a town square...

She waves her wand. The lights change and...

Scene 1: The square

A traditional village square, including a cute little well. CITIZENS enter, going about their business.

FAIRY
Jesus it's like Dean Street Express[15] round here today.

The CITIZENS sing

SONG: THE TOWN SQUARE

In the shadow of the palace
Our square is positively regal
Full of children playing ball games
Call the cops cos that's illegal.

Tickets! Get your tickets to the latest shows and raves!
Admire our statues of great heroes who kept slaves
See the skater boys flash their tummies as they pass
While vendors sell you everything from hot-dogs to ass

We're in the square where life is easy
And rosy and breezy
You'll be met with a nod and smile
In the happiest friendliest borough on this little green isle

Cock fights, card games, gamble all your hopes
Come to be seen, and sometimes to be groped
And leave your phone at home, it isn't safe to bring it
God, shopping takes so long when you have to fucking sing it

Me oh my! It's time to do some miming,
Perhaps pretend I've seen a friend or two
Act as though we're gossiping and laughing
When really it's just crap we learned to do at drama school

We're in the square where life is easy
And rosy and breezy
You'll be met with a nod and smile
It's the luckiest liveliest fairest homeliest happiest friendliest borough
On this little green isle

---

[15] Sexual health testing centre.

The PRINCE enters.

PRINCE
Greetings, townspeople.

The CITIZENS stare at him in an unfriendly manner and exit. The FAIRY remains.

PRINCE
Right...!

A CITIZEN (off)
Go back to where you came from!

PRINCE
Excuse me old woman.

FAIRY
Old woman? I'm thirty.

PRINCE
Gosh! I expect to be dead by 27.

FAIRY
You'll be dead by elevenses if you carry on like that.

PRINCE
Pray tell me the way to the palace, and I shall tip you some change that you might find a hostel for the night. Then you can think about getting back on the market – the job market, I'm not unrealistic – and stop being such a burden. There's a good girl.

He gives her coins.

FAIRY
This is sterling!

PRINCE
Isn't it just.

FAIRY
The currency. You're from the United Kingdom! How did you pass into Lumley-by-Gosh?

PRINCE
Can you keep a secret?

FAIRY
No.

PRINCE
Neither can I. I'm an undercover reporter from a London paper, writing an exposé on this most guarded of nations. Being a master of disguise, I was waived through the border crossing in the guise of a skilled

manual worker. For it is well known that skilled labour has been in demand since your independence.

FAIRY
How did you do that?

PRINCE
I simply slipped on a hi-vis jacket.

FAIRY
I'm surprised you didn't see it, they're bright enough.

PRINCE
What impoverished minds women have.

FAIRY
You won't find a girl with an attitude like that!

PRINCE
I don't want a girl with an attitude like that. No, it's boys for me. Of course I don't blame you for your lack of education. I know girls don't go to school. At least there weren't any at mine.

FAIRY
I went to fairy school.

PRINCE
In a way, so did I. But I don't believe in fairies.

FAIRY gasps.

PRINCE
Do we all have to clap our hands now or something.

FAIRY
Nah we can't do Peter Pan stuff or you have to give Great Ormond Street a royalty, the cunts. I can prove I'm a fairy.

PRINCE
How.

FAIRY
I shall turn yonder tree into a diamond.

PRINCE
It's impossible.

FAIRY
Just close your eyes... and open them again in one billion years.

PRINCE
Don't waste my time, ignorant woman.

The FAIRY produces a bunch of flowers or white dove from nowhere.

PRINCE
You are a fairy! I didn't come here to meet silly frivolous people.

FAIRY
Yes, I see. You're at that age.

PRINCE
What age?

FAIRY
People seem stupid or blind or both.

PRINCE
Yes!

FAIRY
There must be *someone* out there who understands you if only you could find him.

PRINCE
How did you know?

FAIRY
And you heard of small state walled off from the world. A place that's turned its back on the games of the dying old west. A place brave enough to try something different... And then you heard rumour of a beauty. A royal with looks so fair, the very ice caps should melt and burst forth with wildflowers were he to turn his gentle gaze upon them.

PRINCE
And a lovely flat tummy with cum-gutters on either side.

FAIRY
Such a man would see you for the beautiful soul you spent your childhood being told you were, and yet which you struggle to believe yourself to be.

PRINCE
Stop it! Enough.

FAIRY
I'm done now, so: tough.

PRINCE
I say, there must be something fun over there. What are they all queuing for?

FAIRY
They're queuing for bread. Look about you. This is supposed to be our market, there's hardly two sticks of rhubarb to rub together.

PRINCE

I see. And the palace? *(The FAIRY points)* Thank you. I'm going to adopt the persona of a foreign prince and inveigle my way into life at court.

The PRINCE exits.

FAIRY

Off he goes with a big old smirk on him,
If that's our "prince" we'll just have to work with him,
For sure he's but young and he means no malice,
Now, follow him close, to the royal palace.

Scene 2: The palace

The palace used to be the town hall and civic centre of Lumley By Gosh. TALEESHA enters with a mop and bucket. A huge mirror hangs on a wall.

TALEESHA

Alright boys and girls! I said alright boys and girls! Yeah that's better, I thought you'd died. Cos that did happen last year with a matinee audience - combination of old age and G[16]. Welcome to the palace! It dates from the 1930s when it was built as the Lumley-by-Gosh town hall and civic centre. Here, you must think I'm a princess or something what with living in a palace. Nah, I'm his majesty's PA. "Poor arsewipe". I just been mopping his bedroom floor. It gets a bit sticky.

She lifts the mop and the bucket rises with it, attached.

Shit me though, where are me manners! My name's Taleesha.

She approaches the person at the end of the front row.

What's your name? (She moves along). What's your name? Fuck we shoulda done name badges. Tell you what, to save time, I'm gonna count all the way to three, and you can shout your own names all at once. You got that? Right. One, two, three...!

Yeah I think I got 'em. Now, bit of admin yeah, has anyone asked you lot to be their friends yet? No? Get in! Will you be *my* friends? I'm a bit lonely see. But listen right, cos friendship comes with responsibilities yeah? So here's the situation, any time you see me come on – don't pull that face mate, nothing to do with periods - every time I come on stage, I'm gonna shout "Hi hoes!" and you're gonna shout "oh heyyyyyyyy". Let's give that a practice.

TALEESHA exits and returns.

TALEESHA

Hi hoes! *(O hey!)* You can do better than that! I've heard more enthusiasm for Theresa May.

They try again. BABS enters

BABS

What's this fucking racket!

Boo

BABS

Christ, you'd think Taylor Swift[17] had just walked on. Give me a hiss as well. That's it, hiss all over me. Taleesha you lazy slattern! Summon the court painter immediately to sketch me while my chest is still pumped from the gym. I want something hung in the royal gallery by noon, and I don't just mean the delicious art student who frequently makes eyes at me while making his frenzied strokes.

TALEESHA

Yes your majesty.

BABS

Your majesty!? I've told you, call me Babs! We're a happy family here! Now run along. But first...!

TALEESHA starts to exit, running backwards.

BABS

What are you doing?

TALEESHA

I'm running along, butt-first.

BABS

It is time for my magic miroir! Miroir! Show thy face.

Magical sounds and lights. In the mirror, a man appears. He's looking at a puzzle book. He looks up.

MIRROR

Oh it's you! I was just thinking about you.

BABS (pleased)

Really?

MIRROR

Yeah well, I don't have a very wide social circle.

BABS

I do.

MIRROR

Yes you do, you had to get stitches in it after one memorable party.

BABS

You think you're so smooth.

MIRROR

That's natural in mirrors.

[16] GHB, a drug most commonly used at sex parties.

[17] Whether people like or hate Taylor Swift seems to fluctuate monthly. At the time of publishing she seems to have been well liked for some time at least within the gay community but presumably in late 2017 we thought she wasn't.

BABS
You're in a reflective mood ahaha! Taleesha, that was funny.

MIRROR
Oh no it wasn't.

BABS
Oh yes it was! Taleesha, the royal artist.

TALEESHA
Yes Babs. See you later boys and girls!

BABS
Mirror, mirror on the wall, who is the fairest of them all?

MIRROR
Your majesty, I swear it's true
The fairest of them all is-

BABS
Adadadadada! Let me have a guess first. Where's your sense of fun!

MIRROR
Of course.

BABS
Be quiet then! I'm trying to think! Honestly, you set me these silly games at least be quiet for long enough to give me a chance. Now. Oh, gosh. Right. Now is it Sam who does the gift shop, - is that his name? Sam? - Because now his hair's grown out you don't notice the nose as much do you.

MIRROR
It's not Sam.

BABS
(Shouting pointedly offstage) Not Sam! (To the mirror) Well he'll be very hurt when I tell him and you'll only have yourself to blame. Right... well it can't be one of these cretins can it? Oh except! Mirror mirror say hello, he's rather cute in the second row. Is it him?

MIRROR
Bingo!

BABS
What!?!??

MIRROR
You got it it's him. (Re the puzzle book) Now can you help me with this. Two across, "Tree house". Four letters.

BABS
Miroir, you have got to be shitting me, look at him. All of you, look at him. He's barely a six! If this were an orgy, he'd be the host. (beat) Alright stop looking at him now! What *have* we started, you'll get set upon in the toilets. (To the mirror) You're not looking so well yourself these days you know, miroir. Bit of wear and tear. Rather dated. I might trade you in for something younger and funkier.

MIRROR
Sir.

BABS
Yes?

MIRROR
I'm joking! It isn't him.

BABS
Ah! Ahahaha. Of course you were joking! Well miroir, I have to say you've got me stumped! I mean, unless - I mean obviously it's not this, I'm saying this entirely for a joke, clearly, but - well I feel silly even going there but it's not - I mean it couldn't be - little me?

MIRROR
Yes sir.

BABS
Oh mirror mirror in the palace, buy me pearls and call me Alice! What a surprise! But I should say a few words. Some thank-yous. My parents. My late brother King Geoff the Handsome who died so sadly and mysteriously in his prime.

TALEESHA enters

TALEESHA
Hi hoes! (To Babs) The royal artist is ready for you.

BABS
Fuck. Two ticks.

BABS drops to the floor and does some hasty push-ups.

BABS
Not the first time I've been horizontal on stage in front of an adult audience in Vauxhall but certainly the first time at this hourly wage. Oh, and miroir. It's nest.

MIRROR
Sorry?

BABS
Tree house. Four letters. Nest. Bye bye munters.

BABS exits.

TALEESHA
You're only enabling him.

MIRROR
It's harmless.

TALEESHA
He's a psychopath.

MIRROR
It keeps him happy. Anyway. "Beauty." It's subjective isn't.

TALEESHA
I dunno.

MIRROR
Course it is! Listen, one day some girl's going to look at you, and then keep looking at you for the rest of your lives, thinking you're the most beautiful woman in the world.

TALEESHA
Oh mirror! Do you think so?

MIRROR
I know it. Isn't that right boys and girls? And you're blatantly not, so you see? It's subjective. Here, I've got a smudge, I can feel it. Can you give me a little wipe?

TALEESHA spots the smudge on the lower half of the mirror – near where the mirror's "crotch" is. She gives it a rub.

TALEESHA
What here?

MIRROR
Yeah that's it - oh yeah that's good. Go on, bit harder.

TALEESHA
Pervert!

She punches the mirror in the "groin" and the man disappears – it's a normal mirror again. TALEESHA closes the mirror's curtain.

TALEESHA
Here boys and girls you ain't seen my only other friend Snow White have you?

SNOW enters. He has a baggy grey jumper with too-long sleeves and mop of hair over his eyes.

SNOW
Morning Taleesha!

TALEESHA
Morning Snow. These are the boys and girls.

SNOW (shy)
Oh hey.

TALEESHA
"Oh hey"?! Come on, it's a panto and your name's on the poster, you got to own this. It'll cheer you up.

SNOW (very panto here)
Hiya boys and girls!!

Hiya!!!!

SNOW
What happens now, am I supposed to feel happy?

TALEESHA
No mate, the dwarves don't come into it till later.

SNOW
Do you need a hand? Nanny said I'd find you up here moping.

TALEESHA
No, mopping, that was a typo remember? Snow's a prince boys and girls. His dad used to be king of Lumley. You should see the pictures of him as a little boy, proper little poofy outfits.

SNOW
The boys and girls don't want to hear about that.

TALEESHA
You should be on the throne. Not your uncle Babs.

SNOW
The rules changed.

TALEESHA
He changed them. I always say, if a ruler wants to change the rules by which decisions are made about who gets to rule, they shouldn't get to put those rules into play until the end of their own rule.

SNOW
You don't always say that.

TALEESHA
Well no can you blame me?

SNOW
I don't want to be in charge. I'd be scared of power.

TALEESHA
That's why you should be in charge. He treats you like scum.

SNOW
That's ok. One day my prince will come and take me away and love me and none of this will matter.

TALEESHA
You got to stop with all this rubbish. What if he doesn't come?

SNOW
Well he'll have to because I'm not allowed to leave the borough and there aren't any princes here. Babs won't let me travel because he thinks I'd lead an uprising or invasion or something.

TALEESHA (re: a man in the audience)
I think you've given this one an uprising.

SNOW
The truth is I couldn't lead a round of Happy Birthday. I say, Taleesha! Do you think we might have any birthdays in the audience?

TALEESHA
I honestly couldn't give a shit, Snow.

NANNY (off)
Knock knock!

SNOW
Ooh it's Nanny!

SNOW/TALEESHA
Who's there?

NANNY
Mel and Sue.

SNOW/TALEESHA
Mel and Sue who?

NANNY enters. She has a glass of wine and has a handbag.

NANNY (entering)
Exactly![18] Hello boys and girls! I can see you're overawed but let's try that again shall we? (they do)

Goodness I haven't heard so many working-class voices since Grenfell[19]. Hello boys and girls! I'm Nanny. Nanny Fanny. Welcome to my palace! Try not to eat any of the pot pouri it plays havoc with a blue-collar intestine. I know what you're thinking. Yes. I have something of the dear departed Tara Palmer Tomkinson about me. Well you'd be right, it's her handbag. eBay, three pounds. Coincidentally also the weight of the drugs that were hidden inside it. *(She approaches someone).* How do you do sir? No don't tell me how you are, just ask the question back to me, we're in a palace it's not Trisha. Let's try your friend. What's your name? Hello [name], that's it, take my hand, don't be shy, I'm sure you've taken many a hand before. *(She surveys the audience)* Do you know boys and girls, stacked up like that you look not unlike a life size game of Guess Who. Why don't we play. You think of someone Taleesha and I'll have a guess. Have you chosen?

TALEESHA
I have.

NANNY
Now, is he gay, receding and a little rosy-nosed?

TALEESHA
He is.

NANNY
Well this is going to take all day and we simply do not have the time! No, there is cleaning and cooking and gardening and washing and polishing and recycling to do! Oh yes. Glass, plastics, jokes, you name it. Snow, Taleesha, come at once, there is a situation in the kitchen.

SNOW
The kitchen? What is it?

NANNY
It's a room with a stove and a sink but that's not important right now. Fact is, I can't open the oven door

---

[18] Against expectations the Channel 4 incarnation of *The Great British Bake-Off* proved a success, in spite of original presenting duo Mel Giedroyc and Sue Perkins having quit the show when it transferred from the BBC.

[19] We cut this reference to the devastating Grenfell Tower fire after a few performances when an audience had been so appalled by it that Matt (playing Nanny) had to work very hard to get them back on board. The line came too early in the show - Nanny's extreme snobbery hadn't yet been established so it just felt like a crass dig.

and slide a dish in and hold onto my Chablis at the same time, I'm not made of hands! And I've a savoury lasagne to get cooking. (beat) I do know my *height* in hands, incidentally. That's not uncommon in girls of my breeding. (To her man) [Name], you look like you've enjoyed a good breeding. I can picture you on the golf course. Three swings and a firm little nudge and it's straight into the hole I'll bet.

SNOW
Nanny!

NANNY
Quiet Snow, I'm trying subtly to flirt. You'll notice I narrowly avoided splitting an infinitive there. (To her friend) Would you like to split mine? *(A quite word with Snow)* If I play this right we could soon find ourselves ensconced beneath this fine gentlemen's roof.

TALEESHA
Like a gargoyle.

NANNY *(ignoring this, talking to her friend)*
Yes you've the sniff of the quad about you! *(to his neighbour)* Whereas with you sir it's more the stench of the exercise yard. *(To everyone)* Oh but this place would fall down without me! That's why his Majesty calls me the buttress, he holds me in very high regard. He'd do anything for Fanny. Now, on with our chores! Let's turn that to-do list into a ta-dah list. I read that on a fridge magnet in the kitchen of a lower middle-class acquaintance and I thought it rather jolly. Quite right too, smile in the face of adversity. Poor woman had so little space she'd taken to keeping her washing machine in the kitchen.

SNOW
Nanny was born into nobility.

NANNY
I think that's apparent, Snow. It's true! But relegated many years ago when my father was banished for high treason and his lands were seized, since when I've been nanny to young Snow White here and slowly accruing responsibilities. It's alright for you! One day a prince will come to this palace and lower you onto his great throbbing steed and you'll shoot off without a second's thought.

TALEESHA
(Weary of this bullshit) Oh my god.

SNOW
It's true.

TALEESHA
You ain't the first slave to console himself with ridiculous dreams of an afterlife.

NANNY
A fairy told us that Snow was destined to marry a prince and thus one day rule a kingdom.

SNOW
She was definitely a real fairy because she said "thus".

The PRINCE enters

NANNY
May I assist?

PRINCE
I'm looking for an introduction.

NANNY
An introduction! Marvellous.

She clicks her fingers. The intro to Donna Summer's "I feel love" plays loudly. NANNY, SNOW and TALEESHA dance.

PRINCE
No! I wish to- I wish to be introduced to his majesty!

The music stops.

NANNY
I see. Have you your papers?

PRINCE
I'm afraid I don't smoke. You girl, fetch him.

TALEESHA
Yes sir.

TALEESHA exits

NANNY
You'll take tea with us. Snow, keep him on the simmer.

NANNY exits

PRINCE
Well young chav, what do you do?

SNOW
Oh er, very well thank you.

PRINCE
Yes, I – you're a servant?

SNOW
Well, yes, I am really.

PRINCE
Enjoy it?

SNOW
In a way... It's good really because the experience will keep me grounded and humble when I'm living in a palace of my own with a prince far far away. But listen to me rabbiting on! What do you do?

PRINCE
I'm a prince.

SNOW's jaw drops and he sort of goes to pieces at this. For quite a while.

PRINCE
Are you alright?

SNOW nods – it's all he can do.

SNOW
Boys and girls! My Prince! Or *a* prince, at least. Is it to be any old prince, or a specific one?

He returns to staring at the PRINCE for a while, speechless.

PRINCE
You're... not unattractive you know.

SNOW
Oh God, am I unattractive?

PRINCE
I just said you weren't.

SNOW
But you thought I thought I was.

PRINCE (warmly)
Honestly! I bet all your cute bedroom selfies are captioned "looking rough this morning".

SNOW
What's a selfie?

PRINCE
Now while we're alone, I'd love a little tour of the palace. What say we-

NANNY enters

NANNY
At ease! I'm back!

PRINCE
No tea?

NANNY
A watched kettle never whistles! My maid used to say that when I was a young girl of excellent breeding. *(To her friend, in the manner of Lauren Bacall)* You know how to whistle, don't you [name]? Now listen boys and girls, although his majesty dotes upon me, being a professional he prefers not to show favouritism and he will be a little angry if he finds us stood here shooting the birds.

SNOW
Breeze.

NANNY
Well where's the fun in that? Anyway, should you see Queen Babs will you give us a heads up? Thank you. (To the PRINCE) Young man, you mentioned a tour.

BABS enters followed by TALEESHA. The audience shouts. NANNY and SNOW instantly drop to their knees and pretend to be polishing the floor.

NANNY
Babs!

BABS slaps SNOW's arse pulls him up and gets him in a playful headlock.

BABS
There you are Snowflake you naughty little tramp! Don't forget, wrestling practice this afternoon.

PRINCE
Your majesty.

BABS
What's your business, we don't take visitors *(Now he looks at the Prince properly)* Oh hello take a seat, my face is free. Now, what would a fashionable young man fancy, an aperol spritz? A portion of piri piri chicken? Nanny, at once.

NANNY
I'm sure I don't know what those are.

BABS
Nanny's rather naïve.

NANNY
He thinks me innocent!

TALEESHA
He called you naïve.

NANNY
Well it's all part of the dance.

BABS
Young man, join me in my salon. Walk this way.

He flounces out.

PRINCE
I'll certainly give it a go.

The PRINCE exits, mimicking BABS' walk.

TALEESHA
That's it, someday your mince will come.

NANNY
He's quite the sight for sore eyes.

SNOW
Sore something. Nanny, he's a prince!

NANNY
A prince!

SNOW
But I don't think he'd be interested.

NANNY
Well that's nice! I'll have you know there are men who'd leap like a show pony at the chance of a refined but worldly lady with a considerable... well let's call it a CV shall we? To think I wet-nursed you! Breast fed you like you were my own. (To the audience) Until he was eight, nine, ten. Only occasionally, for a treat. Usually on birthdays. Usually on mine.

SNOW
Nanny, I meant me. He wouldn't be interested in me.

NANNY
Oh! He's not... Do you think?

SNOW
Course.

NANNY
Why do you say that?

SNOW
Well the venue for one thing.

NANNY
Well I dare say no he wouldn't be interested in you. Look at you with your stroppy hair and sulky knitwear, slumping about like an ostrich.

SNOW
Ostrich?

NANNY
Emu.

TALEESHA
Emo?

NANNY
That's it.

SNOW
It doesn't matter anyway, he's probably not *the* prince. One day *my* prince will come, and it wouldn't look very good if I had a boyfriend would it!

TALEESHA
You're scared.

SNOW
What?

TALEESHA
You're using this bullshit about a prince coming so you don't have to make an effort with actual real life boys who actually exist in all their actual complexity and might actually fancy you without being blind to your actual flaws and who you might actually have to make an actual effort for, and occasionally actually be let down by, such is the rough and tumble of actual romantic and sexual adult life, actually.

SNOW is really discombobulated by this. NANNY glares at TALEESHA.

TALEESHA
Aaaaaand... when your prince does come it 'd be nice to look good for him yeah?

SNOW
He won't be shallow!

NANNY
What you need is what the television-watching classes call a makeover. You want him to woo you don't you? I've been wooed on many occasions. Oh yes [name]. As wooed as you can imagine.

SONG: THE FAIREST IN THE LAND

NANNY
Sometimes I fear I've let myself go

126

What with having so much to do
So dear be a treasure and grant me this pleasure
Let Nanny live vicariously through you
Parade yourself in a tiny vest
I've bought you loads but you just let them fester
Pluck those eyebrows, Get shaping
And smoking's rather sexy, why not take that up - no vaping

Wear your denims low and your knickers high
So your fine upper bottom can catch the eye
With confidence perhaps you'll learn to charm
By why take the risk - you could just flash some arm.

You'll be in fashion, you'll transcend
You'll straddle all the trends
You'll take friends who are lovers and lovers who are friends
Yes you'll look quite the man about town

Look at the gays in the magazines
White's a nice colour but try tangerine
Pose for a portrait topless with a kitten
Or with wine in the bath, hashtag thirsty, they'll be smitten!

NANNY & TALEESHA
You'll be in fashion, you'll transcend
You'll straddle all the trends
Get yourself a fella, gotta make like Cinderella,
You'll look quite the man about town

SNOW
And some day my prince will come
In my hot little... heart I know it Watch this space, you won't regret it
See this face? You won't forget it
I'll make you understand
I'll be the fairest in the hood

NANNY
In the land, understood?

ALL
In the land in the land!

NANNY, SNOW and TALEESHA exit as BABS and the PRINCE enter

PRINCE
I'm a Prince on a diplomatic mission from the People's Democratic Republic of Rottenluck. Like Lumley we are held in contempt by the wider world but I come with an offer of friendship, and a request that you might offer me two weeks' internship.

BABS
Internship! Is that what it sounds like?

PRINCE
Work experience.

BABS
Ah, right. We are a sufficient and efficient nation with no need of assistance.

PRINCE
Of course... And a monarch as beautiful as you probably receives all the offers of help you can manage.

BABS
Ahahahahahahahahaha naughty! I'll have a bed made up. Start you off in a room of your own and see how things progress. Snowflake!

SNOW WHITE enters. Quite a transformation. His hair is nice and he has an expensive and well-fitting t-shirt on.

SNOW
Yes Babs.

BABS
Have a bed made up in the east wing.

SNOW
The east wing?

BABS (wearily)
The former department of highway maintenance.

SNOW
Of course.

PRINCE
I don't believe we've met.

SNOW
Oh.

PRINCE
I mean, I'm sure I'd have remembered! I'm, er... Rupert! That's it. Prince Rupert.

SNOW
Snow White.

NANNY and TALEESHA poke their heads out to watch, making encouraging gestures to SNOW. Maybe doing French kissing faces with their tongues.

PRINCE
A name as fair as your beauty.

SNOW (distracted and annoyed by NANNY and TALEESHA, who retract their heads)
Stop it!

PRINCE
It was only a little banter.

SNOW
Oh not you sir! Banter away. Give me a proper bantering.

The PRINCE gets his phone out.

PRINCE
I say, what's your Instagram.

SNOW
My what?

BABS
He doesn't have one.

PRINCE
Then you'll make a guest appearance on mine.

He takes a photo and posts it online.

PRINCE
Your majesty, what a fine son you have. *(Glances at his phone again)* Look at that! Eighty-five thousand six hundred and thirty-two likes already! And an aubergine. And a poo[20]. (To BABS) Are you on the old insta?

BABS
Well I... I have an account but I'm barely on it what with all the ruling I have to do, so I don't get quite as much er... reach as I might.

PRINCE
Snow, are you free to show me to my room and perhaps give me a tour?

SNOW
I am. After you.

PRINCE
Are you indeed!
SNOW
See you later boys and girls!

The boys exit, leaving BABS seething with jealousy.

---

[20] Future digital archaeologists are going to look at the poo emoji and think us very odd.

Scene 3: The woods

The FAIRY sits on a tree trunk drinking a mug of tea, she has another mug and a tea pot beside her. On her knee is a badger which she is petting.

FAIRY
Don't get up boys and girls, I wouldn't. I'm just enjoying a cup of nettle and hawthorn. Will you join me?

She puts the badger on the floor, pours some dark murky liquid into a mug and offers it to some audience members.

That'll take the hairs off your back. I wonder how that prick of a prince is getting on - but what do I care? Mustn't get involved. Doctor's orders. No, if I see the chauvinistic arsehole, I'll tell him to jolly along.

Unseen by the FAIRY, the PRINCE enters, hearing her and creeping until he accidentally treads on the badger.

FAIRY
Get your foot out of my badger!

PRINCE
I'll watch out for the skunk as well.

FAIRY
There's no skunks in these woods.

The PRINCE sniffs.

PRINCE
Are you sure? (He sniffs again) It smells like there is. Are you clean?

FAIRY
Am I clean? This isn't Grindr![21] I washed in the lake this morning.

PRINCE
Listen I've had spiffing day and I don't wish to spoil it.

FAIRY
I'd say you've the glad eye for a fella.

SONG: THERE'S A BOY
(Sung by the Prince)

There's a boy, there's a boy and he's lovely,

And although we didn't really speak,
In my head we are already wed with a pug
Hosting pool parties twice a week

He makes me forget the crushes of my youth
Like the lad on the District line,
And the twink who takes coats in the nightclub booth,
Surely this one must be mine

There's a boy gives me such frisson
I can't wait to take him home,
And my parents won't guess that we'll have a threesome
When they let us use the flat in Rome

I won't neglect him, after I've wrecked him
No ghosting or looking over his shoulder
Maybe it's just I'm getting older,
There's a boy I've undressed in my mind and I'm impressed -
I'm obsessed, and I have to make him mine!

The FAIRY is becoming invested, in spite of herself.

FAIRY
Ooh! So, what are you going to- Never mind.

PRINCE
Well

FAIRY
No, no. You do what you like.

PRINCE
You wouldn't understand anyway! What do you know of young love! (*He sniffs the air again*) I was wrong, it's not your armpits. You have a mangy minge.

FAIRY
I sprayed this morning! With a potion of bluebells and bog orchid. I don't mention the smell of old parmesan emanating from your britches do I.

PRINCE
Well, no time to stand about gossiping like an old washer woman.

FAIRY
That is enough. It's time for a spell. I'll cast you out of the borough.

PRINCE
But my boy! He lives here!

---

[21] "Are you clean?" is a euphemism for "are you HIV negative" and sometimes other sexually transmitted infections.

FAIRY
Alright. You can stay. But you will live as a woman.

PRINCE
What?

FAIRY
You shall live as a woman and know what it is to live in a man's world.

PRINCE
Now really, it's hardly a man's world when there are more women than men in it. If anything you have the advantage.

FAIRY
In this case, I do. Now listen. Change your ways and the spell will be broken. Reveal yourself to be a man before then and you'll wake up back in London, banished forever. So, what's it to be?

PRINCE
A little Ralph Lauren number?

FAIRY
Primark it is! Gentlemen, start your engines. I feel a spell coming on.

Scene 4: The palace

TALEESHA and NANNY are cleaning.

TALEESHA
Hi hoes!

NANNY
Do work quicker Taleesha, we've still to do the bedrooms.

TALEESHA
All twenty of them. I'll take the odd ones.

NANNY
Well they're none of them exactly normal. To think I once had someone to 'do' for me.

BABS enters.

BABS
Anyone would do for you, Nanny.

NANNY
Oh haha Babs darling... Little Babyliss... Babaganoush... Babylon Five... Now, might I have a word? It'saboutourworkload. Taleeshawascomplaining-

TALEESHA
We work night and day,

BABS
And still the place is filthy. Your work is poor yet you have the audacity to ask favours.

NANNY (flirting)
I'd make it worth your while.

BABS
I'll hire someone.

NANNY kisses him.

NANNY
Thank you.

BABS
The two of you can head for the dungeons.

TALEESHA
We cleaned them yesterday, did you have another snuff party?

BABS
The dungeons are where you will spend the rest of your earthly lives. If I hire someone else, you two will have to go.

TALEESHA
That don't add up.

BABS
Don't start looking for logic now, Christ.

The man in the mirror appears, now wearing a fluorescent puffer jacket and shades. NANNY, behind him, admires them both in it.

NANNY
Look at us. Aren't we suited.

BABS
I'll have you belted. Mirror mirror, round and grand, who is the fairest in the land

TALEESHA
I wouldn't kick that girl from the bakers out of bed.

NANNY
Crumbs!

BABS
Miroir!

MIRROR
Yo man.

BABS
Yo man??

MIRROR
I'm trying something younger and funkier innit.

BABS
Answer me!

MIRROR
You're well vexed bruv!

BABS
Get on with it!

MIRROR
Alright! It's Snow.

BABS
I didn't ask for the fucking weather.

MIRROR
Snow White. He's well peng.

BABS
Have you had some sort of stroke?

MIRROR
He's been working out innit. Scrubbing up. New treads, new threads.

BABS clicks his fingers and the mirror returns to normal.

BABS (to NANNY)
Nanny, a cup of Lapsang Souchong.

She trudges out.

BABS
Taleesha, you know you're my favourite and best employee.

TALEESHA
Am I?

BABS
There's something I must tell you. It's about Snow White.

TALEESHA
Oh, yeah he told me himself, but did you know he can only do it if he hasn't eaten in 24 hours and even then he can only reach the tip.

BABS
He's plotting to kill me and take over the throne.

TALEESHA
Oh no he isn't.

BABS
Oh yes he is!

TALEESHA
Oh no he isn't.

BABS
I have intelligence.

TALEESHA
You kept that hidden.

BABS
I'm afraid it gets worse. He hates women.

TALEESHA
He doesn't hate me.

BABS
A front my dear! He hates you and when he takes charge he's planning to kill you all.

TALEESHA
No!

BABS
But you can stop that. You can be a heroine. Imagine all of Lumley's women worshipping you as a heroine! You could have all the... breasts in the borough.

TALEESHA
That might take some juggling.

BABS
You just need to do one teensy thing.

TALEESHA
And I'll be a hero?

BABS
Absolutely. All you must do is take Snow White into the woods and kill him.

TALEESHA
Yeah alright.

BABS
You'll do it?!

TALEESHA
Yeah sound, it'll do me good to get out.

BABS
You'll take Snow White into the woods and kill him?

TALEESHA
Oh! No, I missed that bit. I can't do that!

BABS
Then I'll find someone who *can* do it – and do it painfully.

TALEESHA
No! I'll do it!

BABS
There is one condition. Bring me proof of his death! Once you've killed him, cut out his heart and bring it to me.

TALEESHA
But that's-

BABS
Yes, heartless. *(He passes her an ornate heart-shaped box).* Bring it to me in this box. Off you go, find Snow White and kill him. Break a leg!

TALEESHA
I don't think that'd do it.

TALEESHA exits. The doorbell rings.

BABS
Door!

NANNY enters with the PRINCE. The PRINCE is dressed as a woman.

132

NANNY
Queenest Babs, there's a lady to see you.

PRINCE
Good afternoon. I'm Lady Rhianna Perry-Swift, a diplomat from the state of Rottenluck.

NANNY
How nice to receive guests of quality.

BABS
Rottenluck? We had chap from there.

PRINCE
I'm afraid he's been recalled. But we're still keen to nurture strong relations.

BABS
My grandmother could crack coconuts between her thighs.

NANNY
Lady Rhianna is hoping for a poke.

PRINCE
A post. Unpaid of course.

BABS
Perfect timing, I was about to take tea.

PRINCE
Wonderful!

BABS
The kitchen's through there. Two sweeteners, a slice of lemon and a drizzle of manuka honey.

NANNY
He never calls *me* honey.

The PRINCE starts to exit. TALEESHA and SNOW enter. TALEESHA is carrying an axe.

TALEESHA
We'll be off then.

She stops, staring at the PRINCE. SNOW also stares. The PRINCE curtsies.

NANNY
Where are you going?

SNOW
A walk in the woods.

NANNY
Then put a jacket on. You'll catch your death.

The PRINCE exits

TALEESHA
Who was that? She's gorgeous.

SNOW
Yeah. She is.

TALEESHA
Snow?

SNOW looks confused.

SNOW
Yeah, I know...

BABS
Hurry along! You'll miss the best of the light! And Snow White?

SNOW
Yeah?

BABS
Goodbye.

SNOW
Er, bye.

BABS
Oh, and Snow White?

SNOW
Yeah?

BABS
Sorry, before you go you couldn't quickly write down one more time exactly how to programme the Tivo could you[22]?

SNOW
Um-

BABS
No! No, don't worry. Have fun!

---

[22] Tivo was a gadget that let you digitally pause, rewind and record live TV.

Scene 5: The woods

The woods. There's a large log on stage. The FAIRY enters.

FAIRY
That's a big log. I'll have to make a note of that. In me log book. (She sits on it) There we go, rest me legs and in a minute I'll brew meself some cabbage and cowslip. (beat) Oooh I've got a tingle downstairs. I bet it's that thrush again.

She reaches under her skirt and removes a bird.

Yeah thought so. No I'm still tingling – I know what it is. It's me fairy senses. Me hairs are all on end. It means someone's in danger! (She stands, heroically.) No, you're here to relax. (She sits. She can't bear it) Tell you what, I'll just have a little walk and if do happen to spot anything then that's as may be. (To the audience) If you see anyone about to get killed or anything, try and stop it alright?

The FAIRY exits. SNOW enters with TALEESHA who has the axe, and a bag with the box in.

SNOW
Hello boys and girls!

TALEESHA (sadly)
Hi hoes.

SNOW
This was a great idea! It's so nice to spend some time just you and me.

TALEESHA
Yeah...

SNOW
Are you ok?

TALEESHA
Yeah! Yeah.

SNOW
You know when we were in the square... People seemed to be staring at me... Do I look funny?

TALEESHA
No, it's cos you're fit now. (beat) Let's chill a bit.

SNOW
We've come so far.

TALEESHA
And we've reached so high.[23]

SNOW
What's the axe for?

TALEESHA
In case... we wanted to chop some wood. (She points at the log) Bring that over will you?

SNOW goes over to the log and bends down to grip it. Behind him, TALEESHA nervously raises the axe. The audience shout. SNOW looks up.

SNOW
You lot are noisy aren't you! What's up?

Shouts back from audience

SNOW
What?! Taleesha's my best friend! Right, let me move this log.

SNOW bends down again. TALEESHA raises the axe. The audience shout. The FAIRY runs in.

FAIRY
I can't bloody bear this!

TALEESHA freezes, SNOW looks up.

SNOW
Taleesha!

TALEESHA
I'm exercising! (she lifts the axe up and down) Triceps!

FAIRY
Oh no you weren't.

TALEESHA
Oh yes I was.

FAIRY
Oh no you weren't.

SNOW
Oh fucking hell Taleesha - you?! So I don't even get a sexy huntsman to kill me? Some gay pantomime this is. I thought you were my friend.

TALEESHA
Babs told me what you're planning.

SNOW
My Friday night wank with poppers and hummus?

_____
23 Take That's *Never Forget*.

134

TALEESHA
No! To become king and kill us women.

SNOW
Jesus that's mental!

FAIRY
That's not very PC.

SNOW
Alright, Mohamed that's mental!

TALEESHA
It's not true?

SNOW
No!

FAIRY
My fairy senses tell me that Snow White here is a good man, pure as... as snow.

TALEESHA (rather charmed)
You're a fairy?

FAIRY
That's right.

TALEESHA (flirty)
I bet you can work magic.

FAIRY
Well, nothing to write home about.

TALEESHA
Oh I wouldn't write home about it. Far too shocking.

FAIRY
Oh....!

SNOW
Er, guys, my life's at stake here, it's kind of a key plot point. I'm a wanted man am I? Right. I'm going to the palace.

FAIRY
Don't go to the palace! It's ever so pricey and they don't even let you see the bedrooms.

SNOW
I'm going to have it out with Babs.

TALEESHA
He'll kill you.

SNOW
You can talk!

FAIRY
Go deeper into the forest. You'll find somewhere to shelter and hide.

SNOW
I guess...

TALEESHA
Bye Snow

SNOW
Bye boys and girls!

He heads off stage. As he passes her:

SNOW
Judas!

He exits.

TALEESHA
I'm going to be in trouble.

FAIRY
Just tell Babs you killed him.

TALEESHA
But I got to bring proof.

FAIRY
His head! In a sack! So he knows you really killed Snow White!

TALEESHA
Oh... No, that would make way more sense. Shit man, this is a piece of piss. Can you help me kill an animal and cut its heart out?

FAIRY
I could not!

TALEESHA
You're vegetarian?

FAIRY
Well, yes.

TALEESHA
Alright, Jesus, don't go on about it.

FAIRY
Ok... Now, what about if we-

TALEESHA
Do you wear leather shoes?

FAIRY
Excuse me?

TALEESHA
Leather underwear?

FAIRY
No!

TALEESHA
I bet you eat chicken.

FAIRY
The animals are my friends! I find it very soothing petting badgers and stroking beavers and holding little tits in my hand.

TALEESHA
Say that again.

FAIRY
No.

TALEESHA
Is there really nothing you can do?

FAIRY
You got into this mess.

TALEESHA
Please?

Eye contact. She's irresistible.

FAIRY
I suppose I could try and *magic* up a heart.

TALEESHA
Sweet!

FAIRY
Listen, it's pretty high-grade magic this, I can't say it'll work. Have you got something to put it in.

TALEESHA
Yeah, he gave me a wooden box thing.

FAIRY
Ok.

The FAIRY concentrates hard with her eyes shut and is about to cast a spell.

TALEESHA
Here...

FAIRY
What?!

TALEESHA
Do you want to get a drink sometime?

FAIRY
A - a drink? I – er I – I don't go out with axe murderers! (beat) Or with anyone much. I'm happy with my company. Now, come on. Get your box out.

BLACKOUT

Scene 6: The cottage

We're in a tiny cottage. There is a bowl and spoon on the tiny table, at which there are tiny chairs. Somewhere there is an opened tub of Quality Street chocolates. There is a tiny fridge. On an upper level, reached by a little ladder, are seven tiny beds. The front door is very short and has a little hole in it at crotch height. It is quite dark. The door opens and SNOW enters, nervously.

SNOW
Hello...?

He finds a light switch and the place becomes much cheerier.

SNOW
Hello boys and girls! I ran deep into the woods and suddenly I saw this little cottage. Oh my, this is adorbs! I wonder who lives here, it must be children! Gosh, I'm really hungry.

He sees the Quality Street. He takes one, eats it and puts the wrapper back in the tub.

They've got Sky! That's banned in Lumley, they must get signal out here in the forest. Seven tiny beds! With adjectives carved on them – they must be their names. Let's see. High, Horny, Top, Bottom, Sleazy, Sweaty and Philippa. Poor Philippa.

A great crash of thunder. It rains heavily.

SNOW
Bollocks! I left my cagoule at the palace. (He sits) I'm so tired and those beds do look soft. Do you think anyone would mind if I had a snooze here?

He notices a little curtained doorway leading further into the cottage.

Ooh I wonder what's through there.

He exits, neatly ducking so as not to bang his head.

BLACKOUT. A clock ticks over the rain. Lights up on the same. The external door opens. GRIZZLY BEAR squeezes through, banging his head on the doorway in the process. He is in considerable pain. A large open umbrella now fills the doorway, its owner unable to get it through. The umbrella disappears and HONEY BEAR enters, backwards, holding the umbrella's handle. The umbrella is still up and won't come through the door after him.

HONEY BEAR
(Singing) De dum, de dee, we're back in time for tea.

The umbrella is still stuck.

GRIZZLY BEAR
Take it down!

HONEY
You're right. (Singing in a lower key) De dum, de dee, we're back in time for- oh I see!

The umbrella contracts and HONEY BEAR pulls it through the door.

HONEY
Home sweet home! Hello boys and girls! I said hello boys and girls! I'm Honey Bear and this is my companion, Grizzly Bear. We're back from a hard day's work at our little cannabis plantation in the forest. It makes us happy, dopey, sleepy and in a certain someone's case just a little bit grumpy. Oh Grizzly Bear, did you bang your big sexy head?

GRIZZLY
Don't fuss, Honey Bear! I'm fine!

He walks into the table which is at knee height and yelps.

HONEY
Why don't you sit your big sexy self down.

GRIZZLY
I'm not a child!

HONEY
A big sexy child!

GRIZZLY
That's weird.

GRIZZLY sits moodily in a tiny armchair, getting his bottom wedged in it.

GRIZZLY
We should never have bought this cottage. Fucking estate agents, their cameras make everything look enormous.

HONEY
A bit like the men on Scruff[24]. We'll get used to it, you'll see. You're just tired from a long day's work. Just think, we finally have a place of our own! My Cath Kidston

---

[24] A gay dating and hook-up app.

dressing-gown hanging next to your Tom of Finland pyjamas... The dwarves moved out to pursue a career in acting, boys and girls.

GRIZZLY
Short films, mainly.

HONEY
One of them called in yesterday to collect some mail. Touchy little fellow. He told me he was working on an exciting project and when I asked him if he'd like to expand he said, "how fucking dare you" and punched me in the knee.

GRIZZLY (pointing at the door)
The only upside to the place is that the dwarves' spyhole is the perfect height for a glory hole.

HONEY
Now why don't I make us a nice cup of tea.

HONEY busies himself. GRIZZLY looks in the bowl.

GRIZZLY
Someone's been eating my porridge!

HONEY
No one's been eating your porridge!

HONEY absent-mindedly picks up the open tub of Quality Street.

HONEY
I've told you not to leave it out all day, it sets like concrete and it's not you that ends up washing it up. (Beat) Oh now really! Someone's put empty Quality Street wrappers back in the box!

GRIZZLY
Is that an accusation?

HONEY
Get the milk would you?

GRIZZLY
Yes...

HONEY
In the fridge.

GRIZZLY
The fridge...

HONEY
The "cheese cupboard".

GRIZZLY

Right-o. (He can't get up from the tiny chair) Fuck's sake.

HONEY
I'm here I'm here.

HONEY tries to pull him up. When he does, the chair is still wedged onto his bottom. HONEY offers a hand to someone in the front row.

HONEY
Hello what's your name? You're going to have to help me.

He brings the audience member on stage.

Don't worry, you're perfectly safe. It's not the Old Vic[25].

He gets the audience member to help him separate Grizzly from the chair.

HONEY
(To Grizzly) Right. You – milk. Me – kettle. (To the audience member) You – sit. We'll have to pay Equity minimum if you're up here much longer. That's funny because it isn't true.

GRIZZLY opens the little fridge.

GRIZZLY
Someone's been drinking our milk!

HONEY takes the milk bottle from him, as GRIZZLY stomps off deeper into the cottage, banging his head loudly on the door as he goes.

HONEY
Oh look at that, it's not even completely empty it's just *almost* empty. I couldn't glaze a garibaldi with that!

GRIZZLY enters, banging his head again.

GRIZZLY
Not only has someone used up all but one sheet of bog roll, they've also left the biggest floater I have ever seen.

HONEY
Oh really! Why can't you flush.

GRIZZLY

---

[25] In 2017 the Old Vic Theatre said it had received 20 personal testimonies of alleged inappropriate behaviour by its former Artistic Director Kevin Spacey.

Flush? You'd need a crane to lift the bastard out. It's like the Mary fucking Rose.

HONEY
Let's have a nice sit down and watch telly. Enjoy our new life together. (He picks up a remote and points it) Oh heavens sake. Who's played silly monkeys with our Sky box settings!

GRIZZLY
Someone's been here!

HONEY
In my little cottage! Boys and girls! Have we been burgled? Is there a murderer here? Grizzly Bear, search the house.

GRIZZLY (a bit scared)
Why don't you search the house?

HONEY
We'll both search the house. I'll start here in the kitchen and you can look upstairs.

GRIZZLY (still a bit scared)
Why don't we both go upstairs?

HONEY
Darling it's hardly the moment.

GRIZZLY
It never is. Come on.

They climb up to the bedroom and gingerly touch the heap of bedding.

GRIZZLY
Something's here.

HONEY
Kill it!

GRIZZLY
I'll get a knife.

HONEY
A knife?! There'll be blood all over my stairs! Use something blunt.

GRIZZLY picks up a candlestick. SNOW enters casually in vest and underpants, or perhaps oversized pyjamas, brushing his teeth. The BEARS are mesmerised. SNOW doesn't notice them. He takes his time. He stretches. He slips a hand in his pants and adjusts his balls. The BEARS sigh.

HONEY
Right. Kill it.

SNOW screams.

GRIZZLY
It's a boy!

SNOW screams again.

GRIZZLY
It's alright, we won't hurt you.

HONEY
Won't hurt him!?

SNOW
Sorry!

HONEY
Explain yourself.

SNOW
I'm from the palace. Babs sent me into the forest to be killed, but I escaped. I only wanted somewhere safe to rest. (beat) I'm afraid I ate a few of your chocolates.

HONEY
And drank our milk. And diddled with our telly.

GRIZZLY
...And you finished off the last of Honey Bear's special white chocolate and raspberry ice cream that you knew he was looking forward to!

HONEY BEAR looks furiously at GRIZZLY, who looks very guilty and shifty.

HONEY
Well, we're glad you're safe. Good luck on your way.

GRIZZLY
On his way? You shall stay here with us.

HONEY
We only moved in together a week ago! Darling, please. This is meant to be our special time.

SNOW (sweetly)
Oh you're a couple!

GRIZZLY
Well it's very casual.

SNOW
I'll get out of your way.

GRIZZLY
We wouldn't dream of it. You nearly got killed!

HONEY
You're not far off. There's no space.

GRIZZLY
We've got seven beds.

HONEY
In one bedroom.

GRIZZY
Well....

HONEY
Oh, I see!

GRIZZLY
What?

HONEY
The boy doesn't want to be lying next to you while you fart your way through your night sweats.

SNOW
Oh god!

HONEY
Now what?

SNOW
Don't look in the toilet.

HONEY
Too late.

SNOW
Cringe!

GRIZZLY
There's no need to be embarrassed! Only the finest little botty could produce a turd as noble as that.

HONEY
Oh my living soul.

SNOW
I could go on the sofa?

HONEY
We are not into that!

SNOW
To sleep, I mean. But don't worry, I'll be fine. I just – well I don't know the forest at all. And if I go back to town, Babs might find me and kill me. And I've nothing warm to wear. Or money to buy food. And no phone...

The bears look on at this sad tale. A moment.

HONEY
Right well best of luck.

SNOW
And I'm sure this isn't remotely of interest but I am actually the fairest in the land.

GRIZZLY
He's staying.

SNOW
Yay! Right, before anything else can I get the wifi password and borrow a lightning charger?

HONEY
I thought you didn't have a phone.

SNOW
Yeah I was making a sex party joke, but it didn't really land.

HONEY
There's the door. Mind your head.

GRIZZLY
Honey!! This isn't the kind, sweet bear I fell in love with.

HONEY
Oh, Grizzly.

SNOW
It won't be for long. One day my prince is going to come along and carry me away. I'd make it up to you.

GRIZZLY
What you got in mind?

SONG: THREE OF A KIND

SNOW
I'll clean the lube you spill on the stairs
I'll clean the shower when it's full of hairs
It's natural when you live with bears
You'd barely know I'm here

I'll clean in my pants, oh yes I will
Even if it's cold and I catch a chill
I'll bend over to clean the window sill
Oops sorry there's my rear,
I'm only talking temporary
I'd bring a touch of class like Mary Berry

We're three of a kind, two bears and a twink
And if we can get on well it makes you think
If the world could be like we three

There'd be nothing but harmony!

I'll be your sous-chef if you'll be mine
I'll make you tea and pour you wine
I'll get out of your hair on Valentines
Unless you want me to stay...?
I'll beat your rugs and scrub your floors
Picture me down on all fours
Or cleaning your chimney like a twink Santa Claus,
Did I mention that I'm gay?

I'm happy to sit in the kitchen peeling
I'll bring a little edge like Noel Fielding

ALL
We're three of a kind, two bears and a twink
And if we can get on well it makes you think
If the world could be like we three
There'd be nothing but harmony.

SNOW
While I serenade you, can I persuade you?
Baked goods and apple puds and lemonade you?

BEARS
Together's better than alone,
Welcome home!

Scene 7: The palace

BABS is talking to the MIRROR.

BABS
Mirror mirror, don't let me down
Who is the fairest queen in town?

MIRROR
Dude! That face! That hair! Those abs?
The fairest in this town is Babs

BABS
Does mirror have a crush on his little queen?
I've never asked which way you lean.

MIRROR
It's academic, Babs, cos I'm stuck behind glass
But at boys *or* girls I'd make a pass

BABS
Oh so you're a two-way mirror!
Well now, while I've time to dither,
And as I'm beautiful, buff and healthy
I'll celebrate with a little selfie.

BABS takes a few photos of himself in the mirror with his phone. A range of poses and expressions.

BABS
It's harder than it looks, whichever way you turn,
You think you're looking sultry but you end up looking stern.

He takes a few more then turns around, pushing his bum out.

MIRROR
Work it, work it.

BABS takes a shot over his shoulder to get a rear view. Then bends to take one through his legs. TALEESHA enters with the box.

BABS
Taleesha! Have you crossed the Rubicon? Is this his heart?

He takes the box and holds it aloft.

The boy lies dead, cross forest and field
My fate as Lumley's pin-up is sealed!
Now behold, his vital organ revealed.

He opens the box and looks inside.

A penis?! Is this a joke? I wanted his heart, not just his penis!

TALEESHA
Well that's men for you!

BABS
I wanted him dead!

TALEESHA
I killed him sir, honest.

BABS
Oh no she didn't.

Oh yes she did.

BABS
I see.

TALEESHA
It's just ain't easy cutting a corpse's heart out, especially as I'd lost me axe in the brouhaha.

BABS
The brouhaha? I told you take him to the forest, not Lumley's only hipster pub!

TALEESHA
No sir, the ruckus. The commotion. So all I had to do the dissection with was a plastic spoon out of a pasta salad what I'd bought on the way.

BABS
It can't have been pleasant.

TALEESHA
You're telling me. They'd put tuna in it and I hate tuna.

BABS
Yes... You don't seem especially traumatised.

TALEESHA
Well I've eaten worse.

BABS
By the killing.

TALEESHA
I know but it probably had a long and happy life swimming about in the ocean until it was caught.

BABS
Snow White's killing!

TALEESHA
Oh that! I expect it's shock. It won't have hit me yet. (beat) Oh God what have I done?!?! (beat) There it is.

BABS
Well done Taleesha. Severing a penis and smuggling it all this way! Who'd have thought you'd have it in you!

TALEESHA
I didn't take it out of its box!

BABS
Nanny! Rihanna! Staff meeting at once!

NANNY and the PRINCE arrive.

PRINCE
My first staff meeting!

NANNY
I've brought your favourite shortbread, Babs. (To the prince) What did you bring? Oh, nothing. Very bold.

BABS
I'm afraid, my dear ones, I have sad news.

NANNY
Has Trump cancelled his state visit to Lumley?

BABS
It's more of a personal nature. You see – I can barely find the words – our young Snow has died.

NANNY
No!

PRINCE
No!!!

NANNY
You can pipe down with your virtue signalling, you barely knew him. My poor snow! And just as he was filling out so nicely in the chest and shoulders.

PRINCE
He was so beautiful.

BABS
(tetchy) Yes all right! Don't be so hysterical!

NANNY
You never call me hysterical.

BABS
Now, this brings me to item one. As you were Snow's Nanny, Fanny, there's no longer a position for you here. You'll pack your bags immediately.

NANNY
But Babs!

BABS
We're not a care home. The days of having a job for life are long gone.

NANNY
But- but who will cook for you?

BABS
I haven't touched a mouthful of your hideous food since I found a toenail in the Christmas dinner.

NANNY
You asked for all the trimmings!

BABS
I've survived quite well on Deliveroo – they've such delicious cyclists, too. Off you go.

NANNY is very sad. "Ahhh"

NANNY
I think we might do a little better than that.

Ahhhhh.

NANNY
I've no place to go! But I shan't stay where I'm not wanted. May I take a little something of Snow's to remember him by.

BABS passes her the box containing the penis.

BABS
Well as it's you.

NANNY opens it, curious. She stares into it, confused.

NANNY
I don't understand.

BABS
Oh please, if you laid all the ones you'd seen end to end they'd reach to Uranus and back.

NANNY
I know what it is. But *this* one isn't-

TALEESHA nudges her hard and urgently to shut her up.

NANNY
Taleesha! We're all shaken and I know I conditioned my hair this morning but control your urges. I was merely pointing out that this particular-

TALEESHA slaps her.

TALEESHA
She's distraught.

NANNY
I am now!

NANNY raises a fist to TALEESHA.

BABS
Enough! Leave my staff alone and get out!

NANNY pulls a sad face and trudges off. BABS picks up the box.

BABS
Ungrateful bitch. Well, such excitement, I'm off. Toodle-oo.

PRINCE
To the loo?

BABS
To my sunbed. Ciao.

BABS exits.

PRINCE
Poor innocent Snow!

TALEESHA
Come here. *(She hugs him)* Do you want to go for a walk in the secluded orchard?

PRINCE
A glass of champagne might help.

TALEESHA
A glass of champagne and a movie curled up together under a duvet on the sofa with a bowl of low fat corn chips and salted caramel popcorn?

PRINCE
First Wives Club?

TALEESHA
Thelma and Louise?

PRINCE
Double bill?

TALEESHA
Perfect!

They exit, as BABS enters. He sings to the tune of Seven Nation Army/Oh Jeremy Corbyn: Ohhhh Quee-ee-een Ba-abs, Ohhhh Quee-ee-een Ba-abs.

BABS
Yes it's all worked out just as I planned,
Yours truly is the fairest in the land!

I'll have new banknotes printed in my honour! My visage and chest adorning the front. A tasteful bum shot on the reverse... Perhaps a hologram of my hole. Ah, commoners, what bliss!

An owl hoots.

And so peaceful without Snowflake and his monstrous nanny! You can hear everything ticking over. The London traffic safely in the distance... Your bowels resettling sir after a lengthy bottoming session.

He spots a newspaper. He looks at it.

A newspaper!? We have no newspapers! Oh it's British! Strange. *(He flicks through it. He gasps, delighted)* There's a picture of me! *(He reads)* "Lumley's insane, despotic ruler, the self-styled Queen Babs, is said by some to be the fairest in the borough". I'm adored! Adored! Look! There's a whole story about Lumley! "... Your intrepid reporter found a once great country on its last legs, and appalling human rights abuses..." We have the best gay pride parade in the world! What more do they fucking want! "While trains grind to a halt and hospitals strain to cope, vain Babs-" Fake news! "-spends every waking hour preening and grooming. If only the true heir to Lumley's throne, the even fairer Snow White, was in charge."

He hurls the paper away.

Well he's not in charge! He's dead! Haha!!! Miroir! Wax my balls and get my ring done, who is the fairest in the kingdom?

The MIRROR comes to life.

MIRROR
Always this question! It's never politics is it. It's never literature over a nice glass of Malbec.

BABS
If you want to get smashed that can be facilitated. Indulge me!

MIRROR
Right... To withhold such a thing would be travesty, the fairest in town is our very own majesty!

BABS
(Dancing with glee and singing) He stirs your loins! His face is on the coins! It's Babs! Queen Babs- Wait!! I asked who was the fairest not in the town but in the kingdom.

MIRROR
Well it's all the same.

BABS
Then answer me.

MIRROR
You're putting me on the spot!

BABS
I will put my fist through you.

MIRROR
Sir I'm blushing!

BABS
Mirror!

MIRROR
Very well you sexy pup, you're our noble runner up.

BABS
Runner up!?

MIRROR

For on this peaceful, balmy night, the fairest in the land is Snow White.

BABS
Traitors! Plotters!

MIRROR (unconvincing)
Your portraits always have the healthiest throng about them in the gallery.

BABS
If you want something done properly, do it yourself! Snow will fall! I will hunt him down and kill him - myself!

The FAIRY appears

FAIRY
What earthly horrors lie in wait!
Warm beer, that wine, the pervs in the loo,
But as for our young Snow White's fate
Be sure to join us for part two!

INTERVAL

Christopher Lane as Queen Babs in *Snow White: Rotten to the Core*. Photo by PBGstudios.

Andrew Truluck as the Town Crier in *Snow White: Rotten to the Core*. Photo by PBGstudios.

Scene 8: The forest

FAIRY
Welcome back boys and girls, we're more than half way!
Now previously on "Snow White - The Play"
One boy went into hiding, another's in drag,
And Babs learnt that victory's not in the bag,
The girl seemed to think I'm a bit of alright,
But what of poor Nanny, cast out in the night?

The FAIRY exits. A wild wind howls. NANNY fights against it, plodding on with a little suitcase. Perhaps she wields an inside-out, wind-torn umbrella.

NANNY
Boys and girls! Here I am alone in the forest, vulnerable to wild animals and predatory men. (louder) I said, vulnerable to wild animals and predatory men!

A squirrel puppet appears.

NANNY
Disappointing. What is it? A squirrel! Are they dangerous? What do squirrels eat? I'm sorry, squirrel, I'm afraid I don't have nuts. (To the audience) I see we've found your level. (She sits on her suitcase). Now boys and girls, I'm very tired and need a nap but I've heard that this forest is inhabited by big fuck-off scary wolves. Will you keep watch while I rest? If you should see a big fuck-off scary wolf creeping up behind me, I'd like you all to shout "Nanny Fanny, there's a big fuck-off scary wolf creeping up behind you". Got it?

She snoozes. A fearsome wolf pokes its head from the vegetation. They shout.

NANNY
Boys and girls really I'm trying to rest! What is it? A wolf? Where? Over there?

The wolf retracts when she turns to it.

NANNY
Boys and girls I think you're mistaken, settle down.

She naps again and the wolf appears in another place. The audience shouts. The wolf vanishes.

NANNY
I don't think that's very funny boys and girls. Here I am alone and vulnerable and all you can do... is to cry wolf.

The wolf appears again, this time with a fake nose and moustache. The audience shouts. This time Nanny sees it. She goes to it.

NANNY
Good evening sir, we're looking for a wolf, have you seen one?

The wolf shakes his head.

NANNY
Will you keep a look out for it?

The wolf nods.

NANNY
Such a gentleman, let me kiss your snout.

The wolf screams and vanishes. The FAIRY enters.

FAIRY (sung)
Into the forest diddly dee,
A snooty lady has to flee
She stops a while to catch her breath
Before she meets her certain death!

NANNY
Certain death? Who are you?

FAIRY
I'm a fairy and I live in a forest.

NANNY
Well I'm a Nanny and I live in a... nice palace. Or rather I did. I was born into nobility, spent years as a servant and now I'm homeless and penniless.

FAIRY
You'd have a much happier ending if you told that story backwards.

NANNY
I've had the most trying day.

FAIRY
Well that's life sometimes. N'night.

NANNY (almost in tears)
Please!

The FAIRY can't help it.

FAIRY
Right... What do you usually do when you're feeling down?

NANNY
I beg your pardon!?

147

FAIRY
I'll tell what I do when I'm in the dumps.

NANNY
What, apart from scavenging for clothes?

FAIRY
I sing a little song. Here why don't I teach you the chorus! Here we go.

> When I'm sad, when I'm blue
> When I don't know what to do
> I know a little trick,
> When I'm in a nasty slump
> When you'd say I've got the hump
> Well please don't think me sick
> Don't be weary, don't be annoyed
> Try a little schadenfreude.

Got it?

NANNY
Oh I expect so! But shouldn't the waifs and strays join in too?

FAIRY
That's a good idea!

NANNY
I expect we'll need some sort of song sheet, not to mention ear plugs.

The FAIRY magics a song-sheet. They sing the chorus again.

FAIRY
Oh yes very good! Why don't we do the song and the boys and girls can join in the choruses.

NANNY
How many choruses are there?

FAIRY
Three.

NANNY
Well! Why doesn't everyone on my side sing the first chorus, because they look like better singers!

FAIRY
And why doesn't everyone on my side sing the second chorus, cos they're more like the headline act after your warm-up.

NANNY

And we'll all sing the third together! How does it start?

FAIRY
It starts with a chorus.

NANNY
Marvellous! Are you ready team Fanny?

They sing. NANNY and the FAIRY sing the verses and all join in with the choruses.

SONG: SHADENFREUDE

When I'm sad when I'm blue
When I don't know what to do
I know a little trick
When I'm in a nasty slump
When you'd say I've got the hump
Well please don't think me sick
Don't be weary, don't be annoyed
Try a little schadenfreude.

Have a chuckle when someone's card gets cloned
While they're holidaying overseas
It's a laugh if a friend says he got boned
Only to find the bastard gave him fleas

When I'm sad when I'm blue... [etc]

When someone sees a drag race spoiler
Spends two grand on a faulty boiler
Sees their naked selfies leaked
Just laugh because your day just peaked

When I'm sad when I'm blue... [etc]

NANNY
Oh boys and girls thank you! That's completely taken my mind off the fact that I'm tired and lost and scared and hungry.

FAIRY
Hungry she says!

NANNY
I'll thank you not to narrate me.

FAIRY
The forest is full of food.

NANNY
I haven't a gun.

FAIRY
There's blackberries.

NANNY
One can't kill a stag with blackberries.

The FAIRY picks a mushroom.

FAIRY
Have a mushroom.

NANNY
It's filthy!

FAIRY
Garnished with the good earth of the land. *(She spits on the mushroom and rubs it on her skirt).* Here. Go crazy.

NANNY eats it.

FAIRY
How is it?

NANNY
Bitter. And grittier than a play about chemsex at the King's Head Theatre[26]. Goodness, look at those trees swaying.

FAIRY
Swaying?

NANNY
In time to the music.

FAIRY
Music?

NANNY
I think you might be coming down with something, you've gone a little green. (beat) Red (beat) Purple. Oh God what's happening to me?

FAIRY
Ooops! It's ok, you're in a safe place. Sit it out. Enjoy it.

NANNY
Enjoy it? When the trees are chasing me? Oh, mercy!

NANNY runs off into the forest.

FAIRY
And just like that, off she went!
Now let's see how Snow White's been paying the rent.

---

[26] Islington's King's Head Theatre had recently staged gay sex-themed shows including *The Chemsex Monologues*, *Five Guys Chillin'* and *The Clinic*.

Scene 9: The cottage

SNOW WHITE sits on GRIZZLY's knee. HONEY BEAR is pointedly getting ready for work.

GRIZZLY BEAR
And there was one time at Honey Bear's old place he got so upset at putting too much paprika in the goulash he locked himself in his bedroom and left me to host the dinner party!

SNOW
Really!?

GRIZZLY
Nobody would have cared, they'd only come over to play the hat game and have a go on the sling.

SNOW
How did you meet?

GRIZZLY
In a dark room. There he was under a low watt bulb with his knee pads and his little bottle of anti-bacterial.

SNOW laughs far more than this warrants.

HONEY
PrEP does not protect you from day-to-day household germs! Are you ready for work?

GRIZZLY
Yeah yeah just a minute. (to Snow) You will stay safe?

HONEY
Oh I think he'll be safe enough out here in the cottage. After all, *you'll* be at work.

SNOW
Let me get your packed lunches!

HONEY (opening the fridge)
Too late.

He retrieves a large picnic hamper. He gives it to Grizzly.

HONEY
There's yours.

He retrieves another large hamper.

HONEY
Here's mine.

GRIZZLY
I might just take a salad.

HONEY drops his picnic hamper.

HONEY
What?

GRIZZLY
It don't hurt to be a bit in shape.

HONEY
If you don't eat properly you'll end up like this Twigletty little stick insect, present company excepted, and we wouldn't like that, would we.

GRIZZLY goes to him, a little way away from SNOW.

GRIZZLY
You're just a bit tired.

HONEY
Tired! I didn't expect our bedroom to be infested with a *louse* quite this early into our cohabitation!

GRIZZLY
You started it.

HONEY
I started it?! You invited him to sleep with us, and then proceeded to talk inanities until 3am because you didn't know how to instigate anything. If I hadn't given him the old spit and knuckles we'd have been swapping coming out stories till sunrise and had no sleep, and then where would we be?

GRIZZLY
You looked like you were enjoying it.

HONEY
Oh but darling I always *look* like I'm enjoying it with you.

SNOW
Welcome back boys and girls! The bears have been so kind to me, you know I think they'll be quite sad to see me go when my Prince turns up. It was a bit of an unexpected night... (Confiding) First I tried Grizzly bears, but Grizzly Bear's was just a little too large. And then I tried Honey Bear's but that was just a little too small. Then they shoved some poppers up my nose and both dived in at once and that felt just dandy. I mustn't make a habit of it, I need my beauty sleep what with being the fairest in the land.

HONEY (To GRIZZLY – warmer)
Oh come here. Who's my big hunky chunky monkey?

SNOW WHITE: ROTTEN TO THE CORE

GRIZZLY (also softening)
I am!

They kiss, a nice little moment.

HONEY
Right, we're off. Snow, you need to refill the generator, clean out the cess pit, polish the bed heads, give the rugs a shake, iron the curtains, clean the toilet including the underside of the seat because it's got some awful brown mottling, compost the window boxes, put the scraps in the compost and then the day is yours. Grizzly, ready?

GRIZZLY clears his throat. The BEARS sing.

SONG: HO HO HO

Ho ho ho! Ho ho ho!
We're chopping wood for market
The finest wood you've seen
But inside each little bundle
We hide an ounce of green
Sure as someone buying roses
Is hoping to get boned,
If someone says they're getting wood
they're likely getting stoned!

They exit with their lunches, possibly banging their heads on the door frame. SNOW is suddenly very alone. He sings.

SONG: ONE DAY A PRINCE WILL COME

One day a prince will come
And the worst of my days will be done
He'll be charming and gay
And he'll know straight away
that he loves me
One day a prince will rescue me
No more fear or hard labour he'll set me free
He'll kiss my weird feet,
Hold my hand in the street
cos he loves me

He'll wake up and shower, bring me breakfast in bed
And feed me with pancakes while he gives me head
He'll love me as I am, but he'll go to the gym
And have lovely friends who like me more than him

One day I'll stand proud and tall
In a house where the chairs aren't too small
And I don't bang my head
And no one wants me dead at all

He'll tell me he only has eyes for me
But won't mind me pointing out guys on tv
And maybe we'll have the occasional fight
But at least I won't cry on my own late at night,
When he comes.

There is a knocking at the door.

SNOW
There's somebody at the door! Could it be my Prince? Or could it be Babs?! I know! I'll peek through the glory hole.

As he bends to do so, a flesh-coloured dildo is thrust through it at great speed and wiggles about.

NANNY (off)
Come on! Open up! I can hear you in there!

SNOW opens the door.

SNOW
Nanny!

NANNY
I knew it! Hello boys and girls! (Re the dildo) This was stood up in the garden next to the gnome, its nose in the air like a meerkat. I thought it was another fungus. Oh Snow! I've been de-employed! Un-homed! I've walked for hours! Days! Possibly weeks, we never quite agreed on a timeframe did we. Now come here.

She pulls SNOW'S waist band and looks inside the front of his pants.)

I knew it wasn't yours! You might want a trim, darling, where are the scissors?

SNOW
No! They like me furry.

NANNY notices the tiny chairs. She picks one up and stares at it.

NANNY
You may have misread the Ikea instructions.

SNOW
Oh, no, they were left by the dwarves.

NANNY
Dwarves? I once knew a cottage of dwarves. I wonder...

SNOW
But now it's bears.

NANNY
Bears?!

SNOW
Gay bears! Not real bears.

NANNY
Snow! Just because a bear happens to be gay it doesn't make him any less of a bear.

SNOW
No it's a type. Like otters.

NANNY
I see! (She peruses the audience) What are you, a spaniel? ...A wallaby? ...Pangolin... Shrimp... Right, pop the kettle on while I freshen up, it's been quite the ordeal. I might as well familiarise myself if I'm to be living here.

She starts to exit but bangs her head on the door violently.

SNOW
Poor Nanny!

NANNY (upset)
You might have warned me! Run me a bath would you?

SNOW
I can't, they've only got a shower.

NANNY
Only a shower!? How can you bear it here! If I wanted to live in a rabbit hutch with barely half a bathroom I'd move to Haggerston and pay four hundred grand for it! I'm tired, I'm cold, I'm god-knows how far from civilisation! *(A beat. Then happy)* Oh look, they've got Sky!

Scene 10: The square

There are now large banners with a heroic portrait of Babs on them. The FAIRY has a fishing rod and dangles it in the well. The PRINCE enters, still in drag.

FAIRY
Morning miss.

PRINCE
I already give to charity.

FAIRY
Do you?

PRINCE
Of course. I have youth membership of the National Trust. It's been marvellous this year with all the gay celebrations, absolutely crawling with screamers. Prowling through the ornamental mazes like it's the Hyde Park rose garden at midnight. I couldn't tell you the number of times I've been taken aback at a priest hole. *(looks at her)* Oh it's you.

FAIRY
How's it hanging?

PRINCE
It's not, it's all bunched up between my thighs. And these shoes are excruciating but Babs insists they're required uniform. This morning he squeezed my bottom and when I shrieked he said he was gay so it was just for a laugh and I wasn't to get prissy about it. Why do you wear such ridiculous things? Well not you. Proper women. A skirt like this, I'm asking for trouble. I passed a building sight on my way from the palace, and I heard a wolf whistle from above.

FAIRY
At last! I've been teaching that wolf to whistle for months.

PRINCE
I looked up to see a handsome builder with deliciously awful tribal tattoos, and I made to give him a wave, only to realise said whistle had come from his unfortunate friend, who had the appearance of one who's been beaten about the face by a shovel before having part of his brain removed with it. I scowled at him, in response to which he shouted that I was too ugly to be fussy! I'll ask Babs to find out who they are

and have the pair of them sacked. *Please* can I stop now?

FAIRY
Well yeah, you are going on a bit.

PRINCE
I wish to be a man again.

FAIRY
All in good time. What are you doing this fine morning?

PRINCE
My young man died two weeks ago! So I'm going for a walk to be alone with my all too brief memories of him.

FAIRY
Ah, mourning.

PRINCE
Yes good morning. Now excuse me.

The TOWN CRIER enters. He has a handbell.

TOWN CRIER
Hear ye, hear ye!

He rings his bell but it is silent.

FAIRY
Your bell is busted.

TOWN CRIER
Little Ben is silenced! Democracy would fall apart, were we a democracy[27].

FAIRY
Get on with it!

TOWN CRIER
Snow White is wanted for treason! All Lumleyans are hereby instructed to keep their eyes peeled for him. By order of Queen Babs.

The TOWN CRIER exits.

PRINCE
What do you make of that?!

FAIRY
He was better as the mirror.

---

[27] In August of 2017, to the dismay of Prime Minister Theresa May and other senior MPs, Big Ben's chimes were silenced while a four-year restoration programme was begun on the tower. The decision to silence the bells was to protect construction workers' hearing.

153

PRINCE

Snow White's alive! I must find him! The last I saw of him, he was going for a tramp in the woods.

FAIRY

He didn't *seem* the violent sort. Well, good luck. But don't forget – you must stay in disguise until the curse is lifted.

The PRINCE exits. The FAIRY starts sliding the wishing well into the wings.

FAIRY

Into the forest, dum de dum,
A young man strode in search of bum,
Has life for our foresters turned a page?
We'll see once I've got this well off-stage.

Scene 11: Outside the cottage

Basically the forest. SNOW WHITE, HONEY and GRIZZLY. There is a hog roast on a spit over a fire which HONEY bear is turning. SNOW and GRIZZLY are sat down drinking and laughing.

SNOW
Hello boys and girls!

GRIZZLY
We're having a "bear-be-cue".

SNOW laughs

HONEY
Grizzly, are you going to take a turn on the pig, or does the poor creature remind you too much of your selfies from leather week?

GRIZZLY
It's nice and sunny Snow, why don't you take your top off.

SNOW
Why not.

He takes his shirt off. GRIZZLY shows a bottle of suntan lotion.

GRIZZLY
I'll do your back if you like.

GRIZZLY starts to rub sun tan cream into SNOW's back. The PRINCE enters.

PRINCE
Snow White!

SNOW
Lady Rihanna Perry-Swift!

PRINCE and SNOW WHITE (simultaneous)
(S)he remembers me! But of course (s)he does!

PRINCE
Thank God you're alive! What a charming little place.

He sits down, smooths his skirt. He's become very naturally feminine.

SNOW
Lady Rihanna, this is Grizzly Bear and Honey Bear, we're just friends.

GRIZZLY
Can we help you?

PRINCE
I expect you get up to all manner of naughtinesses out here in the woods!

SNOW (flirting)
Wouldn't you like to know!

The pig is now cooked.

HONEY
Pork anyone?

PRINCE
Not recently. Oh! No, thank you.

SNOW
There's tea.

PRINCE
Oh but swill my pot out, slap your bag in and bring me to the boil! I meant to say: you're in danger! Babs wants you for treason.

SNOW
Can't he do it himself?

PRINCE
He means to make an example of you.

SNOW
Well... we'll just have to stay here then, won't we.

GRIZZLY
We ain't got room.

HONEY
Nonsense, it's right that the boy has a companion his own age.

PRINCE (looking at the cottage)
Father has a folly rather like this cottage. I used to sit alone there in my formative years, the rain falling about me, wondering if I'd ever dare tell him that I was- but it doesn't matter.

SNOW
That you were what?

PRINCE
It's nothing.

SNOW sits next to the PRINCE. An intimacy.

SNOW
I used to sit out in the conservatory when it was raining. Wondering if I would ever dare tell *my* father that I was...

155

PRINCE
Yes?

SNOW
Hungry! I used to get very hungry. All that growing you do, as a teenage boy. But anyway, he died, so that story has no ending.

PRINCE
Your father?

SNOW
King Geoff the Handsome.

PRINCE
You were the late King Geoff the Handsome's son? (Aside) He's a Prince! A real prince!

TALEESHA (off)
Lady Rihanna!

PRINCE, SNOW
Taleesha!

TALEESHA enters, running.

TALEESHA
Hi hoes!

SNOW
Taleesha! You came to warn me!

TALEESHA
I'm so glad you're okay Lady Rihanna! I thought you'd got lost!

PRINCE
I went for a walk.

TALEESHA
I coulda joined you.

PRINCE
A man must be allowed alone with his thoughts!

They look at him. A man?

PRINCE
A man, in the er, generic sense.

SNOW
Well, it's nice to see you Taleesha, but I expect you'll want to get back.

TALEESHA
Oh! (Takes PRINCE's hand) Yeah, I expect you don't want us girls hanging about, cramping your gay little home.

SNOW
Gay?! Oh, yes! It is gay isn't it! Jolly and gay!

PRINCE
Might *I* still stay for tea?

SNOW
You're not going anywhere.

PRINCE
How forceful!

TALEESHA
Well I suppose I *could* stay.

SNOW
No no.

NANNY enters she wears a bathing costume and large ornate sunglasses. She carries a cake.

NANNY
Glorious day!

HONEY
That's my swimming cossie!

NANNY
Yes thank you Sherlock, I hardly thought it was Kate Moss's. Incidentally, one is supposed to remove the plastic lining from the gusset upon purchase. If things get any more tropical down there I'll start producing orchids.

She hands the cake to the bears.

NANNY
There you go, chaps. Don't worry, I'm not stopping.

She sits down.

GRIZZLY
Right. Only you have been saying that every day for two weeks.

NANNY
No no, you see some day soon a Prince is going to turn up and take Snow and I away.

SNOW and PRINCE
And you?!

NANNY
Now, goodness, it's quite the party, who wants to fill me in?

PRINCE
Babs knows Snow White is alive.

156

SNOW
He wants me for treason.

NANNY
Can't he do it himself? Look, we can't hide out here forever and if have to eat off your Wilko's crockery for another week I shall likely get gum disease. We must take revenge on Babs and restore ourselves to a home befitting our social standing.

TALEESHA
Don't get mad...

PRINCE
Get everything!

They both laugh.

SNOW
What?

TALEESHA and PRINCE
First Wives Club!

SNOW
Oh I haven't seen it.

TALEESHA and PRINCE (disappointed and dismissive)
Oh...

NANNY
So, here's the plan. Taleesha, *Lady* Rihanna, you two pop back to the palace where you're still welcome and kill Babs.

TALEESHA and PRINCE
Yes!

SNOW
Good luck! Hurry back, Lady Rihanna.

TALEESHA and the PRINCE exit.

NANNY
Do I detect a young man on the turn?

SNOW
I don't know. It seems such a fucking waste turning straight now that I know how to look good in a more obviously thirsty way and attract men.

NANNY
If only you had another, older woman with whom you might safely experiment... Do you know, I've realised why I've been here before! It was the little woodsman's cottage on daddy's estate. I don't remember the name

of the little woodsman. Or woodsmen, I think we had a succession.

SNOW
You had a suck session?

NANNY
Yes, a succession. Understandably so, there was a lot of wood to handle.

DILWYN DAVIES enters He is all got up in hiking gear.

DILWYN
Hello, sorry to intrude but I think I'm lost. I'm Dilwyn Davies. I'm on holiday. I'd never been to London see, so I thought I'd take my little tent and see what all the fuss was about.

SNOW
London! What's it like?

DILWYN
Well I wasn't disappointed by M&Ms World, but otherwise the place isn't for me. Very hectic, you know. A bit flashy. Buses every three minutes! And every time I pitched my tent the police would move me on. So, I packed myself up and headed to Ealing forest.

NANNY
Mr Davies, this is all very dull I'm sure but you're blocking the sun, I expect it's down to your lack of breeding, but if you really must complete your tale, for goodness sake sit down next to Nanny. Don't worry, now that I've got that off my chest I shan't hold it against you.

DILWYN
Your chest?

NANNY
Don't draw attention to it!

NANNY plumps up her chest and displays it.

DILWYN
Right! Well. After a day's perambulation I saw through the trees a mighty wall topped with barbed wire! Left and right it went as far as the eye could see. I suspected it must have some political function because there was a Banksy mural on it. Well now. Dilwyn I said, Dilwyn you'll have to turn back. Next thing I knew a branch snapped underfoot and I fell into a tunnel.

HONEY
The smuggler's tunnels!

SNOW
Babs said they'd all been filled with land mines.

DILWYN
No! I crawled through and here I am. Where am I?

SNOW
You're in Lumley-by-Gosh.

DILWYN
By Jove! Wait until I get back to the valleys and tell my customers about this.

NANNY
You have a business. An empire!

DILWYN
Oh no nothing like that. I work for the dairy farm. I'm a milkman. You could say I "keep a float".

NANNY (disappointed)
I see. How exciting for a lowly milkman to encounter a gentlewoman. Now these strapping chaps are Honey and Grizzly, and this is Snow White. They're homosexuals.

DILWYN
Yes I see it now! Like on the Bake Off.

NANNY
So you see your unrefined heterosexual energy is liable to cause all sorts of sparks to fly.

DILWYN
How fascinating. Can you advise me on any, ahem, "camp" sites?

NANNY laughs her tits off at this.

DILWYN
I say, you're the boy on the posters!

GRIZZLY
Posters?

DILWYN unrolls a poster. It has a picture of SNOW and says "Wanted: Snow White"

GRIZZLY
"Wanted. Snow White."

HONEY
Oh Grizzly, they must be auditioning for a pantomime! Can we?! I'll read the Ts and Cs. "A reward of fifty thousand Goshes is offered to anyone who can provide information to his worried uncle, Queen Babs."

DILWYN
He must be missing you. Shall I go and let him know you're safe?

NANNY
No! Mr Davies, stay with us for a few days. I'll show you where you might whack a peg in. The turf about my frontage is as yielding as any and should offer plenty of grip.

DILWYN
How incredibly kind of you.

NANNY
Did I mention my other house is a palace?

DILWYN
No! Why don't we go for a little stroll and you can tell me all about it.

NANNY smiles.

SNOW (to NANNY)
If I didn't know you better I'd say you've fallen for an untitled milkman.

NANNY
A milkman, really!

DILWYN
Shall we go for our stroll?

NANNY
If you insist but don't pester a lady.

SNOW
Don't get cream down your swimsuit.

They exit

GRIZZLY
Why don't we go for a walk in the woods too Snow.

SNOW
Ok! I'll get my shoes.

SNOW exits. HONEY picks up the "Wanted" poster.

GRIZZLY
That's a nice photo of him isn't it.

HONEY
Fifty thousand Goshes!

GRIZZLY
Babs must be desperate. Let's hide that.

HONEY
Of course. Just think though, what a couple of bears could do with that kind of money. Buy a house that's big enough for bears! Apply for an extremely expensive exit visa and go to bear week at Sitges!

GRIZZLY
A weekend on a cheese farm.

HONEY
Yes! Cadbury World!

GRIZZLY
A Celine Dion concert!

HONEY
Just the two of us.

GRIZZLY

Just the two of us...

SNOW enters with his shoes on.

SNOW
Well boys, shall we?

HONEY
Oh! Yes why not.

As HONEY follows them off...

GRIZZLY
Honey dear, we can't leave the pig unattended.

HONEY
Oh I'm sure you'll look after him.

GRIZZLY and SNOW exit. HONEY is dejected. He reads the poster again, puts it into his pocket and exits.

Scene 12: The palace

TALEESHA *is cleaning. The PRINCE is giving BABS a pedicure. TALEESHA removes a shotgun from the wall and creeps up behind BABS. He turns around and she hides the gun behind her back.*

BABS
What's the matter with you?

TALEESHA
Nothing. I was just thinking how beautiful you are.

PRINCE
As ever! Look in the mirror.

BABS
No! The wretched thing belongs in a skip! Well perhaps a little glimpse. Mirror mirror, in whom I groom, who is the fairest in the room?

MIRROR (with DILWYN's voice)
Now that's a new one.

BABS, TALEESHA and the PRINCE all shake their heads.

MIRROR
Sorry! I said this would happen. I had more downtime between parts when I spent an afternoon in the sand dunes on Gran Canaria. Right... You look delish, but if I may dare, you seem to have a nasal hair.

BABS
No!!

PRINCE
He's right you know. Get a closer look.

BABS gets up and looks in the mirror. The PRINCE picks up a knife and starts creeping up behind BABS.

PRINCE (whispering)
Come on!

TALEESHA
What?

PRINCE
While his back is turned!

TALEESHA
You want to creep up behind him, unseen, while he's looking in a fucking mirror?

BABS
What are you two doing?

PRINCE
Nothing!

TALEESHA
Just... getting the feel of it! I was planning on shooting a pheasant for your dinner tonight.

PRINCE
I was... going to carve it for you!

The door chimes. TALEESHA exits and returns with HONEY BEAR.

BABS
Go away! I'm very busy trying to extract a (whispers) nasal hair.

HONEY
Have you tried twisting it?

BABS
Twisting it?

HONEY
Yeah. It hurts less than pulling it and it'll be out in a second.

BABS tries this. It works. He presents the hair proudly. TALEESHA, the PRINCE and the MIRROR make a happy little gasp, "ahhhh!", as if having learnt something delightful.

TALEESHA
Right thanks for the life hack but his majesty's busy.

HONEY
I know where the boy is.

BABS
My dear little beanbag.

PRINCE
The man seems deranged.

BABS
Haven't you a pheasant to shoot?

He ushers them out forcefully. The mirror has faded to normal.

BABS
You're not hoaxing are you? Fifty thousand Goshes is an awful lot of money and in spite of the wealth and happiness I've brought to the kingdom, greed still abounds.

HONEY
Oh no sir.

BABS
Really, it breaks my heart, I'm all Snow White has. That's why I'm increasing the reward to one hundred thousand Goshes. Just think! You'll be able to buy iPhone Xs for your wife and children.

HONEY (thrilled)
Oh my God you thought I was straight! Ha! Wait till I tell my boyfriend.

BABS looks HONEY BEAR up and down.

BABS
You're gay? Good god, what happened? Depression or something? Well, I'm sure your boyfriend is very proud to have such a beefy little treat to call his own. Can't take his eyes off you I bet.

HONEY
I don't know about that any more... *(Decisive)* He's in our cottage in the woods.

BABS
How do I get there?

HONEY
You look for the tallest chestnut tree. Go past it and keep going in that direction.

BABS
Honey Bear, was it?

He takes out a chequebook, scribbles quickly, tears out a cheque and hands it to HONEY.

BABS
Don't spend it all on biltong you fat fuck. Off you go, I'll get my coat.

HONEY
Boys and girls! Did I do the right thing? Have I ballsed things up on a scale not seen since two successive Tory leaders thought they'd stake their party's future on their own dismal popularity? Oh dear.

He exits. BABS picks up a black cape. He sings.

SONG: DEAD PRETTY

Some are born to greatness
Some seize it with both hands
It's time to free myself and be
Greatest and the fairest in the land

I could have him sent away,
To Chechnya let's say,
But what if even they
Come to love the wretched gay...

But how to do it? What device will I employ
To give the boy his final day?

A cock ring that tightens as soon as it's worn
A tablet that zaps him when he watches porn
A guitar that explodes when struck by a plectrum
A dildo with spikes that pop out in his rectum

Prosecco so gassy he'll swell like a ball
Or magical shoes that cause him to fall
As he climbs up the stairs, or hey what the heck
A chic little scarf that cuts right through his neck

You'll be pretty, dead pretty!
And soon pretty dead
Your gorgeous cadaver won't trouble my head
And gentlemen callers will call to demand
To see me, cos I'll be the fairest in the land

A hair gel that poisons the skin underneath
At least he'll look stylish when I lay his wreath,
A gadget built badly, could that be the answer:
A microwave oven that fills him with cancer!

You'll be pretty, dead pretty
And soon you'll be gone
You're hardly Diana, they shan't mourn for long
The crowds will gasp and bow down and admire
When yours truly appears in his funeral attire

I'll be pretty, so pretty
And loved left and right
They'll crowd round the palace
For one little sight
I'll be Macron, Obama and Trudeau combined
And the star of this whole little show:
The whole of mankind!

Scene 13: The cottage

The Cottage, SNOW and NANNY are cleaning.

NANNY
Snow, start on the washing up then see what you can do to the oven with a steel brush. I'll give the surfaces a spritz, a woman's work is never done.

There is a knock at the door. DILWYN enters.

DILWYN
Excuse my entering Fanny.

NANNY
Mr Davies!

DILWYN
Might I use your privy? You see I've been jumping in the bushes but now I need a number two, I do.

NANNY
It would be an honour.

DILWYN
Thank you.

NANNY
But goodness, wipe your feet.

DILWYN
Wipe my *feet?* That's not how it works in Wales.

He runs through the house.

SNOW
"It would be an honour!" He only wants to use the bog.

NANNY
Loo, Snow!

SNOW
You fancy him!

NANNY
What rot. Imagine, my Lady Chatterley to his Mellors, it's unthinkable. In any case, an unrefined, uncouth, working class, rugged outdoorsy type would never dare think to be interested in me. I shall make that very clear.

DILWYN enters

DILWYN
That's lightened the load. When I got out my little stove last night I realised I hadn't much left in the way of supplies so I ended up making a prune and baked bean stew. Very nutritious but rather eager if you catch my drift.

NANNY
You're clearly incapable of looking after yourself! I suppose you shall have to dine with us henceforth. I can easily stretch for another man.

DILWYN
I'd not want to bother you.

NANNY
If it was a bother I wouldn't have offered. I'm sure I can spread things out to accommodate you.

DILWYN
That's very kind.

NANNY (Impatiently)
Well are you going to stay for a cup of tea or not? I really don't have time for your plebbish dithering. Snow, make a start on the bathroom, I can only imagine the state Mr Davies has left it in.

SNOW
I thought-

NANNY
Off you go!

She pushes SNOW out of the door and starts to make a cup of tea.

NANNY
Well, here we are.

DILWYN (to audience)
Boys and girls, I don't meet many lush ladies like Nanny Fanny. You look like men of the world, I bet you've all had plenty of experience chatting up women haven't you boys?

NANNY passes him a biscuit tin then presents two mugs of tea.

NANNY
There, pop your bottom down on that chair and I'll pop my bottom on this one.

DILWYN
But it's tiny.

NANNY
Why thank you!

There is a knock at the door

NANNY
Never a moment's peace!

She answers the door. BABS enters. He is disguised as an old woman and carries a cake box.

BABS
But my dear, I hope I'm not interrupting.

NANNY
Go away you grimey beggarwoman, it's teatime and I was about to offer Mr Davies a finger.

BABS
Forgive me young lady, I'm looking for sweet Snow White.

DILWYN
He's in the bathroom. I'll call him will I? He's only cleaning, not pooing or anything

BABS
I've baked him a lovely cake. For I wish to pay homage to his somewhat high street good looks.

NANNY
Snow!!

BABS (to audience)
It's me, in a cunning disguise. And this isn't a cake, it's a bomb. As soon as Snow White opens it, bang.

DILWYN
Why don't I put it on a plate?

He takes the box from BABS and walks towards the kitchen sink.

BABS
Don't open it!! I mean, I'd like Snow to do that. It will give me such pleasure seeing the look on his face (aside) as it separates from his skull and hits the ceiling.

NANNY
I trust the bears have cake forks.

She bends down and opens one of the lower cupboards. She is practically inside the cupboard bent over, her underwear can be seen. DILWYN looks and gasps and in excitement he drops the cake into the sink with a splash.

DILWYN
Oh cripes, clumsy me. I've dropped this lovely cake into a sink full of water. It's saturated.

BABS
Luckily I have a plan B.

He pulls a pair of fancy boxers out.

BABS (to audience)
Stitched inside the lining of the crotch is a deadly scorpion.

SNOW enters

NANNY
Snow, you have a fan come to see you.

SNOW
Well the thing is Nanny I'm very attractive now.

BABS
Young man, these fine knicky-knockers are a gift from a company who will sponsor you to wear them.

SNOW
Wow cool!

BABS
Put them on and I'll take a photograph.

A large mouse appears from behind a sofa (or whatever is available). NANNY screams.

NANNY
A mouse! It went behind the sofa! I told the bears we'd get mice with all their mess.

DILWYN snatches the boxers and runs behind wherever the mouse appears.

DILWYN
I'll get the blighter.

NANNY
So brave!

DILWYN bashes the unseen mouse repeatedly with the pants. When he shows them again they're a bloody mess.

DILWYN
These will need to go in the wash I'm afraid.

BABS
Not to worry, luckily enough I have a plan C.

He takes an apple from his pocket. It glows strangely. A magical sound effect.

BABS
Snow White, I've bought you a delicious apple from my orchard.

SNOW (unimpressed)
An apple?

BABS
Yes...?

SNOW
Right. Woo! An apple! Um thanks that's... kind.

He takes it.

DILWYN
What a tasty looking orb.

SNOW
You have it Dilwyn.

NANNY
No! I don't think he should eat any more fruit.

SNOW
I'll save it for later.

BABS
These apples are best eaten as soon as they're picked.

SNOW
I'm not really hungry.

BABS
Eat it!

NANNY
Snow White, eat the blasted apple and she might go away.

SNOW
Of course.

BABS
That's it...!

SNOW gives the apple a rub on his top to polish it clean. He does this for a tediously long time.

BABS
A little pesticide isn't going to fucking kill you!

SNOW bites into the apple. He reacts instantly and falls to the floor.

DILWYN
Boyo?

NANNY
Snow!

BABS pulls off the disguise and starts laughing.

NANNY
You murderer!

BABS
It's not my fault the little snowflake has an allergy! Hahaha! Once again I am truly the beauty of the borough!

He laughs and exits. NANNY is crouched over SNOW.

NANNY
Snow!

DILWYN is feeling for a pulse.

DILWYN
There's no pulse. He's dead!

He puts his arm around her to comfort her.

Scene 14: The town square

TALEESHA *enters with heavy shopping bags.*

TALEESHA
Hi hoes! I'm looking for Lady Rihanna. Have you seen her?

She moves to the back of the stage with her back to the audience still looking. The PRINCE enters still dressed as a woman, with a tiny bag.

PRINCE
I'm looking for Taleesha, we're doing the household shop. Have you seen her?

He moves to the side of the stage, Taleesha is now on the opposite side of the stage. They both walk into the centre with their backs to each other, they crash into each other.

PRINCE
There you are!

TALEESHA
Lady Rihanna Perry-Swift!

PRINCE
Honestly, have some spatial awareness.

TALEESHA
Have you done any shopping?

PRINCE
Yes! I found a darling pair of swimming trunks.

TALEESHA
Swimming trunks?

PRINCE
Er yes... I believe in gender neutral clothing. Let's get back to the palace and see if we can kill Babs.

TALEESHA
Why don't we chill a bit eh? Have some us time. We could go for a wander in the woods. Those woods are lovely, dark and deep.

PRINCE
But we have promises to keep.

The FAIRY enters.

FAIRY
There you are! I was settling down to a nice cup of bluebell and cyclamen, when my rocks started throbbing.

TALEESHA
Throbbing?

FAIRY
And clacking.

PRINCE
Your rocks?

FAIRY
My balls. My crystal balls. It's a sign of danger. Then I saw it, a vision of Snow White on the floor of a cottage.

PRINCE
I say! Did you get a screen shot?

FAIRY
He's been killed by Queen Babs! But there's hope. I know a spell that will bring him to life if within one hour he is kissed by someone who is destined to love him.

PRINCE
Then let's go!

TALEESHA
Oh Lady R P-Hyphen-S, ain't he told you? He bats for the other side.

PRINCE
That may not be a problem.

FAIRY
Have you redeemed yourself?

PRINCE
Come on, you're a smart, intelligent woman, you must see that is the only way we can help Snow.

TALEESHA
What's going on?

PRINCE
Taleesha I am not Lady Rihanna, I am working undercover to find out what it is like to live in Lumley by Gosh.

TALEESHA
Well it takes all sorts but he still bats for the other side.

PRINCE
And I'm a man. This was all a ridiculous- no, a *smart* sort of test. And colour me woke but I see the error of my ways. It's me that's the dummy! I mean that silly plan of mine to pounce on Babs as he looked in a mirror! You saw straight through it.

FAIRY
That sounds more like a window. Anyway yeah, you've changed. Get changed.

PRINCE
Sorry?

FAIRY
You can take those clothes off.

The PRINCE pulls his blouse and skirt off and stands in his pants.

FAIRY (To Taleesha)
Sorry. I didn't mean for you to be fooled.

TALEESHA
That's alright. (beat) What you thinking about?

FAIRY
I'm thinking there's a half-naked young man on stage - Arianna Grande could come on with Fifth Harmony as backing dancers and this lot wouldn't notice so there's not much point us doing any dialogue.

PRINCE
Um excuse me. Clothes.

FAIRY (pointing)
There's a TK Maxx just opened.

PRINCE
We've got an hour, not an afternoon. Can't you magic me some?

The FAIRY waves her wand, nothing happens. She waves it again, still nothing.

FAIRY
Sorry, seems I'm all out. Maybe the boys and girls will help. Boys and girls would you like to help say a spell so the Prince has some clothes to put on.

"No!"

FAIRY
Oh well! We off then?

PRINCE
Ladies, follow me and we'll be there in no time. This way!

FAIRY
I don't think so!

PRINCE
Look it's not sexist to acknowledge the fact that I happen to be rather good at navigating. (beat) The cottage is the other way isn't it.

TALEESHA /FAIRY
Yes.

PRINCE
Right!

TALEESHA
You can still lead the way if it makes you feel better. Now, let's save Snow White.

They exit. BABS appears from hiding – perhaps from inside the well.

BABS
Save Snow White? That's what they think! I'll sequester a horse, beat them to it and finish him off. Ha ha ha!

Scene 15: the cottage

The cottage. SNOW's lifeless body is propped against a chair. GRIZZLY has two cans of beer.

GRIZZLY
Here you go little one.

He puts his beer down and tries to give one to SNOW but his hand won't grip it, so he wedges it between SNOW's thighs. GRIZZLY sits on another chair. He has a beer too. He clinks the tins together: "cheers". GRIZZLY brushes SNOW's fringe out of his eyes.

GRIZZLY
Come on, sit up straight for Grizzly Bear. If you're good you can sit on my knee later.

HONEY enters with a spade.

HONEY
What the hell are you doing?

GRIZZLY
Spending some quality time before I give him his bath.

HONEY
Right... Look, I'm heartbroken too, but this isn't healthy.

GRIZZLY
It's one beer, Jesus.

HONEY
He's starting to smell!

GRIZZLY
You used to like a bit of body odour. You got something sticking out your pocket. *(He extracts the cheque)* A cheque for one hundred thousand Goshes! Wait a second. That's exactly what was offered as a reward for Snow White, working on the assumption that at the last moment, Queen Babs doubled the amount from that which had been advertised.

A moment.

HONEY
I'm sorry! I thought I was doing the right thing.

GRIZZLY
The right thing?

HONEY
I did. And... and alright, I thought it would be better if the boy went home. Cos then you might start loving me again. (a pause) We need to bury him. I've dug a hole.

GRIZZLY
You certainly fucking have! Bury him!? His beautiful little face hidden from the light. I thought we might build him a sort of box-

HONEY
A coffin?

GRIZZLY covers SNOW's ears.

GRIZZLY
Sshh! A *showcase*, made of glass. With some little lights in it.

HONEY
Oh my god.

GRIZZLY
I suppose you think it's a bit much.

HONEY
I think it's a bit Dennis fucking Nilsen! (beat) Cover him up at least. I'll let some air in.

GRIZZLY puts a tablecloth over SNOW. HONEY opens the front door. He walks over to the sink where the cake tin containing the bomb still sits.

HONEY
Ooh! The cake's probably dried out now! That'll cheer us up.

HONEY starts to open tin, he peeks inside.

HONEY
Well goodness me! It's not a cake. I think it's a bomb!

He throws the cake tin to GRIZZLY who catches it and screams.

HONEY
The grave! Throw it in the grave!

GRIZZLY throws the tin through the open door.

GRIZZLY
We're not burying him with a bomb.

BABS enters, gun in hand.

BABS
With aplomb? Show me the Snowflake or I'll give you both barrels.

HONEY
Your majesty, he's dead!

BABS
Ha!

HONEY
He's in his grave. It's just outside.

BABS
Hahahahaha!

BABS runs outside. We hear him jump in the grave. An enormous explosion. BABS screams. GRIZZLY takes the tablecloth off SNOW. DILWYN enters

DILWYN
There's been an explosion!

NANNY enters. She wears a black Victorian dress and has a black veil over her face, like Queen Victoria in mourning.

NANNY
Oh howl! Howl! Howl!

She can't see a thing and gropes her way along the front row before reaching DILWYN. Her hands end up on his crotch.

DILWYN
My Fanny!

NANNY removes her veil – and her hands from DILWYN.

NANNY
What on earth was that noise? It's disrespectful.

HONEY
It was a bomb. And it took Queen Babs with it.

NANNY looks at SNOW

NANNY
Grizzly Bear! What on God's green earth!

DILWYN
I think it's part of the grieving process.

NANNY
That's no excuse for drinking straight out of the can like a tramp in a doorway. One can't abandon standards because somebody's licked the bucket.

HONEY
Kicked the bucket.

NANNY
Now really, haven't we had enough violence? We had best make preparations.

GRIZZLY
We could get him a nice little suit.

SNOW half falls off his seat and rests at an awkward angle.

GRIZZLY
Oh! Someone's tipsy!

DILWYN
Perhaps I could assist with the funeral arrangements.

NANNY
It will only be for family and close friends.

DILWYN
I see. I thought we had become close friends. Perhaps more than friends. At least let me sleep in with you tonight to comfort you.

NANNY
There's no room! This stupid tiny house with its stupid tiny furniture.

DILWYN
I can give you something big to sit on!

NANNY
Mr Davies! My dear Snow is dead and you turn into Harvey Weinstein! How could you!

DILWYN
I'm so sorry.

NANNY
Leave at once.

DILWYN
But I...

NANNY
Go on! Pack up your tent and leave.

DILWYN exits, dejected.

There is a knock at the door. TALEESHA, the FAIRY and PRINCE enter. GRIZZLY has been propping SNOW up but at the sight of the PRINCE he stands up leaving SNOW to fall over.

GRIZZLY
Hello hello.

NANNY
A young man has just passed away and you gad about in your underwear!

168

PRINCE
Forgive me.

NANNY
Not at all, it was merely an observation.

TALEESHA
Go on, kiss him.

GRIZZLY puts his face in front of the PRINCE and goes to kiss him.

FAIRY
Not you, you muppet. Go on. Kiss Snow.

The PRINCE walks over to SNOW. He bends down and kisses SNOW. Nothing happens.

PRINCE
We must be too late.

TALEESHA
Try again. A proper snog.

PRINCE
His mouth actually stinks.

HONEY
I'm not surprised, the places it's been.

A kiss. Eventually SNOW wakes.

SNOW
Hello. (He looks at the PRINCE) Hello!

PRINCE
Hi.

SNOW
You look familiar.

PRINCE
Yes, we've met.

SNOW
The Prince! My Prince! Oh mate, I proper fancied you!

PRINCE
And I you.

SNOW
I nearly went with some posh girl but I can see now I am definitely gay, she had nothing on you.

NANNY
Snow, Queen Babs is dead! You can take your rightful place as king of Lumley-by-Gosh.

All cheer

SNOW
Nanny, the first thing I'll do is restore you to former glory. You'll have back the property and titles Babs took from your family.

NANNY
Oh Snow! (To the bears) This my cottage now. Rent will be due on the first of the month.

HONEY
What?

SNOW
Don't be mean Nanny.

PRINCE
You're a king! That's even higher than a prince. I'll have to start calling you Daddy.

SNOW
My Prince!

He kisses the PRINCE. They embrace. All cheer except for the FAIRY and TALEESHA who cough. The PRINCE gives them a panicked glare.

NANNY
Now Snow, before you consider copulating I think you might check his lineage. You are royalty after all.

SNOW
Says the woman who's gagging to have it off with the milkman.

NANNY
Snow White! You're not too old for me to put you over my knee. (beat) Though now I'm a woman of property and leisure it seems sad not to have somebody to share it with. *(She approaches the man she flirted with in scene two.)* We might have had fun darling but I can't possibly make a life with somebody who celebrates Christmas at a fringe theatre.

DILWYN enters. SNOW nudges NANNY.

NANNY
Haven't you gone!

DILWYN
I've barely got my fly down.

SNOW
Your fly?

DILWYN
My flysheet.

NANNY
I asked you to get off my property.

SNOW
Nanny! What were you just saying about sharing your life?

NANNY
I doubt Mr Davies knows many eligible aristocrats.

SNOW
You don't need an aristocrat! You've got a whole suite at the palace, you've got land. Love's what matters.

NANNY
Oh Snow you're right. Mr Davies, will you have me?

DILWYN
Dilwyn, please. It would be an honour.

All cheer.

NANNY
Is there room for two under that tarpaulin of yours?

DILWYN
Well I'll have to get it up again.

NANNY
Nanny can help with that. Goodbye boys and girls!

They exit.

SNOW
To be honest I don't care if you're a Prince or not. When you find someone special, it doesn't matter about their status.

PRINCE
Well that's good but just so you know, I'm positive undetectable.

SNOW
Oh that's alright.

The FAIRY coughs.

PRINCE
But I'm... not a prince.

SNOW
Fucking what?!

PRINCE
Except, I would be, if you married me...

The PRINCE kneels.

SNOW
Yeah go on!

All cheer.

SNOW
Honey, Grizzly. Thank you so much. You've both shown me so much kindness. I hope that me and Prince Rupert...

PRINCE
Um... It's Gavin actually.

SNOW
Oh. Really?

PRINCE
Yes.

SNOW
No, it's fine, we'll make it work... (to the Bears) I hope Prince... Gavin and I can build something as special as you have. You both deserve each other. Look after each other.

GRIZZLY
I will learn to treasure you better you beautiful bear, starting today.

HONEY
And I'll let you have a gangbang on your birthday.

GRIZZLY
Will you provide a casserole?

HONEY
Oh Grizzly!

They hug.

HONEY
Make up time.

The bears run off excitedly pawing at each other.

TALEESHA
What are you doing now?

FAIRY
Back to my clearing I suppose. There's animals will want petting. After all this excitement I'm gonna need a whole year off fixing people's problems.

TALEESHA
Can I come with you?

FAIRY
I think it's high time you met my beaver. We can show those rabbits a thing or two.

TALEESHA
You are def my kind of girl.

They exit. We hear the bears having sex.

PRINCE
Sounds like someone's having fun.

SNOW
Shall we join them?

PRINCE
No! I want you to myself.

SNOW
Me too.

PRINCE
Come back to London with me.

SNOW
I can't.

PRINCE
Nonsense, you'll love it. There's a bar in Shoreditch that has a ball pool for adults!

SNOW
But I'm the king now. I'm responsible. I have to try and undo all the damage Babs did to Lumley. Open our borders. Spend taxes on the people instead of the palace. Let women drive again. Release the political prisoners. Fix the new Routemasters so people can hop on and off at the back between stops again as was originally intended. [28]

PRINCE

Lumley could become a London borough again?

SNOW
Maybe. We'll have a referendum. Tomorrow. But first, we've a royal bedroom to try out.

BOTH
Hi ho, ho, it's off to bed we go.

They kiss and exit. The FAIRY returns for the epilogue.

THE FAIRY

Some people go on endless first dates,
Some people sleep around,
But in panto, for true love you just have to wait -
Just play with a broom and wear rags till you're found.
Gavin and Snow had a great Royal Wedding,
Giving hope to gay kids all over the place,
There are souvenir mugs, even souvenir bedding -
You can drink out of Gavin, and cum on Snow's face.

Queen Babs, it turns out, wasn't killed by the blast,
But his face was so badly disfigured, he passed
Many months in the forest, in hiding, and poor -
But now he plays Lloyd-Webber's Phantom on tour.

With Snow White as king, Lumley became
A kinder, more liberal state,
As sanctions were quashed they got merrily sloshed,
And their pride parade's still first rate,

And whether you're pretty or have other blessings
Be grateful and kind but not proud,
It has been our great honour to stand here addressing you:
Safe home now, you beautiful lovable crowd.

THE END

---

[28] One of Boris Johnson's pet projects as Mayor of London was to introduce a new version of the classic Routemaster bus with an open platform at the back so people could hop on and off between stops, but as this would require a conductor as well as a driver, the buses have never functioned in this way.

Beauty on the Piste

Ross Tucker as Mac, David Moss as Morag and Joshua Oakes-Rogers as Beau in *Beauty on the Piste*. Photo by PBGstudios.

Beauty on the Piste

2016. Americans voted for Donald Trump to be their new President, the British voted to leave the EU, and *X Factor* fans voted controversial rapper Honey G all the way to the quarter finals in spite of her being labelled a joke and having been accused of appropriating black music culture. Sadiq Khan was elected Mayor of London, beating Conservative candidate Zac Goldsmith into second place after the latter's campaign of dog-whistle racism.

Having worked our way through most mainstream pantomimes we turned to Beauty and the Beast, which is occasionally staged but is certainly second tier. We wanted to keep true to the original 18th Century French fairy-tale while playing with elements of the classic Disney film: a Gaston-style villain and in particular the castle's population of living household items. A limited cast size meant thinking laterally, which led to a superb turn from Ellen Butler – one of our most frequent panto performers – as the shapeshifting Heidi.

Most pantomimes feature a romance, but it is rarely the focus of the story and the lovers-to-be are often kept apart for much of the plot. So it was fun to tackle a fairy tale in which the protagonists spend a lot of time holed up together in the beast's castle, and in which the object of the story is for Beau (our male Beauty) to somehow fall in love with his cruel and grizzled captor. It gave us an opportunity to write our second act as a traditional romantic comedy, in which the obstacles to true love come as much from the characters' personalities as they do from outside circumstance.

Our title *Beauty on the Piste* (subtitle – a Tale of Old Alpine) was suggested by Peter Bull, which prompted us to invent the fictional Swiss skiing resort of Les Dennis - pronounced, of course, "Ley Denii" by our French-Swiss characters. At the same time as our show was running, the actor and comedian Les Dennis was appearing in *She Loves Me* at the Menier Chocolate Factory in Southwark. Understandably thrilled to discover that we'd honoured him in such a way, he sent our cast a funny if bemused video wishing them a happy new year.

Beauty on the Piste

By Jon Bradfield and Martin Hooper
Songs by Jon Bradfield

Characters

Mabel, a fairy. Very Chelsea/Sloaney.
Sebastian, the villain, a landlord and former ski champion.
Morag, the dame, a middle-aged Scot. Proprietor of a tea-room.
Mac, her son.
Beau, a young waiter at the tea-room.
Gustave, Beau's father, in love with Morag.
The Beast, a yeti, formerly a nobleman.
Heidi, his housekeeper.

The play is set in the French-Swiss Alps, in and around the minor ski resort of Les Dennis. British characters always pronounce the town "Les Dennis"; Swiss characters pronounce it "Ley Denii".

Beauty on the Piste was first performed at Above The Stag Theatre on 24 November 2016 with the following cast and creative team:

Mabel, a Fairy: Briony Rawle; Sebastian St Moritz: Simon Burr; Mac Trump: Ross Tucker; Morag Trump: David Moss; Beau: Joshua Oakes-Rogers; Gustave: Andrew Truluck; The Beast: Jamie Coles; Heidi: Ellen Butler

Director: Andrew Beckett; Designer: David Shields; Lighting Designer: Jamie Platt; Musical Director: Aaron Clingham; Choreographer: Carole Todd; Costume Designer: Brigid Guy; Sound Designer: Luke Johnson; Production Photographer: Gary Sherwood; Poster illustration: Leo Delauncey; Produced by: Peter Bull for Above The Stag Theatre

Scene 1: Outside Les Denise

The Swiss Alps. Mountains, pine trees, a twinkling ski town in the distance. Everything is white with deep snow. MABEL, a fairy, enters.

MABEL
Gosh hello boys and girls! What jollies we have planned!
Here in glittering French Switzerland
There'll be cheers! There'll be boos! There'll be ahhhs! But before we
begin, Let me tell you a little back story.

A young nobleman once lived in these parts,
A beautiful face but the coldest of hearts,
He lived in a castle alone with his wealth,
And cared for no-one except for himself.

The queen of the fairies sent me to test him,
If he couldn't be good I must teach him a lesson,
I dressed myself down so he'd think I was poor,
And I knocked and knocked at his great oak door,

"Please help me" I trilled, "I'm barely alive,
I got lost in the woods, it's been days - four or five,
Please see me safe through this treacherous weather,
Just an apple I beg, and a Twix or whatever".

He narrowed his eyes which were pretty as pearls,
And said, disappointed, "oh - you're a girl,
I've a Gaydar shag coming, he's quite a blinder"
- This was still a couple of years before Grindr.

"I've got to get ready, I must douche and trim,
Put out the cocaine and the humous for him.
So you can't navigate? You're stupid or lying,
Find some other castle - or die while you're trying."

I reached in my pocket and drew out my purse,
Took out my travel-wand and gave him a curse:
"You cold young man, so bitter and petty
You'll live evermore as a big ugly yeti!

The curse is strong and will hang above you,
Until you can find a young man to love you."
The yeti roared loud, but I said "Let me stop you,
There's another condition: you must get him to top you!"

Now back to the present, we can't sit here chilling
This is all very pleasant but this show needs a villain!

A snowball is thrown at her from the wings. As she squeals and brushes herself down, SEBASTIAN enters. A puffed-up chest, chiselled jaw and brightly-coloured ski-wear.

SEBASTIAN
Ha ha ha ha ha!

Boo...

SEBASTIAN
Don't tell them I'm the baddie! It isn't fair or kind,
I'm sure they can make up their own, tiny minds.

MABEL
Oh how darling, someone's been down the Sports Direct sale.

SEBASTIAN
You're looking at a former Olympic ski champion.

He gives her his business card.

MABEL
"Sebastian St Moritz". What sort of prat puts his photo on his business card?

SEBASTIAN
One who looks like me. Keep it. I hear it's popular as a masturbatory aid.

MABEL
I'd be scared of getting paper cuts. Now, help a girl. I'm looking for Les Dennis.

SEBASTIAN
Who?

MABEL
Les Dennis – I think that's the place.

SEBASTIAN
You ignorant tourist. It's pronounced "Ley Denii".

MABEL
That's the sausage. A rather dreary third-rate ski resort somewhere in the environs. Do you know it?

SEBASTIAN
Know it? I own it!

MABEL
Awkward.

SEBASTIAN
Most of it anyway. I'm trying to turn Les Dennis into a resort befitting a man of my tastes, status, charm and

looks. (Points at the audience) We're getting too many of this sort of Pontins rabble. The kind of repressed lower middle classes who say "apres ski" in a funny voice because they think it's an innuendo and they're going to spend every evening getting classily banged on a sheepskin rug instead of trying to sponge their own vomit out of it. The trouble is, a couple of tedious locals are refusing to budge from their hovels, but I'm going to trick them into selling up and fleeing the place.

MABEL is looking at something in her handbag.

SEBASTIAN
Are you listening?

MABEL
I find exposition tedious darling, but it's important the boys and girls hear it so do jolly along.

SEBASTIAN
One of them is Gustave, the batty old goat herd who also runs the local rag. The other, Morag, is the old crone who runs the tea shop where the goat herd's son works. Now, the son, that's a completely different story.

MABEL
Why, is he called Aladdin or something?

SEBASTIAN
His name is Beau.

MABEL
Bo? Bo as in peep?

SEBASTIAN
Beau as in peep. As in gaze. As in gawp. As in ogle. As in stare through his bedroom window for hours at a time with my nose pressed against the cold glass and my erection pressed against the frosted clapboard wall until both are frozen fast and have to be prised unstuck with a combination of hot brandy from a hip flask and my own salty tears... Oh, I see what you mean – Little Bo Peep. No, Beau as in male beauty. B-E-A-U.

MABEL
So, you're gay! I should have known,
Half of my chums are gay back at home.

SEBASTIAN
Yes, you have the desperate smell of the Fag Hag.

MABEL
Oh stop being a knob,
Cards on the table,
Being a fairy's my job
And my name is Mabel.

SEBASTIAN
Right I'm bored now. I'll visit the tea room. I'll see if I can make the old bat see sense and try my charms with young Beau while I'm there. Fuck two holes with one cock, as it were. I'll transform Les Dennis into the most exclusive resort in the Alps. Mark my words!

MABEL
Alright, I give you about 6 out of ten. I'll stop you and your evil schemes!

SEBASTIAN
Oh no you won't!

MABEL
Oh yes I will!

SEBASTIAN
How, precisely?

MABEL
Gosh no it won't be precisely. It'll be approximately, haphazardly and I dare say pretty cack-handedly too. Thought I'd manage everyone's expectations there.

SEBASTIAN
I can't wait. Right. Must dash.

MABEL
Ciao.

SEBASTIAN
No no. *Moustache.* You might want to try bleaching. Au revoir. Ha ha ha ha ha ha.

SEBASTIAN exits.

MABEL
I fear with that one I might come a cropper
But good will win out boys and girls, yes it will!
So now to Les Dennis for the story proper
A ski town where everything's going downhill...

Scene 2: Trump's tea room

A cosy café with the pine walls of an alpine lodge but a touch of Scotland in its décor – tartan tablecloths and so on. A chalk-board menu hangs on the wall, and the place is decorated for Christmas, including a Christmas tree. Perhaps there's a moose head on the wall.

MAC enters, a likeable young Scot.

MAC
Hullo! Welcome to Trump's Tea Room. You lot look new, you must be fresh off the funicular! I'm not sure I can do you a table for seventy-five - I'll just have to split you up arbitrarily like a bored 20th century western power drawing lines through a map of the middle east. Don't worry, it's all knob jokes from now on. I can't tell which of you's come with which of you. There's a bit of sexual tension going on over here... and I can sense with these two there's an argument that's been temporarily parked because it's supposed to be a special night out even though *somebody* was meant to book tickets for the Palladium panto instead.

Where are my manners?! My name's Mac. As you can probably tell from the expensive accent coaching I'm Scottish. Aye that's right, the ones that voted to remain. Well I didn't, I was playing Mario Cart. This is my mum's tea-room. We moved here a few months ago, so I'm a bit lonely. (Ahhh) I'm lonelier than that. (Ahhhh!) Alright steady on. I'm not at the mad loner stage yet. I haven't downloaded the Isis application form. But I had to leave all my pals behind and I don't have many friends yet. Would you be my friends? Would you? Aw thank you.

I'm trying to integrate. I'm learning to yodel! I think you guys should integrate too. I tell you what, whenever I come on, I'll give you one of my yodels, and I want you to yodel it back to me. Alright? Shall we have a wee practice? Alright. I'm going to go off what I call stage right. Also known as muggle left. I'll be back in a moment.

He goes and comes back. They yodel.

I have got one friend actually. You'll meet him, he works here. His name's Beau. He's a bit of a jobbie jabber if you know wha' a mean. Aye, he's gay. But he's actually alright.

MORAG (off)
Mac!

MAC
That's me mam. She can be a bit frosty but she's ok. She just needs a bit of affection. I'd love her to find a nice man.

MORAG (off)
Mac Trump!

MAC
I should get back to work. Mam what is it?

MORAG (off)
MacDonald Trump!

MAC
Are you coming on mum, or were you just going to keep shouting my name from the wings for what barely constitutes a gag?

MORAG (off)
I'm preparing my entrance.

MAC (To someone in the audience)
Don't mate, she's my mum.

MORAG (off)
Right, I'm ready.

She enters, in a tartan apron, arms raised in greeting.

MORAG
Hello boys and girls! I said Hello boys and girls! No I've forgotten what I was going to say now. Aye that's it.

She exits. She enters with some clothes. They are completely stiff like they're made out of cardboard.

MORAG
Mac! I told you, hang the up the washing *indoors*. These are frozen. *(She hits him with them).* And nobody wants to see my undergarments flailing madly about like a Clapham homosexual at a Jack Wills sale.

MAC
I dunno mum. Old Gustave might.

MORAG
Gustave!? Really! If a woman and a man can't be simple friendly neighbours at my time of life then I don't know what we're coming to – I'm older than I look, boys and girls, though younger than I dress. Hang these over the bath.

MAC exits with the clothes.

MORAG
How do you do, my name's Morag. Morag Trump. Welcome to my tea-room. I see you've thought fit most of you to leave your dirty shoes on. Well, here I am in Switzerland! All the way here from my little west highland village of Suchmacoch at the foot of Scotland's tallest mountain-climbing and outdoor activities shop. I've been adapting my traditional Scottish cuisine to the local expectations. I call it fusion food.

MAC enters

MAC
She gets it stuck to the pan a lot.

MORAG
I'll stick it to you young Mac. *(To the audience)* I've been melting a lot of cheese. Red Leicester mainly. The cheese round here has a tendency towards holes, not unlike today's bar staff. I see you've met Mac, he's a bit daft in the head but he's a decent one aye, he just needs a bit of affection. You're looking for a girlfriend aren't you?

MAC
Mum!

MORAG
For years I thought he was gay but you don't have the panache for it do you son. Perhaps we'll find a nice lass for you here.

MAC
Mum!

MORAG
(To a woman in the audience) You look respectable enough, considering what I've heard about the venue.

BEAU enters

BEAU
Morning Morag, morning Mac.

MAC
This is Beau. The gay one.

BEAU
Hi boys and girls!

MORAG
Beau! What time do you call this.

BEAU
Why?

MORAG
Because I've not learnt the times in French yet.

BEAU
Am I late again?

MAC
It's cos he comes from a different house every morning.

MORAG
Were you born in a barn?

BEAU
Oh sorry.

BEAU shuts the door.

MAC
He's used to leaving the door ajar...

BEAU
You won't embarrass me Mac. I'm living my truth. You're just jealous

MAC
Aye, I am. I don't know how you do it. Mum's right boys and girls - I'd love to meet a girl and settle down.

BEAU
Oh I don't want to settle down!

MAC
Beau's had more men than I've had hot suppers.

MORAG
You can't say that in front of the boys and girls! They'll think I don't feed you properly. (to BEAU) Well I trust he gave you breakfast.

SONG: SLEEPING AROUND
Sung by Beau (italics = sung by rest of the characters in the scene)

Six o'clock the town awakens
Lanterns gleam in the snow
Eight o'clock my phone goes off
Oops! Where am I today? I don't know!

The butcher and the baker
I've had them all
And tourists from Jamaica,
Latvia and Senegal

I could embark on a real adventure
But it's harder, it's harder when you're poor
So I get my validation
With my knees and my elbows on the floor

I'll do old, young, butch or femme
I'll do sober, drunk or chems
I'm a happy slut but I'm in a rut
And the question is, what then?
I'm good at what I do,
And what I do is "it",
But maybe I need bigger goals
Than "look at him, he's fit"

People speak of love so highly
It sounds such a faff
Trust me, I'll take the golden shower
Before the candle-lit bath

I could widen my horizons
Like I've widened my little hole

He'll do bears, cubs, otters and twinks
He'll do black, brown, white and pink
He'll do dinner too if the bill's on you
But he's happy with a drink

There's more to life as well
But hell,
There's loads of guys about
I'm scared of missing out
If I don't put out
And I put out well!

BEAU
Why did you move here Morag?

MORAG
That bloody vote is what clenched it.

BEAU
Clinched it.

MORAG
Auch, my French, it's a bit crusty. Aye. I didnae want to leave the EU did I. Stronger in and all that.

BEAU
Is Switzerland in the EU?

MORAG
No. I know that now, don't I.

MAC
But you voted out in the Scottish referendum.

MORAG
That was different. Scotland's a more... socialist country. I liked the idea of building a more kind-hearted nation. A place where you look after each other. Where you share what you have.

BEAU
That sounds nice.

MORAG
Beau, get your hands away from my biscuit barrel, those are for paying customers. (beat) And I felt like an adventure. Once you've bagged every Monroe and cultivated a friendship of sorts with the Loch Ness monster you've pretty much done with a place.

BEAU
Nessie??

MORAG
He hates that name. It's largely why he avoids purple.

BEAU
Purple?

MORAG
No, wait... *People*. My French! It's no' easy taking new things on board at my age.

MAC
I bought her a spiraliser for her birthday this year. You never got the hang of that did you.

MORAG
I don't like new kitchen gadgets. Better the Breville you know.

GUSTAVE enters clutching some newspapers.

GUSTAVE
Morning Morag.

MORAG
Gustave! Gustave these are the boys and girls, boys and girls this is Gustave. Gustave's a widower and he has a tendency toward sentimentality that doesn't quite sit with his rustic demeanour. What are you doing here?

GUSTAVE
Oh I er, I was bringing the boy to work.

MORAG
Beau? He's here

BEAU
Hi dad.

GUSTAVE
Ah! Yes. I er... Well I thought I'd hand deliver your paper.

MORAG
Thanking you. Will you have a drink? A coffee?

GUSTAVE
How kind!

MORAG
Beau, get Gustave his coffee.

BEAU goes. GUSTAVE flicks through the paper.

GUSTAVE (faux-casual)
Why don't I read you your horoscope?

MORAG
Horoscope! Get away with you.

GUSTAVE
Here we are. "Now's the time to seize the day, take the plunge and embark on a romance."

MORAG
Romance!

GUSTAVE
"You will meet a handsome, loyal middle-aged local man who could make you very happy."

MORAG
I don't know how people can think of such things in these temperatures.

GUSTAVE
You're from Scotland.

MORAG
I felt the same there. When Mac here was conceived - which was only because the cat had eaten the Uno cards - his father and I were sporting 22 pieces of thermal clothing between us. I've still got three of them on now. Leave sex to the Mediterraneans I say. They've the colour for it and their television's atrocious. I'll get you a franc for the paper.

GUSTAVE
For you Morag, its complimentary.

BEAU enters with a coffee.

BEAU
Here's your coffee dad.

MORAG
That's three francs and ten. You can leave it with Beau, I've work to do.

MAC
Mum you should take some time off. Get out and about a bit.

MORAG
I go to church. Three miles there and back it is.

GUSTAVE
There's a church here in Les Denise.

MORAG
Not a proper one. Not a protestant one. I don't take to your bells and whistles and statues and cushions and heating. Give me long slow dirge and a good hard pew.

GUSTAVE (beside himself)
Good God.

MORAG
Gustave you've gone quite the colour. Will you excuse me. Mac.

MORAG and MAC exit. GUSTAVE smiles after her.

BEAU
Dad, please. You're embarrassing yourself.

GUSTAVE
Embarrassing myself?

BEAU
Pining after her like that. You need to sort yourself out first if you want a chance with someone. You've got worse every day since mum died. Look at you. You don't cook, your hair's a tangle, the house is a tip, you dress like a tramp.

GUSTAVE
It doesn't sound like it's me who I'm embarrassing.

BEAU
I'm sorry dad. I care about you that's all.

GUSTAVE
Perhaps if you were at home more often I wouldn't be as lonely.

BEAU
Aw come here dad.

They hug. SEBASTIAN enters.

SEBASTIAN

Ahahaha! Beau, Beau Beau, it is such a treat to see me isn't it.

MORAG and MAC enter.

MORAG
Mac, look, it's Mr St Moritz.

MAC
I know what a dickhead looks like.

SEBASTIAN
Well Trump, don't stand there grinning like a Cheshire twat. You know why I'm here.

MORAG
Is it for my cheese trifle?

SEBASTIAN
I'd rather eat my own intestines. I'm here to sign for the deeds of this place.

MORAG
I've decided not to sell.

SEBASTIAN
I see. Well then, while I'm here, as chair of the Les Denise Tourism Guild, I'll collect your overdue membership fee. Six months' worth.

MORAG
Oh Mr St Moritz.

SEBASTIAN
Sebastian, please.

MORAG
Sebastian, please.

MAC
Sebastian, please. A smart businessman like you knows what it is to get a business up and running. The investment, the debts, the advertising, the unnecessary and inaccurate adoption of words like "pop-up". We're trying to build a great café here. Please, give us a window.

BEAU
We've got a window.

SEBASTIAN
Isn't he cute when he tries to speak adult. Gustave, you've a fine son.

GUSTAVE
He gets all that from his mother, long may she rest.

SEBASTIAN
I dare say she will. She's dead, it's hardly a power nap.

GUSTAVE
Morag, may I use your toilet.

MORAG
Aye go on. The first three sheets are free.

GUSTAVE exits.

SEBASTIAN
I'm afraid you've had your chance. If you can't pay up I'll take the tea-room on a compulsory purchase order. I'll replace you with something more upmarket. Ha, not that that would be difficult. Perhaps a branch of Chicken Chalet.

MORAG
Pah, Chicken Chalet! With its secret blend of one herb or spice.

SEBASTIAN
Perhaps I could be lenient. With the right incentive... Beau, we've waited so long, dine with me this evening.

BEAU
I'm washing my hair.

SEBASTIAN
Is that the best you can do.

BEAU
It sounds better than douching.

SEBASTIAN
I know it must be overwhelming, someone like me interested in someone like you but you really mustn't feel inadequate.

BEAU
That's it! I'd feel inadequate. I mean, imagine, me on your arm.

SEBASTIAN
Well I wouldn't normally go that far on a first date.

MAC
Beau would. He's got a tattoo on his bum that says "now wash your hands".

MORAG
Auch go on Beau. Take one for the team. He's a champion skier.

SEBASTIAN

I've got medals for going down.

BEAU
I'm not for sale!

MORAG
Mr St Moritz... Will I get you something to eat. A sporty gentleman like you must get hungry.

SEBASTIAN
There's no use you flirting with me. You've as much taste and warmth as the coffee you serve.

MAC
She wasn't flirting with you!

MORAG
No I was Mac, I'm just a bit awkward with it. Sebastian, let me rustle your little something up. That didn't sound quite right. I serve good traditional fare, with my own wee twist.

SEBASTIAN
A twist? What is it?

MORAG
It's a variation or improvement but that's not important right now. I do a very moreish tempura.

SEBASTIAN
Tempura what.

MORAG
Mars bar. Haggis balls. Have some soup?

SEBASTIAN
Your soup goes right through me.

MORAG
That was the cockaleekie.

GUSTAVE enters

GUSTAVE
I'm a fool! I just remembered! I was a founding member of the Tourism Guild and the rules clearly state that members pay nothing in their first year of business. I've got the papers at home.

MAC
Ha!

MORAG
You can't make the rules up as you go along. It's not a Labour Leadership Election.

SEBASTIAN
Well! An easy mistake to make eh? But if you won't be reasonable, I'll destroy you. Just you wait and see!

SEBASTIAN exits

GUSTAVE
Excuse me. I must go and feed my goats.

GUSTAVE exits.

BEAU
He makes my skin scrawl.

MABEL enters

MABEL (very slowly and deliberately)
Excuse me, is this the tearoom?

MAC
It's ok you can speak English in here.

MABEL
Oh thank God. (Normal speed) Excuse me, is this the tea-room?

MORAG
Aye it is. Welcome to Trump's Tea room. I'm Morag Trump and this is my son, Mac Trump.

MABEL
No relation I hope.

MORAG
I just told you, he's my son. Sadly.

MABEL
When did you come to Les Dennis?

MORAG
We've done the chat love, this is where you buy something. What will I get you?

MABEL
I'll have a tea.

MAC
I'll get it for you!

BEAU
Ooooh. Someone's keen!

MABEL
What did he say? I didn't catch it, my French...

MAC
Nothing! Um... I'm Mac.

182

MABEL
And I'm Mabel.

MORAG
Aye I bet you are, you look the sort.

MABEL
Mabel. It's my name. Have you Earl Grey?

MAC
We got English breakfast.

MORAG
That comes with an egg and sausage in it.

MABEL
I'll have an Irish tea. That comes with whisky in it.

MORAG
Whisky's Scottish, and being respectable we don't serve alcohol at this hour.

MABEL
You know what, I'll have a juice.

MORAG
Get her a juice Mac.

MAC gives her a can of Irn Bru.

MABEL
Um

MORAG
Mac! What are you thinking. (beat) Get her a chilled one from the fridge.

MABEL
I'm actually here to see you. That chap who was here before me, he's a bit of a tyke. He wants to see you leave Les Dennis.

MORAG
You're kind. And about as much use as a marshmallow canoe. We know all about Sebastian and I'm sure we'll be fine. Now if you'll excuse me I've things to do - it's been like Morrisons at yellow sticker time in here this morning.

MABEL
I might give the cable car a try.

MAC
You cannae, it's suspended.

MORAG
Aye, that's how they work. Some mothers do 'ave 'em!

MABLE
Is there a bar open? (To Beau) Sorry, I should try my French. (Slowly and deliberately) Is there a bar open?

BEAU
There's a hotel across the way.

MABEL
Thank you.

MAC
Wait! I'll walk you.

MABEL exits. MAC goes to follow but is stopped in the doorway by GUSTAVE who enters in a panic.

GUSTAVE
Disaster! Disaster! Your penguin has let my goats out!

MORAG
Well I don't like to say but they were a bit tight on you.

GUSTAVE
What?

MAC
Goats mum! Not coats, goats!

GUSTAVE
He broke the fence and they've disappeared. Think of the little things, all frightened and lost.

MORAG
It's alright it's alright, don't panic. It'll be fine.

GUSTAVE
I don't see how. I feel terrible.

MORAG
You mustn't! I can take goats cheese off the pizza menu it's no bother. I'm no real fan of posh toppings.

BEAU sighs happily.

MORAG
Beau?

BEAU
Posh toppings. Reminded me of those Cambridge lads we had in a few weeks ago.

GUSTAVE
What am I to do!

MORAG
The poor wee lambs.

GUSTAVE, MAC, BEAU
Goats!

183

GUSTAVE
I must go and find them.

BEAU
I'll help.

MAC
Wait - why don't you go and help Gustav mum? Keep him company.

MORAG
Me?

MAC
That's it. (suggestive) You and Gustav.

MORAG
I cannae be chasing off up the mountains I've scones to batter and low price caterers' ketchup to decant into Heinz bottles.

MAC
We can do that.

BEAU
Course. We'll look after the place.

MORAG
Alright. (She takes off her apron and gives it to Beau). Beau, I'm leaving you in charge.

MAC
That's not fair.

MORAG
If life was fair, I wouldn't be here every night while Sarah Harding swans about on tour in Ghost the Musical. Auch Gustav, what a pullover.

GUSTAVE
Oh, thank you Morag!

MORAG
No – palaver, that's it. I'll get there. Now, Gustave. Take me up the valley.

GUSTAVE
I will, Morag. I will.

They exit.

BEAU
Right, come on. Get to work?

MAC
What do we do? You're the boss.

BEAU
You clean the oven, I'll choose the music. See you later boys and girls!

BLACKOUT

Scene 3: Outside the castle

Tall wrought iron gates, their stone gateposts a mess of ivy. A dark, overgrown void beyond them. MORAG enters.

MORAG
Here goatie goatie! Auch I'll take a breather, we've walked miles. Och it's nice to be up on the hills and into the forest. I couldn't live in a city. Neither could my mother – she was banned from the three nearest ones. She was a country girl though. One of the saner pieces of advice she gave me was, dinnae pick your blackberries after Michaelmas because that's when the devil pisses on them. I assumed she was being metaphorical until three years later on Michaelmas night itself she was found steaming drunk in a hedgerow shouting "feed me Satan". (beat) I'm looking for Gustave's goats. Have you seen one? Well keep an eye out for the little devils.

A goat is thrown on stage.

MORAG
What was that? A goat behind me. But I've only just asked you to look for them. (To a man in the audience) I think you're just trying to impress me. Well there's no need, young man. You won't.

The goat bleats.

MORAG
You were right!

She picks the goat up.

MORAG
Gustave! Gustave I've found one.

GUSTAVE enters

GUSTAVE
You pretty little thing.

MORAG
She's not that pretty.

GUSTAVE
I mean you Morag.

MORAG
What?

GUSTAVE
You're a remarkable woman.

MORAG
Gustave...

GUSTAVE
It's true. To up sticks and move to a new country and make a success of yourself. It's quite the upheaval at your ripe- your perfect age.

GUSTAVE
It's good of you to come out here with me. Were you not frightened?

MORAG
Gustave, you wouldn't scare a sheep.

GUSTAVE
Up here though, by the old castle.

MORAG
Who lives in it?

GUSTAVE
They say it's abandoned now. Nobody goes in there and nobody comes out. There have been rumours of a fearsome beast who prowls this forest. It's all nonsense of course.

MORAG
It's getting cold.

GUSTAVE (offering a hip flask)
Have some of that.

MORAG
Och! A hip flask.

GUSTAVE
No, just an old fashioned one. (beat) That tree looks like it's got a face in it.

MORAG
It's just the light. You'll be picturing faces in bushes next.

He gets out a hip flask, hands it to her. She swigs and passes it back.

GUSTAVE
Morag... Well this won't be a surprise to you but the truth is, the truth is I don't just come to your tea room to sink my teeth into your scones. You know, I'm just a lonely goat herd, I'd sit each morning high on a hill and-

MORAG
Gustave I've no great objection to drugs but I find the discussing of them invariably tedious.

GUSTAVE

I'd sit there each day and think I'd never again meet anyone to make me happy. And then one day I wondered past the tearoom, and there you were in the window, putting up your handwritten notice: Under New Admonishment".

MORAG chuckles.

MORAG

I'll get there Gustave. I'll get there.

Behind them, the BEAST appears in the shadows beyond the gates. A fearsome sight, his arms held up, threatening. He silently opens the gates... The audience hopefully shout.

MORAG

Button it a minute boys and girls, Gustave's trying to tell me something.

GUSTAVE

You are a wonderful woman Morag.

MORAG

Oh Gustave...

They move closer about to kiss, the BEAST puts his head between them and they kiss him. MORAG and GUSTAVE scream.

BEAST

Stop it! Hurt a beast's pride why don't you.

They scream again.

BEAST

Stop screaming! My ears!

MORAG

They're not your worst feature by any stretch.

GUSTAVE

My dear, we may have stumbled on the local cruising area. Keep an eye out for a Boston Red Sox baseball cap, Beau said he'd lost his somewhere. My dear chap we were only going to embark on a little kiss.

MORAG

Gustave! Shush! I'm not ashamed, but you don't need to hire a bloomin' skywriter. Now, now Mr-

BEAST

Mr! Mr?? Do I sound like a mere Mr?

MORAG

Oh give it a rest, I don't care what bathroom you use.

BEAST

I mean, I am a... *(Aside)* But no, that is in the past. *(Back in)* I am a beast. I am a yeti.

He roars. They are a little more scared.

MORAG

I'm very sorry if we annoyed you. (She pats her pockets) Muffin?

BEAST

You have stolen from me.

MORAG

We've got plenty of witnesses who'll say we haven't! Boys and girls we haven't stolen anything have we?

BEAST

You've got my goat!

GUSTAVE looks at the goat. He checks the tag on its ear.

GUSTAVE

He's right! It's not one of mine. I'm very sorry sir, our mistake.

BEAST

Thieves. You will pay the price for your atrocities.

MORAG

Now listen, Mr Alphabetti Spag-yeti, I'm not one for new age mumbo jumbo but if you don't mind me saying you seem to have anger issues.

BEAST

You will be my prisoners, locked in my castle for eternity!

GUSTAVE

But that's ages!

BEAST

Take one last look around you. You will never see daylight again.

He gets them both on a headlock and leads them away.

Scene 4: Trump's tea room

BEAU is dancing and looking at his phone. MAC enters with a tray of scones cut in half, and puts them on the table next to a can of squirty cream and a jar of jam. Carly Rae Jepson's "I really like you" is playing. They have beers on the go. MAC yodels, and the audience responds. The song comes to an end. The same song starts up.

MAC
That's the sixth time!

BEAU
Yeah it's my favourite playlist! My Carly Rae Jepson I Really Like You playlist.

MAC
What are you doing?

BEAU
"Networking"

MAC
Networking! You're meant to be serving scones not buns. My mum pays you to work.

BEAU
And she put me in charge. Look, this is tourist town right? If you make the visitors feel welcome, they come back for more.

MAC
More what, non-specific urethritis? Beau, what do you put on first, jam or cream?

BEAU
I usually let the other guy decide.

BEAU picks up an empty tray.

MAC
These are ready.

BEAU
Alright. Boys and girls, who'd like a scone? You sir, coming right up! Mac, chuck us a scone.

MAC
Coming right up.

MAC chucks a scone, underarm, to BEAU who bats it into the audience with the tray.

MAC
I think you might have sent that to the wrong table.

BEAU
I think I did, Mac.

MAC
We'd better try again.

MAC throws another scone which is batted into the audience by BEAU. MAC squirts cream onto a couple of scones and holds them.

BEAU
Oh we're doing that are we?

MAC
I think we are.

SEBASTIAN enters.

SEBASTIAN
Beau!

BEAU turns and walks into MAC getting cream all over his face.

SEBASTIAN
(To audience) You really can't take your eyes off me can you. Beau! You've started shaving!

SEBASTIAN licks the cream off BEAU cheeks.

BEAU
That's gross.

SEBASTIAN
Quite right, who puts squirty cream on a scone. It's meant to be clotted. Or whipped...

He gives BEAU's bum a slap. He removes the remainder of the cream from BEAU's cheek with his finger, goes to lick his finger, then offers it instead to an audience member.

SEBATIAN
Now Beau, we must stop ignoring the elephant in the room, and I don't just mean the big fat trunk in my sexy mesh undies. Don't you want to see the world? Enjoy the high life? Feel my unexpected item in your gagging area? Be my beau, Beau.

BEAU
We're busy.

MAC
What do you want?

SEBASTIEN
Other than this little Alpine alpaca, I want the establishment.

187

MAC
Beau's had half of them already.

SEBASTIAN
The tea-room.

BEAU
Morag won't sell.

MAC
I wish she would. I wouldn't be stuck here all day. I could get out, meet people. Find a girlfriend. Get a job with prospects!

SEBASTIAN
Prospects eh? Then you might be in luck. I need a man.

MAC
You gays dinnae stop.

SEBASTIAN
I need a chap. A wingman. A side-kick. A deputy. An assistant.

BEAU
Do you need a number two?

SEBASTIAN (not getting it)
Urgently.

BEAU and MAC high-five

SEBASTIAN
(Aside) If this idiot takes the job, perhaps he can get me the deeds to this place. (To MAC) What say you?

MAC
Me? I'm very flattered but I don't think I'd better.

SEBASTIAN
Cockswallop. I can see you're a man of ambition. Yes, you and me we're like two balls in a sack. You're not an obvious candidate I know, but a piss in the mouth is worth two in the bush. Say yes.

MAC
What do you think boys and girls?

Don't do it Mac!

MAC
Sorry the boys and girls say no.

SEBASTIAN
Your loss. But remember I always have an opening for a bright young man. (*He picks up a silver spoon.*) Your mother's not about is she?

MAC
No they've been gone ages.

SEBASTIAN
Well tell her to put her lenses in when she's washing up, she's missed a- (*he sees his reflection*) Fucking hell though look at me. I'd better go before I get a lob on and break something. (*He ruffles the hair of someone in the audience*) Or someone. Love you!

SEBASTIAN exits.

BEAU
They *have* been gone ages! It's nearly dark. Do you think they're alright?

MAC
Aye, I'm sure.

BEAU
Do you think something could have happened to them up on the hills?

MAC
Naw, they'll be grand.

BEAU
It's easy to get lost up there you know, especially in the forest. Do you think they could have got into trouble?

MAC
I shouldnae think so.

BEAU
But do you think for the sake of the plot, we could go and look for them anyway?

MAC
Aye ok! Come on.

BEAU
See you later boys and girls!

Scene 5: Inside the castle

A grand and gloomy castle hall. The BEAST enters with MORAG.

MORAG
Where's Gustave? What have you done with him?

BEAST
He is in the dungeon.

MORAG
The dungeon!

BEAST
Don't be hysterical! It is very comfortable. It is mainly used as a home cinema.

MORAG
Still it's no very welcoming.

BEAST
You are my PRISONERS!! You will never leave.

MORAG
We'll be missed! Someone will rescue us.

BEAST
Nobody comes near this place.

MORAG
I'm not surprised. It's filthy.

BEAST
Then you will clean for me!

MORAG
I spend my life cooking and cleaning.

BEAST
Or your friend will die.

MORAG
Die! And in a pantomime! What kind of monster are you? (beat) You've cat hairs everywhere too.

BEAST (embarrassed)
They're not cat hairs.

MORAG
Are you moulting? Is that why you're so tetchy?

On the mantlepiece she notices a strange and very phallic plant. It's rather limp. She goes to touch it.

BEAST
Take your hands off my penis.

MORAG
I beg your pardon!

BEAST
The plant. It is a penis flytrap. A rare and magical plant that was... given to me.

MORAG
It's a bit limp.

BEAST
It is the only thing that will break the curse that was put on this castle.

MORAG
What curse?

BEAST
I cannot tell. But if the penis grows firm the curse will be broken.

MORAG
I'll put my hands to it and we'll have it up in no time. I'm known for my brown fingers.

BEAST
Excuse me?

MORAG
Something like that. I'm still learning the colours. All it needs is a squirt.

BEAST
No! The penis shrivels in water. It will only rise if I fall in love with someone and they love me in return.

MORAG
Why don't you do that then?

BEAST
You mock me!

MORAG
Grow up you big bairn. What are you talking about?

BEAST
Who would ever love me like this?

MORAG
Now, now! I'm sure...

BEAST
Would you??

MORAG
Oh! Well now, see, because of the unfortunate moment at which you chose to interrupt me and Gustave earlier I'm not altogether sure of my relationship status.

BEAST
People are fickle.

MORAG
Some are, aye. Fortunately for you, you have a castle. Many girls go for that sort of thing. Not me. As my mother used to say, dinnae marry for money, you can borrow it cheaper. (beat) The debts that cussed woman left me.

BEAST
Girls do not interest me.

MORAG
No. Naturally it's a *woman* you'll be after. *(a thought)* oh! Have you brought me here to be some sort of love slave? Have me whenever your whim takes you? Get me Dysoning the dining room in my goose-down knickers?

BEAST
Your what?

MORAG
Because if that's what this is I'd rather you were upfront. You'll not find me the love-starved loon but I'm not an immovable feast and nor am I lacking in either imagination or pragmatism when backed into a corner.

BEAST
What are you talking about?

MORAG
I'm no sure myself, I was hoping you'd interrupt me. You wouldn't have a piece of shortbread? I usually permit myself an indulgence at this hour and I'm a little weak.

BEAST
I am gay.

MORAG
I see. Still I'm sure a wee bite won't kick your diet too far into the long grass.

BEAST (getting very angry now)
My point is, I am attracted to men!

MORAG
Aye, men, well now, they *are* fickle. You're in a pickle. Good luck.

A flurry of flapping wings.

MORAG
What in God's good name was that?

BEAST
Bats. I like them. They are nearly blind, you know. They cannot see what I am.

MORAG
That's a very common misconception. The average bat can see as well as you or I. So you see, they like you well enough just as you are.

She goes to the drinks cabinet.

MORAG
Why don't we have a wee dram. I've earned it, and you can't be any worse drunk than you are sober.

She starts to pour a drink. HEIDI enters - she is giant toilet brush.

HEIDI
Be our guest why don't you I'm sure.

MORAG
Is there a party going on? Why didn't you say! I won the fancy dress three years in a row at the Suchmacoch village hall Diwali knees-up. And not with anything indecent, mind. Not even when the theme was slutty Pixar.

HEIDI
Fancy dress? If it was fancy dress would I be dressed as a bleeding bog brush.

BEAST
Heidi, as long a Morag is my prisoner for all eternity she will be treated with respect. This is Heidi, she's cursed.

MORAG
So you're a... toilet brush are you my dear?

HEIDI
No I'm Cher. Yes I'm a bog brush. At least until I go through the change.

MORAG
The change?

BEAST
She changes into a different household item every two hours.

HEIDI
Only this time I've really hit the skids. Still, mustn't grumble. A candle, a clock, a saucepan, you name it I've been it.

BEAST
Heidi is my housekeeper. She makes an excellent cherry fruit cake.

MORAG
Genoa?

HEIDI
Of course he does, we live together. If only I'd answered the door that fateful day! He beat me to it. Thought it was going to be some boy he'd ordered. I thought it was going to be my girlfriend Sofia coming to meet me from work, but it wasn't it, was an old enchantress come to test him. He fucked it up royally, didn't you eh with your nonsense and kaboom ka fuckity boom I got turned into a mug tree.

MORAG
When you say girlfriend...

HEIDI
I mean vaginal companion, yes.

MORAG
No well I think that's wonderful.

HEIDI
Which bit? The disappearance of the love of my life, or terrible curse that means any time now I could evolve into the kind of overly elaborate corkscrew that wankers buy each other for Christmas? I don't need your blessing thanks all the same. Dunno where Sofia is now. Probably shacked up in Geneva with a banker and a cat.

MORAG
Have you seen a doctor?

HEIDI
A doctor? "Doctor doctor I think I'm a pair of curtains" "You are a pair of curtains". This isn't some yeast infection.

MORAG
Or beast infection

HEIDI
It's a curse love, a curse.

MORAG
Can I go now?

BEAST
NO! You'll get to work.

HEIDI
Somebody's getting tired and hungry! You'd best get used it. You're stuck here for good.

HEIDI gives MORAG a broom, and HEIDI and the BEAST leave.

MORAG sings

SONG: SOME GIRLS

Some girls dream of fairytale weddings
And princes and palaces, gowns like Grace Kelly's
I was the girl with mud on her skirt and they'd laugh at me

Some girls get all the prettiest toys
They learn how to spellbind the loveliest boys who had been your best friends
So that comes to an end and you're left watching.

Some mothers say, no don't be an actress
I need you at home and that life's not for us
You don't make a fuss and it's true what they say
Your dreams fade away.

And then life happens
Too fast to understand
Till you find yourself here with a mop in your hand...

But...
Cooking and cleaning ain't such a hassle
Now those girls live in tenements and I live in a castle!
Give me a leg up, stand over here
Watch me swing from the chandelier

I've even got myself a fella
Where I want him - in the cellar!

Show me the cobwebs I could dust till I'm dead
I'll reach them bouncing on a four poster bed
I'm not here by choice but my smile isn't fake
When life gives you lemons make a lemon drizzle cake

I'll sunbathe nude out of his gaze
Between the hedges of the maze

Such fabulous things, you can tell that he's gay
The coffee table could be in the V&A
I'll put my feet up upon on the chaise longue
And do my corns with the fireside tongs

Some girls dream asleep in slums,
And some girls take it as it comes.

191

Scene 6: Outside the castle

BEAU and MAC enter. BEAU is staring avidly at his phone.

MAC
Yodeladyodeladyyodeladyyodeladyyodelady
yodeladyooo!

BEAU points at something.

BEAU
There he is!

MAC
Who? Where?

BEAU
Pikachu! Got him![29]

He notices a baseball cap and picks it up.

BEAU
Look! I found my cap! Oh wow! This must be the old castle!

BEAU puts his hat on.

BEAU
Ugh!

MAC
What?!

BEAU
I think there's a slug in it. *(He takes it off and looks inside.)* Oh, nope.

BEAU removes a used condom from inside the hat and replaces it. He drops the condom on the ground.

MAC
Why would guys still go cruising? You've got Grindr. You've got gay marriage.

BEAU
Well, I guess growing up gay still makes you associate sex with secrecy, you know? Also it's the only way you're likely to nosh off a celebrity.

MAC
Look. Prints.

BEAU
A prince!

MAC
No, prints - tracks, here in the snow. Here see? Those are from mum's shoes.

BEAU
Those must be dad's boots. And that footprint is from a goat.

MAC
Then what the hell made that one?

They both scream.

BEAU
I'll try the gates.

MAC
No!

BEAU
They must be in there, the tracks stop here. *(He tries the gates)* They're locked.

MAC
Of course they're locked it's not the nineteen fifties.

BEAU
But it looks abandoned... Oh my god! Maybe they went inside somehow for a canoodle.

MAC
A what?

BEAU
It's like a fuck but jollier.

MAC
You think they're in there going like the clappers?

BEAU
Don't call them that, they're the boys and girls. *(He looks up)* There's a light on. Up there. We need to get in. If only there was someone who could help us get inside the castle...

MABEL appears in a puff of smoke. BEAU and MAC scream.

MABEL
Stop screaming! You sound like a provincial gay who finally got retweeted by Britney.

BEAU
How did you do that?

---

[29] The newly launched augmented reality smartphone game Pokémon GO was the year's big craze.

MABEL
I'm actually a fairy.

MAC
No but seriously.

MABEL
Don't worry boys, no need to yelp,
I'm on your side and here to help!

BEAU
Oh my god!

MAC
You *are* a fairy!

BEAU
We need to get inside the castle. Our parents are inside and something's happened to them. Look at the ground.

MABEL
Oh yes, they left a condom!

BEAU
Please, help us. Can you cast us a spell to get inside.

MABEL taps on the castle wall.

MABEL
Truthfully, no. It's beyond my abilities. In spite of appearances the walls are thicker than a teenager's sixth ejaculation of the day.

BEAU
But we're nearly halfway through the show and you haven't cast any spells yet.

MABEL
Neither true nor fair. Only an hour ago I changed the taps in the hotel's bathrooms from hot and cold to Coca Cola and slimline tonic. So now they're mixer taps.

BEAU
You're shit.

MAC
I don't think you're shit.

MABEL
Thank you Mac. Have you tried the doorbell?

She indicates the doorbell.

MAC
We don't know who's in there with them.

MABEL
I can't get you through the walls but I'll tell you what, I'll magic you a disguise so you can knock at the door with no risk of harm. Let me think. Someone who everyone would let into their home...

MAC
Desmond Tutu.

MABEL
...You want me to disguise you as a black man?

BEAU
Yeah idiot. Michelle Obama!

BEAU and MAC
David Bowie!

MABEL
He's dead.

BEAU
There'd be less chance of the real one turning up...

MABEL
Come on now, think.

BEAU
This is bullshit we're better off without you. So long, farewell, auf wiedersehen goodbye.

MABEL
The Sound of Music! Bingo! That's given me an idea for the perfect disguise. Oh my god seriously this is fucking brilliant. Alright lads. Stand there together. He we go.

Scene 7: The castle

MORAG is cleaning and humming her song. GUSTAVE is handcuffed to a chair.

MORAG
It's nice he let you out of that dungeon a while.

GUSTAVE
Your feminine charms persuaded him!

MORAG
Och you silly old flatterer! Did he hurt you Gustave? Were you violated? I'll not think less of you.

The door bell rings. They look at each other.

MORAG
I'll get it will I?

GUSTAVE
We're unguarded! This could be our chance! Go and answer the door to whoever this is, and while the yeti's distracted by his guest you run home, whip up a mob and bring them here to rescue me! You'll be back in your little kitchen by supper time.

MORAG looks about at her grand surroundings.

MORAG
My little kitchen.

The doorbell again.

GUSTAVE
Well? Go on.

MORAG
Och I know you're right. Wait there. *(She sings as she goes)* "Supper time.... and the livin' is easy..."

She exits.

MORAG (off)
What on earth?

She returns with MAC and BEAU, who are dressed as Nazi storm troopers.

MORAG
Please don't hurt me! *(Whisper)* I'll hide you, Gustave. (She sits on Gustave) It is just me, all alone, a poor lady of indeterminable age. With barely a pot to piddle in. In my humble castle.

GUSTAVE moans. MORAG stamps on his foot. GUSTAVE screams.

BEAU
Shhh! Listen. It's us.

MORAG (a whisper)
Bite my shoulder if you can't contain yourself.

The BEAST enters. BEAU and MAC scream.

BEAST
Who goes there?

BEAU
Shit!

MAC
What do we do?

BEAU
You rescue your mum and find my dad. I'll distract him. (To the Beast, a German accent) Er... Ve are here to collect for ze party!

MORAG
I'll do you a plate of cheese and pineapple, I'm sure we can stretch to that.

BEAST
I said leave. NOW!

BEAU
It's alright if you don't have much cash... You can give us something for the, for ze bring und buy sale! We... Ve could look for something together. *(looks about)* Wow you place is wicked mate. Er, I mean, zis place is vicked...

MAC
Freund!

BEAU
Freund! Thanks. Tell me about zis painting.

MAC tries to pull MORAG from her chair.

GUSTAVE
Don't stand up!

MORAG
I would never betray you!

GUSTAVE
It's just that you've given me a... gentleman's condition.

MORAG
Oh Gustave!

MAC
Gustave!

MAC hauls his mum from the chair and falls over.

MAC
Bollocks and shite!

BEAU
Dad!

BEAST
You think you can fool me!

GUSTAVE
Beau! You came! Why are you dressed like that. Are you off to that club in Geneva again?

BEAU
The fairy's an idiot, she got her Nazis and nuns confused.

BEAST
You are not Nazi storm-troopers! You are village people.

BEAU
No but I can see where you're going with that. We've come to get our parents back!

GUSTAVE
Beau! My brave boy! I'm proud of you.

BEAU
Thanks dad!

MAC looks at MORAG. A beat.

MORAG
Mac, did you remember to turn the oven off?

BEAU
Let them go!

BEAST
Never! They stole from me. They would have kept that goat forever. Therefore, I will keep them here forever!

MORAG
It was a mistake! Have you never made a mistake?

BEAU
He's my dad! Please!

BEAST
Never!

A moment.

BEAU
I tell you what mate, I'll make a deal with you. If you let them go – both of them – I will stay here as your prisoner.

MAC
Beau!

BEAU
Think about it. I'd be useful. You could put me to work. I'm younger. I'm fitter. I'm-

MORAG
Alright that's enough

GUSTAVE
Son, I can't let you do that. You've your whole life ahead of you! A whole world to explore.

BEAU
Dad, all I do is serve food and have meaningless sex. It's not like I'm gonna find a cure for cancer or write a great novel or get a million Instagram followers.

GUSTAVE
It would break me heart!

BEAU
Dad, you said it yourself. I've not been a good son to you since mum died. I've been selfish. This way I can do right by you. So, Mr...

BEAST
Sir.

BEAU
Sir. *(Aside, a bit excited)* Sir! *(To Beast)* Sir. So. Are you up for swapping?

BEAST
Very well. You will stay.

The BEAST removes a key and unlocks GUSTAV's handcuffs.

MAC (to Morag)
Do you reckon Beau fancies him?

MORAG
He'd no be Beau's type would he?

MAC
He's got a head and elbows.

BEAST
I will escort the prisoners out.

MAC, GUSTAVE and MORAG hug BEAU. They exit with the BEAST, BEAU looks around, sees the plant, is puzzled. HEIDI enters, she is a giant Teapot.

HEIDI

We don't see a soul in ten years and suddenly it's like a coach party's turned up. I hope his knobs don't expect me to cater for them is all.

They look at each other. A moment.

BEAU

You're a teapot!

HEIDI

Give the boy a coconut. What are you doing here?

BEAU

I'm to be a prisoner. Forever.

HEIDI

It might not be forever. I wonder...

The BEAST enters

BEAST

You will go to the dungeon.

BEAU

Isn't it enough that you're keeping me here forever?

BEAST

To the dungeon! That way. I will be down in a minute to lock you up.

BEAU exits.

HEIDI

Sir, if I may, we talked about you having a tendency to take things a bit far. He's young sir - and he's easy enough on the eye... We need to hurry up and find someone to fall in love with you and pop his brush up your chimney so we can all go back to normal. If your penis doesn't start perking up soon, one of these days it could die and then we're stuck. Don't you want to break these curses?

BEAST

I will find someone.

HEIDI

How? You went on Gaydar the other day – oh yes, I know what you're up to. You had that Pentium out and you left Internet Explorer open. You know how many men were online? Yes, you do. Four. In the whole of Europe! Two total bottoms, one top who thinks body hair is unhygienic so that's you out, not least because your body hair IS fucking unhygienic, and a fourth who didn't specify his preferred role but you ain't meeting

him because his profile includes the phrases "just a normal guy", "I tell it like it is" and "Be a man, if wanted someone feminine I'd have a girlfriend lol" and there is no way am I going to risk having to go to a wedding where someone like that has any say in the planning of it. So either the gays all died and went to Fire Island, or technology has moved on in the ten years we've been holed up here.

BEAST

What do lesbians use?

HEIDI

I use me hands but some like a dildo. There was a girl in the next village along who got herself the nickname Rolling-pin Rebecca. If I ever find myself turned into one I'll pay her a visit. (beat) I know that's not what you meant I just wanted to see if you'd get all queasy. (beat) Let the boy out, eh? He's done no wrong. Lock the front door but give him the run of the place.

BEAST

Perhaps you're right. I will tell him.

HEIDI

And maybe hunt down some deodorant first eh?

MABEL enters.

MABEL

Two lonely hearts, both stubborn, and yet
It seems there's a spark – could something take off?
Could love find a home, could our beast even get
As royally fucked as Channel 4's Bake-Off?[30]
Now! Off to the bar or queue for pee,
But return - for the curse has yet to be lifted,
I don't know about you but I can't wait to see
If the snow in a yeti's cold heart has drifted.
Go refresh yourselves before our final ascent, oh
Sweet boys and girls, until then, À bientôt!

INTERVAL

---

[30] It had just been announced that Channel 4 had acquired the BBC hit The Great British Bake-Off. People predicted a disaster. We were wrong.

Ellen Butler as Heidi in *Beauty on the Piste*. Photo by PBGstudios.

David Moss as Morag and Jamie Coles as the Beast in *Beauty on the Piste*. Photo by PBGstudios.

Scene 8: Outside the village

GUSTAVE and MORAG enter, looking for goats,. MAC has an enormous trekking rucksack on. They're wrapped up warm. MAC yodels and the audience respond.

MAC
Och hello boys and girls. We're looking for Gustave's goats.

MORAG
Coooeee!

She searches under a couple of seats

GUSTAVE
Where are you my precious little ones.

He bursts out sobbing.

MAC
It's alright Gustave, chin up.

GUSTAVE
No goats, and no Beau, I'll never see any of them again.

MORAG
Nazis! Of all the stupid, stupid...

GUSTAVE
It's alright, it's alright. But why did you not go for something more innocuous?

MORAG
Aye. Like the Ku Klux bloody Klan. At least they hide their faeces!

GUSTAVE & MAC
Faces.

MORAG
I'll get there I'll get there. Why didn't you get done up as pizza delivery boys?

MAC
What if he hadn't ordered pizza? He'd have been suspicious!

MORAG
Mac, everyone knows if someone turns up with pizza you didnae order you accept it with good grace and a prayer of thanks and ask no questions. It's God's little thank you to the meek.

GUSTAVE
Poor Beau. Things look bleak alright.

MORAG
Now now, why don't we cheer ourselves up with a wee singsong. Here's a catchy one my mother taught me[31].

Up the airy mountain, down the rushy glen,
We dare not go a-hunting for fear of little men,
Wee folk, good folk, trouping altogether
Green jacket, red cap, white owl's feather!

Are ye cheered up yet? There's another 65 verses if we need to continue but a lot of them aren't nice about the English or the Catholics, or those of darker skin tones, or the French, or Jews.

GUSTAVE
Perhaps if we all sang the first verse together.

MAC
That's it! You'll help us cheer Gustave up won't you boys and girls. You look like you've had a dram or three at the interval.

MORAG
Will I teach them the words?

MAC
I think we can do better than that!

A songsheet appears. It has slightly different words...

MORAG
Splendid! Right Mac, you lead them, off you go nice and loud!

They sing:

Up the airy mountain, down the rushy glen,
Here we go a-hunting for hairy little men,
Wee folk, good folk, cruising altogether
Shirts up, pants down, all in leather!

GUSTAVE
Very good!

MORAG
Very good? I'd expect such smut of you Mackety Mac Don't Talk Back but I thought better of the boys and girls.

[etc.. they have a singing competition]

GUSTAVE
That's a nice backpack, Mac.

---

[31] Jon: It's a catchy one that my own Scottish granny taught me.

MAC
Cheers. Huh? Where'd that come from?

GUSTAVE (looking).
Millets.

MORAG
You didnae have that on earlier.

MAC
I think I picked it up and put it on without thinking when we stopped for a rest in that clearing.

MORAG
Put it down! There might be a bomb in it!

MORAG and GUSTAVE escape into the audience. MAC take it off and has a look.

MAC
No it's just a little camping stove... Some hiking socks...

MORAG and GUSTAVE sigh with relief.

MAC
An asthma inhaler... Someone's insulin wand...

MORAG
That's alright then.

MAC
...Something called Truvada[32]... Oh! And sweets! Would anyone like a sweet boys and girls?

He dishes them out.

MORAG
Oh that's right, we've been trudging for miles but you dish them out to these lot.

It starts to rain

MORAG
Come on. It's starting to rain.

GUSTAVE
My poor brave boy! The beast won't really keep him there forever will he?

MORAG
Of course not.

GUSTAVE
We're not close you know. Not really. I didn't notice it

when his mother and sister were with us. I should have made more of an effort to bond with him. Joined in with whatever it is he likes to get up to.

MAC
You were probably best out of that.

GUSTAVE
But to think of him there at the castle. We could have done more. I mean, when I look back at it, there were four of us and only one beast.

MORAG
Oh now you mustn't feel guilty! I mean, who knows how many other beasts lived there with him? He could have all sorts. Flying monkeys, a sharknado.

GUSTAVE
Poor Beau!

MORAG
And he was very charismatic. Oh it should have been you Mac.

MAC
Mum!

MORAG
Well it should. I'm sorry but I've said it now and there it is.

MAC
Then you won't miss me if I'm not around, will you!

GUSTAVE
Mac?

MAC
I've had a job offer. One with prospects! One with perks! *(Goes to leave)* I'll see you in court!

MORAG
You'll- you what? Mac where are you going, tell us the truth.

MAC
You want the truth? You can't handle the truth.

GUSTAVE
Well don't get lost for goodness sake. Stick to the roads.

MAC
Roads? Where I'm going we don't need roads. Good day.

---

[32] A brand of PrEP (Pre-exposure prophylaxis). This was just becoming popular.

MORAG
But-

MAC
I said good day!

MAC exits. They look puzzled.

MORAG
I've got a bad feeling about this.

GUSTAVE
Oh now you're at it you silly bean. Let's get you out of this rain.

MORAG (Romantic)
Is it still raining? I hadn't noticed.[33]

Exit.

---

[33] A nice thing about writing panto is you can write a page of movie clichés just because you feel like it..

Scene 9: The castle

It's evening. BEAU is on stage.

BEAU
Well boys and girls, I suppose I wanted a change of scene. An adventure. There's nobody here apart from those two, it's dead weird. *(He reaches for his pocket, stops).* Oh yeah. He's taken my phone.

The BEAST enters.

BEAST
What are you doing?

BEAU
Nothing.

BEAST
You have been here a night and a day. You have barely left this room. You have a whole castle to explore. Except for the forbidden tower which you must never enter on pain of death.

BEAU
Ok.

BEAST
Well?

BEAU
I have forever to explore. (beat) What do you do all day anyway? Stuck here alone.

BEAST
I manage the estate. I read. I hunt, I watch films. Recently I have mastered the art of topiary.

BEAU
That's hedges right? *(He goes to the window and looks out).* Oh yeah! (beat) I like the mouse.

BEAST
The mouse?

BEAU points

BEAST
Ah. Yes that one's a recent effort.

An awkward silence

BEAST
Well, this has been...

He goes to exit. HEIDI enters unseen by BEAU dressed as a standard lamp. She raises her lampshade and whispers in his ear.

HEIDI
Ask him what he likes to get up to.

BEAST
Ask him yourself you nosy bitch.

HEIDI
Sir! Remember what you're trying to accomplish.

BEAST
I don't even know if he's gay!

HEIDI
Then ask him!

BEAST
It's embarrassing! Alright, I'll try and be subtle. But for fuck's sake, a mouse!?? Does it look like a mouse to you?

HEIDI
I expect the boy is tired and out of sorts. And he's only the moonlight to go on. It's clearly not supposed to be a mouse.

BEAST
No?

HEIDI
No!

BEAST
No. Quite. Because it looks like a...?

HEIDI
It looks like a...

BEAST
A ca...

HEIDA
A ca... a cat!!

BEAST
A CAMEL. God's teeth!

The BEAST grabs her wrist, marches her to BEAU, grabs his wrist too, marches them to the window.

BEAU
Ow.

BEAST
Look at it. It's got a hump, what did you think that was?

BEAU
A rucksack?

He lets go of HEIDI's wrist but neglects to let go of BEAU's. They both look at his hand on BEAU's wrist,

201

both privately enjoying the moment, and the BEAST holds it a little longer before awkwardly releasing it.

HEIDI
If you'll excuse me sir I'd like to be alone. I can feel a change coming on and it brings me out in a right flush.

BEAST (whispered)
Don't leave me with him!

HEIDI
Take a deep breath and stay calm. You can do it.

BEAST
Peasants are so boring!

HEIDI
Talk to him. Excuse me.

HEIDI exits. A moment.

BEAST
This... this situation, it reminds me a little of Jane Eyre. The house, the master... Have you read Jane Eyre?

BEAU
What did she write again?

BEAST
She's a character.

BEAU
That's what people say about me when they're trying to find a nicer word than slag.

BEAST
Men cannot be slags.

BEAU
That's a very old-fashioned attitude sir. You just have to put your mind to it.

Pause.

BEAST
So... How do *you* like to spend time?

BEAU
I dunno. I work in the tea-room, I see a bit of telly-

The BEAST yawns. BEAU looks slightly upset.

BEAST
Ugh, sorry, sorry. Go on.

BEAU
I dunno. Bit of Netflix, quite a lot of chill. I ski a bit, obviously.

BEAST (Disappointed)
Oh. You're sporty. You like... football?

BEAU
Nah not really. I mean I like Ronaldo and whoever that blonde French one was that was in the Euros and- (checks himself, more butch) I mean, yeah it's er... Yeah mate it's alright.

BEAST
Mate??

BEAU
Sir. (Then an aside, rather excited) "Sir!"

BEAST *(Hopeful)*
Or perhaps you are a man of more... cultural, artistic pursuits?

BEAU
Well... I tried to like Christine and the Queens for a couple of weeks.

BEAST (frustrated rage)
Jesus Christ this is impossible! DO YOU HAVE A GIRLFRIEND??

BEAU laughs hysterically.

BEAST
What's so funny?

BEAU
Sorry it's just, oh my god – girlfriend! The last time I saw a vagina was from the ins- (aside) But wait, what if I'm locked up with a homophobe? (To the Beast) Sir, no, I don't currently have a girlfriend.

BEAST
Currently. He said currently! What does he mean?

BEAU
It means not right now.

BEAST
That was an aside!

BEAU
Do you? Have a... girlfriend or whatever you call them. Are you... betrothed?

BEAST
Me? A girlfriend? Ha! The last time I saw a tit I was sucking on- (Checks himself) No, Beau, I... I prefer a solitary life.

BEAU
Yeah, course.

BEAST
Who wants to be tied down?

BEAU
(Puts his hand up enthusiastically) Me! Oh – right. Yeah, no. Still. You're doing alright for yourself. How did you get to live in a castle?

BEAST
I'm an aristocrat. I inherited it.

BEAU
Oh! So that's why you look all... like you do. Cos aristocrats are a bit "sandwich paste" ain't they.

BEAST
Sandwich paste?

BEAU
Usually inbred.

BEAST
GET OUT!

BEAU
I'm so sorry!

BEAST
That was a terrible joke! I haven't always looked like-(aside) but I mustn't tell him anything. (to BEAU) How astute, it is indeed my inbreeding that has left me so very beastly, and... manly! With such an impractically large penis and such a freakishly pretty bottom.

The plant stirs and rises very slightly.

BEAU
You could, you know. Have a girlfriend I mean. You're not all that unattractive... mate.

BEAST
Well it is getting late.

BEAU
Yeah.

BEAST
I will go to my bed. My enormous bed.

BEAU
Me too.

BEAST
You are comfortable I trust. The mattress.

BEAU
Well I woke up a bit stiff this morning.

BEAST
Isn't it always the way.

They laugh awkwardly, then stop laughing, also awkwardly.

BEAST
You were not cold?

BEAU
I was a bit.

BEAST
It's growing increasingly hard.

BEAU
You what?

BEAST
To heat that wing of the castle... And when you sleep alone, with no other body heat... Look, my bed really is enormous you'd barely know I was there.

BEAU thinks for a moment, decides to go with it.

BEAU
You'd know *I* was there.

A moment. BEAU takes the BEAST's hand for a second. It's going to happen. It's definitely going to happen. The plant stirs some more. BEAU notices it.

BEAU
Here, your plant could do with watering.

BEAU takes his drink towards the plant, thinking he'll pour it into the pot. The beast pushes him roughly out of the way.

BEAST
Don't touch the plant! Ever! You IDIOT boy!!

BEAU
Oh fuck off you total arsehole! I don't know your stupid shitty house rules do I? Stop shouting at me every two minutes you spoilt prick!

BEAST
That's it! Back to the dungeon!

BEAU
I've done nothing wrong!

BEAST
You will stay there forever. Your meals will be slid under the door.

BEAU
Don't bother! I'll starve to death, and when I die with a six-pack you better take a photo.

BEAST
Come. Now.

The BEAST leads BEAU away.

BEAU
And a blind man with potatoes for hands could do a better camel than that heap of shit out there.

They exit.

Scene 10: Trump's tea room

GUSTAVE enters with cups of tea. He's wearing pyjamas. MORAG is dressed.

GUSTAVE
Morning my darling.

MORAG
Alright you old softie, no need for fruity language before noon. That's kind bringing those teas all the way from yours in your pyjamas.

GUSTAVE
Perhaps one day you might actually let me stay the night here?

MORAG
Keep your voice down! The church is only in the next valley and the organist claims to have perfect pitch.

GUSTAVE
You're ashamed of me.

MORAG
Gustave, if I ever feel shame it's for my own occasional wrongdoings. Not on account of other souls and especially not kind gentlemen who think to bring me tea. In my tea-room. How's business?

GUSTAVE
I haven't sold a single paper this morning.

MORAG
And I've not sold a single cheese éclair. Gustave, something's up.

GUSTAVE
I can't help it around you.

MAC enters with a pile of newspapers

MAC
Read all about it! Read all about it! Oh hello boys and girls. Yodlediddle-yodlediddle-yodlewubbawubbawub!

MORAG
Mac, what are you doing?

MAC
I told you... I got a job! With prospects!

MORAG
As a paper boy?!

GUSTAVE
Well one has to start somewhere eh lad... Are those my papers?

SEBASTIAN enters

SEBASTIAN
No! They're my papers. The first edition of the Les Dennis Debacle, hot off the presses! Mac, give them a copy.

MORAG
I'll not buy your nonsense.

SEBASTIAN
They're free. Please. Take one.

GUSTAVE
No wonder I haven't sold any papers. How did you get an interview with Tom Daley?

SEBASTIAN
Connections. Ah now there's a boy whose little bronze medallion I'd like to slip over my head.

MORAG
The headline! "Hygiene scare at Trump's Tea Room! A penguin and raw fish have been seen at Les Dennis's foreign-run eatery." Foreign-run! I'm Scottish!

SEBASTIAN
Yes it's funny that because my new restaurant is heaving. Partly the celebrity factor of course, partly because of my full-page advertorial on page 5 complete with two-for-one voucher. Where's Beau? I was going to ask him to dine with me.

GUSTAVE
It's terrible. He's been taken from us.

SEBASTIAN
What? Oh god! Departed! (he drops to his knees) Poor innocent Beau... I don't suppose he's still warm?

MAC
He's not dead.

MORAG
We think.

GUSTAVE
A yeti has taken him prisoner. Up in the forest.

SEBASTIAN
A yeti! Ha! With my charm and charisma it will take no time to persuade the monster to let Beau go, and if he

205

does kick up a fuss we'll have his head mounted on the wall like a moose.

GUSTAVE
It's worth a try.

SEBASTIAN
And then Beau will marry me!

GUSTAVE
Oh no! He doesn't want to marry you. We'll think of something ourselves.

SEBASTIAN
Fine, throw the bottom out with bathwater, you crazy old man.

MAC
Sebastian sir... Could we no help them a bit. If we put a story about it in the paper, maybe enough people would see it and go and rescue him.

SEBASTIAN
I don't know.

MORAG
Oh Mr St Moritz, please. I'll give you an interview if you think it'll help, but I'll not pose in swimwear, unless you've a burkini to hand. Just give me a couple of inches.

GUSTAVE
I can't imagine you swimming.

MORAG
That's intentional. Though I enjoyed a few good lengths as a lass. We were on the shores of a loch where I grew up. Wee place called Lichmanochers, it had a remarkably balmy microclimate. On a quiet morning I'd be out there wearing nothing but a clothes peg to keep the hair out of my eyes.

SEBASTIAN
But really! A yeti in the Alps! Would anyone believe such a thing? *(aside)* But of course they wouldn't! *(Back in the room).* Mac, continue on your rounds. Gustave, I know good copy when I see it. Tell me everything!

MAC exits

MORAG
You won't regret it! Now if you'll excuse me I've got to peel a ton of Laughing Cow cheese triangles for today's salad.

MORAG exits.

GUSTAVE
This is very generous of you Sebastian.

SONG: READ ALL ABOUT IT
(Sung by Sebastian)

A community leader must always do his bit,
Society's great pillar ought to help the village twit...

Read all about it! Old Gustave has seen
A yeti in the woods! What next? A dragon on the green?
Centaurs at the cinema, mermaids at the baths?
If you weren't so fucking dull I'd say you're playing us for laughs

Read all about it! Our lovely safe resort
So popular with tourists - I hope the beast is caught!
A yeti on the prowl! Well gosh it sounds like hell
Our bookings will drop off, they'll all fuck off to Meribel

Read all about it! Really it's quite sad
The only sane conclusion is that Gustave's gone quite mad!
Perhaps because his wife died, or because his son is gay
We must do best to let you rest - safely locked away!

You're mad, Gustave you're mad
But I'm bad, And I'm dangerous to know!
You're mad like Tom Cruise or Hitler
Without the wild charisma
I think you'd better go!

Read all about it! Shout it from the steeple
Gustave is the enemy of hardworking people
They'll pitch up with their pitchforks, they'll form a motley crew
They won't come for the yeti mate, oh no they'll come for you!

BLACKOUT

Scene 11: The castle

A great dinner table is set. Beau sits at one end of it but not facing the table. He's reading a book. The BEAST enters. BEAU ignores him.

BEAST
There you are.

BEAU
Ta-da!

BEAST
Don't be sarcastic!

BEAU
I'm a prisoner in your castle. Where did you expect me to be, Lego Land?

The BEAST hands BEAU a drink.

BEAST
I let you out of the dungeon. You might show gratitude,

BEAU (mumbling)
Cheers

He carries on reading.

BEAST
You have the run of the place.

BEAU
(angry) I'm not a house rabbit! *(beat. To amuse himself, quietly:)* I'm a techno bunny.

BEAST
Well. You must feel free to explore. Keep yourself entertained. You've discovered my library. Good.

BEAU
"Library"

BEAST
It is a library.

BEAU
Library. You'd be adorable if you weren't such a wanker.

BEAST
It is a room full of books. Some very fine, rare manuscripts.

BEAU
Yeah but it's not a library is it, there's no scratched DVDs or mad homeless people or ancient beige computers with all the porn sites blocked off them, or-

BEAST
It is the best fucking library IN ALL OF SWITZERLAND!

BEAU
Ok.

BEAST
Say it!

BEAU
It's the best fucking-

BEAST
DON'T PUT THAT BIT IN!!

A moment.

BEAU
You'll give yourself a heart attack. With any luck. *(He knows this is too far)* Sorry.

BEAST
Forgive my temper. I spend so little time with other people.

BEAU
Well that's considerate of you.

BEAST
Anyway, you're welcome to browse.

BEAU
Have you got anything less wordy.

BEAST
I have most of the Taschen books. They're art books. A few of them are really quite, um, quite erotic if you, if er... Heidi! Heidi!! Where are you?

The BEAST sits at the table. He fiddles with his cutlery. An awkward pause. BEAU giggles.

BEAST
Something amuses you.

BEAU
I bet you've got a cupboard under the stairs that you've put a little desk in and now you call it your "study".

BEAST
I have got a study! I have ten bedrooms, two kitchens, a great hall, an alright hall, three pantries, a buttery-

BEAU
A what?

BEAST
A buttery. Where butts of wine are stored.

BEAU
Ahahaha butts!

BEAST
A library, a study

BEAU
"Study"

BEAST
A conservatory, a billiard room, a Cluedo room, two sitting rooms, a forbidden tower into which you may never venture on pain of death, a laundry and utility room, a drawing room, an atrium, a B-trium and two dining rooms.

BEAU
Great. We can use one each.

BEAST
Heidi!!

HEIDI appears, she is a set of bellows.

HEIDI
You bellowed sir?

BEAST
Where have you been?

HEIDI
Oh you know. Shooting the breeze. Having a blast. Evening Beau. Now, have I got a lovely Christmas supper for the pair of you!

BEAU
Christmas?

HEIDI
It's only right to have a special supper on Christmas eve.

BEAU
Oh my god! It's Christmas eve? Is this it? Where's the tree? Where's the tinsel? I wish I was back in Les Dennis. I'd be drinking glühwein by the fire, all snug and cuddled up with someone and trying to remember his name.

HEIDI coughs and nudges the BEAST who awkwardly removes a Christmas cracker from a pocket. He offers BEAU an end.

BEAU
You'll only have a tantrum when it snaps.

HEIDI
Put your book down for dinner love.

BEAU
I'm fine, thanks.

BEAST
Why won't you sup with me?

BEAU
"Sup"

BEAST
Excuse me?

BEAU
'Sup dude.

BEAST (lost)
Heidi...?

HEIDI
Why won't you join the master to eat?

BEAU
I have dietary requirements.

HEIDI
I'm sure I can accommodate.

BEAU
I can't eat with an arrogant prick in the room.

HEIDI
Beau!

HEIDI frowns then forces a smile. She nods at the window.

HEIDI
It's snowing.

They both stand and go to the window. HEIDI, behind them, places BEAU's hand on the BEAST's shoulder. After a moment he awkwardly removes it.

BEAU
It's not snowing.

HEIDI
Made you look. Now, sit. Eat.

HEIDI presents a dish.

HEIDI
Asparagus? There's er.... there's some says as how it's an aphrodisiac. I wouldn't know of course.

BEAU
I'll get myself something later.

BEAST
I will send you back to the dungeon!

HEIDI
Sir...!

BEAU
It's fine if it gets me away from you!

A moment.

BEAST
(To HEIDI, whispered) Aphrodisiac! Could you *be* any less subtle?

HEIDI
Course sir. (She presents another dish). Oyster?

BEAU sulks

HEIDI
I'd have been grateful having such luxuries when I was growing up. (She breaks down) Is it too much to ask that you get on!

She drops the dish she's holding and it clatters to the floor, hitting the BEAST'S foot. He roars in agony and hops about clutching his toe.

HEIDI
Well if you won't put decent shoes on.

BEAST
It's broken!

HEIDI (picking up the dish)
Nonsense. Bit of a dent is all. I'll pop it in the kitchen.

HEIDI exits.

BEAU
Let me see it. Come here. Stay still. Morag made me do a first aid course. You know, the kiss of life and stuff. It's a bit like when you give a guy a blowback.

The BEAST sits in a chair and raises his foot. BEAU examines it.

BEAU
Nothing broken. You could do with some ice on it.

BEAST
Why not just leave your hand there, you have been cold enough with me.

BEAU
Oooooh!

BEAST
You have had many men. Yet you have not settled down with one of them.

BEAU
Settled down! Even my old man stopped trying that one with me. I'm strictly about the fun.

BEAST
I am not your type. You think me too hairy.

BEAU
Oh is that your hair? I thought you'd made yourself a nest. How does it feel now?

BEAST
It is getting better. Keep your hand there.

BEAU
Ok.

He does. He shifts his weight to get more comfortable and ends up leaning against the BEAST's leg.

SONG: A YETI AND A YOUTH
(Regular = Beau; Italics = Beast; Bold = Both)

Maybe it's the snow
Maybe it's the setting
Or maybe I'm forgetting something hidden in my heart?
Maybe it's the fire
Maybe it's the music?
But I feel like I'm losing it here with him in the dark

Maybe it's the light
He looks so vulnerable and young
He's such an animal,
I bet he farts and growls when he comes

One two three four hours we spent just talking in the room
One two three fortune lights a candle in the gloom
A little nervous like we wished we could rehearse
Could it be that all an ugly beast needs is a slut who's been with worse?

Making little plans
Tour the castle gardens

209

Notice how he hardens when my hand touches his side
But could he treat me kindly?
He's such a mindless twink
I've barely seen him think but God I'd like to see inside,

Maybe I'm a fool,
He's here for punishment and duty
Getting to his private parts
Would be like the prince hacking away
Trying to get to Sleeping Beauty

One two three four hours we spent just walking through the halls
Two Three forever wouldn't feel too long at all,
This all seems more like a dream than a curse,
Could it be that all an ugly beast needs is a slut who's been with worse?

They'd mock me in the village
His fur smells of the damp
And he could be less camp
Hey bitch I'm living my truth

But looking from a distance
The castle seems to sparkle,
And somewhere in the dark'll be a yeti and a youth
Yes somewhere in the dark'll be a yeti and a youth.

The intimate moment is interrupted by HEIDI

HEIDI
Mind-me-scuse-me. It's late sirs. Beau, I meant to put fresh sheets on your bed but I didn't get round to it what with one thing and another... I did the master's though. Lovely and soft. Hashtag just saying.

BEAU
How do you know about hashtags? They're not ten years old.

HEIDI
If Shakespeare could have a clock chiming in Anthony and Cleopatra, I can have a bleeding hashtag. Well, I'll turn in if I may. Night night.

HEIDI exits.

BEAST
It is late.

BEAU
It is. Here, I think your plant needs watering-

BEAST
---!

BEAU
Only joking only joking. I think I'm gonna crash too. Night.

BEAST
But... I thought perhaps.

BEAU
We got forever ain't we? Let's see how tomorrow goes.

BEAU gives him a smile, and exits. The BEAST is crestfallen. After a moment, BEAU runs back on with a look that says "what am I like?", grabs the BEAST's hand and leads him off to bed.

Scene 12: Trump's tea room

MORAG enters.

MORAG
Hello boys and girls! It's been a whole two months! Well one whole month plus February. Poor Gustave's locked up in the loony bin! They took him away on the high security snow plough. And that's not the end of it. I'm down to my last few Euros. Times are tough boys and girls. (*Ahh*) They're tougher than that. (*ahh!*) Nailed it. It's a relief young Mac's supporting himself even if it is with that man.

MAC enters

MAC
Yodeladywaydeewoo! Hi mum.

MORAG
Auch I see. Just walks in here like it's a... like it's a...

MAC
Cafe? He's sacked me mum. He's replaced me with an actual proper newspaper editor who has real world experience beyond assisting in a tearoom. It's not fair. Can I come back?

MORAG
You millennials! Now Mac, I'm afraid we need a little talk.

MAC
Mum I've told you, google that stuff if you're confused.

MORAG
I'm going on the market. See what offers I get.

MAC
What? Are you lonely with Gustave banged up?

MORAG
I'm talking about the tea room. I need to sell before we go under. We're moving back to Scotland.

MAC
We? But I like it here. I see that fairy about sometimes. She beat me at pool last week. I didn't even have to let her.

MORAG
I'm sorry Mac, my minds made up. It's back to the highlands for us.

MAC
You once said you wished your mam had let you follow your dreams.

SEBASTIAN enters

SEBASTIAN
Ahahahaha!

MORAG
Mr St Moritz, you've arrived at a very opportune moment.

SEBASTIAN
I have?

MORAG
Have a seat. (Offering a tin) Have a flapjack. Just a plain one, don't take the mickey. The Stilton ones are for paying customers. You'll want a pen and either your chequebook or a modern downloadable equivalent.

SEBASTIAN
I will?

MORAG
You'll be delighted to hear I'm in a position to add a special something to your portfolio. Now, how much was it you offered.

SEBASTIAN
Oh but Trump, I quoted that price months ago. Property prices have plummeted.

MORAG
They have?

SEBASTIAN
Let's say 50,000 francs.

MORAG
50,000 francs? That's nothing like what I paid.

SEBASTIAN
You bought a thriving business but look at it now. Well, your choice. It will sell for even less when you're bankrupt.

MORAG
Boys and girls what shall I do.

SEBASTIAN
How about 50,000 *and* I take the boy back.

MORAG
That's kind but I looked into taking him back once and you can only do that with adopted ones.

MAC
It means I can stay here. I don't want to go back to Scotland. I'm making friends. You can go. Let's do it mum.

MORAG
I see. Very well I'll speak to my legal people.

SEBASTIAN
Legal people?

MORAG points to a couple of people in the audience.

MORAG
Aye. These pair. (a stage whisper) What are your surnames? (They tell her). That's it. [name] and [name], legal people. See.

SEBASTIAN
Well go on.

MORAG
What do you say boys. Should I sign?

SEBASTIAN
You won't get a better offer.

MORAG
I don't know.

SEBASTIAN
You're flogging a dead horse here Morag. I am your saviour.

MORAG
You're right. It was a mistake coming here, it's back to bonnie Scotland for me. Get me a pen, I'll sign.

Scene 13: The castle

A Scrabble board is on the table at which the BEAST and BEAU it. HEIDI is a blackboard and is keeping the scores on herself with a stick of chalk.

BEAU
So anyway the whole prison's in lockdown cos Vee's managed to escape out the greenhouse. And Roso comes back from her chemo thing and they've told her she's only got a few weeks to live! And she doesn't wanna die in prison y'know? So with all this shit going on she steals the prison van and burns it off down the highway. Anyway she's driving along and who does she see? Vee! Sees her and drives straight into her! Kills her. And she goes "Always so rude, that one". Boom. Fade to orange. So that's season two. [34]

The BEAST and HEIDI are now glaring at him.

BEAU
Now season three starts with- what?

BEAST and HEIDI
(Wearily) It's your go.

BEAU
Oh! Yeah soz.

He returns to the table, glances at his pieces, puts some down. He counts.

BEAU
So that's four, five six seven, eleven... and it's triple word so that's... Three times eleven.

HEIDI
Eighteen then.

BEAU
Yeah.

HEIDI writes the score down. The BEAST leans forward and reads.

BEAST
"Hunty"?

BEAU
Hunty.

BEAST
That's is not a word.

BEAU
Oh yes it is.

BEAST
Oh no it isn't.[35]

(etc)

BEAU
It's a mixture of hun and cunt. Like, you're being nice, but in a sassy way.

BEAST
You can't have abbreviations.

BEAU
It's an-

BEAST
YOU CAN'T HAVE ABBREVIATIONS

BEAU
IT'S NOT AN ABBREVIATION! It's a... What's that word you put down. *(Looks at the board)* That's it. An elision.

BEAST
IT'S NOT A FRENCH ONE!

Pause.

HEIDI
It's more of a portmanteau.

BEAST
GOD DAMMIT!

The BEAST angrily upturns the board and the pieces fall off onto the floor.

BEAST
For God's SAKE. (beat) Heidi! Pick these fucking tiles up.

BEAU
Oi! No. It's alright Heidi. We'll sort it.

BEAST
Excuse me?

BEAU
She's got enough to do.

HEIDI
It's alright Beau.

---

[34] He's talking about the TV series *Orange Is The New Black*.

[35] Which of them the audience joined in with depended on how familiar they were with American drag slang and RuPaul's Drag Race.

BEAU
No. Come on. You knocked them off you can pick them up. I'll help you.

Pause.

BEAST
Very well.

BEAU
And apologise to Heidi.

BEAST
Apologise?

HEIDI
Beau.

BEAU
Be a bit kinder.

BEAST
I am the lord of this castle!

BEAU
Gosh I am tired, I think I'll go to bed.

BEAST
I'm sorry! I'm sorry Heidi.

HEIDI
Thank you sir. Right well, I might turn in. Leave you two at it. I mean, to it. Night night.

BEAU
Night Heidi.

HEIDI exits.

BEAST
I... my hands, they're clumsy.

BEAU
So long as you try yeah?

They kneel and begin picking up the tiles.

BEAU
Thank you

BEAST
Sorry.

The BEAST is too embarrassed to make eye contact. After a while he chuckles. Slowly, he smiles in spite of himself and looks briefly at BEAU.

BEAST
Hunty.

Beau allows himself a little smile back.

BEAST
Were you trying to drop hints?

BEAU
What?

BEAST
When you were talking about Orange is the New Black. About not wanting to die in prison. You were talking about your situation.

BEAU
Oh my God I'm such a dumb cunt! I didn't even think about that lol! No, no I wasn't. I wasn't.

They look at each other. They kiss.

BEAST
You're the best sex I've ever had.

BEAU
You're definitely in my top ten.

BEAST
Your top ten men?

BEAU
Top ten percent.

BEAST
I must ask Heidi to change those sheets.

BEAU
No! It's embarrassing, they're like something out of a field hospital. I'll do it.

BEAST
Very well. (Beat) You know...

BEAU
Yeah?

BEAST
No it's nothing.

BEAU
Oh my god who does that. What?

BEAST
It's just... we don't have to... You mustn't feel that we always have to do it that way round.

BEAU (sweet)
Oh! Oh my god I'm sorry. Course!

BEAST (happy)
Really?

BEAU
I just like it that way cos I can watch us in the mirror but yeah whatever, on my back or against the window whatever you like.

BEAST
JESUS CHRIST!

BEAU
We talked about your temper.

BEAST
Sorry, sorry. (beat) You mustn't feel you always have to be the bottom.

BEAU finds this hilarious.

BEAU
Dude. You are like 1000 percent masc-for-fem power top. Embrace it. (Seeing him look awkward) I haven't done it in years. I wouldn't be very good at it. I'd be nervous.

BEAST
I would like it.

BEAU
Um. Ok. Ok, I tell you what. Do something for me, and I'll do that for you.

BEAST
Anything! Anything!

BEAU pauses at this. Gets a cocky look about him.

BEAU
Oh yeah? Anything? You begging for it bitch? Are you? (He cracks up with laughter) Sorry. I can't do dom.

BEAST
That was dom? I assumed you were acting out a favourite moment from La Cage Aux Folles.

BEAU
I'll practise. But. I want to see my father. I want to visit him. I miss him. At least, I feel like I should miss him, you know? I want to see if he's ok.

BEAST
You want to escape!

BEAU
No. No I don't. I want you to let me go, for a few days, and trust me that I want to come back to you.

BEAST
I cannot allow it.

BEAU
Then I'm just a prisoner to you. You know where the conservatory is. Help yourself to a courgette.

BEAST
What?

BEAU
That's what I use when I want something up me in a dry patch.

BEAST
You will return?

BEAU
Yes. I promise. I just want to see my dad. Also I got some knock-off viagra at home and I think I'm gonna need it.

Scene 14: Trump's tea room

MORAG enters carrying a tartan suitcase. MAC brings out a tartan hat box for her. SEBASTIAN paces up and down.

MAC
Here you go mum.

SEBASTIAN
That's it Trump! Time to leave.

BEAU enters

BEAU
Morag! Mac!

SEBASTIAN
You came back to me!

MORAG
Beau! But- but how?

BEAU
What's happened to dad? I went by our house, but it's now an electronic cigarette store called Vape Me Up Before You Gogo.

SEBASTIAN
Beau you mustn't be upset, he's in the best possible care.

MORAG
He's been sectioned.

BEAU
Oh my god that sounds horrible!

MAC
It means he's in the looney bin.

BEAU
Oh right. Still.

SEBASTIAN
I suppose I'm to blame. The road to hell is paved with good intentions. But really, he was ranting and raving about a yeti taking you prisoner!

BEAU
But there is a yeti!

SEBASTIAN
Beau, a little poem to welcome you back. You're as mad, As your dad.

BEAU
And it's kind of moved on from the prisoner sitch.

MAC (eye-rolling)
Oh my god.

BEAU
He's really nice. I miss him already.

MAC
It's called Stockholm Syndrome!

MABEL bursts in out of breath. She is holding a mirror.

MABEL
Beau you arsehole!

SEBASTIAN
Are you still a thing?

MABEL
I've been calling after you the last half hour! I have this for you.

BEAU
A mirror?

MABEL
A mirror, yes, but it's magic,
Invented for sweethearts whom fate kept apart.
Back in the days before Skype, it was tragic
And this offered solace to lonely hearts
It's called a lovers' looking glass,
It's surface as dark and deep as a pond
Look into the mirror, your reflection will pass
And you'll see the one of whom you are fond!

BEAU
Wow

MABEL
Yes. I mean don't know how reliable it is, it's an Alcatel[36].

SEBASTIAN takes it

SEBASTIAN
Well how about that! There I am!

BEAU takes it. The mirror glows magically.

MORAG
That's him! The beast!

_____

36 A cheap brand of smartphone.

SEBASTIAN
It's true! He's a brute! But what's- what is he doing? Oh.

We hear the beast moaning sexually

MORAG
Mac! Avert your gaze.

She looks away. Then looks back.

MORAG
Well they've got bigger since I last saw one.

MAC
Why's he holding a courgette?

MORAG
Look at the time! I'll miss my flight. Beau, help me get the rest of my luggage will you?

BEAU and MORAG exit. We hear the BEAST moan Beau's name a couple of times.

SEBASTIAN
In love, ha? This dangerous monster must be found and killed before he harms anyone! Mac!

SEBASTIAN grabs MAC and they run out.

MABEL
Mac! Where are you going?

MAC
Sebastian wants to slay the yeti.

MABEL
Is that like spank the monkey?

MAC
No.

MABEL
And you're going to stop him! My hero!

MAC
Oh. No.

MABEL
Are you serious? What has he ever done to you?

MAC
He kidnapped my mum.

MABEL
Tragic, yah. But that was months ago darling, I should know I've got through most of a Hilary Mantel the amount of time I've been offstage. And he didn't kill her. Beau loves him, and he's your best friend. You

can't shoot your best friend's chap. Bros before hoes. Or bros' hoes before other bros. Or-

MAC
It's not really applicable.

MABEL
No.

MAC
And Beau's not really my best friend anymore.

MABEL
You're not the man I thought you were Macdonald Trump. I always thought you were a decent sort.

MAC
Aye. Decent.

MABEL
There's nothing wrong with that.

MAC
I thought girls liked a bad ass guy.

MABEL
Well you're the expert. Off you go. You go and kill that poor creature and totally ruin Beau's life at the same time.

SEBASTIAN enters

SEBASTIAN
Hurry up!

SEBASTIAN exits

MABEL
Haven't you ever been in love?

MAC
Me? Nah. (shyly, looking at her) Maybe. You?

MABEL
Haha behave! Not me.

MAC
Ok. See you.

MAC exits

MABEL
Well that was totally awkward. Mabel, you really are bloody awful at this sort of thing. Also don't talk to yourself. Talk to the boys and girls. Bye boys and girls!

MABEL exits. MORAG and BEAU enter, BEAU carrying a suitcase.

MORAG
Where have they gone?

Audience shout.

BEAU
My beast! Morag, we have to stop them.

MORAG
Hold on laddie, I've a flight to catch.

BEAU
Please! And you can't go while Dad's locked up. You think Morag should stay and help don't you boys and girls?

MORAG
Och well I'd better respect the will of the people! Step to it!

They exit

Scene 15: The castle

The BEAST is pacing up and down. HEIDI, now a pot plant, is watching.

BEAST
I should not have let him go. He will not come back.

HEIDI
Did you ever hear such nonsense! Course he will! The way he looks at you, he loves you, the idiot. Like you love him. I mean look at your penis, the size of it! The curse'll be broken sooner than a hymen on A-level results night.

The doorbell rings.

HEIDI
You see? That'll be him.

HEIDI goes to exit.

BEAST
Wait!

The BEAST pulls a comb from a pocket and tidies his hair – starting with the hair on his head but giving the rest of it the once-over.

BEAST
I should cut my nails.

HEIDI
I ain't got time to fetch the secateurs You look... fine.

BEAST
Go then. Let him in then.

HEIDI exits and returns with SEBASTIAN who carries a gun and MAC.

HEIDI
It's some posh bloke and the Scottish Nazi.

SEBASTIAN
God! It's hideous!

BEAST
How dare you!

SEBASTIAN
(looking about him) No really, get an interior designer, I don't know how you can bear it. *(He looks at Heidi)* What a strange attire.

HEIDI
It's not attire you skidmark. It's me. It's who I am.

SEBASTIAN
Identity politics, how 2015.

BEAST
What do you want? Who are you?

SEBASTIAN
Who am I!

HEIDI and the BEAST look at each other blankly

SEBASTIAN
Sebastian St Morritz. I was merely out hunting and I thought, that looks a friendly place to call in for cup of something. Didn't I, Mac, didn't I just say that very same thing. Mac. Wasn't I just saying?

MAC
Er, yeah.

BEAST
Hunting for what?

SEBASTIAN
Whatever comes my way as I stroll through the woods.

BEAST
You are on foot?

SEBASTIAN
Yes! My steed is ill.

BEAST
Your horse.

SEBASTIAN
Am I? Drat, it must be catching. You wouldn't have a brandy to warm me up would you? It would be a shame to go home without snaring some prize beast.

The BEAST turns away to get some brandy. SEBASTIAN raises his gun. The doorbell rings. The BEAST turns around again and SEBASTIAN lowers his gun.

BEAST
Door, Heidi.

HEIDI stomps out

SEBASTIAN (to MAC)
Distract him, get him to turn his back.

MAC
I, I, I dunno. Maybe we-

SEBASTIAN
Do it moron! Or this yeti won't be the only thing that gets it today.

MAC
Mr Beast

BEAST
Sir!

MAC
Sir... I like your art, sir. What's the story behind this painting of a young gay nobleman.

BEAST
What makes you think he is gay?

MAC
Oh, please sir. Look at it. The pose. The hair. The Kylie poster in the background.

As the BEAST is distracted, SEBASTIAN raises his gun. BEAU rushes in followed by MORAG and HEIDI.

BEAU
Noooooo!

The BEAST turns around and sees SEBASTIAN, who holds its nerve.

SEBASTIAN
Stand back! You know you'll get in a tiz if you get blood and fur all over your clothes.

BEAU
You can't shoot him! It... it doesn't work on Yetis.

SEBASTIAN
Well let's find out shall we?

The BEAST roars and leaps at SEBASTIAN. SEBASTIAN goes to shoot. BEAU leaps at him knocking the gun to the floor.

MORAG
Beau! Be careful!

MORAG picks up an ornament or vase and tries to hit SEBASTIAN over the head with it but SEBASTIAN pushes the BEAST in the way and she hits the BEAST. The BEAST falls to the floor.

SEBASTIAN
Mrs Trump, how helpful of you! Now to finish the job.

He goes to pick up the gun. BEAU wrestles him for it.

SEBASTIAN
Mac help me you idiot.

MAC
I'm not an idiot!

MABEL enters.

MAC
I'm not an idiot! (beat) Everyone says I am but I'm not. I coulda gone to university you know. But I didn't know what I'd do, so I stayed and helped mum, just like mum stayed and looked after her mum. Though that was different cos granny couldnae manage to consume anything that didn't pass through a straw or have moonshine in it. But I coulda gone. To Glasgow, or Edinburgh.

MORAG
Well maybe not Edinburgh Edinburgh. But Edinburgh Napier.

MAC
I'm not an idiot. A coward though, aye, maybe I'm that. That's why I'm up here in this castle with Sebastian isn't it. Now Beau – I mean, Beau's really dumb. You'd play "Guess Who" with Beau and he'd likely come third. But he's no coward. He knows what he wants and he does it. Beau's brave. And that's why he's up here in this castle too.

I'm not an idiot - I just get a bit stumped by the world and when I do have something to say I think what's the point? It's just another bloody voice. What does it matter what I think about, I don't know, whether Syria's better off being a stable dictatorship or a hopeful but bloody mess? Or whether the Labour party should play the long game and build a mass social movement, or do whatever it can to get into power right now so it can actually change things? Or whether Shakespeare's Globe should have natural lighting, or whether Honey G's an offensive appropriation, or whether Zac Goldsmith's a pragmatist with noble environmental principles or just a racist cunt who'd sell his fellow man down the Thames just for a view of it from City Hall.

What is there to say, when shouting it over and over doesn't stop you living in a world that's run by people who think being powerful means you can shove your tongue down a lassie's throat, or grab her by the pussy. If someone did that to my mum I'd smack his teeth in, but it shouldnae be just about your mam, it should be about any lass. I want a girl. But I want a girl who wants me to kiss her and who lets me touch her pussy cos it's what she really wants too. You know?[37]

_____

[37] We needed to buy time here, and Mac's long speech was the very-last-minute solution. Jamie, who played the Beast, was

MABEL
Oh Mac!

She kisses him. It's a proper Hollywood movie kiss. He breaks off.

MAC
Beau! I cannae fucking distract him any longer - get the fucking gun!

SEBASTIAN and BEAU continue to fight. It's a proper full-on wrestle. Eventually SEBASTIAN knocks BEAU to the ground. He points the gun at him.

SEBASTIAN
Beau, my darling, we might as well formalise this. You want to save Harambe?[38] Marry me.

BEAU
Never!

SEBASTIAN
Then it's bye, bye, Beastie and it's bye, bye, Beau.

MABEL
Mac! Do something!

MAC
Me? I'm not the fairy in the room.

SEBASTIAN, BEAU
Oi!

MAC
Can't you do something magic?

MABEL
I've told you, I'm at advanced beginner level. I can't do life or death stuff. Fancy dress spells, I'm your girl.

MAC
Balls!

MORAG
MacDonald, you and your language. It's the sign of a stunted mind! Always grasping for a twat or shoving a dick into it.

MAC
But that's it! Snowballs! Mabel.

MABEL
That's my name, don't set up a fan account just yet.

MAC
Can you magic up loads of snowballs.

MABEL
Darling, there's snow outside.

MAC
Just do it! Eh?

MABEL
When things look bleak and doom befalls
Send to me a load of balls

A load of snowballs appear.

MAC
Snowballs! Help me give them out to the boys and girls.

MORAG, HEIDI and MABEL hand out snowballs to the audience.

MAC
Boys and girls we need your help! Hold your balls up in the air and on the count of three, lob them at Sebastian.

SEBASTIAN
As if a few snowballs can hurt me.

MAC
Are you ready? One! Two! Three!

The audience throw the snowballs at SEBASTIAN, they knock him off balance, he falls. BEAU picks up the gun and points it at Sebastian.

SEBASTIAN
My sweet, think about it we could be so happy together. You'd be the envy of the world. I have access to finest clubs. I can self-suck!

ALL
Can you?

SEBASTIAN
Well technically. Technically I can iron a shirt but why risk injury and do someone out of a job.

---

offstage getting changed for his final transformation. When the Beast fell, partially hidden by a chair, he exited and his "body" (or at least his legs) was played by Andrew, who played Gustave. Then while Beau and Sebastian fought, Jamie swapped back into the scene, ready to wake up.

[38] The previous May, a three-year-old boy had climbed into the zoo enclosure of a gorilla called Harambe, who proceeded to drag the boy around the enclosure. A zookeeper shot the gorilla dead.

BEAU
There's only person here I'd marry. Now. You'll pay for what you've done.

SEBASTIAN
You'll have to catch me first! And let me tell you, a former Olympic champion will be a lot faster than a twink who only did P.E. once; a mother and son who think Tunnock's Teacakes make for a healthy crouton alternative; and a fairy slowed down by the weight of an upper lip that's a permanent Freddie Mercury tribute.

By now, the others have surrounded him.

SEBASTIAN
Drat!

MAC
Mabel, can you manage a spell to get rid of him.

MABEL
Bloody Nora fucking Jones do you actually get off making me feel inadequate? No I can't. Tell you what, I'll do a nice rhyme for you, you do the hard labour.

This arrogant sausage has caused too much hassle
Now throw the cretin from the roof of this castle!

Well go on.

MORAG, BEAU, MAC and MORAG grab SEBASTIAN

BEAU
This way! The stairs!

They exit. MABEL listens as we hear lots of footsteps climbing the stone stairs getting quieter and quieter and higher and higher. A pause. A long scream. A splat. We hear them go "ew!" They all re-enter, and we hear the smash of a window..

MABEL
If that's Sebastian this is going to look a little far-fetched.

GUSTAVE enters, holding a goat.

MORAG
Gustave!

MABEL
I thought you were locked up!

GUSTAVE
My goats, my missing goats! They found me and broke in and helped me escape! They're outside. Sebastian nearly landed on this one.

MORAG runs to him.

MORAG
I was all set to bake you a Dundee cake with a knife inside it for smuggling into the loony bin!

BEAU
Are you alright? What was it like?

GUSTAVE
The things I've seen!!

MAC
Like what?

GUSTAVE
Daytime television! Other than that it was a perfectly nice bit of sheltered housing with on-site care and well-tended gardens. I was just starting a pottery class when my furry friend here turned up and overwhelmed the young nurses.

MORAG
That's quite enough about the nurses.

BEAU (To the BEAST)
He's still sparked out but at least he's safe.

MAC
Yeah! Three cheers for Mabel!

MABEL
Hip hip-

BEAU
Three cheers?! She didn't do anything!

MAC
She helped us believe in ourselves. Turns out it's all we needed!

A satisfied cheesy sigh from all. BEAU is leaning over the BEAST. HEIDI enters.

HEIDI
Lawks!

BEAU
He's breathing but he won't wake up.

HEIDI
Try talking to him.

BEAU
I have.

HEIDI

No, but... You must have a few sweet words you're dying to blurt out. From inside your heart?

BEAU
Kinda. It's a bit public...

MAC
Mate, I've seen you give head on the ski lift. That poor girl walking underneath thought a bird had scored a direct hit.

BEAU
Well that's blates not true! I never spill a drop.

HEIDI
Come on! Say the words! Home stretch! Happy ending! Bows! Lights up! The bar! Some nice tweets about my performance in particular.

BEAU
Ok. *(Clears throat)* Sir. You know I'm kinda into you and all, and I... Well, what I'm about to say I never said before, not to anyone, except a couple of times when it woulda been awkward not to. But the thing is- Hang on, fuck, what are we thinking? I know we've been all bants about chucking Sebastian off that roof but I'm a murderer now.

GUSTAVE
Beau you daft sod. I'm sure he just slipped while you were up there stargazing. Barely worth thinking about.

MORAG
And if anything it was Mac who gave him the final shove.

MAC
What?!

MORAG
I'm just saying.

HEIDI
Jesus, I can't stand this, you're never going to say it are you.

HEIDI storms out

BEAU
Sir. I want to tell you... To tell you... The thing is, I, I-

SEBASTIAN bursts in, a mess but alive. He's holding a goat that he's started to eat. He takes a manly bite and roars. BEAU picks up the gun and shoots him. He dies instantly, collapsing.

MORAG, GUSTAVE, MAC
(proudly) Now you're a murderer!

All laugh heartily.

BEAU
Oh you big sexy yeti. From the bottom of my slutty heart, and the heart of my slutty bottom, I love you man. I love you!

The plant stirs a little. Magic begins to happen – lights flicker, then return to normal.

MABEL
I think we need more love in the room. Boys and girls, help me please. I need you to turn to your neighbour, take their hand and say I love you. After three. Three! That's it. Bit of a hug maybe.

BEAU
Stop. It's no use. He won't wake up! Oh god! What if never wakes up! I never even got to...

HEIDI, MORAG, GUSTAVE, MAC
What?

BEAU
I was going to top him! I'd never topped him before and he really wanted me to and it was going to be really special.

MABEL
Why don't you give it go now?

BEAU
What??

MABEL
Go on. Turn him over. I'll help.

She helps turn the BEAST over.

MABEL
That's it, tug his pants down a little.

BEAU
He's asleep!

MABEL
Oh go on. It only needs a little dip.

BEAU
No!

The plant starts to die.

HEIDI
The plant!

MABEL
The plant! Beau, if that plant dies... well never mind. But this is the only way to save it.

223

BEAU
What?

BEAST
(As if in his sleep) ...Do it...

BEAU
What?

MABEL
You heard.

BEAU
He's awake![39]

BEAST
...Do me now!

BEAU
Alright. Dad can you – can you look away? Right (He tries) I've gone soft now.

MABEL
Fear not! I've a spell, I do beg your pardon.
Abra-viagra. I give you a hardon

MABEL casts a spell.

BEAU
Wow! Um. Ok.... Wait I haven't got a condom.

MABEL
Easily fixed, it's the logical step,
Abracadabra you're now full of PrEP!
...Expensive spell that one. Quick!

BEAU
Right. Ow. Ow he's.. you're really tight... It's not going to... OH!

MABEL
Yes!

BEAU
Oh!

BEAST
Yes!

BEAU
There it is!

Magic. HEIDI enters, dressed as a maid. She's human.

HEIDI
I'm human! I'm human again! You broke the spell!

BEAU
What spell?

BEAST
Seeing as everyone else knows, I'll fill you in later.

BEAU
Oh no. I'm going to fill you in later. Oh my god.

The BEAST stands. He is now human too.

BEAST
How do I look?

BEAU
You look beautiful! But I thought you looked beautiful before. I love you!

BEAST
You do?

BEAU
So much!

BEAST
I thought I would never hear these words!

BEAU
I love you and I fancy you and I like you and... And, look, I'm just what I am you know? I'm not smart. I'm not cultured. I don't know about politics or nothing.

BEAST
But you're just magical. I love you!

They kiss.

MORAG
And Gustave, I love you!

They kiss.

MAC
And Mabel, I really fancy you.

He kisses her.

MABEL
I need a lie-down Mac.

MAC
Oh.

MABEL
Want to join me?

---

[39] This line was our timid attempt to avoid having Beau fuck the Beast while he's unconscious, which would of course be non-consensual and hence a Bad Thing.

She takes MAC's hand and they go to leave.

BEAST
But not the forbidden tower!

HEIDI
Fuck mate will you chill out about that forbidden tower. It's where he keeps his hair curlers and dildos. You use wherever you like.

MAC
Bye boys and girls!

MAC and MABEL go.

GUSTAVE
Morag, until you arrived in the village I thought it would be a betrayal to Beau's mother to be with anyone else. And I was shy. Who would want me? But I couldn't get you out of my mind. I would like the rest of my days with you. Will you do me the honour of becoming my wife?

MORAG
Och Gustave! Nothing would make me happier!

GUSTAVE, BEAU & BEAST
Hooray!

MORAG
But I can't.

GUSTAVE, BEAU & BEAST
Oh.

MORAG
I'm on the brink of bankruptcy and I'll never find work here, not with my lunging skills.

A beat. Puzzlement.

BEAST
Language skills!

MORAG
Yes! I'll get there I'll get there. Gustave, I have to go back to Scotland.

GUSTAVE
I've got a few francs stashed away.

MORAG
It won't be enough. I'm sorry Gustave I can't marry you.

BEAST
Morag. I have been rattling around in this castle alone for too long. I have come to think that one day I should

like to open the place to the public. Guided tours and a working kitchen garden that sort of thing. And also have tea-room here.

MORAG
A tea-room.

BEAST
It would please me greatly if you might deign to run it. What do you say?

MORAG
Aw laddie! I say yes!

She gives him a huge hug, then slightly embarrassed pulls away.

MORAG
Now if you'll excuse me, Gustave and I have a wedding to plan.

HEIDI
Strange, all them years I longed to be normal again so I could go out and about in the world. And now, well after so long I don't know what I'm going to do.

There is a clash of thunder and flash of light. They run over to the window.

BEAU
That old tree! The one that looked like it had a face staring out of the trunk.

GUSTAVE
It's fallen... It's transforming.

BEAU
Into a person. Into a woman.

HEIDI
Sofia! She must have got caught up in the curse too. She's not in Geneva, she's been here all along! Sofia I'm coming.

HEIDI runs out

MORAG
Come on Gustave. Take me home.

They exit

BEAU
Just you and me then.

BEAST
It looks that way.

CH: BEHIND YOU: ELEVEN GAY PANTOMIMES

SEBASTIAN wakes up with a roar.

BEAU and BEAST
Fuck off!

SEBASTIAN dies.

BEAST
Beau, I...

BEAU
Yeah yeah enough talk. Man I'm well pumped after that fight earlier. I felt proper butch. I saved your life and shit!

BEAST
Yes?

BEAU
Yeah mate. I think... I'm going to take you upstairs.

The BEAST laughs.

BEAST
By my guest!

They exit. The plant produces a flower. MABEL enters.

MABEL
It's late spring, a bright morning, and the last of the snow,
Fills the streams which babble past the town below,
But nobody's there to hear their sweet notes,
For Les Dennis is empty, except for the goats.

They're all at the castle - the butcher, the baker,
The tourists from China, from Wales or Jamaica,
To bestow on three marriages all kinds of luck,
Now it's long after dawn and they're still drunk as fuck.

And if there's a moral it's this one I'll wager:
Be true to yourself, but let good people change you,
So seek validation but value yourself,
And keep your heart open, it's good for your health.

Les Dennis, you see, is not such a flop,
If a sweet slutty bottom can come out on top,
But search on a map and *[click fingers]* it's gone - at least for you;
With a smile, and our love, safe home now: adieu!

THE END.

Tinderella: Cinders Slips It In

Joseph Lycett-Barnes as Prince Charming and Grant Cartwright as Cinders in *Tinderella: Cinders Slips it In*. Photo by PBGstudios.

Tinderella: Cinders Slips It In

The very first pantomime we wrote together in 2006 was based on the Cinderella story and was written for a Christmas party of the LGBTQ running club we belonged to, London Frontrunners. We won't be sharing that script here but one of its characters, Nicole Ferrari, survived to make it into this version.

For *Tinderella* we invented the Eastern European country of Slutvia, complete with its own currency, the Slutvian Twink. Cinderella is one of the most popular pantomimes and the story is bursting with famous moments and characters – the "ugly" sisters, the pumpkin coach, midnight striking, the trying on of the glass slipper – and we were determined to preserve its special magic. And it's the panto that features Buttons, an archetype character you'll find in various incarnations in many of the scripts in this book – Taleesha in Snow White, Will Scarlet in Robin Hood and Josh the Footman in Sleeping Beauty to name three.

It was 2015. Donald Trump and Hilary Clinton began their presidential election campaigns, civil war continued to rage in Syria and on a dramatic day in March, Zayn Malik announced that he was leaving One Direction. Earlier in the year, Disney had released their new live action Cinderella and the creative team incorporated little references, such as the beautiful blue dress that Cinders wore to the ball.

Tinderella: Cinders Slips It In

By Jon Bradfield and Martin Hooper
Songs by Jon Bradfield

Characters

The Fairy, a New Yorker.
Countess Volga
Buttons, a young man in his twenties.
Cinders, a young man, our hero.
Miley, a human-sized mouse.
Maude Escort, Cinders' step-sister. Podgy, common and fairly smart.
Nicole Ferrari, Cinders' other step-sister. Skinny, posh and fairly stupid.
King Ludwig
Prince Charming, his son.

Miley's costume should include a full headmask. She can be played by any actor not on stage.

Because unmarried men are not allowed to wear trousers in Slutvia, Buttons should wear baggy long shorts, Cinders should wear ragged cut-offs, and Prince Charming should wear tights.

Tinderella: Cinders Slips It In **was first performed at Above The Stag Theatre on 26 November 2015 with the following cast and creative team:**

The Fairy: Rebecca Travers; Countess Volga: Ellen Butler; Buttons: Lucas Meredith; Cinders: Grant Cartwright; Maude Escort: Louie Westwood; Nicole Ferrari: Christopher James Barley; King Ludwig: Andrew Truluck; Prince Charming: Joseph Lycett-Barnes

Director: Andrew Beckett; Designer: David Shields; Lighting Designer: Chris Withers; Sound Designer: Phil Hewitt; Projection Designer: Jack Weir; Associate Costume Designer: Nina Morley; Production Assistant: Lucas Livesey; Musical Director: Aaron Clingham; Musical Arranger and Incidental Music Composer: Daniel Johnson; Choreographer: Aaron Jenson; Producer: Peter Bull for Above The Stag Theatre; Poster illustration: Matthew Harding; Marketing: Jack Bowman; PR: Katherine Ives

Scene 1: A clearing in the woods.

Sunshine and birdsong. In the clearing stand three grave stones. The oldest is the grandest, the newest is the most humble. The FAIRY appears. She is a New Yorker.

FAIRY
On Europe's farthest, eastern edge
Where cities have names that won't mean much to ya
The morning sun rises hours ahead
On a small, proud country known as Slutvia

There are no cheap flights there, no guide books
Their media's censored, the food is hearty
There's no gay bars - just knowing looks
To tell you where to find the party

The local schnapps flows cheap and free
But Christ, avoid the wine
The capital's called Slut on Sea
Which is bold, cos there's no coast line

From the old-fashioned trains with wooden compartments
You'll see little white churches with onion domes
Jostling with concrete, Cold War apartments
And a few run-down, but grand, old homes

By day it's mainly factories and farming
And at night, while they all get shit-faced,
The river Slut glows bright – it's alarming -
With the glimmer of nuclear waste

Let's follow the Slut as it shimmies its way
To a wooded suburb on the edge of town
Where I'm on a mission to save a young slave
It's my last chance to earn back my wings and my gown

Boys and girls! Will you come with me to Slutvia?
Can you cheer? And can you boo? You'll be fine!
If you'll help me I'll take good care of the lot of ya,
As we offer: our pantomime!

There is a rumble of thunder. It begins to rain. The COUNTESS enters with a black umbrella.

FAIRY
Fuck's sake lady, you've made it rain!

COUNTESS
It's just spitting a little on my entrance.

FAIRY
When you put it like that.

COUNTESS
It will pass in no time. The king has been testing his magnificent nuclear missiles again and it plays havoc with the weather.

FAIRY
Who are you?

COUNTESS
You may call me Countess. *(The sun comes out)* There, see?

THE COUNTESS throws her umbrella offstage; a parasol is thrown back to her.

FAIRY
That's one hell of an underarm you got there lady.

COUNTESS
I ran out of deodorant this morning.

FAIRY
I'm talking about your throw but I'm sure you smell great. Want me to check?

COUNTESS
Are you making advances?

FAIRY
I'm that way inclined, if you want to let me stretch out in your little clearing.

COUNTESS
Disgusting! (At the audience) And look, refugees! FAIRY
These ain't refugees, these are the boys and girls.

COUNTESS
Although this one looks vaguely eligible. He might persuade me to open my borders... Why are they here?

FAIRY (pointing around the audience)
This row came for the show. This little clump came for the warmth. These four got lost on the way to The Hoist, this gentleman thought we were still performing Rent Boy The Musical[40], and these little piggies came for the free sweets.

COUNTESS
What free sweets?

---

[40] The Hoist was a gay fetish club in Vauxhall, close to Above The Stag. *Rent Boy - The Musical* had played at Above the Stag earlier in the year.

The FAIRY reaches into the COUNTESS's bag or pockets and pulls out a handful of sweets. She throws them to the audience.

COUNTESS
How - how did you do that? You witch! Leave, now! I'm here to pay my respects to my late husbands.

FAIRY
I'm sure they'll be along any minute.

COUNTESS
They're dead, dyke. This was my first husband, Ernest number one.

FAIRY
How did he die?

COUNTESS
Generously. He left me my house and land and the first of my beautiful daughters. It was a tragic accident. He was enjoying a bath when into the water slipped his radio. And a toaster. And an electric lawnmower. I wore a veil for a month.

FAIRY
I've never worn a veil.

COUNTESS
But you must, if only as a service to mirrors. This was my second husband, Ernest number two.

FAIRY
What's the line... To lose *one* husband...

COUNTESS
Another tragic accident. Run over by his own limousine. I only took my eyes off the driveway for a split second to check my lipstick. I wore a veil for a week. And this was my third husband, Ernest number three. I would have had them cremated but then I'd have three Erns in three urns and it would have been just too funny.

FAIRY
Was he another "tragic accident"?

COUNTESS
Suicide.

FAIRY
This is a jolly old panto ain't it boys and girls.

COUNTESS
So sad, I was behind him when he jumped. I wore a veil for a minidress, got royally drunk with a gang of workmen and vowed never to marry again. Except Ernest number three left me only my title and a wretched stepson.

FAIRY
Ha, do you remember Madonna's cowboy phase when all the queens were wearing those stupid pink hats.

The COUNTESS stares at her.

FAIRY
Oh a *step*son. A wretched *step*son. *(Aside)* The boy!

COUNTESS
I should have known he had no money from the day I married him. We had a worse reception than Kanye West got at Glastonbury. *(She looks into the audience)* So I'm on the look-out for a rich husband.[41]

FAIRY
I can think of at least two reasons why you might be looking in the wrong place.

COUNTESS
Are you Sluttish?

FAIRY
There's no shame in it.

COUNTESS
Your accent. You're not from Slutvia.

FAIRY
I'm American.

COUNTESS
You're a spy!

FAIRY
I've been sent to protect a young man from a terrible life.

COUNTESS
You made Zayn leave One Direction?

FAIRY
No...

COUNTESS

---

41 Performing at Glastonbury that year, Kayne West forgot lyrics and made other musical mistakes. He later admitted to having messed up and said that it had put him in a depressed state..

231

You stopped Nick Grimshaw from spiking Harry Styles' vodka?

FAIRY
No! Course, the kid I'm looking for could be anywhere.

COUNTESS
Yet here you are.

FAIRY
Who lives in the big crazy mansion over there?

COUNTESS
That's Annie Hall, and it belongs to me. A leaking, creaking gothic monstrosity according to some.

FAIRY
I bet they only call you that cos they're jealous of your house.

COUNTESS
Away, now.

FAIRY
Make me.

COUNTESS
I will.

The COUNTESS pulls at the handle of her parasol and slides a sword out from its stem. She throws the parasol offstage and points the sword at the FAIRY.

COUNTESS
Work your magic on that.

The FAIRY tries. She can't.

FAIRY
Dammit! I can't use my magic to save myself. Only others.

COUNTESS
Then die!

FAIRY
It would be a very short pantomime.

COUNTESS
These little peasants don't care about you! They're only here for the boys in scene two.

FAIRY
You don't want me to die do you boys and girls?

COUNTESS
Oh yes they do.

Oh no we don't

COUNTESS
Oh yes you do

Oh no we don't

Thunder. Lighting. The heavens open.

FAIRY
You made it rain again!

COUNTESS
What's a spot of rain? *(She goes to open her parasol but it is now just a sword).* Fuck! Have a pleasant stay in Slutvia. I hope it was the last thing on your bucket list. Hahahahahahaha!

The COUNTESS exits

FAIRY
It's my first job in years - well I ain't very good
But the queen of the fairies came down to my hood
She said "half of my fairies are off, it's a pain
They're interning for free on the Clinton campaign"

But fuck me, I think I found my man
I best be off to make a plan
I got to get him to a royal ball
Now off you go – to Annie Hall!

Scene 2: The kitchen of Annie Hall

Cinders spends most of his life in this kitchen-cum-utility room. It should have a decent-sized cupboard in it that will be used to transform things magically just before the interval. There is an entrance into the rest of the house, perhaps with stairs glimpsed. Another entrance leads outdoors. There is a knock at this door. When nobody enters, BUTTONS opens it slightly, peeks in, then enters holding a parcel, and some flyers for a club night.

BUTTONS
Delivery! Delivery! (silence) Cinders! Cinders? You about? (nothing) Oh hello boys and girls! My name's Buttons. Are you alright? Are you sure? No put your hand down sir, we can talk about it later if it's still flaring up. I think we're gonna be mates you know! Will you do something for me? Whenever I come on and say "Hello boys and girls", will you go "Hey Buttons what's up how's it going nice one"? Let's give that a go.

They do.

Well! Welcome to Annie Hall. I do a few deliveries here see. I don't know what this is...

BUTTONS puts the parcel on a surface. It starts vibrating. He manages to stop it and goes to the front row with his flyers.

I run these secret underground parties in the old tin-mine on the way into town. It's the best gay night in Slutvia. I call it The Veal Crate, cos it's packed and half of them are under-age and the next day everyone feels pretty tender. Sometimes, Prince Charming himself comes! I like to get all the cutest and best dressed lads into my parties.

So here's a flyer for you sir, half price entry. And for you Mr, and one for you... *(at the next one he doesn't hand out a flyer, just shakes their hand)* Nice to meet you sir. *(Moves on)* Flyer for you mate. *(Goes back to the one he didn't give a flyer to)* I'm only joking. Oh I had you pegged for a Slut but you're not are you.

I got all sorts of jobs going on but I like delivering to here cos I get to hang out with Cinders. He's the Countess's step-son but she treats him like a slave. When Cinders was 12 his dad died, see, and straight away the Countess dragged Cinders out of boarding school and put him to work. Can I tell you something? I... I really like Cinders. I don't know what it is. *(As if this is unique)* I think it's a sort of combination of his looks and personality.

CINDERS (off)
Is that you Buttons?

BUTTONS
That's him!

BUTTONS spits in his hand and straightens his hair. CINDERS enters with rubber gloves on, holding a plunger. They're neither clean nor dry.

CINDERS
Buttons!

BUTTONS
Morning Cinders! *(He gives him a hug).*

CINDERS
Careful, I've been helping the Countess with her constipation again.

He puts aside the plunger and gloves.

BUTTONS
Have you met the boys and girls?

CINDERS
I don 't meet anyone do I. Hey boys and girls! Are you alright?

BUTTONS
Yeah they're fine, apart from him at the back.

CINDERS
Oh no! Should we-

BUTTONS
No leave it, I think it's a bit personal.

CINDERS
Did you meet the Countess yet boys and girls?

BUTTONS
Even though there's thirteen bedrooms she makes him sleep in the linen cupboard.

CINDERS
She does! Still at least I got a roof over my head. And a shelf. And a spiders nest. (He gets a phone out of his pocket and checks it).

BUTTONS
You're getting addicted to that app.

CINDERS
I'm not! It's called Blunder boys and girls. Buttons invented it.

BUTTONS
I bet you get loads of messages.

CINDERS
I keep getting confused in conversations. My reading and writing's rubbish boys and girls cos I stopped school at twelve. Yesterday I wrote some man a whole poem cos I thought he'd said he was really into rhyming. I don't know why I bother with it really, I'm not allowed out and I can't have someone back here to sleep with me can I, cos the spiders are homophobic.

BUTTONS
We're not meant to have mobiles. The King thinks the Americans use them to spy on us.

CINDERS
Buttons gave me this one. (A noise) Here I got a message! (checks phone). "Are you still there?" Wait, I'll just reply. (Typing) "No mate, I'm not still here, I've gone round to your dad's to blow him and I left my phone at home". This is dead exciting, you're the first people I've met in ages!

BUTTONS
I'm your only friend ain't I?

CINDERS
Even if you weren't you'd still be my best friend. I got a pet though. Do you want to meet her? I don't think they're sure are they. Alright let's try again, do you want to meet her? Alright. Help me call her ok, she's called Miley. One two three! Miley!

MILEY enters. She is a human-sized mouse. She stares at the audience.

CINDERS
Are you being shy Miley? I don't know if you can tell from there boys and girls, but she's actually a bit bigger than a normal mouse cos she was born in the basement of the king's nuclear laboratory. It's affected her genes.

BUTTONS
She can't fit into them!

CINDERS
I'll give you some cheese in a minute girl. Miley loves cheese. Come on Miley don't be shy, come and meet the-

MILEY has been sniffing the air. She goes up to a man in the audience and starts sniffing his crotch hungrily.

CINDERS
Miley! I think she can smell cheese boys and girls. I'm so sorry sir, she thinks you've got a Mini Babybel in there. Come here Miley.

BUTTONS
How's it going with your boyfriend Miley?

MILEY shakes her head.

BUTTONS
Same old trouble?

CINDERS
Her boyfriend doesn't satisfy her.

The mouse uses her paws to indicate something very small.

CINDERS
It's very sad. Do you want to meet him too? Billy Ray! Where are you? Billy Ray?

A tiny finger puppet mouse appears. He has a little daisy in his paw.

See what I mean, he's tiny.

CINDERS picks him up and passes him to MILEY who nuzzles him.

I know it's a bit weird. They're girlfriend and boyfriend and they got the same names as a father and daughter and it's not even just a coincidence, cos they're mice, they don't naturally have names. I named them. I get really fucking bored boys and girls.

He looks at MILEY

Aw don't they look cute. Can I get an "ahh" boys and girls?

MILEY starts rubbing her boyfriend against her crotch.

Miley! You'll get his fur all matted.

Miley waves goodbye and exits. BUTTONS hands CINDERS an envelope.

BUTTONS
Here Cinders, can you give this to the Countess?

CINDERS
Oh my god how much is that?

234

BUTTONS
Ten thousand twinks.

CINDERS
Ten thousand Sluttish twinks! Can you imagine what you'd do! What's that for?

BUTTONS
It's from my friend. If you give the Countess ten grand she sorts you a fake passport and smuggles you to London.

CINDERS
Why does your friend want to go to London?

BUTTONS
Well, cos it's ok to be gay there.

CINDERS shrugs

BUTTONS
Hmm. That's a point...

CINDERS
It was more of a shrug but go on.

BUTTONS
Well it's just, another friend of mine, he saved up for a year for one of your mum's passports, and she sent him off in a truck to London, and I never heard from him again. I didn't even get one of those cut-out postcards of Prince Harry's face I asked him for. I was gonna wear it for pulling.

CINDERS
Oh my god look at this guy!

BUTTONS
Whatever.

CINDERS
But look! He never shows his face of course, but he's really charming and I really like his body and look how nice that chair is it's like a throne or something.

BUTTONS
Cinders, that's- Never mind.

CINDERS
Who?

BUTTONS
It doesn't matter. Where are your sisters?

We hear MAUDE singing as she enters.

MAUDE
Davey Davey, give me your answer do
I ain't waiting, I'm busting for a poo
It won't be a stylish marriage, we'll do it in your garage
We'll all get drunk, we'll share a bunk
And I'll get off with half your crew!
(Spoken) Morning Cinders!

CINDERS
Morning Maud. This is my stepsister. Maude Escort.

MAUDE
Hello boys and girls. I thought I'd come and move things along. People don't come to fringe pantomimes for the plot. (She sits on someone's lap and fondles him). No they come for the intimate experience. Hello, I'm Maude, the Countess's second daughter. And you must be... well, tied to a bedroom chair if I had my way. What's you name? (She repeats his name)

CINDERS
Where's Nicole?

MAUDE
Oh she's surpassed herself this morning that one.

NICOLE (off)
Help!

CINDERS
That sounds like Nicole there now.

BUTTONS
Is she alright?

NICOLE (off)
Help me someone! I'm blind!

NICOLE enters. She's a bit of a rake. She is wearing a sleeping mask, over her eyes.

NICOLE
I've gone blind! I woke up and I couldn't see a thing! I had to dress without looking in the mirror.

CINDERS
You don't look worse than normal.

NICOLE
Oh how kind Cinders. Cinders that was you wasn't it?

CINDERS
My step-sister, boys and girls. Nicole Ferrari. Product of Slutvia's finest finishing school.

Nicole gropes about, feeling audience members including MAUDE's new friend.

MAUDE
Oi not him he's mine.

NICOLE
Darling they're never yours are they, you just borrow them for a few minutes. Ooh, it's true what they say about being blind - your other senses start to compensate. *(She sniffs dramatically)* What am I getting? *(She sniffs again)* Nervous sweat and a particularly dreadful new-world pinot grigio. No really *(she points toward the bar)* it's a fiver for a large glass and twice that for a small one. *(She wiggles her fingers)* Gosh, I expect my sense of touch is through the roof too. *(She goes to an audience member and feels him through his clothes.)* Yes, now what's this...? *(She screams)* That's right, static. Is there doctor in the house?

BUTTONS
No we don't get doctors here, they go to the posh panto in Wimbledon.

CINDERS
It's alright Nicole I know a cure for this.

BUTTONS
What you know a cure for stupidity?

MAUDE
Oi.

MAUDE clips BUTTONS round the ear. CINDERS puts a hand over NICOLE's masked eyes.

NICOLE (sniffing)
What am I smelling now... Disinfectant... Rubber... and.... oh, God!

CINDERS
Shush, listen, you've got to say the magic words. Now, close your eyes tight and repeat after me, Eenie Meany Minie Mo

NICOLE
Eanie Meanie Minie Mo

CINDERS
Erm...

BUTTONS
I'm a scrubby old scarecrow

NICOLE
I'm a... scrubby old scarecrow

CINDERS *(sliding the mask off her)*
There we go.

CINDERS
Open your eyes.

NICOLE
A miracle! *(Sees the audience)* Oh yes! A miracle.

MAUDE
Quite a haul this morning.

NICOLE
And so clever how they've put the tallest ones at the back so everyone can see. They do pack them in don't they. Are you comfortable?

MAUDE
I was just saying they've come for the intimacy. Here, everyone lean forward and give the person in front a reach-around.

CINDERS
That'll ruin your dress.

NICOLE
Her figure did that years ago. You're chirpy this morning.

MAUDE
Yeah the futile shitness of it all doesn't hit me until I've had me breakfast. Talking of which, where is it Cinders?

NICOLE
Yes I must keep my strength up, I'm doing my pilots at 11.

MAUDE
You mean Pilates.

NICOLE
Sadly. I'll have an egg white omelette. I'm on a diet.

MAUDE
I'm on a mission. I'll have a Doritos pizza and you can slip her yolks in me coffee. Now clear off Buttons, Mum don't like you hanging about with Cinders.

NICOLE
She thinks you're a bad influence.

MAUDE
She says you've had more cheap men and vodka inside you than the Yumbo Centre.

236

BUTTONS
I don't know what that is but probably. I'll see you later boys and girls. I got to go to my other job at the palace.

CINDERS, MAUDE and NICOLE
The palace!

NICOLE
Give Prince Charming our love.

BUTTONS
Bye Cinders!

BUTTONS exits.

CINDERS
Bye Buttons. I'm sorry boys and girls, I got to do the table, see you later.

CINDERS exits.

NICOLE (sadly)
Intimacy.

MAUDE
Into your what? I knew you were feeling lonely. You spooned me in your sleep last night.

NICOLE
Spooned?? Did I dip into your yoghurt pot?

MAUDE
No you numpty. It's a hug from behind.

NICOLE
My Sven used to do that to me. I'd feel him poking me in the small of my back. I didn't mind it on the whole.

MAUDE
On the where? Look I told you, you got your own room, stop sleepwalking. I could tell you were feeling down.

NICOLE
Oh God was I doing that too? I hope my manicure didn't scratch you. The indignity of being back in the family home after one's husband has left one for the snooker boy.

MAUDE
The pool boy.

NICOLE
No, I'd have understood if it was with him. With his trunks on he looked like he'd just come back with the weekly shop. Oh but it's my Sven I miss. In spite of it all. That man bled me dry.

MAUDE
Bled you dry? He was loaded.

NICOLE
Yes but he was even more well-endowed than the pool boy. *(She looks about cautiously)* Just between you and me-

MAUDE
And the boys and girls

NICOLE
And the boys and girls, I asked a very expensive plastic surgeon about tightening things up a little. He said the best he could do at this stage was give me a drawstring.

MAUDE
I got touched up by a surgeon once. Still. We got our looks.

NICOLE
We have.

MAUDE
I don't know why we're not more popular.

NICOLE
We're popular! You should have come to that new cocktail bar the other night. Emojis.

MAUDE
Who was there?

NICOLE
All the usual faces.

MAUDE
We never get invited to the prince's balls do we.

NICOLE
One day.

MAUDE
A gentlemen friend of mine had a masked ball. Well I say masked, it was just very small and hidden behind the other one.

NICOLE
Perhaps the Prince considers us too young for his balls.

MAUDE
Too young? Please! Woke up this morning, I thought Joan Rivers' ghost had staggered in.

NICOLE
I'm only two years your senior. And you're-

MAUDE
Seventeen.

NICOLE
Is that your age or your weight?

MAUDE
Neither pet, it's your IQ.

NICOLE
I'm sorry, I'm just tetchy. You're very pretty. And you know how I envy your lovely hair.

MAUDE
Cheers Nicole.

NICOLE
The way it sprouts from your chest like a vine. Oh, to go to a ball at the palace! To dance! To meet Prince Charming...

SONG: THE PRINCE'S BALLS

Picture a palace with candles and lights,
Sparkling like summer rain,
Bottles and barrels of wine, red and white,
Magnums of champagne,
They'll be buffing up the dance floor, polishing the halls,
There's such a lovely smell of wax about the prince's balls,
But the marble tiles are slippery, I say this unamused,
The prince's balls have often left a bottom badly bruised,
Yes the prince's balls have often left a bottom badly bruised.

Picture the carriages, picture the band,
Dressed in their penguin suits,
Look! there's a nobleman taking your hand,
He's filthy rich and cute,
But be careful with your cocktail if he takes you for a spin,
When the prince's balls are swinging you could get a sticky chin,
Yes they're tightly packed and sweaty, they spill out onto the lawn
They say the prince's balls are always bursting full till dawn,
Yes they say the prince's balls are always bursting full till dawn.

Obama's balls and Putin's balls are not as big as his,
The Queen of Norway privately says they get her in a tizz,
And President Assad brings his entire entourage,
(It's partly down to him the prince's balls have grown so large)
Does any royal banquet offer such a spread? It's doubtful!
They queue up at the prince's balls for mouthful after mouthful.

Imagine the music, the light on our pearls,
Garlands of flowers arranged,
We'd be the cutest most popular girls,
Our lives would be changed,
All the guests are given goodies so the journey home won't drag,
Yes the nicest thing about the prince's balls might be the bag,
But the man who does the guest list, he won't return our calls,
How I'd like to slap the little arse behind the prince's balls,
Yes we'd like to slap the little arse behind the prince's balls.

And there he is, the prince himself - he's seen us!
However will he ever choose between us?
He's beckoning - oh could he really mean us?
If we play this right then late tonight we'll get to see his royal gardens.

As you might have gathered we'd really like to go,
We're tired of seeing the prince's balls in Tatler and Hello,
But they say the royal bouncers lack a certain grace,
If you try to crash the prince's balls they'll slap you in the face,
Yet we're sure if we attended, the crowd would fall quite hushed,
And they say Prince Charming likes to have his balls a little crushed,
Yes they say Prince Charming likes to have his balls a little crushed.

The COUNTESS enters

COUNTESS
Cinders, stop that racket! Oh it's my beautiful girls, what enchanting baritones you have.

NICOLE
Morning mama.

MAUDE
Alright mum.

NICOLE
Do you think we should revive our musical double act?

COUNTESS
Why not! You'll want a hobby when you're married to rich gentlemen.

MAUDE
Yeah but... What about as a career. Instead of pinning all our hopes of happiness on finding a husband.

COUNTESS
Where's your ambition, Maude!

NICOLE
I wish Slutvia wasn't banned from Eurovision. We could win that.

COUNTESS
Where is the brat? Cinders?

CINDERS enters.

CINDERS
Yes Countess. Breakfast is served in the morning room.

MAUDE
Wicked! Come on Nicole.

NICOLE
Maude.

MAUD
Yeah?

NICOLE
Do you think you might stop making jokes about my intelligence?

MAUDE
Your what?

NICOLE
That's just what I mean.

MAUDE
Yeah alright, sorry. Come on.

MAUD heads towards breakfast. Nicole goes to the opposite side of the stage.

MAUDE
Nicole. This way.

Nicole realises her mistake. They exit.

COUNTESS
Cinders! When you've washed up the breakfasts and ironed our dresses and cleaned the bedrooms I have some work for you.

She holds out a toothbrush.

CINDERS
A toothbrush?

COUNTESS
A lawn polisher. I want every blade to sparkle.

CINDERS (offering the envelope)
Here, this is for you.

COUNTESS
Ah, yes.

The COUNTESS pulls forward the neckline of her dress and waits for CINDERS to wedge it between her breasts. He has done this many times before. She enjoys it.

COUNTESS
A little lower. That's it. Aren't you curious about what it's for? Would *you* like to go to London?

CINDERS
Slutvia's the envy of the world isn't it?

COUNTESS
Oh it's fine for decent folk. But not for dirty little dicky-lickers. They love your sort in London. Imagine, walking down the street, hand in arse with the man you love... Now if you stop being a lazy little twat-dodger and work hard for one more year, I'll send you to London for free! Would you like that?

CINDERS
Well yes! Yes I would! Countess... I wanted to ask, would you very kindly get me some new clothes?

COUNTESS
New clothes? You've had those barely a month.

CINDERS
The holes are a bit revealing.

COUNTESS

Yes, I had them made like that especially! Cinders, the lawn. But before you begin, a task. There is a roundel of cheese in the hallway, and twenty new mousetraps. Set them about the house.

CINDERS (sad)
Yes Countess.

COUNTESS
Now, breakfast. Just in time to listen to the King's morning radio broadcast.

CINDERS
Can I listen to the King's broadcast?

COUNTESS
Why would a wretch like you want to listen to things that don't concern you! Oh and Cinders, you've dropped something.

The COUNTESS leers over CINDERS as he bends over searching. There is nothing there.

COUNTESS
My mistake. Have a lovely morning.

COUNTESS exits.

CINDERS
Cow.

COUNTESS (off)
I heard that!

CINDERS
I bet she didn't.

COUNTESS (off)
I am not a harridan!

CINDERS (muttering)
Deaf old loser.

COUNTESS (off)
That's better!

CINDERS
I'd better be getting on. See you later boys and girls!

Scene 3: The national palace

If there's a phrase to describe the décor it's "military camp". A desk is set up with a microphone and a tiny keyboard or xylophone. BUTTONS enters.

BUTTONS
Hey boys and girls! Welcome to the National Palace. I work here too. I'll do you a tour if you like, I charge more than the official one but then I've got keys to the wine cellar.

KING (off)
Buttons!

BUTTONS
That's his Majesty the King! Right...

BUTTONS pulls out a remote control and points it into a corner. A fanfare plays. The KING enters, amiably.

KING
Good morning subjects, good morning Sluts.

He takes the remote control.

KING
I do like a fanfare.

He points it into a corner and presses a button. Instead of the fanfare, a burst of Heroes (the 2015 Eurovision winner) plays. He tries to stop it, and eventually succeeds. He stares at the remote.

Now what have we here. A coach party?

BUTTONS
These are the boys and girls sir.

KING
The boys and girls... Well I can't promise I'll remember all that but I'll give it a bash. *(To an audience member)* Good morning, where are you from? And what do you do? Well I'm a king so I think I win that round. Ding ding! Do visit the gift shop. You're just in time to hear me speak to the nation!

BUTTONS
Here's the post, sir. An invitation.

KING
Goody!

BUTTONS
From the Slutvian State Opera.

KING
Oh drat.

BUTTONS
And a letter from the European Commission.

KING (reads)
"Your majesty, thank you for your latest letter of application to join the ew." [Literally: ooooh]

BUTTONS
I think it's "the EU" sir.

KING
Ah yes. "Your majesty, even if Britain were to leave the union, it is not one-in-one-out. Slutvia has never signed the Geneva Convention, and you continue to proliferate nuclear weapons." All flattery so far! "Finally, we are a separate entity to Eurovision and are unable to take forward your request to be reinstated following your behavioural incident in 2008, which we note has received 38 million views on YouTube." What the hell's YouTube? I don't even want to take part! It's my son that keeps insisting. Give me a military marching band any day.

BUTTONS (yearning)
Oh and me sir...

KING
Or a bit of pomp from our national composer. The royal firework music. The royal water music. The royal elevator music. The royal hold music. The royal I'm trying to get to bloody sleep music. I've had to lock the bastard up. He's in the tower with that fucking artist and those gay rights protestors. Now, it's time for my broadcast. Bring my office throne.

BUTTONS
Yes sir.

BUTTONS exits and enters wheeling himself on a lavish throne that is also a swivel chair. The KING hauls him out of it and sits, spinning a full circle. BUTTONS hands him a sheet of paper.

BUTTONS (handing over some sheets of paper)
The headlines sir. From the state news agency.

KING
Anything I should read through first?

BUTTONS
Oh no sir, keep it fresh. Thank you sir.

BUTTONS exits. The KING sits at the table with the microphone. He looks at his watch or a clock. At the right time he plays a very tinny little jingle on the keyboard.

KING
Good morning subjects, good morning Sluts, it is I, your loving king Ludwig here. First, the headlines. Right. Ah, yes, our largest national clothes retailer has released its quarterly figures. Shirts are up, trousers are down and bras are holding steady. Now, thought for the day.

A slight pause.

That's enough of that. For I have an announcement! My dear and only son Prince Charming is to come of age and to celebrate I will throw the biggest ball for him Slutvia has ever seen! My son needs a wife – a future queen no less! - and so every eligible young Slut in the land will be invited! That's all for today. Coming up, the cookery programme. Our national dish – Miss Slutvia - will guide you through some traditional recipes..

PRINCE CHARMING enters. He is angry.

CHARMING
Daddy!

KING
Wait!!!!!!

THE KING shushes him and points to the microphone.

KING (Quiet and polite)
Thank you for listening.

He fumbles to turn off the microphone.

KING
Wait wait wait.

CHARMING
Daddy, what is the meaning-

KING
Back back back!

He brandishes his remote control. CHARMING reluctantly exits backwards hovering in the entrance. The KING presses a button. From the speakers we hear I Like My Men Like I Like My Coffee by Supersister.

KING
That'll do that'll do. Good morning Charming.

CHARMING
I don't want a wife!

KING
I thought you'd be pleased!

CHARMING
I don't want to get married!

KING
Your mother brought me such a lot of pleasure. To watch her playing with her pretty hair, her pretty breasts, her pretty ladies in waiting...

CHARMING
Then perhaps it's you that needs a wife. (He sees the audience). Oh I say what fun, hullo. And what are you into? Er, I mean, what do you do? *(on the reply)* Scandalous!

KING (a peace offering)
Look, this was meant for me but why don't you take this very special invitation.

CHARMING
Ripping!

KING
The Slutvian State Opera

CHARMING
Oh fuck.

KING
Now look here, Charming, one day you'll be king and you need a wife. There are three countries with whom we still have diplomatic relations. These are highly traditional nations. They like to do business with royalty. And they'll expect you to have something pretty on your arm.

CHARMING
Then buy me an Apple watch.

KING
Alright alright. Frankly you could come home of a morning with an arse like a trodden-on doughnut and a willy like a chocolate-dipped banana, but you need a wife. The church won't stop banging on at me about it. (To audience) The Slutvian Unorthodox Church broke away from the Catholic Church 300 years ago over an unresolvable theological dispute. The virgin Mary appeared in a vision to a Sluttish nun. She told her

she'd always hated the colour blue and wouldn't have been seen dead in it. *(To Charming)* Come here son. Look at that. *(He gestures out front as though at a view)* One day, all this will be yours. These hills, that forest...

CHARMING
That's a painting, daddy.

KING
Right, right.

He shuffles them both sideways.

KING
One day, all this will be yours.

CHARMING rather likes the look of someone in the audience.

CHARMING
Oh I say. How explosive, what.

KING
What?

CHARMING
What?

The KING sees a woman he likes the look of.

KING
Hello young thing. Do you have any royalty in you? Would you like some? You must come to the ball. (To the Prince) Don't you want to wear trousers one day? In Slutvia, only married men are allowed to wear trousers.

CHARMING
I like wearing tights.

KING
But I only made that law so you'd want to get married! In any case, you'll have a party the like of which has never been seen before! I'm having a new suit made! Buttons!

BUTTONS runs on with a box.

BUTTONS
Yes your majesty. (To Charming) Morning mate. How's your head.

KING
Mate?! Your *royal highness*.

BUTTONS
You don't have to call me that sir.

KING
My suit will be made of the finest fabric money can buy! Isn't that right?

BUTTONS
That's right sir, I got a sample here. Woven in Kashmir from the silk of the Himalayan yak. They say it's magical.

KING
Must be if it comes from a talking yak!

BUTTON
They say, sir, the cloth is so fine, that only people of the most refined sensibilities can see it.

KING
Did you hear that! Well, I won't be able to see it, old military duffer that I am. Open it up!

BUTTONS opens the box. It is empty. The KING gasps.

KING
Nope, not a sausage! How clever. I'll have a feel.

BUTTONS
Go on then sir.

The KING lifts the "fabric" out of the box, weighing it appreciatively.

KING
It's like there's nothing there! You can see it can you?

BUTTONS
It wouldn't be very special if an oik like me could see it sir!

CHARMING
The boys and girls can see it can't you?

Yes!

KING
Marvellous! *(He claps his hands in excitement)* Oh fuck I've dropped it. *(To someone in the front row)* Be a sport young man and pick it up.

BUTTONS offers the box to receive the cloth.

KING
You know about these sort of things Charming. Would you wear it?

BUTTONS
He was wearing something very like it at the Veal Crate.

KING
Have one made up too Charming. All the young ladies admiring you in your birthday suit... Well, royal duty calls. It's time to inspect the palace guards.

CHARMING
I could do that daddy!

KING
That's the spirit! Taking on responsibilities. They're a rambunctious lot so don't be afraid to show them some discipline. Yesterday they were being so loud and naughty in the showers I had to knock one out. Don't worry. He soon came to. Now, what's say we have a bit of a lads' night in tonight. Some beers, a curry, watch a match. A bit of a, bit of a "chill-out".

BUTTONS and CHARMING stare at him.

KING
Oh come on, the Slutvian basketball team is playing. Nice little slamming session!

BUTTONS
I can't sir.

CHARMING
It's not really my thing.

KING (sad)
Oh. Well, I have lots to do, I'm sure... At ease, lads.

The KING exits. BUTTONS pulls a magazine from his pocket.

BUTTONS
Here I got you some more porn.

CHARMING
Spaftacular. I wish we could crack the internet firewall though. I want action.

BUTTONS
Just turn the pages fast. Listen, can I give you some advice? I'd lay off the old Blunder a bit.

CHARMING
I'm very discreet.

BUTTONS
With respect mate it's not discreet to send pictures of your royal behind. It could spread.

CHARMING
It can and does, Buttons. What am I going to do? I can't get married. Not to a girl.

BUTTONS
You never know, you might be straight. You've been with girls.

CHARMING
I'm a Prince. Girls throw themselves at me all the time. Occasionally one lands in the right place. No, I have it all worked out. I'm going to find a boy. Not some dreary Lord, someone real. Someone common. And he and I shall fall in love, a love so pure that daddy will see how happy I am and make him my consort and introduce gay rights to Slutvia! I'm tired of slagging it about! I want something more, something deep, something noble! (pause) Right, let's go and inspect those saucy guards.

BUTTONS
Yes sir! See you soon boys and girls!

Scene 4: A clearing in the woods

The FAIRY GODMOTHER wanders in disguised as an old woman. She is also smoking something which looks like a home-made cigar.

FAIRY
I know what you're thinking, she's aged fucking quick!
It's just a disguise kids I'm playing a part
See before we can get our young Cinders some dick,
I need to find out if he has a kind heart.

She smokes the cigar, a contented dazed expression crosses her face.

I been foraging. I made this myself. See, if Cinders helps an old coot like me, it means he's a good person and the Fairy Queen will make me his Fairy Godmother! Hell boys and girls why is life so complicated. I was hoping to get lucky with a local girl by now but turns out the Sluts are all prudes. We want to have fun don't we girls?

The FAIRY hides behind the gravestones as CINDERS enters with a small bouquet of wild flowers.

CINDERS
Hello boys and girls! I've finished polishing the lawn and sneaked way to lay these on my Dad's grave. Only a few months til I can get away to London! I can't wait. Gay bars, the Shrek Experience, Chariots Roman Spa, do you know anything about that sir? And I'm definitely going to the Olympic Park and have someone take me up the Arcelor.[42]

MILEY runs on goes over to the grave, crouches and pisses.

CINDERS
Miley! Not on Dad's grave.

MILEY hides behind a tree.

CINDERS
What's wrong now? Silly thing. (Gets his phone out). While I've a moment... Oh hello. It's the hottie! He's...

---

[42] Chariots is a gay sauna which in 2015 had several branches in London. The Shrek Experience opened in July 2015. The ArcelorMittal Orbit is Anish Kapoor's 114.5-metre tall sculpture-cum-viewing tower in the Olympic Park.

50 metres! (Looks about). That can't be right... 30 metres!

CINDERS wanders off. CHARMING enters. Sunglasses on his head.

CHARMING
Hullo sweeties! I had to get away from the palace, father won't stop banging on about weddings... I meant what I said about settling down you know. I've had half of Slut on Sea – the prettier half, natch – but I can't even make proper friends. I can hardly have a load of camp scamps lounging around the palace in fabulous belts where daddy might trip over them. It's a brutal shame, I've the country's only copy of Death Becomes Her on BlueRay and nobody to watch it with. (Ahhh) No, no, it's sadder than that. *(Looks about)* Charming little place, I'll catch a few rays before the weather changes. *(He takes off his shirt and stretches. He gets out his phone)* While I've a moment... Oh! 20 metres!

CHARMING prowls about looking at his phone and trying to find the boy. CINDERS backs onto the stage.

CINDERS
10 metres!

CHARMING
5 metres!

They crash backwards into each other. CHARMING falls over in a heap. CINDERS turns and sees him. CHARMING puts his sunglasses on and tries to look cool.

CINDERS
Hi

CHARMING
Hi!

MILEY pokes her head out, her nose twitching. She can control herself no longer. She runs over to the PRINCE and starts sniffing at his crotch. The PRINCE screams.

CINDERS
Miley! I'm so sorry, she gets like this at the slightest whiff of cheese. I'm Cinders.

CHARMING
Hello Cinders.

There is an awkward silence.

CINDERS
And you?

CHARMING
Ahaha very good! (Aside) He's bold, I like it.

CINDERS
(Aside) He's laughing at me, I don't like it.

CHARMING
Oh! You can see them too can you? (Aside) I'll have to be more discreet with my asides!

CINDERS
What are you doing? (aside) He thinks you're watching a show about *him*!

CHARMING
You really don't know who I am?

CINDERS
No!

CHARMING
Charming.

CINDERS
There's no need to be sarcastic.

CHARMING
It's my name. Aren't you a Slut?

CINDERS
Since birth!

CHARMING
Do you not read the papers? Watch TV?

CINDERS
I'm not allowed. Are you from the village?

CHARMING
Well actually I'm a... Yes, yes! Rather. I'm just a boy from the village. I love this ragged look of yours, is it All Saints? Tell you what, I've had a splendid idea.

CINDERS
I'm having several right now.

CHARMING
Why don't I pop off and get a bottle of fizz - hashtag thirsty - and something to eat and we can have a picnic and a chat and help each other out with the sun cream, it'll be a fucking riot.

CINDERS
That would be literally the best thing that happened to me ever in my entire life, but I've got to go and give Maud and Nicole their baths.

CHARMING
Oh... (Aside, sad) They're his daughters, he's straight.

CINDERS
No...

CHARMING
Ah! (Aside, happy) They're his dogs, he's gay!

CINDERS
They're my sisters, they're just lazy with the loofah.

CHARMING
Ask me what a loofah is.

CINDER
I know what a loofah is.

CHARMING
But just ask me.

CINDERS
What's a loofah?

CHARMING
Well if you don't know that, stay off the carpets when you come round for dinner! Ahahahahaha...! Wait here for me.

CINDERS
No, I'd get a right thrashing.

CHARMING
Nonsense, I'll be gentle. Back in a tick.

He starts to run off, then runs back and kisses CINDERS on the cheek.

CHARMING
Don't go anywhere.

CHARMING exits. CINDERS is beside himself

CINDERS
I want to stay but if I do the Countess will never let me out again. I feel so lonely all of a sudden. What should I do?

Stay!

CINDERS
Alright. I suppose I could stay a bit longer. Can I say you told me to? Oh I nearly forgot about these.

CINDERS goes to place the flowers on the grave, putting his phone down as he does. The FAIRY pops up from behind the grave. CINDERS and MILEY leap in the air in terror.

246

CINDERS
Jesus Fuck!

FAIRY (Old lady voice)
Geez Louise there's an old woman struggling here.

CINDERS
With what? Stalking tendencies?

The FAIRY limps out, stooped over.

CINDERS
Are you ok?

FAIRY
Fuck kid do I look OK? *(Changing back to an old lady voice and over acting)* Young man, I'm gathering wood for my cottage. I can't afford the electric. Thing is with my old back I can't take much.

She picks up a small stick

This should keep me warm for an hour.

CINDERS
Let me help.

CINDERS picks up some logs. He goes to hand them to.

FAIRY
I can't carry them dear. My neck, my back... (She twinkles at the audience) My pussy and my crack

CINDERS
What?

She fiddles with something around her waist.

FAIRY
Nothing. Just adjusting my colostomy. I made it myself from a fanny-pack and a Macdonalds straw and it leaks like a power bottom after a bank holiday weekend.

CINDERS
Wait – fanny pack? Where are you from?

FAIRY
The nineties.

CINDERS
Well it was nice to meet you.

FAIRY
(In her regular voice) The logs!!!!!

CINDERS
Oh yeah! I'll drop them off later.

FAIRY
(In old lady voice) I'm getting pneumonia...

CINDERS
But I was meant to-

The FAIRY coughs

CINDERS
I'll help you with your logs.

CINDERS starts to exit. MILEY pees again, this time on CINDERS' phone.

CINDERS
I'll just send that guy a message... Miley, Miley! Don't piss on my phone! *(He runs, snatches it and wipes it dry.)* It's fucked! You killed it!

FAIRY
Come along now. You're a good 'un! From now on you will have a Fairy Godmother!

CINDERS
Yeah whatever. Come on Miley.

CINDERS, MILEY and the FAIRY exit. CHARMING enters from the opposite side with a picnic basket carrying an open bottle of champagne.

CHARMING
Cinders we are going to make this place a fucking disaster zone! Cinders? Where are you you scamp?

He looks behind some of the gravestones. He looks sad. He sits down, glumly.

CHARMING
And he seemed so nice. Picnic for one, then.

We hear the Blunder/Grindr message noise. CHARMING forgets his woes and grabs his phone.

CHARMING
Now *he's* cute!

BLACKOUT.

247

Scene 5: The kitchen at Annie Hall.

NICOLE is applying make-up with a small mirror. MAUDE is sat backwards on a chair, her lags straddling the back, reading a book but mainly watching NICOLE.

MAUDE
You'd be quicker getting a plasterer in love.

NICOLE
Stop watching me! I have remarkably youthful skin

MAUDE
You do! More acne than a mosh-pit. What is that, magnolia?

NICOLE
Yes. (She looks at the make-up) With an all-weather silk finish. (pause) Stop watching me!

MAUDE
Just think, the Prince coming here! *(looking at her hands)* I was gonna do me falsies but last time I stuck em on with No More Nails. Appropriate name it turned out, they've only just grown back.

MAUDE watches NICOLE.

NICOLE
Shouldn't you be getting ready?

MAUDE
I am ready, I'm posing ain't I. *(She waves her book)* I don't want Prince Charming to think I'm just some sexy airhead. That happens a lot.

NICOLE
Well darling you know best. I don't suppose you've seen the tweezers?

MAUDE
Yeah they're upstairs.

NICOLE
Good, you might want to glance at your upper lip. I wonder what my invitation will be like. Elegant, I expect, and ever so thick.

MAUDE
I don't think they personalise them to that degree. You'll be on the B-list love. And all of us what's on the A list are gonna say yes so you ain't got a chance.

The COUNTESS enters.

COUNTESS
Girls! They're minutes away! King Ludwig and Prince Charming! Maude darling, I know you're shy but don't hide your pretty face behind that book or he'll notice your bottom. Why aren't you practising?

NICOLE
Practising?

COUNTESS
The national anthem of course.

The girls practice the national anthem, which they turn into an audience sing-along with the help of a song sheet.

SONGSHEET SONG: THE SLUTVIAN NATIONAL ANTHEM

Oh Slutvia, oh Slutvia, we rise up for our king,
Our heads erect, as loyal subjects, we proudly kiss his ring,
When picking fruit out in the fields,
Or reaping what the harvest yields,
I will sing it out and sing it loud:
I'm a Slut and I am proud.

The KING and CHARMING enter.

COUNTESS
King Ludwig, Prince Chow Mein, welcome to my humble mansion your majesties. I am Countess Volga, I'll let my daughters introduce themselves.

NICOLE (indicating herself and Maud)
Oh mama, we already know each other!

MAUDE
I'm Maude your hotnesses.

NICOLE
Oh I see. Nicole. Sixteen.

MAUDE (stage whisper, outraged)
What the fuck! That makes me fourteen! He won't be able to sleep with me.

COUNTESS
Darling relax, he's an important man, they'll turn a blind eye.

KING
Greetings, subjects.

NICOLE curtsies, MAUDE bows. The COUNTESS coughs. MAUDE curtseys. As they stand, MAUD stays down longer than she should looking at the PRINCE's crotch.

NICOLE

I've heard such things about your balls your highness.

PRINCE

Oh they're nothing compared with some. When Daddy bought me my degree at the London School of Economics I had a taste of Prince Harry's balls. Destroyed me. But we're going to have Beyonce aren't we daddy.

KING

Ah... I'm afraid Beyonce's put her fees up for performing for despots.

NICOLE

We could sing!

MAUDE

We know some good old naughty music hall numbers. Do you know A threeway isn't incest if you use a different johnny?

KING

How does it go?

MAUDE

Oh no that ain't a song your Maj I was just saying.

KING

Before I issue your invitations, are you both indigenous?

NICOLE

She gets indiginous when-

MAUDE

We're both proud Sluts your Maj.

KING

Then here we are.

He hands them invitations.

CHARMING

Daddy, let's go.

COUNTESS

Your majesty, may I say, even the photos in the paper don't do justice to how handsome you are in real life.

KING

What? I'll have the picture editors arrested!

COUNTESS

Every time I see your handsome face on the front of a twink I find it very hard to hand it over. Who is to be your escort at the ball?

KING

Escort?

COUNTESS

You must have an escort. Someone of good breeding.

KING

Like a cow?

COUNTESS

Like a Countess. I'll be there at eight.

BUTTONS enters

BUTTONS

Hello boys and girls! Hello your majesties.

CHARMING

Buttons! Does anybody else live here?

BUTTONS

Yeah there is.

COUNTESS, NICOLE, MAUDE

Oh no there isn't.

Oh yes there is!

COUNTESS, NICOLE, MAUDE

Oh no there isn't.

Oh yes there is!

COUNTESS

Your majesties. Why don't the girls and I show you our upper quarters.

MAUDE drags CHARMING away.

NICOLE

Have some decorum darling.

She pulls the PRINCE away and starts to drag him.

NICOLE

She wants to show you her itchings.

CHARMING

You mean etchings.

NICOLE

I'm afraid not. No talent in that department. Give her a crayon she eats it.

249

MAUD
Give her a steak and she tries to make friends with it.

NICOLE
Your highness, I should tell you, my desires are... unconventional.

MAUDE
She likes being beaten.

CHARMING
Really?

MAUDE
Yeah, so give her a game of Junior Scrabble and she'll purr like a fingered cat.

CHARMING
Ladies! I need a little tête a tête with Buttons. Take father upstairs.

COUNTESS
Your majesty.

The COUNTESS, MAUDE and NICOLE practically carry the KING out. CHARMING gives BUTTONS some invitation.

CHARMING
Give these to some of your gay friends will you. It'll be unbearable otherwise.

BUTTONS
But, but the whole point is to find you a wife.

CHARMING
Don't be obstructive. Give them to boys who might be, you know, grateful to be asked eh? God, I met a perfect one yesterday. Sidney? Cindy? Something like that, proper wheeze.

BUTTONS
I'll see if I can think of anyone.

The KING enters followed by MAUDE, NICOLE and The COUNTESS. His clothing is dishevelled.

CHARMING
Daddy?

KING
Time to go.

COUNTESS
But we haven't heard your army stories yet.

MAUDE
I bet you know your way round a trench.

KING
Many more young women to meet.

NICOLE
You won't find any like us.

KING
That's it, be positive. Come along, Charming.

MAUDE
I'll get me handbag.

KING
My *son*.

COUNTESS
We'll see you out.

CHARMING, The COUNTESS, KING, NICOLE and MAUDE exit

BUTTONS
I think Charming's met Cinders somehow! I should give Cinders an invite, he'd love a night out. Few drinks, bit of a dance, meet the prince... Aye but there's the fucking rub. What if they meet again? What if they pull? What if they.. I dunno, get a Boston Terrier and sign up for a circus skills course together? They'd have no time for me. Should I give him the invitation? You're right, I will.

CINDERS enters, sweaty and dirty. BUTTONS screws up the invitation and puts it in his pocket. They air-kiss.

BUTTONS
You're glistening.

CINDERS
I'm sweating. I nearly put my back out doing the stables.

BUTTONS
You probably want a, a massage...

CINDERS
Oh probably. But Buttons, did you hear? If I'm good for another year the Countess is going to send me to London!

BUTTONS
Babes you don't wanna go to London, Gypsy closed already[43].

---

[43] Imelda Staunton as Rose. Savoy Theatre, transferring from Chichester. Brilliant.

CINDERS

You could come with me!

BUTTONS

I can't can I. What would me mum do without me? And me little brother Velcro and me sister Toggles and little baby Poppers. And then there's the Veal Crate, and the Palace... Anyway I can't say I'm off to London with a boy. Mum doesn't know about me. And listen you need to be careful. My mate's a trolley dolly, he gave me this yesterday.

He takes out a newspaper cutting from his pocket and hands it to CINDERS.

CINDERS

You know I can barely read.

BUTTONS

Look, it says there's rumours that gay men are being trafficked to the UK on the promise of West End musicals and Cereal Cafes and Saudi sugar daddies and streets paved with cock, only to be enslaved and forced to work on a kale plantation.

CINDERS

I'm used to hard work. What's a musical?

BUTTONS

They're like plays but with songs in and generally based on films about the British working classes. So er... you know the Prince invited Maude and Nicole to his ball.

CINDERS

I wish I could go the ball.

BUTTONS

You won't even come to my club nights.

CINDERS

I spend my life in dirty cellars. This is the palace! A boy can dream. I best get on.

CINDERS grabs a mop and bucket and starts to mop the floor.

BUTTONS

Boys and girls I feel mean. Should I give him his invite? (*Yes you should!*) I should. If I don't I'm just as bad as the Countess. I just... no, you're right. I'll do it.

He takes out the invitation from his pocket.

BUTTON

Cinders.

CINDERS

Yeah? God it's got hot again hasn't it.

CINDERS pulls up his top to mop his face, exposing his stomach. BUTTONS stares at him admiringly.

CINDERS

Well what is it?

BUTTONS stuffs the invitation back in his pocket.

BUTTONS

Nothing man. See you later.

BUTTONS runs out. CINDERS carries on cleaning.

Scene 6: The kitchen at Annie Hall

MILEY is asleep in the corner with Billy Ray. CINDERS enters. He carries a bag with vegetables including a courgette and a pumpkin. He plonks them on a surface.

CINDERS

Hello boys and girls I've been shopping. They're organic. (He waves the courgette) This one especially.

NICOLE enters she has a face pack on and a long flowing silk dressing gown. She is in a state of utter panic. MILEY covers her ears.

NICOLE

Ahhhhhhhhhhhhhhhhhhhhhhhhhhhhh.

CINDERS

What's wrong?

NICOLE

Where's my dress I can't find my dress Cinders get me my dress.

CINDERS

It's in your bedroom I hung it over your mirror.

NICOLE

Oh! Silly me, I've been staring at it for twenty minutes wondering if I needed a boob job.

MAUDE enters. She is wearing a very short animal print dressing gown and also has a face pack on.

MAUDE

What time is it?

CINDERS

Oh it's-

MAUDE

It's time to partaaaaaaaayyyyyyyyyyyy. Hello boys and girls. We're getting ready for the ball! I know we only just got the invites but if we stuck in another scene we'd be here till Easter. I fucking love Easter.

NICOLE

She does, she spends the whole weekend face down in her eggs.

MAUDE

I bet you can't tell who's who with us wearing these can you. Like a lucky dip ain't it [name of the man she chatted up earlier].

NICOLE

You asked his name? Things *are* serious. It'll be on a tattoo by tomorrow. Come on.

MAUDE

I'm naked under this, [name].

NICOLE

Cinders, set an extra place for breakfast in case Prince Charming prefers to come back here.

MAUDE

Aw that's thoughtful of you Nic but if he does get hungry halfway through the business I keep some takeaway menus under me pillow.

Cinders starts to unpack the shopping, putting the courgette and pumpkin on a table.

COUNTESS (off)

Girls! Our carriage is here! Are you ready?

NICOLE

Just going to slip our dresses on mummy!

MAUDE

Two minutes!

NICOLE

Ha, I won't tell Maude she still has her face pack on. *(realises she also has one on)* Ahhhhhhh!

NICOLE and MAUDE look at each other, scream and run out. MILEY sits up,

CINDERS

Looks like it's just going to be me and you here tonight girl.

MILEY nods. BUTTONS enters.

BUTTONS

Hi Cinders. Hi boys and girls.

CINDERS

Buttons! What are you doing here?

BUTTONS

I'm taking the girls to the ball aren't I. Buttons taxis at your service. But I er... I got something for you.

He takes the invitation out of his pocket and hands it to CINDERS.

CINDERS

An invitation to the ball! Oh Buttons!

CINDERS gives BUTTONS a friendly kiss. The COUNTESS enters

COUNTESS
Buttons! We're waiting.

BUTTONS (To Cinders)
See you later!

BUTTONS exits.

COUNTESS
Why are you not cleaning you disobedient little deviant? What is that?

CINDERS
Oh Countess! I'm going to the ball.

COUNTESS
Oh no you're not.

CINDERS
Oh yes I am.

COUNTESS
Oh no you're not

She snatches the invitation from CINDERS

CINDERS
Oh yes I am.

COUNTESS
Oh no you're not.

She tears the invitation into tiny pieces.

COUNTESS
Just for that I'm locking you in. And if I play my cards right tonight, who knows when I'll be back! Hahahahaha!

She locks the outside door then exits into the house. We hear a key turn in another lock.

CINDERS
That's so unfair isn't it Miley! Will you help me raid the wine cellar and get pissed together?

MILEY shakes her head.

CINDERS
Oh yeah. Date night isn't it?

MILEY nods and stands exits.

CINDERS
Alright don't do anything I wouldn't do. No I mean it stop eating your own shit it's gross.

MILEY exits

CINDERS
I best finish the washing up.

He takes an object from the sink and dries it. It's a dildo. He looks at its base.

CINDERS
I wish they'd put name tags on them. And I wish I was going to the palace. Silly idea I guess. Well boys and girls, I guess that's me for the night.

CINDERS sits, glum. He stands, finds a corkscrew. He looks in the cupboard. He pulls out a bottle of white spirit.

CINDERS
White spirit, that'll do. Cheers.

CINDERS settles himself down with the wine. After a moment, a knock at the door.

CINDERS
It's locked!

FAIRY (Off)
Oh no it ain't! But you gotta let me in yourself it's the rules.

CINDERS tries the door. It opens.

CINDERS
That's incredible!

FAIRY
Incredible? Incredible is how much hate the gays have for Sam Smith in world that's got the Catholic church, Isis and Putin in it.

CINDERS
Who are you?

FAIRY (Brandishing a bible)
Your Fairy Godbotherer!

CINDERS
Sweet Lord.

FAIRY
That's the spirit! Cheer up, I'm having a laugh with you. The only Jesus I'd bring into your life is my cheeky young Puerto Rican neighbour who goes splits with me when I can't afford an eighth. Look, it's me you space cadet (She does her old woman voice) Young man...

CINDERS
The old woman! That's uncanny!

FAIRY
Uncanny? Uncanny is how realistic my sofa in the shape of Kim Kardashian's ass is. Sometimes I spend the whole night on it and wake up with a tongue covered in lint. Listen kid, I'm your fairy godmother and I'm going to get you to that ball if I pop a tit doing it. Now, something for you to wear... Get your kit off.

CINDERS
I...

FAIRY
Honey you're safe with me. I'm such a dyke I broke the Kinsey scale while headbanging to The Indigo Girls.

CINDERS
But the boys and girls-

FAIRY
Have paid good money.

CINDERS begins to undress to his underpants. They have holes in too.

FAIRY
There we go. And I'll need some shoes.

The FAIRY gathers up the clothes and puts them in a cupboard. She closes the cupboard. CINDERS picks up some old slippers.

CINDERS
There's these old slippers...

FAIRY
What an unusually shaped left foot you got. I'd almost say it was unique.

She puts them in the cupboard too and closes it.

FAIRY
Now, all I need to do is say the magic spell, and we'll have you fit for a Prince.

CINDERS
A prince! I might meet the Prince!

The FAIRY gets into a magic pose. A long wait.

CINDERS
What's wrong.

FAIRY
I forgot the fucking spell! *(She laughs)* Agh, I smoke too much it messes with the little grey cells. Come on girl... Nope. It's gone. What could it be?

CINDERS
Fuck.

FAIRY
No that ain't it.

CINDERS sits down, defeated.

CINDERS
Fuckety fuck.

FAIRY
Now that's not bad.

CINDERS
Fucketyfucketyfucketyfuck.

FAIRY
I like it!

CINDERS
What?

FAIRY
(Sings) Fucketyfucketfucketyfuck... (Speaks) That'll do just nicely.

They sing. In the ensuing song the fairy bundles Cinders into the cupboard with his clothes, and he reappears wearing a ballgown. She transforms his scruffy shoes into high heels, and transforms the head of a mop into a wig.

SONG: FUCKETY FUCKETY FUCKETY FUCK

FAIRY
We'll get you to the palace,
We'll just have to improvise,
Like when there's nothing in the fridge,
And you got guests,
And all your clothes are out to dry.
It's nothing you ain't handled really,
Just on a bigger scale,
Just like a fairytale!

CINDERS
I'm going to the palace,
To play at being someone else,
Play at being someone special,

Someone normal,
Who don't sleep beneath a shelf.
I've done it in my dreams but really,
Now I'm not asleep,
It feels like quite a leap...

FAIRY
And when your confidence is waning,
And in your heart it's raining,
Better quit complaining say the magic words:

(CHORUS)
Fucketyfucketyfucketyfuck!
Fucketyfucketyfucketyfuck!
Try it when you're feeling out of luck,
Pick yourself up, wash your face and tuck your shirt in,
Now who's hurtin'?
It's the magic word for intercourse,
Sing it till you're hoarse.

CINDERS
Perhaps I'll bag a man there,
Perhaps we'll fall in love,
Perhaps we'll run away,
I won't spend every day,
In rags and rubber gloves.
I keep a house quite well but really,
I wanna be kept well too,
After this life wouldn't you?

And when your confidence is waning... [etc]

FAIRY
Back in the game!

CINDERS
A dress??

FAIRY
You got more chance getting in this way. More chance getting near the prince.

CINDERS
Don't I look a bit manly?

FAIRY
Kid, even magic can't do that for you. Now hop in your carriage and sail up that drive and get yourself a noble knobbing!

CINDERS
What carriage? There's a car, but I can't drive... Can you?

FAIRY
Only New York style.

CINDERS
What's that?

FAIRY
Taxiiiiiii!!!!! Well we gotta get you a carriage. Let's see...

CINDERS
Boys and girls, what can we turn into a carriage?

"Pumpkin!!"

FAIRY
Pumpkin! Aw is that what they call you? I'll try my best. Vegetables are tricky fuckers. I can make it bigger and make it golden but it's going to stay pretty much pumpkin shaped. So let's turn that thing into a big beautiful golden pumpkin-shaped coach. You know what to do kiddos! After me, Fuckety Fuckety Fuckety Fuck!

"Fuckety fuckety fuckety fuck!"

Lights flicker and briefly black out. When they settle the pumpkin is still there.

FAIRY
Dammit!

CINDERS
It's ok. You did your best but I was never destined to go to the palace was I.

FAIRY
I'm sorry kid.

CINDERS
Wait. The courgette.

FAIRY
The what?

CINDERS
The courgette. The green thing.

FAIRY
The zucchini?

CINDERS
It's gone!

CINDERS opens the door and looks out. Snow blows in.

CINDERS
Oh my god.

He runs out.

FAIRY
I'm all of a tingle, I'm getting the feels
I think we just got our hero some wheels!

CINDERS appears in a carriage the shape of a giant golden courgette, pulled by Miley with a plumed headdress like a horse. The FAIRY has a laughing fit.

FAIRY
Well it sure ain't a pussy wagon!

CINDERS
I love it!

FAIRY
It sure is a ride!

CINDERS
Thank you! Oh, the music, the men, the dancing – the food! - watching the sun rise...

FAIRY
Oh yeah about that. The magic don't last so long. It only works on the day the spell is cast, and at midnight the spell breaks!

CINDERS
Midnight?

FAIRY
That's right. You'll be stood in the great ballroom in your rags with a mop on your head while a footman asks who's double-parked their zucchini on the lawn. So get outa there in good time.

CINDERS
Midnight? That's shit! I'll barely be coming up by midnight. Fuck's sake!

FAIRY
Take it or leave it kiddo. Now, have a great night and don't do anything I wouldn't do!

CINDERS
I want some Princely peen and you're a lesbian.

FAIRY
Yeah but I get very drunk... Miley, get set go!

The carriage leaves. Epic music underscores this.

FAIRY *(spoken to similar rhythm as the last song)*
Perhaps he'll meet a Prince there,
Perhaps they'll fall in love!
Perhaps they'll run away, spend every day in bed
With rags and... rubber gloves
It's working out quite well but, dearies,
The bar and the toilets call,
I'll see you at the ball!

INTERVAL

256

Louie Westwood as Maude and Christopher James Barley as Nicole in *Tinderella: Cinders Slips it In*. Photo by PBGstudios.

Ellen Butler as The Countess in *Tinderella: Cinders Slips it In*. Photo by PBGstudios.

Scene 7: The palace ballroom

A string quartet can be heard playing. As the audience returns from the interval, BUTTONS asks some of them names and announces them as if arriving. He can give them titles. The PRINCE, next to him, politely welcomes people. MAUDE and NICOLE are the last to arrive. They have dance cards. BUTTONS takes their names.

BUTTONS
Lady Nicole and Lady Maude!

MAUDE (putting her hand up)
Yeah we're here Buttons! Didn't know there'd be a register.

NICOLE is writing on her dance card.

MAUDE
What are you doing?

NICOLE.
Darling we need to get some names on our dance cards, we'll look more popular if we've a few on there already.

MAUDE
Oh, a man filled me in in the queue. (She spots a man in the audience) Look, this one's fit, you should put him down.

NICOLE
Very well. Sir, your wardrobe's out of date, your hair's out of fashion and your face is out of a medical textbook. What do you think?

MAUDE
I think people in glass houses shouldn't throw orgies. *(Spots her favourite in the audience)* Oh you got in! Now [name] you know I would nom you down with chips and prosecco but I need you to give me a bit of space tonight.

CHARMING
Buttons, did you manage to get me anything?

BUTTONS *(slipping him a little bag of white powder)*
Yeah here you go, happy birthday.

CHARMING
(Excited) And oh my god fiasco! You managed to drag a few gays along! Not one showed up last time.

BUTTONS
Well I told you not to clash with the Bette Midler gig. (To the room), Ladies and Gentlemen!

MAUDE
Ooh get that, you were just the boys and girls before, did your balls drop in the interval?

BUTTONS
May I humbly present his majesty, Commander in Chief of the armed forces, Protector of the Sartorially Correct Virgin Mary, and winner of the nicest despot competition 2012, King Ludwig!

The KING enters, gracefully and proudly in nothing but underpants, socks, shoes and a bowtie.

KING
Greetings, greetings, welcome to my son's birthday ball! Now, I promised I wouldn't embarrass him - didn't I Charming - but I'm sure he won't mind my reminding you all that we're hoping for a little royal romance! Why are some of them laughing Buttons?

BUTTONS
You're a king, sir. They're nervous, so they're imagining you naked.

KING
I'm glad I had the shirt made from the same stuff. Light as air. (To MAUDE and NICOLE) Ladies, are you sophisticated enough to see it?

MAUDE
If you wanna show us it your Maj, you go ahead.

THE FAIRY enters.

FAIRY
Hey kids, turns out a fairy can swoon,
Some of the girls here, I'm dripping!
I left young Cinders in the ladies room,
He's fixing his breasts, they keep slipping.
I wish I'd made more effort in fact,
Though I ain't one for salons and facials,
I expected a barn dance in some old rundown shack
But this palace is fucking... palatial!

BUTTONS
Welcome m'love, can I take your name?

FAIRY
It wouldn't suit you honey.

BUTTONS
I need to announce you.

FAIRY
No worries kid, The Duchess of Cambridge.

The FAIRY enters the ballroom and passes immediately to the other side, exiting.

BUTTONS
The Duchess of Cambridge! (Realising this isn't true) Hang on. Wait! Wait!

BUTTONS exits following the FAIRY. NICOLE goes towards CHARMING.

MAUDE
Where are you going? Wait!

MAUDE runs after her.

NICOLE
Your royal highness, many happy returns.

MAUDE
Ain't you got a lovely pad.

CHARMING
You're kind. (He takes a hand each) Have you had a nose about?

NICOLE
Oh, your highness, the gallery!

MAUDE
You even got a rare Blue Mary.

CHARMING
Sometimes it feels as though the portraits are following me round the room.

NICOLE
And who can blame them ahahahahaha!

NICOLE laughs far too hard and for too long. MAUDE smiles with weary patience. CHARMING tries to retrieve his hands, they won't let go. BUTTONS enters with a tray of food crossing the stage, exiting the opposite side.

BUTTONS
Canapés!

MAUDE
Yeah see you, bye.

MAUDE follows BUTTONS, exits.

CHARMING
Well it's been a pleasure to meet you.

NICOLE
Likewise.

BUTTONS enters with a now-empty canapé tray waving a hand in pain. MAUDE follows, chewing.

BUTTONS
She bit me!

BUTTONS exits the opposite side of the stage. MAUDE approaches the KING. The COUNTESS enters

KING
Oh! I was wondering where you'd got to.

COUNTESS
Just settling in - I mean, looking around, my darling. (To MAUDE) Go and mingle, Maude. Remember, smile and don't talk too much.

MAUDE joins NICOLE and CHARMING.

MAUDE
I tell you what your Maj, I'll let you marry me if you can find my gag reflex.

NICOLE
It's funny because she doesn't have one.

MAUDE
I know but maybe it's like only a real prince can find it.

CHARMING
Ah, like the Princess and the pea.

MAUDE
Well, whatever it takes.

COUNTESS
I know how challenging it is to be a single parent. My daughters, sir, well, two finer young women Slutvia has not seen. (a pause) Are you alright?

KING
Yes sorry I'm just trying to make sense of that sentence, it was a bit oddly structured.

COUNTESS
Either of them would make Charming the perfect consort.

KING
He does like a cocktail.

THE FAIRY enters

FAIRY
Will you look at this place, it's insane.
Everything's gorgeous and old – (to an audience member) like you sir!
I guess that's the thing when you reign
Look, even the switches are gold!

She shows a light switch she's stolen.

The Prince might be pretty but don't get erected
They're taking you all for fools
They don't know hard work, they ain't even elected,
They just rule and rule and-

KING
Young lady.

FAIRY
Oh my god oh my god he's coming this way – I can't help it, I'm American we go nuts for em - how do you do your royal highness?

KING
You're enchanting. May I have this dance?

FAIRY
Sure, I ain't using it.

KING
Where is your accent from?

FAIRY
Drama school. And I'm from the States.

KING
America! You let men marry men and women marry women. What next!

FAIRY
Well you definitely see more chihuahuas in bridesmaid dresses.

KING
We only invited Sluts but I'm glad you snuck in. What brings you here.

FAIRY
Oh I heard such... things about your country.

KING
Beats the so-called land of the free I'll bet!

FAIRY
You should give democracy a go.

KING
It's hard enough keeping the critics at bay when you can't be voted out.

FAIRY
Yeah but think how you'd feel if people actually chose you.

KING
And if they didn't? (They dance) This is nice. You know, I'm told I should find a wife of my own.

FAIRY
Who told you that, the husband?

KING
My son

FAIRY
Are you close?

KING
Not quite but if you hold me like than any longer things might get sticky... Are you married?

FAIRY
Me? Hell no. Though we're finally allowed to.

KING
How backward! We've always allowed women to get married. I say, have you ever seen a missile?

FAIRY
Oh my god honey you gotta work on your lines.

NICOLE walks over to CHARMING waving her dance card.

NICOLE
Your highness, I have a little space right here and it would be an honour to have your squiggle in it.

MAUDE waving her dance card pushes her out of the way.

MAUDE
Oi! I got two gaps and I want him to fill them both.

She pulls CHARMNG close, holds him so he can't escape and starts to dance. CINDERS enters now dressed as a woman.

CINDERS
Hello boys and girls! How do I look? I hope they're not too tricksy on the door.

BUTTONS enters and walks over to him. He does not recognise him.

BUTTONS
Welcome m'love. What's your name?

CINDERS
Oh that's easy, I'm Cin- oh, uh, um...

BUTTONS
You don't know your own name?

CINDERS
Course I do! It's just foreign and hard to pronounce. I'm Princess... yes, Princess Elsa.

BUTTONS
Ladies and gentlemen. Princess Elsa!

MAUDE has now released CHARMING and everyone looks at CINDRS.

MAUDE
Look at that.

NICOLE
Bit manly if you ask me.

MAUDE
Big hands. You know what that means.

NICOLE
Mmm. Good at pottery.

The KING walks over to CINDERS

KING
My dear, welcome, welcome. Did you travel far?

CINDER
A fair distance, yes.

KING
You must be frozen.

CINDER
Let it go, I'm fine.

KING
Let me warm you up.

The COUNTESS marches over and pushes CINDERS away, she takes the KING's hand.

COUNTESS
Why don't you go over there and meet the Prince dear?

CINDERS wanders over to CHARMING.

CINDERS
(Aside) It's him! (To CHARMING) Your majesty. What's a girl got to do to get a drink round here?

PRINCE
Oh yes allow me.

The others are now talking, CHARMING walks to the side of the room, CINDERS follows, he taps CHARMING on the shoulder. CHARMING turns around. CINDERS takes off his wig.

CINDERS
It's me.

He replaces his wig.

CHARMING
You poor thing is it chemo? Are you here with the My Last Wish people?

CINDERS removes the wig again.

CINDERS
It's me!

CINDERS replaces the wig.

CHARMING
Good lord you're a fellow. Ah! One of those drag thingies I saw in England. Place called the O2. Taylor something.

CINDERS
It doesn't matter. It was nice to meet you.

CHARMING
Wait! The boy with the enormous mouse! Audacious! But you disappeared that morning.

CINDERS
An old woman made me get wood for her.

CHARMING
(Aside) He's bi, this is monumental! (Beat) Princess Elsa, allow me to show you around the palace.

CINDERS
Fucking hell. I mean, it would be a pleasure your... um

MAUDE
I wanna see the palace.

NICOLE
And I.

CHARMING
Sorry ladies, tonight's tour is full. Come back tomorrow at fuck off o'clock.

He holds out his hand. CINDERS takes it. They exit. The KING slaps his hands ever so excitedly.

KING
It's worked. It's worked! Buttons!!

BUTTONS enters

KING
My son has found the perfect princess!

BUTTONS
What? Brilliant! Ladies and gentlemen, please join us on the terrace for the fireworks!

All exit. CINDERS and CHARMING enter.

SONG: A LOVE SONG

This feels like an accident,
Destiny could not have meant
For me to stumble into you twice.
And because we're gay,
We've had to steal away
The secret somehow makes it twice as nice.

And in the morning I'll remember you,
Wonder how soon I should text you,
I can imagine saying I love you, some day...

I want to hang with you, enjoy your kiss your laughter,
Finger you, and smell my finger after,
And every part of you could be my favourite feature,
I want to rim you like I'm some kind of burrowing creature.

Right now you're my only thought,
I don't care if we get caught,
You make me want to break all the rules.
Might be because I'm high,
I want to feel your thigh,
Until I find your lovely Crown Jewels.

And in the evening I'll see you again,
You can choose the where and when,
But don't you dare wank before then, okay?

I want to hang with you, enjoy your kiss your laughter,
Finger you , and smell my finger after,
And every part of you could be my favourite feature,
I want to rim you like I'm some kind of burrowing creature.

I would eat your shit for breakfast,
You could split me clean in two,
You can fuck me till my hole's a wreck first,
Then I'll take both fists for you,
I'll be your prince and I'll be your slave,
If you'll be my wettest dream,
I won't let you leave my bed,
Til it looks like a murder scene.

I want to hang with you... [etc]

CHARMING
And do you know the best thing, Cinders? In the theatre, a song like that is really a metaphor for a sexual encounter.

CINDERS
So... we've had sex?

CHARMING
I just came all over your chest.

CINDERS
Brilliant.

CHARMING
You're not leaving till dawn!

CINDERS
Of course! Wait, no, shit, I can't.

CHARMING
Of course! You probably have one of those job thingies don't you. How exotic.

CINDERS
It's not really a job. I just have a load of duties and in return I get a roof over my head.

CHARMING
But darling, that's exactly same as me!

CINDERS smiles, takes CHARMING's hand and goes to exit.

CHARMING
Where are we going?

CINDERS
You're going to find me a metaphorical towel.

They exit.

The lights come back up. Empty bottles on stage. MAUDE is slumped on the floor in a very unladylike position holding a keg of ale from which she drinks.

NICOLE is holding a bottle of champagne and is seductively dancing around a pole or statue. Or maybe she's sat on some stairs and crying. The FAIRY GODMOTHER enters.

FAIRY
Hey kids I been searching out there,
But Cinders is nowhere to be seen... (looks around her)
Fuck me, it's like a Williamsburg house-share
On the day after Halloween.

The KING and COUNTESS enter.

COUNTESS
Such wonderful fireworks. I do enjoy a few good bangs on the terrace of an evening. (to the FAIRY) It *is* you, you tipsy gypsy! Your majesty, this woman is a wi-

KING
Not now, dear. (He prods MAUDE) Are you alright? It must be Buttons' home brewed vodka. Good lord, it must be late. (He looks at a clock) Oh, it's only just coming up to midnight!

FAIRY
Fuck! Where'd he go boys and girls?

The FAIRY exits the way they point. CHARMING and CINDERS enter holding hands

CHARMING
Daddy, thank you. The ball was a fabulous idea.

KING
Don't they look happy! Could there be wedding bells? I can't wait to retire.

COUNTESS
What??

KING
Oh yes. As soon as Charming marries I intend to resign. Hand things over. Let him be King.

COUNTESS
Abdicate???

KING
Thank you yes that's the word! I'll probably get an allotment.

The FAIRY enters. She coughs gently next to CINDERS who ignores her. She coughs louder, still nothing. She coughs very loudly - no change. She kicks CINDERS, he turns around. The FAIRY taps her watch. CINDERS assumes she's asking for the time.

CINDERS
I've no idea sorry, I don't have watch. (Beat) Shit! (To CHARMING) Sorry. Sorry.

CINDERS runs, he does not look where he is going and runs into the COUNTESS.

COUNTESS
You! I knew it!

CINDERS runs, the COUNTESS rugby tackles him. CINDERS falls. He pulls away. The COUNTESS grabs his feet, CHARMING joins her and pulls off a shoe. CINDERS pulls away and exits.

KING
Good effort, Countess. A little violent...

COUNTESS
We can't have your son's true love disappearing into the night.

CHARMING
Why would... she do that?

MAUDE
Plenty more fish, your maj.

CHARMING
I don't eat fish. I think you'd all better leave. The ball's over.

The FAIRY exits, NICOLE drags MAUDE out.

COUNTESS
If there's anything-

CHARMING
There isn't. No one can help.

COUNTESS
Then goodnight. I'll see you soon.

She starts to exit but hovers by the door. CHARMING picks up the shoe.

CHARMING
How will I ever find... her?

KING
Perhaps she left some token behind? Something that might lead you to her.

CHARMING
I don't think so.

KING
Are you quite sure...?

263

CHARMING
Oh! Of course! Daddy you genius! I've still got the condom! It's bloody filthy, I'll place it on a cushion and take it from house to house until I find- No, wait, that won't work, this is hopeless.

Unseen, the FAIRY appears briefly from the wings holding a torch which she points at the shoe. CHARMING looks at it as though it is magic.

CHARMING
This shoe, it's such an unusual shape. Almost unique... Father if I find the owner of this shoe can I marry them?

KING
Yes, yes of course you can my boy.

CHARMING
Then that's what I'll do. Whoever this shoe fits will be the one I marry.

The KING and CHARMING exit.

COUNTESS
Oh will you now. There's only one person you're going to marry now, Prince Chargrill. We'll live in bliss as king and queen – until you go the same way as my other unfortunate husbands. Then, Slutvia will be mine!

She laughs and exits.

Scene 8: The sisters' dressing room

NICOLE and MAUDE are on a daybed having collapsed there. Nicole is asleep, Maude in a hungover stupor. Birdsong. NICOLE's hand goes a-wandering along MAUDE's body. MAUDE looks perturbed. In the distance, church bells.

NICOLE (dreaming, drowsily)
Darling we'll be late for church. Late for our wedding. How naughty to spend this night together.

MAUDE lifts an arm and gently hits NICOLE without looking. NICOLE wakes with a grunt.

NICOLE (in hungover pain)
Oh god my head.

MAUDE
Oh god my stomach.

NICOLE
Yes dear I'm surprised you only just noticed it.

MAUDE
That buffet was sat out for too long... Can you get pregnant from a quiche?

NICOLE
At least we can say we've been to the palace. At least we can say we danced!

MAUDE
Yeah that's true. For what it's worth, you led me very well.

NICOLE
Thank you.

MAUDE
Those canapés were massive I nearly choked on one.

NICOLE
It was a hog roast and you know it.

MAUDE
I know, I'm just being cute.

MAUDE starts patting the bed around her, searching.

NICOLE
What are you looking for?

MAUDE
Just double checking.

NICOLE
What for?

MAUDE
Dunno. The prince. An aristocrat. A waiter. The taxi driver... The pizza boy... Pizza...

NICOLE
May I knife you?

MAUDE
What the fuck?

NICOLE
No not knife.

MAUDE
Spoon, you prick. Yeah go on. (pause) I didn't think we'd *both* come home empty handed. I mean I didn't expect marriage or nothing. Not really. Just a bit of sex with someone who can string a sentence together. Someone who's seen a bit of the world, you know? I ain't expecting a sunset but I'd like some bigger horizons. I'm tired of putting me ankles in the air just for tradesmen and village boys.

Nicole contemplates this.

NICOLE
What ankles?

The COUNTESS enters.

COUNTESS
Time to get up!

The COUNTESS opens the curtains. The girls scream.

COUNTESS
I'll open the window too, that'll blow the cobwebs from between your thighs. Go and have breakfast. Get Cinders to knock up something fatty.

NICOLE
Mummy don't call her that.

MAUDE
I might cook.

NICOLE
Are you quite alright?

MAUDE
I was listening to them recipes on the radio. Sounded fun. Learn a skill. Be self-sufficient.

COUNTESS
Cinders will cook for you. Now, quickly, we're missing the king's broadcast.

265

NICOLE fumbles for the radio. We hear the jingle, then the King.

KING (VOICEOVER)
What a marvellous night, thank you all for coming to the ball! Now, somebody left something behind didn't they! That's right. We've found some keys, a USB stick, and something called a Nandos Card, so if anyone- What is it, Charming? - Ah, yes! And the shoe! The beautiful thief who stole my son's heart ran away and a left a shoe in its place. That was rather good wasn't it. Charming and I will travel the land seeking the lovely foot it belongs to.

The women gasp.

KING (VOICEOVER)
We'll see you very soon. Mine's a milk and two sugars and my son likes a frappucino.

COUNTESS
Girls, breakfasts.

MAUDE
I'll see you down there, I need a shit.

MAUDE goes to the en-suite, NICOLE exits the other way. The COUNTESS fantasizes.

COUNTESS
Good morning my Prince, what a night we've had together. The servants have brought our teas. Here, let me sugar them. What? I'm sweet enough already? You silly thing. Alright, just one, just one little kiss...! (Snapping out of it) We all know who that shoe belongs to don't we. Well, he wants to go abroad, it's the least I can do to help hurry him on his way.

She goes to the door.

Cinders! Be an angel and pop up here.

She goes to the telephone and speaks into it. It's a very old-fashioned phone.

Slutvia 352. (Pause) No it's not a crime show, it's a number, connect me. (Pause) These fingers don't dial darling. (Pause) There you are. It's me. Make the lorry ready. I need to do an extra trafficking. Today.

She hangs up. CINDERS enters.

CINDERS
I've put out the rubbish and cooked breakfast and I've cleaned the stables and groomed the horses.

COUNTESS
You work yourself too hard. Sit down with me and let us talk.

CINDERS
But I've had my one-minute break.

COUNTESS
Nonsense, come and sit next to step mummy.

CINDERS sits. The COUNTESS places a hand rather intimately on his thigh. A long pause as the COUNTESS forgets everything apart from said thigh.

CINDERS
Countess?

COUNTESS
Oh! Yes. I promised that one day I would pay for you to go to London. Well, today my dearest boy. Today is the day.

CINDERS
Today?

COUNTESS
I thought you'd be happy.

CINDERS
I just... I don't have anything nice to wear.

COUNTESS
Head to Lewisham or somewhere, you'll be fine. But perhaps you'd rather stay and work here. Although I mean, it's not as though some, I don't know, some prince or something just for example is really going to come along and risk everything for a tattered, illiterate servant is it?

CINDERS
No, you're right. I should say goodbye to Buttons.

COUNTESS
No! No time, come along, keep the plot moving, piss off.

CINDERS
Who'll look after Maude and Nicole?

COUNTESS
Why should you care? They wouldn't care about you. No, sometimes life just doesn't work out. Better to cut your losses and leave. Your transport is outside.

CINDERS goes to the window, bends over to look out.

COUNTESS
I will miss that view.

CINDERS
An old lorry?!

COUNTESS
A *whole* lorry!

MILEY enters holding a wedge of cheese. The COUNTESS screams MILEY drops the cheese.

COUNTESS
A mouse! A horrid hairy mouse!

CINDERS
Oh! Yeah, little tiny mouse I didn't see her there. Come on Miley you better find Billy Ray.

COUNTESS
No no, no mice in the UK! Some woman called Theresa was on the news, frothing about vermin[44]. Off you go. I'll see she's taken care of.

CINDERS exits.

COUNTESS
I'll take care of her alright.

---

[44] Theresa May's reign at the Home Office is remembered for her obsession with curtailing immigration. Her "hostile environment" programme, aimed at forcing out people without leave to remain, was rolled out with such haste and zeal that it resulted in the harassment and deportation of Windrush Generation UK residents who were legally entitled to live in the country they'd called home for decades.

MAUDE pulls aside a curtain and watches from the toilet she's sat on as the COUNTESS takes from her pocket a little bottle of green liquid. It glows. She picks up the cheese.

COUNTESS
You poor thing you dropped your cheese!

MILEY wipes her eyes. The COUNTESS spills a few drops of the potion on it.

COUNTESS
Cinders has gone to London but we can be friends. Look, I have your cheese. Go on, downstairs I'll bring it with me.

MILEY exits.

COUNTESS
Well I don't want her vomit on the carpet.

She laughs and exits. MAUDE emerges still clutching a loo roll.

MAUDE
Boys and girls! I got no time to lose!

MAUDE goes to exit, pauses.

MAUDE
Oh hang on.

MAUDE goes back to the toilet. We hear a flushing sound.

BLACKOUT.

Scene 9: The clearing in the woods

Posters are stuck to trees on either side of the stage with a picture of the FAIRY on them. Beneath the image, the words Wanted: Witch.

FAIRY
My fairy sense is in overdrive!
I don't even know if the boy is alive,
And this hangover, Christ, go fuck the world,
But at least I'm safe, ain't that right boys and girls?

The audience hopefully point out the poster.

FAIRY
Oh! Look at that they're recruiting for a fairy! I might apply. Wait - what the furry fuck?

She takes the poster down. She goes to the other tree to remove the other poster. The COUNTESS enters carrying more posters and pins one to the first tree. She stealthily crosses the stage at the back as the FAIRY crosses the front to the new poster.

FAIRY
What's going on boys and girls?

Lots of "Who?" and "Where?" and "Behind you". Eventually she sees the COUNTESS.

FAIRY
What the hell?

COUNTESS
Hell is exactly where you should be you satanic sorceress. These are all over town. People are talking. There are men with tuning forks!

FAIRY
Do you mean pitchforks?

COUNTESS
There are men with pitchforks! You'll be hunted. You'll be found. You know what the king thinks of witchcraft.

FAIRY
Actually I don't, we cut that bit of dialogue but I get the picture... How did you get *my* picture?

COUNTESS
That ridiculous photo booth at the Prince's party.

FAIRY
Dammit.

The COUNTESS shows some more wanted posters with funny pictures of the FAIRY pulling faces, snorting coke, wearing the King's crown, doing a sexy pose, etc.

FAIRY
You won't get away with it.

She waves her wand, The COUNTESS leaps forward and grabs it.

COUNTESS
Au contraire, you little shit.

The FAIRY punches the COUNTESS. They fight. The COUNTESS pushes her against a tree. The FAIRY is groggy and does not seem to know what is going on. MAUDE enters.

MAUDE
How could you mummy?

COUNTESS
Go home you silly girl, I didn't raise you to question me.

MAUDE
Let her go!

COUNTESS (bored)
Come and stop me then.

MAUDE walks over to her. Once she is there the COUNTESS kneecaps MAUDE in the groin. MAUDE screams. The COUNTESS pushes her against a tree with the FAIRY. The COUNTESS gets some rope and a gag out of her bag.

COUNTESS
I heard these are *de rigueur* in Vauxhall.

She ties the FAIRY and MAUDE to a tree trunk.

MAUDE
Mummy how can you do this. I'm your daughter.

COUNTESS
Are you? I mean, really, are you? Sometimes I swear they got the babies mixed up at the hospital. I mean how on God's earth did something like you come out of someone like me.

MAUDE
Well I was a lot smaller...

COUNTESS
Shut up!

She gags her.

268

FAIRY
Give me my wand, it's expensive and rare!

COUNTESS
Don't be defensive, I really don't care.
You can have it as soon as you've cast me a spell.
You've seen Cinders' weird foot? Make mine like that as well!

FAIRY
You gone completely wackadoodle lady? He's got horrible feet. If that's all you want no problem.

MAUDE is furiously shaking her head but the FAIRY takes no notice. The COUNTESS stands behind a tree stump, she waves the wand over her foot as the FAIRY casts a spell.

FAIRY
Come on spirits, make like Harry Potter,
Give the bitch one of Cinder's trotters.

The COUNTESS stamps and dances as if her foot is hot. She then steps out from behind the tree stump. It's the same shape as CINDERS' foot.

COUNTESS
Excellent.

FAIRY
My wand?

She throws the wand in the opposite direction.

COUNTESS
Oh fuck-a-woopsie look at that I've dropped it. Sorry! But I will give you this.

She gags the FAIRY

COUNTESS
As if we hadn't had enough terrible gags already. Righty-ho, now, I'd better spruce myself for Prince Chinless. What do we think he'd prefer - flats, heels or just a strap-on? Fear not, I'll be back later with some angry townspeople. Yes, I think it will be a nice evening for a barbecue! Hahahaha!

She exits.

BUTTONS enters from the opposite side. He is dishevelled. He does not the Fairy Godmother. The FAIRY GODMOTHER moves around trying to attract his attention but he does not notice.

BUTTONS
Hello boys and girls. I've been in the woods all night with a couple of the King's footmen. *(He indicates something big)* And now I know why they're called footmen.

He indicates a length of twelve inches with his hands, then tidies up his clothing.

BUTTONS
Cinders never turned up at the ball you know.

He sees the poster the COUNTESS put up.

BUTTONS
Witchcraft? She looks familiar... I might take this, I could earn myself a few twinks as a reward if I find her. You haven't seen her have you boys and girls?

She's behind you! BUTTONS turns around and sees the FAIRY. He looks at the tree with the FAIRY tied to it, then the tree with the poster on it and back again a few times. The FAIRY moans.

BUTTONS
Shush love I'm concentrating. Oh! Should I take the gag off them?

He takes the gag off the FAIRY and MAUDE

FAIRY
Untie me, Cinders is in trouble.

BUTTONS
Cinders?

MAUDE (to the FAIRY)
What did you do that to her foot for! The Prince is going to marry whoever the shoe fits!

FAIRY
Ohhhhhhh fuck. She's after the Prince!

BUTTONS
Charming.

MAUDE
I know, right?

BUTTONS
Ha she's got no chance. He's drained more gay dick than The Stag's urinals.

FAIRY
Everyone help, or I'll never get my wings back. Listen, we got to get Cinders and the Prince back together.

BUTTONS
Cinders don't even know him.

FAIRY
They did a whole song about bumsex and everything. We have to help him. Pick my wand up. Over there.

BUTTONS does.

BUTTON
You're not a witch, you're delusional. It's just a myth to control people. It's tosh.

FAIRY
Yes but I'm a fairy! Wave the wand, and watch.
Honey, this fairy don't have to fake it,
Take a look at the boys and girls naked.

BUTTONS looks at the audience, he is shocked.

BUTTONS
Oh my god. *(To one man in audience)* I had one like that mate but I had to get it taken out cos it went septic.

MAUDE
Hello *(To her favourite audience member)*. Nice to see you let grow out all natural.

FAIRY
Hey. Untie us so we can save Cinders.

BUTTONS
But then he'll go off with the Prince.

FAIRY
Yep. Cinders don't love you kid. Sorry.

BUTTONS
But we've fooled around and everything.

FAIRY
That's how gays make friends. Attenborough did a thing on it. Boys and girls, if by any chance we got any gays in tonight, put your hands up if you're here with a friend you've slept with.

BUTTONS
All right.

BUTTONS unties the FAIRY and MAUDE. She grabs her wand.

FAIRY
Come on.

The FAIRY exits

BUTTONS
Yeah I guess...

MAUDE
Chin up duck. I know it's crap when you love someone and he don't love you. We can't all be as lucky as me and [audience member's name]. But there's plenty of boys out there.

BUTTONS
I know.

MAUDE
It just ain't your story this time. Come on.

MAUDE and BUTTONS exit

Scene 10: The sisters' dressing room

Nicole has bare feet and is admiring them.

NICOLE
Why does it have to be a shoe boys and girls? I have such pretty feet. Perhaps he'll take one look and decide he needn't bother with the shoe palaver.

The COUNTESS enters.

COUNTESS
Darling are you trying to count to twenty again? Look sharp, they're here!

NICOLE pulls her slippers on. The KING and CHARMING enter. CHARMING has the shoe.

COUNTESS
King Ludwig, Prince Charming. You remember my daughter Nicole.

NICOLE
Lovely bash.

COUNTESS
Shall we get down to business.

KING
Quite right. Now, I've still got the USB stick.

CHARMING
Oh look really must we go through this?

NICOLE
I feel the same!

NICOLE grabs the shoe and flings it across the room.

NICOLE
Why let our love be decided by a silly shoe!

KING
Sorry dear thing, you must.

NICOLE fetches the shoe.

NICOLE
I can see you're nervous but don't worry, if it doesn't fit we can come to some arrangement.

CHARMING kneels reluctantly offering the shoe. NICOLE extends a foot.

COUNTESS
Take off your slipper, child.

NICOLE
I'm ticklish.

She removes a slipper and tries to put the shoe on, screaming as it tickles. She cannot get her foot into it, and she tries to walk around as if it fits.

COUNTESS
Ah well, worth a try. Take it off before you put a joint out.

NICOLE
Nonsense mummy, it's like a reunion with an old friend!

COUNTESS
Yes, one that's aged rather better than you.

CHARMING
Look, if there's nobody else.

COUNTESS
Actually there is.

All gasp

CHARMING
There is? Who?

COUNTESS
Moi!

NICOLE
Oh! (beat) Who?

COUNTESS
Yours truly.

NICOLE
Oh! (beat) Who?

CHARMING
I'd remember if we'd spent time together at the ball.

COUNTESS
But darling! That scene was just the edited highlights. The ball lasted for several hours and there were 500 guests, we could hardly stage the whole thing in a railway arch.[45]

CHARMING
Dammit she's smart.

She takes the shoe and tries it on. It fits.

CHARMING
It's impossible!

---

[45] The theatre was housed in a railway arch. In 2018 it upsized, taking over two connected arches.

COUNTESS
Sweetheart, there are only about six common shoe sizes it's hardly a revelation. Still, you made the rules.

KING
You've found your bride!

COUNTESS
(Girly) Gosh this all so sudden! (beat) Right, shall we?

CHARMING
But-

COUNTESS
I won't hear of it, you can buy me a ring later

CHARMING
We can't just marry, we need a church.

COUNTESS
Your father can make a decree to change that.

CHARMING
Only a priest can conduct marriages.

COUNTESS
Then let's change the rules so that a [audience member's job from scene 3] can conduct a marriage[46].

KING
Ah! But *this* man's a [ditto]!

COUNTESS
And your majesty, if you could make one final decree, making the Prince's new wife the official joint ruler of Slutvia, it would be appreciated. Think of your retirement – your allotment...

KING
I, I don't know...

CHARMING
There must be a mistake

COUNTESS
Perfect fit I think.

She waves her foot in the air

KING
Very well. I decree that a [*audience member's job*] can conduct a wedding, I decree that weddings can now be

conducted at Annie Hall, and I decree that whoever marries Charming will be joint ruler of Slutvia.

CHARMING
No! Cinders where are you? When will I see you again?

COUNTESS
That's the three decrees. Let's get on with it.

BUTTONS, MAUDE and the FAIRY rush in

BUTTONS
Stop!

MAUDE
Hold it!

COUNTESS
Hurry up there's a biological clock ticking here.

MAUDE
It's just your pacemaker. Where's the shoe, I want a go.

COUNTESS
The last thing I want in my shoe is your improbably-named athletes foot.

MAUDE ducks and pulls the shoe off the COUNTESS

KING
Strictly she ought to have a go.

CHARMING
Oh please really daddy, that's enough, I told you, it's not going to be the ugly sisters.

MAUDE
You what?

NICOLE
Who's he talking about?

MAUDE
The ugly sisters? What a shitty thing to say.

CHARMING
Forgive me.

NICOLE
Does he mean us?

CHARMING
It - look I'm sorry I didn't mean it. I'm just-

MAUDE
Fucking hell. I'm winded by that I am.

KING
It was just a little bit of harmless...

<hr>

[46] On some nights, watching our fabulous countess Ellen trying to remember what job the audience member had said was a bonus delight.

NICOLE
Banter.

KING
Exactly!

MAUDE
Banter? I'll give you banter you cunt.

NICOLE
Maude!

MAUDE
Check your fucking privilege, twinkle. You wouldn't talk about boys like that. I mean, you'd think with your schedule you might find time for the gym, I seen a perkier arse on a month-old snowman but I don't say nothing, do I your maj? Jesus. I might become a republican now.

NICOLE
You haven't pulled a pint in your life. And for god's sake it's highness for a prince, majesty for a king.

COUNTESS
I could have sworn you had two shoes when you got back from the ball.

MAUDE
I carry a spare. Now!

She prepares to try on the shoe.

NICOLE
Oh I see.

MAUDE
Well he's cute and he lives in a palace. In for a penny, in for a pounding.

MAUDE tries to put the shoe on.

MAUDE
Ha! Like a glove.

NICOLE
It's a bit bloody tight.

MAUDE
Not something you'll hear her say often.

NICOLE
How dare you!

MAUDE
She's like the loading bay on the Death Star.

COUNTESS
Give me my shoe!

BUTTONS
It's not your shoe!

FAIRY
She made me change the shape of her foot.

COUNTESS
Your majesty. I hate to spoil the occasion but I insist this woman is removed. She practices magic.

KING
A witch! Yes - she enchanted me at the ball.

FAIRY
Your majesty. Your son is in love with someone who is miles away.

MAUDE (nudging Nicole)
Miles away - maybe it is you, Nic.

FAIRY
I can cast a spell to bring that person here.

CHARMING
Yes!

KING
Magic is banned! We're a modern nation!

FAIRY
Oh please, I seen your wallpaper.

CHARMING
Why don't you ask the people daddy? See if the Sluts think magic should be allowed.

KING
Well... I suppose we can call it an experiment in democracy. Sluts, would you like this witch to cast her spell?

Yes!

COUNTESS
Oh no they don't.

Oh yes we do.

COUNTESS
Oh no they don't

Oh yes we do.

KING
Marvellous stuff! What happens now, I'm a little confused.

BUTTONS
You go with the majority.

KING
What if they're wrong?

BUTTONS
Then it's not your fault.

KING
How clever! Go ahead young lady.

FAIRY
Cinders, we're getting you out of that van,
Get yourself home to marry your man!

KING
Was that it?

FAIRY
It was either that or the one where I rhyme truck with fuck.

CINDERS enters, he has his top off and his shorts are around his ankles. He has one slipper on.

CHARMING
Cinders!

CINDERS
Charming!

CHARMING
Why are you...?

CINDERS
I was thrown in the back of a dark lorry with a load of young gay men. It's like calves to a teat, we don't need instructing.

COUNTESS
Your spell is quite useless, now what's your plan?
This is no princess, just a sad little man!

CHARMING
What's going on?

BUTTON
Try the shoe on mate.

CINDERS
You found it! Wonder why it didn't turn back into a slipper like the other one.

FAIRY
Yeah it's a bit inconsistent that.

CINDERS picks up the shoe which the COUNTESS took off. It fits. All gasp.

KING
But he's a he.

CHARMING
Yes daddy. I'm marrying in a man. I'm gay.

KING
Sluts can't be gay.

BUTTONS
But gays can be Sluts. Equal rights innit.

NICOLE
Cinders, congratulations you darling darling boy.

CINDERS
Eh?

MAUDE
You won't forget your adoring sisters I hope.

NICOLE
It's wonderful news.

BUTTONS
(Sadly) Yeah. Wonderful news.

CINDERS
Buttons. Don't be upset. We'll still be mates.

BUTTINS
Mates...

CHARMING
Even better Buttons, you'll be his servant! I'll tell you what old chap. You can do the PR for the wedding. It will be a world first! A gay royal wedding.

KING
The fucking left-wingers won't know whether to protest or celebrate. I'm game.

BUTTONS
My two best mates are getting married and they want me to be the PR?

CINDERS
And the entertainment.

BUTTONS
I can pre-program a DJ set and all if you got any celebs coming that want to have a go without any skill or previous experience.

CHARMING
Out of the park!

BUTTONS
Right... Well, I'll get started. See you later boys and girls.

NICOLE
For god's sake you bloody fools!! He's your best friend!

CINDERS and CHARMING
Ohhhhh.

CINDERS
Buttons, will you be my best man?

CHARMING
And will you be *my* best man?

BUTTONS
I'd love to!

CHARMING
But if you could still do the PR.

BUTTONS
My pleasure, Charming.

BUTTONS exits.

KING
Gay! But we sent you to such a good boarding school. Well so long as you're not just confused. Some men are very impressive. *(Wistful)* Donald Trump...

CINDERS
Wait! I must tell Miley I'm back! Miley!

COUNTESS
Oh! I hate to break it to you but poor Miley passed away.

CINDERS
What...? Miley!

MILEY runs in. The COUNTESS screams and lets go.

FAIRY
Oh yeah I forgot to mention why we were late.

MAUDE
She dumped Miley in the woods.

BUTTONS
She was poisoned!

FAIRY
So I made her a little potion out of herbs and pine nuts. And hey pesto.

COUNTESS
It was an accident!

MAUDE
I saw you!

COUNTESS
Oh please it's a fucking mouse.

KING
They're always a little larger than you remember aren't they. Countess Volga, you're an evil woman. You are not wanted in Slutvia.

FAIRY
Hey your magistrate if you'll allow me I know a spell.

KING
Be my guest.

The FAIRY waves her wand. We hear a truck approaching.

COUNTESS
The lorry! No!

FAIRY
It's time for you to face damnation,
You'll spend your life on that kale plantation.

There is a gust of wind. The COUNTESS is blown away screaming. The truck revs and leaves.

NICOLE
Mummy!

MAUDE
Good riddance. She was holding us back.

NICOLE
But what will we do?

MAUDE
I dunno. Get a job.

NICOLE
We can't do anything.

MAUDE
We got a 13 bedroom house in a country with zero inheritance tax. We'll sell it, buy a nice little two-bed and get ourselves an education.

NICOLE
An education...?

MAUDE
Yes.

NICOLE
...Frat boys!

CINDERS
Would you like to be my bridesmaids?

MAUDE
Always the bridesmaid.

NICOLE
But bridesmaids on TV! Come on Maude.

MAUDE
Where?

NICOLE
We have a new squats regime and it starts now.

MAUDE
Can you spot me?

NICOLE
Yes darling, in the dark and a mile off. Follow me.

MAUDE and NICOLE leave. CINDERS gets out his phone and starts looking at it.

CINDERS
It's working!

CHARMING
What are you doing?

CINDERS
Sorry, old habits

KING
That's a mobile phone!

CHARMING
Oh Daddy. Everyone's got one, there are illegal networks all over Slutvia! I used mine to find men. Look *(he gets out a phone and uses it as a torch to look at the audience)* There, see? Dozens. You could find yourself a girl. See, with this app. Wait, let me change the settings.

CHARMING shows the KING his phone. The KING looks at the screen.

KING
Good heavens. Maidens just metres away. That's the lady over there - nice use of props, madame. And this one here, dressed as a schoolgirl, is that you? *(He approaches another woman then turns to a man close by)* Oh, no it's you sir.

FAIRY
Listen kitten, I'll be back for the wedding, try and seat me next to a girl with a bit of personality and either a drinking problem or low self esteem. I'm outta here if everyone's happy.

CHARMING
I don't think your mouse looks very happy.

FAIRY
Oh everyone's an expert.

MILEY is crying

CHARMING
What's up with her?

CINDERS
I think I know. Fairy Godmother, I don't suppose you could manage one more spell.

FAIRY
Alright. But I'm kinda spelled out so boys and girls I'll need your help. Can you do that? Yeah you can. Ok, say after me.

I saw a mouse, well it's hardly surprising,
Let's give our Miley a proper downsizing.

MILEY twirls around. She falls behind the bed.

CINDERS
Miley. Miley are you ok.

He runs to the bed, pulls it aside. Miley has vanished.

CINDERS
Miley... And Billy Ray!

He picks them up: both normal, mouse-sized mice, snuggling together.

CINDERS
(To Charming) We don't have to announce it yet, you know. The wedding. If you want to make sure first. I'm not stupid.

KING
Rubbish! Now, go out into that sunshine and stroll hand in hand to the palace. That'll show em.

CINDERS
It'll show them where to throw stones.

KING
Nonsense! You're courting a Prince now.

CHARMING
See you later boys and girls!

CHARMING and CINDERS exit

FAIRY
You ain't got a daughter knocking about I suppose.

KING
Afraid not. I only ever wanted a boy but I haven't been very good at bonding with him. I er, - I don't suppose you'd like to come back to the palace with me and-

FAIRY
Honey you're sweet, but I was kinda planning on finding a bar, sinking a beer and watching some women's tennis.

KING
I have a microbrewery, and a home cinema screen the size of Croatia.

FAIRY
I'll be right along. Go on. Wait in the coach.

The KING exits.

FAIRY
And that's how it ends, with a fabulous wedding,
Well it's never the fights in Ikea over bedding,
Or the threesome that one of them wants to revisit -
That ain't what the marriage campaigns mentioned is it?)

And the world looked on, though the Beeb and CNN,
Saw the crowds and the flags and two nervous young men,
Who grinned from a coach that I made them - so posh!
Till it turned back into a butternut squash.

And a country we laughed at as backward and dumb,
Took a look at itself and what it had become,
And partied and danced in the streets and the bars;
Boys and girls, thanks for coming; with our love - au revoir.

Then a blackout. Then a voiceover.

ANNOUNCER
Ladies and gentlemen! Following a full apology from young King Charming, we are delighted to welcome back to the Eurovision Song Contest... Slutvia!

Dry ice. Epic lighting. Maude and Nicole enter, and perform the following song supported by the rest of the company. It begins ethereally Celtic, before turning into energetic Europop. The rest of the company enter and join in for the last chorus.

SONG: SLUTS ON THE DANCEFLOOR

On the frontiers of Eastern Europe,
Where the sun sets so far ahead,
And the mountains give way to wheat fields,
There our homeland makes its bed,
When the mist clears in the morning,
Hear the song of the Slutvian folk begin,
In our homeland a new day dawning,
God they'll kill us if we don't win,
Please let us win...

I'm gonna be famous,
A citizen of the world,
I'll make you a citizen of me,
Yeah get in me!

I wanna be global,
We're not just two pretty girls,
We're the Keisha and Mutya of Slutvia,
Come on thrill me!

And if you come here just a little bit
Stay just a little bit
See just a little bit more,
We'll make Slutvia right here
Like sluts on the dance floor!

And if you can dance just a little bit
Shout just a little bit
Lunge just a little bit more,
We're gonna burn it up right here
Like sluts on the dance floor!

My face is my passport,
My ass is my invite,
My heart is just bursting out with pride,
And it's so fun!

I got one foot on the stage here,
I got one foot on the moon!
We're gonna be conquering Europe better
Than Napoleon.

And if you come here just a little bit
Stay just a little bit
See just a little bit more,
We'll make Slutvia right here
Like sluts on the dance floor

And if you can dance just a little bit
Shout just a little bit
Lunge just a little bit more,
We're gonna burn it up right here
Like sluts on the dance floor

We're gonna burn it up right here
Burn it up right here
We're gonna burn it up right here
Like sluts on the dance floor.

THE END

Treasure Island: The Curse of the Pearl Necklace

Hugh O'Donnell as Ethel in *Treasure Island: The Curse of the Pearl Necklace*. Photo by Derek Drescher.

Treasure Island: The Curse of the Pearl Necklace

Neither of us had seen Treasure Island adapted as a pantomime. It is occasionally done, and there are plenty of film adaptations, but we revisited (or in Jon's case, visited) Stevenson's thrilling original novel to adapt it directly. Jim's mother became our dame and we threw in a prince, a lot of smut and a sub-Shakespearean story of separated siblings, but hopefully we salvaged enough of what makes the book special, from Jim's yearning for adventure to Ben Gunn's reincarnation as our savage, Miranda. We tried to give the island-set second act, in which the characters are separated from each other in pairs, a continuous farcical momentum in tribute to Stevenson's choreographing of the warring factions on his island.

An inevitable sacrifice on the altar of panto was John Silver, as least as he functions in the book. Silver is one of the greatest literary creations: a mysterious and romantic figure, as seductive as he is terrifying. Stevenson keeps his cards close to his chest, and as a result, the fatherless Jim Hawkins' evolving relationship with the enigmatic Silver is one of the novel's chief joys. But pantomimes need a villain to be overtly wicked from his first appearance – and Silver was the obvious candidate for our villain.

Our pantomimes have tended to go on sale before we've written a single filthy line, which means we decide on a title before we have a script. The subtitle, (a nod to the movie Pirates of the Caribbean: The Curse of the Black Pearl) was Peter Bull's suggestion, and it suggested a way of introducing a touch of the supernatural to the plot.

We tend to call our shows adult pantomimes or gay pantomimes, and slightly resist the "LGBT panto" label they're sometimes given because it makes them seem more representative than they are. But Treasure Island features a trans character, Ethel the Merman, and we hope that - some years on - he doesn't seem too naïve or insensitive an invention. This was also the first of our pantomimes to feature original songs written and composed by Jon.

2014 was the year of the ice bucket challenge, the UK Independence Party were the most successful party in the European Parliament Elections winning 27% of the vote, the much-hyped X Factor musical I Can't Sing opened at the London Palladium only to close after six weeks and two days, and Michael Gove became the Chief Whip, moving from his role of Secretary of State for Education.

Treasure Island: The Curse of the Pearl Necklace

By Jon Bradfield and Martin Hooper
Songs by Jon Bradfield

Based on the novel by Robert Louis Stevenson

Principal Characters
Ethel Merman, a merman called Ethel.
Long John Silver, a pirate and keen gastropub chef.
Sally Hawkins, proprietor of the Royal Bumboy Inn. The Dame.
Jim Hawkins, her son.
Marina, the cook at the Royal Bumboy Inn.
The Captain, a former sea captain, and long-term guest at the Royal Bumboy Inn.
Daryl, the crown prince of Atlantis. He has an Essex accent.
Josephine, the Captain's glamorous actress daughter.
Miranda, the Captain's long-lost, island-dwelling daughter.

Other Characters
Silver's Parrot, who primarily resides on Silver's shoulder
Gorilla
King Neptune, Daryl's dad, heard briefly as a voiceover
Seadogs and Wenches

Josephine and Miranda are to be played by the same actress. The Parrot speaks occasionally. In our production she was voiced by Su Pollard.

The scenes on Treasure Island are theoretically in a number of locations but can be played on the same set.

Treasure Island: The Curse of the Pearl Necklace was first performed at Above The Stag Theatre on 28 November 2014 with the following cast and creative team:

Ethel: Hugh O'Donnell; Long John Silver: Alex Wood; Marina: Briony Rawle; Jim Hawkins: Lucas Livesey; Sally Hawkins: Philip Lawrence; The Captain: Andrew Truluck; Josephine/Miranda: Ellen Butler; Prince Daryl: Luke Webber

Director: Andrew Beckett; Designer: David Shields; Lighting: Elliott Griggs; Musical Arranger/Director: Daniel Johnson; Projections: Maximilien Spielbichler; Associate Designer: Zoë Hurwitz; Poster illustration: Matthew Harding

Scene 1: A rock off the Cornish coast

It's the sort of rock a seal or three might take a nap on, but on this rock sits a merman called Ethel. He has a fish's tale and a man's upper body. His hair is long and unkempt like a surfer. Ethel is Australian.

ETHEL

On a wind-beaten coastline some miles from Penzance
The locals share rumours of lost treasure troves!
And tell tales of adventure, brave deeds and romance -
In a small fishing harbour that's called Michael Cove

It's far old cry from our dizzying streets
Disney don't sponsor their Christmas lights
And if you went on Grindr your nearest meet
Could be three towns away with no bus back at night

No this ain't the Cornwall of toffs with two houses
Or surfers in wetsuits all gleaming and tight
Or ladies in trendy yet hideous blouses
In galleries full of bland seascapes and shite

Still, these few weathered palm trees, and pebble-dashed streets
The old concrete jetty and salt-rusted cars
Are our very own Bethlehem! Cos here you will meet
Your young hero, Jim Hawkins, who's born to go far!

So give us have a cheer? And can you say boo?
And can you go "ah"? Oh sublime!!
Then welcome my dingos, with no more ado
To our nautical pantomime!

SILVER (off)
Ahaaaaarrrrrrrrrrrr!!

ETHEL puts a hand to his ear.

ETHEL
Strewth boys and girls! It sounds like I've lured another sailor! I never mean to. Last week it was three posh fella's on their daddy's yacht. They ran aground on my little rock, well, they looked so disappointed when they got a proper look at me I felt obliged to help pull them off.

SILVER rows on in a battered little rowing boat. He has a beard, and a large bird on his shoulder. If it resembles anything it's a mangy pigeon. The boat has a flagpole on the back of it. He wears an eyepatch which has the little Apple symbol on it.)

ETHEL
G'day mate.

SILVER
Ahaaar! I be Long John Silver! My father was Pajama Bottoms Silver and his father was Mad Meggings Silver. You be looking at the most infamous, most fearsome, most formidable head chef of that there yonder gastropub on the shore.

ETHEL
Oh yeah I see it. All the twinkly coloured lights.

SILVER
They were my idea. It be the little touches what count.

ETHEL
It's certainly what counted with Dave Lee Travis[47]. I'm not one for a gastropub. I prefer a barbie on the beach so I can slip back into the sea. You see, if I'm kept out of the water for more than 30 minutes, I die! It's a pain in the backside alright. I've never seen a complete episode of Orange is the New Black.

SILVER is staring into the water

ETHEL
What are you doing?

SILVER
Looking for the plughole, ahaaaar.

ETHEL
I've heard of you. You used to be a pirate.

SILVER
A pirate I'll be again, mark my words!

ETHEL (sceptical)
I heard you had twelve terrifying beards.

SILVER
I do have twelve terrifying beards! I just don't wear 'em all at same time.

ETHEL
And I heard your parrot could talk.

SILVER
She can talk! She's just quite reticent.

_____
[47] In September 2014 radio DJ Dave Lee Travis was found guilty of indecent assault, having been arrested as part of Operation Yewtree.

PARROT
I feel seasick.

SILVER
You're hungover!

PARROT
Don't be reductive. And get some Head and Shoulders it's like a skiing holiday up here.

ETHEL
And I heard you had a metal hook for a hand.

SILVER
Arr now, that be but a legend.

SILVER opens his coat to reveal a metal hook poking out of his groin where his penis would be.

ETHEL
Fair dinkum, I've heard of copper-bottomed, but that's a first.

SILVER
It be handy for tea-towels. I've heard of you too. Ethel the Merman. So you're the token trans.

ETHEL
And you're the token twat. It ain't a secret boys and girls. To all appearances I was born a little Sheila. Spent my childhood praying for a change... just not one quite as surreal as this. I'm sure the boys and girls are all very chilled out about gender aintcha? You know, I once took part in a competitive drinking session with the Dalai Lama, and he told me, fuck 'em Ethel, it doesn't matter if people... No I still can't remember what he said, he holds his drink very well. Anyway here's the thing. King Neptune has told me, if I prove my worth to him in some special way, he'll turn me back into a human. So I'm looking for an opportunity.

SILVER
What will he turn you into? A man or a woman?

ETHEL
A man, of course! I think... Why have you got a little apple on your eye patch?

SILVER
Because it's my Apple iPatch

ETHEL points to the pole sticking up from the back of the boat.

ETHEL
What's with the dodgem car business?

SILVER
This be my flagpole, so as I can fly my flag!

He tugs on a string and the Cock and Balls flag winches up the little flagpole. It is black but instead of the traditional skull and crossbones it has the simple, commonly graffitied symbol of a cock and balls.

ETHEL
That's the Islamic State flag, he's a flaming jihadist!

SILVER
It be the infamous pirate flag, you waterlogged wanker. The Cock and Balls. I also got the Cornish Independence one in here somewhere.

ETHEL
How are you going to become a pirate again?

SILVER
Can ye make out yonder old tumbledown inn on the cliffs in the shadow of them there clay heaps? The innkeeper be a poor woman by name of Sally Hawkins-

ETHEL
Like the actress?

SILVER
That's it.

ETHEL
I liked her in Blue Jasmine.

SILVER
I liked her in that Mike Leigh thing but I fear we be straying from the point. This Sally Hawkins has let the place go nearly to ruin. The hard work and running about be done mainly by her son Jim, a comely young lad I'd gladly bait my hook for. Now, the inn be called the Royal Bumboy. It used to be just the Bumboy, plain and simple. The Hawkins were inspired to give it the Royal prefix some years back when they took in a guest who they were convinced were none other than Her Royal Highness the Princess Royal, Princess Anne, staying incognito under a false moniker.

ETHEL
What name did she use.

SILVER
Monica. Well now. As I expect you've fathomed, it turned out not to be Her Royal Highness Princess Anne. It were just an ordinary lass who happened to favour wearing a unique and very strange-looking hat. Now,

I be approaching the point of my tale. Did thee hear tell of a ruthless pirate, long dead now, called Captain Cunt?

ETHEL
That's unusual... How are you spelling that, c-u-n-t is it?

SILVER
I think that's it. He did many a pirate out of a fortune, yours truly among them. Rumour has it his treasure is buried on a far-off island, and the map what reveals its location is hidden somewhere in the Royal Bumboy Inn.

ETHEL
Gotcha mate! You're going to help poor Sally and Jim find the treasure, split the proceeds fairly, help them out of poverty, put a bit aside for your pension and put the remainder towards the humanitarian relief efforts in Syria.

SILVER
Ahahahaha! No! I'm gonna screw them over something rotten! Hahahahahahaha!

ETHEL
You want to chill out mate. Doesn't this gastroboozer pay you a fair wage?

SILVER
I don't like a fair wage. Right, I be buggering off. I left a bouillabaisse simmering and I'll get violent if it spoils.

ETHEL
Don't let it see your face then. I'll see you later, Prick Stein.

SILVER
Is that right.

ETHEL
What do you reckon you dingo? Scene one, a mythical creature in need of a task meets a raving lunatic in an unusual location? You and me, we're destined to be on opposite teams.

SILVER
Then may the best "man" win. Ahahahahaha!!!

SILVER exits. There is a shift, in the lighting – a shift somehow in time.

ETHEL
In a village called Upshit Creek, down under,
Young Ethel felt more like the boys that she knew,
And her folks kicked her out when one day they found her
In her father's old suit with her hair shaved grade 2

And still in that big silly suit Ethel ran,
Ran away from the house and jumped in the sea
To swim far away - but the suit became tangled
And heavy, and Ethel just couldn't get free!

Ethel thought strewth! This is taking the piss,
As she found herself pulled deep under the waves
To a magical kingdom of legend and myth
The realm of King Neptune! Could Ethel be saved?

King Neptune offered Ethel a position:
"You'll be my Valet! How's that for a plan!
It's good money" said Neptune, "there's just one condition
You must lose those young tits and become a merman!"

And so Ethel was turned into this manly ride!
This hunky Merman you've got as your host
Now buckle your lifebelts, watch out for the tide,
It's time we set foot on that Cornish coast.

Scene 2: The bar of the Royal Bumboy Inn

It's fairly spit-and-sawdust and has lots of nautical décor: a fish in a glass case, fishing nets and buoys strung up on the walls, a ship's wheel, rope. There are glasses and old-fashioned tankards on the bar. On a shelf is a stack of battered board games including Risk. There should be lots of places where a treasure map might be hidden.

It is night. As the Royal Bumboy set is brought into place by rough seadogs and wenches, they sing as many verses as is necessary of an old sea shanty...

SONG: I KNEW A SAILOR

I knew a sailor from Plymouth Town
He used to sail with his trousers down
And round the harbour he would stroll
He liked to feel the wind on his hole

Sailor sailor boy
Sailors be perverts ahoy ahoy

I knew a sailor from Dublin Port
He used to get his trousers caught
On things around the harbour walls
And all of Dublin had seen his balls

I knew a sailor from Anglesey
He right leg ended at the knee
And when the harbour girls he'd pass
He'd use his crutch to poke their arse

I knew a sailor from old Torbay
We used to ask him if he were gay
We caught him doing the harbour cat
No-one asked him much after that

I knew a sailor from John O'Groats
He'd come to the harbour to sow his oats
But no girl got a kid in her tum
Cos he'd been doing 'em up the bum

I knew a sailor from Berwick on Tweed
He liked it when the drunk lads peed
He'd take a tankard to the harbour
And ask them to splash a bit into his lager

I knew a sailor from Marloes Sands
He had the most enormous hands

The harbour girls they thought him buff
But one finger was quite enough.

When the scene is set we hear the unmistakable tune of an ice-cream van. As one, the drinkers run off in excitement leaving the bar empty. The lights change: it's the next morning. Tankards are left lying about. MARINA rushes in with a plate of very badly made fondant fancies and a bottle of cleaning spray.

MARINA
Jim – cakes!

She sees the audience

MARINA
Hello there! I'm Marina. Welcome to the Royal Bumboy Hotel, here in our little tiny fishing harbour. It's called Michael Cove, and it's best days are behind it. Are you waiting to check in? It's alright you can talk back that's how you know you're not at the National. Obviously that's not the only difference. Alan Bennett's never been found in *our* toilets on his knees with his face in an understudy. Oh hang about, you're the boys and girls ain't you! Are you alright? I'm not. It's morning and I've been up hours. I'm the cook here at the Bumboy. It's no life. The landlady's my mate Jim's mum, but me and Jim do all the work. She's a bit of a drunk. (Calls) Jim! Cakes! (To the audience) I'm practising to get on next year's Bake-Off. Would anyone like a nibble of my fondant fancies?

She hands out cakes.

MARINA
I'm trying to save up to buy a boat and go sailing around the world like my fantasy woman Dame Ellen MacArthur. You lot can be my crew if you like! When I shout "Ahoy there shipmates" I want you to shout "Ahoy there Marina!". Come on, let's try it. "Ahoy there shipmates".

Audience shout back.

MARINA
You can do better than that! "Ahoy there shipmates".

Ahoy there Marina.

MARINA
I might meet a girl if I went travelling. I've never had a girlfriend. The local cattery's stopped doing its singles

night, and the only lesbians I meet are couples from Stoke Newington on glamping holidays with tents from Habitat. Jim has loads more luck than me. Me and him are old school mates. We're always playing tricks on each other. Let me know if you see him.

She brandishes the spray like a gun and creeps about.

MARINA
Cakes Jim!

MARINA looks in corners and off stage and in the audience. Eventually she stands in front of the bar, facing forward, leaning back on it. JIM pops up from behind it with a mop in one hand and a soda syphon with which he hoses MARINA, who screams.

MARINA
Jim Hawkins! I thought you lot were my mates. What you up to Jim?

JIM (sarcastic)
I'm re-watching season two of Desperate Housewives and cracking off a cheeky little wank over the gardener.

MARINA
Are you?

JIM starts picking up glasses.

JIM
No. I been mopping out the cellar haven't I.

MARINA
Mopping? How much did you wank?

JIM
Hello boys and girls! Welcome to the Royal Bumboy!

MARINA
I've already done this bit.

JIM
I know but it's more impressive coming from the owner's son. Take these glasses through will you. Is mum up?

MARINA
Sort of.

We hear her bang into something.

JIM
Mum?

We hear a loud smash of pottery

JIM
Was that you mum?

SALLY (off)
No. *(a pause)* It was a flowerpot.

JIM
Mum!

SALLY (off)
I'm coming Jim. I'm coming.

SALLY enters holding a Bloody Mary, complete with celery stalk.

SALLY
Hello boys and girls!

Hello!

SALLY
How lovely, did you hear that Jim, a gentle sea breeze I think it was. Now come on, you're at the theatre, try projecting. I said hello boys and girls! (They do) That's it! That's much more forceful, I think I heard Marina's little hymen snap. (About an audience member) You take this one's lead boys and girls, he looks like he knows what he's doing, he's been going to pantomimes since they were in black and white. And in Sanskrit. *(Points to her face)* I know what you're thinking. You didn't know Renee Zellweger was going to be it. Now my name's Sally, are you alright my loves? Let's have a look at you. (to Marina) Go tidy the kitchen. Did you meet our cook, she's called Marina. Like the Stingray puppet but shitter at cooking. You won't get a girlfriend if you don't get better in the kitchen my love.

MARINA
We'll just eat out.

SALLY
That's too much information. Here you just should try that Tinder, it's very addictive. I been playing on it the last half hour sat on the bog.

MARINA
Did you swipe right at all?

SALLY
No love, front to back, even I know that. Off you go.

MARINA (exiting)
See you later shipmates!

MARINA exits

SALLY
(downing her drink) Cheers.

JIM
Bloody hell.

SALLY
Bloody Mary. Two of my five a day, that. By which I mean I've had two so far... (To a man in the audience) Welcome sir, what's your name? (he replies. She repeats his name excitedly.) Years back, a fortune teller told me I'd meet a handsome stranger called [name]! Can you believe that? She was right, I met him a week later, we had a hoot.

JIM
You're hammered.

SALLY
I don't like that word. I like bladdered, it's not so violent. Now my lovelies, welcome to the Royal Bumboy Inn!

JIM
I've done all this.

SALLY
I know but it's more impressive coming from a six-foot bombshell. Do you know there's been seamen spilling out of the Bumboy come midnight for centuries. I'd show you around, but that'd take more complex a staging than we've got at our dispersal. We did ask the set designer if we could have a revolve like in Les Mis. He told us to swivel. (She picks up a couple of tankards). Glass bottoms see. You know what that's for? It's so you can have a sly little check-out of the totty while you're taking a sup. They been here since my great grandfather's time, they're probably due a wash.

Over Jim's next few lines SALLY "subtly" holds the tankards up to her eyes and starts cruising the audience. She gets right into the face of one or two handsome men.

JIM
That's not right mum. The captain told me.

SALLY (distracted by the boys in the audience)
Oh did he.

JIM
He said, the reason they have glass bottoms is so you couldn't be press-ganged into joining the navy by

having someone drop the King's shilling into- Mum! I think he can see you!

SALLY
No point being too discreet. Fix me a nice drink will you Jim.

JIM looks at his watch.

SALLY
Alright alright. Just to steady myself.

JIM
What do you want, a rum? Whisky?

SALLY
No, it's been a tough old morning, I'll have something stronger.

JIM looks puzzled, sniffs a few unlabelled bottles. Pours something.

JIM
"Tough morning"!

SALLY
I got a pounding headache.

JIM
Some of us have been working since seven!

SALLY
I'll have a sit down and then I'll help you.

SALLY goes to sit on the chair, misses it, lands on the floor, where she settles. JIM goes to help her up.

SALLY
Don't, don't. I'm comfy. And don't look at me like that, I don't have a problem. I saw Dr Hackett yesterday, he said I was a, a high functioning alcoholic.

JIM (concerned)
What? You went to the doctor mum?

SALLY
No, bumped into him in the market didn't I.

JIM
What else did he say?

SALLY
"Mind where you're bloody going" I think it was! I'm a bit damp I squeezed passed Marina earlier and she spilled her breakfast juice down me thigh. Cheer up my boy, I don't like seeing you all glum - have you swept this floor you've missed a bit there if you have.

She licks a finger and wipes away some muck she's spotted. She tastes her finger.

SALLY
It's bingo and cabaret tonight! You should bring your young man. You're still seeing him aren't you, lovely Billy?

JIM
No. He left me.

SALLY
Oh Jim.

JIM
What an arsehole.

SALLY
Yes I remember you saying it was nice.

JIM
He's gone to London. To study.

SALLY
Him? Are you sure?

JIM
Yeah, fashion.

SALLY
Oh, right. Well, invite your friend Bobby along.

JIM
Bobby's gone off as well. He's doing musical theatre...

SALLY (sings, to the tune of *Getting To Know You*)
Getting to grope you, getting to grope all about you...

JIM
I'd love to do something like that boys and girls.

SALLY
You got two left feet.

JIM
Well. Not musical theatre. Straight acting.

SALLY
Haha you. Straight acting.

JIM
I'd just like to get away from this place for a bit.

SALLY
You have your little gay nights in Truro.

JIM
That club has more pasty and oddly shaped gay men in it than the shy corner at a Sam Smith concert. I want to go travelling, I want to have adventures.

SONG: THE WHOLE WIDE WORLD
(Plain text: Jim. *Italics: Sally*)

I wanna see the whole wide world
I want my life to begin at last
I wanna make it my world
Sleep with a guy from every page of the atlas
Sail the Danube, Amazon and Nile

I'll climb hills in Bavaria
Spend Christmas in Rio - and New Year
Take pills for malaria
Take my fill of a surly gondolier
Rent out my room, I'll be gone a while

I wanna fly away like Dorothy and Toto
You'll only get all vain about your passport photo...

You'll get mugged in Marrakesh
Get Delhi-belly in Bangladesh
I think I heard in Budapest they're always hungry
Get Tsunami'd in Japan
Eat chickens' feet in Vietnam
Pull a whitey in Amsterdam
You're better off at home

I wanna see Istanbul with someone prosperous
So he can have me on his boat upon the Bosph'rous

But I know where I'll begin
I'll go clubbing in Berlin
In just a harness and a grin
I've seen the pictures
Fall in love with a Spanish youth
Watch the moon from a Paris roof
Catch syphilis in Magaluf
I've seen the pictures

I'll get stoned on a rocky ridge
With some tosser from Cambridge
He'll have dreadlocks
And nits
We'll get dinner
And the shits
But it might be nice, Yes it might just a bit...

Crossing rivers and mountains,
Throwing coins in Roman fountains
And getting out in
The big wide world.

SALLY
I don't know what's got into you.

JIM
Mum voted Ukip in the Euros this year.

SALLY
I did not. It was raining. We had that Farage in swigging a pint for the cameras. And Miliband. We had them all in, didn't we. I asked them why, they said it's cos you got a swing seat here. We do, it's in the garden. Now, I ought to practise my bingo calls for tonight. Legs eleven, I know that one. Thirty-three, knobbly knees. Eighty-eight, too fat to fuck...

The CAPTAIN enters from outside.

SALLY
Look what the wind's blown in. Morning Captain! Sleep alright did you?

CAPTAIN
Like I was back in my berth on a gentle sea, Sally. Ah lass, you look even finer than yesterday.

JIM
Have you been for your morning constitutional Captain.

CAPTAIN
I have, Jim.

SALLY
I wish you'd use the indoor one like the other guests. Would you have a word with young Jim, he's got ideas in his head about going off on dangerous adventures. I blame Marina.

CAPTAIN
A boy has to have adventures Sally! See the world. Sow his oats.

JIM
I bet you were a wild one.

CAPTAIN
I had a girl in every port I sailed to.

SALLY
One in Dover, one in Calais. I expect they could wave to each other on a clear day. "Oi, Amelie! Tell him to bring me back 200 Marlborough and a Toblerone once he's pulled out and spritzed."

JIM
Will you take me in your boat one day?

CAPTAIN
I don't know Jim. I haven't sailed her in a long time.

JIM
Please?

CAPTAIN
I tell you what, I'll take you if your mum comes along too.

JIM
But mum doesn't like the sea!

SALLY
I do. To look at. To listen to. But I've seen the movies, I know happens at sea. Sandra Bullock comes shooting out of the sky at you in a space capsule.

JIM
You can't even swim.

SALLY
I told you, my phone stops working. Did Marina cook your breakfast Captain?

CAPTAIN
She did but it's alright, I got something up at the fisherman's mission.

SALLY
Jim lad. I've got something to tell you. I was fingering through my drawers earlier, blimey the dust, and well, I found this from the brewery.

She puts her pulls out a piece of paper from between her breasts and hands it to JIM.

JIM
A final demand! For seven grand!

SALLY
I know, it rhymes. Nice touch.

JIM
Mum!

SALLY
I sort of forgot about it. I sort of forgot about this one too.

She pulls out another bill and hands it to JIM

JIM
Unpaid council tax...

SALLY
And this one.

JIM
Two grand on Botox!

SALLY
He said he'd fill my creases.

JIM
Mum we've got no money. There's only one thing for it. You'll have to downsize.

SALLY hits JIM

CAPTAIN
Your mother has an hourglass figure.

JIM
She does, Captain. Everything's going downwards. Think about it Mum. We've only got two guests apart from the captain. We're overcharging and the bar's doing awful. You can't keep a place afloat on a handful of alcoholics.

CAPTAIN (looking about the theatre)
I'm not so sure about that.

JIM
The Fisherman's Mission does fish, peas and mushy chips for three quid, and then there's that bloody gastropub. We're being squeezed from both ends. Like that young man on the back row - leave him alone! Talk about audience interaction.

SALLY
There's one thing we can do Jim. We can get rid of Marina.

JIM
But Marina's my best mate!

SALLY
We can't afford her wages can we. I'll have a word with her later. Go and help her.

JIM exits.

SALLY
I got something with your name on it too, Captain.

CAPTAIN
"With my name on" eh Sally?

SALLY
A letter.

CAPTAIN
"A letter" eh Sally?

SALLY
Good grief. Here.

CAPTAIN
Well blow me with a fine south-westerly! It's from my daughter.

SALLY
Your long-lost daughter! Your poor daughter that you lost to the sea in a sudden tempest when she was but a toddler? Your daughter what's been a source of grief and guilt for so many a year?

CAPTAIN
No. No, my other daughter.

SALLY
Josephine! The actress!

CAPTAIN
It's very strange. She never writes to me.

SALLY
Josephine's a proper famous actress boys and girls. Two years on Corrie she did. And more recently the lead role in Talentless, the Britain's Got Talent musical that closed after two and a half performances at the London Palladium[48].

CAPTAIN
I didn't even get an invitation. (Opens the letter) She wants to come and stay!

SALLY
A star of stage and screen! Here in the Royal Bumboy! Oh Captain! Where can I put her! I haven't got a suite. She can have my room, there's the Teas-maid if she can get it working and I'll give my toys a rinse.

CAPTAIN
Nonsense! My room's the nicest room, she can stay there and I'll bunk up with you.

SALLY
No you don't, I remember that palaver with you pretending to have nightmares if you sleep alone. You're as bad as Krzyzsztof. He's the local taxi driver boys and girls. I'm not saying he's all hands, but his nickname's Uber-familiar.

---

[48] *I Can't Sing – The X-Factor Musical* began previewing at the Palladium in March 2014. It closed in May 2014.

CAPTAIN
She's coming today!

SALLY
What?

A knock at the door. SALLY goes to answer it. She can't open it however hard she pushes. She gets into a drunk panic.

CAPTAIN
You have to pull it.

SALLY
I was going for suspense!

She opens it. SILVER is in the doorway.

SILVER
Hahahaha!

Booo!

SILVER
Pipe down you shitlicking bottom-feeders or I'll fill your pots with a gill-full of me plankton. Ahoy there, comely wench!

CAPTAIN
Wench?!

SALLY
Comely?!

CAPTAIN
(To Sally) That's not what you think.

SILVER
Such words are a part of my seagoing culture and heritage! But hand on heart I come in friendship. HAHAHAHAHA! I mean, (girlish giggle) a ha ha ha ha ha.

SALLY
What a lovely little budgie!

SILVER
A budgie? Have ye never laid eyes on a parrot before?

SALLY
No, but I've had me hands on a cockatoo. Should I let him in boys and girls?

Noooo!!!

SALLY
Sorry Mr Silver but I'm operating a fledgling democracy here and the people have spoken.

SILVER
You owes me, Hawkins! I nearly got shipwrecked just now all thanks to thee! I was out yonder on the briny for a paddle in my little rowing boat, fishing for ingredients for my award-winning fish stew, next thing I know a mighty wave takes me and I find meself bashed repeatedly against your rocks. (To a boy in the audience) I wouldn't mind being bashed repeatedly against *your* rocks. (To SALLY) Why isn't your bastard lighthouse working?

SALLY
Shit, sorry, I unplugged it last week it so I could use me epilator.

CAPTAIN
It's daylight!

SILVER
Put a cork in your blowhole, you crusty old crabstick.

JIM enters

JIM
Don't listen to him Captain, he's all Muller Light and no Crunch Corner.

SILVER
Alright, calm down Jim lad.

JIM
Stop hassling my mum then. *(He looks at the hook poking from Silver's crotch)* What happened to you anyway, did you get fingered too hard by Captain Hook?

SILVER
I be here on business. I'm here to see thy much-maligned chef, see. I'm starting a union for all the kitchen-workers of Michael Cove.

SALLY
Well that's only you and Marina and the pregnant Bulgarian lady what's doing maternity cover at the Mission.

SILVER
That's why we need representation. I want words in private.

JIM
I'll get her.

JIM, SALLY and the CAPTAIN exit. MARINA enters, nervously.

MARINA
Ahoy there shipmates!

SILVER
Don't be afeared, Marina lad. Listen good. Did ye ever hear tell of an old map showing the spot where the notorious seadog Cunt buried his treasure? (To a favourite in the audience) I'd let you bury your treasure deep enough.

MARINA
I don't know nothing about a map.

SILVER
Many have spoke of the treasure map hidden here in the Bumboy. I'll make you an offer. That treasure's said to be worth a king's ransom.

MARINA
A king's ransom!

SILVER
Find the map, and we'll sail away thick as thieves and recover the treasure.

MARINA
The treasure!

SILVER
Stop repeating me parrot-fashion. (to the parrot) What is parrot fashion?

PARROT
Don't ask me, I'm a nudist.

SILVER
Once we got the booty we'll split it according to the rules of the pirate's code! (To his man in the audience) Whereas I'd split your booty from the first light of dawn till the last sweet stroke of midnight. What do you say. Come and be my first mate.

MARINA
I got a mate. I'm happy here and I don't want to be a pirate.

SILVER
Leave me high and dry eh? You'll change your mind if that's not too grand a name for what you got in your skull, but until then I leave you with this terrifying warning. I be working on a new winter specials menu for the Fister's so damn tasty it'll sink this poxy tavern for good. Hahahaha!!

SILVER exits.

MARINA
A treasure map! Here! I heard rumours boys and girls but I never thought it was real. If we found the treasure we could share it, Jim wouldn't have to work so hard, I could do a course in how to not cook so shit, and Ms Hawkins wouldn't be so hard up. Here, boys and girls, maybe you can help me find the map! And we could share the treasure with you too. Will you help me? Where will I try?

They make suggestions and MARINA looks. After a while, MARINA spots something under someone's seat.

MARINA
Here it is! Oh no it's a leaflet I think it's come out of your bag sir. (She reads) "What you should know about chlamydia".

MARINA tries the shelves. She gets down the board games and opens the Risk box. She takes out the board.

MARINA
Oh my god! I found it! This is it, isn't it? (They tell her: no) Oh well I give up then... hang on!

She pulls something else out of the box... a large, creased, yellowed sheet of paper folded up. She unfolds it. It's the map!

SALLY (off)
Marinaaaaa!

She enters with JIM.

JIM
Has he gone?

MARINA
Yes, but Jim, listen!

SALLY
Not now Marina. Get going on the lunches.

MARINA
I know, but this is really exciting, listen

SALLY
Hey. Less chattering, go and get battering.

MARINA
All right...

MARINA leaves the map with the games box on the bar and exits.

SALLY
Well! You were a fat lot of help!

JIM
What?

SALLY
I thought we were going to sack her.

JIM
She's my best mate. You're her boss! You said you'd have a word with her.

SALLY
Alright I will. Give me a drink to steady me nerves.

JIM
No.

SALLY
Alright! Marinaaaaaa!

MARINA comes back.

SALLY
Jim wants a word.

JIM
You're such a coward.

SALLY
I can't can I. Look at her there. Her little face! Never been kissed.

MARINA
I have been kissed... Guys, I left a baked Alaska out of the freezer...

SALLY
Alright alright. It's awkward that's all. And you standing there listening. Alright. Marina *(She breathes deeply)*. When a man and a woman love each other very much-

JIM
Mum!

SALLY
Oh you do it Jim.

MARINA
No, I don't like the version he tells, it's disgusting. *(To the audience)* I don't know what they're on about shipmates! Do you know?

They tell her

MARINA
You're... you're getting rid of me?

SALLY
Oh no we're not!

Oh yes you are [etc]

MARINA
You are! After all these years we've been friends Jim. Me and you. Us pair. We two. We were going to show each other the world, and now you're showing me the door. And to think I was going to tell you about...

JIM
What?

MARINA
It doesn't matter now.

She wipes away a tear. SALLY sobs loudly, briefly and drunkenly emotional.

JIM
I'm so sorry, there's just no money. But there's no rush to leave. Ain't that right mum?

SALLY
Oh, yeah. Course! Wait till you done the lunches.

MARINA
No thank you. There is a rush. There's a very big shiny rush with my name on it. *(She goes to the door and opens it)* Mr Silver! Wait for me!

MARINA exits. They watch her go – JIM walking to the door, SALLY staying put. A moment.

SALLY
She'll be back.

JIM
We just sacked her.

SALLY
Oh right yeah.

JIM tidies a bit, putting the games box and the map and maybe other thing into a cupboard.

JIM
Come on. I'll teach you how to use the hob.

SALLY
You and your fancy gadgets. "Hob". See you later boys and girls!

BLACKOUT.

Scene 3: A rock off the Cornish coast

PRINCE DARYL is asleep on the rock. He wears a flamboyant outfit that might be seen on the singer Prince. He has a sack with gold bars visible in it and a backpack adorned with a royal crest. He wakes up, sees the audience and stands up.

DARYL

Awight there boys n' girls? How you doing? My name's Daryl, Crown Prince Daryl! Can you guess where I'm Prince of? Atlantis! That's it, Atlantis, the city under the sea! I decided to leave Atlantis cos I want to see the world and I want to meet men. It ain't easy for gay Atlantans right now. Me old man – that's King Neptune – he thinks he'll be more popular if he has a bit of a crackdown. Family values and all that. So I can't go about being all gay in public any more. I'm well excited though. I heard there's loads of fitties on the surface world. And I'm looking at you lot and thinking, you might be able to point me to them.

ETHEL emerges from the sea.

ETHEL

G'day your highness!

DARYL

Ethel Merman! What you doing here?

ETHEL

This is my rock. Also, your olds might have asked me to keep an eye on you.

DARYL

Spy on me! That is bang out of order.

ETHEL

Spy?! Look after! Keep you safe! On which note... *(he hands him some condoms)* You don't want to bring any unwanted "souvenirs" back from Cornwall.

DARYL

I was only going to pack some fudge. This ain't fair, you'll cramp my style.

ETHEL

Me? Haven't I wiped away your tears? Put you to bed? Sung your favourite songs? Bounced you on what would be my knee if I had knees?

DARYL

I suppose.

ETHEL

That was a bonza night actually we should get hold of some more of that stuff. Look, I like you. You got spunk.

DARYL

(checking his trousers) Aw crap...

ETHEL

But - you need my special merman sense. When I got turned into a merman I was granted a special sense. Not gonna lie I'd have preferred a cock, but it means I can tell when folks are in trouble.

DARYL

Nothing scares me son.

ETHEL finds a squid in his hair or in some seaweed and throws it at DARYL. He screams.

ETHEL

Wuss. What's in your bag?

DARYL

Got me some Atlantan gold ain't I. And this.

DARYL takes out a pearl necklace.

ETHEL

Strewth mate get that back in the water.

DARYL

It's the old girl's! Thought it'd be nice to have it with me while I'm on my travels. Don't you like it?

ETHEL

Worse. It's cursed.

DARYL

Cursed? Beeee-ave! Mum used it wear it.

ETHEL

Yeah, underwater. Up here in the air it releases a curse on whoever's got it.

DARYL

What a load of cobblers.

He takes the necklace and holds it, looking around.

DARYL

See?

We hear a seagull fly over. DARYL looks up, and a large dollop of seagull shit lands on his head.

ETHEL

Told you.

DARYL hands the necklace back to ETHEL. ETHEL climbs back into the water.

ETHEL
I'll see you around mate.

ETHEL swims off.

DARYL

I need me beauty sleep boys and girls. While I'm having me shut-eye, keep a look over me Atlantan gold for me will you? It's all I got. If you see anyone near it gimme a shout.

DARYL stretches out and goes to sleep. SILVER and MARINA enter in SILVER'S boat. MARINA rows furiously.

SILVER
Ahaaar. Marina lad, we'll make a seaman of you yet. Now, let's have look at that map and make a plan.

MARINA
Shit! I left the map! Sorry, I didn't have time to think.

SILVER takes one of the oars and hits MARINA round the head with it.

SILVER
Time or capacity? Idiot. We'll have to go back and get it.

They see the DARYL and the gold.

SILVER
But looky, looky me hearty. Gold! We could use that to buy a proper boat to sail to Treasure Island!

MARINA
That's stealing.

SILVER
Arrr it be. Now keep quiet. If no one makes a noise I can creep on to the rock and take it.

SILVER climbs out of the boat on to the rock indicating to the audience to keep quiet. They don't. As SILVER is about to the gold the DARYL wakes.

SILVER
Curses! (To the parrot) How do I look?

PARROT
Get me a cotton bud, I'll do your lugholes. It's like staring into a baby's nappy.

DARYL
Awight mate. Prince Daryl of Atlantis.

SILVER
A Prince? Long John Silver at your service. This be my number two.

MARINA
Don't call me that. Miss Marina here.

SILVER
I'd be careful telling people you be a prince, me worship. There's people would take advantage, it be quite a fortune for you that you met us first. We was just admiring your fat little ingots there.

DARYL
It's pure Atlantan.

SILVER
And be that a pure Atlantan outfit you're wearing, sir?

DARYL
Nah mate, in Atlantis we go about naked. I had a look on Gurgle – that's like Google but underwater - to see what Princes wear on the surface. This is from the Purple Rain era. I know you surface dwellers are funny about nudity.

SILVER
Oh no we're not.

DARYL
Oh yes you are.

"Oh no we're not!"

DARYL (to the audience)
I will if you will mate. I'm looking for adventure and men.

SILVER
You'll be needing a guide sir, to show you about and protect you from Cornish knockers.

DARYL
Knockers?

MARINA
Goblins that live underground[49]. The tin miners used to keep 'em happy by tossing them the crusts off their lunches, but there's less mining these days so the knockers come out into daylight all hungry with grasping fingers and haunted eyes.

---

[49] This is a "real" Cornish myth.

SILVER

You won't get the reference sir, but it's like a Sunday at noon in Vauxhall.[50]

ETHEL sticks his head up.

ETHEL

Silver! You're a bullshitting bandicoot.

SILVER

Sorry Ethel, EU fishing regulations. You gotta throw the unwanted ones back in.

SILVER kicks ETHEL, he screams and falls back into the water. He drops the necklace on the rock.

SILVER

Now, will we explore Michael Cove together.

DARYL

We got to shift this gold first. Atlantan gold only lasts a short while in the air before it turns to dust.

SILVER

Then what say we buys a boat? That'd impress all the men!

DARYL

Sick!

---

[50] In case you don't get the reference either, Vauxhall is popular for all-night gay clubbing.

MARINA points at the necklace.

MARINA

Aw nice, a necklace!

DARYL

Throw it in the water! It's cursed.

MARINA

You're having a laugh!

A seagull is heard.

DARYL

Hold the necklace and stand there.

He pushes MARINA to the centre of the rock, he and SILVER move to the side.

MARINA

A cursed necklace! That's stupid.

A seagull flies over. DARYL laughs pointing at MARINA. A large dollop of seagull shit lands on DARYL's head.

SILVER

I got some old jam-jars in the boat I been collecting for a batch of quince jelly. You fill one up with water Marina lad and put the necklace in it. A cursed necklace could be useful me hearties. Very useful indeed. Ahaaaaaaarrrr!!!

Scene 4: The bar of the Royal Bumboy Inn

The bar at the hotel. SALLY is just finishing murdering "New York, New York". She has a garish cocktail. JIM is behind the bar. There are a few bar snacks. The CAPTAIN applauds loudly.

SALLY
Thank you, thank you! Welcome to cabaret live at the Royal Bumboy.

She downs the cocktail in one.

SALLY
Jim.

JIM appears not to hear.

SALLY
Jiiiiiiiiiiiiiiiiiim!

JIM takes ear plugs out of his ears.

JIM
Yes mum?

SALLY
Fix us another. (she points at the empty glass).

JIM
Mum had a reviewer in from the local paper last week.

SALLY
He wrote that my voice was quivery.

JIM
She phoned him up.

SALLY
I did. I said, quivery, I think you're referring to my vibrato.

JIM
He said no he was referring to the whiff of cheesy crisps.

SALLY
Time for another song!

JIM puts the ear plugs back in.

SALLY
Now, ladies and gentlemen. Shirley Bassey's done it. Bette Midler's done it. Freddie Mercury did it at Wembley and even Lana del Ray's had a stab at it. But I'm not here to talk about the perils of dogging on a full stomach, I'm here to sing for you.

SALLY starts to sing Big Spender. JOSEPHINE bursts in carrying a bag and brandishing a spray of mace. She wears a fur coat.

JOSEPHINE
Stop! Police!

CAPTAIN
Josephine!

JOSEPHINE
(At SALLY) Thank goodness, you're alright, I thought someone was being attacked. Daddy darling! (She looks about) Well, isn't this just... What would you call it, shitty chic? (To an audience member, taking his hand) My other bag's just by the door there. Would you? That's it, chop, chop.

She ushers the audience member to the door to fetch her case then points him back to his seat. She leaves the mace spray on the bar.

SALLY
Welcome to the Royal Bumboy! Sally Hawkins at your cervix.

JOSEPHINE
I've misread your postcards Daddy, I thought you wrote that the place was charming and the landlady gave you the hots, but you must have said the place was alarming and the landlady gave you the trots. My own silly fault for losing my prescription Guccis.

SALLY
I was gonna get a pair of them but I heard the silicon pops at high altitude and I like a turn on the big dipper at Flambards. (She strokes Josephine's coat) Now I like this, very glamorous, what is it? (She has a peek at the label) Ooh, genuine fox fur! Spelt the French way, F-A-U-X.

JOSEPHINE runs a hand along the bar, it is filthy. She looks disgusted. SALLY spits on the bar and wipes it with her hand.

JIM
What can I get you?

SALLY
Don't say pregnant he's not that way inclined!

JOSEPHINE
I was going to say a taxi. Darling daddy, how are you?

CAPTAIN
Well let's see, I was a wee bit poorly a couple of weeks ago

JOSEPHINE
Was it serious? Terminal?

CAPTAIN
Just a gippy tummy.

JOSEPHINE
Oh. (BEAT) Daddy, about the trust fund...

CAPTAIN
Now Josephine, your mother, God rest her soul, said that the money was to be held in trust until you were twenty-five in case we found your sister. It can only be released to if your sister hasn't been found by your twenty fifth birthday.

JOSEPHINE
The brat drowned at sea!

CAPTAIN
I must respect your mother's wishes.

JOSEPHINE
But daddy I have this tremendous opportunity. There's this film for me to star in. It's a bio-pic: "Nicole". It's about a Hollywood actress who turns her back on adoring audiences and critical acclaim in order to play Princess Grace of Monaco[51]. But we need a teensy cash injection.

CAPTAIN
I'm sorry Josephine.

JOSEPHINE
It could make me an international star. God, the thought of setting foot in another fringe theatre. I must lie down, I feel a migraine coming on.

JIM
Breakfast's from eight in the Waterloo dining room.

JOSPEPHINE
Like the sea battle?

JIM
Like the Abba song. Here's your key. You're in the Chiquitita room.

JOSPHINE
The what?

JIM
Mine's the Dancing Queen.

SALLY
And I'm in the Take a Chance on Me Boudoir.

JOSEPHINE
Daddy darling, take my cases.

The CAPTAIN picks up the cases, he wheezes JOSEPHINE marches out, he follows.

SALLY
I expect she's narky from the journey. Right, back to my song!

SILVER enters

SILVER
Ahhaaaaarrr!

JIM
Saved by the bell-end.

SILVER
Come along, Princey Sir.

DARYL enters. DARYL is now wearing a tight fitting sailors suit, he also carries a bag.

DARYL
You said this outfit would help me fit in.

SILVER
And you fit in it beautifully. This be where the map is hidden. I'll distract them by getting a drink and chatting up the old urchin.

DARYL starts searching around. JIM stares at him, his eyes following him around.

SILVER
Ms Hawkins you could turn a boy.

SALLY
Oh thank you Mr Silver *(points at DARYL)* I hope it's that boy.

SILVER
Jim lad, a glass of your strongest liquor to warm me insides and clean me out. (To his boy in the audience) While I'm about it, would *you* like a strong liquor to warm your insides and clean you out? Jim lad, a run.

[51] Grace of Monaco, starring Nicole Kidman, had just flopped.

298

JIM pays no attention he watches DARYL. SILVER squirts JIM with a soda syphon. JIM starts to pour a drink.

SILVER
Are ye responsible for the charming décor?

PARROT
Where's the charming décor?

SALLY
It's just what washed in when we had the floods[52].

SILVER
Might I have a tour?

PARROT
Well that's subtle, you might as well just ask her where the map is.

SILVER slaps the PARROT

SILVER

And a pint of scrumpy for the Parrot. (To the parrot) One word from you, you bladdered blackbird and I'll have you drinking J2Os for a week.

He picks up a pint and sticks the parrots' beak in it. JIM walks over to the DARYL.

JIM
Hi. Jim.

DARYL
No it's Daryl. Awright.

JIM
Are you performing later? Mum didn't mention a hen night.

DARYL looks confused.

DARYL
I'm Prince Daryl.

JIM
A Prince?!

DARYL
Me Dad's in charge of Atlantis.

JIM
Is that the nightclub in St Austell that got closed down

because the toilet attendant was doing burgers on the side in the ladies?

DARYL
It's a city under the sea. Thousands of years ago, it was a city off the coast of Southend, where the pier is now. One day there was an earthquake. It shook the whole of Essex, but Atlantis broke away, floated out to sea a bit and sank. Our people have lived under the water ever since.

JOSEPHINE marches in followed by the CAPTAIN.

JOSEPHINE
I am not happy with my room.

SALLY
The Chiquitita? Tell me what's wrong.

JOSEPHINE
The bed's swarming with bugs and the loo seat wobbles. Shall I go on?

SALLY
Depends how good your balance is, love. Do you like the complimentary toiletries?

JOSEPHINE
They're not complimentary, they're offensive. Did they come free with your dress?

SALLY
You can go elsewhere of course but this is high season. You won't find anyone as vacant as me.

JOSEPHINE
That I can believe.

SALLY
Seventy-five quid in advance then please.

JOSEPHINE takes out a credit card.

JOSEPHINE
Do you take plastic or just wear it?

SALLY snatches the card. Weighs it as though it's a wallet.

SALLY
Ooh heavy.

She goes. SILVER has now joined DARYL.

JIM
I'll sort your room out for you.

JIM exits

---

[52] There'd been terrible flooding in Cornwall caused by storms at the start of the year.

SILVER (to DARYL)
Go with him!

DARYL
Yeah alright, he's fit. You're a great guide, mate.

SILVER
Look for the map!

DARYL exits. SALLY marches over to JOSEPHINE brandishing her card.

SALLY
Declined. And the machine ain't broke, so you must be.

JOSEPHINE
Daddy! There seems to be a fault with my card. You couldn't pay for my room could you?

CAPTAIN
I don't have much money Josephine. I only have my boat.

SILVER and JOSEPHINE
Boat!

CAPTAIN
I suppose it's a, haha, a liquid asset haha.

Everyone stares at him coldly.

SILVER
'Scuse me Cap'n sir, did I hear you say you were thinking of selling your boat?

JOSEPHINE
Yes he is.

SILVER
I'll take it off your hands for you. And in these uncertain times, what better payment than solid gold!

PARROT
It's a lovely boat though Captain.

SILVER
I will tar you and de-feather you, you twaddled tit.

PARROT
Bring it on! I'm descended from the dinosaurs.

SILVER
Then brace yourself for extinction.

JOSEPHINE
Imagine Daddy, what we, what you could do with a lot of gold.

CAPTAIN
What do you think boys and girls?

SILVER
Cap'n Sir...

SILVER shakes the CAPTAIN's hand.

SILVER
That's sealed the deal. Princey lad sir!

DARYL stumbles down the stairs, doing his trousers up and wearing Jim's shirt. JIM follows buttoning his flies and wearing the Daryl's top.

SILVER
I've bought us the Captain's old tug. Second hand, but it's decent. Go fetch your sack of gold. (To his audience boy) I be sure you'd get your sack out for me in exchange for a decent old tug.

DARYL takes the bars of gold from his bag and hands them to the CAPTAIN. JOSEPHINE grabs them. SALLY un-crumples a carrier bag, puts them in it and gives the gold back to the CAPTAIN.

SILVER (to DARYL)
I don't expect you found the map while you had your hands inside Jim's clothes did you? I tell ye what, take him out tonight. (To the audience) And I can turn this place upside down....

DARYL walks over to JIM and SILVER to SALLY.

DARYL
Mate, let's go out tonight.

JIM
Ok! Wow. I guess we could go to the Oily Otter. There's... there's one other thing. There'll probably be quite a lot of guys there that I know...

DARYL
I'm well up for meeting your mates.

JIM
Right, well, just, don't feel you have to ask every single one of them how they met me.

SALLY
Off out are you?

JIM
Mum, this is Daryl. He's a prince.

SALLY

Good evening your majesty. (She bows, low, her face in his crotch. Impressed) He's got very big feet Jim. Now remember, keep him keen. Don't put out before the end of cloakroom queue. Give me a kiss before you go.

JIM goes to give her a kiss, she walks past him and kisses the Prince.

SALLY
Have a lovely night.

SALLY returns to the bar. JIM points at his shirt, then at DARYL's. They giggle a bit and take off their shirts as they about to hand them back to each other they look at each other and kiss. SILVER coughs. They replace their shirts.

JIM
I reckon things are starting to look up! The Captain's got all that gold and I've got a date with a prince. What can possibly go wrong?

SALLY
Well something will have to or it's going to be a fucking short pantomime.

DARYL and JIM exit.

JOSEPHINE
Come along Daddy let's go and put all that lovely gold somewhere safe. My suitcase has a very strong padlock.

The CAPTAIN goes to pick up the gold. JOSPEHINE grabs it.

JOSEPHNE
Allow me. You don't want to injure yourself.

JOSEPHINE and the CAPTAIN exit carrying the gold.

SILVER
Hawkins, you're looking quite the siren.

SALLY
You should see me flashing. You've polished yourself up nice too.

She plays with his hook. He giggles. She plays with it some more. JOSEPHINE enters still with the gold.

SALLY
Can I help you love?

JOSPEHINE
I forgot to ask. Are there more towels?

SALLY
More towels, what are you doing up there, a nativity play?

JOSEPHINE
For goodness sake I'll find them myself.

She opens a cupboard, it is full of junk.

JOSEPHINE
Towels, where are the towels.

She kicks the cupboard, a few things fall out in including the map.

SILVER
What be that there.

JOSPEPHINE
Some old map.

She looks at it.

JOSEPHINE
An old map of Treasure Island!

She starts to exit. SALLY grabs the map. SILVER tries to get it from SALLY.

SILVER
You don't be wanting that mangy old map! I got something far better. How would you like a pearl necklace?

SILVER produces a jam jar full of water, with the necklace in it.

SALLY
No man ever gave me a pearl necklace! Why's it in water?

SILVER
To keep it shiny for you.

JOSEPHINE
What if the map belongs to my father?

SALLY
Ooh, love, I think – I think your nose is slipping.

JOSEPHINE scrams, grasps her face and exits.

SALLY
(To Silver) Will I get you a drink?

SILVER
I don't want your mucky mixes! We got what we came for! We be off! Ahaaar!

SILVER exits. SALLY looks briefly sad then finds a bottle of wine. She takes it to a chair, taking a swig. She puts the bottle down, takes the necklace out of its jar and puts it on.

SALLY
I feel quite the lady sat here with a bottle of Spanish and a fresh pearl necklace.

SALLY She swigs. Something falls off a shelf close to her head. She jumps.

SALLY
I'll have a little nap so keep it down.

SALLY settles into the chair and goes to sleep. A clock starts ticking. SALLY opens an eye.

SALLY
That's to show time passing boys and girls.

SALLY sleeps again. A wind picks up and there is a rumble of thunder. The wind howls. The captain enters looking windswept and cold.

CAPTAIN
Sally! Wake up!

SALLY
What is it? You look terrible

CAPTAIN
What's the difference between me and the roof of the inn?

SALLY
I don't know, what's the difference between you and the roof of the inn?

CAPTAIN
I didn't get blown off in the night.

SALLY
What??

CAPTAIN
I woke up and I could see stars. A storm lifted it clean off.

SALLY
The Royal Bumboy!!

CAPTAIN
No, he's still out with Jim. I don't feel right. It must be the food poisoning.

SALLY
What food poisoning?

CAPTAIN
The other guests were complaining about it. They're going to sue.

JIM enters looking exhausted.

JIM
I've had a terrible date boys and girls! No it was worse than that! We got to the club and the Prince disappeared into the pop-up dark room and never came out again! Then I lost my wallet, and I had to walk all the way home! I found these letters outside. They look like more final demands...

SALLY opens one.

SALLY
Oh mercy!

CAPTAIN
What is it?

SALLY
It's a human quality like forgiveness or compassion but that's not important right now. We got bailiffs coming round!

CAPTAIN
If it's any help... I have all that gold,

SALLY
Our sweet Captain!

CAPTAIN
I'd do anything for you Sally.

SALLY
Yes yes just go and get it.

The CAPTAIN exits.

SALLY
It's like we been cursed! This is all your fault and your talk of going away. The gods don't like it!

The CAPTAIN enters with the carrier bag of gold.

CAPTAIN
Careful, it's heavy.

They open the bag. They look shocked. JIM reaches in and pulls out a handful of powder.

SALLY
Dust! It's turned to dust!

CAPTAIN
I've been made a fool!

302

JIM
There's only one thing for it! We're going to get our hands on that treasure!

SALLY
We don't know where it is.

CAPTAIN
We know where the map is.

JIM
If the boat's still at harbour we can climb aboard and stowaway.

SALLY
I'm not getting on that boat!

JIM
You stay here then. You can mop up the vomit in the bedrooms, you can sleep in a room with no roof on and you can give the bailiffs a hand too. I'm going.

CAPTAIN
And I.

SALLY
What do you think boys and girls? And will you come too? Alright I'm game! Captain, lead the way!

Scene 5: The deck of the Mardy Cow

It is still dark, the very early hours of morning. The sky is streaked with stars and there is moonlight. On the deck is a large crate, and next to it is a barrel with a sign on saying "apples". (Or it could just be two barrels) Note: if possible it would be helpful for an actor to be able to cross from one wing to the other in this scene.

SILVER and MARINA enter, MARINA carrying a lantern.

SILVER
Ahar!

MARINA
Ahaaar! Ahoy there ship mates.

Ahoy there Marina!

SILVER
Now you lot try. Ahaaaar! *(They try. To a man in the audience:)* Christ lad, it's not "ah ha", it's not Alan Partridge. Welcome aboard the Mardy Cow! Now that I be back at sea, I be as happy as Lance Black's busy little tongue. Now, hear me well and I'll learn ye the special names for the parts of the ship. We got an old sea shanty does the job o' that. (To Marina) What are you looking all thoughtful about?

MARINA
I was wondering whether pirates live in shanty towns.

SILVER looks at her for a few seconds then slaps her so hard she falls over. MARINA looks sad.

SILVER
She'll be fine she's got her winter fat on her. Now, you have a listen and I'll teach you the song because you need to know the proper nautical names for things.

> Oh... the front of the boat's called the front of the boat
> And rear of the boat's the fucking rear
> And the left's the fucking left and the right's the fucking right
> And middle bit we just call "here"
> Oh! The middle bit is just fucking here.

You won't remember that but that's alright because we got a sail cloth here with the words on.

SILVER pulls a cord and a sheet unfurls with the chorus lyrics on.

SILVER
We bought it like that from John Lewis already printed. Now, I'll sing me song and when we get to the chorus, you'll join in.

During the first verse, SILVER pulls out various knotted ropes to illustrate (or has a chart with pictures on). The "Boris" has a lot of frayed ends over the knot.

SONG: A PIRATE'S LIFE

> *Now the first thing a pirate learns, Is how to do his knots and lashings*
> *This knot's called the twink's restraint, so you can give him a thrashing*
> *And this one's called the Boris cos it looks a bit like him*
> *And this one's just a mess, we call it "Mother needs a trim"...*

> *Oh a pirate's life is a gay old life, And a gay old life is his.*

> *Oh... the front of the boat's called the front of the boat*
> *And rear of the boat's the fucking rear*
> *And the left's the fucking left and the right's the fucking right*
> *And middle bit we just call "here"*
> *Oh! The middle bit is just fucking here.*

(Spoken) I've heard a lot worse. Not from humans...

> *Now the next thing a pirate learns, is how to grab his booty*
> *We steal it from innocent cargo ships and we smuggle it home, no duty*
> *The third thing a pirate learns, is how to hold his grog*
> *Cos if he gets sick, he'll feel a prick, when we fuck him while his head's in the bog*

> *Yes a pirate's life is a gay old life, And a gay old life is his.*

> *Oh... the front of the boat's... [etc]*

SILVER
You better give th'selves a round of applause. Now Marina lad, be we shipshape and Bristol fashion?

MARINA
What's Bristol fashion?

304

SILVER
Tracksuits I think. And do ye know boys and girls the very most important thing to prepare for a voyage? Always bring something tasty and long lasting to eat!

SILVER opens a hatch to reveal DARYL, tied up inside. SILVER chuckles.

SILVER
If you're good we can play sardines later, would you like that? (DARYL nods vaguely and sadly) You might not know my version. In my version I give you a handful of sardines to swallow and then I go fishing for them with my hook. It's a bit like football. In that I change ends at half time. *(SILVER closes the door)* I can't wait to get him in me crow's nest boys and girls. Now, you keep a watch Marina lad, I be off to chop some salad.

SILVER exit.

MARINA
I guess I'm a baddie now boys and girls. Sad face. But I'm dead excited. I haven't seen the world. I wonder where we'll visit. Trinidad and Tobasco. The United Arab Immigrants. The Costa del Skol... I might meet a nice girl. Imagine if I got with someone like the captain's daughter. I've seen her on telly. We'd go to premiers and parties like Ellen Degeneres and whatsername and take selfies with Jennifer Lawrence and have our nude photos leaked.

JOSEPHINE enters, dressed for travel.

JOSEPHINE
What an early departure, I nearly missed you!

MARINA
But... Josephine Fishbeard!

JOSEPHINE
I'll take an en suite with a portside window and a seat at the captain's table for tonight's dinner, you'll advise me on the dress code?

MARINA
But – I – are you coming with us?

JOSEPHINE
Of course if there's no room for me you can drop me at the port of the next major tax haven... me and the three tiny bikinis I've packed. Now, where's the spa?

MARINA
You don't need a Spar! We got groceries, and I can lend you a tampon. You should do films you know, you got a great face for cinema.

JOSEPHINE
So have you. (aside) Or any darkened room.

MARINA
Have you ever had *your* breasts leaked?

JOSEPHINE
I beg your pardon?

MARINA
Sorry, that came out a bit messy, as the Bishop said to the choirboy.

JOSEPHINE
Just take my luggage to my berth. I'll be sure to tip you. (Aside) Right over the side.

MARINA
Wow. These are real Louis Vuitton boys and girls, like you get down the market! Follow me.

JOSEPHINE and MARINA exit. JIM emerges from the shadows.

JIM (stage whisper)
Aye aye boys and girls! Mum! Captain! It's all clear.

SALLY emerges. She wears a figure-hugging sailor suit, wearing sunglasses and pulling a mini suitcase. She has a book and a net of oranges.

SALLY (not remotely a stage whisper)
Jim!!

JIM
Shhh!

SALLY gropes about and bangs into things.

JIM
Take your sunglasses off.

SALLY
(Loud) What? (Quieter) Oh right. That's better. Do you want an orange? They stop you getting scurvy, I've had twelve already. I'm getting acid reflux. Mind the pips, they're full of them, I'm going to be like a road-gritting truck tomorrow. Hello boys and girls! (Indicating her outfit) You're wondering how I found it, we've been hiding in the ship's lost property box what they have

for when sailors forget their kit. Christ the smell, crotches and armpits! What was it like Jim?

JIM
Yeah it was brilliant.

SALLY
I've brought some holiday reading. Lord of the Flies. It's about teenage boys gallivanting in shorts on an island. I had a quick flick while we was hiding but I had to stop cos the captain said he could hear my lips moving.

The CAPTAIN enters.

CAPTAIN
It's monstrous, monstrous!

SALLY
(Indicating her outfit) It's just a bit tight.

CAPTAIN
Silver's hoisted his cock and balls up my mast, look!

They look up.

CAPTAIN
How's my girl? First time on a boat

SALLY
I'm calm as a millpond. When do you think it'll set sail?

CAPTAIN
Set sail? We're already miles out.

SALLY goes to the edge of the boat and looks out. She screams. JIM puts an orange in her mouth.

JIM
Just breath.

SALLY
Mmmf mmm. *(She removes the orange)* I can't bloody breath. *(She gives the orange to someone in the audience)* Here. I'd say mind the pips but you look like you can stomach a bit of seed.

JIM
You two stay here. I'm going to have a snoop around. I'm not in the mood for company.

CAPTAIN
Now stop mooning my lad.

JIM *(pulling his trousers up)*
Sorry. Boys and girls, keep an eye on them will you?

JIM exits.

SALLY
I need a drink.

CAPTAIN
There should be some grog here somewhere...

He finds a bottle and offers it to her. She drinks.

CAPTAIN
That'll put silt in your slit.

SALLY
I don't know how you coped with life on a boat. I'd get lonely.

CAPTAIN
I had my crew.

SALLY
I don't think you should be attempting urban slang at your age.

CAPTAIN
My shipmates.

SALLY
But the same people day in day out. Like Big Brother. I used to enjoy that when it was on Channel 4, I don't see it now that it's only on Twitter. The nice thing about keeping an inn is you've plenty of company but they fuck off again before you've run out of your best conversation.

CAPTAIN
You're scared of letting people get close to you. (He gets very close to her)

SALLY (retracting herself)
I think we're going to need a bigger boat.

CAPTAIN
I expect you've been hurt?

SALLY
A woman's heart is an ocean of secrets. (To a boy in the audience) And her mind's a lake of muck, haha. (She drinks). It's a clear old night.

CAPTAIN
I used to like navigating with the stars.

SALLY
Was that a game show? Here, which way's the poop deck?

CAPTAIN
It's up there, why?

SALLY
I might need one later.

CAPTAIN
Don't you get tired of being alone? You've romanced some of guests.

SALLY
Romanced!

CAPTAIN
That actor who stayed the week while he was doing the summer show at Newquay. In and out of his bedroom you were.

SALLY
I was helping him with his lines.

CAPTAIN
They were very monosyllabic lines.

SALLY
It was a very modern piece.

CAPTAIN
I'll find us somewhere safe to sleep. Just remember-

SALLY
I know I know. Never play Jenga with an octopus.

CAPTAIN
Just remember we're stowaways. We got to keep a low profile.

The CAPTAIN exits.

SALLY
I don't like this one bit boys and girls. What if we capsize? I need to take my mind off things.

SALLY downs the rest of the bottle.

SALLY (singing quietly at first)
What shall we do with the drunken sailor
What shall we do with the drunken sailor
What shall we do with the drunken sailor
Early in the morning....

Any suggestions?

(If there is a good suggestion they sing a verse of that. If not she gets them singing one of these...)

Shave all his pubes and write twat on his forehead
Shave all his pubes and write twat on his forehead
Shave all his pubes and write twat on his forehead
Early in the morning

Photograph his cock and text it to his mother
Photograph his cock and text it to his mother
Photograph his cock and text it to his mother
Early in the morning...

Oh thank you boys and girls ever so much, I feel a lot happier now!

SILVER creeps on in the background, looking about. They don't see each other. The audience warn her, "he's behind you!".

SALLY
Who is it? Oh how lovely, Mr Silver oh no wait that's who we're hiding from. Thank you.

SALLY exits quickly and drunkenly.

SILVER
Most strange! I thought I heard something. A pack of wild dogs perhaps, or the live recording of Kate Bush's comeback gigs. Did you see anything? (no!) Oh yes you did! (Oh no we didn't) Very well. I'll get back to my pan-fried scallops.

SILVER exits. JIM emerges from the shadows.

JIM
It's me, mum. Mum? Boys and girls have you seen my mum or the Captain? Ah, that's ok then. You know, I wouldn't mind if they got together. He's a decent man, and she's a... woman. I better find somewhere to hide. Can you see anywhere?

The audience point out the crate and the barrel. He chooses the barrel but moves the "Apples" sign from the barrel to the crate. He climbs into the barrel out of sight. MARINA enter with a large bucket of slops. The bucket should really be full.

MARINA
Ahoy there shipmates. I'm just going to get rid of these slops overboard. (She takes aim for the audience) Three, two one... Oh wait. I don't suppose that's very good for the environment. Where shall I pour them... (she sees the barrel and crate) Now that crate's for the apples, so that barrel must be for the slops.

MARINA pours the lot into the barrel. Jim screams.

MARINA
What was that?

JIM
Albatross.

MARINA
Fair enough. (*She looks over at the crate*). I could do with a nice apple.

She goes to reach into the crate. Jim's arm shoots out of the barrel and across to the crate and puts an apple into Marina's hand. MARINA takes it without thinking.

MARINA
Thank you very much.

MARINA exits. She enters again. She runs to the barrel and looks in. Jim sticks his head out.

MARINA
(loud) Jim!

JIM
Marina!! A pirate! How could you!

SILVER runs on, still armed. He holds the sword to JIM's throat.

SILVER
Ahaaaa! It's ain't that whitebait's wankstain Jim Hawkins! Your minutes be numbered, boy.

JIM
Marina if we ever get back home to Cornwall I will... I will wipe my knob all over your favourite Claudia Winkelman poster.

SALLY runs on

SALLY
No!!!! You leave him!

SILVER aims the gun at her and indicates to MARINA to take hold of it.

SILVER
Train the gun on her.

MARINA
What?

SILVER
Train the gun on her.

MARINA
I don't know what that means.

SILVER
Sixty-nineing sea cucumbers! Just hold the gun and-

The CAPTAIN charges on with a roar and rugby tackles MARINA who falls. SILVER moves from JIM to pick up the gun. JIM climbs out of the barrel.

CAPTAIN
I've got him I've got him, run while you can!

JIM and SALLY run off. SILVER grabs the gun and runs off the opposite side of the stage. MARINA wriggles free and follows SILVER. The CAPTAIN catches his breath. He walks off in the direction SALLY and JIM exited... and as he gets to the side of the stage he gasps and starts walking backwards. SALLY and JIM emerge walking backwards too followed by SILVER walking forwards with the gun.

SILVER
I should make every scurvy one of you walk the plank. Only it might be useful to have an experienced pair of hands such as yours Captain. The finest sailor of his generation.

SALLY
Oh Captain! Did you hear that?

SILVER
Still I needs to assert me authority so someone's going overboard and not overboard in the sense of oh, I've done far too big a buffet haven't I, 12 trifles and three roast chickens and 40 mini quiches is actually quite a lot for five people, I might have gone a little overboard, whoopsydaisy. In case you thought that was what I meant. So who's it going to be.

JOSEPHINE enters in pyjamas and with an eye mask pulled up over her forehead.

JOSEPHINE
Can we please keep the noise down! This really is the worst cruise I've ever been on and I once went on a cruise with Max Clifford.

SILVER comes behind her and holds the sword to her throat. He keeps the gun trained on the others.

SILVER
You're going to take a little stroll my pretty. Think of it as a red carpet. You'll make a right splash!

JOSEPHINE
Daddy!!

The CAPTAIN steps forward.

SILVER
One step and I'll shoot you in your saggy old neck. Marina lad! Bring the you-know-whats!

MARINA enters with bright orange inflatable armbands.

SILVER
Well it is a comedy boys and girls.

MARINA and SILVER slip the armbands onto Josephine.

JOSEPHINE
You can't be serious!

SILVER
Tata now.

They all watch her exit. After a moment, there is a scream and a splash. Everyone is in shock.

SILVER
What is it they say, never meet your idols. Right! Hear me well. Captain you will be our navigator and the ship's cleaner. Hawkins, S, you'll be being the scullery maid and kitchen assistant. Hawkins, J, you'll be being the cabin boy.

SALLY
Sounds better than what I got. What's a cabin boy?

SILVER
No-one knows, it just has pleasingly saucy overtones, I think basically I get to fuck you all kinds of merry ways until we reach our shore.

JIM
No way!

SILVER
Oh man up! Just lie back and think of England.

JIM
I'd rather lie back and think of a man with an actual cock.

SILVER
Jim lad, that hurts. Not as much as this will, granted. Now, go and find yourselves berths.

JIM and the CAPTAIN exit. As SALLY exits the CAPTAIN stops her.

SILVER
Hold it wench.

SALLY
Are you going to make me a cabin boy too?

SILVER
That be the pearl necklace I gave you. I'd better keep that safe. Give it to me.

SALLY takes it off.

SILVER
Off you go.

SALLY exits.

SILVER
I don't really need them as crew so much as I've got a 1996 edition of Trivial Pursuit lined up in yonder officer quarters and the notion of playing it with only Marina and a Prince who left Atlantis two days ago is enough to make me want to put my mouth to a cannon and light the fuse. Course, after that, I'll kill them. Ahaaaaar!!!

He exits.

Scene 6: The deck of the Mardy Cow

ETHEL sits with a bottle of Chardonnay. He pours a glass.

ETHEL
A merman sat on the wooden deck
His tail was all a-quiver
He hoped there wouldn't be a wreck
But there was – it was just his liver. Bottoms up.

DARYL enters. He wears a gold all in one wresting outfit.

DARYL
Ethel! You're meant to be keeping me out of trouble!

ETHEL
Why what have you done, had a run in with the fashion police?

DARYL
Nah, this is what respectable princes wear at sea. Reem or what.

ETHEL
What, I think.

ETHEL looks at his wine glass and at the amount of wine still in the bottle, he starts swigging wine from the bottle. JIM enters.

JIM
Daryl! There you are! What's going on?

DARYL
I been taken prisoner!

JIM
Me too! Silver's working me like a dog. I'm sweating like a glassblowers arse.

ETHEL coughs. JIM looks very confused.

DARYL
Aw sorry. Jim, this is my bodyguard, Ethel.

JIM
How do you do. What's with the shit drag?

ETHEL
Interestingly, where I come from "shit drag" is a very dull and very unhygienic game played by sheep farmers to stop them getting bored or horny. Now listen, you're supposed to be heroes. Right?

DARYL
Right!

JIM
Right...

ETHEL
So behave like it. Take the ship.

JIM
Mutiny!

DARYL
Oh fuck! Where?

ETHEL
You, you dingo. Then I'll lead you to Treasure Island. Good luck.

ETHEL exits

DARYL
I dunno about this...

JIM
I thought you were a hero. Just follow my lead.

DARYL
I don't want to get hit do I. This face is going on coins one day darlin.

SILVER enters with the parrot. He puts the parrot down.

SILVER
Stay there you intoxicated pterodactyl.

PARROT
Oh my god stop flirting with me it's exhausting.

SILVER
Princey lad sir! I can barely wait till we be married!

JIM
Married?! *(Faux sweet)* I mean... congratulations!

SILVER
Most noble tradition! We pirates had same-sex marriage even centuries back![53] How be ye liking my boat.

DARYL
It's *my* boat, and it's shit. There's no extras, no decals. We got to pimp it up a bit.

JIM (slightly flirty)
He's just tired Mr Silver...

---

[53] This be true, arrr.

SILVER
That's to be expected after being force-fed a bag of ketamine the size of an Argos carrier and dragged into a darkroom aharrrrrrr.

JIM
You total bas- *(changing tack again, flirty)* I mean, you clever, devious, powerful man...

JIM drapes an arm around SILVER who runs a hand down Jim's chest.

SILVER
You be mighty sweaty me lad.

JIM nudges DARYL who fondles SILVER's hook. SILVER giggles. JIM looks at DARYL.

JIM
Now!

They grab SILVER either side. There is a fight. DARYL isn't much use. JIM corners SILVER.

JIM
It's off to the brig with you.

SALLY and the CAPTAIN enter.

SALLY
Ooh hello. Intimate moment?

JIM
We've captured Silver! The ship's ours.

SALLY
Oh my brave Prince.

DARYL
Yeah thanks.

DARYL and JIM start to drag SILVER away. JIM feels in SILVER's pocket and pulls out the Treasure Map. He gives it to SALLY.

SALLY
Don't forget his feathered friend.

SALLY picks up the PARROT.

PARROT
What have I done?

SALLY
Guilty by association bird brain.

SALLY throws the PARROT to DARYL.

SALLY
Take them away.

They drag SILVER away. The PARROT sings Close Every Door to Me.

CAPTAIN
Time for a celebration I think. I've a little something tucked away which you might enjoy.

He rummages in a crate and pulls out a bottle of champagne.

CAPTAIN
I didn't want to pop my cork until a very special lady came along.

SALLY
Oh Captain! The finest sailor of his generation!

CAPTAIN
Oh I found your necklace below deck, sat in a jar of water. *(He pulls the necklace out.)* Put it on my dear.

The audience shout.

SALLY
The boys and girls don't seem to want me to. I think this one wants me to take something off.

CAPTAIN
Perhaps one day I can buy you some jewellery myself. Perhaps even a ring...

She takes it out of the jar and the CAPTAIN helps her put it on. The weather changes.

SALLY
It's got ever so chilly all of a sudden.

MARINA rushes in.

MARINA
Captain! Something's rising on your starboard side.

SALLY
I noticed that.

MARINA
Iceberg! Dead ahead! Abandon ship!

SALLY
How lovely, there's a band on ship! I hope they know some Donny Osmond.

An iceberg slides into view.

MARINA
Abandon ship, abandon ship!

MARINA runs off. SALLY and the CAPTAIN do not look around. The iceberg gets closer.

SALLY
Captain! Are we going down?

CAPTAIN
Well I...

There is a terrible thud, the splintering of wood. The lights go out. We hear screams.

MARINA (off)
Abandon ship. Abandon ship.

Ethel appears:

ETHEL

Just as our heroes have taken charge
Along comes an iceberg and skewers the barge
The water looks cold, unfathomably deep
Are Jim and co doomed to their final sleep?

These heroes are cursed, this tale makes me wary
We shoulda done Cinders, I'd make a cool fairy
There's bigger holes now in the boat than the plot
Will these be the heroes that history forgot?

But just as the bulk of an iceberg is hidden
Maybe our Jim and co do have it in 'em
To turn things around as the boat starts to sink
But that's for part two – now go get a drink!

INTERVAL

Luke Webber as Prince Daryl, Philip Lawrence as Sally, Alex Wood as Long John Silver and Lucas Livesey as Jim in *Treasure Island: The Curse of the Pearl Necklace*. Photo by Derek Drescher.

Briony Rawle as Marina and Alex Wood as Long John Silver in *Treasure Island: The Curse of the Pearl Necklace*. Photo by Derek Drescher.

Scene 7: Under the ocean

ETHEL welcomes us back.

ETHEL
My beautiful boomerangs, you came back to me!
I'm glad that you did, we're all at sea
I expect you've been wondering what fate has tossed us
And I see no-one thought to bring me a Fosters.

Now, the same time has passed in our world as in yours
Since we left them sliding about on all fours
We'd best fill you in – it won't take us long
But events such as these should be told in a song…

JIM, DARYL, SALLY, THE CAPTAIN and MARINA are underwater. There is seaweed and fish and old bits of boat. Some lines are sung individually as appropriate.

SONG: Under the Ocean

There are schools of fishes playing
In the seaweed gently swaying
And the surface far above us shines like ice
It's like nothing here can hurt us
In this underwater circus,
It's a colourful and quiet paradise

We've been down here longer than we oughta
I can feel my lungs filling up with salty water

We are drowning, we are drowning
Under water, out of reach
Take me to my bloody beach

Don't wanna die before I get abs
But we're more likely to get crabs
It looks it's all over just like that

I wish we hadn't lingered
I think I'm being fish-fingered
Or a hermit crab has nestled in my twat

We want to go back home and who can blame us?
I think a sea cucumber's slid right up my anus

We are drowning, we are drowning
Under water, out of reach
Take me to my bloody beach.

(Then faster and rockier)

Under the ocean, Under the brine
We got a quibble we're getting nibbled
Throw us a line

We asked the fishes, help us to the rocks?
They said no we're cod fish, You depleted our stocks
Hey Mr Lobster, get us out of this dive?
He said no way guys, You boiled my brother alive

Under the ocean, Under the brine
Before we start tripping, and skinny dipping
Throw us a line

Hey Mrs Sturgeon, show us where to go?
She said get yourself fucked, you ate my children as roe
Now now Mr Sperm Whale, give us emancipation
But all he gave us, was his ejaculation

Under the ocean, Under the brine
Sorry for frowning, but we're all drowning
Throw us a line
Sorry for frowning, but we're all drowning
Throw us a line!

BLACKOUT

Scene 8: On Treasure Island

A sandy island, but not barren - there is vegetation including palm trees. There is a tall pile of rocks to the back of the stage. We can hear ocean waves, and tropical sounds: birds, a monkey.

JIM lies unconscious on the sand, washed up from the shore.

MIRANDA enters. She is played by the same actor as Josephine but should have hair of a different colour, and it should unkempt, matted, messy. Her clothes are torn, made from animal skins or leaves. She drags a fishing line with a fish on the end of it. She puts the fish down and gathers sticks with which to make a fire. After a while.

JIM (unconscious)
Mmmmmnnn

MIRANDA cocks an ear, looks puzzled. Carries on making a fire.

JIM (unconscious)
Mmmn, Daryl....Yeah... Mmmmmmnnnn

MIRANDA again looks alert.

JIM (unconscious)
Wait! Not on my T shirt.

MIRANDA sees JIM. She freezes. Cautiously she approaches. She's curious. She smells him. Touches him. She feels his flat chest, then feels her own, and notices the difference. She feels his crotch. Strange... She smells it. She undoes his fly, lifts his waistband and has a good look. She hasn't seen this before. She puts a hand in for a feel and pulls out a small crab. She puts her hand back in for a proper feel. She feels something stir and plays with it a bit. She retrieves her hand and smells it. She enthusiastically offers a smell to the front row. She returns and looks at JIM's genitals again... She is now reminded of something. She is alarmed.

MIRANDA scuttles into the trees and returns with a bundle of something - a ragged and torn old Cock and Balls flag. She sees that the symbol on the flag is what JIM has in his pants. Does this make him a pirate?

MIRANDA looks like a threatened animal. She picks up her fish and starts attacking JIM with it, beating him about the head. JIM wakes up.

JIM
Stop it! Stop! Help! Stop!

MIRANDA stops but holds the fish, ready to strike again.

JIM
You're supposed to batter the *fish!*

MIRANDA startles at being shouted at. She exits.

JIM
Hello boys and girls! Where can this be? I hope it's Sitges cos I always wanted to meet some real-life mainstream gays from Clapham. Mum! Mum? I lost mum in the sea, and she can barely swim... maybe the captain saved her! Captain! Captain? And Marina? At least Daryl will be alright. But I expect I'll never see him again.

MIRANDA enters.

JIM
She reminds me of someone.

MIRANDA points at JIM. A GORILLA lumbers on, looks at MIRANDA, then looks at JIM.

JIM
What... no. Oh no.

The GORILLA advances on JIM. JIM panics and flees. The GORILLA chases him off-stage. MIRANDA watches them go, then exits too.

SALLY enters looking exhausted, still wearing the necklace. She has a banana. It has a little sticker on it like you get when you buy fruit from a shop.

SALLY
There you are boys and girls! I'm purpled! No not purpled what is it – marooned! I've been walking in circles. The sun's relentless and I lost my factor fifteen, I think it fell out of my pocket when I was pulling myself up after my interval poo. Have you had a nice drink? It's more than I've had, I think we must be in the Middle East because I can't find a fucking bar anywhere. I don't know where Jim is, or the Captain. My sweet, loyal, reliable captain, the finest sailor of his generation! To think I ignored his advances all those years... To be fair, when he first moved in I thought he was more into menfolk because he said he'd been a rear admiral which I took to be slang for something. Not that I got a problem with that, no, I was pleased. After my Jim came out, I used to say, "See that Captain, he's one of your kind Jim, and it hasn't

stopped him growing into a fine, respectable gentleman, now why don't you follow him up to bed and try and wangle a few extra quid out of him." *(She waves the banana)* I found a tree with these on. Funny, I always thought the little sticker was put on after. *(Calls)* Jim? Captain? *(She startles at something and yelps)* There's bugs and creepy crawlies everywhere! Deadly poisonous I shouldn't wonder. I keep getting flashbacks to the time I freaked out at the Eden Project. Well really, twenty-three pound fifty it was!

A spider appears. SALLY screams. It scuttles off.

SALLY
Where did it go where did it go?

They tell her.

SALLY
Thank you, I'll go this way.

SALLY dashes to the other side of the stage, her body out of sight, her head still peering out from the wings.

SALLY
I said to the ticket man, twenty-three pound fifty, who do you think you are, Centre Parks? Has that spider gone? (She creeps out again). Will you keep an eye out for it? That's very kind of you. I've lost that nice Prince Daryl too, I don't understand where he's got to, we been getting along like a house on fire.

Behind her, the spider appears again from somewhere. "It's behind you!"

SALLY
What's that my loves? Now come on don't all shout out at once, put your hands up if you got something to say. That's right, yes, you sir.

The spider disappears.

SALLY
Behind me is it?!?!

SALLY turns around. The enormous spider is now clinging to the middle of her back. She faces front again.

SALLY
I think the heat's getting to your heads.

The PRINCE enters, upstage of SALLY so she can't see him. He is exhausted, a wreck. He carries a stick as a weapon that he barely has the energy to hold. He sees the spider and screams. SALLY screams. She turns her head to see him.

SALLY
Daryl! You scared me!

DARYL
Stay right there.

SALLY
Anything you say your majesty!

DARYL
Don't move!

SALLY
I'm not!

DARYL creeps towards her, mesmerised by the spider. He has his stick ready.

SALLY
Oh! Daryl! I can feel your fingers all over my back! Ooohoohoooo! What are you doing to me you naughty boy! You be careful now, I'm hugely dehydrated. I can't afford to be losing fluids.

DARYL
Nearly there…

SALLY
Me too!

DARYL whacks the spider, hard, nearly knocking SALLY off her feet.

SALLY
Fuck OFF your majesty!

SALLY whips Josephine's mace spray out of a pocket and sprays DARYL liberally. DARYL totters blindly. SALLY snatches his stick and beats him with it.

SALLY
That hurt!

DARYL
There was a spider on your back!

SALLY screams.

DARYL
It's dead now.

SALLY
Oh.

SALLY screams again. DARYL gingerly throws the dead spider offstage – SALLY doesn't see the spider. DARYL is beat. Collapses onto something, sitting down.

DARYL
My eyes!

SALLY
You'll be alright dreckly[54].

DARYL
I feel faint. And hot. And parched. Me head's spinning.

SALLY
I expect you're not used to being out in this hot dry air, out of the sea, with a beautiful woman. (She leans in... the leaps away again) Fuck! What if you got Ebola! And there's me, all- Where is Atlantis, is it in Africa?

DARYL
It's under the Atlantic Ocean.

SALLY
Oh yeah! As you were.

DARYL
I can't go on. I think I'm dying!

SALLY
Dying? How sad. Have you any... unfulfilled wishes you want to try out before you kark it? Anything... at all, your majesty?

DARYL
Where am I? How did I get here?

SALLY
Well, you helped drag me to the shore after the shipwreck, and-

DARYL
What shipwreck?

SALLY
Oh my! You lost your memory, I think he's got ambrosia. Now, concentrate, what's your name and where do you come from and who was at number one the week you were born, I'm not telling you mine.

DARYL
I... I don't know.

SALLY
Alright (she puts a hand up) How many fingers have I stuck up?

DARYL
None darlin', they're all there in front of you.

SALLY
Listen, your name's Daryl, alright? And I'm Sally. And one day, you came wandering into my five star boutique hotel in... in greater Padstow without a penny to your name, asking for shelter and a crust of bread. And being a kind soul I turfed Cher Lloyd out of one of the cheaper suites and nursed you back to health, and that is how you came to fall in love with me.

DARYL
You're having a laugh. Are we an item?

SALLY
Are we an item! (Sally looks up, and...) Look!! A plane! Help! Help!!! (She waves her arms frantically). It can't see us.

DARYL
I don't think I've ever been on a plane.

SALLY
I done it once. It's a bit like Christmas... you all have your tea, you watch Harry Potter 12 with the swears cut out, you get pissed at ten in the morning, you eat a foot-long Toblerone in one sitting, someone vomits, a baby screams, and eventually you hide out in the toilet just to get some peace and have a fag. (Watching the plane, sadly) No. It's gone.

DARYL
Fucking hell I'm famished.

SALLY offers him the banana.

SALLY
Here, I been saving it.

DARYL goes to eat it with the skin on. SALLY peels it for him.

SALLY
Useful tree, the banana. I had to use its leaves as bog roll. It was all a bit slidey slimy mind you, and there was nowhere to wash my hands.

DARYL hands the banana back in disgust.

SALLY
You not hungry? Wait! I know how to find out where we are! The sticker! (She picks up the banana and reads) "Produce of... Treasure Island!" We're on treasure island!

---

[54] Cornish slang: at some point in the future.

SALLY pulls the folded treasure map out of her bra. ETHEL appears from behind a rock.

ETHEL
G'day!

SALLY
Oi! I'm having a private moment here. Oh my lord what the hell are you. It's like RuPaul's Drag race before they had a budget and let me tell you this out of kindness, whatever it is you think you are it sure as hell ain't fishy.

ETHEL
I'm a merman you dick-brained platypus, what's you're excuse? Well, if it ain't my dappy prince Daryl! How's it going mate?

SALLY
My Daryl doesn't know no merman.

DARYL
Hey... I know you.

ETHEL
G'day boys and girls.

SALLY
Wait, what, don't you dare. These are my boys and girls, how do you know them. (To the audience) Do you know this halfway haddock?

ETHEL
(To Daryl) Where's that spunky boyfriend of yours?

DARYL
Wait, I think I remember... a beautiful, handsome young man... In a mirror... Me! I was getting ready for a date! But who with?

ETHEL sees the necklace

ETHEL
Shitsticks Sheila what's that necklace you're wearing? Give it here, pronto.

SALLY
I will not! You're just jealous because I'm here in my finery with this young man.

ETHEL
Jealous of who? I'm not gay and I'm not blind. Hand it over or I'll take it from you.

SALLY
You and whose shoal? You've not got a leg to stand on. Typical Aussie, descended from thieves!

ETHEL
That necklace is cursed.

SALLY
Cursed!

ETHEL
How did you get it?

SALLY
It was given to me! It was the night everyone got ill and the storm blew the roof off and Jim had his wallet stolen and we had to sail away on the boat and got hit by an iceberg and nearly died, why do you ask?

DARYL
When I had it, I had some bird do a shit on my head.

SALLY
The things a woman will do to earn a crust.

DARYL
Ethel's right.

SALLY
I know I know. But it's so pretty. It's the only proper nice thing I ever got given.

SALLY takes it off.

ETHEL
Cheer up. It's just a pearl necklace. Easy come, easy go.

SALLY
I never had a pearl necklace before. A man did give me a lemon drizzle cake one time. It was the gentleman from coeliac bakery, it's called Wheat Free Kings.

DARYL
We've got a map of the island Ethel. But we don't know where we are.

SALLY
So we were wondering would you mind having a look at it and pointing us to somewhere we can get a gin and tonic.

DARYL
No, the treasure.

SALLY
Don't bicker with me in public me 'andsome.

ETHEL
Very well. *(Looks at the map)* This is where you are. And here's where the treasure's meant to be. And you cross a stream here, look, where you can get water.

DARYL *(Pointing at the map)*
It says "here be dragons"!

ETHEL
They put that on every map for a laugh mate. It's even on the tube map, top left bit of the Metropolitan line that no bugger looks at. Right, my time's up. I'm getting weak. I need to get back in the water or this fish is fucked. See you later.

ETHEL exits. SALLY looks at the map. She turns it round. And round. She's confused. DARYL takes it. He scans the horizon.

DARYL
You see that hill over there that looks like a you-know-what.

SALLY
Oh yeah! It's very geo-graphic...

DARYL
I think that's that hill here. Those are the trees next to it... Come on. We need water.

SALLY
You lead, I'll follow. (Aside) This way I can watch his royal jelly while he walks. See you in a bit boys and girls.

They exit.

Scene 9: On Treasure Island

MIRANDA has a fire going. She settles her fish on it to cook. There is a rustle from offstage. JIM and the GORILLA enter. The GORILLA has an amorous arm draped around JIM and they both have cigarettes dangling from their mouths. The GORILLA has a garland of tropical flowers which he hangs round JIM's neck. JIM is walking funny. They have had sex. JIM's face is resolutely expressionless. After few moments:

JIM

I don't want to talk about it boys and girls. (pause) I will say two things. Firstly, you'll notice, he didn't kill me. Secondly, after what he did just do to me, you could put me on a crazy golf course and use me as one of the least challenging holes. (To the gorilla) Alright alright, don't fuss me. I'm all hot and sweaty. Big boy. I thought gorillas were meant to have small penises.

The GORILLA strolls off, happy. He blows Jim a kiss as he exits. Jim calls after him.

JIM

This is not to go on Facebook alright?

MIRANDA points at a pile of wood.

MIRANDA

Get!

JIM

She speaks!

MIRANDA

You get wood!

JIM

I might have had a semi.

MIRANDA

Wood! Fire!

JIM

Ok, sorry. Calm down.

JIM starts to carry logs to the fire.

JIM

Wait a second... Josephine!

MIRANDA looks confused.

JIM

I should have known when you started hitting me you uptight cow. Ha! Well you're not so chic now are you!

MIRANDA

(points to her cheek) Cheek?

JIM

Maybe you're not Josephine. What is your name?

MIRANDA

My name is Miranda. What is your name?

JIM

I'm Jim. You stay away from me with that fish.

MIRANDA

Do you like crazy golf?

JIM

What? Everyone likes crazy golf. But I only mentioned it by way of making a joke about how having anal sex with that gorilla had left me with an abnormally stretched arsehole.

MIRANDA

Mr Jones likes crazy golf.

JIM

You what?

MIRANDA

I like cooking. Sometimes I go swimming.

JIM

Wait, who's Mr Jones?

MIRANDA

Mr Jones lives in Wolverhampton. He works in a bank. He lives with his wife in a semi-detached house. Thy have three children. Wolverhampton is an industrial town in the midlands. It has approximately 250,000 inhabitants. There is a cinema and a town hall and lots of shops. Where do you come from?

JIM

You wouldn't know it. Look I don't know what you're on about. Who are these Joneses, I can't keep up with them.

MIRANDA looks impatient. She exits and returns with an English language textbook. She opens it and shows JIM a page.

JIM

Oh! You're learning English! Where are *you* from?

MIRANDA

I don't know.

JIM
Well what other languages do you speak?

MIRANDA shakes her head. Points at the book.

MIRANDA
Ethel.

JIM
Ethel... Oh Ethel! You know her do you? Did she give you the book?

MIRANDA hits JIM

JIM
He! Sorry, did *he* give you the book?

MIRANDA nods.

JIM
You're very fucking progressive for a savage. He's been teaching you has he?

MIRANDA
A-B-C-D-L-G-B-T-Q-I-A...

MIRANDA inspects the fish and takes it from the fire.

JIM (flinching)
Not the fish!

MIRANDA offers the fish to JIM who takes a couple of bites.

JIM
Oh god thank you. Thank you. I'm so weak.

MIRANDA
Week... Monday Tuesday Wednesday Happy Days Friday I'm in love Craig David.

JIM
(laughs) No. Weak as in tired. Tired? It's very hot, and I've swum a long way, and your friend just... aped me.

MIRANDA holds out her hands for the fish. JIM gives it to her. MIRANDA eats it in a violent blur until there's a cartoony fishbone left.

JIM
I'm probably an orphan now. I expect you're an orphan too are you? We'll probably die orphans. Right here. Sat wondering what Mr Jones and his family are getting up to.

MIRANDA looks in a washed up crate and pulls out a bottle of rum.

MIRANDA
It's rum.

JIM (still melancholic)
It really is.

MIRANDA
Rum!

JIM
Oh. (takes a swig) Thanks.

SILVER (off)
Ahaaaarrghhhhhhhhhh!

MIRANDA stands alert, grabs JIM's wrist, cocks an ear, points a "wait, listen" finger in the air.

JIM
Ow, get off. I don't know why you're doing the whole child-of-nature thing. We all heard the noise.

MIRANDA pulls him by the arm and they hide in a corner, half hidden. SILVER enters

SILVER
Aharrrgh! But what's this? There be a whole school of whales beached and stranded, I shall have to rescue 'em and push them back into the sea, oh no wait, I'm a bastard I don't have to do that, also oh no wait it's not a whole school of beached whales it's you lot. Present company excepted. If I do see a beached whale I'll eat it Japanese style, raw on a bed of sticky rice. (To his boy in the audience) I'd have you raw on a sticky bed lad. Well now boys and girls you'll see I be on dry land. I happened to see the Mardy Cow's little lifeboat floating free. I swam to it and I've brought it to this little island. Lady luck's a prick tease alright, but on this occasion she was drunk and she put out.

MARINA enters

MARINA
Ahoy there!

SILVER
There you be, Marina lad.

MARINA
You know I'm a girl, right?

SILVER
That's alright Marina lad, girls can be pirates too. Did ye never hear tell of Cornish Patsy? The most afeared

pirate of her time. There goes a story of how she arrived one evening at the castle of the Duke of Penzance, but the duke would not make time to see her for he and his family were at dinner, nor did he invite her to sup with them. Offended, Patsy torched the castle till it were naught but charcoal. Henceforth and to this very day, the duke's descendants keep a spare frozen vegetarian moussaka for one in the freezer lest her ghost turns up hungry. I don't fear much, Marina lad, but the legend of Cornish Patsy's ghost being still abroad, lurking in her old island haunts, wailing and shrieking and doing unspeakable things to seamen, it makes my spine shiver[55]. Now, I told you don't go wandering off. I'm glad my one companion be safe and sound.

MARINA
Aw thanks Mr Silver.

SILVER
Not you!

SILVER exits and returns with the parrot.

SILVER
There she be.

PARROT
Put me back! I'm on the pull, there's a whole tree full of parakeets back there.

MARINA
What's a parakeet?

SILVER
I think seeds, mainly. I wish I'd married that pretty Prince when I had the chance. In his sailor suit - I likes a young sailor. Did ye ever see that film with a young Ryan Phillipe in it about teenage boys trapped on a ship in a storm? It be called White Squall, which was also my response to it.

MARINA
You er... you think a handsome young Prince is going to want to marry you?

SILVER
Why ye little-! It be what's inside what counts. (To his boy) And I'd have you so firmly inside, your dick'll think he's Oscar Pistorius[56].

MARINA
Do you know where we are?

SILVER
I have a hunch.

MARINA
You should try Pilates for that.

SILVER
You see that there hill that's shaped like a, you know

MARINA
Oh yeah!

SILVER
And those trees there? That be the same arrangement as was on the map! Wait about. I recognise this place... I been on this island before and I don't like it. (Whispers) This be where my penis got bitten off by a native during a grog-fuelled encounter. If I find him I'll kill him.

The PARROT hiccups.

SILVER
Talking of grog the Parrot be bloody drunk.

PARROT
Are you starting something?

SILVER
How'd she manage that? Now, if those pesky Hawkinses were here with the treasure map...

MARINA
Look! Footprints!

SILVER
By heck you're right Marina lad! If we find Jim and his maternal liability they can help us carry the treasure to the lifeboat, load it up, and then we'll kill em! Let's follow them.

Before they can move, the CAPTAIN enters. MARINA is about to call to him. SILVER clamps a hand over her mouth and they draw back out of sight.

---

[55] It's possible that Silver was thinking of the fearless 16th Century Irish chieftain Grace or Gráinne O'Malley.

[56] The disabled South African Olympic hero was jailed in October 2014 for the culpable homicide of his girlfriend Reeva Steenkamp.

CAPTAIN
Boys and girls! My poor boat. My poor daughter. My poor Sally! I wish I'd told her how I felt a long time ago. Auch, I hinted often enough, wee suggestive jokes and the like but I should have just come out and said it. I'm not a confident man. I used to be, but after I lost my wee girl to the sea I lost all confidence in my sailing. I should never have set sail in such as storm. And sailing was all I was ever good at so after that I lost all confidence in myself. I think I'm the only survivor, is that right boys and girls?

They tell him he isn't.

CAPTAIN
Are you sure? What a relief. I know what I'll do. An old sea-scout trick, I'll leave a trail of signs so Sally can follow me.

He arranges some twigs into a couple of arrows on the ground.

CAPTAIN
I'll not show you my other sea-scouts trick. You need a sleeping bag, a rubber band, a torch and an erection.

SILVER (to MARINA)
We'll take him hostage.

MARINA
Why?

SILVER
We're pirates! And if the Hawkinses be here with the map, we can use the Captain as bait.

SILVER creeps up behind the CAPTAIN, puts a hand over his mouth and drags him offstage.

MARINA
Dammit boys and girls. I don't want to be a proper pirate! But if I don't stick with Silver I'll never survive out here.

A noise. MIRANDA has rustled something. She appears from hiding. MARINA turns and looks. MIRANDA puts a finger to her mouth.

MARINA
It's a savage! A very pretty savage...

MARINA gives a little wave. MIRANDA returns it.

MARINA
I knew I'd meet a nice girl if I went travelling! (To Miranda) Alright...

MIRANDA
I'm very well thank you, how do you do?

MARINA
Um. I'm alright. But I'm a bit lost and I think three of my closest friends might have drowned today and I'm really really hungry. (pause) Sorry, I'm wittering (pause) I just find you really easy to talk to somehow (pause) I think because you don't say anything back.

MIRANDA runs off. We hear a splash and a thud. She returns with a fish which she presents.

MARINA
Oh! Thank you.

MIRANDA
You're welcome.

SILVER (off)
Marina lad!

MARINA
(Calls) Alright, I'm coming. I'm Marina.

MIRANDA
My name is Miranda. Do you like crazy golf?

MARINA
Yeah I fucking love crazy golf! I'm the Cornish women's crazy golf champion. I'm supposed to be going to the national finals in Bridlington.

SILVER (off)
Marina! Where are you? Stop dyking about!

MARINA
I've got to go. But I'll find you.

She exits. JIM enters. MIRANDA points after MARINA.

MIRANDA
Goodly creature...

JIM
She ain't a creature. She's my mate Marina. Well, she was... I don't know what she is now. You like her do you?

MIRANDA rubs at her crotch unconsciously.

JIM
I wouldn't do that, this heat's so dry you'll start a bush fire. Boys and girls, I couldn't really hear what they were talking about, do they know what island this is? Treasure Island! I wish I had that map. There's a map of

this place Miranda. An old map. You know what a map is?

MIRANDA shakes her head. JIM shows opens the English text book and points at a page.

JIM
A map, this is a map. Like this. It shows where there's buried treasure. It shows where it's hidden, with a cross.

MIRANDA looks at the map.

MIRANDA
Wolverhampton.

MIRANDA starts to wander off in the same direction as MARINA.

JIM
What are you doing? Am I following you?

MIRANDA shrugs

JIM
Alright. Wait – are you taking me to the treasure? You know treasure? Gold, silver, jewels and that.

MIRANDA understands. She points in a different direction.

MIRANDA
No. There.

JIM
Brilliant! She knows where the treasure is! You know the way?

MIRANDA
The way?

JIM
Um. The route... The directions!

MIRANDA
Directions yes! I know all the directions.

JIM
I'm glad I met you!

MIRANDA
Go straight ahead.

JIM
Straight ahead.

MIRANDA (just reeling them off)
Turn left. At the roundabout, please turn right. At the traffic lights, continue-

JIM
No, no... Look, I tell you what, why don't you show me. Here, take my hand.

MIRANDA
How do you do.

JIM
Ok, no, just, like this ok?

They hold hands.

MIRANDA
It feels nice.

JIM
Yeah. It does, it's meant to.

With her free hand MIRANDA touches herself again.

JIM
Er... Yeah. Come on. The treasure.

MIRANDA looks down at herself. JIM doesn't notice.

MIRANDA
My treasure.

JIM
Alright, *"your"* treasure. Show me.

MIRANDA goes to lift her skirt.

JIM
No, no! Gold and silver. I have seen vaginas before boys and girls - mainly on very badly targeted online ads. Come on.

They exit. SALLY and DARYL enter. SALLY has her copy of Lord of the Flies open. DARYL has the map. SALLY is bright red from sunburn. SALLY is singing Craig David's Seven Days as she goes.

SALLY
This is torture boys and girls, I haven't been this sober since I was in single figures. Am I getting a tan? Have you got us lost Daryl? Daryl!

DARYL
Just stop talking!

SALLY
Stop-! How can you say that! Daryl, listen to me Daryl, I don't want to die a virgin, if you catch my driftwood...

DARYL
A virgin? How can you be a virgin? What about Jim?

SALLY
That wouldn't be appropriate, he's my son. (Looking at her copy of *Lord of the Flies*) Look, here. It says the boys built a fire to attract the attention of sailors. They shoulda built a pub. But it's worth a try. *(Notices Miranda's fire)* Look there's a pile of wood over there look, we'll use that. Help me carry it over here.

DARYL
I ain't an expert darlin but I think that's a fire.

DARYL wonders to near the rocks and starts staring at something.

SALLY
Alright, Baden Powell. Wait, if that's a fire that means the island's inhibited! Did you hear me?

DARYL
I found a rock pool.

SALLY
Give me a hand.

DARYL
Oh God.

SALLY
What?

DARYL
My hair's a proper mess.

SALLY
We should build the fire up a bit, look, we can use these twigs.

She picks up the twigs the Captain made into direction-arrows and tosses them on the fire.

SALLY
I'm hungry, is that what happens when you stop drinking?

DARYL
And me. I'm meant to be bulking up! I hate the surface world. All I seen is a shit island, a boat that's seriously lacking in customisation, a shit gay bar and a shit seaside hotel!

SALLY looks aghast.

SALLY
If we make a go of things here young man, I hope you won't spend the whole time complaining.

DARYL
We ain't making a go of things.

SALLY
What did you think of the Oily Otter?

DARYL
I don't remember much about it.

SALLY
I do. Jim took me once. I don't shock easily, but they had a go-go boy, 60 years old if he were a day. He wore a very loose-fitting jockstrap and it was all hanging out of it, swinging between his legs.

DARYL
His penis?

SALLY
His anus. (pause) Here, we might have to populate this island.

DARYL
I'm a prince!

SALLY
So? We're a well-to-do family! I take the Radio Times at Christmas. And I suppose you think my Jim's too beneath you to be beneath you?

DARYL
Jim ain't an idiot, is he. I mean, I'm stupid enough. Back in Atlantis they take the piss out of us royals, they say we're so inbred we don't even have webbed fingers. But you... You're off the scale.

SALLY
I've not had an education have I. My brother he got it all. He don't talk to me now, just a card at Christmas and a bloody round robin letter. Now, slip your top off and sunbathe and let me read.

DARYL slips his top off. SALLY reads, at first distracted every other word by DARYL's toplessness, then absorbed. After a while:

SALLY (quietly)
I think I'm in trouble boys and girls! There's a boy in this story, he starts out nice enough, only the heat gets to him and he starts going mad! He gets all arrogant and bossy and suspicious and won't do as he's told and before you know it there's people dying! (She looks at Daryl suspiciously) He nearly killed me earlier! I never

saw no spider on my back. (To Daryl, too sweetly) I'm just going for a pee my love.

DARYL
Have a shit and all and take your time about it.

SALLY exits. We hear an enormous gushing of piss. We then hear a loud sawing noise. SALLY returns stealthily with a large stick. She picks something out of her teeth.

SALLY
I had to chew through the branch boys and girls. Now, quiet.

SALLY creeps up on DARYL, swings at him and knocks out.

SALLY
Oh lord! What was I thinking! What have I done! It's not him that's gone mad - it's me! There's a lesson to us all! Don't read books. Oh! Tragedy!

SALLY kneels facing away from DARYL, or leans against a tree, in heightened grief and self-disgust.

SILVER tiptoes on, without the parrot, and tries to drag DARYL away. He beckons for MARINA to join him. She does. They take the Prince off behind the rocks.

SALLY
My poor little seahorse! What'll Jim say if he's alive? They could have got married! I could have been surrogate mother for them. I'd have had your babies Daryl! (She turns around) Daryl? Your highness?

DARYL's hand waves from behind the rocks. It's clearly being manipulated by SILVER.

SILVER (impersonating DARYL)
Awight my princess!

SALLY
He's alive! Hello me 'andsome! You're alright!

DARYL
Course I am darlin'. Here, come and have a look behind me rocks.

SALLY
I can't wait! I'm coming!

She goes to investigate. SILVER leaps out and puts a knife to her throat.

SILVER
It's a Kitchen Devil. Finest steel from the ship's galley. Don't move.

SALLY
Oh Mr Silver sir please sir no sir! Let me go.

SILVER
Oh alright then. Tell ye what, instead why don't we be stoking up that there fire, you forage some wild herbs, I'll gather up a few parakeet eggs and we'll whip up a nice fluffy omelette and maybe sing a few camp songs, and sir I don't mean camp songs like what's on your optimistically named Spotify "gone for a run" playlist, I mean songs like you sing around a camp fire, then we'll watch the embers die down to a hypnotic glow and watch the moon come out and say "ooh I wonder if there'll be fireflies I never seen fireflies in real life".

SALLY
Oh, really Mr Silver?!

SILVER
No you lard-arsed limpet! I be taking you prisoner. (He holds the knife close to her throat)

SALLY
If we're doing a hostage video I want make-up.

We hear the PARROT hiccup.

SILVER
Where are you tipsy toucan?

A hiccup. SILVER drags SALLY as they look for the PARROT which they find behind a small rock. SILVER scoops her up.

SILVER
How'd you get drunk out here.

PARROT
I ugh...

SALLY grabs the PARROT and shakes it.

SALLY
Where's the drink?

PARROT
In the pool in the pool get off me you slut.

SILVER
Now that's inappropriate.

They look behind the rocks.

SILVER
It be just a rock pool.

SALLY sticks a finger in it and licks it.

SALLY
It be it gin I think. *(Dips a finger again)* Or some kind of schnapps.

She dips her finger in a third time, screams, and pulls out her hand with a crab on it. She flings it aside.

SILVER
It's those berries what have fallen into it. They've fermented somehow.

SALLY finds a different pool.

SALLY
This one's got a banana in it. (She tastes) Ooh yeah. Daiquiri. The island's a natural distillery!

SILVER
Marina lad! Captain!

MARINA and the CAPTAIN enter. The CAPTAIN has his wrists bound and he is gagged.

SALLY
Captain! Oh my captain!

CAPTAIN
Mmmf mfmfmf mmffff.

SILVER
Right! We got the map, we got you, off we go.

The GORILLA enters. It looks at SILVER. Gradually they notice him. The GORILLA gives SILVER a hug.

SILVER
What's he... I... Wait I know that smell.

The GORILLA runs off and returns with a homemade necklace. On it hangs a shrivelled penis. The GORILLA waves the penis at SILVER.

MARINA
Haha! He was your hairy native.

The GORILLA roars, offended, and beats its chest.

MARINA
Sorry! Sorry! It's ok everyone, I read about this, you're meant to freeze.

The all freeze. One of them farts. The GORILLA roars angrily. They all scream and run off.

ETHEL appears.

ETHEL
G'day! I been hanging about as I thought something was up. Prince Daryl's in trouble isn't he! Can you tell me where he is? Nice one.

ETHEL discovers DARYL behind the rock he was dragged behind.

ETHEL
Your highness. (No reply) Mate. (No reply) Mate you fell asleep for real and missed your cue and got a boner and all the boys and girls saw it.

DARYL
Huh?

ETHEL
Just kidding.

DARYL loses consciousness again.

ETHEL
This might be my chance to prove myself! I'll save him, and Neptune will turn me into a human man with feet and legs and a massive- Wait, now I think about it I don't think he actually said a man... I wasn't really listening. I might be a woman. Either way, the feet'll be a bonus. I always wanted to know whether Crocs feel as shit as they look.

SONG: ETHEL'S SONG

On my rock or treading water
I only wish one wish
To find myself no more this cold-blooded fish
I'd like romance
I'd like to dance
I just want to be like you
And do all the things that people do
Just to catch a movie, watch tv
Don't wanna waste my life here in the sea

So tell me: Do I have to beg?
I'd like at least one leg
And a snake to wake,
And a booty to shake
But when I come back to the world
What if I'm a girl?
Could I live with that?
Could I love my twat?
When you live in the ocean you're always at sea

So I guess I'll just hope when I'm human I feel
like me.

But what if I'm mistaken
Perhaps it's not the plan
For me to be a real hot-blooded man
I'd like to date
And roller skate
So how far must I go
To become a human head to toe?
Just to knock a little ball around
I'd like to feel my feet on solid ground.

So tell me: Do I have to beg... [etc]

And though I don't much feel like starting over
I would love toenails to bite once again,
Please tell me it's the end.

ETHEL
Right where was I – oh, shit, his highness! Fortunately,
your highness, I know a bit of magic merman medicine.
I need a bit of samphire, It's a seaside plant boys and
girls. There's some growing here, bonza. And a little bit
of kelp... There we are. Mix em up with splash of booze
from the rock pool and roll it into a little ball. There!
Can you tell what it is yet? That's right, it's a pessary!

*ETHEL rolls DARYL over and slips his hand down the
back of his shorts.*

ETHEL
I'm only thankful he hasn't had much to eat boys and
girls. Right, excuse fingers.

ETHEL pops the pessary in.

ETHEL
Now we just have to wait while it takes effect. Obviously,
most people would have woken up when it went in...

*ETHEL looks at his finger that he used to insert the
pessary. DARYL wakes*

DARYL
Ethel! I just had an amazing dream.

ETHEL
So er, did you know that the rock pools here have
booze in them? Here, have a taste. Don't get up.

*ETHEL sticks his bum finger into a pool then offers it to
DARYL.*

ETHEL
There you go.

DARYL sucks ETHEL's finger.

DARYL
Oh my days that is lush.

ETHEL
That's it... get it all in you.

DARYL
I'd better go and find Sally. Thanks Ethel!

DARYL runs off.

ETHEL
Wait...

But DARYL has exited

ETHEL (weakly)
Wait... I... I think I've been out of the water more than
30 minutes... I feel really weak... Give us a hand
getting back to the water will you? Your highness?
Daryl...?

ETHEL collapses.

BLACKOUT

Scene 10: On Treasure Island

Elsewhere on the island... MIRANDA enters followed by JIM.

JIM
There you are boys and girls! I feel like we've been walking for days! Why are we stopping?

MIRANDA
Treasure! Gold. I think it is here.

Offstage we hear Silver shout "ahaaar"

JIM
Shit, I can hear Silver. We should be quick. Where shall we look boys and girls?

JIM looks around erratically. At the back corner of the stage MIRANDA grabs JIM to stop him going further. She points.

MIRANDA
Cliff!

JIM
You saved my life!

MIRANDA digs behind a rock. She pulls out a rusty old sword.

MIRANDA
Look! A knife.

She continues to dig and pulls out a treasure chest.

JIM
Miranda, I could kiss you.

MIRANDA goes in for a proper kiss. JIM kisses her forehead. They begin to open the chest, which creaks loudly, when DARYL enters.

JIM
Daryl! I thought you'd gone home!

DARYL
Awright babe! I thought you'd drowned!

DARYL and JIM kiss.

MIRANDA
Hello. My name is Miranda.

DARYL
Awright love. I'm Prince Daryl.

JIM
Have you seen anyone else?

MARINA enters

MARINA
Jim! You're ok! Miranda! You're more than ok! Daryl I'm so sorry.

JIM
Have you seen my mum?

MARINA
Yeah I know, what's she like! (*An impression of Sally*) "Oooh look I'm drunk old Sally Hawkins, I need an Advocaat, oh shit I need the toilet but I'm so lazy and drunk I think I'll just piss myself"

JIM
Yeah... I mean have you seen her here?

MARINA
Oh, yeah! Oh Jim! Silver's got her. I managed to get away and run ahead. He's coming here.

JIM
Right. (Picks up the sword) I'll be waiting for him. Miranda, take Marina to find some good big sticks to fight him with. Wood, remember? Wood.

MIRANDA takes MARINA's hand and they exit.

JIM
I hope you're feeling brave.

DARYL
(*Standing behind Jim*) I'm right beside you love.

SILVER enters, his knife held close to SALLY's neck. The CAPTAIN has his wrists bound with rope.

JIM
Mum!

SALLY
Jim! He's gonna do a wotsit on me. Ibis. Isil.

SILVER
Jim lad. Get your treasure out.

JIM
Never!

SILVER
What be in it then? Gold? Silver? Precious stones for drilling and mounting? (To his boy) You're my precious stone ain't you. You be ripe for drilling and mounting.

329

JIM waves his sword. SILVER holds his knife closer to SALLY. She screams.

JIM
Let her go!

SILVER
She let herself go a long time back. I'll let her go, with one condition.

JIM
Take it.

SILVER
Not the treasure. *(He points to DARYL)* I'll let her go if he'll marry me.

JIM
What? I want to marry Daryl.

DARYL
Do you babe?! But we gotta save your mum.

JIM
Right...

DARYL
I'll do it. To save your mum.

SALLY
Oh Daryl!

DARYL
She's been nothing but kind to me Jim, looked after me all day. Ain't that right sweetheart?

SALLY
That's right...!

DARYL
Come on then Silver.

SILVER pushes SALLY to one side and holds the sword to DARYL's throat.

JIM
Marina!

SILVER
This be the happiest day of my life. I wish I'd brought my most fetching beard.

DARYL
I want gold-embossed menus, right. Oh and pink up lighting. And we can have matching silver tuxedos, and a big purple limo-

SILVER
Shut it. *(to the CAPTAIN)* You, you're a sea captain, you can marry me.

SALLY
How many men does he want to wed? This is what they said would happen after gay marriage. Slippery slope.

CAPTAIN
I've never actually done this before.

JIM
I wish Marina would hurry up.

SILVER
Get on with it!

CAPTAIN
Very well, but you'll have to kneel.

SILVER and DARYL kneel, SILVER still wielding his knife.

JIM
This is so unfair! I wanted to marry him boys and girls. Just imagine what it would be like, going around the world with a royal!

SALLY
Well I think it mainly involves getting your bits photographed by the foreign paparazzi. Poor Kate. The Sun did an advent calendar of her this year, you revealed a different body part every day and on the 24th you get a double door special.

CAPTAIN
Welcome, everyone. We are gathered here today to celebrate-

SILVER
Get on with it!

CAPTAIN
Very well. I'll cut straight to the poem.

SILVER
Copulating cuttlefish!

CAPTAIN
Understood... Do you Prince Daryl take Long John Silver to be your awful wedded husband.

SILVER
Awful, I like that! Arr, he does.

JIM
Where the hell is Marina?

CAPTAIN
And Long John Silver-

SILVER
Buggering barnacles!

CAPTAIN
What is it?

SILVER
I just realised I'm going to be a royal! I wish my old mum were here to see this. Suppose I shoulda thought o' that before making her walk the plank. We live and learn. Well, she didn't.

CAPTAIN
Do you take Prince Daryl as your lawful wedded husband.

SILVER
Arrr I do.

CAPTAIN
Then you may now kiss the, er, you may now kiss each other.

JIM
Seriously, where the hell is Marina?

SILVER leans in to kiss DARYL. From offstage, MARINA moans... a very loud, sexual moan. The all freeze. She moans again higher and louder. And again.

SILVER
By God!

MARINA is definitely having some sort of sex.

JIM
Oh God...

SALLY
That sounds like-

SILVER
The ghostly wailing of Cornish Patsy!!! She be coming for me!

Taking advantage of SILVER's distraction the CAPTAIN brings his wrists down on SILVER's knife, cutting his bound wrists free. He kicks the kneeling SILVER who falls backwards to the ground. DARYL jumps up. JIM leaps for SILVER with the sword, but SILVER springs up in time. JIM and SILVER fight, knife versus sword.

DARYL
Fight! Fight! Fight!

JIM
Oi!

SILVER knocks the sword from JIM's hand and has him cornered. MIRANDA appears with a stick behind him and wallops him on the head.

CAPTAIN
A noble savage!

Silver passes out and collapses. JIM and DARYL pick him up by either arm. He wakes. JIM and DARYL drag SILVER to the edge of the cliff.

SILVER
Please no! Not the cliff! Let me go! My fiancé ...

DARYL
Nah mate.

SILVER
Give a man chance!

JIM
What do you think boys and girls. Shall we let him go?

No!

JIM
Time to fly, Silver. 5, 4, 3, 2... 1. Jump Silver.

SILVER screams and jumps out of view. There is a loud splash. JIM kisses DARYL. MARINA runs on.

MARINA
Sorry sorry sorry.

JIM
You could have come earlier.

MARINA
I really couldn't. *(She wipes her hand on something)*

CAPTAIN
Now! The treasure chest!

JIM opens the treasure chest which creaks again. SALLY delves inside. She pulls out some old 1970's style jewellery.

SALLY
Ooh it's lovely.

JIM
Is that it?

DARYL
I've worn better jewellery than that on my dick.

JIM
Like what?

DARYL
A few tongue piercings. (He winks. He looks in the chest) It's empty.

MARINA
We've spent two hours farting about for this?

JIM
We're as poor as ever and now we're stuck on a fucking island.

SALLY slumps to the ground.

CAPTAIN
I have all the treasure I need right here.

He takes SALLY's hand.

SALLY
Oh Captain.

They kiss.

MARINA
And I think I've found the girl of my dreams.

MIRANDA burps. They kiss

JIM (to MIRANDA)
Wait. Miranda, if you've lived here since before you could speak, how did you know what your name was?

MIRANDA scrabbles behind another rock and pulls out a torn and faded birth certificate.

JIM
A birth certificate! But how did you know it was yours?

MIRANDA pulls out a little necklace with a tag on it. She points.

JIM
It's your name! Was this washed ashore with you?

MIRANDA pulls out a mug with "Miranda" on it, a teddy bear with Miranda on it, and a babygrow with "Miranda" on it.

CAPTAIN
Miranda... let me see. (He takes the birth certificate and reads) "Miranda Fishbeard. Parents Agnes and Alan Fishbeard". Fishbeard? Miranda Fishbeard?! My child! My little daughter! (He hugs her)

MIRANDA
Daddy?

CAPTAIN
Will you ever forgive me! But you're safe, you're safe!

SALLY
Davina McCall'll be popping out from behind that rock in a minute[57]. Well I never!

CAPTAIN
I know.

SALLY
It's Alan then is it? Look, this is all very nice but we're still stuck here we've got no money.

CAPTAIN
My child now that we've found you, the trust fund will be yours. You're rich. What will you do with it?

JIM
She won't know what a trust fund is.

MIRANDA
Holiday resort.

JIM
Fair enough.

SALLY
I never want to go on holiday again in my life.

MIRANDA
No! Holiday resort. Here! Rollercoaster ice cream lifeguard hotel swimming pool Madeleine McCann restaurant sex-on-the-beach.

MARINA
She wants to build a holiday resort!

SALLY
A hotel! Now that I understand!

CAPTAIN
An undiscovered tourist spot.

SALLY
Unlimited booze.

MARINA
Crazy golf in the sand dunes.

JIM
Let's turn it into a gay resort!

---

[57] McCall presented a TV show, Long Lost Family, which probably doesn't need further explaining.

ETHEL staggers in. He is breathless and looks unwell.

SALLY
Our first guest! Oh it's you.

ETHEL
I', I' I've been out of water too long. I, I, I'm not going to make it.

DARYL
No! Jim we gotta do something.

JIM
What?

ETHEL
Jim! Look after Daryl for me. Daryl, tell your Dad I did what I could for you.

JIM and DARYL take ETHEL off behind some rocks.

DARYL (off)
He's stopped breathing!

As they return...

JIM
I'm so sorry.

A solemn pause.

SALLY
He's gonna stink. What do you do with a half man half fish? Burial or barbecue?

Sounds. A thundercrack. Waves hitting the shore.

SALLY
Another storm!

We hear the booming voice of KING NEPTUNE. He has a strong Essex accent.

NEPTUNE
Awright there.

DARYL
Dad! It's me old fella, King Neptune.

SALLY
Your highness!

NEPTUNE
Dazza. I see you got yourself a bloke! I'm sorry I made things so hard for the gays. I'm sorry I had to send you away. I only did it because I'm a massive closet case.

DARYL
What? Dad, it's Ethel.

NEPTUNE
Oh yeah. All I can think of at night is riding bareback with Vladimir Putin, topless over the Russian Steppes.

DARYL
Ethel's dead!

NEPTUNE
Behave! He ain't pegged it. He saved your life. Now I'll do as I promised, he'll be a merman no more.

There is loud bang and smoke. ETHEL appears. He wears a smartly cut suit. He is a man. They all stare at him.

ETHEL
What you staring at?

SALLY
I only ever seen an Aussie in a suit once before and that was Rolf Harris in court. Tell you what boys and girls, Two Little Boys was a red herring and a half wasn't it.

DARYL hugs ETHEL.

ETHEL
How do I look?

DARYL
The old fella ain't done a bad job. Have you, er, had a peak at the downstairs?

ETHEL
Flaming funnel-webs, it ain't just about the old snag. *(He has a little look)* Maybe I'm a grower.

MARINA (to MIRANDA)
Will you give me a tour of your island?

MIRANDA
Come and see my little creek.

They exit. A massive wave. A Coke bottle is thrown on stage with a message in it. JIM picks it up and tugs out the piece of paper.

JIM
"Dear reader, please get this message to Captain Alan Fishbeard, The Royal Bumboy Hotel, Michael Cove, Cornwall..."

CAPTAIN (taking the letter)
"Daddy, I'm alive! After that horrible man made me walk the plank..."

JOSEPHINE (off)
"...I was rescued by a Brazilian naval ship. We have moored, just me and 200 sailors, at a strange little island, the most remarkable feature of which is a hill shaped like a you-know-what! It really is most fortunate. This evening I'm performing cabaret for the sailors and a number have suggested we make a film together tonight!"

CAPTAIN
She's here! Ah, my two daughters!

DARYL
And 200 sailors! Jim, we should go and make them feel welcome...

JIM
Do think it's a bit early in our relationship for us to start having threesomes?

DARYL
Who's talking about a *threesome*?

They exit. SALLY watches them go. The captain puts his arms around her.

SALLY
I think I just want to go home.

CAPTAIN
Well of course we must go home. We have lots of packing to do.

SALLY
No, home. To stay. I'm rubbish at abroad.

CAPTAIN
But who's going to run the hotel?

SALLY
I think we both know I'm rubbish at that too.

CAPTAIN
Sally Hawkins. It's been many a year since I first entered the Bumboy and I've not wanted to lay my head anywhere else since. You must have been doing something right.

SALLY kisses him.

SALLY
Finest sailor of his generation. We should see if that warship's got supplies. And see how the next generation measures up-

The CAPTAIN lays a finger on her lips

CAPTAIN
My lass. No - my lady. Would you do me the honour of having me as your husband?

SALLY
Yes, Captain. Yes I would. "Lady!"

CAPTAIN
I'm afraid I've no ring to hand, but in the sand I found this charming necklace.

He takes the pearl necklace from his pocket. SALLY takes it and starts to put it on. She stops.

SALLY
Isn't this the cursed necklace?

CAPTAIN
Auch no!

He throws it to ETHEL who screams. ETHEL throws it to SALLY who screams.

PARROT (who is drinking from a pool)
Calm down woman it's only a pearl necklace. Throw it out to sea and let and let a girl drink in peace.

SALLY
Here goes. One. Two - oh I don't know, can it really do any harm?

There is a clap of thunder

SALLY
Three!

She throws it over the cliff. The thunder stops.

CAPTAIN
I'll give you a pearl necklace of your own. Now, come. Let's choose a site for your hotel.

SALLY
See you later boys and girls!

They exit. ETHEL rounds things off in verse.

ETHEL
It's time to leave them, boys and girls
With 200 sailors and a horny primate
Now – it turns out the island was just off Wales
But blessed with a bonza micro-climate

For Jim, island life was too small by far
So now he and Daryl live in Peckham Rye

Saving money for travels doing shifts in a bar
- And next year they'll open a gay bar in Mumbai

And what about me, no passport, no degree
No trace of my former self?
Well pop into Walkabout soon and you'll see -
I'll pour you a pint, and toast your good health

You can travel the whole wide world to find treasure
But it might not be buried in sand
You can travel the world in search of pleasure
But it might take a helping hand

And now it's your turn to return to the world,
Slip into our dark little alley without fear[58],
And wind your way home with your dreams unfurled
Taking with you our love, and the season's good cheer.

Blackout. Curtain call. And:

---

[58] The entrance to this incarnation of Above The Stag Theatre was along an alley off Miles Street.

SONG: OVER THE OCEAN

Come for the beaches, and the palm trees
Come for the sand dunes, and the STDs
Come for the bingo and the cabaret
The bar's free-pouring and it's open all day

Over the ocean, right on the shore
Come to relax, get sand in your cracks
And come back for more!

And when the sun sets at the end of the day
Sit by the pool and feel your cares fall away
We've got rooms for singles couples or groups
And the bar TV is showing Mean Girls on loop

Over the ocean, right on the shore
Come to relax, get sand in your cracks
And come back for more!

Come to relax, get sand in your cracks
And come back for more!

THE END.

Jack Off the Beanstalk

Ian Hallard as Fleshcreep and Joseph Miller as Cillian in *Jack Off the Beanstalk*. Photo by Thomas Jewett.

Jack Off the Beanstalk

A scratch and sniff panto! We gave audience members cards with scented panels to scratch off when prompted by numbers which were revealed from time to time within the set or on a prop, adding an extra, pungent dimension to the show's events and characters - including Kylie, our pantomime cow.

2013: Michael Gove was Secretary of State for Education, Iain Duncan Smith was Secretary of State for Works and Pensions, Edward Snowden leaked classified information from the National Security Association revealing the scope of its security operations, and Above The Stag Theatre moved to a brand new venue in Vauxhall, home to a number of gay bars and clubs and a sauna.

Jack Off the Beanstalk is set in the fictional Yorkshire village of Upper Jumper, and it was first time we'd really worked at creating a real sense of place, something we've also tried to do in our versions of Cinderella, Beauty and the Beast, Mother Goose and Pinocchio.

This was the last year we used reworked versions of existing songs. Writing your own means you can better use them to tell your story, but using existing ones meant we got the spectacle of Matthew Baldwin as Dame Trott rapping his way through a rustic version of that year's controversial Robin Thicke hit, Blurred Lines.

Jack Off the Beanstalk

A scratch-n-sniff pantomime for adults, by Jon Bradfield & Martin Hooper

Characters

Fairy Fanny Goblin, the teacher at the village school and secretly a fairy.
Lord Fleshcreep, an evil landlord. Posh northern, a hereditary peer.
Simon Trott, "Simple" Simon, a young village lad.
Jack Trott, his brother.
Maisie, Fleshcreep's niece. Late teens. From London.
Dame Trott, Jack and Simon's mother, a dairy farmer. Very Yorkshire. The dame.
Kylie, a Friesian cow.
The Giant, aka Herbert Skeselthwaite. Self-made Yorkshireman.
Cillian O'Connell, a young Northern Irish lad with a good voice and good looks.

Jack Off the Beanstalk was first performed at Above The Stag Theatre on 29 November 2013 with the following cast and creative team:

Miss Goblin: Stephanie Willson; Lord Fleshcreep: Ian Hallard; Simon Trott: Toby Joyce; Jack Trott: Chris Clynes; Maisie: Rosie Bennett; Dame Trott: Matthew Baldwin; Kylie: Herself; Cillian O'Connell: Joseph Miller; The Giant: Steven Rodgers

Director: Andrew Beckett; Designer: David Shields; Lighting Designer: Elliott Griggs; Musical Director: Daniel Johnson; Choreographer: Angela Nesi; Stage Manager: Will Hunter; Poster illustration: Matthew Harding; Production Photographer: Tom Jewett; Front of House: TJ Chappell; Produced by Peter Bull for Above The Stag

Thanks to Robert Carvill, Elaine Devlin, Zoë Hurwitz, Lauderdale House, Joel Ormsby, Out of Joint, Dan Timms.

Scene 1: The road into Upper Jumper

We're in proper English countryside in Yorkshire. Green, rolling hills, hedgerows, farmland. A signpost tells us that the road leads into the small and not particularly picturesque village of Upper Jumper. The other way it leads to farms, including the Trotts'; and to Fleshcreep Hall. There are a couple of trees, which later in the show people will hide behind. The FAIRY, Miss Goblin, enters.

FAIRY
In the shade of a green and far-off vale
Is the ugliest village you've seen
It's called Upper Jumper, and that's where our tale
Takes place; Now I'll set the scene.

The wind here, it chills your very bones
The houses they're half of them wrecks
For those who like watching Game of Thrones
It's Westeros without all the sex

When Prince George were born we baked special pies,
The streets are still hung with bunting,
And we're not what you'd call worldly wise -
We think drag is a kind of hunting.

We've all the usual suspects, like
A blacksmith and a farrier
And a barmaid who's less the village bike
More the village people carrier

They call it God's own country here
But it's not all kindness and love
Lord Fleshcreep rules us with cunning and fear
He's as slippery as a farm vet's glove.

But somewhere there's a hero round whom we can rally,
A strapping lad we can put to the test!
He'll bring emancipation to our valley
And later, maybe he'll get out his chest.

Will you help us tell our strange little play?
Can you cheer? And boo? Oh yes, to a tee!
And let's have all phones off, we don't want the NSA[59]
Listening in - as they do - for free.

Oh lads and lasses! With your kind consent,
I think we've had enough rhyme
So hold on tight as we humbly present
Our magical pantomime!

FLESHCREEP enters

FLESHCREEP
Fee fo fi fum, I smell the shit on a city boy's bum.

FAIRY
Fee fo fi fum..? I don't think that's your line

FLESHCREEP
Of course it's mine. Everything is mine. The fields, the farms, half the village, and the land from here all the way to the Jodie Marshes. (To the audience) Get off my land. Go on. *(To a man in the audience)*. But not you. You can stay. It'll be pheasant season soon, I could use a young lad beating in my bracken. Only wear something bright, you don't want me shooting in your face by accident. (To FAIRY) Is my niece keeping out of trouble at your laughable village school?

FAIRY
She's doing well. You know I was reluctant to take her on as an assistant, you know, what with you being such a bastard, but I think she'll do very nicely.

FLESHCREEP
Enjoy it while it lasts. When I was last in parliament, which was admittedly only for the subsidised quiche, I persuaded Michael Gove to let me sell your school and get a Tesco's built on it. Not even a good Tesco. A really shit one.

FAIRY
You'll get your comeuppance one of these days. I can tell with my sixth sense.

FLESHCREEP
Your sixth toe. I shan't keep you, I've the monthly Ukip meeting up at the hall. They're a gaggle of dribbling wombats but they bake an excellent fruit-loaf. (To the audience member he liked) You can come and serve. I sacked my last boy for spilling cream all over my Chesterfield. Goodbye you old witch.

---

[59] In June 2013 The Guardian reported that the US National Security Agency had been collecting the telephone records of tens of thousands of Americans. This was followed by further reports in the Guardian and Washington Post that the NSA tapped directly into the servers of nine major internet companies including Facebook, Google and Microsoft.

He goes.

FAIRY

I'm not a witch. But I am a fairy. Oh yes. I use a combination of magic, suggestion, psychology, misdirection and showmanship[60]. You know, you've timed this well. It's not so bad a day for Upper Jumper. Everything smells so fresh after the rain.

SMELL 1: HONEYSUCKLE (A number 1 appears somewhere)

FAIRY

What could that mean? I know. Get your cards and scratch your first sticker. No, your sticker, sir. That's it. Ah, smell the honeysuckle in the air.

SIMON enters. He has a ferret on a lead (one of those joke dog leads that stays stiff as if it's being pulled) and another lead that dangles empty at his side. He wears bicycle clips. A dead rabbit hangs on a string from his belt.

FAIRY

Oh look it's Simon Trott. Say hello Simon.

SIMON

Hello Simon.

FAIRY

No love.

SIMON

Right! Hello boys and girls!

FAIRY

Simon doesn't exactly wear his brains on his sleeve. Oh, Simon! You've lost a ferret!

SIMON

Oh shit!! Dec! Dec where are you? I'm sorry boys and girls, this is my ferret, Ant. But it looks like Dec's run away. He'll be about here somewhere, be careful of your trousers they're like rats up drainpipes. That's why I wear these ferret clips.

FAIRY

Those are bicycle clips.

SIMON

You're having me on Miss Goblin. You can't get a bicycle up a trouser leg. Dec!

---

[60] This was how Derren Brown used to introduce his TV shows.

FAIRY

Everybody, check your neighbours to see if they've got a bulge they shouldn't have.... And try under your chairs?

Simon goes looking in the audience. He looks in quite intimate places.

SIMON

Oh I can feel the furry little... oh no that's not him, sorry miss!

Someone finds Dec.

SIMON

Dec! Oh thank you. Come here Dec. Oh..! It's our Jack coming.

There's a beep-beep, and Jack comes in driving a milk float. This needn't be spectacular but it should be cute. It should say "Trott's" on the side.

JACK

Eh up everyone!

Eh up!

JACK

No come on let's have it loud. Eh up!

Eh up!

JACK

That's grand! Well lads and lasses, I'm Jack. Jack Trott. Simon, mam said to come find you. It's time for milking. Hello Miss Goblin.

FAIRY

You don't have to call me miss now you're all grown up, Jack. Not like at school. Call me Fanny.

JACK

Fanny Goblin. Aye I will do.

FAIRY (taking his hands)

Hello Jack darling. Ooh look at your fine hands, Jack. I'll do a reading shall I? Let's see. Oh! Jack this crease here says you'll be a hero!

JACK

A hero!

FAIRY

And this crease says you're going to find love! Have you got yourself a boyfriend yet?

340

JACK
How am I going to do that? I can't even afford the ride to Leeds to get to any bars or owt.

SIMON
You don't ask me if I've got a girlfriend yet.

FAIRY
I know love but we've never had a gay couple before. The whole village is looking forward to it. Now, this crease here says you'll come into great wealth.

JACK
It's probably a typo. I'm not going to come into wealth, am I. I'd be happy with just a bit more so mum didn't have to work so hard. Then she could concentrate on her cheeses.

FAIRY
Hands never lie. (To a member of the audience) You've got good hands for reading. Now you see this very pronounced crease here, that means you should vary your hand position more when you're pleasuring yourself. (she pulls out a handkerchief and gives her hands a wipe). Give my regards to your mother boys.

She goes.

JACK
Are you coming then?

SIMON
I was going to do some fishing and have a think. I've met a girl Jack.

JACK
A girl?

SIMON
Well, not met her. Seen her. Oh I tell thee she's dead nice boys and girls. She makes me all soft on the inside and all hard on the outside. I think she's new here.

FLESHCREEP enters, running.

FLESHCREEP
Jack Trott! You were this close to running me over back there.

JACK
I don't know how that happened, my aim's usually better.

FLESHCREEP *(pointing at Simon's rabbit)*
Have you poached that?

SIMON
I haven't even skinned it. We need it for dinner.

FLESHCREEP
And don't be fishing round here. I'll be over later to collect the rent. Make sure you have it. I'll see you later. And if you see my niece tell her to come home, I've told her not to mix with the serfs. Hahaha.

He goes. We hear thunder.

SIMON
The Smurfs?

JACK
So what's so special about this girl?

SIMON
Everything. Her hair, her smile. This little red hat she wears. I don't even know how to describe how I feel about her Jack.

MAISIE walks on, unseen. Wearing a red hat. She nips behind a tree, and listens.

SIMON
I mean, she... I just basically want to put my entire head in her vagina and leave it there. I don't suppose there's a gay equivalent to that.

JACK
Only at a stretch.

SIMON
I'd probably stay there inside her till my cheeks were all wrinkled like after a bath.

MAISIE
Oh my God.

The boys slowly approach the tree and find MAISIE

JACK
Eh up!

MAISIE
Alright...

JACK
I'm Jack. This is my brother Simon.

MAISIE
What's up?

SIMON stares at her.

SIMON
Is she black?

MAISIE
Do I look black? I'm from London.

SIMON
Are you a princess? We're farmers.

JACK
Dairy farmers.

SIMON
Our mum makes the best cheese in the country. She's teaching us.

JACK
You should try Simon's blue veiny hard one.

MAISIE (pointing at the rabbit, joking)
You got a hair on your trousers.

SIMON
That's a rabbit.

JACK
Why are you here if you're from London?

MAISIE
My rents sent me here. They said I'd got in with a bad crowd, which I had. And they said I'm too interested in magic. Which I am. So they said I have to live here with my uncle, Lord Fleshcreep. He's well important.

SIMON
You're Fleshcreep's niece? But she's so nice Jack! You wouldn't have thought she'd come out of him. Imagine being from London and coming to live in a place like this. You must be thanking your lucky stars!

MAISIE
No. It's shit. And weird. There's nothing to do, and I got no mates.

SIMON
We'll be your mates

MAISIE
And strangers talk at you in the road and try to be your mates. No offence. And the weather's crap all the time. (She looks up) See that cloud? It hasn't moved since I've been here.

JACK
It's been there since we were little.

MAISIE
Really?

JACK
It's why the farming's so hard round here. The grass doesn't get enough light. The cows hardly produce any milk... We're the only village in Yorkshire to give a prize for the year's smallest marrow. Blimey, London though... Have you seen Wicked?

MAISIE
Yeah. It's about magic. And strong women. Have you?

JACK
Aye....

SIMON
The Village Players did it.

JACK
Sort of...

SIMON
They couldn't get the rights properly so we did Macbeth instead but the witches sang Defying Gravity and Lady Macduff did Dancing Through Life just after they killed her.

JACK
Our Simon had the best role.

SIMON
Aye I did. I was the castle dog.

MAISIE
In Wicked...?

SIMON
No. Macbeth. There isn't a dog in wicked.

MAISIE
So... are you both, like, "into musical theatre".

JACK
Yeah!

SIMON
Yeah!

MAISIE
Oh. I see.

JACK
What?

MAISIE
Oh nothing, it's just... if a boy's into musical theatre... Alright, how did you feel about Girls Aloud breaking up.

JACK and SIMON look at each other

SIMON
What????

JACK
Do you want to come back to the farm for tea?

MAISIE
I'm not allowed to mix with surfers.

SIMON
We're not surfers.

MAISIE
Ok then. Yolo. But don't just sit about and play on your Xbox or whatever you do.

JACK
We ain't got one of those.

SIMON
We make our own entertainment.

JACK
She doesn't want to see that. Come on, before it rains again. We'll tell you about Upper Jumper.

SONG: THE WAY TO UPPER JUMPER
(To the tune of The Way to Amarillo)

When the day is dawning
On a rainy Yorkshire morning
A massive cock awakes you
Crowing loudly, god it breaks you

But when the harvest
Is in for the year
We make the largest
Batch of local beer

This is the way to Upper Jumper,
Line your tractors bumper to bumper,
And make your way to Upper Jumper,
We'll give you Parkin for your tea!
This is the way to Upper Jumper,

May all our harvests be bumper,
And make your way to Upper Jumper,
Grab your coat we'll wait for thee

When the day is over
The sun sets on fields of clover
You muck out the stable
And dream that one day we'll get cable

But when you've cleared the land
On market day
You can find a stable hand
And tumble in the hay.

This is the way to Upper Jumper... (etc)

SIMON
It looks like it's going to rain. We'd best head back t'farm. See you later boys and girls!

They exit

Scene 2: Dame Trott's farm

The kitchen and living space of Dame Trott's little farmhouse. It is run down and a little chaotic. On one wall, the ubiquitous three ducks. There is a kitchen unit with sink and cooker.

A window, which can be opened, leads out onto hazy farmland. On one side of the stage, a practical front door, on the other a door or passage leading to bedrooms. There is a battered little armchair and a small table beside it with an old laptop on. A shot-gun is propped up against the wall.

The sound of wind and rain. TROTT enters. She has a wet waterproof coat on and wellies. She is carrying an egg in her hand. NB. The egg must be very convincingly real. Or actually real. Although there are lots of stage directions here the words should keep flowing as she does things.

TROTT
Farming in winter boys and girls! I've been slopping about in piss and shit wi' barely any light for t' best part of 8 hours. *(at a man in the audience)* There's a young man here who's eyes have just lit up all nostalgic, I can't think why... Ello lads and lasses! I'm Dame Trott. I won't ask all your names because I don't want to get attached, you learn that when you look after livestock. But it's reet good to meet you. Can I have big "Reet good to meet you"?

They shout.

TROTT
Can we turn the rain down a bit, I can barely hear this lot. We've had that much rain the village has been put on shark alert. Right, let's try again. *(They do)* Aye that's more approaching it. *(She puts the egg down on the chair).* Keep an eye on that for me, I'll get this off.

She takes her coat off, and gives it a good shake to dry it, water spraying all over the audience.

TROTT
Oh what a day. It's blowing glass donkeys out there.

She picks up a bucket, looks into it. It's full.

TROTT
There's been so much rain me poor ceiling's dripping like a sow that's come into season.

She pours it out of the window to empty it. We hear chickens protesting.

TROTT
I'll have to patch the holes up. I've been up on the roof looking for them but it's like trying to find a poodle in a nutsack.

She picks up another bucket, looks into it. Reaches in and pulls out a frog. She empties the bucket and isn't sure what to do with the frog. She puts him in the sink. A badger appears at the window.

TROTT
Now who's for a cup of- what? (She sees the badger) Oi! You stay right there!

She opens the window, grabs the shotgun, shoots the badger. It falls from view. She leans out of the window to retrieve the now dead badger.

TROTT
We're in a trial culling zone. They're riddled with TB.

TROTT pops the badger into a cooking pot on the stove and replaces the lid.

TROTT
We'll have that for supper. Oh I can see we've a few familiar faces from the village here! Look, it's our vicar *(she approaches someone in the audience).* He's quite new so I've forgotten his name, what's your name sir? Aye, it was on the tip of me toes. That's it! Reverend [name]. He was parachuted out of his last parish at short notice after he got into a spot of bother about women vicars. Three of them at once.

She puts a dog collar on him, and approaches someone else.

TROTT
And here's our barmaid. The Tart with a Heart – it's a crude name for a pub if you ask me. Remind me your name? That's right, I don't know why I forget, it's the most requested design at the mobile tattoo parlour.

She approaches another member of the audience

TROTT
Here's the stable boy look! He's not unpleasant to look at, but you know what they say about him. A moment on the lips, a lifetime of cold sores.

She goes to sit on the chair, realises – hopefully prompted – that the egg is on it. She puts the egg on the little table.

She flops into the chair. She lifts her legs and stares at her wellies. She tries to pull them off. She stands up again and approaches the man in the audience that she first spoke to (when she mentioned slopping about in piss and shit), taking his hand so as to get him on stage.

TROTT

Hello sir, as you clearly like getting close to nature come and give Dame Trott a hand with getting my wellies off. I used to have one of those whatnots you shove your boot heels into. A husband, haha. *(She sits down)* What's your name my love? *(She lifts her legs)* There, grab them both and give them a good tug. *(It's a bit of a struggle)*. It's like the enormous turnip this. Pull hard enough it'll come eventually. Don't snigger. Sorry love my ankles swell up sometimes but keep tugging it'll be good for your arms.

The boots come off. She has bright stripy woolly socks with huge holes through which her toes protrude.

TROTT

That did something quite interesting to my hips. I'll take them *(she takes the boots)*. That's very kind, give him a clap boys and girls. "How was the theatre?" "Aye it were alright I pulled a couple of old boots".

She goes to put the boots on the side table, where the egg is, and again realises last minute.

TROTT

I'm sorry reverend, your being here and me with my extremities out. Right I'd best do me accounts. I still haven't worked out how to get my subsidies.

She hauls the laptop onto her lap. She bashes a few keys and occasionally swipes at it as if hitting return on a typewriter. She closes it.

TROTT

Not a clue. I should probably think about getting the internet. I'm going to share something with you lads and lasses, it's nothing airborne. The farm's doing ever so badly. *(ahhh)* Oh no it's doing much worse that. *(AAHHHH!)* *(Then at someone in the audience)* Ee look, you've got lovely strong sharp molars sir. I bet you get through your pillows quick.

She puts the laptop down on the table, almost gets the egg, stops. She rescues the egg, the laptop goes on the table and she slips her egg into her bra. JACK and SIMON

enter from the front door. They come to the front of the stage.

SIMON

You embarrassed me!

JACK

You nearly killed us driving like that, I had to take over.

MAISIE enters quietly from the same door and stands in the doorway. She pulls her hat off.

SIMON

You always make me look stupid.

JACK

I don't *make* you look stupid. You volunteer. You were trying to impress her cos you fancy her.

SIMON

You were trying to impress her because you want her to think you're sophisticated and not a country bummer.

TROTT

Hey hey calm thissen down. Monkey's in brass houses shouldn't cry wolf.

MAISIE coughs.

TROTT

Who's this? Is it you that's got them fighting? Not that it takes much, they once spent the whole of Christmas arguing over a box of cheap chocolates. Talk about the war of the Roses.

SIMON

This is Maisie.

MAISIE

Nice to meet you Mrs Trott.

JACK

She's from London.

TROTT

(Appalled) That Janet Arkwright went to London once and when she came back she had a shower installed. And it's Dame Trott to you. Now listen, coming in here with your city ways and your come to bed thighs. Let me tell you, *(indicates Jack)* you're barking up your own bush with that one. And don't start on our Simon, he's got enough to worry about without your hurling romantic misadventures into his way. We're good simple folk here.

Maisie walks into the room properly, puts her hat on the chair, upside down. When she speaks it's a bit provocative and directed more at Jack and Simon

MAISIE
Is it true that people learn about sex earlier in the country?

TROTT
Aye that's right; and they teach us to shoot from the age of 6. *(points to the ducks on the wall)* You see those ducks? They just flew in through the window like that one day in formation and I took a lucky shot. They've been there since.

MASIE (unsettled, then friendly)
Wow... When we did drama at school Miss Fraser told us that Chekhov said, if you show a gun in Act One it has to go off in Act 3.

TROTT
You just worry about making it to the interval my girl. Get that rabbit off Simon and pop it in t'pot.

MAISIE takes the rabbit, lifts the lid of the pot, looks in sees the badger, screams. TROTT chuckles.

JACK
Mum's a bit stressed. The farm's not doing well.

TROTT
Now Jack that's our business. Oh but he's right, I'm caught between a rock and two hard stools. We're behind on the rent and the landlord's a cruel, cruel man.

JACK
Mum.

TROTT
Oh but he's a pig he is, Maisie. King of the bastards and Lord of the pricks. He's called Fleshcreep. Flush-crap we call him. Fleshcreep by name, utter cunt by nature.

SIMON
Mum, Lord Fleshcreep's Maisie's uncle. She lives with him.

TROTT slowly forces a rictus smile. She panics somewhat.

TROTT
Why don't I fettle us all a nice cup of tea! Maisie, how about a nice brew.

MAISIE
Have you like got anything herbal?

TROTT
Tea is herbal what do you think it's made from, Jelly Babies?

MAISIE
Unless you've got skimmed milk.

TROTT
Sk- sk- ski- Jack what is this THING you have brought into my home?

JACK
Maisie's working at the school with Miss Goblin mum.

TROTT
You watch your way with her. There's those who say she's a witch.

MAISIE
A witch?

TROTT
You've seen that cloud that hangs over the place, keeping us in perpetual winter. Some think it's her doing.

JACK
Mum that's rubbish.

TROTT
The day it appeared she was seen crying and shaking her fist at the sky. I'm just saying.

MAISIE
What is it you don't like about uncle Fleshcreep?

TROTT
That's like asking what it is you don't like about a kick in the teeth with a shit-covered boot. He's driving the rent up so's no-one can pay it. He's bought up all the local abattoirs and dairies and pays a pittance... Sir don't get excited an abattoir's got nowt to do with Swedish pop music. And he sold me my last herd of cows. Useless they were. *(She gets out a grubby handkerchief)*. I've had to get rid of most of them. Now there's just one cow left. *(She blows her nose good and hard)*

JACK
My favourite cow. Kylie. I named her. By eck boys and girls I hope we don't have to sell her too. Only I couldn't get her to milk this morning and she looked ever so sad

with her big melancholy eyes like a... cow. She's been like it since we sold her friend Liza-with-a-Z. Liza-with-a-Z is another cow.

MAISIE
I'll speak to my uncle. I'll ask him to give you more time for the rent.

TROTT
Oh no pet really.

JACK
Honestly mum don't be so proud.

TROTT is staring, gently fascinated, at the contents of her hanky

TROTT
You're right, it is a failing. (To Maisie) Oh you are an angel, come here.

TROTT goes to give Maisie a big hug, remembers the egg at the last possible minute, fishes it out from her chest and hands it to Jack who places it absent mindedly into Maisie's hat on the chair. TROTT hugs MAISIE properly and then releases her. MAISIE starts coughing at the farmy smell of her.

SIMON (going to hug Maisie)
You can have one from me and all.

TROTT
You, behave. All priapic he us. And take yer coat off lass.

MAISIE takes her coat off. She is wearing a T shirt that says "Meat is Murder". TROTT gasps and doesn't know what to do with herself.

TROTT
I think I'm having a turn. She's a barbarian. Meat is Murder!

JACK
Mine is, it's massive.

TROTT
See? You've corrupted them.

MAISIE
But-

TROTT
Jack, let's have a bit of radio on. *(JACK switches it on. The Archers theme plays.)* Oh no we'll get that nonsense

right off. (Turns it off). I was hoping for a bit of news I like my current affairs. There might be developments on the Fame Factory.

MAISIE
Oh my days I hate Fame Factory. I like Jake Bugg. He's authentic.

TROTT
We never miss the Fame Factory do we Jack? Or Strictly Come Off It. Nice bit of glamour. I'm less keen on the housework ones like Pimp my Cake or the Great Bloody Sewing Fiasco. Mind, if they did one on cheese-making I might submit my prizewinning Dairymaid's Secret for inspection. It has a natural crust to it but once you prise it open it's wet as curds. It went down a treat with the Young Farmers at their annual ball and buffet. Oh you should have seen those lads going at it, it were dried out something terrible by the end of the night, what was left of it. Let's try for some news.

She turns on the radio again

NEWSREADER (SFX)[61]
And finally, there has been new controversy over top TV pop talent show The Fame Factory.

TROTT
Ooh shush shush shush.

NEWSREADER (SXF)
Popular contestant Cillian O'Connell has been thrown off the show, just days before his appearance in the grand finale.

TROTT
Cillian O'Connell! You like him don't you Jack. He's got that Irish charm. They're the salt of my loins, the Irish.

NEWSREADER (SFX)
Sorry, I was just pausing there to take a sip of water. Series creator Simon Shallow said they were left with no choice after O'Connell, the favourite to win, was caught with cocaine for the second time in a week.

TROTT turns off the radio.

MAISIE
Oh my God, who gives a shit.

---

[61] Su Pollard recorded the voice of the newsreader for our production.

TROTT
If my boys were found with drugs they'd go into hiding too! (She rummages and finds a framed signed photo of Cillian). Here he is. Cillian O'Connell. That's going straight in the bins.

JACK
No!

JACK tries to grab the picture but MAISIE gets it first.

MAISIE (Reading)
"Dear Jack, lovely to hear from a fan, love from Cillian".

TROTT
I'm going aback to start up the milking machine. Though it's hardly worth it for one cow.

TROTT exits

MAISIE
Talking of herbal... Do you boys know where I can get some grass?

JACK and SIMON both look out of the window.

MAISIE
No. You know. Weed. For smoking.

JACK
Oh! Course. Simon grows it in the old polytunnel.

MAISIE
Is that the thing in the field that looks like a big condom?

JACK
No that's probably a big condom, the village kids chuck them over the hedge.

SIMON
Will I fetch you a handful?

MAISIE
No because that's gross.

SIMON
No, the weed.

TROTT enters

TROTT
Weed? What weed?

SIMON
Erm... Maisie was just saying... (JACK punches him discreetly) saying she weed herself.

MAISIE
No I didn't!

TROTT
Happened to me once, Eurovision 1997, I got all excited when Katrina and the Waves won it. I was knocking back a lot of tea. Right the parlour's up and pumping but I can't find Kylie.

JACK
(He looks out of the window). She's there!

TROTT
Kylie? Where?

JACK
Standing by the edge of the slurry lagoon. I think she's suicidal. That slurry's like quicksand. If she jumps in there'll be no saving her.

TROTT
She'll be fine Jack. Cows can't jump.

SIMON
But she don't know that!

JACK
Why don't we bring her in?

TROTT
In here? The lads and lasses don't want some heifer barging about like a bull in a chinaman do you?

JACK
Of course they do don't you!

TROTT
Oh no you don't...

Oh yes we do... etc

JACK
I'll go and get her!

He exits. As he opens the door we hear the cold wind from outside. He leaves the door open.

TROTT
Close that door, it's parky! Were you born in a barn?

JACK (off)
Aye!

TROTT
It's true, he was. Oh it were like the nativity Reverend, you'd have loved it if it weren't for all your allergies.

"The stars in the bright sky looked down where he lay,
And little Jack Trott did a sick in the hay".

JACK (entering)
Come on girl... That's it...

KYLIE follows in behind him. A cow[62]. She looks at the audience. MAISIE is scared at first. She steps back, and quite near to Simon.

JACK (to Maisie)
Go on. You can touch her.

SIMON
All right! (He puts an arm round Maisie)

JACK
Like this.

Jack gives her a rub. Maisie does the same, tentatively. KYLIE moos and wanders to the front row of the audience. She has a bit of a sniff in a few laps, especially women.

JACK
She's only after something salty to lick.

TROTT
Stupid cow. Jack, if she starts shitting, you'll have to help me turn the carpet other way up. We'll be in awful trouble if Fleshcreep hears we've brought animals in t'house. Will you keep an eye out for him lads and lasses? Maisie, grab that bucket for me and pop it under her.

MAISIE does. TROTT crouches at KYLIE's udder. She milks. Nothing happens.

TROTT
You lot, gimme a hand.

They each take a teat and start yanking. No good. KYLIE begins to get very distressed.

JACK
Sometimes we play music in the milking parlour to relax them. We could try that. (He grabs some CDs and goes to the laptop). These are her favourites. She likes Tracy Chapman, Pink, The Indigo Girls... Here we go. Kelly Clarkson.

He puts a CD in. "Since You Been Gone" plays. KYLIE looks very sad. She responds physically to Jack's questions.

JACK
What's wrong girl? Are you sad? Poor Kylie. Are you missing someone? Are you missing Liza-with-a-Z? She's just gone somewhere nice for a little holiday.

TROTT tries milking again. Nothing.

TROTT
I think she's got a blocked teat, Jack. That or mastitis.

She bends the teat up to look at it. She squeezes. It shoots milk into MAISIE's face. MAISIE shrieks.

TROTT
Calm thissen girl I'm sure it's not you're not used to.

FLESHCREEP appears at the window. The audience hopefully shout "He's behind you". When they look, he goes out of sight. This happens a couple of times.

JACK
Quick! Let's hide her.

They all line up between Kylie and the window, hiding the cow. FLESHCREEP appears. They wave. MAISIE gasps and turns to face forward, away from the window.

MAISIE
Don't let him see me!

TROTT
Alright, now, after three we all shuffle along and get Kylie out of the room. Three. Come on.

They all, including KYLIE, shuffle along to the door that leads into the rest of the house, apart from Simon who starts shuffling the other way.

MAISIE
Simon! This way!

She holds out her hand, which he takes. He looks at the audience over his shoulder and grins.

TROTT
That's it. Out we go.

They shuffle all the way to the door so KYLIE can exit. JACK, SIMON and MAISIE also exit. There's a knock at the door. TROTT panics, steadies herself. She opens the door, sees Fleshcreep. She closes it again.

---

[62] Kylie was a traditional pantomime cow played by two actors in a suit – the actors changed from scene to scene depending on who was not on stage at the same time as Kylie.

349

TROTT

I thought I heard a knock at the door. I was wrong. It was a prick. (opens floor, smiles) Oh Mr Lord Flush er Fleshcreep!

FLESHCREEP

Afternoon, serf!

TROTT

Don't just stand there like Tom Daley.

FLESHCREEP

What do you mean.

TROTT

Half in, half out.[63]

FLESHCREEP

I was passing by your window and I said to myself oh gosh, there's that useless, past-it old cow.

TROTT

No!

FLESHCREEP

And here you are!

TROTT

Yes...!

FLESHCREEP

Is that an animal I can smell, or is it just me?

TROTT

I wouldn't like to comment. There's not been animals in here has there lads and lasses?

FLESHCREEP

These urban urchins wouldn't know an animal if David Attenborough poked them up the hole with one. You know the rule, Trott.

TROTT

I don't, I've never seen Fight Club.

FLESHCREEP

You let animals in my farmhouse, you're out on your heel.

The frog croaks, unseen, from the sink.

---

[63] We'd begun previews for this show when Tom Daley posted a video on his YouTube channel announcing he was in a relationship with a man but still fancied girls. We added this joke in time for the performance that evening.

TROTT

Frog in my throat.

A badger pops up at the window. TROTT grabs the shotgun and this time bashes the badger over the head with the butt of the gun. It drops out of site.

FLESHCREEP

What was that?

TROTT

Postman. *(Aside)* He nearly saw me badger there.

FLESHCREEP notices the milk bucket, picks it up

FLESHCREEP

Do you always drink milk out of a bucket?

TROTT

Not always. Usually it's cider.

FLESHCREEP goes to sit on the chair. TROTT manages to grab Maisie's hat, containing the egg, before he sits on it.

FLESHCREEP

And I think I saw my niece in here!

MAISIE is seen creeping past the window. TROTT sees her, opens it and slips her the hat.

TROTT

Your niece? Never.

MAISIE pulls the hat onto her head, the egg inside it. She rams it down. MAISIE screams. Chicken noises in reaction. FLESHCREEP jumps up.

TROTT

The sounds of the countryside. Now, if you're here about the rent-

FLESHCREEP

I'm here to tell you about my new venture.

TROTT (looking into his mouth)

Oh aye very nice, you can hardly tell.

FLESHCREEP

I'm going to stage a festival! Like Glastonbury but without all the charity shit. Look.

He unfurls a poster. On it is written in big type, LIVESTOCK FESTIVAL.

FLESHCREEP

Naturally I'll have to get rid of a few of the smaller farms to make room for it.

TROTT
This has always been farming land!

FLESHCREEP
It will only be the troublesome tenants, I'm sure you've nothing to worry about. Now, while I'm here. The rent.

Offstage, KYLIE moos.

FLESHCREEP
What was that? I can smell something. I think it's a... number two.

SMELL 2: MANURE

FLESHCREEP
I think I can smell manure.

TROTT
That's just me *(she farts)*. Terrible wind I've been having, I think it's the gulf stream.

JACK enters

JACK
What's he want? *(Smells the fart)* Oh fucking hell mum.

TROTT
Yeah alright I had to.

FLESHCREEP
I need the rent, Jack.

TROTT
Give us time? Please? Just this month. My artisan cheeses are bound to pick up, We've just been so busy.

FLESHCREEP (shudders)
Bleaurgh. Hardworking families... Well, you've a week or you're out of here. I must dash, I'm expecting a call from Fiona Bruce. They want to film an Antiques Roadshow up at Fleshcreep Hall.

TROTT
The Antiques Roadshow!

FLESHCREEP
You hear that Jack? You should take your mother. She might fetch a few bob if they find a few interesting marks on her bottom. Hahahahaha!!!

He exits.

JACK
Aye get out! We don't want to come to your stupid festival. (He looks at the poster again) I really want to go to the festival... What we gonna do for money?

TROTT
It pains me to put you through it, Jack, but you'll have to get married. I read about it, the government give you money, it's bit like a farm subsidy except you have to let the animal in your bedroom.

JACK
Mum it's only £200 and they give it you in Asda vouchers.

TROTT
Don't joke. No, there's only one thing for it. We'll sell Kylie.

JACK
No! Boys and girls we can't do that can we?

TROTT
She's not right; you know she's not. She's barely milking. We've tried every bull in the area she won't breed with any of them. It's market day tomorrow. You take her down there and make sure you get a good price. Alright? *(She looks out the window)*. Do you know, son, I think the weather's clearing. There's a glimmer. Red sky at night, angel delight.

JACK
Shepherd's delight.

TROTT
No love it's Shepherd's pie. Right come on you can help me dig out some veg. Bye boys and girls!

JACK
Bye!

Scene 3: The village green

This can be the same set as the road to the village but without the signpost. Instead there is a sort of market stall. It has a sign advertising strawberries, and tourist information. There are strawberries in punnets. (You shouldn't be able to see under the stall because the ferret puppets appear behind it later in the scene). The stall belongs to the FAIRY, who enters.

FAIRY
Strawberries! Tourist information! Fine juicy strawberries! Lovely enticing Tourist Information!

I'm not just the village teacher my dears
I do the visitor centre too
But we hardly get any visitors here
Cos there's nothing for them to do!

MAISIE enters

SMELL 3: STRAWBERRIES

FAIRY
Can you smell them boys and girls? Maisie darling! Can I interest you in some strawberries?

MAISIE
I'm alright thanks.

FAIRY
They're-pick-your own.

MAISIE (looks at them)
No they're not...

FAIRY
How about some tourist information?

MAISIE
Yeah ok. I could do with some tips.

FAIRY
Alright. Well I can really recommend the strawberries.

MAISIE goes to leave

FAIRY
Why don't you be a lamb and do a shift for me?

MAISIE
I'll do a shift for you if you teach me magic.

FAIRY
What have you heard? It's that Trott woman isn't it.

The Fairy hands Maisie a book

FAIRY
Now, you must practice and have patience. If you concentrate you might be able to magic up your very own prince.

MAISIE
So if you can just magic up princes how come you haven't got a man?

FAIRY
That's very personal.

MAISIE
Oh soz, is it a hygiene thing?

FAIRY
I had a soul mate once... He was a successful man, a brilliant man, but he became greedy and slowly he let greed take over his life.

MAISIE
Was this Mark Zuckerburg? Cos he's a bit young for you.

FAIRY
But one day he crossed the wrong man, and that man got a wicked revenge on him. He ended up with a terrible curse.

MAISIE
A curse?

SIMON runs in holding the ferrets.

SIMON
Eh up boys and girls. Eh up Maisie.

MAISIE
Eh what?

FAIRY
Get those ferrets away from my strawberries Simon Trott. Health and safety.

SIMON
No, Ant and Dec.

Simon puts the ferrets behind the stall.

MAISIE
Where's Jack?

SIMON
He's gone to flog Kylie.

FAIRY
He's selling the cow? The poor lamb. Right well I'll be off. Will you mind the stall Maisie?

FAIRY exits.

MAISIE
How's it going?

SIMON
Very well thank you. (A pause) How's it going?

MAISIE
Yeah alright. (Pause) They're having a movie night at the village hall next week.

SIMON
Oh aye?

MAISIE
It's a double bill of Shortbus and Despicable Me 2.

SIMON
That sounds nice.

MAISIE
So...

SIMON
So...?

MAISIE
So I'll have to find someone to take me.

SIMON
Oh. Will you?

MAISIE
Well yeah I don't wanna go on my own.

SIMON
No I know but I thought.

MAISIE?
What?

SIMON
I doesn't matter.

MAISIE
Say it.

SIMON
I can't remember now you got me all confused. (Aside) Oh heck boys and girls I'm useless at this. Oh wait I've had an idea.

SIMON sort of crouches and shakes his bum very fast.

MAISIE
Er. What are you doing?

SIMON continues. He moves towards her as he does it.

MAISIE
Simon..? Oh my God are you twerking?[64]

SIMON
No. Yeah.

MAISIE
Oh my god.

SIMON
It's meant to be- it doesn't matter.

MAISIE
Do you reckon Jack'll call by later? After he's sold Kylie?

SIMON (disappointed)
Jack? I dunno.

The FAIRY enters. She takes stock of the scene.

FAIRY
Do you know Maisie I've left my purse in the post office. You wouldn't pop over and rescue it?

MAISIE exits. The FAIRY takes her purse out of her pocket. She makes it vanish.

FAIRY
You look don't look right darling.

SIMON
It's always about Jack ain't it.

FAIRY
Jack? Oh come on. He's not into girls.

SIMON
He's dabbled though.

FAIRY
In what, glitter?

SIMON
No one notices me unless it's to laugh. I've seen QR codes that get more attention than I do. "Simple Simon".

FAIRY
But we all love you! You're sweet.

SIMON
Sweet!

_____

[64] Twerking emerged in 1980s New Orleans but reached new levels of awareness partly thanks to a 2013 Facebook video of Miley Cyrus doing it.

The FAIRY waves a hand as if casting a spell.

FAIRY
This town needs a hero. Maybe you could be a hero? One day, at least. Darling, all it takes is just one person to believe in you and soon, soon everyone will.

Here we had the song Just One Person from Snoopy the Musical. The Fairy and Simon were joined by Maisie part way through the song; then the ferrets joined in too.

SIMON
Thanks Miss Goblin.

He starts to run out.

FAIRY
Haven't you forgotten something.

SIMON comes back.

SIMON
Oh yeah.

He picks up the ferrets from behind the stall and leaves. THE FAIRY and MAISIE laugh heartily but not cruelly.

FAIRY (warmly)
That boy is so stupid, if you asked him to jump off a cliff he'd ask you what a cliff was. Mind the stall again will you my dear. You're so good at it. I've some business to attend to.

The FAIRY pulls a shawl or cape from behind the stall and exits.

MAISIE
Strawberries. Lovely strawberries. Anyone want any strawberries. (She gets out the bag of weed) Rizlas! Rizlas! Anyone got any rizlas!

Blackout

Scene 4: The road into Upper Jumper

Cillian enters, he has a small back pack and is carrying a tabloid newspaper. He is whistling. He gets his phone out and takes a selfie. He takes a couple more with different expressions. He is pleased at what he sees. Then he sees the audience and runs behind a tree. The tree doesn't need to be wide enough. After a moment he leans his head out cautiously.

CILLIAN
Hello boys and girls! Wait, you're not the paparazzi are you? Are you sure? Ah all right then! How's you all doing? It's me so it is, Cillian O'Connell, disgraced Fame Factory contestant and almost certain winner. I've come here to the fucking Shire to hide from the papers *(he shows his newspaper, he's on the front of it)*. I'll tell you what, it's a big ol' fuss about nothing. You know how it is, I went out in Vauxhall, three days later I stumble out of some doorway after a chill-out after a slamming party after an afterparty after a party and I just forgot to wipe under me nose before I got into daylight. I really wanted to be a popstar! Shite, there's someone coming.

He drops the paper on the ground and hides behind a tree. JACK and KYLIE enter. KYLIE has a "For Sale" sign on her.

JACK
Eh up lads and lasses. We're off to town, it's market day.

KYLIE gives a sad moo. JACK spots the paper.

JACK
Bloomin tourists leaving litter all about. That's Cillian! They still haven't found him. I wonder where he is?

The audience start to shout. KYLIE looks around and sees CILLIAN and starts to Moo and nudge Jack.

JACK
Here Kylie, you've spun around. What's that? Behind me?

He looks around as he does CILLIAN hides behind another tree.

JACK
You're having me on guys. I thought we were mates!

He starts to read again. CILLIAN comes back out JACK looks round again as he does CILLIAN hides. KYLIE sees

him again and this time charges at the tree and head butts CILLIAN forcing him out.

CILLIAN
How's it going? I'm Cillian.

JACK
I know. It's me! Jack!

CILLIAN
Jack?

JACK
Jack Trott. You sent me a photo.

CILLIAN
Was this on Grindr?

JACK
No.

CILLIAN
Jackd?

JACK
Not since this morning. You, you sent me a signed photo. You said it was lovely to hear from me.

CILLIAN
Oh! It's nice to meet you. Listen I'm supposed to be in hiding but do you have any cocaine?

JACK
No.

CILLIAN
Can I kiss you?

JACK
Yes.

CILLIAN kisses JACK

JACK
You don't hang around.

CILLIAN
Not when I see something I want mate.

JACK
You don't want a cow do you? I'm taking her to the market.

CILLIAN
And later he's taking her to the pictures! (Slaps his thigh) Hello girl.

KYLIE moos. CILLIAN and JACK kiss again, KYLIE looks on. It gets very heated. JACK removes CILLIANS shirt. CILLIAN pauses to take a selfie of himself topless.

FLESHCREEP (Offstage singing to the tune of English Country Garden)
How many farmers can a man evict in an English country village

JACK
Someone's coming!

CILLIAN
Well it's not me! I haven't come in three weeks from all the chemicals.

FLESHCREEP enters still singing

FLESHCREEP
I will reclaim what rightfully is mine so I may resort to pillage ---

CILLIAN
Shite.

CILLIAN runs behind a tree leaving his shirt and bag.

FLESHCREEP
Good afternoon young Jack. Afternoon Dame Trott, oh my mistake. (sees the For Sale sign). You're pimping your girlfriend out.

JACK
We've got to sell her to pay your rent.

FLESHCREEP
Why then, allow me to make an offer.

JACK
No way! You'll flog her to the sausage factory, just like you did with her mate Liza-with-a-Z.

KYLIE starts to cry

FLESHCREEP
A magnificent breeding animal like this? No, I'll put to the bull to her.

KYLIE becomes even more upset

JACK
I don't know. What do you reckon boys and girls?

FLESHCREEP
Young Master Trott, in my trousers there's a fat old packet with your name on it.

JACK
Ok. I'll sell her. Sorry girl.

FLESHCREEP hands JACK two £20 notes

JACK
Forty quid?!?

FLESHCREEP
What do you expect for this broken bovine?

The FAIRY enters. She has a coat on and a shawl over her head, in disguise.

FAIRY
Young man young man. Are you selling that cow?

FLESHCREEP
She's yours for eighty pounds.

JACK
Eighty..?! She ain't yours to sell yet.

FAIRY
I'd like to buy her.

FLESHCREEP
This Faulty Friesian? Oh no you don't.

JACK
Oh yes she does.

FLESHCREEEP
Oh no you don't

JACK
Oh yes she does. What can you pay? I want her well looked after but I haven't a bean.

FAIRY
Now that's very fortuitous.

She holds out a handful of beans.

JACK
Beans? I wish I'd said I haven't a 12 inch penis.

FAIRY
These are magic beans lovey. They'll bring you more riches than you can ever imagine.

JACK hesitates. FLESHCREEP rolls his eyes and adds another note to his offering. The FAIRY responds by rolling her eyes and adding another bean to the handful.

JACK
Who would you like to live with, girl? Fleshcreep?

KYLIE shakes her head and moos

JACK
Or this lady?

KYLIE nods and dances

FLESHCREEP
The well-known bovine dance of displeasure.

JACK
What do you know about animals? Ok old lady I'll sell her to you.

FAIRY *(Hands him the beans)*
You won't regret it lovey.

JACK
(To Kylie) Sorry girl. We'll miss you. (To the FAIRY) Well. Maybe our paths'll cross again.

FAIRY
Maybe they will. Come along Kylie I'll look after you.

She goes.

JACK
How did she know Kylie's name?

FLESHCREEP
It's in the script.

JACK
Eh?

FLESHCREEP
Those beans aren't going to pay the rent are they. You have until the end of the week.

He starts to exit, looks down and sees CILLIAN's shirt and bag. He picks up the shirt.

FLESHCREEP
Curious.

JACK
Oh... that's mine!

FLESHCREEP picks it up

FLESHCREEEP
And how, pray, can a poor farmer afford something like this?

JACK
It's just cheap off the market.

CILLIAN
Fuck off is it!

FLESHCREEP
There's someone here.

JACK
No no! Just thee and me.

CILLIAN sneezes

FLESHCREEP
What was that?

JACK
Hay fever. Trees.

FLESHCREEP
It's not even a real tree. (Taps it) It's made of wood.

JACK
That's normal with trees.

He pretends to sneeze

FLESHCREEP
You should get yourself indoors. Off you go.

JACK
Ay ok. *(shouts in the direction of the tree Cillian hides behind)* I'll be off back to me farm. The one about a mile outside the village on the northern side on the road to Harrogate. The one where we love having people visit us.

CILLIAN's arm extends from behind the tree giving a thumbs up to JACK. JACK exits. CILIAN sneezes again. FLESHCREEP wanders up to the tree and looks behind it.

FLESHCREEP
Well, well, well. It's the drug-disgraced delinquent from Fame Factory.

CILLIAN
What? No.

He picks up his bag and goes to take his shirt and make a dash for it. JACK sneaks back on and slips behind the tree unseen.

FLESHCREEP
Not so fast. I could be the answer to your prayers.

CILLIAN
James Franco's never gonna come out.

FLESHCREEP
I can make you a superstar.

CILLIAN
Keep talking big man.

FLESHCREEP

I've got an opening for you. I'm organising a festival on my land. And you, young man, could be top of the bill. Think of it, super-stardom overnight. Stay with me at Fleshcreep Hall. There's plenty of room... *(aside)* in my four-poster. Come with me.

CILLIAN

I don't know. I thought I might hang about here and wait for...

FLESHCREEP

Jack? He's not going to protect you from the press or make you a star. He's poor. Also, he... *(he whispers in Cillian's ear)*

CILLIAN

Really?

FLESHCREEP

Help me out about the place, clean my niknaks, and I'll ensure you're locked away, I mean hidden, from the press until the festival. What say you?

CILLIAN

I say lead the way.

FLESHCREEP

I feel this is just the start the start of a beautiful friendship.

CILLIAN starts to exit. FLESHCREEP follows still holding CILLIAN'S shirt and using it to hit him across the back as if he is whipping him. JACK steps out.

JACK

I could hardly hear them... Where's Cillian gone? To Fleshcreep's? Oh shite. Thanks Boys and girls!

He exits in a hurry.

JACK OFF THE BEANSTALK

Scene 5: Fleshcreep Hall

A grand, old fashioned, dusty and slightly camp mansion. MAISIE enters. She has a book of spells. He also has headphones in and is singing random phrases. She notices the audience. She pulls out her earphones.

MAISIE
Alright. This is my uncle's place. Oh my days though it's massive. It's bigger than any of my mate's houses back in London, even Katie's and her mum's a tax evader. I'm meant to stay in my bedroom but Fleshcreep's given me the smallest, coldest room right up in the roof. Listen I'll kill you if you say anything but I'm a bit lonely up here in Upper Jumper. *(Waits for the audience to say "ahhh")* I'm lonelier than that! Check this out though. Miss Goblin gave me a book of spells. If I learn magic, right, I can make the world a better place and make Ed Sheeran fall in love with me. I don't fancy him, I just want to lure him to a painful death

FLESHCREEP enters. He wears a slightly feminine dressing gown and is a little camper at home than he is in public. He is carrying a magazine called "Goodbye!"

FLESHCREEP
This is my favourite magazine. Goodbye! It's like Hello! but they show you inside the homes of the recently deceased. Last month's was a special on David Frost, they didn't tell you it was his house you had to guess from the clues. Aha! Welcome all to Fleshcreep Hall. Every corner teems with ancient history and rather less ancient stains. (To Maisie) Oh, it's you. The trash in the attic.

MAISIE
Why are you doing really shit drag?

FLESHCREEP
This is my smoking jacket! It was my grandmother's. I'm glad to see you're making you're keeping busy, we strapping country gents aren't much suited to girlish homely fun. (Sighs) My skin looks dry and old doesn't it?

MAISIE
Yeah

FLESHCREEP
What do you recommend?

MAISIE
Distance and 40 watt lightbulbs.

FLESHCREEP
Oh but oh but guess what your uncle has found!

MAISIE
A lump.

FLESHCREEP
Oooh you're frosty the fucking snowman you are. I have found treasure, in human form! And what a form. I have uncovered Cillian O'Connell! Or at least I intend to.

Halfway through MAISIE's next line, CILLIAN enters.

MAISIE
Cillian O'Connell?! That over-groomed, manufactured idiot with the stupid hair and the *(she sees him)* and the twinkly eyes and wait fuck that I'm not falling for it.

FLESHCREEP
My niece, Maisie.

CILLIAN
Charming to meet you! (To Fleshcreep) I love your pad.

FLESHCREEP
It's not a pad, I'm just naturally bootilicious. Do you know, the house is haunted! On stormy nights, in the 2nd floor bathroom, one hears the screams and rattling chains of a rent boy who passed away in a game that went horribly wrong. His ghostly form sometimes appears when I'm at my ablutions, though it's never for long enough to get a proper wank in. Now, how would you like to make your uncle a cup of tea.

MAISIE
I'd rather go for lunch with Charles Saatchi. What did your last slave die of?[65]

FLESHCREEP
I just explained all that. Oh, boys and girls, I was scarred for life! Literally! You can still see the rope burns.

MAISIE
You wouldn't ask a *nephew* to make your tea.

CILLIAN
Maisie, I'd kill for a cuppa. Would you be very kind?

MAISIE
Alright. Do you want sweetener or are you artificial enough already? Seriously though, he can't headline Laughing Stock.

---

[65] In June, the Sunday People newspaper had published photos of Charles Saatchi grabbing the throat of his then wife Nigella Lawson as they lunched outside a restaurant.

359

He's Behind You: Eleven Gay Pantomimes

FLESHCREEP
Livestock!

MAISIE
What did you try Bonnie Tyler but she wasn't available?

FLESHCREEP AND CILLIAN
(Gasp) Don't insult Bonnie![66]

MAISIE
It's a festival! You need bands, someone with a following.

CILLIAN
I played G-A-Y!

FLESHCREEP
You're among friends, Cillian, you don't have to spell it.

MAISIE
People who go to G-A-Y won't come up here! They'd struggle to navigate the train timetable. They'd struggle to navigate the two times table...

CILLIAN
That's my fan base you're talking about.

MAISIE
They won't hear will they, they're deaf.

CILLIAN looks very wounded.

MAISIE (slightly protective in spite of herself)
Oh. Oh god don't do that. I'm not going to fall for that. I'll get the tea.

MAISIE exits. CILLIAN looks at his surroundings.

CILLIAN
You must work hard.

FLESHCREEP
It's been in the family for generations. I've managed to keep the National Trust at bay so far. I work so hard for this little jewel of a valley. And yet I'm held back at every turn by my useless tenant farmers. The Trotts are the worst! But I have a plan, and it involves the festival!

CILLIAN
What is it?

FLESHCREEP
It's a big outdoor concert with overpriced noodle stalls, but that's not important right now. My plan is this:

---

[66] Bonnie Tyler represented the UK in Eurovision in 2013 finishing in 19th place.

when the Trotts are out of their farm enjoying the festival, I'll send the bailiffs round, and have them change the locks while I'm at it! (To his favourite in the audience) Could you see yourself as a bailiff? I'd let you seize *my* jewels in lieu of cash...

FLESHCREEP goes to slip an arm round CILLIAN but turns into a more innocent gesture as MAISIE enters

MAISIE
Tea.

FLESHCREEP
That was quick.

MAISIE
(Aside) He's going to evict the Trotts! I need to warn them not to leave the house tonight!

MAISIE makes to leave

FLESHCREEP
Where are you going? We must prepare for Livestock. Come to the study.

MAISIE (Picking up her book)
Can I finish my page off?

FLESHCREEP
Some of my happiest moments have been spent finishing a page off. Very well. Cillian, come with me. I'll show you my little Botticelli.

CILLIAN
I don't know what a Botticelli is.

FLESHCREEP
I was hoping you might say that.

FLESHCREEP and CILLIAN exit.

MAISIE
If I can't go and see the Trotts, how can I send them a message? (*Hopefully the audience will suggest magic*). You're right! Magic! I'll use a telepathy spell to send a message to Simon. (*looks through book*) Here we go. Ok. (*She closes her eyes, screws up her face for bit*).

CILLIAN enters he has his shirt off and wears a harness

CILLIAN
Maisie, Fleshcreep says can you bring us a clean towel. What are you doing?

MAISIE
Er... Nothing! Coming uncle! *(Aside)* I'll have to do it later.

MAISIE exits.

Scene 6: The Trotts' cottage garden

There's a garden bench and a few pots. JACK enters. He is wearing an animal onesie. It is unzipped to the waist, allowing a glimpse of torso.

JACK
Eh up boys and girls! (Eh up Jack!) We're going to the festival! We're going to find a hole in the fence and sneak in for free. (Shouts off) Come on Simon! Come on mum!!

SIMON enters. He is also wearing a novelty onesie, he is wearing it the wrong way round. It should have a tail, so that it hangs from his crotch. He has those "poi" balls on strings that people swirl around at festivals and so on. He is swinging them about.

JACK
We're late! What you got there?

SIMON
They're for swinging about like this.

JACK
Why?

SIMON
Cos I can't be fucked to learn how to juggle. And I want to impress Maisie! Do you think there'll be hippies at the festival?

DAME TROTT enters in a fabulous, yet ill-fitting onesie. She has wellies on, flowers in her hair.

JACK
Mam, come on.

TROTT
I know what you're thinking lads and lasses. Catwoman. I've been an hour putting meself into this boys and girls it was like changing a pillowcase. Jack! You'll catch your death (doing his zip up). Simon are those love eggs? Don't be shocked, I got sent the wrong catalogue once, it was supposed to be seeds.

SIMON
I bet all this takes you back eh mam?

TROTT
Truth be told I've never been to a festival. Closest thing we had was the County Show in 1972. They had a steam fair, you could guess the weight of a goat, there was a parade of all the latest tractors, and then The Who played and I got off with Keith Moon.

SIMON (pointing)
There's a man selling hotdogs. Can I have five pound?

TROTT (looking)
Five pounds for a hot dog! Has it won Crufts or something?

Coloured lights flicker

JACK
Oh look mam! Fireworks!

TROTT
Oooh! It's either that or the lights are about to blow[67]. Grab your pints in case boys and girls, the firemen have stopped responding to our calls.

SIMON shrieks

JACK
What's wrong?

SIMON
I heard a voice. Inside me own head!

JACK
They're called thoughts Simon, other people have them.

SIMON
No it sounds like Maisie. It is! It's Maisie! Well you remember, Jack, she said she liked magic. Maybe she's communicating. She's saying something... She says, we're not to go to the festival.

JACK
You're just nervous. He's worried he looks stupid.

SIMON
What?? (To TROTT) Do I look stupid mum

TROTT
Oh no pet, you'd never know from looking at you.

SIMON (listening)
Hang on... She says we'll lose the farm if we go!

JACK
Come on!

---

[67] Later changed to "the ceiling's about to fall in", after part of the ceiling at the Apollo Theatre in the West End collapsed during a performance of *The Curious Incident of the Dog in the Night-Time*. Thankfully, no one was seriously injured.

SIMON
She means it!

TROTT
Now listen Simon! I've never been superstitious and it's done me no harm so far, touch wood.

SIMON
She says we'll lose everything!!

JACK
What are we supposed to do else?

TROTT
We'll have our own festival! Right here in our cottage garden.

JACK
It sounds shite. I wanted to see Cillian!

TROTT
Oh I know pet. Still, every clown has a silver spoon. Here, Jack. You still haven't told us how much you got for Kylie.

JACK
Aw mum let's not talk business tonight. Let's enjoy ourselves.

TROTT
Go on our Jack. What did she fetch? Let's see.

JACK reaches into his onesie and pulls out a handful of beans. TROTT and SIMON lean in.

TROTT
Beans?!?!?!

JACK
They're not just any beans.

TROTT
What are they Marks and bastard Spencers Beans? Oh you fool Jack! Right. (She reaches into her onesie and takes out some paper).

JACK
What are you doing?

TROTT
It's a festival isn't it. I'm going to roll them up and smoke them, it's all they're good for.

SIMON (pulls a large spliff out)
You could put them in this.

TROTT
Simon Trott!!

SIMON
Don't be cross. (He takes the beans and puts them into the joint)

TROTT
I'm not cross. It's not you what sold our fine cow for a handful of beans. I'm proud of you, Simon. It's been a privilege getting to watch you grow up from a boy to a man, as if you were my very own Daniel Radcliffe.

SIMON lights the spliff. TROTT takes a toke.

TROTT
I don't know what the fuss is about, I can't feel a thing. I'll go get the radio.

TROTT exits with the spliff. SIMON pulls a flask out from somewhere and puts it on the floor.

SIMON
Here Jack. I made magic mushroom tea. We can share some later.

CILLIAN enters from the opposite side.

CILLIAN
Jack!

JACK *(unzipping his onesie again)*
Cillian!

CILLIAN
Did you see my gig?

JACK
I'm sorry. We missed it.

SIMON
We're having our own festival.

CILLIAN
I was amazing! I'm definitely going to be a pop star. I like your... *(pointing at Jack's onesie)* what do you call it. Torso.

TROTT re-enters with radio and spliff and a flask identical to Simon's. She is now stoned off her tits.

TROTT
(Singing) Be sure to wear some flowers in your hair, If you're going to San Fransisco... *(Speaking)* I've made us all a nice flask of tea! *(She sees Cillian)* Oh.

362

TROTT faints. JACK goes to help her. TROTT slaps him out of the way.

TROTT
Not you not you.

CILLIAN helps her up.

TROTT
You're Cillian O'Connell. We liked you before your fall from grace. You've got a lovely arse. Voice. Arse. I'm Dame Trott.

CILLIAN
A dame!

TROTT
School nickname, it stuck. Jack you've come undone again.

CILLIAN
That's how all the hotties wear them.

TROTT
Oh well. In for a penny, out for the count

TROTT unzips her onesie revealing a bra and the top of rather lot of pubic hair. SIMON offers the joint around that now has the beans in.

TROTT
I'm a bit peckish somehow.

She passes the joint on to SIMON. It gets passed about during the scene. CILLIAN takes a selfie then takes JACK aside.

CILLIAN
How's my hair?

JACK (laughs)
I haven't stopped thinking about you.

CILLIAN
Me neither. Do you wanna take me inside?

JACK
What?

CILLIAN
This is your house no?

JACK
Oh...! Aye. Do you want to?

TROTT
Cillian will you have a cup of tea?

CILLIAN
I'd like that very much.

TROTT
Simon give the lad a swig.

SIMON picks up his flask. Stops. Looks confused. Picks up the other. He repeats this. He takes a wild and hopeful guess. Offers it. CILLIAN takes it and swigs.

TROTT
Proper Yorkshire tea.

CILLIAN
It's quite bitter...

SIMON and JACK
Shit.

CILLIAN
Why are you having your own festival?

JACK
Exactly. It's rubbish. We haven't got any bands.

TROTT
Why doesn't Cillian sing.

CILLIAN
I don't know...

TROTT
Well if you won't, I will...

SONG: BLURRED LINES[68]
(Dame Trott sings lines in regular type, Cillian sings lines in italics.)

VERSE [1]

If you can't sing I will sing with you
Cos I'm feeling that I'm into you
Maybe you're going mad
Maybe you're getting stoned
Maybe I wanna get boned...

Ok now come get close, I will domesticate ya
Like an animal, I'll even milk you later
Come on I'll liberate ya
Will this get in the papers?
Hell with that pretty face yeah.

---

[68] This is a parody of Robin Thicke, Pharrell Williams and T.I.'s controversial 2013 hit (original songwriting credit: Robin Thicke, Pharrell Williams, Clifford Harris Jr and Marvin Gaye)

CHORUS

And now I'm gonna take a bad boy
I know you want it / *Hey hey hey!*
I know you want it / *I'm pretty gay*
I know you want it
I'm a gay boy
But hey it's early / Ee by gum
You're getting flirty / Ecky thump
Are we getting dirty?

VERSE 2

This ain't what I dreamed of
Until I got chucked off
Come here get your shirt off
You're the hottest stud in this place
I wanna squeeze you
Until you're purple
What rhymes with purple?
Pretty lady what do you want from me
You tryin'a get me in your onesie
Is it alarming how
When I'm farming now
I wanna pull on you plough...

(Chorus, then...)

RAP

We're only livestock, we're only animals,
I'd like to eat you and I'm no cannibal,
You're the Green Man, I'm mother nature,
That don't mean I'm too old to mate you,
I'll give you some work to get your ass into,
There's a hay barn you can shovel grass into,
You'd look reet fine in just boots and a Barbour,
When I hose you down in the milking parlour.
You can stay til spring when the river's high,
And the snow comes up to your lean young thigh,
And the lambs are up on their shakey little legs,
You can come in my henhouse and feel for my eggs.
From Bridlington to Harrogate,
They'll want a piece of my tup well they can wait,
Come on lad, shake it, you turn me to jelly,
You got me so damp I need to drain my welly.

FLESHCREEP enters

FLESHCREEP
At home, Trott? I'd have thought you'd be at the festival supporting your village. After all, you're sturdy enough. Why are you all dressed up like Elton John's toddlers?

SIMON
We're doing our own festival.

FLESHCREEP
Aha! An illegal rave?

JACK
It's not a rave, it's a...

TROTT
Tea party.

SIMON
Yeah. (panics, grabs flask from Cillian) Do you want some?

JACK (Snatching the flask)
No!!!

TROTT
Oh, oh Lord Flushcrap we wanted to come but we couldn't afford it. We're being responsible and thinking about your rent.

FLESHCREEP
Don't call him that, he's my protégé.

JACK
What's the festival like...?

FLESHCREEP
I haven't seen so many stupid hats since the Village Players attempted My Fair Lady.

TROTT
Our Simon did the costumes for that. Is he being nice or mean, I can't tell.

SIMON
Mean. Mum, most people think I'm stupider than you think I am.

TROTT
I'm sure that's not true.

FLESHCREEP
Why don't you all come to the remainder of the event on free passes! Get you out of this little hovel. For a while, I mean.

JACK
Aw I really want to! What do you think boys and girls? *(They say no...)* We're all right here thanks. Anyway, Cillian sang for us here. Your... protégé is very talented.

SIMON
Aye he's grand. I thought he'd suck.

FLESHCREEP
Oh he does that. Very well. You hear that Jack? Very well indeed.

JACK
What?

CILLIAN
He's... I... I didn't want to. How are you Fleshcreep? (Approaches) Holy god you look beautiful tonight.

TROTT
Eh?

CILLIAN
Your lips are so red and big and like a beautiful big SPIDER! SPIDER! Ahhh spider's everywhere! With teeth and ears and massive dicks! Help! Heeeelllllp!!

CILLIAN runs off.

FLESHCREEP
Drugs! You've given him drugs.

TROTT
Oh no Flushcrap! no!

FLESHCREEP (pointing at her joint)
What's that then?

TROTT
What, this? Boomerang. (She lobs it behind her. Waits) Oh. Well that's what the man in the shop said. What a crook.

FLESHCREEP
Dealing drugs on my land!

SIMON
What's he mean, dealing?

JACK
He means selling.

SIMON
People sell drugs? Shit. I just give em away.

FLESHCREEP
A confession! You'll be out of here by sunrise. For good. Get packing!

TROTT
Oh please sir! It's just a little cottage but it's home. Where will we go?

FLESHCREEP
I couldn't give less of a shit. Right. Well I'm off to round up Cillian and fuck him back to sobriety in what used to

be the pear orchard but is now apparently the "drum and bass fairy glade". I feel positively rejuvenated. Of course, that might just be the coke. You don't have any of that going spare do you boys? Of course not. You can't afford it. I'll just hope there's a few grains left on Cillain's arsehole. If there are, I'll snapchat you picture. Hahahaha!

He goes. A long pause.

TROTT
Bedtime.

JACK
Mum!

TROTT
I'm sleepy. We'll pack in the morning. Come on boys.

They trudge off. It gets darker. The Christmas tree music from the Nutcracker starts to play. A beanstalk starts to grow from where the spliff got tossed. It grows and grows. The sky lightens. It is dawn. We hear TROTT snoring.

The FAIRY enters. She calls off, trying to wake Jack through the cottage window.

FAIRY
Jack. (No response) Jack...!

JACK pokes his head out of the house.

JACK
Miss Goblin?

FAIRY
Beanstalk!

JACK enters.

JACK
Oh! That's where mum threw the beans. It's... it's gone all the way up to that cloud!

FAIRY
Perhaps, young man, those beans were magic
And worth their weight in gold or cow
Unless you want this tale to be tragic,
Get on that stalk and climb it, now!

JACK
I'm gay, I can't climb trees for toffee.

FAIRY
Didn't I always say to you

You're just as good as the other guys?
Now at the top, besides the view
There waits for you a great surprise
I'm sure a hunky boy like you
Can take that stalk between his thighs.

JACK
It looks ever so high. Alright. I'll do it. I'll do it!

JACK begins to climb the beanstalk...

FAIRY
Jack's been nimble, Jack's been bold
What will he find? Perhaps there'll be gold,
A land of plenty high up in the air!
Why ever else would I send him up there?

And, from off, in a fearsome, booming voice we hear:

GIANT (off, amplified)
Eee.... Bye.... Gum!

INTERVAL

Rosie Bennett as Maisie, Chris Clynes as Jack and Toby Joyce as Simon in *Jack Off the Beanstalk*. Photo by Thomas Jewett.

Stephanie Willson as Fanny Goblin and Matthew Baldwin as Dame Trott in *Jack Off the Beanstalk*. Photo by Thomas Jewett.

Scene 7: The top of the beanstalk

JACK at the top of the beanstalk, at the door.

JACK
Welcome back lads and lasses! Are you alright? I decided to wait for you because being a pantomime here I can't make a decision without asking for your approval.

GIANT (off, booming)
Ee... By... Gum...

JACK
He sounds right terrifying. Shall I run? Or should I go in? Alright. I'm going in. Wish me luck.

He opens the door, lights come up on the rest on the rest of stage to reveal the giant's front room. It is very 90s. There is a large television and a VCR, and some VHS tapes. JACK switches it on, the theme to Friends plays. He turns it off. A giant gold penis appears through the door. Herbert, the "GIANT", enters. It is his penis.

GIANT
Ee By Gum. Heh heh. Evening lad.

JACK
It's... it's morning... sir.

GIANT
Right. Well. I wasn't expecting visitors. Been a while since I've seen anyone. 3rd of August 1996. What is it now?

JACK
What? It's 2013.

GIANT
2013? That's not even a year it's just some number from the future. Bloody hell. Seventeen years. Tories are still in I hope?

JACK (indicating the chair)
Aye I think so. You know your flies are undone mate?

GIANT
Very funny.

JACK
That's a right whopper.

GIANT
It's a bleeding curse.

JACK reaches out to touch it.

GIANT
Don't touch, christsake! What are you, a queer or a male nurse? Though if you're the one you're probably t'other heh heh.

JACK
I'm not a nurse.

GIANT
Oh. Well. I'm not prejudiced me. Can I get you a doily?

The GIANT turns the TV on. The Eurotrash theme plays.

GIANT
Eurotrash. It's bloody marvellous. Have you seen it? Swedish birds with their knockers in meatballs and German men getting their fat arses spanked in Brummie accents, it's a right hoot. You'd like it, it's got one of your lot presenting it. Hang about. (Turns it off) I've seen this one. (He sees JACK staring at his penis). Hey me eyes are up here you know. Well, two of them are.

JACK
Sorry.

GIANT
Look. Thing is, I had a curse put on me been stuck up here years.

JACK
It's a bit whiffy in here aint it?

SMELL 5: FART.

GIANT
Sorry lad, I've been sustaining myself on tinned foods for years, it's been building up like a turd in a pressure cooker. I think there might be another on its way. (he farts again). Christ that one were like Findus Crispy Pancakes... Can you still get them?

JACK
I don't know. Mum's distrusting of foreign food.

GIANT
So. What brings you here?

JACK
Riches, I think. Riches would be grand. We're broke, see.

GIANT
Riches ain't the answer lad. That were me downfall. I were filthy rich. Mills and factories scattered all over

the place, like a special Yorkshire edition of monopoly. Course I outsourced the work abroad when it got cheaper. Devastated the place but it made no odds to me. Everyone were doing it, I had to. Thing is, I'd trod on too many toes on t'way up until a rival of mine thought I was getting too successful. So they put a curse on me with a magic potion. I grew this chap, and everything it touches turn to gold! I'm a changed man now. Had time to think like. I just want to help others.

JACK
How?

GIANT
I don't know. Help make the dreams of little kiddies come true or something. You know, give them a hand like that Jimmy Savile chap.

JACK
Never mind that. Your cock turns things into gold? That's amazing!

GIANT
I was a danger to society! I couldn't go anywhere. Then this fairy I knew had a suggestion.

JACK
I bet.

GIANT
Don't be a fool, there were no queers in Upper Jumper. This lass I were courting, she were magic see. And for my own sake and the safety of society she froze me in time up in this magic cloud.

JACK
Right. Come with me.

GIANT
I can't go back down there. As soon as the cock touches anything it will turn to gold. People and all.

He belches

GIANT
Sorry about that.

JACK
You're having a laugh.

GIANT
No that were a burp. Here, I'll show you. Give me something,

JACK
I've only got the clothes I'm standing in.

GIANT
Give me your shoes.

JACK does, the GIANT rubs them against his huge penis. They turn to gold.

JACK
Fuck me.

GIANT
Watch it.

JACK
Here try something else.

He takes off his top and hands it to the GIANT. The GIANT rubs it against his penis, it turns to gold.

JACK
She were right! This could bring us riches. Here.

He pulls off his trousers and hands them to the GIANT, they come back gold.

GIANT
You going for the set then?

He points to JACKS pants.

JACK
Naw.

GIANT
I seen it all before, Saturday afternoon in the rugger club changing rooms.

JACK
Oh ay?

GIANT
Don't get funny ideas. There aren't no gays in rugby.

JACK
I'm not taking these off. The lads and lasses'd feel awkward if I stood here with my arse out.

The audience shout.

JACK
Ay alright, fuck it.

He turns his back to the audience takes off his pants. They come back gold. He puts his new golden pants on and grabs the rest of his gold clothes and shoes.

JACK
Mate, this is amazing - will you wait here a bit?

GIANT
I was hardly about to bugger off to Benidorm.

JACK
Can I go fetch some stuff to rub on your cock.

GIANT
It's a bit late for antibiotics. Look lad, being rich ain't all it's cracked up to be.

JACK
It's got to be better than being poor. See you later big boy.

JACK exits and starts climbing down the beanstalk.

GIANT
I don't know! Gays in rugby. If they had gays in rugby it'd make all the buggery very awkward indeed. Now, I should be able to catch TFI Friday.

He switches the TV on. The theme from Men Behaving Badly

GIANT
Oh, no, Men Behaving Badly. Jackpot!

Blackout

Scene 8: The road into Upper Jumper

THE FAIRY, MAISIE and KYLIE enter. The FAIRY has a mail bag.

FAIRY

Welcome back boys and girls! We're doing the post round. Not that I need to work since I sold off my Royal Mail shares[69]. What's wrong lass? You look as grumpy as Kylie.

MAISIE

Why I have to do the post round just so I can learn magic.

FAIRY

Hard work keeps you grounded. Are you sure that's all that's troubling you?

MAISIE

Have you seen the Trotts lately? They seem to have got their hands on some money. What if Simon won't like me now he's rich?

FAIRY

Listen to me. You're clever and you're kind and he'll be lucky to have you.

MAISIE

Clever and kind?

FAIRY

Aye.

MAISIE

Oh my god, you think I'm ugly.

FAIRY

It doesn't matter what I think.

MAISIE

I shouldn't have played hard to get.

FAIRY

Oh is that what you were doing! I thought you were just a bit mardy. Listen darling, when you meet that special someone you'll know.

MAISIE

It hasn't worked for you has it. Yours got cursed. You didn't finish telling me about him.

FAIRY

Oh well. This was back in the nineties.

MAISIE

Oh he's probably dead then.

FAIRY

It were all my fault. I was working on a new magical potion and I left it lying about. Well, one day your uncle Fleshcreep came a-calling – they were bitter rivals you know. My Herbert were a self-made bastard and Fleshcreep was a bastard by birthright. Anyway, while I had my back turned, Fleshcreep laced my Herbert's tea with some of my potion.

MAISIE

What kind of potion?

FAIRY

It were deadly poison! I only made it for precautions - I was never going to use it. Same as with my handgun and my stash of chemical weapons. Don't look at me like that, this is the countryside. Anyway, there was poor Herbert gasping for breath. I tried to save him with a spell, but the spell had certain... side effects. But I still loved him, see. So I used my magic to imprison him in a magic cloud... The beanstalk's rather complicated things. Oh I am careless. When I bought Kylie with those beans, I accidentally gave Jack a special magic one.

MAISIE

Accidentally?

FAIRY

That's right. Dizzy old thing aren't I. Who'd have thought we'd have all this trouble from one flick of my little bean.

MAISIE

I think you wanted something like this to happen.

FAIRY

Destiny finds a way.

A pause

MAISIE

I know Simon's not very bright.

---

[69] The Royal Mail was privatised and floated on the stock exchange in Autumn 2013. Share prices shot up soon afterwards leading to accusations that the Government had undervalued it. Postal workers were given shares as part of the process.

FAIRY

The boy's that daft, if you kicked him in the arse it would go over his head. But the village girls like him enough, on account of his having a very big heart. He gave you those drugs for free didn't he, even though he was broke.

MAISIE

You knew about that?

FAIRY

I know a lot. I don't know what's up with her though.

MAISIE

Come here Kylie.

KYLIE joins them.

MAISIE

What's wrong? Why are you so sad?

FAIRY

Listen girl. To be happy, all you need to do is be true to yourself. Do you want to be happy?

KYLIE nods.

FAIRY

Then like I say lass. Be true to yourself.

MAISIE

What does that mean?

KYLIE

She understands, don't you girl?

KYLIE nods.

MAISIE

Whatever. I'm going home. Fleshcreep's out so I can smoke in the bath.

FAIRY

See you tomorrow.

MAISIE exits.

FAIRY

Come on you. Come with me. It's home time.

KYLIE wanders off in the opposite direction, away from the Village.

FAIRY

Hey! Kylie! This way.

KYLIE exits the wrong way.

FAIRY

I really don't know what to do,
You'd get more obedience from a cat
But I'd do what the hell I liked too,
If I'd been blessed with tits like that!

The FAIRY scuttles behind a tree and hides as FLESHCREEP ENTERS. He has a rope that leads offstage.

FLESHCREEP

As I was walking to St Ives
I met a man with seven wives
Each wife had seven sons, between
The age of twenty and fifteen
We had an orgy the road,
How many of them took my load?

He allows a moment's calculation/response

FLESHCREEP

Ah ah you see it's trick question. The boys took turns to fuck me, the father kept a look out and the wives popped over to the M&S services to get bits and bobs for a picnic. Welcome back you southern softcocks. *(To his favourite in the audience)* Have you got squiffer or have I got more attractive? I'm looking for a security guard by the way. So if you think you can handle my back entrance with a light but insistent touch, drop me a line.

FLESHCREEP yanks the rope. Cillian is on the other end of it.

CILLIAN

Ow! This is embarrassing.

FLESHCREEP

Shall we hang pants on it and pretend you're a washing pole? This is the spot where we first met. I laid eyes on your straining little bag and instantly I knew you'd come a long way. Now, it's time for your vocal training.

CILLIAN

What, here?

FLESHCREEP

Do you want to be a world famous star? Do you want the gold disks? Nick fucking Grimshaw photobombing you at any opportunity like an over-keen orphan in a Comic Relief film?

CILLIAN

It's all I ever wanted! But I want to write my own songs.

FLESHCREEP
I want to wear Ryan Gosling's thighs around my ears like the flaps of a deerstalker but we don't always get what we want.

CILLIAN
And I need new clothes and a personal trainer.

FLESHCREEP
You have a personal trainer! What's wrong with him!

CILLIAN
He doesn't understand the Alexander technique, and he's just you in a pair of fake glasses.

FLESHCREEP
Don't be ungrateful. As we speak an engineer from Abbey Road is installing a state of the art studio in the basement next to the dark room. I can't wait to get you in the booth. It's completely soundproof.

CILLIAN
What kind of dark room? For developing things?

FLESHCREEP
Well yes, if you count a couple of fleeting crushes and a drug-resistant strain of chlamydia. But! We shall get nowhere unless we practise. Now, stand up straight. After me. (Sings like Cher) "Do you believe..."

CILLIAN
"Do you believe"

FLESHCREEP
No no that's flat, here use your diaphragm. (Places hand on Cillian's lower stomach) "Do you believe"

CILLIAN
"Do you believe"

FLESHCREEP
Better (shifts hand lower down Cillian's body) "Do you believe"

CILLIAN
"Do you believe"

FLESHCREEP
Yes nearly (slips hand into Cillian's trousers and squeezes) "Do you believe"

CILLIAN
"Do you believe"

FLESHCREEP
Yes! Sing my angel of music!

FLESHCREEP withdraws his hand and sniffs it.

<u>SMELL 6</u>: MUSK

FLESHCREEP
Have good musky sniff boys and girls of Cillian's crotch. What is that, is that Lynx?

CILLIAN
It's Hugo Boss.

The FAIRY comes out from behind the tree.

FAIRY
Here's our squire, the country bumpkin
Stinking in his tweed
His arse is like a massive pumpkin,
His head's a mouldy swede.
His willy's just a tiny bean
He wants to grow it more
And that is why he's often seen
Shoving it in manure!

FLESHCREEP puts his hand over her mouth. She pulls it away.

FAIRY
What is that, is that Lynx?

CILLIAN
It's Hugo Boss!

FLESHCREEP
Where did you spring from.

FAIRY
Out of thin air!

FLESHCREEP
Thin air? With that arse?

FAIRY
Honestly boys and girls, a face like that on him and he complains that wind-farms are an eyesore! Now I'm here with my post-woman's hat on.

FLESHCREEP
I think it's blown off.

The FAIRY magics a cap from behind the tree and puts it on. She hands him an invitation and exits.

FLESHCREEP
Oh my, an invitation! (Reads) Your company is warmly requested at a posh tea. There will be champagne from three-thirty and music from five. Yes I heard they were

reforming[70]. (reads again) Lots of love from... The Trotts! RSVP! but that's impossible!

CILLIAN
No it's easy you just write back to the address here. Oh can we go? Please?

FLESHCREEP
I see! You want to see Jack! Has he built you a recording studio? I don't think so! But perhaps I should pay a visit. I don't know where they've suddenly got money from, but if they've struck oil or something, it's mine! Hahahahaha!

FLESHCREEP exits with the end of the rope. CILLIAN stays on stage...

---

[70] The pop band Five reformed in 2013, albeit with only four members.

CILLIAN
If Fleshcreep wants to make me rich and famous who am I to argue. If he wants to throw his fat wad my way, I'll sat back and take it.

We transition into the next scene with a song, "We're In The Money" from 42nd Street[71]. CILLIAN sings the first verse before being yanked offstage by the rope. JACK and SIMON then enter and complete the rest of the song. They're wearing gold clothes.

---

[71] In fact – musical fans – it was originally performed by Ginger Rogers in the 1933 film *Gold Diggers of 1933*, but was included in the stage musical adaptation of *42nd Street,* which premiered in 1980. Our rewritten version included couplets like "We've got new wellies/And widescreen tellies".

Scene 9: Dame Trott's farm

It is the same room as in scene two but it is smarter (though not particularly tasteful) and there is a lot of gold. The ducks on the wall are now gold now for example.

JACK
Eh up boys and girls! I'm just back from a night out, living it up amid the bright city lights of Leeds. I met a boy online! I took him to the finest restaurant, then to the ballet, and then it was back to the 5-star hotel for four-way cocaine sex with a pair of twin rent boys. I was going to round it all off with a Kitkat from the hotel minibar, but it was really fucking expensive. Hey, our Simon, make us a brew.

SIMON
You make us a brew, I want to play with my new Playstation 4.

JACK
Oh aye, how's it going?

SIMON
I don't know what I'm doing with it. What's it for? It doesn't bounce, it doesn't roll and you can't put your dick in it.

JACK
It's probably broken.

SIMON
It feels alright.

JACK
Go on. Make a brew. I'll pay you.

SIMON
Alright.

JACK
Idiot.

SIMON
Idiot.

KYLIE enters.

JACK
Kylie! Er... what are you doing? You don't live here anymore.

KYLIE moos. Off, we hear TROTT singing "The Rain in Spain".

JACK
Oh god it's mum coming home.

SIMON
If she finds you in here now that we've got the place all smart she'll tan your hide.

KYLIE moos

JACK
It's just a phrase! Quick, get in there until I can distract mum. Go on.

KYLIE exits through into the rest of the house. Jack looks casual. DAME TROTT enters from outside. She is dressed in the way she would imagine a lady of means would dress.

TROTT
Oh you're back lads and lasses that's a relief, we sometimes lose a few down the secret passage that runs between the toilets and Chariots[72]. Simon, has that Maisie been round? It smells like a vegetarian's dropped a sly one.

JACK
I can't smell anything.

TROTT
Well, as long as we're all singing from the same spreadsheet. I've been shoe-shopping! The shop was called "bootique" which I thought was very clever. I even had a pair of heels made *(She lifts her wellies – horse shoes are stuck to the soles)*. The blacksmith did them. He said, Dame Trott, I'll be able to hear you coming a mile away in these. And then he winked. I think he spends too much time alone bashing away in his lean-to.

JACK
You look great mum. It suits you being a lady of leisure.

TROTT
A lady of leisure! I like that I'll use it. Now, you haven't been telling people how we came by all this money have you?

JACK
No mum.

---

72 As mentioned elsewhere in this book, Chariots is a gay sauna with a large venue in Vauxhall.

TROTT

Only we'll have the world and his dog up that beanstalk else, and there's no fun being rich if everyone else is loaded too. I've been relaxing at Harrogate Spa! Eventually. Once someone pointed out I was expected at the pump rooms and not the convenience store. I had afternoon tea with a group of society women. Posh little tarts. And sandwiches, the ones where they lop the crusts off. Spent three hours filling my hole with buttered cucumber. My hands are still all tacky from confectioner's cream...

She wipes her hands on an audience member. FLESHCREEP enters. He looks about the place.

FLESHCREEP

Good God.

TROTT

Tasteful, isn't it.

FLESHCREEP

It's about as tasteful as Cher's comeback wig.

JACK

If you've come to mock.

FLESHCREEP

I've come to RSVP.

TROTT

Well help yourself but put the seat down when you've finished.

FLESHCREEP

Although I can't help but be curious, from whence has come all this newfound financial security...?

TROTT

Oh, didn't you hear? Ian Duncan Smith's been putting benefits up all over the show. He were round earlier in a jesters hat with bells on doing a camp little money dance, you can't help but warm to him. It's none of your business. We got lucky that's all! Like you got lucky. You might not have inherited your father's kind heart or benevolent ways but you inherited his money and his halitosis.

FLESHCREEP

What about that monstrosity in your garden?

TROTT

Beanstalk. It were meant to be a bonsai but Simon planted it wrong way round.

FLESHCREEP

(To his favourite boy) That reminds me, I'm on the lookout for a gardener. So once I've trimmed my little thicket perhaps you could see your way to giving it a liberal seeding. (To Trott) Might I pop up for a look?

TROTT

No! I mean, it isn't safe. Well. I expect I'll be seeing more of you now we're in similar social circles.

FLESHCREEP

Similar circles! Oh yes. I can just see the cream of Yorkshire society gathering for Bellinis under your classy golden ducks! Well I shouldn't be surprised, I can hardly see you with a Canaletto.

TROTT

I'll drink what I like.

FLESHCREEP

I'll find out your game.

TROTT

I am not! Get out and leave us in peace. You were happy enough accepting a year's rent up front.

FLUSHCRAP

Well as I say I was here to RSVP. Partial though I am to an Iceland prawn ring I'm afraid I will be otherwise engaged with Cillian's ring. Good day.

FLESHCREEP exits. Unseen by the Trotts, KYLIE pokes her head through the door.

TROTT

I've said it once and I'll say it with flowers, I don't miss farming one bit. Stupid useless creatures, cows. That Kylie! Oh what a waste of good feed she was. (She spots Kylie) Oh...! Kylie. What are you doing you tyke? Have you come for a glimpse at my glitz? Everyone wants a piece now don't they. Haven't forgotten you Reverend, I can see you're eyeing me up for a contribution towards having your organ fixed.

KYLIE wanders sadly into the room.

TROTT

Is she alright? I hope she's been taking her tablets Jack.

JACK

What's wrong Kylie? What is it girl?

KYLIE nudges a CD on table.

JACK
Yeah I know, it's that Indigo Girls CD you used to like.

KYLIE walks over and looks longingly at a calendar on the wall, It is a Beautiful Cows calendar 2013.

TROTT
Do you think she's lonely jack? Don't worry love now we're loaded you can have your choice of all the bulls in Yorkshire.

KYLIE starts to fret. She is distressed.

JACK
Steady on girl, what's up?

KYLIE nudges the CD then the calendar.

JACK
Hold on are you saying that you're the type of cow who'd rather munch on bunch of curly kale rather than nibble a carrot?

KYLIE nods

JACK
She's a lezza mum! Good on you girl.

TROTT
Oh my bras and garters. A gay cow!

SIMON
That's why you were so nice to the cat!

TROTT
We never could get you breeding.

SIMON
I've seen the size of bull's willies. They're terrifying.

TROTT
I can't say I've noticed. I certainly didn't notice all through my impressionable teenage years.

CILLIAN enters. JACK isn't quite sure what he feels about this.

CILLIAN
Knock knock.

TROTT
Cillian! Have you come to give me access to all your areas now I'm a, what was it, lady of the night.

CILLIAN
A what?

TROTT
I think my clothes speak for themselves. The skirt's a bit itchy mind, I think it's herpes. *(She checks the label)* Hermes, that's it. Have a sniff of my perfume, it's one of your modern ambiguous scents that doubles as a lady's perfume and a cover-up for pet smells. Here you can all have a sniff... That's it. There's a gentleman back there sniffing his through a rolled-up banknote note.

SMELL 7: MILDEW

KYLIE is looking dreamily at the calendar again.

CILLIAN
What's with her?

TROTT
Some cows are gay, get over it. Alright enough, get out Kylie, this is a nice house now. Simon, take her out.

SIMON leads KYLIE off. CILLIAN and JACK are a bit awkward.

TROTT
Right, well. Two's company, three's a mouthful. I'll be out back.

TROTT exits.

CILLIAN
Your party sounds fun.

JACK
It will be. Loads of hot lads coming.

CILLIAN
Oh. *(Not happy)* Nice one.

JACK
I've met so many fit men since we got rich.

CILLIAN
Oh. So where did all the money come?

JACK
We... we inherited! We had a long lost relative. Then we found him again. And then he died, it were right sad.

CILLIAN
Sorry. Do you want to get a vodka and lilt down at the Tart?

JACK
I dunno. Where've you been? I haven't seen you since the festival.

CILLIAN

It's only been a week! Which was long enough for you to rim half of Leeds apparently.

JACK

What was I meant to do?

CILLIAN

I've been busy.

JACK

Busy? It's Upper Jumper, there's nowt to do. It's not fucking.... Bradford.

CILLIAN

Fleshcreep doesn't like me going out on my own.

JACK

You don't have to act like his slave just so you can make a record, you're either good or you're not. Have some dignity. You can't sing with a cock in your mouth.

CILLIAN

That's bullshit, Enya made three albums like that. At least I've got some ambition. *(He takes a selfie)* Ambitious selfie. I'm going.

JACK

Go on then.

SIMON enters

SIMON

Jack, Jack, is it your turn to go up the magic beanstalk to rub normal stuff on the giant penis to turn it into gold stuff or is it my turn to go up the magic beanstalk to rub normal stuff on the giant penis to turn it into gold stuff?

CILLIAN and JACK both look at Simon.

Blackout.

Scene 10: Fleshcreep Hall

FLESHCREEP, MAISIE and CILLIAN

FLESHCREEP
I love these moments when we're at home together, one happy family! The father figure. (To Cillian) The surrogate and protégé. (To Maisie) The drudge. I know! Tonight why don't I treat us to a takeaway and a movie night. There's a curry house two villages away. Sidebottom's. Mrs Sidebottom went to Goa in 2008 when she had her affair, so it's very authentic. She does a pork dhansak in an oversized Yorkshire pudding, you can have it with or without grated cheese.

MAISIE
Does she do vegetarian?

FLESHCREEP
She used to but the council stopped her on account of it not being in keeping with the character of the local area.

CILLIAN
I should get my own nutritionist if I'm going to be a big star.

FLESHCREEP
You have a nutritionist, what's wrong with him?

CILLIAN
Well, he's never heard of any special diets, and it's just you in a beard and a novelty apron.

FLESHCREEP
Shush shush. Now, have you heard my latest venture? No, you haven't. I've had an epiphany. You see if that beanstalk grows any higher it will burst through that cursed cloud and sunshine will return to Upper Jumper.

CILLIAN
So that'll be good for the farmers?

FLESHCREEP
No! Haha! No. I've decided to create the country's largest, finest private sailing lake on my doorstep! We'll be surrounded by the boats of the rich and famous, and pride of place will be my yacht, the Lesbian Queen! There's only one problem. To make the lake I need to flood the valley.

MAISIE
What about Upper Jumper?

FLESHCREEP
Vanished! Submerged! Lost! The thing is, I've looked into it. To get compulsory possession order on the remainder of the village I'd have to bribe the parish council, the county council, the local media, and five bloody cabinet ministers and they're all fucking millionaires as it is. George Osborne would notice the average cash sweetener about as much as this gentleman *(he points at someone)* would notice a pat on the arse six hours into a bank holiday special at The Hoist. Still. One has to have a dream. Changing the subject: The Trotts. What's going on? Is it oil? I should have drilled that woman's back garden when I had the chance.

CILIAN
It's not oil. It's gold.

FLESHCREEP
Gold!

CILLIAN
There's a man at the top of that giant beanstalk with a massive penis, and everything it touches turns to gold.

FLESHCREEP
Gold!

MAISIE
How massive?

CILIAN
I don't know. But everything it touches turns into gold.

FLESHCREEP
Gold!

FLESHCREEP
You're lying. Lying to protect Jack.

CILLIAN
I don't want to protect Jack.

FLESHCREEP
Then there's no time to waste. We must get our arses onto Jack's stalk. We'll kidnap the man with the golden schlong, get rich, flood the valley and Upper Jumper will be drowned hundreds of feet beneath the sparkling waters of the new Yorkshire Riviera, lapping gently at my perimeters. And that's not a euphemism, it's just a bit sexy. (To his audience favourite) you could be a lifeguard. The number of times I've been found clinging desperately to a buoy after swallowing a lung-full. I'm

sure you could bring me to the edge with a couple of tugs.

MAISIE
You can't flood the valley! People will protest.

FLESHCREEP
"Ooh help, a petition from change.org." They can try and protest. I've been stockpiling Turkish tear gas for months! Anyway, you hate Upper Jumper. Right! In haste! Cillian! To the basement!

CILIAN
Are we going to make a plan?

FLESHCREEP
Oh yes! We'll do that after.

FLESHCREEP and CILLIAN exit.

MAISIE
The man is nuts. I'll warn Simon again. Maybe the Trotts can stop Uncle Fleshcreep getting to the beanstalk!

MAISIE's spell book is thrown to her from the wings. She flicks through it.

MAISIE
Oh here's a good one. Gain a flat stomach in three easy steps.

FLESHCREEP enters with a rope

FLESHCREEP
You traitor! Stop your own uncle would you?

He grabs her and starts tying her up.

MAISIE
Let go of me!

FLESHCREEP
Interfering little bitch! *(He grabs the book)* This can't be so hard. *(reads)* I say, gain a flat stomach in three easy steps! But first! Mind control. Here we are... "Mind Control Spell. Works best on a very small mind." I know just the fellow! Mr Simon Trott!

Blackout

Scene 11: The top of the beanstalk

In the Giant's lair at the top of the beanstalk. DAME TROTT and the GIANT are drinking tea from gold mugs and admiring the view from the top of the beanstalk. TROTT has a sort of climbing harness and hard hat and has some rope about her. There is an undercurrent of mutual interest running through the scene. Trott gazes out at the view. After a little while...

TROTT
My, it's a hell of a sight though isn't it. Goes on for ever.

GIANT *(looking at his penis)*
It *is* bothering you.

TROTT
The view, man. *(Looks at her harness)* Oh damn... I've lost my little dangly thing.

GIANT
Carabiner?

TROTT
No thank you, I'm fine with my tea. Look, that village by the hill. Middle Finger. I spent my wedding night there at the Slippit Inn. (She points out into the audience) Oh there's the upper common, the lower common, the terribly common...

GIANT
You're married?

TROTT
In theory. He ran off with a hygiene inspector.

GIANT
I'm sorry.

TROTT
I don't expect you meet many women.

GIANT
No... I used to be engaged.

TROTT
Well. I wanted to say, we're ever so grateful.

GIANT
You keep sending up your delicious food and you can have all the precious metal you can carry.

TROTT
Alright but stop turning my Tupperwares into gold, it won't seal properly. You know, if you liked, you could come down and have a cuppa sometime. Or a glass of champagne. We're only down there.

GIANT
You're kind, lass. But people would... I could come down at night I suppose.

TROTT
You could. I don't go to bed very early now I've not got the morning milking to do. You can't stay up here forever.

GIANT
I'd be lonelier down there. What if I met my fiancé?

TROTT
I expect she's aged terribly

GIANT
Or, or someone else, and if I took a shine to her... I wouldn't be able to satisfy her.

TROTT
Size isn't everything. I think it's the companionship I miss the most. I sort of forget that sex is something humans do.

GIANT (looking down)
Is that a condom?

TROTT
It's the polytunnel, but you might just squeeze into it.

SIMON enters, with Trott's shotgun. He's holding it back to front.

SIMON
Jazz hands!

TROTT and the GIANT make jazz hands.

TROTT
Wait I think he means "hands up". Simon you'll do yourself an injury!

SIMON
What? *(He notices the gun is pointing towards himself)* Oh aye. *(Corrects it)*

GIANT
Shite!

TROTT
Get it off him. Wait until you can see the whites of his eggs.

SIMON
Mum, you get off home. (To GIANT) And you're coming with me.

TROTT
Simon what are you playing at!

SIMON
I can't help it.

TROTT
Were you put up to this? Oh hell, did you tell someone about the beanstalk? Oh you stupid, stupid boy!

SIMON
Aye. Stupid. That's all you think of me.

TROTT
You listen to me, son. Blood's thicker than water, and you're thicker than both. I love you. Now give me the gun.

SIMON
Sorry mum. Off you go.

TROTT exits fearfully. SIMON has the GIANT in his sights.

SIMON
Right you. Come with me. And keep your cock where I can see it.

Blackout

Scene 12: Fleshcreep Hall

Maisie is tied up.

MAISIE
Help!!!

CILLIAN enters

CILLIAN
Oh my god! Who did this?

MAISIE
Fleshcreep.

CILLIAN
The bastard!

MAISIE
I know right.

CILLIAN
I thought he only did this to me!

MAISIE
Untie me before he gets back!

CILLIAN goes to take a selfie.

CILLIAN
Jealous selfie.

MAISIE
Oi! Back in the room.

CILLIAN (putting his phone back in his pocket)
Sorry.

MAISIE
See? Wasn't that hard was it.

CILLIAN whimpers but starts to untie MAISIE. FLESHCREEP enters. CILLIAN runs off.

FLESHCREEP
Cillian? (Calling off) Bring Fleshcreep a drink dear boy! Scotch with a splash. And perhaps a little water too. A drink, Dozy? But how insensitive, you're tied up.

SIMON enters.

SIMON
Sir.

FLESHCREEP
Aha! But you're alone. Where is he?

SIMON
The man with the massive penis?

FLESHCREEP
No, Edward Snowdon, who do you think? Yes, the man with the massive penis!

SIMON
I tried to make him climb down but he couldn't reach the stalk with his hands to hold on because of his massive penis.

FLESHCREEP
I see. Then stand guard over my vile charge here. I'll get my hands on that massive penis and milk it for all it's worth.

He gives an evil laugh and leaves.

MAISIE
Simon you wanker, untie me.

SIMON looks like a zombie and says nothing.

MAISIE
Wanker. Fuck's sake. Simon. It's me. Maisie. I wish Miss Goblin was here, she'd have a spell. Simon please, you don't want to hurt me. Simon I never told you this and I wish I had in a way but, I, I think I've fallen in love with you.

CILLIAN (*sticking his head out of where he is hiding*)
Ah! (He takes a selfie)

MAISIE
I love you Simon.

SIMON's face twitches, then his body starts to move as if he is doing some unusual hip hop dance.

SIMON
Do you? Do you really love me?

MAISIE
Yeah. Now untie me.

SIMON starts to untie MAISIE, CILLIAN also comes out to help. FLESHCREEP enters. CILLIAN returns to hide.

FLESHCREEP
Simon!

SIMON
I'm going to save Maisie.

FLESHCREEP
Oh no you're not.

He picks up a large vase and is about to hit SIMON over the head.

MAISIE
Wait! Isn't that priceless?

FLESHCREEP
No! But this will be!

He swings it hard at SIMON's head. SIMON is knocked out.

FLESHCREEP
And now my dear it's time to get my chopper out.

MAISIE
You are vile.

FLESHCREEP
My helicopter of course! Get your mind out of the gutter you filthy tramp! Come along.

He leads MAISIE out. CILLIAN comes out and runs over to SIMON.

CILLIAN
Completely glazed over and out of it. It's like chucking out time at Fire[73].

There is a helicopter noise, and the appropriate music from Miss Saigon. Dark. Dramatic searchlights. Smoke. And: a tiny little helicopter appears bobbing about on a fishing line.

FLESHCREEP (heard from off)
We were going to use the one from Miss Saigon but the cunts are bringing it back[74]. To the beanstalk!

_____

[73] A big gay club in Vauxhall.
[74] Miss Saigon was revived in the West End in 2014.

They fly off. Lighting returns to normal.

CILLIAN shakes SIMON, who does not wake. He picks up a soda siphon and squirts it in SIMONS face – nothing.

CILLIAN
Will I try mouth to mouth? Alright.

He does. Eventually Simon wakes.

SIMON
What are you doing?

CILLIAN
Sorry. I had to wake you.

SIMON
Thanks. Give us another one.

CILLIAN
What? Are you gay and all?

SIMON
No mate. You're just really pretty.

CILLIAN gives him a peck.

CILLIAN
Listen. Your man Fleshcreep's going to get the man with the massive penis and flood the valley.

SIMON
That's disgusting.

CILLIAN
No, with water! And he's got Maisie.

SIMON
Maisie? Maisie! I'm coming to save you!

Scene 13: The Trott's cottage garden

There is a sound of a helicopter in the distance/ overhead. KYLIE and JACK are looking out of the window. The beanstalk is wobbling.

TROTT enters, bouncing on an inflatable space-hopper toy and singing Miley Cyrus's "Wrecking Ball". She throws the space-hopper offstage.

TROTT (now speaking)
Oh my bras and garters there's a helicopter flown up to the top the beanstalk!

SIMON and CILLIAN run in.

TROTT
Simon! Get away from him everyone!

SIMON
It's ok mum! I was under Lord Fleshcreep's spell but I'm ok now. I'm so sorry!

TROTT hugs him

MRS TROTT
Oh my brave boy.

SIMON
Cillian saved me.

TROTT let's go of SIMON quickly so he nearly falls. She hugs CILLIAN pushing his head between her breasts.

TROTT
Oh my brave boy!

CILLIAN
Listen! Fleshcreep's taken Maisie up there as a hostage.

TROTT
I knew she were trouble.

SIMON
She's not trouble mum. She undid me spell!

TROTT
Aye I bet she undid your... spell.

CILLIAN
He's going to use the power of the penis to take over the whole valley.

SIMON
I'll save her!

Simon runs and starts climbing the beanstalk.

JACK
Simon! Be careful. Let's go after him.

TROTT
What if it's dangerous?

CILLIAN
What if he captures you both?

JACK
So what can we do?

CILCIAN
The beanstalk is magic so it is. Maybe we need magic to defeat Fleshcreep.

TROTT
I got one of those Paul Daniels magic kits last year from the village fête. It's mainly balls and hankies but there might be something.

JACK
Mum we need proper magic.

CILLIAN
We need a fairy.

TROTT
You won't find any fairies round here love.

KYLIE moos urgently.

JACK
Kylie! Hold on are you saying there are fairies round here?

KYLIE nods.

JACK
Boys and girls, do you know the name of a fairy we can call?

The audience shout.

JACK
Fanny Goblin? Ok, we're going to shout "We want Fanny" three times and hope she appears. Ready? One, two, three. "We want fanny, we want fanny, we want fanny..."

The FAIRY appears wearing a sweatband.

FAIRY
This had better be important darlings. I was in the middle of Davina's thirty minute workout.

TROTT
Thirty minutes? Add a couple of noughts and you might get somewhere.

FAIRY
I see. You heard about my being magical.

MRS TROTT
We used to burn the likes of you round here.

FAIRY
We used to breed the likes of you round here. Woman, the magic won't work on the beanstalk any more than it'd work on your face. It will only regenerate. Unlike your face. The only way to destroy it is to chop it down. Let me get you an axe.

JACK
What sort of an axe?

The FAIRY magics a small plastic ace which she hands over to JACK.

TROTT
An anticlim-axe.

JACK starts to chop at the beanstalk. FLESHCREEP enters

FLESHCREEP
Not advisable! My nauseating niece and your brainless brother are up there. I would hate to see them fall to their deaths and besides you have no right to be here. I'm evicting you for multiple transgressions.

TROTT
Transgressions?? I'll have you know I am all woman.

CILLIAN
Miss Goblin, we have to save Maisie and Simon. Have you got a spell?

JACK carries on chopping.

FAIRY
Plenty my dear. But I'll need help. And a kiss.

CILLIAN
A kiss? Alright... *(Gives her a peck)* What did you need that for?

FAIRY
Everyone needs a little kiss sometimes. But now I need help.

TROTT
The boys and girls will help again. They helped get you here, didn't they?

FAIRY
Join hands boys and girls. Join hands and repeat after me. "Fe fi fo fum, Simon and Maisie, down they come!"

SIMON and MAISIE appear.

CILLIAN
Keep chopping Jack.

MAISIE
Hold on. Herbert's sill up there!

FAIRY
And there, I'm afraid, he must stay. His massive penis is a danger to us all.

JACK
I'll get this beanstalk down.

FLESHCREEP
Oh no you won't.

He pushes JACK. There is a fight. FLESHCREEP gets the axe. He grabs TROTT and holds it to her throat.

TROTT
Just take an inch off and thin me out on top.

FLESHCREEP
Leave, now. All of you. Or the old goat loses her head.

The FAIRY is in a trance like state.

FAIRY
The last spell took all my power, I'm spent. Maisie, you'll have to do it.

MAISIE
Me?

FAIRY
A spell to banish your uncle.

FLESHCREEP
I am here you know.

MAISIE
I can't.

SIMON
You can, Maisie! You can do it! I believe in you.

FLESHCREEP
Bored now! You've got five seconds.

TROTT
Maisie, please!

FLESHCREEP
Five.

MAISIE
Alright. But I'm going for something more modern. Not a verse.

She gets out her wand

FLESHCREEP
Four.

MAISIE
Spoldgecamonius!

Nothing happens.

FLESHCREEP
Three. Two.

SIMON
Come on Maisie!

FLESHCREEP
One –

He raises his axe about to chop off Mrs Trotts head.

MAISIE
Spoldgecamonius!

FLESHCREEP screams and lets go of Mrs Trott. He starts to move backwards as MAISIE continues to wave her wand. He is dragged off stage by invisible forces.

CILLIAN
Where's he gone?

There is a scream followed by an enormous muddy splash, then the sound of bubbles.

TROTT, JACK, SIMON
The slurry lagoon!

JACK
It's like quicksand!

TROTT
The easier they fall the harder they come.

SIMON
That was amazing! A-maisie-ing! You're my hero.

MAISIE
You're my hero!

SIMON
I thought maybe you only said what you said back at mansion so you could break the spell on me.

MAISIE
Yeah I did mainly. But then when I said it, it sort of felt true.

They kiss.

JACK
You saved my brother! You're my hero Cillian.

JACK and CILLIAN kiss. CILLIAN takes a selfie, of them both.. There is a creaking sound. The beanstalk starts to wobble.

MAISIE
Cool it, Jack! Your stalk's going to kill someone.

TROTT
It's going to fall!

They all run to the sides as it crashes down. TROTT exits and returns holding one of the ducks from her wall. It is no longer gold.

TROTT
Look! What's happening to the gold?

CILLIAN
What about yer man with the penis.

The FAIRY is quietly crying.

MAISIE
Miss Goblin, are you alright?

FAIRY
Aye, aye of course I am. I just miss him so much, but I never worked out how to reverse the curse.

The GIANT enters. He no longer has a giant penis.

GIANT
Still so beautiful!

TROTT
I do what I can, it's only been a couple of hours.

FAIRY *(looking up)*
Herbert Skesselthwaite!

GIANT
Fanny Goblin!

The FAIRY and the GIANT kiss.

TROTT (sad)
Oh...

MAISIE
Aw Miss Goblin! It's so romantic!

TROTT
Oh no it isn't!

TROTTS' phone rings.

TROTT
How do. (pause) Aye this is she. (pause). HRH who? I'll never guess from your initials lad, just spit it out. Prince Charles! Your royal highness!

She curtsies

TROTT
Yes! (pause) Yes! (pause) Yes!

She puts her phone away.

TROTT
It was Prince Charles!

Everyone gasps

TROTT
He tried some of my Dairymaid's Secret at that all-organic farm show in t'summer and now he wants me to make a cheese in honour of Baby George.

Everyone gasps.

FAIRY
Your Dairymaid's Secret isn't organic.

TROTT
I know, that's the secret. But that's not all. He wants me to manage a dairy farm in the grounds of Highgrove!

Everyone gasps.

TROTT
And I'm going to be a dame!

Everyone gasps. The GIANT's gasp turns into an awful choking cough.

GIANT
Sorry. I swallowed a fly. Well done lass.

TROTT
I've forgotten who you are sir, have we met?

JACK
Are you going to go?

TROTT
Still waters run amock, Jack. I'd better get packing.

CILLIAN
Mrs Trott - Dame Trott. Before you go. When I went on the Fame Factory I just wanted to be rich and adored by millions. But after just a couple of weeks here I've seen that you don't need money to be happy and you only need to be adored by one person, so long as that one person is someone very, very, special.

TROTT
Cillian, you're vision and a half but I can't rock up at Highgrove with a toyboy, I'm practically royal now.

MAISIE
Awkward.

CILLIAN (Humouring her)
Dame Trott you break a boy's heart sure you do. But you'd console me if you'd grant me your permission to marry Jack.

TROTT
Oh. Well, sauces for horses. Be my guest.

CILLIAN
That's if you want me.

JACK takes CILLIAN in his arms and kisses him

TROTT
A wedding! But I haven't got a hat.

JACK
Perhaps Camilla will lend you one.

TROTT
I'm not without admiration for the woman but I'm hardly going to turn up at my own son's wedding in an adulteress's hat!

TROTT exits.

GIANT
Come on Fanny love, we've twenty years of lost time to make up. Shall we go to the school house?

FAIRY
The school house? There's a perfectly good barn just there.

They run off.

SIMON
Maisie, do you want to come and see my polytunnel.

MAISIE
If I can help make something grow.

SIMON and MAISIE run off.

JACK
Did you mean what you said about not wanting to be a star anymore?

CILLIAN
Well, no. But I meant what I said about you. And before I try to become a star, how about we go on a tour all of our own.

JACK
What, Leeds? No, London?

CILLIAN
No, silly. I was thinking of the whole world.

They start to exit. KYLIE moos.

JACK
Oh Kylie. I won't leave you too long.

KYLIE starts to cry.

CILLIAN
She must be missing her mates so she must. Specially as Fleshcreep had them turned into burgers.

JACK
Burger! Don't be daft. It'll have been something much nicer. Like a steak bake.

KYLIE looks more upset.

CILLIAN
She needs to be with other cows... What's the smell? Even I can smell it and my nose is fucked.

SMELL 8: CHEESE

TROTT enters with a case and a cheese.

TROTT
(Singing) I'm as corny as Carlisle in Autumn, High as me tights on the fourth of July... (Stops singing) Have a sniff of this lads and lasses! Fit for a king. HRH has just called back and said I can graze me cattle at Highgrove. That's you Kylie. You'll get to mix with hundreds of royal cows. You might even find a lover. Would you like that?

KYLIE nods. TROTT and KYLIE exit.

JACK
Come on lad we've got a wedding and world tour to plan.

JACK and CILLIAN exit. The FAIRY takes back the stage.

FAIRY
Now picture, my darlings, a marvellous erection
A great marquee on the village green
And a party to cheer evil Fleshcreep's ejection
All because of my little bean!

The school trio will give us Vivaldi out of tune,
And the band will play ill-advised covers
And there beneath lanterns and a kind, pale moon
On the grass we'll marry our lovers

And yes, there'll be arguments along the road
And yes, maybe even affairs
But first there'll be dancing and when the drink's flowed
There'll be love and good cheer without cares.

If one day *you* find yourself lonely and down
In a far-flung part of this isle
Or a stranger appears in your own part of town
Keep your arms and hearts open, and smile:

For strangers are friends that you haven't yet laid
And the fool can be as kind as the bright,
Now with thanks that you came – and with thanks that you stayed -
Safe home, you fine people, good night.

CURTAIN CALL

SONG: UPPER JUMPER
(To the tune to Proud Mary)

Living here in Upper Jumper
Working on the land just to earn a bean
Ee by gum, the days were glum,
Man, the life was mean mean mean

Magic beans a-sowing *(sowing)*
Jack's stalk keeps on growing *(growing)*
Climbing, climbing, climbing up a beanstalk
Climbing, climbing, climbing up a beanstalk

Made a lot of cheese in the village
Made a little time just to shoot the breeze
Have no pity when your back in your city
And only send the hottest tourists *(please please please)*

Get your beans a-sowing *(sowing)*
Get that beanstalk growing *(growing)*
Climbing, climbing, climbing up a beanstalk

(Feels like) Climbing, climbing, climbing up a beanstalk

If you come to Upper Jumper
Mind you drop by for a brew
We've waved bye bye to raining skies
And we're miles away from High Speed Two *(Choo choo choo)*

Get your beans a-sowing *(sowing)*
Get that beanstalk growing *(growing)*
Climbing, climbing, climbing up a beanstalk
(Feels like) Climbing, climbing, climbing up a beanstalk

Ee bye gum, Ee bye gum, Ecky thump
We love Upper Jumper, yeah!

THE END.

Get Aladdin!

Lucy Gill as Wishy Washy and Josh Rochford as Widow Twankey in *Get Aladdin!* Photo by Derek Drescher.

Get Aladdin!

2012. The Olympics were an outstanding success with the armed forces stepping in at the last moment to support security company G4S. A scaled back World Pride took place in London in July. Greece needed a second bailout loan and there were serious concerns about what would happen if they won Eurovision as they would not be able to afford to host the contest the following year. Having successfully mentored Little Mix to victory the previous year, X factor judge Tulisa found herself in a media storm after her ex-boyfriend Justin Edwards leaked a sex-tape of them. And the first series of Big Fat Gypsy Wedding aired on Channel 4.

On screen, Aladdin is usually set in the Middle East but in pantomime it's set in China. In fact it's a Middle Eastern story set "in one of the cities of China" but that could well have been vague exoticism on the part of its tellers. Ours is set in the fictional Chinese province of Hao Hung - the first time we had set one of our pantomimes anywhere fictional, something we've done ever since. There's something special about being able to create a "whole new world"...

One of the most important ingredients in a pantomime is taking an audience on an adventure. That comes from creating a setting, and it's also about creating highly contrasting worlds within a show: the familiar and the exotic; rich and poor; city and country; magical and mundane. You can do that with words alone, as Shakespeare did, but our worlds have been immeasurably enhanced by the talents of David Shields, the brilliant designer of most of these shows. We've probably got better over the years about thinking what is and isn't possible in a fringe theatre but we like to throw the creative team a few curveballs, such as Aladdin's magic flying carpet.

Looking back at *Get Aladdin!* while preparing this book we were a bit startled by the number of jokes about race and racism, and remembered an audience member getting in touch after seeing the show to tell us that his minority-ethnic boyfriend had found it quite unpleasant. (He was generous enough to engage in an illuminating email conversation about it.) Some of the references are valid targets, such as Aladdin's blasé, Grindr-esque declaration that he's "not into Asians" shortly before he falls for an Asian prince - though whether pantomime is the place for satirising that is another question. Others were more gratuitous and while nothing stood out as particularly racist in itself, cumulatively the script felt at times like a couple of white writers trying to have their cake and eat it by being both woke and provocative. Our shows are escapism – audiences come in groups for their big Christmas night out. If you're a person of colour, it's clearly not very escapist or fun to be casually reminded of racism every ten minutes, however knowing the humour. We've cut a couple of lines from the script accordingly.

Get Aladdin!

By Jon Bradfield and Martin Hooper

Characters

The Genie of the Lamp, female, an older Mary Poppins with an eye for young men.
Abanazer, the villain, a slick East End gangster type.
The Gimp of the Ring, a lad from Colliers Wood, now Abanazer's slave.
Aladdin, a street thief from Clapham.
Police Woman, from Scotland Yard (seconded from G4S).
Wishy Washy, Aladdin's female monkey.
Widow Twankey, Aladdin's mum, proprietor of a laundry.
The Prince, heir to the throne of the province of Hao Hung.
The Emperor, his father.

Get Aladdin! was first performed at the Landor Theatre on 7 December 2012 in a production by Above The Stag, with the following cast and creative team:

The Genie of the Lamp: Sarah Dearlove; Abanazar: Matthew Baldwin; The Gimp of the Ring: Toby Joyce; Aladdin: Greg Airey; Wishy Washy: Lucy Gill; Lauren, a Policewoman: Elaine Holbrook; Widow Twankey: Josh Rochford; Prince Char Ming: George Bull; The Emperor of Hao Hung: Philip Lawrence

Director: Andrew Beckett; Designer: David Shields; Lighting and Video Designer: Richard Lambert; Musical Director: Matt Randall; Choreographer: Jodie-Lee Wilde; Stage Manager: Andres Jimenez; Lighting Assistant: Matt Wright; PR: Katherine Ives and Target Live; Production photos: Derek Drescher; Rehearsal photos: Jon Bradfield; Poster illustration: Leo Delauncey; Producer: Peter Bull

With thanks to Out of Joint theatre company, Ku Bar, Lauderdale House, LAMBCO, Konstantins Rogovs of Atlantic Star, Maximilien Spielbichler and Fabrice Arfi.

Scene 1: The piazza in Hao Hung

The GENIE OF THE LAMP appears, magically. She addresses the audience.

GENIE
Have you heard of the tale of 1001 nights?[75]
A girl called Scheherazade got wed,
To a jealous prince - but then learned with a fright,
That that the next day he'd chop off her head!

Our heroine's smart, she devises a plan
To escape this fate so gory
Post coital, she snuggles up to her man
And begins a long bedtime story

Romances! adventures you wouldn't believe!
Crimes of avarice, crimes of passion;
Of Sinbad, Ali Baba and 40 thieves,
It's like stories were going out of fashion

So gripping were Scheherazade's bedtime thrillers,
The prince became quite vexed,
Morn after morn he declined to kill her
He wanted to know what came next!

Her last tale was set round the crumbling plaza
Of an old Chinese province, Hao Hung.
Where lives the ruthless, uncouth Abanazer
A villain since he was young!

In Hao Hung's green and pleasant land
He's built dark satanic mills,
Where his slaves make phones, clothes, fireworks and drones
Or whatever the West wants for thrills.

But Boys and Girls! Welcome! My what a fine sight,
It really is time we began
So phones off, let's all sit alert and upright,
Oh! That's not what I meant, young man!!

We're only poor players, and though we are tragic
We'll conjure a world for you here
We need your kind help to make our tale magic
So let's hear you boo, hiss and cheer!

---

[75] Aladdin wasn't part of the original Arabic text of *One Thousand and One Nights* but the French writer Antoine Galland included it in his popular translation 300 years ago, having heard the story – and that of Ali Baba and the Forty Thieves – from the Syrian writer Hanna Diyab.

That's perfect! My dears you would all win an Oscar!
Here's our play, both a happy and sad 'un
All the joy of Twelfth night, all the tears of Tosca,
Are here, in our story, Aladdin

ABANAZER enters. He is sharply dressed and speaks like an East End gangster.

ABANAZER
Hahahahaha! Here, have a fucking cobblers at this. What's a pretty young woman doing in such a rough neighbourhood.

GENIE
That's hardly appropriate, I'm a respectable lady
And you, like this theatre, seem a little shady

ABANAZER
Alright calm down. Let me walk you home, I'll see you safe. I can look after meself. I once had a Tesco delivery man kneecapped just for bringing the wrong sized bag of Icelandic prawns. *(He looks at the audience)* Talking of rough neighbourhoods, what have we got here? Is this a fucking Workfare placement or something? (To the GENIE) Where do you live?

GENIE
One might say I'm homeless, but I'm not a tramp
It's rather conceptual, I live in a lamp

ABANAZER (aside)
The lamp! I knew it. I'm gonna get it back!

GENIE
My time is up, it fades like a flower
It's almost enough to make your heart bleed
I'm only allowed out for half an hour
Each year, on my birthday, till I am freed

ABANAZER
Jesus nail me, she's like Lana del fucking Ray.

ABANAZER toys with his ring.

GENIE
You can't think a lady won't notice a thing
If you insist on flashing your grubby old ring

ABANAZER
Do you have to rhyme all of the ti- Bugger, it's catching. I been waiting for the opportunity to give my ring a little rubbing. It's magic you see.

GENIE
You're clearly demented, your ring is quite dented.

ABANAZER

Decades of abuse from clumsy fingers. I acquired it while relaxing in a Syrian souk with an oil sheik. Disgusting drink, I wouldn't recommend it.

He holds out the ring to someone in the audience.

ABANAZER

Be obliging and spit on my ring.

The audience member spits on the ring. Abanazer rubs the ring.

ABANAZER

Now... (He rubs the ring) behold the Gimp of the Ring!

Smoke. The GIMP OF THE RING appears. Coughing. Northern. Collapses on the floor. ABANAZER helps him up.

ABANAZER

Get off your Aristotle and stand on your fucking plates.

GIMP

Man that's better.

GENIE

I wish a young man like you would pop out when I rubbed my trinket.

GIMP

Hello. Are you a genie too?

GENIE

Yes! Are you?

GIMP

Yeah, sort of.

GENIE

Are you going to conference this year? We could bunk up.

ABANAZER

Alright alright. Shut your boats.

GIMP

Where are we?

ABANAZER

Hao Hung

GIMP

You first.

ABANAZER

Hao Hung is the name of this tiny Chinese province.

GIMP

Oh man alive are we still here? Who are you again?

ABANAZER

I'm your master ain't I. The fucking boss. Abanazer.

GENIE

Abanazer!!

GIMP

That don't sound Chinese mate.

ABANAZER

"Mate"? Do I look Chinese? I'm a citizen of the world. I been on more planes than she's had hot flushes. I'm a powerful man. I once got the whole population of a South American country addicted to lethal crack just cos their tinpot airline tried to put me in premium fucking economy. I'm from London. East London. Back before it started looking like a blind kid's fancy dress party. Lately I been spending most of my time avoiding tax in the United Arab Emirates, but I recently acquired a number of Chinese factories. So I said "so long, farewell, auf wiedersehen Dubai" and moved meself here to Hao Hung.

GIMP

So this Hao Hung? What's it like then?

GENIE

I haven't seen much of it dear but I am not impressed.

[Here we went into a song: rewritten version of One Night In Bangkok from the musical Chess. "One Night In Hau Hung" didn't drive the plot much but it introduced us to Aladdin, who attempts to pickpocket from Abanazer; and we learnt that Abanazer is a cruel and exploitative tycoon. By the end of the song, Aladdin had left the stage again.]

GENIE

The battle begins, the magic unfurls,
I'll see you again soon, boys and girls!

She exits

ABANAZER

That genie and her lamp are more powerful than the International Olympic Committee. I had the lamp stolen from the British Museum. It was the star exhibit in their History of the world in 100 objects display.

GIMP
So they got 99 objects but the lamp ain't one?[76] What happened to the lamp?

ABANAZER
I left it in my coat pocket when I sent it to the laundry, along with my Tate Membership card... I like art. I once had a Picasso painted over cos it was looking at me funny. Right, come on you magic gimp, where's the lamp?

GIMP
How do I know?

ABANAZER (gently)
Come here.

GIMP
What?

ABANAZER
Just come here.

GIMP
I think he's a bit mad boys and girls. Do you think I should go to him?

No!

GIMP
I've been advised to stay here, sir.

ABANAZER
Oh what's lovely smell over here, oh I think it's chips and curry sauce!

The GIMP scampers over to him. ABANAZER slaps him.

ABANAZER
Don't mess with me sunshine. (To the audience) Or you. I once made a goat cry. Permanently. Tell me where the lamp is.

GIMP
I've no idea mate. Can we get some food, I like Chinese.

ABANAZER
Food? You've got a ring to squeeze your muffin tops into. Go on. Back inside.

The GIMP disappears. ABANAZER taps his ring.

ABANAZER
Poor fucker. (Taps his ring) Are you alright in there? (Listens) There, he's as cosy as crabs in a darkroom.

_____
[76] Misquoting Jay-Z's song 99 Problems

ALADDIN enters, picks a wallet from ABANAZER's pocket and scuttles off. ABANAZER notices.

ABANAZER
I've been robbed! Police!!!

The POLICE WOMAN enters immediately, very fast.

ABANAZER
If you set off earlier you wouldn't have to rush. He went that way.

The POLICE WOMAN blows her whistle and runs off. ALADDIN reappears. There is a chase. The POLICE WOMAN catches ALADDIN, takes the wallet from him, and holds his hands behind his back.

ABANAZER
I know you!

ALADDIN
Well, we all look the same round here innit.

ABANAZER
You escaped from my factory.

ALADDIN
Better to be a thief on the streets than one of your slaves!

ABANAZER
Slaves? I been audited. I even had those expensive safety nets installed under the windows. You wanna watch your step boy. I once snapped a man's fingers off just for using the wrong kind of lube. I got a reputation.

ALADDIN
Yeah. Abanazer. "Hung like a butterfly and stings like the clap". Banter.

ABANAZER
What's your Cheryl, boy?

ALADDIN
Cheryl?

ABANAZER
Cheryl Cole looks like she's on the game, name.

ALADDIN
Aladdin. Don't forget it.

ABANAZER
If I do I'll just read it off your gravestone. Take him away and smash his baubles.

ALADDIN
Wishy Washy!

WISHY WASHY enters. She is a monkey. She has enormous hairy breasts.

ABANAZER
What the hell's that?

ALADDIN
Wishy's my monkey.

ABANAZER
What is it, a boy or a girl? I like monkeys. Their brains are delicious.

ALADDIN
Wishy, tickle time.

WISHY WASHY looks embarrassed and holds her arms up to expose her armpits.

ALADDIN
Not you. Her!

WISHY WASHY tickles the POLICE WOMAN, she laughs and lets go.

ALADDIN
Come on, run!

ALADDIN and WISHY WASHY run off. ABANAZER turns on the policewoman.

ABANAZER
You'll be out of a job and upside down in the canal when my mob takes over. Piss off, you pleb.

The POLICE WOMAN exits. ABANAZER rubs his ring. The GIMP appears.

GIMP
What is it now I was just having a sing song.

ABANAZER
I didn't mean to summon you, my ring's a bit sensitive. What do you know about the thief?

GIMP
You what?

ABANAZER
The kid. Aladdin.

GIMP
Right, hold up... (He waves his hands and stares into a vision) He lives with his mother in the Chinese laundry.

ABANAZER
They're all Chinese you dickhead, we're in China.

GIMP
The one by the Palace. They've only been in the province a few weeks.

ABANAZER
Where'd they come from?

GIMP
A long way away.

ABANAZER
I'll never get the hang of these Chinese place-names. A laundry, I wonder... Right, come on. I need a vagina.

GIMP
Eh?

ABANAZER
Vagina and clit - a shit.

They exit. The POLICE WOMAN enters.

POLICE WOMAN
Step back everyone, nothing to see here, nothing to- (looks about her, takes off her hat). Ello ello ello! Boys and girls, can I entrust you with a secret? Are you sure? I'm not Chinese at all! I'm an undercover inspector from Scotland Yard, on secondment from G4S. The name's Lauren. Lauren Order. I'm on a secret mission to recover a valuable lamp that was stolen from the British Museum in London, England. On the voyage over I managed to intercept a drugs haul. Would anyone like some?

She throws some sweets to the audience.

POLICE WOMAN
Our little secret. The thing is, I'm really lonely out here. In return for the drugs, will you keep me company? Let's have a try. Ello Ello ello! ("Ello ello ello") Ello ello! ("Ello ello") Ello, ello, ello ello ello (again they repeat). You're so friendly! I'd better fill you in. I've tracked down our prime suspect - a washerwoman who fled from London to Hao Hung with her son, Aladdin... Wait! Aladdin! That thief was called Aladdin! I'll infiltrate this criminal ring, adopting a range of cunning disguises!

ALADDIN creeps on, lifts Abanazer's wallet from the POLICE WOMAN's pocket and hides.

POLICE WOMAN

Fortunately, I'm the sharpest mind in the force. But remember, keep my secret, these are highly dangerous criminals!

The POLICE WOMAN exits. ALADDIN comes forward.

ALADDIN

Wishy!

WISHY WASHY enters.

ALADDIN

I think it's all clear, Wishy!

WISHY WASHY

Well I'd get it looked at anyway.

WISHY WASHY

This is my monkey, Wishy Washy.

WISHY WASHY

And this is my ape, Aladdin.

ALADDIN

And this is my new patch, my little adopted Chinese province. I ain't been here long. I'm a Clapham boy you see, but I had to emigrate at short notice. I even had to leave my sexily named boyfriend Tyler. ("Ahhh") It's sadder than that! But he's saving up and one day he'll come and live with me here. Me and mum found Wishy in a restaurant on the Piazza.

WISHY WASHY

They *ordered* me.

ALADDIN

We didn't know what we were getting. I mean, monkey brains? Grim. Listen, I ain't got any friends here yet. Will you be our mates? Wishy, we got ourselves a crew!

WISHY WASHY

A crew?

ALADDIN

Yeah a crew. Peeps. Posse. Gang. Chumz with a z. Bredren. Fam.

WISHY WASHY

Don't do this.

ALADDIN

Bitches?

WISHY WASHY

Fuck my life. I told you, this street talk doesn't suit you.

ALADDIN looks embarrassed and crestfallen. WISHY tries to perk him up.

WISHY WASHY

...Your T shirt does though.

ALADDIN

Thanks!

WISHY WASHY

Anyway I'm going now.

ALADDIN

Ok I'm coming. See you later everyone!

They exit.

Scene 2: Widow Twankey's laundry

A clutter of drying clothes on lines, tubs, machines, powders, liquids. The Laundry also doubles as Twankey's main living space, so there would be homely touches, and a radio or tv perhaps. WIDOW TWANKEY enters. She has a London accent. She carries a laundry basket with clothes and various objects.

TWANKEY
Hello! Welcome to my bubbly boudoir, my soapy salon, my detergenty den, my own Palace of Persil: Widow Twankey's Chinese Laundry! Let's have a look at you all eh... (She talks to a few people) That could do with an iron mr, "crumpled" went out a few years ago... That top wants a dry cleaning my love, you could do a whole Attenborough series on it. (Sniffs someone) You could just do with a bath.

She spots a handsome gentleman in the crowd.

TWANKEY
Hello me old mucker, sir, matey... what's your name? Very nice to meet you, I'm Twankey. Widow Twankey. That means I'm single but experienced. Just so's you know, I do a full service wash so if you ever want to pop by and dump a load before work I'm your lady. (Sings) "There are 9 million bicycles in Beijing..." Oh I'm in a spin boys and girls, I'm all of a lather. I miss London! The parks. The skyscrapers with stupid names. The drinking culture-slash-problem... It's no life, boys and girls. I've only got 500 Yuan to my name and I haven't mastered the exchange rate so I don't know if that's tonight's dinner or the month's rent.

Still, I've done what I can with the place. Do you like it? I've always tried to keep my interiors welcoming but it's not glamorous. I used to get celebrities in my little Chinese laundry back in Clapham SW4. I had Tom Daley in once with a bag of sopping wet Speedos. So I squeezed them out for him, and he said that's nice, but could you wash my trunks now? I told him of course I can but would you mind standing on some newspaper cos you're dripping all over my floor. He said no I'm not, and I said well one of us is my love. Haha. I tell you, moist is not the word, I was like used teabags.

TWANKEY hits a little shop bell that sits on the counter. It doesn't ring.

TWANKEY
That bell needs looking at, as the actress said to bishop. Will you lot do me a favour? Till I get that mended, if anyone comes through that door and I'm not here can you all shout "Ding Dong"? Let's have a practice.

She exits to the street, comes back in. "DING DONG"

TWANKEY
Alright, I'm coming who is it? Oh, yeah, me! No that was very good, very convincing. Right, excuse me a moment I need to go out back to separate the sheets from the coats.

TWANKEY exits out to the back of the shop. ABANAZER enters from the street, wearing a fake beard. "DING DONG"

TWANKEY (off)
Yeah that's right, you've got it nailed now.

ABANAZER
Ahem!

TWANKEY (off)
Ooh custom, be with you in a moment, who is it?

ABANAZER
Me, your long lost brother in law.

TWANKEY (off)
Oh! Can it be! My poor, long lost brother in law!

ABANAZER
That's him!

TWANKEY
We wondered what happened to you after you lost your leg in that rickshaw pile-up on Frith Street. Seriously boys and girls, if you thought World Pride was a car crash...

ABANAZER panics and somehow affects to have one leg.

TWANKEY (off)
Still. I remember saying at the time, I suppose a leg ain't such a great loss, what with you already being a dwarf.

ABANAZER looks around frantically. He spies some shoes and some shoe polish. He takes the shoes and kneels down, putting his knees into the shoes as though his knees were his feet. He then remembers he is one-legged and ditches one of the shoes.

ABANAZER
Well, I muddle along.

TWANKEY (off)
Or waddle along... You were always dear to my late husband you know. Even though you were adopted from that little Kenyan orphanage.

ABANAZER panics, sees the shoe polish and takes the lid off. He is about to apply it to his face when:

TWANKEY (off)
Quite unusual, a Caucasian baby in a Kenyan orphanage.

ABANAZER puts the polish down as TWANKEY enters.

TWANKEY
Oh Charlie! Look at you all dressed up in your Tesco Finest. Hang about, you're not Charlie.

ABANAZER
Oh yes I am!

TWANKEY
Oh no you're not

(etc)

ABANAZER
Very well. There's been a mix-up...

TWANKEY
You're not joking, you wouldn't think you could stain a sheet paisley would you?... That joke works a lot better if I remember to bring the prop on.

ABANAZER
I'm your even longer-lost brother in law, Rick Shaw.

TWANKEY
(Fingering his suit) This is lovely.

ABANAZER
Thanks. I like a nice whistle.

TWANKEY
There's not many who can pull off a suit like that. (Flirting) Though I'd give it a try... You'll be needing it dry cleaned.

ABANAZER
Why, what you gonna fucking to do it? I mean, how nice to see a lady who appreciates elegance.

Abanazer starts looking for something in the piles of clothes and sheets and curtains.

TWANKEY
Oh yeah, I love elegance. Very noble animals. Oi, don't go fingering my curtains. Can I help you with something?

ALADDIN and WISHY WASHY enter. ALADDIN has brought the post in.

ALADDIN
Hey guys! Hey Mum.

TWANKEY
Your long-lost uncle called to see us!

ALADDIN
He can get lost again, he ain't my uncle. This is Abanazer.

TWANKEY
Abu Hamza???[77]

ALADDIN pulls off ABANAZER's beard

ALADDIN
Abanazer. The bastard who runs the factories. Getting rich on everyone else's misery.

TWANKEY
I didn't know you were political.

ALADDIN
I bought that Chavs book.

WISHY WASHY
Only to wank over.

TWANKEY
TMI darling, TMI Friday.

ALADDIN
He's after something.

TWANKEY (flirty)
He can have it.

ABANAZER
Where's the lamp?

ALADDIN
Leave my mum alone and get out!

---

[77] Famous for the hook he wore in place of his missing hand, Abu Hamza was the former imam of Finsbury Park Mosque, jailed for inciting murder and in 2012 extradited to the US on terror-related charges.

ALADDIN
You might own half the province, but this laundry is on the palace estate, so scarper.

ABANAZER
Nevertheless… You wouldn't want anything to happen to this place, would you?

ALADDIN
Like what?

ABANAZER
Who can say, who can say. Arson? Burglary? You wouldn't believe the sorts we get round here. What you need is some bulging.

TWANKEY
Bulging what?

ABANAZER
Bulging erection – protection. Shall we say 500 Yuan?

TWANKEY (hands it over)
That's cleaned me out like prune curry.

ABANAZER
I'll see you, you and (stroking WISHY's head) the walking dinner later. Hahaha!

He exits.

ALADDIN
Here's the post, mum.

TWANKEY
They're all bills.

ALADDIN
No, they're yours.

TWANKEY (flicks through them)
I don't know how we're gonna pay these. (hands it to him). How was work?

ALADDIN
Oh… you know.

WISHY WASHY
He quit.

TWANKEY
He what? Stupid boy! How are we gonna live-slash-eat! And all you've brought me back is a handful of useless magic beans!

ALADDIN
What?

TWANKEY
Nothing. (hands him a letter) Oh there's one for you.

ALADDIN
Mum I can earn more from half an hour's picking pockets at the market than I can from a week in that place.

TWANKEY
I knew that lamp were trouble.

ALADDIN
It's just a lamp mum. We shoulda just sold it on eBay.

TWANKEY
It was in the paper's the next day boys and girls. 3000 years old. Stolen from the British Museum. An ancient lamp. You'd think they could afford proper lighting… Anyway, they said on the news, because the lamp's got mystical powers, anyone found with it would be done for terrorism.

ALADDIN
So we did the only thing she could think of.

TWANKEY
Emigrated. Well, I'd forgotten this, but I'm actually one sixteenth Chinese, so we claimed asylum at the Chinese Embassy and they shipped us out on a banana boat.

ALADDIN
We should never have left London.

TWANKEY
London…

The bells of Big Ben chime, as if we're going back in time. We're not.

ALADDIN
Mum. Mum.

TWANKEY
Oh, sorry, that's me phone alarm. (she stops it) I do miss my little Clapham Chinese Laundry. Even though it were an 'orrible summer. The poor gays. The pavements were ankle deep in rained-off hair product and they were always bringing in jeans with muddy knees for some reason. Mind you, it was the only business I was getting. Everyone was broke, nobody was washing their clothes, the whole city stank like the toilets in the Two Brewers.

WISHY WASHY (to Aladdin)
That's where you worked yeah?

ALADDIN
Yeah.

WISHY WASHY
In the toilets of the Two Brewers.

ALADDIN
Yeah. It's where I met Tyler!

ALADDIN has opened his letter.

ALADDIN
Shit! I been dumped.

TWANKEY
Dumped? Oh my boy, who would do such a thing?

WISHY WASHY
His boyfriend...

TWANKEY
Oh him. I liked him. Gorgeous he was. Would it be weird if I poked him?

ALADDIN
Facebook's banned mum. I don't want to talk about him. *(He picks up a magazine and flicks through it.)* He was special, mum, I'll never meet anyone like that again!

TWANKEY
Oh nonsense. There's about five young men to every girl out here. Something I plan to exploit boys and girls... Some of them are bound to turn gay just for the maths of it.

ALADDIN
Yeah but I'm not even into Asians... *(spots a picture in the magazine)* Oh my god! He's cute!

TWANKEY
Let's have a beaver.

ALADDIN
Gander, mum.

TWANKEY
He's very photorealist isn't he.

ALADDIN
He's beautiful. It says he's the Prince! The son of the Emperor of Hao High.

TWANKEY
Hao Hung.

ALADDIN
It's hard to tell from the photo. I have to meet him! Wishy, you'll help me break into the palace. Let's go and make a plan!

Scene 3: Abanazer's lair

ABANAZER enters

ABANAZER

Alright boys and girls, welcome to my pad at the top of Hao Hung's only skyscraper. It's called the George Michael cos it's ridiculously fucking high. (To a hot man) Ello. You can stay. I'd have your clothes off before you could say "OMG Katy Perry!" Yeah I'd have them right off, it's not the sweatshop stitching that's offensive it's the sweatshop design. (Talks to the next audience member) Is this your boyfriend? Here's a travel tip, the plastic surgery's cheap as marmite out here. Gimp!

The GIMP enters out of breath.

ABANAZER

If you got asthma I'll have you put down. Just look out there at the piazza. All the little people.

GIMP

That's a bit racist mate.

ABANAZER

Toiling away in my factories by day. Spending their tiny wages in my bars at night. And then they go to sleep and dream of being me! But me with a weird fish head or something. And my mum's in it too but she's speaking French and getting angrier and angrier cos I can't understand her and I won't give her back her knickers...

GIMP

Do you wanna go for a beer? I've not been abroad since Magaluf 2009. Me and the lads had t shirts printed.

ABANAZER

A beer? I've got evil plots to make and not enough time. Come here and suck me off while I perfect my scheme.

GIMP

A scheme? What is it?

ABANAZER

It's like a plan or a plot, but that's not important right now. (undoes flies) Come on.

GIMP

I got a cold sore coming.

ABANAZER

Don't worry, I got worse than that already.

GIMP

I wish I'd never got stuck in your ring. You're not a very nice man.

ABANAZER

Listen, I been thinking, I ain't involved in current affairs enough for a man of my station. Get me the Hao Hung Gazette.

GIMP *(pulls a newspaper out of nowhere)*

Here you go.

ABANAZER

I don't want to read it. I want to buy it. *(Hits the GIMP on the head with it)* The whole paper. Have the shareholder's killed and the editor softened up. *(Looks at the paper)* We'll get a new sub-editor too, Christ the spelling, it says here there's been protests in the middle east over "a carton of Mohammed". And don't make me wait, I once had a postman's van blown up with his cat still in it cos he left a "while you were out card" on my birthday. I hate people spoiling my birthday. I had Justin Bieber play at my party last year. He went and did it without autotune, it was fucking horrible so I had him castrated. Now, how are we gonna get the lamp? That laundry's on palace land. I'll have to ingratiate myself with the Emperor. No, the Prince! We had a thing going once. How do we get in?

The GIMP is reading the sports pages. ABANAZER slaps him.

ABANAZER

Read me the court circular.

GIMP

You what?

ABANAZER

It's like the gossip column, but it says what the Emperor's up to instead of what colour Kristen Stewart's last shit was.

GIMP

Here we go. 10am. The Emperor will meet for coffee with the Danish Ambassador. 12.30pm. The Emperor will inspect the palace militia. 4pm. The Emperor will play host to the Olympic gold medal winning Chinese Women's table tennis team.

ABANAZER
Chinese table tennis? Do they have fucking highchairs?

GIMP
I got an idea mate.

ABANAZER
Why do I feel like an apprehensive Peter Jones only less punchable.

GIMP
No it's a good plan. What are your legs like?

ABANAZER
Haha. I knew I'd get you out of the closet. Great, you can tell me about it while I fist you, and then later you can cut my fingernails.

GIMP
Can I have a few minutes to myself first?

ABANAZER
All right, two minutes, but don't finish, save yourself. See you in a cunt.

GIMP
Eh?

ABANAZA
Countryfile - while.

ABANAZER leaves.

GIMP
I haven't always been a genie you know. It's not like you can do a BTEC. My name's Colin. Colin Culverhouse from Colliers Wood. I was backpacking through the middle east when I had a curse put on me by way of having my sheesha pipe spiked with magic tobacco. Next thing I know, I wake up and I'm sliding out of his ring with a hangover. And now he's my master and the only way to break the curse is if I find my first love again and kiss her. Her name's Lauren. She's back in England, she didn't want to come travelling cos she's concentrating on her career. She's a police woman. I'll never see her will I? How will I see her? That's very kind of you boys and girls! But I don't want to get my hopes up.

ABANAZER (off)
Gimp! This WD40 won't stay slick forever!

GIMP
Right, I'd best be off. See you later boys and girls.

[For a few performances we had Abanazer and the Gimp singing "When You're Good To Mama" from Chicago at this point but we cut it as it didn't really serve a purpose. Which could be said of most of our use of songs in this show...]

Scene 4: The emperor's palace

The Palace. The Prince is drinking tea and reading a book on astrophysics. There is a pot plant. After a while, he talks to it.

PRINCE
Oh Robert, I'm bored. But one day all this study will be worth it. When I'm Emperor, I won't be like daddy. No, I'll be educated. I'll get involved. I'll apply my learning; be influential in, oh I don't know, architecture and agriculture and organic prawn crackers. Well I'm not going out anywhere, yawn, as per every day. I might as well get into my pyjamas.

He starts to drop his trousers then notices the audience. He grabs the plant which he holds in front of his pants.

PRINCE
Intruders! I'll call the guards! What's that Robert? You think they could be friendly? Well, you are my dearest and only friend so maybe you're right. Hello. (Hello!) They're not very loud are they? Hello! (Hello!!) Welcome to the Magic Palace. I'm Prince Cha-Ming. This is my friend, Robert.

THE EMPEROR enters. He is plump.

EMPEROR
I say look lively old bean. Those fine young fillies from the Olympic gold medal winning Chinese Women's table tennis team will be here shortly.

PRINCE
Daddy, must I meet them?

EMPEROR
I need to find you a bride.

PRINCE
You didn't invite them here for my benefit.

EMPEROR
I don't know what you mean.

PRINCE
I know you miss mummy. I know you're lonely but wouldn't you be happier finding a companion your own age?

EMPEROR
At least I can find companions of my own species. Open a window it smells like a Taiwanese toilet in here.

PRINCE gasps and clutches the plant close to him, stroking its leaves.

EMPEROR
To be frank old chap, the cost of my jubilee celebrations has cleaned me out. I haven't a Yuen to my name. Think of the publicity! A prince marrying a gold medal-winning sportswoman! We'll earn a fortune once we get the pair of you into magazines. I tell you what, once you've seen them, take them upstairs for a bit of a test drive, dabble your dipstick so to speak... take your car in for a tuning. Lift the bonnet and-

PRINCE
Have sex with them?

EMPEROR
Well why not! You're a Prince! You can practically click your fingers.

PRINCE (he can't)
Well actually I-

EMPEROR
I know, son, I know you can't.

PRINCE
I'm not interested in women.

EMPEROR
They do witter on a bit.

PRINCE
No daddy. I'm gay.

EMPEROR
Good heavens! A homosexual?

PRINCE
Yes father.

EMPEROR
A queerling?

PRINCE
Yes...

EMPEROR
A tinky winky? An arse wrangler?

PRINCE
Yes

EMPEROR
A grouter of men's tiles?

405

PRINCE
Ye- What?

EMPEROR
A fagnostic?

PRINCE
...Yeah

EMPEROR
An Alleyway Annie? A changing room Charlie? A patron of the buttock ballet? A quiche-eater? A molly? A left-handed teapot? A secret uncle? A steward of the anal airline? A... A... let's see, boys and girls do you have any?

PRINCE
I knew you wouldn't understand.

EMPEROR
Of course I understand.

PRINCE
Really?

EMPEROR
Yes! You're the dormitory sponge!

PRINCE
You just made gay marriage legal! Elton John played at your jubilee! You've dined with William Hague!

EMPEROR
Princes can't be gay.

PRINCE
Then I'll leave Hao Hung!

EMPEROR
You can't.

PRINCE
What do you mean?

EMPEROR
We're in a rather unusual position here in Hao Hung. Think about it. China is a communist country. At least that's what we tell the world. And here we are, an Emperor and a Prince in a luxurious magic palace! Power of disbelief boys and girls, power of disbelief. The party only keeps Hao Hung as it is as a sort of secret retro experiment for their amusement - and only on condition that we never leave the province.

PRINCE
Like in that Jim Carey film!

EMPEROR
Haha! That's us alright. "Dumb and Dumber".

There is a knock at the door.

EMPEROR
The girls are here! We'll have you swimming two abreast in the hairy harbour in no time.

The EMPEROR answers, the POLICE WOMAN enters, she wears a short table tennis skirt and top, she has a wig and a medal around her neck. She carries a table tennis bat.

POLICE WOMAN (in a bad Chinese accent)
Hel – lo.

EMPEROR
My dear! What a pleasure to welcome you to my Palace. Now what's your name?

POLICE WOMAN
Doe Ray. (To audience) Ello ello ello! It's me, the Police Woman. I'm disguised as member of the Olympic gold medal winning Chinese Women's table tennis team so that I can search the Palace for the missing lamp.

EMPEROR
You don't sound Chinese.

POLICE WOMAN
I've had a cold.

EMPEROR
Doe Ray, meet my son, Prince Cha-Ming of Hao Hung.

PRINCE
Hiya.

POLICE WOMAN
Ello ello- er, I mean, velly pleased to meet you.

The PW starts to search around, the Emperor pats her backside.

EMPEROR
You're a frisky little filly eh what?

There is another knock at the door, the EMPEROR answers. ALADDIN enters. He also wears a short skirt, a top and an identical wig to the policewoman's, and carries a table tennis bat.

EMPEROR
My what a corker! And you are?

ALADDIN
Me Far. (to audience) It's me, Aladdin, disguised as member of the Olympic gold medal winning Chinese Women's table tennis team. I'm here to see what I can nick and to hopefully meet that hunky prince.

EMPEROR
Me Far, meet my son, the Prince.

The PRINCE does not look up from his book.

PRINCE
Hiya. (He starts writing a letter)

ALADDIN
Hi! (Realising he is meant to be Chinese he then bows) Hello.

The EMPEROR grabs ALADDINS bottom while he's bowing, and pinches it.

EMPEROR
Arse like Chinese apples.

As Aladdin rises from his bow, the Prince catches a glimpse of him. He puts his book down, intrigued.

ALADDIN
You're beautiful.

PRINCE
I – I'm not into girls.

ALADDIN
Neither am I. You must get so lonely here.

PRINCE
I have Minecraft, it's very extensive. And I have Robert.

ALADDIN
Oh…

PRINCE
My plant.

ALADDIN (at a loss for conversation)
Yes… Do you like Buffy?

PRINCE
I love Buffy!

ALADDIN
Gypsy Wedding?

PRINCE
Tibetan Bride but it's the same thing.

EMPEROR
Doe Ray, your friend Me Far is here!

ALADDIN and the POLICE WOMAN bow to each other.

POLICE WOMAN (to audience)
I'll never find this lamp boys and girls. I wish I was back with me fellow Colin. I wish I knew what had happened to him. Still, no time to dwell, I need to expand me search.

The POLICE WOMAN exits to search elsewhere. ALADDIN is going round looking at ornaments and puts some in a bag. There is a knock at the door. The EMPEROR answers. ABANAZER and GIMP enter. They wear short skirts, tennis tops fake breasts and similar wigs. They carry table tennis bats.

EMPEROR
Aha, best in show! Now that's what I call a pretty pair.

ABANAZER (in a bad Chinese accent)
Thank you (nudges GIMP)

GIMP
Thank you

ABANAZER
We do our best.

EMPEROR *(squeezing ABANAZER's breasts)*
Very pretty.

GIMP (to ABANAZER)
I told you they weren't too much.

GIMP has a feel himself. ABANAZER slaps his wrist.

EMPEROR
Carry on carry on we're not prudes here. And who might you be?

GIMP (in a bad Chinese accent)
So La. (to audience) It's me, Colin, disguised as a member of the Olympic gold medal winning Chinese Women's table tennis team.

EMPEROR
Doe Ray, Me Far, So La… so you must be-

ABANAZER
Far Tee.

EMPEROR
Now tell me, have you brought your balls or will I dig mine out? *(To the PRINCE)* Show some manners old

chap, these lovely young ladies have come to meet you.

PRINCE
They don't look very ladylike.

ALADDIN gasps, offended. GIMP gasps, offended. ABANAZER gasps, offended.

EMPEROR
He's not himself.

ALADDIN
I know how he feels. Your highness, you must have lots of velly velly valuable antiques here.

EMPEROR
Sneak upstairs with me and I'll give you a peak at my vintage ming.

ALADDIN
Can I hold it?

EMPEROR
I don't see why not, it survives the Hoover twice a week,

ALADDIN and the EMPEROR exit. The PRINCE goes to follow, ABANAZER stops him. He giggles girlishly. He encourages the GIMP to do the same. They both giggle.

ABANAZER
Sweet Prince, don't go. Stay and talk to So La and myself.

PRINCE
Oh all right... Wait, I know you.

GIMP
Oh no you don't.

PRINCE
Oh yes I do.

ABANAZER
Oh no you don't.

A knock at the door.

GIMP
I'll get it.

He exits. A door opens. It slams shut again. The GIMP returns.

PRINCE
Who was it?

GIMP
It's the Olympic gold medal winning Chinese Women's table tennis team.

ABANAZER
I'll deal with them later.

PRINCE
What??

ABANAZER (awkwardly)
Ahahaha...

He pulls off his wig. Talks as himself.

ABANAZER
I thought we could pick up where we left off that night.

PRINCE
It was a tragic mistake.

ABANAZER
Googling Tulisa's sex tape with Safe Search on is a tragic mistake. Our fling -

PRINCE
It wasn't a fling!

ABANAZER
Well someone was flung.

PRINCE
That's true...

ABANAZER
Listen. I got very good security. Plenty of privacy. You and me could have a romantic and mind-bendingly disgusting affair well away from the prying eyes of the people. We could travel the world incognito.

PRINCE
In what?

ABANAZER
In my private jet, Cognito... It must be frustrating not being able to see the world, or to find a man...

PRINCE
Oh it is, it is! Oh Robert. Oh boys and girls, do you think I should... succumb?

ABANAZER
See if I care, I got more dumb twinks queuing up than an iphone launch. I give Ivan Massow my cast-offs. Come on gimp.

PRINCE
Wait!

The PRINCE and ABANAZER kiss. It gets full on. The Prince's top comes off. The GIMP gets out a phone and takes a picture.

ABANAZER
Marry me and move me into the palace or this picture's on the front page of my Gazette tomorrow. So my student prince. Are you going to propose?

ABANAZER pushes the PRINCE to his knees in front of him. ALADDIN enters carrying a bag which is now full. He drops it.

PRINCE
It's not how it looks!

ALADDIN
Get away from him!

ABANAZER
The little street urchin.

He turns on Aladdin holding out his table tennis bat, ALADDIN faces him and they start hitting each other with their bats.

GIMP
Fight! Fight! Fight!

ALADDIN gets a hit in.

GIMP
Back of the net!

ABANAZER
You're supposed to protect me.

The GIMP picks up his bat and starts hitting ALADDIN. ALADDIN realises he is beaten and starts to run out. The PRINCE picks up his sack.

PRINCE
Wait! Your sack!

ABANAZER
It ain't *his* sack you'll be weeping over tonight.

PRINCE *(looks in the sack)*
Hey! These are our things.

ABANAZER
He's just a dirty little thief. I'll catch him. And he'll tell me where the lamp is.

ABANAZER and the GIMP exit

PRINCE
I... I think I've just met the man of my dreams!

The POLICE WOMAN enters

POLICE WOMAN
(to audience) I can't find the lamp. Have I missed anything?

The EMPEROR enters

EMPEROR
Ah Doe Ray! Where are Me Far, So La and Far Tee?

PRINCE
They've... they've gone, Daddy.

EMPEROR
Dammed shame. Well at least Doe Ray is still here, though she's a bit manly don't you think? Those other three though... What do you reckon, is there one for you.

PRINCE
You know what Daddy? I reckon there is.

Scene 5: The laundry

TWANKEY enters with a washing basket.

TWANKEY
Oh would you Adam and Eve it boys and girls, I'm still working. I thought, China, it's coming up in the world. I thought we'd join the new middle classes but I'm not even the squeezed middle. Still, keep cats and carry on as they say. I think I took my life for granted in Clapham. I was even doing One Direction's laundry. Little five-packs of M&S briefs, a different colour each, I'd switch the name tags around for the erotic confusion of it all.

ALADDIN rushes in

TWANKEY
What have I told you!

ALADDIN
There's men after me!

TWANKEY
Yeah so why you running?

ALADDIN
They'll be here any minute! Where can I hide?

TWANKEY
In here.

TWANKEY opens the door of a washing machine for Aladdin to dive into. She closes the door on him.

TWANKEY
Oh my giddy aunt. Angry men, coming here!

She finds a lipstick and quickly touches up.

TWANKEY
I feel like that time Paul McCartney came to my little Clapham Clotherama. He was having trouble getting hair dye out of his sunhat. I soon got the stains off his rim.

ABANAZER
Twankey!

TWANKEY
I didn't hear the doorbell.

ABANAZER
I'm on the rampage.

TWANKEY
Well give us a swig then.

ABANAZER
Where's your son? He's a fucking Amanda.

TWANKEY
Amanda?

ABANAZER
Amanda Redman. Dead... man.

TWANKEY
Oh Abercrombie my sweetie possum. "Aba". "Ab". "A". " ". We haven't seen him have we boys and girls?

WISHY WASHY enters carrying a bucket full of foaming soap suds. She walks over to the machine Aladdin is in and pours the bucket in through the top. Aladdin shrieks.

ABANAZER
What was that?

TWANKEY
What was what? I didn't hear no shrieking.

ABANAZER
Yes, what shrieking?

WISHY turns the machine dial from slow to fast.

TWANKEY
Don't do that!

ALADDIN screams. TWANKEY panics, kicks the machine.

TWANKEY
Squeaky old thing, I should get it oiled, but you know how it is.

WISHY WASHY gets a can of oil, pours it into the machine.

TWANKEY
Do you know I just heard on the radio, the Olympic gold medal winning Chinese Women's table tennis team's just been found tied up behind the palace? And before they could tell their story, someone from the Gazette found a load of steroids on them and they were carted away!

ABANAZER
How *could* that have happened.

ALADDIN bangs on the inside of the machine.

ABANAZER
There! Banging!

410

TWANKEY
Some silly bugger's left a coin in their pocket. Money laundering haha. So. Tea? Little snack?

ABANANZER
Why don't I teach you to cook deep fried monkey brains?

He creeps up behind WISHY, hands ready to strangle him. The audience shout. WISHY scampers and hides behind TWANKEY.

ABANAZER
I'll have your brains on a fucking plate.

WISHY WASHY
I'll have your dick on a beer mat and there'll still be room for the glass.

ABANAZER
But wait! Who better to lead me to the lamp than the moronic mother...! Widow Twankey, bereaved so young, have I ever told you how scintillating you look in certain light.

WISHY WASHY
An eclipse.

TWANKEY
Ooh you cheeky monkey.

ABANAZER
Come dine with me tonight.

TWANKEY
Perfect! What channel's it on over here? I took part in that show once boys and girls. They never broadcast mine. They said it was cos of what I done for the after-dinner entertainment. *I* say if you're filming someone recreating Sunset Boulevard in a side split dress you shouldn't have your camera pointing up from the bottom of the stairs... Anyway, your sofa or mine?

WISHY WASHY
He's inviting you to a restaurant, woman.

TWANKEY
Extraordinary how potent cheap perfume is.

ABANAZER
There's a charming little place I know, it overlooks the Yangzte.

TWANKEY
Well, it's easily done. Shall I, boys and girls?

WISHY WASHY
No.

TWANKEY
It's been an age since a man asked me out. Alabama, my little toffee pie, it would be an honour.

ABANAZER
I'll see you at nine. I'm counting the minutes already.

ABANAZER exits

TWANKEY
This could be it Wishy! I could soon have some serious bling on these fingers. I've heard his willy has its own postcode.

WISHY
I heard your bum has its own embassy.

There is a knocking from the washing machine.

TWANKEY
Aladdin!

She runs to the machine and opens, water squirts in her face. Aladdin scrambles out, he is soaked, his clothes have shrunk till they're tiny, and he is covered in foam.

TWANKEY
God it's like that episode of One Born Every Minute when the home birth went tits up.

ALADDIN
Look at my clothes!

WISHY
Yeah, you got that stain out.

TWANKEY
Aladdin, guess what. Your mother is going on a date. With Abadabadoo.

ALADDIN
What? Mum you can't!

TWANKEY
Now you don't begrudge your old, sorry, well preserved mum some happiness! I may be pushing 28 but that doesn't mean a girl stops having needs! It's alright for men! Oh yeah, Bill Nighy can dribble his cornflakes down his piss-stained slacks and it's the hottest thing since the diet coke man, but we women, no, no, lock us up.

ALADDIN
But he's up to no good.

TWANKEY
Ooh I hope so. Anyway I'm a big girl.

WISHY
That's true.

TWANKEY
I'll be good. At least until he takes me back to his, then I'll make like a rabbit on Benzo Fury[78]. Now wish me luck.

ALADDIN
Oh Mum. I love you.

He hugs her, he gets her wet. She screams.

_____

[78] Benzo Fury is a synthetic drug that was briefly popular as a legal high. In 2012 a young woman reportedly rampaged naked through a Tesco in the middle of the day before karate-kicking a policeman in the face after ingesting it.

TWANKEY
You've got me all wet! As I expect I'll be uttering by midnight tomorrow.

ALADDIN exits

TWANKEY
Come on Wishy help me get ready for tonight. I have to look my best.

WISHY
It won't be easy.

TWANKEY lifts the lid of a washing machine, it becomes a dressing table and mirror.

TWANKEY
That Mr Abu Dhabi is one lucky man.

[Here, Twanky and Wishy Washy sang "I Feel Pretty" from West Side Story. By the end Twanky had changed into eveningwear and the set had been transformed into a restaurant.]

Scene 6: A restaurant

POLICE WOMAN
Ello Ello! Ello ello ello ello! It's me! I've disguised myself as a waiter and taken a job in this restaurant to see what I can glean when Twankey comes for dinner. Perhaps the wine will loosen her ruthless tongue. Oh boys and girls I'm so far from home. I was going to move in with my first love, Colin Culverhouse from Colliers Wood. But one day he said he needed to find himself, off he went backpacking and I never heard from him again. Not a postcard. Not a skype. Not even an Instagram of a beer and a sunset.

TWANKEY and ABANAZER enter. TWANKEY uses an erratic posh accent when she remembers to, and speaks to the "waiter" like a Brit talking to a foreigner.

POLICE WOMAN
She's here!

ABANAZER
This is the Emperor's favourite restaurant.

TWANKEY
Oh my, a genuine h'authentic h'ethnic Chinese restaurant! How does it work, do I spread myself on the floor?

ABANAZER
That's Japaneze.

TWANKEY
No it's English, I'm just mumbling cos I'm nervous.

ABANAZER
A table for two, and quick about it.

POLICE WOMAN
Of course sir, there's one over there by the restrooms

ABANAZER
By the rest rooms?? Do you know who I am? Where's the usual geezer?

POLICE WOMAN
He's off sick, sir. Something he ate.

ABANAZER
(He looks at Twankey) I'm not sure I want to be seen tonight anyway. But make it good. I once ripped a sommelier's tongue out for giving me an oaked wine with a seafood fucking lasagne.

ABANAZER removes his jacket and places it on the back of his chair. They sit. The POLICE WOMAN hands them a menu each.

TWANKEY
This is ever so romantic Mr Avabanana.

ABANAZER
We'll have champagne. Your largest bottle.

TWANKEY
I get ever so frisky on champagne.

ABANAZER
We'll start with a glass.

POLICE WOMAN (scheming...)
May I take your handbag for you?

TWANKEY
Ooh no no no no no, I never let it out of my sight. There was a mix-up in a bar once where it got swapped for some other girl's handbag, I popped to the lavs to give my nethers a freshening and ended up spraying mace right up myself.

POLICE WOMAN *(pulls a notebook out of her pocket)*
Theft! She's a criminal mastermind.

TWANKEY
What's she writing?

ABANAZER
She's taking our order.

TWANKEY
On a police notebook?

POLICE WOMAN goes. TWANKEY looks at the menu. She can't understand a word.

TWANKEY
(Aside) I can't read this. (Louder) What *shall* I order! Here look! I got that word as a tattoo. As you'll discover if you play your cards right. It means "strength and harmony".

ABANAZER
It means "All major credit cards accepted".

TWANKEY
Waiter! These bread sticks are stale.

ABANAZER
They're chopsticks.

413

TWANKEY
Right. Shit. What?

ABANAZER
You do know how to use chopsticks?

TWANKEY
(She doesn't) Oh yeah. Course! What are all these numbers? I don't know how to choose it's all foreign. Why don't they have photos of the different meals like they do on holiday, and facebook.

POLICE WOMAN enters with champagne and serves them.

ABANAZER
I suggest you have a couple of delicious dumplings.

TWANKEY
Oh thank you! You make me blush! I'll have noodles. (Overly loud and clear) *NOO-DLES!*

ABANAZER
That's a number fifteen for the lady.

TWANKEY
What are you having?

ABANAZER
I'm going for a number two.

TWANKEY
Well the rest-rooms are just there (cackles with glee).

ABANAZER
It's the speciality, monkey brains.

TWANKEY
Don't call me that, I had limited schooling. Well, my mother was banged up in the Harry Ramsbottom home for battered fishwives.

POLICE WOMAN
I'm afraid the monkey's off today.

ABANAZER
Off?

TWANKEY
Something he ate? Haha!

ABANAZER
I was so looking forward to monkey brains.

ALADDIN and WISHY WASHY enter

ABANAZER
Aha!

WISHY WASHY
Hello boys and girls! I've heard that they serve monkey brains in here. If someone tries to take my brain, I need you to shout "Watch out Wishy". Let's have a go! ("Watch out Wishy"!) Why are we here Aladdin?

ALADDIN
We're keeping an eye on that cretin.

WISHY WASHY
How are we going to pay for anything?

The POLICE WOMAN comes over.

POLICE WOMAN
It's the boy! They must be collaborating on a dastardly plan... Yes, sir. Are you ready to order?

ALADDIN
Give us a minute, please.

She exits. WISHY WASHY gets a book out. TWANKEY has been absent-mindedly spinning the lazy Susan on her table, she spins it so hard her drink flies off. She notices Aladdin.

TWANKEY
Hello my love! Ask if they do those bamboo calendars. They make good rolling mats.

The POLICE WOMAN enters with a large plate of noodles and presents it to Twankey.

POLICE WOMAN
Your noodles, madam.

TWANKEY
The polite word is eccentric. Oh! Yes. Lovely.

ABANAZER
And where's my dish?

TWANKEY
I'm right here love.

She starts trying to eat them with the chopsticks. She's hopeless and can't get them to her mouth. She discreetly tips them into her handbag.

ALADDIN
I'd like noodles please.

POLICE WOMAN
Yes sir, right away.

As she heads to the kitchen she notices Twankey's plate is empty.

414

POLICE WOMAN
You've finished madam, I'll get you more, it's eat as much as you want.

ABANAZER
And bring me a hammer.

POLICE WOMAN
A hammer? We only have the hammer we use for bashing the monkeys' heads in. And the monkey's-

ABANAZER
Off, yes, I know. Just bring it.

She exits, immediately coming back with two plates of noodles. She puts them in front of TWANKEY and ABANAZER and exits again. TWANKEY groans, tries to use the chopsticks and fails. As ABANAZER eyes Wishy Washy up hungrily, TWANKEY scoops what noodles she can down the front of her dress and pushes them down into her bra.

TWANKEY
Delicious. I couldn't be more excited if the Emperor himself was here.

The EMPEROR himself and the PRINCE enter.

ALADDIN
It's the Prince and his dad!

TWANKEY
It's the Emperor and his son!

ABANAZER
Excellent! Just as I hoped.

TWANKEY
Oh look at him. How handsome. How powerful. But he'd never go for some poor lass like me.

PRINCE
Daddy, why must we always come here?

TWANKEY is awkwardly adjusting her breasts as one is now larger than the other.

ABANAZER
You likes your noodles my love! Here have mine.

TWANKEY
How am I going to get rid of these?

TWANKEY distributes her noodles to people in the audience. The POLICE WOMAN enters with a hammer

and two plates of noodles. She gives one to WISHY WASHY and gives the hammer to ABANAZER.

POLICE WOMAN
You've eaten those quickly madam, here have some more.

The POLICE WOMAN swaps TWANKEY's empty plate for the full one.

POLICE WOMAN
Your majesty! Please, take a seat.

EMPEROR
Oh, yes, jolly good, hello. We'll have the 4.99 all you can eat buffet. And bring us a jug of tap water.

PRINCE
Daddy, you're the Emperor.

EMPEROR
I told you, I'm as skint as a Greek. How will I impress the young ladies of the town?

PRINCE
You won't impress them if you keep eating all-you-can-eat buffets.

EMPEROR
You think I'm getting fat.

The EMPEROR goes to sit down but struggles getting in between the chair and table. ALADDIN approaches the PRINCE.

ALADDIN
Your highness.

PRINCE
Aladdin! I didn't think I'd see you here! Are you celebrating?

ALADDIN
I am now.

PRINCE
You're so witty and smart!

ALADDIN
I'm keeping an eye on mum. She's on a date with-

PRINCE
Abanazer!

ALADDIN
I've got something that might interest you.

PRINCE
I expect you have.

He takes Abanazer's phone out of his pocket

ALADDIN
I lifted it from him in the palace. Delete the photos quick and I'll put it back in his pocket.

TWANKEY
That champagne's gone to my head.

ABANAZER
Excellent. Now remind me, why did you flee to Don't-fuck?

TWANKEY
What?

ABANAZER
Don't fuck a minor, China.

TWANKEY
Oh, yes! We'll there was this lamp.

ABANAZER
And where is it?

TWANKEY
I could tell you, but then I'd have to sleep with you.

The PRINCE is still deleting photos on Abanazer's phone.

ALADDIN
There are a lot of photos of you here... Are they *all* from this afternoon?

PRINCE
Well, no...

ALADDIN
Really? Abanazer? What's he like..?

PRINCE
His whole's not as good as his parts.

ALADDIN
Never mind. Come on, you done?

PRINCE
But I like this one of me. I look gaunt.

He finishes and hands back the phone.

ALADDIN
You missed one.

PRINCE
No, I think that's Prince Harry.

POLICE WOMAN
The buffet your highness?

PRINCE
I suppose so. Perhaps there is romance in suffering. But I can't eat wheat. Or dairy. Or nuts. Or anything spicy. And I'm vegetarian.

ALADDIN
I'm Pisces, is that good?

PRINCE
It's a start.

The PRINCE joins his father. ABANAZER takes the hammer and sneaks up behind WISHY WASHY. The audience alert her: "Watch out Wishy!" ABANAZER returns to the table, just as TWANKEY has shoved another plate-load of noodles into a plant pot. She stands.

TWANKEY
I'm just going to touch myself up.

ABANAZER pulls a piece of folded paper from his pocket.

ABANAZER
Wait you er, creature. I want to ask you something. I've always wanted the emperor's autograph, but I'm too shy to ask him for it. Would you do the honours?

TWANKEY
I'll give it a whirl love. What do you want me to write?

ABANAZER looks at her as though she is stupid.

TWANKEY
Oh..! Right, gotcha, I'll go and ask him. I'll just get a pen.

TWANKEY reaches into her handbag, makes a face, removes a pen with a noodle-covered hand, wonders where to wipe it. She wipes it on Abanazer. TWANKEY gets up and approaches the EMPEROR. ABANAZER sees an opportunity, picks up the hammer again and crosses to behind WISHY WASHY. The POLICE WOMAN spies the unattended handbag, reaches into it and finds only noodles. ABANAZER attempts to attack WISHY WASHY but the audience shout. He sits down again.

TWANKEY
H-good H-evening your Travesty.

EMPEROR
Oh MSG!

416

TWANKEY curtsies. Struggles to get up.

TWANKEY
Can you help me up?

EMPEROR
Of course, my cherry blossom. My prickly pear.

TWANKEY
They are not I've had electrolysis!

EMPEROR
You are delightful my little water lily. My rosebush.

TWANKEY
Well you'd better fertilise me then. Oh stop my mouth! How's your night?

EMPEROR
It has only just begun! Please, join us. I feel very relaxed with you.

TWANKEY
Well, I'm a sixteenth Chinese.

EMPEROR
Ah, Eurasian.

TWANKEY
No love, you're Asian, but I don't mind that in a man. No it's my son what's a bit funny about all that.

PRINCE
(Horrified) What??

EMPEROR
But you know the lingo.

TWANKEY
Oh, no. I used to be quite nifty at the Charleston. I'll teach you sometime.

ABANAZER coughs

TWANKEY
Oh yeah. My friend would like your h'autograph.

EMPEROR
Of course.

He signs it and hands it back. She smells it excitedly. She passes it to ABANAZER without looking away from the EMPEROR. ABANAZER snatches it. The EMPEROR is chuckling.

TWANKEY
What's funny?

EMPEROR
I know you wanted the autograph for yourself.

TWANKEY
No, really

EMPEROR
Now, come on my little watermelon.

TWANKEY
You think if was going to come on to you, which is highly probable, I'd piss about with an autograph? Oh shit I said piss to an Emperor. Oh fuck I said shit. Oh felch!

EMPEROR
What is your name?

TWANKEY
Twankey. Widow Twankey. My poor husband was killed when a fridge landed on his head, leaving me unsatisfied but unstoppable. Oh to be wined and dined and royally entwined with you... Why wouldn't you believe me about the autograph?

EMPEROR
Because your friend is Abanazer.

TWANKEY
Azerbaijan yeah. I like how you say it, all posh and with the right letters. Go on.

EMPEROR
If Abanazer wanted my autograph he would ask for it himself.

ABANAZER (laughs)
Yeah I would! But I did not want your autograph. I wanted your signature on this constitutionally binding deed, naming me as your heir, your Emperor in waiting, and the new owner of the magic palace!

PRINCE
Daddy! This is – oh but how exciting! Like in a novel or epic movie. Aladdin will probably risk his life fighting for my entitlements!

ALADDIN
Babe. We just met.

ABANAZER
Oh but your highness, you will live there too, as my consort and lover! Well, that was fucking delicious weren't it, lovely meal, real treat, shame about the company, can't have everything, still it's nice to get out

of the house of an evening ain't it, better than watching Great British Bake Off again, lazily fingering your balls with hands that smell of Pringles. Now listen. You got a choice, your Majesty. Abdicate now, or you'll come to a very sticky end.

WISHY WASHY
Aladdin had one of those, he had to get antibiotics.

ABANAZER
Right. Fuck yourselves a merry little Christmas. Nighty fucking night.

ABANAZER exits

EMPEROR (to TWANKEY)
You tricked me!

PRINCE
Of course! You were in on it!

TWANKEY
Me? How could you think such a thing!

PRINCE
You used your borderline feminine wiles to snare the trust of my father's lonely heart.

TWANKEY
I am utterly as I seem! Well, I might use a bit of help in the chest department.

WISHY WASHY
I can smell the chicken fillets from here.

TWANKEY (very dignified)
They. Are. Salmon!

PRINCE
Aladdin – you too! My once true love turned sworn enemy! And a racist!

ALADDIN
What? Mum-

PRINCE
I'll shed a tear, but just the one. A boy cannot waste all his tears on one love when he is destined for a life of romantic tragedy. Daddy?

EMPEROR (snapping out of a reverie)
Yes my dear boy?

PRINCE
We're leaving!

The PRINCE and EMPEROR exit. Quite a long pause.

ALADDIN
How was your date mum?

TWANKEY
Yeah, lovely. Nice dinner?

ALADDIN
Yeah... Will you see him again?

TWANKEY
I don't expect so, no.

ABANAZER enters

ABANAZER
Wrong! As soon as I'm in that magic palace you'll be my tenants. You got until then to tell me where the lamp is, or you'll be out on the streets.

He goes to exit, manically. He stops, and turns. He retrieves his jacket from the back of his chair.

ABANAZER
I forget me jacket.

Exits.

ALADDIN
There's only one thing for it!

TWANKEY
A song!

ALADDIN
It's time to get the lamp. If that tyrant becomes Emperor, things'll be even worse for people round here, I'll never see the Prince again and...

TWANKEY
And I'll never weedle my way onto the Emperor's four poster. Wishy, you've gone quiet.

WISHY WASHY
Yeah I don't like conflict. (She pulls out an ipod and puts earphones in)

ALADDIN
Where's the lamp, mum?

TWANKEY
Very well. It's in the Magic Cave storage facility on the edge of town.

ALADDIN
Right, come on! Let's get out of here.

TWANKEY
We ain't paid the bill yet. I got some Times vouchers somewhere.

She reaches into her handbag again and gets noodles stuck on her fingers.

ALADDIN
Come on!

ALADDIN, WISHY WASHY and TWANKEY exit.

POLICE WOMAN
The Magic Cave storage facility! I will apprehend the boy and seize the lamp! I'll be famous! I'll be made a dame!

TWANKEY (off)
Oi!

POLICE WOMAN
Aladdin must be planning something terrible boys and girls, is that right? (The audience answer). Hmmm. Now I think of it, didn't sound as though he was planning something evil. It almost sounded as though he was going to stop someone evil... But then, think of the glory restored to the police! I'll get him!

POLICE WOMAN exits

Scene 7: Outside the cave

ABANAZER enters, he is disguised as a beggar.

ABANAZER
Spare us a cigarette? Spare us a few Yuen for a cup of noodle soup? It's me, Abanazer, disguised as an old tramp! *(At an audience member)* Well that that's fucking embarrassing it looks like we both had the same idea.

ALADDIN enters. Abanazer pulls his shawl over his own head.

ALADDIN
(To audience) Alright girls! I'm nearly at the magic cave storage facility. It's dead quiet this side of town. I heard from someone who heard from someone that it's a bit of a cruising ground. Maybe I'll get lucky.

ABANAZER
Young man.

ALADDIN (not keen)
Oh, er, hi mate.

ABANAZER gets closer. ALADDIN looks awkward.

ABANAZER
What brings you out to yonder storage cave.

ALADDIN
Oh... Well bas'c[79], I'm just exploring. Going pot holing in the caves.

ABANAZER
Take my old ring before you go.

ALADDIN (looks about him)
Yeah alright go on, how much you got?

ABANAZER takes off the ring and shows it to ALADDIN

———————————
[79] "Baisk" = basically.

ABANAZER
My lucky ring. It will protect you while you're in the cave.

ALADDIN
I dunno, it's a bit camp for me.

ABANAZER
You fucking what? I've seen you running, it looks like you need a shit but you've just heard Sinita's doing a secret gig across town.

ALADDIN
What? I don't know you. How have you seen me run?

ABANAZER
I told you. My magic ring! My magic, valuable ring.

ALADDIN
Valuable?

ABANAZER
David Dickinson's been sniffing about for my ring for years. It's worth thousands, some say millions.

ALADDIN
I couldn't. What do you think boys and girls?

ABANAZER
I'm sure you've a poor, soon-to-be evicted mother or something who could use the cash.

ALADDIN
I do! Thanks mate! Amaze!

He takes the ring and puts it on.

ABANAZER
The cave's that way. Safe travelling.

ALADDIN enters the cave.

ABANAZER
Soon the power of the lamp will be mine! That little tealeaf will be gone forever!

He laughs and exits.

Scene 8: The cave

Inside the cave, it is dirty and dark. Water drips. ALADDIN enters, crawling. There are ancient artefacts and junk, barely visible.

ALADDIN
Seriously guys I've seen Christopher Nolan films that are less dark and hard to follow than this cave. I just need to find this lamp then I can sell it and me and mum's troubles will be over.

He picks up an old skull.

ALADDIN
To nick it or not to nick? I can't see the lamp anywhere.

The lamp glows in the dark. The audience shout. The light goes out.

ALADDIN
I think you've been on the mushrooms.

The lamp shines again. He pulls it out.

ALADDIN
Fucking hell. Ow. My ring feels like it's on fire.

He pulls off the ring and throws it on the ground. The GIMP OF THE RING appears.

ALADDIN
This ring really is magic. He must have put Grindr on it.

GIMP
Alright mate.

ALADDIN
Who are you?

GIMP
Oh heck boys and girls, how can I nick his lamp? And it's horrible down here. What if there's spiders? I hate spiders. Lauren used to have to get them out the bath for me. Will you tell me if you see one?

ALADDIN *(looking at the GIMP and liking what he sees)*
I don't know how you got here mate, but I ain't complaining. And here we are, just me and you and your outrageous outfit here in a secluded cave…

GIMP
Oh heck boys and girls, I got to hit him and take that lamp. If I don't there's no way the master will let me free.

A large black spider appears, dangling behind the Gimps head. The audience shout.

GIMP
Spider! Did you say spider?

He screams and turns around as he does the spider disappears.

GIMP
No you're having me on.

The Spider appears again.

GIMP
Spider! Agh

He turns, the spider goes

ALADDIN
Mate what's wrong?

GIMP
Spider!

ALADDIN
Haha! Is that all? I can't believe you're that scared of spiders! You fucking wuss.

GIMP
Right you bastard.

He whacks ALADDIN round the head

ALADDIN
Ow! I should have known you like it rough from your outfit.

ALADDIN suddenly becomes dizzy and faints holding his head.

GIMP
Bloody nora! What have I done?!

He dithers between helping Aladdin and getting the lamp. He settles on the latter, picks it up, and the ring too. As he stands up the spider drops on his head. The GIMP screams. He drops the lamp, throwing it towards ALADDIN, and runs out in fear. ALADDIN wakes holding his head.

ALADDIN
You need a safe-word, you fucking amateur! Hey where are you?

There is a crashing sound, rocks falling. ALADDIN runs out then back in again.

ALADDIN

There's been a rock fall. Some kind of landslide. I'm trapped boys and girls. Alone!

The GENIE OF THE LAMP's voice is heard from the lamp.

GENIE

Rub me.

ALADDIN looks about him.

GENIE

Rub me.

ALADDIN

(to audience member) Not now love, we're doing a show.

GENIE

Rub me.

ALADDIN

No that wasn't you your lips didn't move.

GENIE

Rub me!

ALADDIN looks around him confused. Then he looks at his crotch.

ALADDIN *(to his crotch)*

Oh I get it! The magic ring has given me a talking cock!

GENIE *(singing)*

Rub me, rub me, say that you'll rub me[80].

ALADDIN

And it sings! That's amazing, I'll be able to do harmony in the shower. Well, let's give it a bash.

GENIE

No! Be gentle.

ALADDIN

It's a pity you sound like the woman who does the Satnav... Well. Hello my BFF. This could be start of a beautiful friendship.

ALADDIN rubs the lamp. After a while he does. A crash of drums, a flash of light and the GENIE OF THE LAMP appears.

ALADDIN

Oh my God! Another one! It's like that story where the three ghosts turn up. What's it called... The Muppets Christmas Carol. Fuck.

GENIE

Language Aladdin! Please, decorum and tact,
But thanks for releasing me from your artefact

ALADDIN

You came out of my-

GENIE

Lamp, yes the lamp, holed up in that gloom,
I couldn't even knit, there's no elbow room
You're a sight for sore eyes after that claustrophobia!
I can't help but think up some way to disrobe ya...
Ah yes, before I rudely interrupted
Continue what you were doing, don't be disrupted.

ALADDIN

You were in the lamp? You're a Genie?

GENIE *(innocent)*

You've got to rub me the right way.

ALADDIN

But you're- oh never mind, wow mum will be happy!

GENIE

What did you expect, Chris Biggins in a nappy?

ALADDIN

Please, stop with the rapping. It's really annoying.

GENIE

Yes, I see that it could be a little cloying.

ALADDIN

Please?

GENIE

Most people like it. Perhaps you prefer something more modern? But I've been trapped in there for fifty years, three months, five days, twelve hours and thirty eight minutes, not that I was counting.

ALADDIN

So you're... What does that make you?

GENIE

Frustrated. But now that you're my new master you must listen while I explain the rules.

ALADDIN

Your master? Me?

---

80 To the tune of The Cardigans' "Lovefool"

GENIE
I could have done worse. (She smacks his bum) My name is Siri, the Genie of the Lamp. And you have three wishes.

ALADDIN
And they come true?

GENIE
That's really the point.

ALADDIN
So I can wish for anything?

GENIE
Anything at all! But nothing nasty. I won't kill.

ALADDIN
Right, I'll have Channing Tatum and Michael Fassbender. Wrestling in oil. Naked. How many wishes is that?

GENIE
Oh dear. I had high hopes for you.

ALADDIN
There's nothing wrong with being gay!

GENIE
Naked wrestling is hardly going to bring about world happiness.

ALADDIN
It would make me happy. And some of my crew.

GENIE
Who?

ALADDIN
The boys and girls (he indicates the audience)

The GENIE looks at the audience

GENIE
Oh! Well hello again boys! (Then with less enthusiasm) and girls.

She looks at the audience.

GENIE
I think "boys" is stretching it.

ALADDIN
Well you ain't exactly Miley Cyrus.

GENIE
Don't be cheeky. But I confess I do like a younger man.

She looks at the audience and picks out a young looking man.

GENIE
Hello. What's your name?

ALADDIN
You're supposed to be helping me not helping yourself.

GENIE
Charity starts at home. Have some manners, I am talking to [name]. Now, how about a nice cup of tea for me and [name].

ALADDIN
We're in a cave.

GENIE
There's a primus just here, look. Why don't you wish for some tea?

ALADDIN
Alright. I wish for- wait, I ain't stupid. Listen, there's been a landslide. We can't get out.

GENIE
So your first wish will be?

ALADDIN
Channing and Michael...?

GENIE
Where do they educate them these days? Landslide. Trapped. Any idea, dear?

ALADDIN
Oh yeah! I wish we could get out of this cave.

GENIE
Master! Your wish is my command.

She makes gestures with her arms towards the cave entrance and does an odd dance. Nothing happens. ALADDIN slow-claps her.

GENIE
Oh bother. Oh drat. I remember now, my magic doesn't work underground.

ALADDIN
Some Genie you are!

GENIE
Thank you!

ALADDIN
I'm being sarcastic.

GENIE
The lowest form of wit. You'll have to start digging, my boy.

ALADDIN goes off stage. We hear the sound of rocks being shifted. The Genie approaches her friend in the audience.

GENIE
Well here we are! Be polite and make a little space for a lady. I'd make a little space for you.

She sits with the audience. Aladdin is heard panting.

ALADDIN
This'll take years! You could help.

GENIE
More winning, less whining!

ALADDIN
I'm roasting!

ALADDIN's shirt is thrown onto the stage. The GENIE gets up and picks it up. A discreet sniff.

GENIE
This is no good at all.

ALADDIN
What?

GENIE
You're shirtless and I can barely see you.

ALADDIN
I'm sweating like a sniffer dog at Secret Garden Party[81].

GENIE
Why not slip your trousers off for better circulation.

_____
[81] Music festival, held annually from 2005 to 2017. (Interestingly, this reference wouldn't have worked in 2016 when Secret Garden Party pioneered a scheme to offer safe testing of revellers' drugs for them, in collaboration with local police).

Trousers are flung onto the stage. The digging continues.

GENIE
I expect your underpants are terribly warm.

ALADDIN
They will be - they're on the radiator at home.

GENIE
You've stopped wishing for the interval now haven't you boys and girls?

ALADDIN enters. He is naked, and holding a boulder in front of himself to hide his modesty.

GENIE
You should have that looked at. And look you've nearly got us out!

ALADDIN continues to dig as he does there is another landslide, larger he is covered by more rock and gravel and lies unconscious.

GENIE
Aladdin!
Oh what a predicament. What's to be done?
I'd always planned to retire in the sun.
Well there's little point in your hanging about,
While we try to conjure a clever way out,
So pop to the bar or visit the loo,
Or touch up your make-up – yes, and you girls too,
Poor [name of man she spoke to] you seem to have found it quite trying,
Well mine's a brandy and babycham if you're buying,
This seems like a cave one could go quite mad in,
Still at least for the moment, I've got Aladdin!

She bends over ALADDIN as she does more rocks fall, she is hit. She falls to the ground fainting. She looks up, sees ALADDIN and faints again, this time across him. More rocks fall.

INTERVAL

Matthew Baldwin as Abanazer and Toby Joyce as the Gimp of the Ring in *Get Aladdin!* Photo by Derek Drescher.

Greg Airey as Aladdin and George Bull as Prince Char Ming in *Get Aladdin!* Photo by Derek Drescher.

Scene 9: The cave

ALADDIN - now clothed - and the Genie are dusty and bedraggled but just about conscious. Aladdin is clearing rocks. The Genie is sat on a rock with an old guitar. She sings, encouraging the audience to join her.

GENIE (sings)
Kumbaya my lord, kumbaya
Kumbaya my lord, kumbaya
Kumbaya my lord, kumbaya
Oh lord kumbaya

ALADDIN
Help!!

It echoes. No response.

ALADDIN,
Help!!!

GENIE (sings)
Someone's singing Lord, Kumbaya
Someone's singing Lord, Kumbaya
Nobody can hear you Aladdin, Kumbaya...

ALADDIN
I'm not surprised over your din! I'm knackered, I've been shifting rocks faster than Charlie Sheen. Oh hey gang! Welcome back.

GENIE
Yes, welcome back boys and girls!

ALADDIN
Oh my god shut up it's not Daybreak[82]. We're still trapped in the cave boys and girls. I'd better get shifting.

He goes back to clearing rocks. A pause.

GENIE (sings)
Someone's digging lord, kumbaya-

ALADDIN
Give it a rest will you? I mean, it ain't like you're a good

GENIE
Christian?

ALADDIN (looks at her)
Singer.

---

82 Morning TV show.

GENIE (sings)
Someone's moody, lord, Kumbaya...

ALADDIN
Oi! The ceiling's already fallen in once.

GENIE (to the tune of The Lady is a Tramp)
"She hates this cave, it's cold and damp
That's why the lady's in a lamp"

ALADDIN
Hey!

GENIE
Music while you work, dear! If I had a drum I'd bang it. Still, I have you.

ALADDIN
I don't see you doing nothing.

GENIE
With my back, dear? Oooph. You wouldn't give me a teensy rub, would you?

ALADDIN
What happens if I rub you, does a lamp pop out?

GENIE
Well if *you* won't...

The GENIE approaches the young man she was chatting to earlier and sits, ladylike, on his lap.

GENIE
Young man, would you do me the honour? A little higher. Go on man squeeze me. That's it.

She enjoys it.

GENIE
Here's a tip, darling, don't cram so much bulk in your front trouser pockets you'll spoil the line.

ALADDIN
You old tart!

GENIE
Young man. You may be my master but it's a working relationship and I expect you to be respectful.

ALADDIN
Sorry.

GENIE
Unless you think I'm giving out signals in which case take the risk. I hope I've fallen into good hands.

ALADDIN
You have!

GENIE
Show me.

ALADDIN shows her his hands.

GENIE
Fingernails like a crime scene.

ALADDIN
I've been digging, actch. You are a bit of a goer aintcha?

GENIE
I've been out for 30 minutes once a year, I'm hardly Caligula.

ALADDIN
Who's she? You're a bit like my mum.

GENIE
Ouch. There's nothing wrong in having some fun dear.

[Here they sang a reworked version of No time Time At All from the musical Pippin.

ALADDIN
Well I hope we get to start living. But we ain't ever getting out of here.

GENIE
If at first you don't succeed, suck harder.

ALADDIN
What use is three wishes if I can't even use one of them? And after all these miserable weeks, I finally meet someone who might make this tin-pot province feel like home-

GENIE
Thank you

ALADDIN
Not you! The Prince! And he could be anywhere and he probably thinks I'm just a little dirty thief, and meanwhile I'm gonna die in this fucking hole with you. I done nothing with my life. Never been to gay day at Lovebox. Never seen my photo in the clubbing pages of Boyz. Never even got Jake Shears to tweet me back. I don't want to die!

GENIE (rolling her eyes)
Adolescents!

ALADDIN
OMG where?

GENIE
Where what?

ALADDIN
Adolescents

GENIE
Ooh, where? (she looks around the cavern)

There is light from a torch or a lantern. The PRINCE enters, crawling, from another part of the cave.

ALADDIN
Sweet! It looks like one of my wishes might have worked anyhows!

PRINCE
Aladdin!

ALADDIN
My prince!

GENIE
We're actually having a private moment here so-

ALADDIN
Siri!

GENIE
Oh hello...! Boys and girls what a vision! (to her friend in the audience) It's been lovely, no really it's been a lot of fun, but I think I've outgrown us.

PRINCE
You tricked us! You helped Abanazer! I thought you were interested in my well-bred looks and demeanour but you just wanted to get into my palace. I told myself I never wanted to see you again.

ALADDIN
I'm glad to see you.

PRINCE
Of course you are. I'm the handsome Prince. Who's this?!

GENIE presents herself expectantly.

ALADDIN
This is Siri. She's my...

GENIE
I'm his...

ALADDIN
She's kind of my... bitch?

GENIE
Now really!

427

PRINCE
You're a caveman!

ALADDIN
I don't *live* here! Listen, we were tricked! Abanazer's going to evict us too!

PRINCE
But what are you doing here?

ALADDIN
Pot holing, obv. What are you doing here?

PRINCE
There's a secret passage from the palace. We've fled from Abanazer. (Dramatically) We're in exile!

GENIE
Well I'm in head to toe Jaeger but I don't flash it about.

The EMPEROR enters, crawling.

EMPEROR
Thank the goddess Mazu that's over. That passage is as tight as a Scottish schoolgirl, it's taken a layer of skin off my hips. Hello old chap. Oh! Oh! Hello young woman.

GENIE
Oh. Hello.

EMPEROR
What an utter treat. I hope you were blessed with a wider passage than I was.

We hear TWANKEY singing as she enters from another direction with WISHY WASHY

TWANKEY
She'll be coming round the mountain when she comes
She'll be coming round the mountain when she comes
She'll be coming round the mountain, coming like a fountain,
Coming round the mountain when she- Aladdin!

ALADDIN
Mum! How did you get in?

TWANKEY
We was out looking for you. Oh your highnesseses!

EMPEROR
I say, son, we've stumbled into a mythical cave of beautiful women! Which do you like best?

PRINCE
I told you, I'm *GAY!*

He shouts the last word and "Gay" echoes back and forth in the cavern, for a ridiculously long time.

PRINCE
And this is Aladdin, Daddy! My first, doomed, racist love!

ALADDIN
I'm not racist!

EMPEROR
You can't be with an Englishman, you'll end up with round eyes. So, you're a soap-dropper, eh?

ALADDIN
Yeah.

EMPEROR
An after-dinner mimsy? A gentleman's relisher? A muddy flower sniffer? A fairy. A Mary. A drinker of boy's dairy? A lunchbox enthusiast? A yoghurt pot? A shit-nosed reindeer? A biscuit dampener?

PRINCE
God you're so embarrassing.

EMPEROR
A man who likes brown sauce on his hot-dog.

WISHY WASHY
We saw the entrance was blocked. So we searched for another way in.

TWANKEY
I knew me days spelunking with the Workington Caving Society wouldn't go amiss.

ALADDIN
Workington?

TWANKEY
You think you know me son but I've had quite the life.

GENIE
I'm nothing like your mother, Aladdin. Oh forgive me, what a rude assumption, perhaps you're his grandmother. What a charming monkey. Is it a boy or a girl?

TWANKEY
And who might you be when you've done your makeup better?

GENIE
My friends call me Siri.

TWANKEY
Then I won't.

GENIE
He's my-

ALADDIN
I'm her client, mum.

TWANKEY
Client?! Oh no he isn't.

She pulls ALADDIN to him and hugs him.

GENIE
Oh yes he is.

She pulls ALADDIN to him and hugs him.

TWANKEY
Oh no he isn't.

She pulls him back.

GENIE
Oh yes he is.

She pulls ALADDIN back.

GENIE
Now, if you were able to get in, I do think we must be able to get out.

TWANKEY
"I do think..." Get back in your rocker, love, and wait for the nice lady to bring your meds round.

GENIE
Goodness it's ever so craggy in here isn't it, oh wait my mistake that's just your face.

ALADDIN (picking up the lamp)
Mum, Siri's the Genie of the lamp. She was inside it the whole time.

TWANKEY
With thighs like that?

TWANKEY takes the lamp, gives it a cautious sniff.

ALADDIN
We carried her all the way from London.

TWANKEY
I... I carried you..? Sorry. I feel kinda maternal now.

GENIE
I'm sure that's just the HRT. Really, you've the attitude of a fishwife.

TWANKEY
Better than the smell of one.

GENIE
I'm just musty.

TWANKEY
Listen here Granny Grunt I grew up on the streets of Clapham and I'm proud of it.

GENIE
Which no doubt is where you earned a living.

TWANKEY
That's it, you ain't too old for me to lamp you.

She moves about to hit the GENIE. ALADDIN prizes the lamp from her fingers. A giant panda appears. Everyone screams. It takes its head off – it's the POLICE WOMAN.

POLICE WOMAN
Ello, ello, ello. What have we here then? (to audience) It's me, and I've done it, I've found the lamp. (To Aladdin) Aladdin, I am arresting you for stealing this ancient, priceless lamp.

ALADDIN
It ain't mine, it's hers.

He throws it to the GENIE. The POLICE WOMAN grabs the GENIE.

POLICE WOMAN
Then I'm arresting you for stealing this ancient, priceless lamp.

GENIE
It's my home!

TWANKEY
Tramp.

EMPEROR
My dear, would the Emperor of Hao Hung be mixed up with criminals?

PRINCE
It's Abanazer you should be looking for. He's swindled us out of our palace and I bet he's planning to use its magic for world domination.

POLICE WOMAN
Life's never easy is it?

ALADDIN
Then we'll stop him!

TWANKEY
That's me brave boy.

ALADDIN
Some us can go in from the front and the rest can sneak in round the back.

WISHY WASHY
It's a rescue mission not a gang bang.

PRINCE
We'll use the secret tunnel.

EMPEROR
I bet you will.

POLICE WOMAN
I'll help. I'll get that evil Abanazer, I can see that you are good people, you didn't take that lamp.

ALADDIN
Emperor, sir, you and the Prince go back in through the tunnel. You know the way.

POLICE WOMAN
I'll come with you. I trained in kung fu.

PRINCE
I have an offer from Harvard.

POLICE WOMAN
Let's go. Go go go!

EMPEROR
I'm right behind you my dear.

The POLICE WOMAN crawls out followed by the EMPEROR a lot closer than he should be.

PRINCE (to ALADDIN)
You don't have to do this.

ALADDIN
I want to – for you. And then afterward I want to take you away from that Palace. I can show you the world.

PRINCE
A dazzling place I never knew.

ALADDIN
Yeah.

They kiss. TWANKEY starts to cry.

TWANKEY (crying)
A prince, in love with my boy!

GENIE
Contain your emotions, there isn't time and we don't have any TENA pads[83].

PRINCE
We should go. Find me. There'll be a reward.

The PRINCE exits

ALADDIN
Fffffit.

TWANKEY
There'll be a royal wedding, I can feel it in me waters.

GENIE
Cystitis I expect.

TWANKEY
Let's go. Gangbang style.

ALADDIN
Gangnam style, mum. Let's go!

They dance their way off stage to "Gangnam Style[84]".

---

83 We probably wouldn't have multiple jokes about women's bodies and ageing if we were writing it now.
84 Pretty much every panto in the country that year would have referenced Psy's hit song Gangnam Style.

Scene 10: The palace

ABANAZER and he GIMP enter

ABANAZER

The palace, the palace, we're in the fucking palace
The palace, the palace, we're going to work some malice
So suck my massive phallus
While we watch a bit of Dallas...

Ha! The magic palace! Offer accepted, keys exchanged, discovery of dry rot expected any minute. Ha. I once gave an estate agent breast implants while he was asleep cos he described a bay window as fucking panoramic.

GIMP

What's so magic about the palace?

ABANAZER

It controls and protects everything within a 5 mile radius! Apparently it can fly and all, but I don't know how. Of course if we had the lamp we'd be able to work it out wouldn't we?

GIMP

I'm sorry mate.

ABANAZER

Christ

GIMP

I'm sorry Christ it's just that there was a-

ABANAZER

Yeah yeah, a spider. I'll pull its legs off. And yours, you council house cunt. Still, look at this place! It's massive. Shame it's so full of gargling.

GIMP

What?

ABANAZER

Gargling with Matthew Mitcham's spunk, junk. There's clutter everywhere.

ABANAZER starts throwing things out of the window. He picks up an old pipe/flute. He plays it brilliantly – but it should be very obvious that it's a recording. It's like the pipe of snake charmer. A snake appears at the window. Abanazer punches it hard in the face and it disappears from view.

GIMP

That was great!

ABANAZER

Were you musical at all? Did you play anything?

GIMP

CDs mainly. I was more into sport.

ABANAZER

I'll have to get you a sports kit. Right, let's finish getting rid of this junk and I'll have the place decorated. Tasteful mind. I heard Kate had Kensington Palace done over in magnolia and IKEA prints.

GIMP

I like magnolia. It's mutual.

ABANAZER

Neutral. And then I'm gonna see how to make the thing fly. Why be stuck in this pissy province when I could have power over somewhere like... like London.

GIMP

London!

ABANAZER

I'll turn the whole city into my personal factory. 7 million slaves! Thing is, China's going upmarket. And the Middle East. And India. All those fucking ethnic places. They need stuff to buy.

GIMP

We're going to London? That's brilliant! I can find Lauren and then I'll be free.

ABANAZER

You harnessed halfwit, you won't be free. After you ballsed up with the lamp I'm plunging you deep into my ring forever!

GIMP

But, but you need me!

ABANAZER

You? I'll have millions in my power! In you get. And don't bang your sloppy arse on the way in.

GIMP

Please!

ABANAZER

Now!

There is a flash. The GIMP disappears.

ABANAZER
Hahaha! Right, let's get this thing out of here (he chucks the carpet out of the window). Now let's see if the rumours are true about the Emperor's collection of rare and ancient erotica.

ABANAZER exits. A secret door opens. The PRINCE and POLICE WOMAN enter. The EMPEROR tries to but gets stuck.

POLICE WOMAN
Freeze! Oh! Ello ello ello! We've just come through the secret passage.

EMPEROR
Help!

PRINCE
Daddy!

EMPEROR
I know I know, a moment on the lips. I've grown an arse like a Caribbean girl.

PRINCE
That's racist.

POLICE WOMAN
And sexist.

EMPEROR
I suppose you're one of these PC women.

POLICE WOMAN
PC? I'm an inspector!!

EMPEROR
Help me? Please?

POLICE WOMAN
Come on, grab an arm. I warn you sir I may not know my own strength.

PRINCE
I'm surprised you even know your own name. Come on.

The POLICE WOMAN and PRINCE grab an arm and pull. The EMPEROR falls over and lands on the POLICE WOMAN.

EMPEROR
A thousand thanks...

PRINCE
I'll stay here and guard the exit. You find Abanazer.

POLICE WOMAN
No, you stay here and guard the exit. *I'll* find Abanazer.

She exits

EMPEROR (still on the floor)
My poor palace! It's like the time we had squatters. Wait... My carpet! My precious magic carpet!

PRINCE
Everything's missing! Help! Police!

The POLICE WOMAN returns

PRINCE
Abanazer's stolen our things! Find him!

POLICE WOMAN
That's what I'm doing!

POLICE WOMAN exits

EMPEROR
Which of us do you think she likes best?...

PRINCE
Come on, Robert needs watering.

EMPEROR
We'll go via the kitchens. I hope Abanazer hasn't been pinching my dim-sums.

They exit

Scene 11: Outside the palace

ALADDIN, TWANKEY, WISHY and the GENIE are ducking the various objects that we saw Abanazer throw out of the window.

TWANKEY
Grab the brolly Aladdin!

ALADDIN gets it and puts it up. They shelter underneath it.

TWANKEY
Why's he throwing all this stuff out the palace window?

ALADDIN
They'll be fighting! My handsome prince'll be giving Abanazer a good slap... Look! I can see him! My prince is at the window!

They all wave.

ALADDIN
He can't see us.

WISHY WASHY
Maybe it's like in Psycho and he's dead.

ALADDIN
Don't say that! Oh, he's gone.

TWANKEY
I hope he doesn't throw the fridge out. That's what did for Aladdin's poor father.

GENIE
He died as he lived. Squashed by a great weight full of food.

WISHY
Yeah what are we going to do then?

ALADDIN
I dunno... break in and attack?

WISHY
You haven't got a plan. You're meant to be the hero.

TWANKEY
You stupid monkey (she hits WISHY) of course he has a plan. Haven't you my brave boy.

ALADDIN
Mum, sometimes I wish you'd shut up.

GENIE
Master, your wish is my command.

She clicks her fingers

ALADDIN
Eh?

TWANKEY suddenly has a large gobstopper in her mouth.

GENIE
Wish one of three! And a wish well spent if I may say so.

ALADDIN
I didn't mean to go that far!

GENIE
And it's only our first date. You should be careful what you wish for dear.

ALADDIN
If you reverse it, is that another wish lost?

GENIE
Usually it would be. But as you're new, I can include it in the same wish just this once. What do you think boys and girls shall I reverse the wish?

The audience shout.

GENIE
Oh very well.

She clicks her fingers. TWANKEY twirls the gobstopper falls from her mouth.

TWANKEY
My mouth's not as stretchy as it once was.

ALADDIN
God. This is really hard.

GENIE
Chin up. Everyone struggles at first.

ALADDIN
Really? We've only got two wishes left. Wishy you're going to have to help me not to waste them. Who was your best master, Siri? I mean, who would you say used your powers the best?

GENIE
I shouldn't break client confidentiality. But Jesus is certainly top three.

WISHY
Aladdin, could I have a word?

ALADDIN
What is it?

WISHY indicates that they should get out of earshot. They move.

WISHY
You've got three wishes right?

ALADDIN
Well two now.

WISHY
Do you think you could use one of them to, you know, reduce the size of my...

ALADDIN
Your what Wishy?

WISHY
You know.

ALADDIN
Oh! Really? I think your nose is perfect.

There is a great noise and a load of smoke.

TWANKEY
The Palace! Blow me, it's flying!

GENIE
Goodness she's right. A flying palace.

WISHY
That's just a caravan with pretentions.

ALADDIN
Abanazer must be using magic. Siri, can you get us in there?

GENIE
But really dear, then we'd all be trapped.

ALADDIN
Well then... I don't know - make us fly so we can follow.

GENIE
That would be five wishes. One for each of us and two to get your mother off the ground.

TWANKEY
I won't rise to it.

TWANKEY unrolls the carpet which was thrown out of the window. She sits on it.

TWANKEY
This is lovely, they must use a good softener. Do you think it's Islamic? *(She looks at the label)* Oh no, Homebase.

ALADDIN
Hold on. That's it! Siri, can you make this carpet fly?

GENIE
Is the pope Jewish?

ALADDIN
Yeah.

WISHY
No!

GENIE
Oh, right. Well anyway yes, I can make the carpet fly.

ALADDIN
Come on everyone, on the carpet.

GENIE
It's filthy.

TWANKEY
She's stalling.

GENIE
Well I've not driven one before.

There is a lurch.

ALADDIN
It's working!

GENIE
What? You haven't wished yet.

Another lurch.

ALADDIN
It must be a magic carpet! They said the palace was magic! Abanazer, we're coming to get you!

The carpet flies off stage. [85]

_____

[85] The producer, Peter Bull, came up with a hilarious and surprisingly effective solution, inspired by those "man riding an ostrich" costumes: during a black-out the carpet was swapped for a special, stiff "magic" carpet with holes in it for the actors' legs to go through, while fake legs were fixed to the top of the carpet – which was held in place at waist-height by shoulder straps. Their legs were masked by black skirting under the carpet. The lights came up – perhaps using UV lighting – and they performed "Go West" as they flew about the stage.

Scene 12: The palace

The PRINCE is asleep. ABANAZER enters and watches him.

PRINCE
Oh Aladdin...! Why are you climbing in through my window? You naughty thief, you merciless bit of rough, what are you going to steal from me?

ABANAZER approaches him on tip toe

PRINCE
My books? My Brian Cox DVDs? Oh..! Oh that's what you're going to steal..!

The PRINCE rolls onto his front. ABANAZER goes for a feel. He leans in close for a kiss. There is a strange noise, rattling, tumbling, and wind blowing. The PRINCE wakes.

PRINCE
Huh!? What was that? What's happening?

ABANAZER
I expect you felt the earth move. How'd you get in here? Did you miss me?

Something falls off a shelf.

PRINCE
We're moving!

ABANAZER
Moving? We've only just settled in, don't be so fucking needy. I'll get you a new kitchen. Where do you want to get married?

PRINCE
I'm not marrying you!

ABANAZER
I'm gonna put a ring on it. Yours.

PRINCE
I... I don't believe in the institution of marriage. I mean it's steeped in the patriarchal system and based on deeply conservative values, and I don't know how I feel about appropriating heterosexual norms...

ABANAZER
Yeah, anyway, I thought Kensington Roof Gardens. We can get the Beckham kids, the Cameron kids and the Murdoch kids and see who we can get to jump off first.

PRINCE
I want to be with Aladdin!

ABANAZER
You and Aladdin? Camper than a row of bishops.

PRINCE
He's not that camp.

ABANAZER
He will be when I've broken his wrists. Now, how about a bit of how's your father.

The EMPEROR enters.

EMPEROR
Not feeling very well actually.

ABANAZER
That'll be the type 2 diabetes kicking in you fat fürer.

The POLICE WOMAN rushes in.

POLICE WOMAN
Ello ello ello! Boys and girls, I have deduced that Abanazer has vacated the premises.

PRINCE
Oh, really, well done.

They all lurch. The PRINCE rushes to a window.

PRINCE
We're really high!

ABANAZER (romantic)
I feel it too my prince.

PRINCE
We're flying!

ABANAZER
Without wings! You are the wind beneath my duvet.

PRINCE
The whole palace is flying...

ABANAZER
Oh that. Yeah. I found the control room.

ABANAZER cosies up to the PRNCE and has a bit of a fondle.

ABANAZER
I can show you the world.

PRINCE
Don't you dare touch my thighs.

EMPEROR
There's water below! Where are we?

ABANAZER
That's the English Channel. Ain't it beautiful.

PRINCE
Abroad!

EMPEROR
Oh goody, where?

PRINCE
I hate heights! I.. I feel sick.

ABANAZER
Don't be such a fucking poof.

EMPEROR
Where are we going?

POLICE WOMAN
London! That's the Thames now! If you listen you can hear it.

We hear a fragment of the EastEnders theme tune. There is a sudden crash. They look out.

POLICE WOMAN
We've taken out the cable car!

ABANAZER
Oh yeah look. There's Boris clinging to our foundations. Should be plain sailing now.

An enormous crash. They judder to a halt.

EMPEROR
We've stopped!

PRINCE
But we're still high up. Are we floating?

EMPEROR
I'll have a look out of the window.

He leans far out of the window. Abanazer sneaks up and tries to push him out.

PRINCE
Daddy!

ABANAZER
Drat.

EMPEROR
We've been skewered! We're stuck on a spike!

ABANAZER
Don't worry, if you were it wouldn't reach your vital organs.

POLICE WOMAN looks out

POLICE WOMAN
I don't believe it! We're on top of the Shard! Oooh that'll be some expensive damage.

ABANAZER
That's alright, I only own the lower floors. The top ones were more expensive but they're fucking tiny. This is perfect! I can rule the whole city from up here!

A lurch

EMPEROR
We're moving again!

POLICE WOMAN
Looks like we're headed to-

ABANAZER
Soho!

EMPEROR
Soho! Is it true what they say about the young women?

ABANAZER
Yeah, I imported most of them.

A crunch.

POLICE WOMAN
We've landed! Oh boys and girls, I'm home! Home! If only I knew where Colin was.

EMPEROR (looking out)
It is true about the young women. Such tight little tops.

PRINCE
Those are men, daddy! Wait – they're men. Gay men! Everywhere!

Everyone screams, like in a horror.

PRINCE
No, no, it's a good thing.

Everyone cheers.

PRINCE
I may be some time. I understand I'm probably now meant to disguise myself as a pauper in these sorts of stories but really, with this face? Don't wait up.

He goes to run out. Abanazer claps his hands.

ABANAZER
Palace! Shut the doors!

The sound of bolts slamming shut.

ABANAZER
Hahaha! You've had your moment, London, welcome to the third world!! Soon you'll be under my myriad fucking charms and slaving away in my factories. (To the audience) And that goes for you too! Hahaha! Haha! Ha!

Scene 13: The carpet

The carpet is flying, carrying ALADDIN, WISHY WASHY, TWANKY and the GENIE. It is very peaceful, apart from the sound of wind and the occasional seagulls. WISHY WASHY has a fishing rod which hangs over the side. The GENIE is standing, wearing sunglasses and a Pussy Riot t-shirt, and seems to be lost in unheard music and is slightly dancing. She and TWANKY have sunburnt faces. Not much happens for a while.

TWANKEY
This is lovely… How long's it been?

ALADDIN
A week.

TWANKEY
I ain't washed me hair in so long it's getting like Medusa's. I ran me hand through it earlier it came out with bite marks. Oh god, a week. My Emperor!

ALADDIN
My Prince! What if he and Abanazer…

TWANKEY
Still what an adventure boys and girls. We seen the pyramids, the Med, Machu Pichu.

ALADDIN
We got lost. (a pause) Wishy, do you want me to do your fleas while you do my blackheads?

TWANKEY
Got some marvellous photographs.

ALADDIN
That one of you in the market in Marrakesh holding those coconuts.

WISHY WASHY
They weren't coconuts.

TWANKEY
I can't believe we'll be back in London. I wonder if Leveson[86] is still going.

ALADDIN
I wonder if Starbucks have got red cups yet.

TWANKEY
Or paid their fucking taxes. Your father would have loved this Aladdin. You don't mind if I marry the Emperor do you?

ALADDIN
Whatever makes you happy mum.

TWANKEY
You'll barely see me I expect, what with me living in the palace.

ALADDIN
What? I'll be living in the palace. With the Prince.

TWANKEY
We'll see about that. How's my tan coming on? I'm so hungry.

WISHY WASHY flicks up her fishing rod. There's a seagull on it. She contemplates it. TWANKY rummages in a pocket and finds a tin of travel sweets.

TWANKY
Forgot I had these. Who'd like a travel sweet boys and girls?

ALADDIN
Mum be careful. If you drop them you'll kill someone.

TWANKEY
I heard that enough from my burlesque instructor.

ALADDIN
I didn't know you did burlesque.

TWANKEY
Nor did I till five weeks into the course. It was meant to be zumba. I only discovered the mix-up when I said I'd do that demonstration for the old folks home. What's she doing? Siri. Siri. (tugs at Siri's skirt) Oi!

The GENIE nearly falls off the carpet. They catch her.

ALADDIN
She's been like that since Aiya Nappa.

TWANKY
Are we going the right way?

GENIE
What a boring thing to say
My dear, there really is no right way

ALADDIN
She's rhyming again. she's still high. I wish-

---

86 The Leveson Inquiry into the culture, practise and ethics of the British press, in response to the phone-hacking scandal.

TWANKEY and WISHY
No!

ALADDIN
Siri, sit still.

GENIE
I can't, it hurts. Those nice boys from Scunthorpe I met in that club got very rowdy.

ALADDIN
Siri. Am I your first gay Master?

GENIE
Well, again, one shouldn't break client confidentiality. But Jesus...

ALADDIN
That's the Shard! What's happened to it?

WISHY WASHY
King Kong?

ALADDIN
We're going down! Where are we?

GENIE (looks)
Old Compton Street. Brace yourselves.

TWANKEY
What for?

WISHY WASHY
The smell of Jupe.

They land with a bump.

ALADDIN
It looks different.

WISHY WASHY
Something's wrong.

TWANKEY
Look at all the people!

They examine the audience.

GENIE
They're like zombies.

ALADDIN
It's probably just Sunday morning.

TWANKEY
The last time I saw people this dead behind the eyes it was on the parliament channel.

ALADDIN looks at her questioningly.

TWANKEY
We downgraded from Sky to Freeview and I got me numbers mixed up.

ALADDIN
They're all under some sort of power.

WISHY WASHY
It might just be the Jupe.

GENIE
(To her favourite) That young man looks like he needs mouth to mouth.

ALADDIN
No look! There's the palace!

TWANKEY
But there's whole streams of people marching past it towards the... what are they?

ALADDIN
They look like factories! But they're enormous. And there's no windows.

WISHY WASHY
Place looks like a Lowry painting.

TWANKEY stares at WISHY.

TWANKY
Look! Billboards with pictures of Mr Abbey national and the Prince on them!

ALADDIN
They're married! Siri. Siri! Get us into the palace!

GENIE
Very well. Your final wish.

ALADDIN
I've got two wishes left.

GENIE
Ah, yes... Well I've been meaning to ask you. You see, I can only be set free if a master – a kind, handsome master like yourself - uses a wish to grant me freedom. I haven't been free in 3000 years. I've come all this way with you. Please?

ALADDIN
Ok. Do this, and I'll set you free afterwards.

GENIE
Really? I'll be free of this curse! I can go out and enjoy myself! Finally lose my virginity!!

TWANKEY
What?

GENIE
A lamp Genie cannot have sex until she is free.

TWANKEY
What about those poor, poor boys from Scunthorpe?

GENIE
I retained my maidenhood on a technicality.

TWANKEY
I lost mine on one.

GENIE
Now, Aladdin...

TWANKEY
You keep your hands off him!

GENIE
The wish.

WISHY WASHY
Wait wait wait... We have one wish, right? We could go anywhere, meet anyone, do anything.

ALADDIN
I know.

WISHY WASHY
Look, Aladdin... what if the Prince really is in love with Abanazer? I mean, he's all university and you're more... Uniclo.

TWANKEY
You, quiet. I'm gonna get me some royal I-beg-your-pardons if it's the last thing I do.

ALADDIN
I wish we could be inside the palace. Beam us up, Siri.

GENIE
Sound the trumpets and deck the halls
My magic will send you through solid stone walls
One more wish, and then I'll be free
For some lovely sex and a nice pot of tea!

They disappear into the palace.

Scene 14: The palace

Abanazer is on the phone. The GIMP is by his side.

ABANAZER
Listen 'ere Barack me old son. I'm in charge of the UK now so how about us doing some business me old china? (pause) He's hung up!

GIMP
Mate, he's the president of America. That's like president of Johnny Depp.

ABANAZER
Take it from me, twinky kinky, the whole fucking world will do what I want once I increase the magic power of the Palace. Place creeps me out if I'm honest. The rooms move about of their own accord and the portraits follow you round the room like a fat lonely emo twink on crystal meth. Right. Let's go and meet me adoring public.

He exits

GIMP
I wish Lauren was here. You must think I'm obsessed but she's brilliant. She'd know how to stop him. When we get outside, I'm going to leg it and try and find her. Wish me luck boys and girls.

He exits as he does the POLICE WOMAN enters followed by the PRINCE and EMPEROR

POLICE WOMAN
Ello, ello, ello! I'm trying to find the control room of the palace but I don't want Abanazer to see me.

She starts creeping backwards looking out for him. The PRINCE and EMPEROR enter, also creeping backwards. They bump into the POLICE WOMAN and they all scream.

POLICE WOMAN
Why are you creeping about?

PRINCE
I'm hiding from Abanazer! I – I can't believe it. He made me marry him!

POLICE WOMAN
Now from my observations...

PRINCE and EMPEROR
Yes?

POLICE WOMAN
We're in London–

PRINCE
We know!

POLICE WOMAN
And everyone is under Abanazer's control.

PRINCE
But we're not.

POLICE WOMAN
Leave this to the expert if you don't mind, sir.

EMPEROR
Perhaps the magic only works outside the palace.

PRINCE
Abanazer won't know that. Let's pretend we're under his power, and when we get the chance we'll overpower him.

POLICE WOMAN
Precisely what I was going to say. But what about the boys and girls?

EMPEROR
I don't think we could overpower them all. Someone caught your eye, eh?

POLICE WOMAN
I mean they'll have to pretend to be under his power as well. Can you do that?

ABANZER enters, talking to his ring.

ABANZER
Trying to get away like that! Consider yourself at home in there. Permanent.

He taps his ring.

GIMP
Let me out!

ABANAZER
No.

GIMP
I'm out of loo roll!

The POLICE WOMAN frowns, recognising the voice.

ABANAZER
Aha! Adoring husband! Father in law! You...! Have you been avoiding me? But no, you're all under me control ain't you? Say yes master.

POLICE WOMAN, EMPEROR and PRINCE
Yes master.

ABANAZER
And how about you lot?

POLICE WOMAN, EMPEROR and PRINCE indicate to audience to speak.

ABANAZER
Let's see... Stand up.

POLICE WOMAN, ABANAZER and PRINCE indicate to audience to stand.

ABANAZER
The power! Right, now everyone shake hands with person on the left of you. (They try...) Ha, this is brilliant. The power! Alright. What next? Now give both your neighbours a kissywiss.

ABANAZER moves so he is next to the PRINCE, the PRINCE looks concerned but kisses him, the EMPEROR kisses the POLICE WOMAN, really going for it.

ABANAZER
Excellent. Now, everyone. Strip! (he looks at the audience) On second thoughts... (To the PRINCE) but you can.

The PRINCE looks unhappy, he starts to remove his shirt.

PRINCE
I'm sorry. I can't.

ABANAZER
You're lying! All of you! You ain't under me control. That don't matter, I still got the power, hey, yeah, heh. Cos I own the Palace.

He clicks his fingers, there is a flash. The PW, EMPEROR and PRINCE can't move.

EMPEROR
God damn it I'm frozen like a Spaniard's pay packet.

POLICE WOMAN
Me too.

ABANAZER
Now, time to tie you up and decide your fate. And you, me very own sugar plum princess. I got an opening for a new gimp.

There is another flash, ALADDIN, TWANKEY, WISHY and the GENIE appear.

ABANAZER
Welcome to the party.

TWANKEY
I've gone right off you Mr Abacus, so slide your balls someplace else (looking around) Ooh lovely place you got. (noticing) Your emperorness!

EMPEROR
I am all stiff Widow Twankey.

TWANKEY
Oh I say! Do you know how to play filthy hoopla?

ABANAZER (*grabbing TWANKEY*)
Just what I need. A washerwoman.

TWANKEY
Get your hands off me Jim Davidson[87].

ABANZER
And a cook, it's dinner time.

He lets go of TWANKEY and grabs WISHY.

ABANAZER
You lucky little chimp. Yours'll be the first head I smashed in since I dropped that fridge on that little man's head all them years ago.

TWANKEY
Fridge! You bastard!

TWANKEY lunges at him. ALADDIN joins in. A fight.

GENIE
Violence is not the answer!

TWANKEY
Why's that, scared you'll pop a hip out?

GENIE
Aladdin, you've still got once last wish.

ALADDIN
You need that last wish, Siri. Don't waste it on him! I can overcome him with my bare hands.

TWANKEY
Say that again?

---

[87] Davidson was arrested as part of Operation Yewtree over allegations of a historic sexual nature in the wake of the Jimmy Savile scandal. In 2013 the CPS decided not to take further action.

ALADDIN
I can overcome him with my bare hands.

TWANKEY
Yeah, I thought I'd misheard you.

ALADDIN leaps at ABANAZER knocking him to the ground.

ALADDIN
Release them and give the Palace back to the Emperor so he can go back to China.

EMPEROR
Oh there's no rush. There's a bar called the Missing Tassle I read about in the Lonely Planet.

ABANAZER
Before you rescue your precious Prince, you might like to have a look at what's on me phone. Before I release it to The Sun. Get it out me pocket will you?

ALADDIN
Ha. Yeah alright. Idiot.

ABANAZER indicates his front trouser pocket. ALADDIN reaches in and has a rummage, which ABANAZER enjoys greatly. After a while he pulls his phone from inside his jacket.

ABANAZER
Oh, yeah. It's in me jacket pocket.

ALADDIN takes the phone and looks at the photos.

ALADDIN
Oh my god!

PRINCE
It's from before! I kept one. I looked so pale and interesting.

ALADDIN
No it ain't. This an orgy! And it was taken last week!

GENIE
Goodness. There must be thirty men there.

ALADDIN
It's like Where's Wally.

TWANKEY
Where's willy.

ABANAZER (snatching back the phone)
Well we've had to entertain ourselves, and the palace dungeons seemed so perfect.

ALADDIN (to PRINCE)
Couldn't you wait for me?! I've broken into this palace twice to find you!

PRINCE
WELL THAT'S REALLY KIND OF CREEPY!

ALADDIN
Don't shout at me!

PRINCE
I CAN'T HELP IT the writers had caps lock on.

ALADDIN
And you married him, you... slut!

PRINCE
He forced me!

The GENIE takes the phone and shows it to him.

GENIE
Forced you to do that?

PRINCE
Wait. I'm not in this photo! Hang on. (To Abanazer) You bastard! Why wasn't I invited?

ALADDIN
Ha. So you would have!

PRINCE
I didn't think I'd see you again! And it's alright for you. You're experienced!

ALADDIN
Not with 30 men at once. (Counts on his fingers, for quite a while.) Yeah, definitely not with 30 men at once. And why wasn't *I* invited?

ABANAZER
You were in a cave!

ALADDIN (*grabbing Abanazer by the throat*)
Let them go.

ABANAZER
Very well.

He clicks his fingers, the PRINCE, POLICE WOMAN and EMPEROR are released from the spell.

TWANKEY
Your empirical regency, you're free!

EMPEROR
You luscious little lychee.

He kisses TWANKEY. The POLICE WOMAN is looking out of the window.

POLICE WOMAN
Looks like the civilians out there are still under his control.

ABANAZER
You think a few cretins like you can stop me? Time to get some help.(He rubs his ring) Gimp!

The POLICE WOMAN is still looking out of the window so doesn't see what happens next. There is a flash and the GIMP enters.

ABANAZER
Get him off me.

The GIMP throws himself at ALADDIN who is still holding ABANAZER down. The POLICE WOMAN turns around. The GIMP has his back to her so she cannot see his face.

POLICE WOMAN
Ello, ello, ello what's going here then. Get off him you bully!

She leaps on the GIMP, pulling him around to face her.

POLICE WOMAN
Colin!

GIMP
Lauren!! Kiss me quick.

POLICE WOMAN
Not now! Oh Colin look at you! I wanted to be your girlfriend not your fag hag! Why didn't you tell me? You said you wanted a gap year, you just wanted your gap filled.

GIMP
Eh?

POLICE WOMAN
Look at you, mincing in here from Old Compton Street dressed like a show pony.

GIMP
I've been stuck in his ring!

POLICE WOMAN
Spare me the details!

GIMP
I had an ancient curse put on me. The only way I can be released is to be kissed by my first love.

POLICE WOMAN
Goodbye, goodbye, goodbye.

GIMP
And you're not just my first love Lauren. You are my only love.

He takes her in his arms and they kiss. A long slow kiss. He lets her go.

POLICE WOMAN (dreamily)
Ello ello ello.

ABANAZER rubs his ring. Nothing happens.

ABANZER
Shit, it ain't working. Back in the ring gimp.

GIMP
Nah, nah de nah nah. I'm free. It's get your own back time Abanazer.

He joins ALADDIN pinning ABANAZER against the wall.

GIMP
Now give the Emperor his Palace and release that lot down there.

ABANAZER
And if I don't?

ALADDIN
You'll be taking the quick route to join him. To the window!

The GIMP and ALADDIN pick ABANAZER up and start to throw him out of the window.

ABANZER
Come on lads. Let's talk about this.

GIMP and ALADDIN
One

ABANAZER
We can work it out.

GIMP and ALADDIN
Two.

ABANAZER
I'll turn meself in. Give back the Palace.

GIMP and ALADDIN
Three

ABANAZER
Alright! The deeds are in me pocket.

He nods down towards his trousers. They put ABANAZER down and put one hand each in each trouser pocket, searching, which ABANAZER again thoroughly enjoys. After a while:

ABANAZER
Oh yeah. Me jacket pocket.

ALADDIN removes the deeds and hands them to the EMPEROR.

ALADDIN
There you go. It's all yours again mate.

EMPEROR
Jolly dee. Widow Twankey, will you live here as my queen?

TWANKEY
Me? A royal?! Do I get tickets to Wimbledon?

ALADDIN
You hate Wimbledon.

TWANKEY
I like it when it rains and you see all the ballboys tent-poling.

She kisses the EMPEROR.

PRINCE
And I'd like you to live here as my queen Aladdin.

ALADDIN
I really like you dammit but I can't be with a married man.

TWANKEY
So, what, did you have the whole civil thingyship?

PRINCE
A what? We got married. In a church. He made the archbishop of Canterbury do it.

EMPEROR
He made me wear a sailor suit.

TWANKEY
Have you still got it?

ALADDIN
Ha. You ain't married!

PRINCE
What?

ALADDIN
Gays can't get married here yet. You ain't married.

PRINCE
That's ridiculous! This is Britain! A modern, progressive, democratic country! Of course they can.

TWANKEY
Nah he's right. And don't question my boy.

PRINCE
Oh, well! Thank god for bigots everywhere and the slow-turning wheels of democracy! (He takes his ring off) I'm not married! Aladdin-

EMPEROR
He can't be your queen!

PRINCE
Then I can't be your son.

EMPEROR
Nonsense. A queen? He's shown himself to be quite the man.

PRINCE WOMAN, TWANKEY, WISHY
That's sexist!

The Prince puts his wedding ring on Aladdin's finger and they kiss.

POLICE WOMAN
Oh Colin! I thought I'd never see you again.

They kiss again. ABANAZER raises his arms and clicks his fingers. The GIMP collapses.

POLICE WOMAN
Colin!!

ABANAZER
Ha! The magic ain't drained away yet.

The POLICE WOMAN feels for the GIMP's pulse. She shakes her head.

POLICE WOMAN
No!

ABANAZER
I'll make a little deal with you. I'll get out of your lives and reverse this spell if you give me one thing.

TWANKEY
No love you missed your chance, I'm a betrothed woman now.

ABANAZER
Oh it's nothing really. I just want a nice little dinner. A dinner of smoked monkey brain.

ALADDIN
No way.

WISHY steps forward.

WISHY
We'd best be off then.

ALADDIN
Wishy, no!

WISHY
Hey. This is my first line in this scene. Let me say it. I'll go. I can't stand in the way of the happiness of these two young lovers.

ALADDIN
Wishy use your head!

ABANAZER walks over to WISHY

ABANAZER
She is doing! Good girl.

He starts to lead WISHY off, the POLICE WOMAN coughs and points at the GIMP.

ABANAZER
Oh yeah.

He clicks his fingers and the GIMP comes back to life. ABANAZER and WISHY exit. We hear a loud noise – perhaps a chainsaw - and a scream from WISHY. ABANAZER enters with a monkey brain on a plate. It has a sprig of holly in the top.

ABANAZER
Brains before beauty!

ALADDIN throws himself at ABANAZER knocking the brain off the plate. The GIMP catches it screams and throws it to someone else, it gets thrown around the stage.

ALADDIN
Get out of here. Siri, I'm sorry. I want to use me last wish. I wish you'd banish Abanazer!

GENIE
As you wish, Aladdin.

There is a crash ABANAZER spins around and drawn out by a dark and mystic force screaming. TWANKEY is now holding the brain.

TWANKEY
My poor sweet monkey!

ALADDIN
Siri, you couldn't-

GENIE
I'm afraid not dear, you've had your three wishes.

PRINCE
What about the magic of the palace dad?

GIMP
Yeah, have a go lad.

EMPEROR
I'm no Harry Potter you know... I could do with a hand.

TWANKEY
Mine would normally be available but I'm holding a brain.

EMPEROR
Then the boys and girls will have to help me. Boys and girls, repeat after me. "Power of the Palace come to me". Come on now everyone: Power of the Palace come to me.

ALADDIN
Has it worked?

TWANKEY (looking at the brain)
I don't think so love.

EMPEROR
Brain surgery is a very delicate business dear boy. We'll need to give someone the power of a brain surgeon.

ALADDIN
So it could be any one of us? Or one of the boys and girls.

GENIE
Can anyone put a brain back?

ALADDIN
Anyone? I know it ain't the kind of request you get on Cam4....

TWANKEY
Oh come on. It's brain surgery. It ain't rocket science. It's simple ain't it. You connect the cranial nerves first, starting with the olfactory, before moving on to the trochlear, then-

EMPEROR
Dear lady it's you! You have the power!

446

TWANKEY
Oh lawks. But I'm just a poor washer woman.

ALADDIN
You've got to save Wishy.

POLICE WOMAN
You've got to try!

GIMP
Yeah, come on love.

TWANKEY
Give us a scalpel then.

PRINCE
I'm not sure we've got one.

TWANKEY
Well... A knife and fork?

PRINCE
Will these do?

He hands her some chopsticks.

TWANKEY
I don't use chopsticks. Well, only when I've run out of ear buds.

ALADDIN
Come on Mum, before the magic wears off.

TWANKEY exits, we hear terrifying sounds off stage – drilling and sawing. When she re-enters she has blood on her hands, she looks worried.

ALADDIN
Mum?

WISHY enters and everyone cheers.

ALADDIN
Oh Wishy!

EMPEROR
My dear, you did it. Now come along everybody. We have a wedding to prepare for.

TWANKEY
Oh your Emperorness. I hope I stand comparison with your last wife. What was she like?

EMPEROR
Very sweet, but a bit of an old-fashioned racist.

TWANKEY
Well I think we're the perfect match.

EMPEROR
Why?

TWANKEY
Because my dildo says "made in China" on it and that's a perfect fit.

She kisses him. They exit.

EMPEROR (off stage)
Come on everyone get your skates on.

WISHY, GIMP and POLICE WOMAN exit. ALADDIN and the PRINCE go to follow them.

PRINCE
Come on Siri.

GENIE
I'm afraid I can't. Now that you have had your three wishes you are no longer my master. And I must return to the lamp.

ALADDIN
Oh yeah. Well cheers, you've been wicked.

PRINCE
Aladdin!

ALADDIN
I'm sorry and all, but what can I do?

GENIE
If you were to give the lamp to someone else as a gift, then they would become my master and I wouldn't be trapped inside.

ALADDIN
I was gonna to flog it. It's well valuable.

PRINCE
Aladdin, look around you. We've got the palace now! And you've got me. What more do you need?

ALADDIN
Meh. Go on then.

He picks the lamp up.

ALADDIN
Who would like this lamp?

The GENIE points at the audience member she was speaking to earlier.

GENIE
He does.

447

ALADDIN

There you go mate.

He hands the audience member the lamp. The GENIE runs over to the audience member and sits on his lap.

GENIE

Master. Your wish is my command.

ALADDIN

You don't seem all that happy.

GENIE

Well. He's very lovely but what happens when he's had his wishes? Back in the lamp, tossed to fortune again. Unless…

ALADDIN

Mate you're the only one who can help her. Will you wish her free?

The audience member wishes her free.

GENIE

Oh thank you! As my parting gift you can have one wish to keep. But save it till you get home. I'll be thinking of you..!

ALADDIN

And we'll take this lamp back to the British Museum in the morning.

PRINCE

Come on, let's help them get ready for the royal wedding of the century. And then we can swap coming out stories! I want to get drunk with you.

ALADDIN

I want to get high with you.

PRINCE

I want to get naked with you.

ALADDIN

I want to get pizza with you.

PRINCE

What?

ALADDIN

I want to show you my city.

PRINCE

Can you show me the world?

ALADDIN

I know a very good place to start.

PRINCE

The beginning?

ALADDIN

The bedroom. See you later boys and girls!

ALADDIN and the PRINCE exit. The GENIE is left alone. The lights fade, except on her.

GENIE

And now it is time to take to your carriages,
For your hearts and your ears we thank you for lending them
For while many tragedies begin with marriages
Everyone knows that comedies end in them!

We hope you've been charmed by our shambolic myth,
There've been no Greek Heroes, King Henrys, or Russians,
Not even a small part for Sheridan Smith -
But we won't make you stay for a post show discussion.

We can't all have genies to make things right,
But we can all make the best of what we've got
So as we fade into the cold winter night
With our love and kind wishes, be gone, that's your lot.

THE END.

Sleeping Beauty: One Little Prick

Ellie Fiore as Aggie, Mitchell Lathbury as Josh, Matthew Ferdenzi as Beauty, Matthew Baldwin as Lady Gargoyle and Philip Lawrence as Angus in *Sleeping Beauty: One Little Prick*. Photo by Derek Drescher.

Steven Rodgers as Sidney, Mitchell Lathbury as Josh, Matthew Baldwin as Lady Gargoyle, Samantha Ridings as Carabosse, Philip Lawrence as Aggie 2, Ellie Fiore as Maggie, Matthew Ferdenzi as Beauty, Greg Airey as Prince Edward and Mandy Dassa as Fairy Glowstick in *Sleeping Beauty: One Little Prick*. Photo by Derek Drescher.

Sleeping Beauty: One Little Prick

2011. Olympic fever and good old British Olympic scepticism had gripped the country with the games to take place in Stratford, London the next year. In February, WikiLeaks founder Julian Assange unsuccessfully fought a Swedish application to extradite him on suspicion of rape. (The following year he would seek refuge at the Ecuadorian Embassy in London.) Tents were pitched in front of various London landmarks as the group Occupy protested for global democracy. The second series of the hugely popular Downton Abbey aired. Tom Daley would not come out as gay for another two years but he gets his first Bradfield-Hooper pantomime joke in this script – it wouldn't be his last.

The challenge with Sleeping Beauty is also its most potent opportunity: the hundred-year gap in the middle of the story. We created a Downton-esque world with the fictional Stratford Manor, before time-travelling to 2011 Stratford where the Olympic Stadium was being built, and found plausible reasons for some of our characters to have lived for more than a century, depending on how plausible one considers a tortoise butler and a vampire prince. (Choreographer Matthew Bourne also went down the vampire route with his Sleeping Beauty the following year). Even for our pantomimes this one gets farfetched at the end but we're pleased with how we used the two periods and the societal changes between them.

The songs were mainly re-written musical theatre numbers including a "straight" version of *I Am What I Am*, and they were better integrated than in Robin Hood the previous year, or indeed Aladdin the following year.

Sleeping Beauty was the first time we worked with Andrew Beckett, who would go on to direct all our subsequent pantos. Andrew was Company Manager but made a brief appearance at the end of the show playing a lusty tortoise. On stage for under a minute, he managed to steal the show every night.

Sleeping Beauty: One Little Prick

By Jon Bradfield and Martin Hooper

Characters

Fairy Glowstick, a good fairy.
Lady Gargoyle, the matriarch of Stratford Manor. To be played by a man.
Beauty, her son.
Carabosse, the Wicked Fairy, Beauty's aunt.
Josh, the footman at the Manor.
Aggie, the chambermaid.
Sidney, the butler at the manor, and a tortoise.
Prince Edward, a pale prince from Tinselvania.
Angus, Aggie's father, a pub landlord.
Aggie 2, Angus's great-great-granddaughter. To be played by the same actor as Angus.
Maggie - Aggie's great-great-granddaughter. To be played by the same actress as Aggie.
Mani, an Indian tortoise.

Aggie 2 is to be played in drag by the same actor as Angus. Maggie is to be played by the same actress as Aggie. Mani may be played by a stage manager.

Act One is set in 1890 and 1911.
Act Two is set in 2011 and 2012.

Sleeping Beauty: One Little Prick was first performed at Above The Stag Theatre on 25 November 2011 with the following cast and creative team:

Fairy Glowstick: Mandy Dassa; Lady Gargoyle: Matthew Baldwin; Beauty: Matthew Ferzdenzi; Carabosse: Samantha Ridings; Josh the Jester: Mitchell Lathbury; Sidney: Steven Rodgers; Aggie/Maggie: Ellie Fiore; Prince Edward: Greg Airey; Angus Steakhouse/ Aggie 2: Philip Lawrence

Director: Paul Taylor-Mills; Set and Costume Designer: David Shields; Lighting and Video Designer: Richard Lambert; Choreographer: Jason Marc-Williams; Additional choreography: Richard Jones; Musical Director: Matt Randall; Stage Manager: Fabrice Arfi; Company Manager: Andrew Beckett; Press and Publicity: Katharine Ives; Artwork and Programmes: Jon Bradfield; Poster illustration: Leo Delauncey; Production photography: Derek Drescher; Front of House Assistant: Alan Clark; Producer: Peter Bull

Lighting equipment supplied by LAMBCO Lighting Ltd. Thanks to Out of Joint Theatre Company, Barbara Williams and Suneeda Maruthiyil.

Prologue

A swirl of music. A spotlight. Into it staggers the FAIRY. She's recognisably a fairy, but dishevelled and clutching a bottle of ale. She speaks with a rough Glaswegian drawl.

FAIRY
There's a story gets told this time of year
Of a virgin, a child and a birth
Now the first two are barred from the pubs round here
But here's our tale, for what it's worth

The year's 1890, the setting the borough
Of Stratford some miles to the east
You'll have heard that they're planning for something or other
But that's decades away at least

For in Stratford's dark streets shineth
The vomit and horseshit and piss
From the drunks and the traders, you'd want to wear waders
Or better still give it a miss

But overlooking the less desolate side
A great manor house stands aloof
Where Lord and Lady Gargoyle reside
In the last dying flush of their youth

In summer their orchard is bursting with fruit
In winter its wood fills the hearth
The servants are many and so fucking cute
You'd have them fill more than your bath

Now our Lord and Lady want a baby so much
But he spends all his time in Soho
Gambling and drinking and smoking and such
So his sperm is at best, well, so-so

But they're having one! He's our hero! You must help him win
And save him from deep, dreamless sleep;
And we've a foul wicked fairy and, well, 'masculine' women
But that's nothing new in this heap

And I'm the good fairy, whose mission tonight
Is to see us to the curtain call
So boo, hiss and cheer, and all of that shite
And I'll see that we all have a ball

Now we actors are easily dazzled
So phones off, you'll not need reminding
And if any young ladies have been vajazzled
Keep your legs closed, we don't want blinding

Oh Stratford, we've waited this moment for years
It's time for good and evil to fight
Cos the hopes and fears of a couple of queers
Begin, right here, tonight

We hear a voice – LADY GARGOYLE's.

LADY GARGOYLE (unseen)
Push! Push..!! That's it, push! Nearly there! Yes, push!

And then...

LADY GARGOYLE (unseen)
Oh, lick my tits!

FAIRY
Boys and girls, there's been a deception
That's not the birth that's the conception
But using the magic of pantomime
We'll whizz forward 7, 8 er... 9 months in time!

Lights up/curtain open. It's 1890, and we're in a bedroom in Stratford Manor, a grand house. LADY GARGOYLE is in bed in a nightgown, giving birth. The fairy assists her. Nearby is a crib.

FAIRY
That's it my lady, push. You've got plenty of stretch left – I bet with you it's not so much sex as hula-hooping. Auch don't mind me, I've seen plenty of open sesames in my time.

LADY GARGOYLE
You've been a midwife a long time?

FAIRY
No love, I just like a bit of pocket.

LADY GARGOYLE shuts her legs

FAIRY
Don't do that! One more push and we've got the fucker.

She pushes and screams. The FAIRY takes the baby, smiles at it.

LADY GARGOYLE
What is it?

FAIRY
It's... it's green.

She holds the baby aloft. It is, indeed, green. Music from the musical "Wicked" plays.

LADY GARGOYLE

Green?!

FAIRY

Maybe it just wants ripening... hold up, this is that animatronic prop they've been looking for down the road[88].

She flings the baby offstage, where it lands with a thud.

FAIRY

Defying gravity my arse. Right, come on love, try again.

LADY GARGOYLE *moans and pushes.*

FAIRY

Here it is... A bonny wee boy. Where do you want it?

She places the baby into a crib, and then turns the crib around so we can see the baby. It has the head of the actor who plays BEAUTY.

LADY GARGOYLE

Is he... healthy?

FAIRY

Auch yes. Lovely soft stubble. What are you gonna call him?

LADY GARGOYL

His name will be "Cutie"

FAIRY

You can't call a boy cutie!

LADY GARGOYLE

My father's name was Gaylord, and my brothers are Evelyn, Dorian and Elisabeth. What about Beauty?

FAIRY

Beauty it is. Give him some tit and I'll summon the fairies for the baby shower.

LADY GARGOYLE

That sounds dangerous.

FAIRY (to the audience)

It sounds like something they found in Michael Jackson's DVD collection.

LADY GARGOYLE

We can't have it now, I'm wearing a nightie and on the verge of lactation.

FAIRY

I've already invited them. They'll bestow magical gifts on him. And with you being on the posher side of things, probably some boring as shite wooden toys

LADY GARGOYLE feeds the baby.

FAIRY

Aw look at that.

LADY GARGOYLE

Who are you anyway?

FAIRY

I'm Fairy Glowstick, your nominated Good Fairy. For some reason I've been sent to keep an eye on the boy. I'm not gonna lie, you could have done better than me, but the powers that be have given me one last chance to prove myself.

LADY GARGOYLE

With my baby?!

FAIRY

If I see your son safe through life, I can retire to the great fairy garden in the sky.

LADY GARGOYLE

What if you don't?

FAIRY

You lot'll shout out if you see the baby in danger won't you? Where have the fairies got to? They should have been here by now... Right, hold on a second.

The fairies all have gone astray
They'll be making merry and flying while pissed
But we don't need them anyway
We've got enough fairies in our midst!

Let's see if that's worked. Have a look under your seats - right under the seat, that's right. Has anyone got a gift?

Three people should have found small gift bags under their seats. The FAIRY invites them onto the stage.

---

[88] Above The Stag Theatre's first venue was a stone's throw from the Apollo Victoria where Wicked was playing (and still is at the time of writing).

FAIRY
Come and join us, there you go. Come on boys and girls, show them your appreciation. (Then towards the back row) Just your appreciation, sir, you filthy bastard. Hello fairies! Oh look at them it's like A Midsummer Night's Dream but without the, you know, fucking depth. Angels from the realms of zone 3. To the first fairy) Right, you love, what's your name? Lovely, now have a look in your wee bag there. What have you got?

In the bag is a little card.

FAIRY
Can you read that out for us?

AUDIENCE MEMBER 1
By the light of the moon, I promise you'll find
The boy will be sweet-natured, soulful and kind

LADY GARGOYLE
Like mother like son. Now go and sit down.

FAIRY
Right, let's try for a bike or something this time. Go on, hen.

AUDIENCE MEMBER 2
By the light of the sun, this sweet young nave,
Will grow up to be noble, strong and brave

FAIRY
Next time you're invited just click "not attending". Off you go. (To the third fairy) What have you got?

AUDIENCE MEMBER 3
By the soft light of Venus
He'll have a big penis.

FAIRY
Well done fairy number three! Give him/her a round of applause.

CARABOSSE enters, behind the audience member, and cackles.

CARABOSSE
Mwah ha ha ha ha! (To audience after they boo) No, no, don't get up. (To the audience member) You can sit down now, we don't need any more amateurs on stage.

LADY GARGOYLE
Cousin Carabosse!

CARABOSSE
A party for my nephew and I'm not invited?! Just because my brother's a good-for-nothing layabout doesn't mean *I* can't play a part in the boy's upbringing. (To the audience) I'm so modern I'm already into James Blake. Spurned! Forgotten! Neglected! Abused!

FAIRY
Abused?

CARABOSSE
I'm holding out, we've got two hours of this. I will pay my respects to the new heir. What a cute lickle baybee! I will give my own blessing. No, not a blessing. A curse! Ha ha ha ha ha!

LADY GARGOYLE
You see, this is why you never get invited to things.

CARABOSSE
Listen up fairies, this'll make you cry
When the boy turns 21 he'll prick his finger and die!

FAIRY
No!

LADY GARGOYLE
No!

BEAUTY
No!

LADY GARGOYLE
Heaven's devils. Can't you do anything?

GOOD FAIRY
I can roll my tongue up at the sides. I call it the clit clutcher.

LADY GARGOYLE
Then you'll excuse me, I need to rid this house of pricks.

CARABOSSE (at audience)
It's a bit late for that. Toodle-oo. Oh and, congratulations!

LADY GARGOYLE exits. The FAIRY looks at the CARABOSSE

CARABOSSE
What?

FAIRY
Prick his finger and die!? That's a shite curse.

CARABOSSE
Oh no it isn't

Oh yes it is! etc

FAIRY
Why not just say, when he's 21 he'll die? What's with shoving a prick into things?

CARABOSSE
Listen, glow worm.
I'm sorry that you
seem to be confused
He belongs to me
The boy will die[89]. Now what have we got here.

FAIRY
These are the boys and girls.

CARABOSSE
I thought someone said we had a sexy crowd in tonight.

FAIRY
They're gonna help me put an end to your evil doings.

CARABOSSE
I told you, I'd had a dodgy stomach. They won't stop me. Look at them, I've seen healthier looking muscles in a Belgo's lunchtime special. Oh but this one's rather

nice. (To a man in the audience) Have you heard? There's going to be hacking scandal. When I hack into your pants. (To someone else) And you, what's your name? How strange! Are you sure it's [name]? Cos you don't look at all like a [name]. You look like a cunt.

CARABOSSE exits.

FAIRY
I hope none of you thought this was going to be arty
Trust the old auntie to spoil the party.
Now we're going to skip two decades on,
Watching boys grow up can't be all that fun
All farting and wanking, B.O in his pits,
And I can't let you see our young hero with zits
So let's catch up with our favourite young whelp
We need some more magic, and you're going to help,
Boys and girls, hold hands, and say after me
"Fast forward, fast forward" – wait - one... two.. three...

"Fast forward fast forward"

Now the manor's still standing, but getting quite shabby
And no longer a place of marital bliss
It's 1911 - that's like Downton Abbey
And here I must leave you, I'm off for a piss.

Exits.

---

[89] The Wicked Fairy quotes or mangles a lot of pop lyrics. *This is The Boy Is Mine* by Brandy & Monica. See notes at the end of this script.

Scene 1: The kitchen of Stratford Manor

1911. A large working kitchen. A stove burns. We hear a car chugging nearer across a gravel drive. It skids and crashes, and moments later the wheel of an old car rolls onto the stage and teeters over. A young footman, JOSH, runs on in pursuit of it. He's friendly-faced with a glint in his eye.

JOSH
Heel! Oh, hello boys and girls! Tell you what, the butler was right, I need to get me ears syringed, I said HELLO BOYS AND GIRLS. That's more like it! I'm Josh the Jester, and nice to meet you it is too.

He high-fives a few members of the audience.

JOSH
I invented that handshake, I reckon it might catch on. I say I'm Josh the Jester but technically speaking I'm Josh the Footman, here at Stratford Manor. That's Stratford in London in case anyone was hoping for a night of thought-provoking theatre. I'd much rather be on stage though than here in the kitchens. I thought of joining the circus but they make you jump through hoops. I'd be great in the music halls. Or in those new moving pictures they got! Have you seen em? The slapstick ones are the best, although *(he looks about him)* you can also get slap and tickle ones. I don't know why they call them that cos it's mainly just fucking. If I got into the movies, Aggie would start to notice me. Aggie's the maid here. She's ever so ream.

Here, I will be in trouble. I've dented the motor. I'm not supposed to drive it really. It's one of the new ones, vintage they call em. Listen, if anyone asks how that wheel got there, you won't tell on me will you? That's great, we'd better have a practise. If anyone asks you how that wheel got there, I want you to say, "I ain't seen nuffin". Got that? Let's give it a whirl. *(He puts on a posh voice).* I say, how did that wheel get there?

The audience answer.

JOSH
Common as muck.

SIDNEY (offstage)
Joshua!

JOSH
Cripes. That's the butler. He'll be here in a minute. He's a bit slow.

SIDNEY enters. He's dressed formally, and is a tortoise.

SIDNEY
What is this? Have you been driving?

JOSH
No sir! I've been talking to the boys and girls.

SIDNEY looks momentarily embarrassed, straightens his tie, fixes his hair.

SIDNEY
Oh, ah, how do you do boys and girls. Can you tell me how this got here?

They do.

JOSH
Anyway I can't drive, the car needs looking at. It made a very funny noise last time I parked it.

SIDNEY
What kind of noise.

JOSH
Sort of a crashing noise. Thing is, Mr Sidney sir, I got to learn how to drive for when I'm famous in the music halls in case I need to get away from hoards of screaming crowds.

SIDNEY
Waving pitchforks, I expect.

JOSH
Or crowds of screaming whores. That motorcar's a right maid magnet. I written a song about it for my act. "Her Bodice on my Bonnet": Do you wanna hear it?

SIDNEY
No.

JOSH
You lot wanna hear it don't you?

SIDNEY
Give up these ridiculous dreams. Work hard and one day you'll be a butler yourself in a fine house. The stage is no place for a respectable man, and in any case you don't have what it takes. If you sing your silly song to these sophisticated theatre-goers you'll only make a fool of yourself.

SLEEPING BEAUTY: ONE LITTLE PRICK

JOSH is crestfallen. He encourages the audience to say "aahhh"

JOSH
No you're probably right sir. After all, it gets a bit filthy.

SIDNEY
Perhaps I should listen to it once, just to see that it rhymes properly, that sort of thing.

JOSH
Well if you insist.

He coughs and sings:

I got distracted from my steering
Cos me cock caught in her earring
When her mouth was heading south just for a bet
She'd never do it with the roof up
So if sometimes we'd pick a youth up
In the rain some double anal she would get

That's as far as I got.

SIDNEY
Is it based on anything I'd know?

JOSH
I don't think so sir, it's based on experience

BEAUTY enters in his pyjamas. He has an erection. His gift of a large penis is apparent.

SIDNEY
Good morning, sir.

BEAUTY
Morning Sidney.

JOSH
Mornin, Beauty

BEAUTY
Oh that's very kind.

JOSH (He notices the erection)
Hello sailor, going fishing?

BEAUTY
What? Oh!

JOSH gives him his cap to hold over his straining crotch.

JOSH
It's usually me what gets sent down here to get wood.

SIDNEY
Boys and girls, may I introduce the young master of the house.

BEAUTY
How charming to meet you – will you stay?

SIDNEY (looking at Beauty's groin)
Well sir, unless there's anything I can assist you with.

BEAUTY
That will be all, thank you.

SIDNEY shuffles off

JOSH
You spend a lot of time down here in the kitchens these days.

BEAUTY
It's so dull in the house. Mother's bored, she keeps trying to arrange marriages for me. And I get lonely… It's more fun down here with you.

JOSH
We've had some fun times ain't we.

BEAUTY
Do you remember when we used to…

JOSH
What, go hunting?

BEAUTY
Well yes, that, but

JOSH
Take the car for a spin?

BEAUTY
Do you remember when we used to fool around?

JOSH
Oh! Haha course I do. Funny isn't it how you never think you'll grow out of it and then of course you do.

BEAUTY (lying)
Yes, haha… Silly, isn't it…

JOSH
Some of them ladies in the village…

BEAUTY
What about them?

JOSH
They got some very dirty daughters sir. I'm quite popular.

BEAUTY
Of course you are… How many have you slept with?

457

JOSH

No idea, I can only count to shitloads. I'm surprised you ain't had a dabble, you're a hell of a catch.

BEAUTY

It's not as easy in my position.

JOSH

Nah, you do it in a different position with girls. Well, you do with the pretty ones... I'll tell you the best thing about girls, they got a hole round the front too, and you don't even have to use spit to put it in that one.

BEAUTY

I didn't have to use much to put it in yours.

JOSH (considers this)

Yeah that's true. Funny how it hurts like hell the first time you do it, but you know what? (to audience) "it gets better"[90]. You finished with my hat?

BEAUTY

Give it a minute.

JOSH

Tell you what though, I'd give all that up for Aggie if she'd have me. She's so special I sometimes think about her if I'm having trouble finishing off.

AGGIE enters. Aggie is clearly in love with Beauty.

AGGIE

Finishing what off?

BEAUTY

Handy little jobs around the house.

AGGIE

Morning sir!

BEAUTY

Morning Aggie. How are you?

AGGIE

Oh, you know sir. Mustn't complain. I will have a grumble though.

BEAUTY

What is it?

AGGIE

It's like a moan or a whinge, but that's not important right now. Poor dad might be evicted from the inn, what with your evil fairy god-auntie putting the rent up.

BEAUTY

That's awful.

BEAUTY takes her hands in his. The cap stays "magically" in its place, suspended on his erection.

AGGIE

Can't you have a word with her?

JOSH

Morning Aggie...

AGGIE

Oh, sorry Josh, I forgot you were there. I better get on. Her ladyship...

SIDNEY enters, saying...

SIDNEY

I have requested that you stop calling me that, Agnes.

AGGIE

Yes Mr Sidney.

She exits

SIDNEY

Sir, there was one thing. Two more of the chickens are dead.

BEAUTY

Poor things. Josh and I will see to the fencing. It'll be that fox.

SIDNEY

That's what I thought too sir – until I found the fox. They seem to have been drained of their blood.

AGGIE re-enters, gives a little sigh, and faints into BEAUTY's arms

JOSH

Aggie!

AGGIE

It's ok, I was just practicing.

JOSH

(To Beauty) You keep that hat good and tight sir. If something's after blood you'll be a prime target.

---

[90] The "It Gets Better" campaign and organisation was founded in 2010 in response to the suicides of teenagers bullied for being – or being thought to be – gay.

AGGIE
Maybe it's a wolf! And I heard down the village that someone saw a strange figure creeping about in the dark.

BEAUTY
That was Josh, *apparently...*

AGGIE
No it was some tall handsome type. Are you looking forward to your birthday?

BEAUTY
Not especially. You'll both come won't you? And you Sidney?

SIDNEY
I shall be in my quarters with a DVD sir.

JOSH
A what?

BEAUTY
A double volume Dickens. Nonsense, you'll enjoy it. We'll soon have you out of your shell.

They all laugh at this, except for SIDNEY.

SIDNEY
Well I'm glad we got that one out of the way early on.

JOSH
Nah, I reckon that one could be a running gag. Well not running, obviously. Shuffling.

Again, they laugh.

BEAUTY
Please come. I don't have many friends. It'll be all snooty young ladies my mother wants to palm me off on.

JOSH
I could palm a few off if that would help.

AGGIE
Disgusting.

BEAUTY
If I really have to marry a girl, I wouldn't want any of the ones mother chooses. I'd rather marry someone nice, like...

AGGIE
Like who sir?

JOSH catches BEAUTY's eye.

BEAUTY
It doesn't matter.

LADY GARGOYLE (off)
Agnes!!

AGGIE
Coming your ladyship

JOSH
Battleship.

LADY GARGOYLE enters and slaps BEAUTY

BEAUTY
It wasn't me!

LADY GARGOYLE
Then pass it on.

BEAUTY slaps AGGIE. AGGIE slaps JOSH. JOSH slaps SIDNEY. SIDNEY slaps JOSH back.

JOSH
What was that?

SIDNEY
A ricochet.

LADY GARGOYLE
What *are* you doing in the kitchen, Beauty? You know it's not safe. You'll have a prick in your hand or worse before you've even swallowed Sidney's porridge. *(She sees the audience).* Oh my, hello. One forgets how many underlings we have down here paddling away keeping this old duck afloat. I won't remember you all I'm afraid. *(To a man in the audience)* Though you seem to be fingering a recess in my memory.

BEAUTY
Mum, these aren't the servants. These are the boys and girls.

LADY GARGOYLE
Have they been searched?

She rolls up her sleeves and heads into the audience rummaging about.

LADY GARGOYLE
I'm just going to have a feel about for any pricks. *(To an audience member).* Even a very tiny prick could see my son stiff on his back.

BEAUTY
Mum!

LADY GARGOYLE

Don't spend all evening in the kitchen pitying my peeling old jugs and damp, musty drawers and Sidney's misshapen utensils will you? You must all attend my son's birthday celebration. *(To a man in the audience)* I have a gaping space awaiting your fulfilment on my dance-card sir. Ah, to be among my own people. What a time it is for a landed lady. I'm broke, I can't inherit, I can't do anything.

AGGIE

That's why we should be supporting these suffragettes, your ladyship.

LADY GARGOYLE

There's no money you see, boys and girls. Only the house. And I would lose that if anything happened to Beauty... I'm all sagging frontage and no hard cash.

JOSH

I'd make a suggestion, yer ladyship, but I don't think this lot are the right punters for a lady's... hospitality

LADY GARGOYLE

Are you suggesting I take a tenant!?

JOSH

You could charge a few pence for a small holding

LADY GARGOYLE

I am rather desperate

JOSH

As would they be

LADY GARGOYLE

I've a champagne palate and a – well, and a champagne cellar. But that'll be gone after Beauty's birthday party. We're down to our last ten bottles

JOSH

Eight

LADY GARGOYLE

Eight?

JOSH

It could have been ten. I was pissed by the time I'd finished counting

BEAUTY

I've had the best idea! We'll have my birthday party at the inn.

AGGIE

Oh, Beauty! Really?

LADY GARGOYLE

An inn?!

BEAUTY

Why not? It would help Aggie and her father out. It's cosy and there's a piano.

LADY GARGOYLE

I patronised the place one Christmas and nearly swallowed a mouthful of pricks when Agnes's father brought out the cheese and pineapple. And his whopping Prince Albert was up and out where anyone could touch it

AGGIE

Prince Albert?

LADY GARGOYLE

Whatever they call them. Ludicrous vulgar balls hanging off it.

BEAUTY

That's a Christmas tree.

LADY GARGOYLE

Nevertheless, an inn! You will not lower yourself to take a pricking from every direction.

BEAUTY

I'm going to be 21, mother. I'll do as I please. I'm going to have a bath.

SIDNEY

I'll be right up, sir.

BEAUTY

Really, Sidney, I can run a bath. If I've grown out of my wooden duck, I can do without a lifeless tortoise.

BEAUTY exits

LADY GARGOYLE

What have I done to deserve this? Boys and girls, you wouldn't be found in the disused function room above a run-down public house[91] would you?

SIDNEY

Perhaps, my lady, you should take your son to examine the place. I'm sure he will see that it is unsuitable. Just let him realise it for himself.

---

[91] Above The Stag Theatre's first venue was a disused function room above a run-down public house.

LADY GARGOYLE
You're not as slow as you appear, Sidney. Now, my watercolours...

AGNES
I wish all I had to worry about was where I was gonna have my sodding birthday party.

LADY GARGOYLE
And what is that supposed to mean?

AGGIE
Nothing, ma'm. Just some of us have it harder than others, that's all...

SONG: SIX TO TEN
(To the tune of Dolly Parton's 9 to 5)

AGGIE
Panic at the bell and tumble out of bed
Make someone else's breakfast from someone else's bread
Don't yawn or stretch or they'll dock my wage again.
No time to bathe so I'm always stinking
Hope this song's got a lot of you thinking
Of folks like me on the job from 6 till 10.

AGGIE, JOSH AND SIDNEY
Working 6 to 10
Though it's often till eleven
Working 6 to 10

LADY GARGOYLE
But on Sundays you start at seven

AGGIE, JOSH AND SIDNEY
It's an upper-class world
And we run it from the bottom

JOSH
It's enough to make your balls ache – if you got em

AGGIE, JOSH AND SIDNEY
6 to 10
It's your parentage that matters
We don't dream my friend
Cos we know our dreams get shattered
They can't clean their house though somehow they got it listed
It's a damn surprise they can wipe their arses unassisted

AGGIE
The only boys I meet are too posh to look at me

JOSH
The girl I really like she just wants to cook for me
AGGIE, JOSH I got no time for love or me or friends.

AGGIE
Things might be better if women had power
But that ain't gonna happen any time now
And we'd still be working here from 6 to 10

AGGIE, JOSH AND SIDNEY
Working 6 to 10,
it's a dawn til dusk existence
Then you start again, ain't no point in no resistance
It's all look-don't-touch at the shiny things around us
Hell with us down here it's quite the miracle you found us

6 to 10
Scrubbing floors and cleaning dishes
Will it never end?
Skinning rabbits gutting fishes
Them that live upstairs, surely they know where the brains are
But we just clean their smalls and wonder what the stains are.

Scene 2: A street in Stratford

We hear a steam train pull away from a station, and a cloud of steam fills the stage. It is night. Cold. An owl hoots. The steam clears revealing PRINCE EDWARD. He is handsome and pale and speaks with an Eastern European accent. He carries a bag.

EDWARD
Good evening boys and girls. My name's Edward. Prince Edward. I'm from a tiny country called Tinselvania, and I've been travelling around Europe on my gap year.

The owl hoots. PRINCE opens his bag and pulls out an owl.

EDWARD
What's wrong, Coulson? Are you getting restless? (To audience) Oh but I tell you, I've never seen anything like London. Harrods! All those pretty pale out of work actor boys behind the counters. And I've taken tea with Asquith. Your Liberal party goes from strength to strength doesn't it? But the delicate romantic in me is hoping for a bit of rough and tumble in the seedier parts of the capital. (To a man in the audience) I'm sure you can guide me to a few seedy parts, my good man. I hope it won't be dangerous for a lonely traveller.

CARABOSSE sneaks up behind him, menacingly. "She's behind you!". EDWARD steps aside and turns to see her. He puts his owl back in the bag.

CARABOSSE
It *is* you!
EDWARD
Carabosse!!

CARABOSSE
I know what you're all thinking. "21 years later and she hasn't aged a bit". But I'm an actor darlings, we spend most of the day googling ourselves, it's not a stressful life. (To Edward) My my, how long has it been since our fleeting, steamy encounter in those delightful Turkish baths in Budapest? You spent hours trying to shake off that young masseur.

EDWARD
You said that, should I ever find myself travelling alone in your country, you might point me in the direction of entertainment.

CARABOSSE
With pleasure. Although I realise this *(the theatre)* seems an unlikely place to find it. But tell me: How is your little... peculiarity?

EDWARD
It's not a peculiarity. I was nervous and inexperienced.

CARABOSSE
Come, come. Ooh I shouldn't say that actually should I, it might set you off again. But I was referring to your other little problem. Your-

There is more thunder and lightning

CARABOSSE
Your-

There is thunder and heavy rain.

CARABOSSE
Some intervention is required. A spell.

The fairy tries to click her fingers but is shit at it.

CARABOSSE
You try.

The Prince also is shit at it

CARABOSSE
"I thought we'd be great together, but we just didn't click." Ah well.

She claps her hands. The PRINCE is thrown an umbrella from the wings. He puts it up. It is black and impressive. CARABOSSE is thrown an umbrella. She puts it up. It is small and flowery. She looks disappointed.

CARABOSSE
Where were we?

EDWARD
I've travelled throughout Europe. I've stayed with crown princes in great palaces. And now I wish to experience something more humble...

CARABOSSE
Then welcome to Stratford! They only built it to put the Martians off from landing, but then you look about (she indicates at the audience) and you see they failed. Now, there *is* someone nearby I think you'll find rather charming.

EDWARD
Are you matchmaking?

462

CARABOSSE
I've been likened to Emma in the Jane Austin novel.

EDWARD
Which Jane Austin novel?

CARABOSSE
I forget the title. But this young man: Beauty by nature and indeed beauty by name.

EDWARD
He would have to be tolerant of my... specific tastes. And he would have to love me forever.

CARABOSSE
Believe me, I know about forever.

She strokes the Prince's face for a moment, wistfully.

CARABOSSE
Now, run along. Why not start with that little pub over there?

EDWARD
Thank you. May I take this? *(umbrella)* You wouldn't want me to arrive with my shirt all wet.

CARABOSSE
Oh yes we would. (etc)

EDWARD
Very well.

CARABOSSE
Don't speak like that, this isn't goodbye.
I much prefer: 'fuck off and die'.
Ha ha ha ha ha ha!!!!

She exits.

EDWARD
What a coincidence, we're so global these days. Goodbye everyone, see you later!

He exits.

Scene 3: The pub

An East End pub. A bar juts into the run-down tavern from the wings. ANGUS enters.

ANGUS
Hello boys and girls. Angus is me name, Angus Steakhouse. Welcome to me humble little establishment 'ere in the east end. Have you met me daughter Aggie? She lives here too but she works at the big manor 'ouse for that beautiful LADY GARGOYLE Bet *she* don't have trouble paying the rent.

CARABOSSE enters

CARABOSSE
Tootlepip Mr Steakhouse.

ANGUS
I ain't got it.

CARABOSSE
Well don't stand too close just in case.

ANGUS
Me rent.

CARABOSSE
What's all this fuss about your rent, there won't be penny to pay.

ANGUS
Oh thank you, I knew what they say about you weren't true.

She hands him an eviction notice.

CARABOSSE
I'm evicting you.

ANGUS
But it's our home. It's my livelihood!

CARABOSSE
It's not been lively enough. I need a dollar, Angus, a dollar's what I need[92].

ANGUS
Madam Carabosse!

CARABOSSE
Breaking up is never easy, I know, but you have to go. Knowing me, knowing you it's the best I can do. You

_____
[92] Aloe Blacc, *I Need A Dollar*

have until the end of the week. Now, I'll survey my property before I reclaim it.

She exits towards the cellar, the entrance to which is behind the bar. She begins to do a comedy down the stairs' walk behind the bar.

ANGUS
If you're going down the cellar mind the-

A clatter as she falls down the stairs

ANGUS
- step. That reminds me boys and girls. If anyone else heads down to the cellar, will you tell them to mind the step for me? You're good people. Oh heck boys and girls what am I gonna do?

The GOOD FAIRY enters.

FAIRY
Evening Angus. A bottle of ye finest malt please.

ANGUS
Really?!

FAIRY
Nah, any old shite.

ANGUS gets a bottle, blows dust off it and hands it to her.

FAIRY
How are things with you?

ANGUS
Takings is bad, Glowstick. The landlords just evicted us and I thought a fox had got me chickens.

FAIRY
And it hadn't?.

ANGUS pulls a dead fox from behind the bar and pops it on top of the bar.

ANGUS
I'll stick it in the steak and kidney later. But it's poor Aggie's little pussy I'm concerned about. *(He reaches behind the bar and pulls out a cat.)* You'll keep an eye on it for me won't you?

FAIRY
Aye, it will be a pleasure.

ANGUS
Play with it a bit, she likes it being stroked.

FAIRY
Now Angus, would I be right in thinking your Aggie had a lively pair of puppies and all?

ANGUS
You would be.

ANGUS pulls out a basket with two puppies in.

FAIRY
And what about her perky little ass?

ANGUS
Time was Aggie's was the most admired ass in Stratford. It won't get through the door now and anyway I don't want shit all over me carpet again. Boys and girls, please give us a shout if you see anyone coming near Aggie's puppies and pussy won't you?

ANGUS and FAIRY turn away and start to talk, EDWARD creeps on whilst they are talking.

ANGUS
Truth is I don't know what I'm going to do.

EDWARD grabs a puppy. When the audience shout, EDWARD drops the puppy and runs out.

FAIRY
Have some respect, gang, the man's got problems and I got a hangover like Caligula.

EDWARD creeps back on as ANGUS continues talking.

ANGUS
We'll be out on the street me and my Aggie

The audience shout.

FAIRY
Keep it down we're only three feet away..

EDWARD takes the other puppy and is about to bite its neck. AGGIE, BEAUTY, JOSH and LADY GARGOYLE enter. The PRINCE drops the puppy and hides under a table.

AGGIE
Hello Dad. Lady G and her handsome son are here to see you.

ANGUS
Oh my! Lady Gargoyle! What an absolute pleasure.

He kisses her hand. She wipes it on Josh.
ANGUS You're ever so welcome to our humble tavern.

LADY GARGOYLE

Beauty, I've seen enough. Just look at the clientele. (*She does look at them, spots a man she harangued earlier*). Hello again young man. You do pop up unexpectedly.

BEAUTY
I think it's perfect.

AGGIE
You can stroke my pussy if you're gentle sir. It's got a bit wet but don't mind that, it needed a clean. I just can't get it to lick itself.

FAIRY (*downing her whiskey*)
You keep talking lass. Got any more Ang?

ANGUS
There's some down the cellar.

The FAIRY starts to exit towards the cellar, doing the 'down the stairs' walk. Then she tumbles out of sight.

ANGUS
You need to be quicker than that boys and girls. LADY GARGOYLE, I can have the place real nice for your boy's party. What an honour it would be to have you on my table.

LADY GARGOYLE
Many men would like to have me on their table but I'd rather do it in our banqueting hall where there's room for so many more. I intend to squeeze the prime minister in and you know what the king's like with his elbows. He comes up from a munch spilling all across his lap and if one catches it in time one can feed the servants for a week.

JOSH
Is there anything I can do to help?

ANGUS
That's kind. You could get us a barrel from the cellar.

JOSH
I'm always ready to help you and Aggie.

JOSH exits down to the cellar. He trips and screams.

BEAUTY (following in haste)
Joshy! Are you all right?

LADY GARGOYLE
Be careful!

BEAUTY runs to the cellar and falls – we hear him and JOSH yelping.

LADY GARGOYLE
Vigorous vicars! He's gone down on the footman.

LADY GARGOYLE, ANGUS and AGGIE move over and gather around the cellar.

ANGUS
Beg pardon my asking, is it true what they say about your son being a bit... (whistles)

AGGIE
Dad!

LADY GARGOYLE
A bit (whistles)?

ANGUS
My mind boggles at it. Bet you can't your heads round that can you boys and girls?

EDWARD sees his opportunity to leave. As he starts to run out BEAUTY and JOSH reappear dirty and dishevelled. EDWARD hides again.

JOSH
It's amazing how you fell right on top of me Beauty!

BEAUTY
Could I borrow your hat again?

JOSH
That fairy's knocking back your whiskey.

LADY GARGOYLE
It's is a pit of debauchery.

ANGUS
Please, Lady Gargoyle, have a look yourself.

LADY GARGOYLE
Very well.

She starts to exit to the cellar. She screams and falls.

JOSH, AGGIE and ANGUS exit after her down to the cellar. BEAUTY goes to follow too but as he does he turns, just as EDWARD comes out of hiding. Their eyes meet. EDWARD puts his finger to his lips to tell BEAUTY to be quiet and gives him a smile. BEAUTY gives him a cheeky smile back.

BEAUTY
Who are you?

JOSH, ANGUS, AGGIE help LADY GARGOYLE back in - she has a large cobweb in her hair. EDWARD hides again, taking one last look at BEAUTY.

LADY GARGOYLE
Get me out of this hellhole.

AGGIE
So you going to have your party here Beauty? I'll lay on something special. Do you a nice spread.

BEAUTY appears not hear, he is thinking of EDWARD.

AGGIE
Beauty? Sir?

BEAUTY
Yes, yes, of course. It's perfect.

LADY GARGOYLE
Landlord, what champagne do you have?

ANGUS
Well there's... there's all sorts of beers down the cellar. Why don't we all go and choose some!

They all walk to the cellar and one by one they scream and fall down the "stairs". The FAIRY emerges, drunk, carrying empty bottles.

FAIRY
Mind the fucking step.

The crashing chords from The Phantom of The Opera. CARABOSSE enters.

CARABOSSE
You can't stop looking me, staring at me, be what I be[93]... I know what you're thinking.

FAIRY
I'm thinking I'm wasted here.

CARABOSSE
Quelle surprise, chap-stick. You're thinking, there's been a balls up. I fell down the cellar and now here I am exquisitely framed in the doorway like a well hung Holbein. Well ha! That's the sort of magic you're up against.

FAIRY
I can do magic.

---

93 Cher Lloyd, *Swagger Jagger*

She does that thing where it makes it look like you're pulling you're thumb off.

CARABOSSE
Witchcraft!! But I'm not scared.

FAIRY
You ain't invited neither.

CARABOSSE
I'll hold my own party for the nincompoop nephew. A special party where he'll finally get the prick he's always dreamed of! The prick that's hung over him, like a purple-headed pendulum! Like the pork sword of Damocles! Hahahahaha!

Exits.

FAIRY
She had a hard time at Roedean. Oh hell's bell-ends. I got to do something.

EDWARD comes out of hiding.

EDWARD
Yes, we must.

FAIRY
Who the fuck?

EDWARD
Who is that boy?

FAIRY
That's Josh. The bad news is he's not into boys. The good news is if you're quick he won't notice.

EDWARD
No, the well spoken one.

FAIRY
Beauty. I'm his fairy godmother. And he's in trouble, his wicked auntie Carabosse wants to kills him so he'll inherit the mansion.

EDWARD
What? When? Where? Why?

FAIRY
Lay off the questions. My heads starting to throb like a dick in a mousetrap.

EDWARD
We have to do something to help him. Come on, let's make a plan!

Edward starts to escort the Fairy out. She stops, returns to the bar, picks up a bottle then follows him.

Scene 4: The orchard at Stratford Manor

Sunshine. LADY GARGOYLE sits in a deckchair, a glass of something nearby. AGGIE hands her a newspaper. LADY GARGOYLE opens it – there is an iron-shaped hole burnt in the front page.

LADY GARGOYLE
Aggie you've burnt a hole in it. But look! A foreign princess has come to Stratford! A perfect match for my son, don't you think?

AGGIE
Yes m'am.

LADY GARGOYLE
Far more suitable than any of you local girls. Tell Sidney to send her an invitation to Beauty's party tonight. No! Even better, she must come and stay here at the manor. You'll make her up a room. Now run along.

AGGIE
Yes m'am.

She runs off.

LADY GARGOYLE
Aggie!

AGGIE
Yes m'am?

LADY GARGOYLE
What have I told you about running?

AGGIE
Sorry m'am.

She goes.

LADY GARGOYLE
Boys and girls, here we are in my beautiful cherry orchard. I used to play here with my three sisters but they're in Moscow now. Such beautiful weather, I may indulge in a spot of sunbathing. One hopes the high walls will put off any opportunistic photographers

She slips off her robe and strips to her undergarments, turning the process into a rather length striptease, then settles into her chair again.

LADY GARGOYLE
Boys and girls, will you wake me up should anybody approach?

EDWARD enters holding a letter and carrying a parasol to keep the sun off. He looks lost. When the audience shouts, LADY GARGOYLE opens her eyes, watches him for a while, and arranges herself seductively. After too long, she screams.

LADY GARGOYLE
Oh!!! A man! And here I am all vulnerable and alone. You could do anything to me and my screams would go unheard. *(pause)* FYI.

EDWARD
Good afternoon.

LADY GARGOYLE
You'll have come to snaffle my apples. How did you get in?

EDWARD
Your butler was kind enough to guide me in behind him. I received an invitation.

LADY GARGOYLE
You must be the princess's chap.

She shows him the paper.

EDWARD
My Lady, I fear your little hole has caused you some confusion.

LADY GARGOYLE
It is not my little hole it is my maid's little hole.

EDWARD
It does not say "Princess coming to Stratford", but "Prince is coming to Stratford". I heard I could find Beauty here.

LADY GARGOYLE
(Delighted) Young man!

EDWARD
Your *son*.

LADY GARGOYLE
Oh. Then you must be my guest at his birthday party tonight. Now, sunbathe with me.

EDWARD
I...

LADY GARGOYLE
I insist.

She begins unbuttoning his shirt.

EDWARD
My Lady

LADY GARGOYLE
Don't be coy, I frisk all visitors lest a rogue prick should arise. Now close your parasol, I can always help you get it up later.

EDWARD
My lady, I do not take kindly to the sun.

LADY GARGOYLE
Clever Sidney has invented a special lotion that protects us fair creatures from the sunshine. Sidney!

SIDNEY enters with a bottle of sun lotion.

LADY GARGOYLE
I thought Sidney had been learning the piano but he was merely polishing his scales. Now Sidney if this young gentleman does me, could you bear to do him from behind?

SIDNEY
With pleasure.

They get into position. Sidney behind Edward, Edward behind Lady Gargoyle. Edward has the bottle of lotion.

LADY GARGOYLE
Grip it hard, give it a good old shaking and paste me all over.

EDWARD puts the bottle down on the floor and rubs lotion into LADY GARGOYLE's shoulders.

LADY GARGOYLE
Don't hold back, I won't break.

EDWARD gasps.

LADY GARGOYLE
What is it?

EDWARD
It was cold when it hit my back.

LADY GARGOYLE
It can't have been the lotion, the bottle's still down here.

SIDNEY (embarrassed)
Forgive me sir...

LADY GARGOYLE
Look at us. It's like that Edgar Allan Poe horror story, the human millipede.

EDWARD
So this house – is it yours?

LADY GARGOYLE
Technically Beauty has been the true owner since my husband died and left me a single, young and potentially available grieving widow. But he couldn't do without me.

EDWARD
Why?

LADY GARGOYLE
You or I might stomach a prick with no more difficulty than a knife slides into warm butter. But Beauty is, alas-

EDWARD
Beauty is, surely, a lad.

SIDNEY
Just a touch from one little prick and he's finished.

EDWARD
I used to be the same.

LADY GARGOYLE
But wait, I have nobody to rub. Now let me see... Who can I rub off on?

She gets some lotion on her hands and goes wandering into the audience in search of someone. Meanwhile, SIDNEY picks up the lotion and applies it to EDWARD. He starts screaming.

LADY GARGOYLE
Whatever is the matter?

EDWARD
My skin`s burning! What's in this stuff?

SIDNEY
It is but milk, flour and garlic.

EDWARD
Garlic?!

LADY GARGOYLE
An aphrodisiac. You're overheating.

SIDNEY
He's overacting.

EDWARD wipes it off hastily then picks up the parasol. BEAUTY enters. He and Edward look admiringly at each other.

LADY GARGOYLE
Beauty, my new friend, Prince Edward.

BEAUTY
(To audience) Fit. (To Prince) Pleased to meet you. And is your... wife travelling with you?

LADY GARGOYLE
He's unattached! And tired, I'm sure, of silly young girls throwing themselves at his feet. (To Edward) Not your type at all I expect. (To beauty) Prince Edward is to escort me to your party tonight! We're having a quail stuffed into a heron stuffed into a badger.

SIDNEY
There's a gentleman's club in Vauxhall where they stuff an otter with a bear.

They all look at SIDNEY. BEAUTY turns to EDWARD.

BEAUTY
Let me show you this.. er... (pointing at someone in the audience) shrub.

They come forward, BEAUTY leading the PRINCE with a hand on his back. He finds it sticky.

BEAUTY
What's this on your back? It smells like turtle soup. And why are you undressed with my mother?

EDWARD
Get rid of these people and meet me back here. I need to talk to you alone.

BEAUTY
Mother, the Prince is tired from his travels. Might we leave him to rest?

LADY GARGOYLE
Very well. Should you wish to make me come it only takes a raised finger.

LADY GARGOYLE and BEAUTY go to leave. SIDNEY stays looking at EDWARD.

BEAUTY
Sidney, come along. We'll find you some radishes.

SIDNEY
Radishes!

They leave. EDWARD sits in the chair with his parasol. The FAIRY enters.

FAIRY
Hey diddle diddle the cat did a widdle all over the kitchen floor. The little dog laughed to see such fun, 'That cat's such a skanky old whore'... Get your shirt on, you, if the boys and girls want to perve at an Eastern European on his gap year they can look at the ads in the back of QX[94]. Have you warned him yet?

EDWARD
I'm meeting him here later... Are you sure he likes men?

FAIRY
That one'd have his mouth round your balls quicker than a hungry hungry hippo. But if you want him to like you for sure, you need to cheat.

EDWARD
Cheat?

FAIRY
Listen up. I get around more than Times New Roman. I've handled more puppies than Cruella De Ville, but only by bending the rules. (She fishes a little bag from her pocket) Here, I got some magic love powder left over from the dyke ball at the Bath assembly rooms. Right.

She slaps his knee, sits on his lap, picks up the drink and gives it to him.

FAIRY
Hold this

She sprinkles the powder into the drink.

FAIRY
Take a swig of this magical potion, you must,
And the first who crosses your path
Will fall madly in love and in lust with you
Don't fear, it's just drugs, they're a laugh.
It may taste a little bit sickly
But the best things in life make you gag
Now the thing is, it wears off quite quickly
So no flirting - get straight to the shag.

EDWARD
You are very kind.

---

94 In 2011 the back pages of weekly gay magazine QX were still filled with ads for rent boys.

FAIRY

I'm the bitch's titties darling. I'm the best hope for singletons until Marks and Spencers food hall starts selling dildos. Right, don't think, drink. I'm off to the pub. Good luck.

She playfully punches his arm. It really hurts. She goes.

EDWARD

Bottoms up, as they say in Berlin.

EDWARD drinks some of the drink then places the glass on the floor. He tries to relax, leans back and goes to sleep. LADY GARGOYLE enters, sees EDWARD asleep and quietly takes a sip of the drink. She fondles EDWARD, who wakes and instantly loves her.

EDWARD

My Lady!

LADY GARGOYLE

Sweet prince. I'm sorry to wake you.

EDWARD

Nothing in my dreams could match the beauty that stands before me.

LADY GARGOYLE

I thought it was just a fold in your trousers.

EDWARD

Touch me.

LADY GARGOYLE

Touch me.

EDWARD

No you touch me.

LADY GARGOYLE

Fucking touch me now.

LADY GARGOYLE and EDWARD sing a very passionate rendition of "Touch-a Touch-a Touch Me" from The Rocky Horror Show, then exit deeper into the orchard.

BEAUTY enters

BEAUTY

Edward! Edward...? Have you seen him? What that way? Was he alone? She's barking up the wrong cherry tree with him. I wasn't even sure if he liked gentlemen but then I saw that parasol... I'll wait for him to come back. Ooh, a drink! Shall I have some, boys and girls?

He settles in the chair, takes a sip of the drink and shuts his eyes. JOSH enters.

JOSH

Hey hey people! I'm trying to find Aggie.

He sees Beauty and is smitten.

JOSH

Oh! Young master Beauty! I tell you what, when you see him in this beautiful dappled sunlight...

He takes a sip of the drink.

JOSH

Don't mind if I do.

BEAUTY wakes.

BEAUTY

Josh!

JOSH

Do you remember when we used to-

BEAUTY

Go hunting together?

JOSH

No...

BEAUTY

Take the car for a spin?

JOSH

Do you remember when I used to bend you over a tree stump and turn you inside out?

They kiss. Edward arrives in a state of undress. He doesn't see them at first.

EDWARD

I don't know what came over me!

He notices the boys kissing and embracing, and is very upset. Not seeing him, they drag each other off into the orchard. Aggie enters.

AGGIE

Oh hello sir. Have you had a nice turn in the orchard?

The PRINCE is about to storm off.

AGGIE

Charming! Oi!

EDWARD

Forgive me?

AGGIE

You posh boys, you look at me and all you see is my apron. It wouldn't hurt to mentally undress a girl once in a blue moon! Go on. Piss off.

EDWARD exits

AGGIE

Beauty's the same. Oh I'm not naive. But I wouldn't mind not shaving me legs and letting him do me the Old Testament way. And if he's got to marry a girl it's not like he's had much luck with the posh ones is it? And then there's Josh. But he'd stick it in the mouth of a lion if it winked at him twice. He's been round the village more times than our paper boy, and that paper boy's a right skank. Josh doesn't really like me in a special way does he? Does he really like me? Has he said so? Maybe I've not given him a chance. I should spend some proper time with him. Will you tell me if you see him? Oh thank you boys and girls. *(She notices the drink).* Ooh. I am thirsty. *(She picks it up and is about to drink...)* Ew it smells worse than Josh's fingers.

AGGIE puts the drink down and wanders to the front of the stage. JOSH and BEAUTY enter on one side of the stage still making out as they cross the stage and exit on the other side. The audience cry "they're behind you".

AGGIE

Sorry, I got totally distracted then thinking about kittens. What did you say?

JOSH and BEAUTY come on again. Aggie sees them but they don't see her.

AGGIE

Beauty! Josh! Oh..!

She runs off. The magic wears off on JOSH.

JOSH

What are you doing mate? I said I wasn't into this anymore.

BEAUTY

I... I wanted to find Edward.

JOSH

Well he's not in my fucking mouth is he? Look, we'll just forget it happened. Agreed?

BEAUTY

Agreed. *(To the audience)* I am so going to wank about this.

JOSH

And you can't wank about this.

BEAUTY

Of course! *(To audience)* I really am going to wank about this rather a lot.

JOSH

Shit! we got to get ready for the party.

BEAUTY

Right, right. See you back at the house....

He exits.

JOSH *(calls after him)*

Beauty! I mean it.

BEAUTY *(off)*

I've already started wanking!

LADY GARGOYLE returns

LADY GARGOYLE

Oh! Josh!

JOSH (backing away)

No no you're alright LADY GARGOYLE. Have you seen Aggie?

LADY GARGOYLE

That young man – I think he tried to bite my neck!

JOSH

Did you pull him off?

LADY GARGOYLE

A lady doesn't tell. Oh Josh he put me in mind of a, a vampire.

JOSH

He ain't a vampire! I got this book on monsters. A vampire can't come into your home unless he's invited.

LADY GARGOYLE

Oh God.

JOSH (folding up the deck chair)

It's been a funny old afternoon. Here, Lady Gargoyle. Would you allow me to escort you to the party?

LADY GARGOYLE

You may escort me back to the house, Josh. *(Shivers)* There's a chill now. I trust Angus has heating. It would be unseemly to spend the entire evening with one's hands never leaving one's muff. Now, will you take a lady's arm?

JOSH

I'd have to work up to it from a finger. Come on m'Lady.

With the deck chair under one arm he offers her his other arm. She takes it. They go to leave. She spots the rest of the drink, picks up the glass to take with her, takes his arm again. They exit.

Scene 5: The pub

A stepladder. A recently painted banner saying "Happy Birthday Beauty" is in the process of being hung up. AGGIE is mopping the floor, wearing trousers. JOSH enters.

AGGIE

Josh, you'll get me floor dirty! And you'll slip. Why don't you take me rug out and give it a banging.

JOSH

What are you wearing?

AGGIE

If you men can wear them why can't we?

JOSH

Cos it's harder to look up trousers. You ain't one of them suffering jets are you?

AGGIE

We just want equality.

JOSH

Listen. We get equality, you get tits. Anyway we're different. We got spatial awareness.

He goes to climb the ladder and, obviously, completely misses the step and falls on the floor.

AGGIE

Come on get working. We've got to get this place right for Beauty.

JOSH picks himself up and pulls a little box from his pocket.

JOSH

I wanted to give you this. See, me Mum, may she rest in peace, she gave it me when I was little and I always said I would give it to a girl who I really liked.

AGGIE opens it and takes out a locket. She opens it and stares sat the picture inside.

AGGIE

Is it a piglet?

JOSH

It's a baby.

AGGIE

No wonder she kept it hidden in here.

JOSH

It's me.

AGGIE

Oh yeah. I see it now. Ta Josh.

She puts the box on the table.

JOSH

Don't you like it?

AGGIE (unconvincingly)

Yeah. It's great. I might put a picture of Beauty in it.

JOSH

What? I'm a catch, you know. Even Betty at the cycle shop says so and she's got a tongue so long she can French kiss me while she's licking my arse.

AGGIE looks at him briefly and continues mopping.

AGGIE

Then you don't need to get jiggy with Beauty, do you?

JOSH

What?! I didn't... It was him... It was laugh.

AGGIE

Who has sex for a *laugh*?

JOSH

I dunno. Fat people?

JOSH picks up a book from the table and tries to read the title.

JOSH

"Tits Androgynous..."

AGGIE

It's Shakespeare. I'm gonna be clever like Beauty, I bet he knows all Shakespeare's plays.

JOSH

I do too.

AGGIE

You.

JOSH

Some of them. A Midsummer's Ice Cream. The Dromedary of Terrors. I've even wrote a song about that Romeo geezer.

AGGIE

Yeah?

JOSH

Where's the piano?

AGGIE

We pawned it. Use the bar.

JOSH sits at the bar and plays it like a piano. He starts to sing "This Can't Be Love" from the musical The Boys From Syracuse. He's uncertain at first but gains confidence as he gets into it. Aggie is really charmed – she takes the locket from its box and smiles at it.

BEAUTY enters with a tray of custard pies. AGGIE drops the locket on the table and runs over to him.

AGGIE
Dad hasn't got you working on your birthday?

BEAUTY
I don't mind. Nice trousers!

AGGIE sticks her bum out as obviously as possible.

AGGIE
They make my bum look like a boy's...

Beauty doesn't react.

AGGIE
Ugh! I better see if Dad needs a hand. See you later Beauty.

BEAUTY
Yes, see you.

JOSH
Bye Aggie.

Aggie appears not to hear.

JOSH (shouting)
Bye Aggie!

AGGIE
Oh you are funny! Bye!

She exits. Josh looks miserable.

BEAUTY
Cheer up. It might never happen.

JOSH
That's just it. She's never going to like me.

BEAUTY
Well I like you.

JOSH
You know what I mean.

BEAUTY
She... she said you were funny. Josh the Jester! Star of music hall, theatre and film!

JOSH
Me?

BEAUTY
Of course! Imagine we're like that vaudeville act we saw at the Theatre Royal on your birthday. You be the funny one, I'll be the good looking one.

JOSH
Yeah! (Frowning, offended) Hang on! (A moment) They did that custard pie routine didn't they?

BEAUTY (chuckling)
Oh yes!

JOSH
Thing is I don't think I'd be no good at that.

BEAUTY
It's simple old chap. You just get a pie *(he picks up a pie)* Hold it like so. (He places the pie in front of Joshs' face, Josh looks at it) And deposit it. *(he pushes the pie into Josh's face)*

JOSH
I, I don't think I quite saw that mate.

BEAUTY
Not to worry. You just pick up a pie and do this. *(he picks up a pie and plants it in Josh's face)*

JOSH
Hold on, I need to practice. So I just get a pie *(he picks up a pie and holds it in front of Beauty)* And then I throw it...

BEAUTY steps aside.

BEAUTY
Not at me old chap. I need to observe you doing it. Check your wrist action and all that.

JOSH
Then who can I throw a pie at?

They both turn to look at the audience, mischievous.

JOSH
I can't throw pies at the boys and girls mate. So stand still will you.

BEAUTY
You really don't want to push a single pie in my face.

JOSH *(Picking up a second pie)*
Yeah you're right there mate. I'm not going to push a *single* pie in your face.

He deposits a pie on each side of Beauty's face.

BEAUTY
That was not funny.

He picks up a pie to throw at JOSH. As he does AGGIE enters and naturally gets hit with the pie.

AGGIE
Josh how could you!

She plants a pie in JOSH's face then turns to BEAUTY.

AGGIE
Come with me, I'll give you a good rub down, get you clean.

JOSH
I need a rub down too!

BEAUTY
I'll do it.

AGGIE
You get this place clean before Dad comes in

AGGIE and BEAUTY exit. JOSH starts to clean up. ANGUS enters. He puts a record on the gramophone[95].

ANGUS
Good lad.

ANGUS goes up the ladder and finishes hanging the banner. SIDNEY enters. ANGUS and SIDNEY start dancing like a bull and a matador. LADY GARGOYLE enters.

LADY GARGOYLE
This horrid modern music. *(She turns it off)*. Now Angus, I don't expect to see any unprotected pricks this evening.

ANGUS
You look ever so lovely tonight. Have a drink.

He hands LADY GARGOYLE a beer. She looks at it unsure but accepts it. Sidney helps himself to a sherry. The GOOD FAIRY enters

ANGUS
What can I get you, you crazy fairy?

SIDNEY
I'm fine with my sherry thank you.

FAIRY
Surprise me.

ANGUS
I'm rich, you're successful and he's got an eye for the ladies.

---

95 We used Billy Merson's 1911 recording *The Spaniard That Blighted My Life*.

ANGUS places a bottle of whiskey and a glass in front of the FAIRY. She ignores the glass and drinks from the bottle.

FAIRY
Where's the sound?

ANGUS
Come over' ere girls and rifle through me selection.

They turn around as they do so CARABOSSE enters disguised as a radish seller. The audience shouts.

LADY GARGOYLE
Please, we're compiling our set list.

She returns to the records.

CARABOSSE
It's me, disguised as a humble radish seller. (Louder, with a bad accent) I am a humble radish seller! Who will buy my lovely radishes, nibble my radishes.

SIDNEY
Radishes?!

CARABOSSE
Delightful, delicious, delectable, de.. deep fried radishes.

SIDNEY tries to eat the radishes. The CARABOSSE puts a bag over his head and starts to drag him away.

CARABOSSE
But I nearly forgot!

She flings a birthday card onto the floor and walks out with a trembling Sidney. ANGUS and LADY GARGOYLE turn around holding records. The FAIRY is slumped in the corner.

LADY GARGOYLE
This should bring the ambassador up nicely.

ANGUS
Where's Sidney?

LADY GARGOYLE
The party pooper!

BEAUTY, JOSH and AGGIE enter.

LADY GARGOYLE
Don't play with the servants darling, you'll get rickets. *(Hands Beauty an envelope)* Here, Happy Birthday.

BEAUTY (opening it)
Tickets.

SLEEPING BEAUTY: ONE LITTLE PRICK

LADY GARGOYLE
I'm taking you on a cruise next year. The maiden voyage of the RMS Titanic. All those well-heeled young ladies for you, and eligible young lords for me.

ANGUS puts on a record.

ANGUS
Let's get this party started then.

AGGIE
Dance with me Beauty?

AGGIE and BEAUTY start to dance. The FAIRY advances drunkenly toward LADY GARGOYLE.

FAIRY
How's about it, corset crusher?

She walks straight past LADY GARGOYLE, walks into the wall and collapses.

ANGUS
May I er, may I 'ave the pleasure?

JOSH
Go on LADY GARGOYLE. It's practice.

JOSH pushes LADY GARGOYLE into ANGUS, they dance.

ANGUS
You're terrific ma'm.

LADY GARGOYLE
One's hips don't lie.

JOSH looks sadly at AGGIE. Then he notices the birthday card on the floor and picks it up.

JOSH
'ere, Beauty.

BEAUTY stops dancing and takes the card.

BEAUTY
Oh lordy, lordy. By golly, by gosh. Sidney's at the zoo!

They stop

LADY GARGOYLE
How ungrateful! (*She takes the card.*) "Come to the zoo now if you want to see your tortoise alive again." Well. Shall we put it to the vote?

JOSH
We got to rescue him.

LADY GARGOYLE
But the Prime Minister is rumoured to come without warning.

BEAUTY (starts to cry)
Poor Sidney.

JOSH (putting his arm round Beauty)
Don't cry mate.

BEAUTY
It's my party, Joshy, and I'll cry if I want to.

BEAUTY gives the sleeping fairy a nudge. She doesn't wake. He gives her a kick.

FAIRY
You bastard! I was in the Magic Fairy Garden in the Sky, face-deep in bush.

BEAUTY
Please, I need your help.

FAIRY
I gave you a belly busting cock, what else do you want?

BEAUTY
We need to go to the zoo.

FAIRY
What a load of fucking pooh, send these morons to the zoo.

She swigs more whiskey and collapses. JOSH, BEAUTY and LADY GARGOYLE twirl round and round.

JOSH
I'll be back, Aggie, I'll be back. Keep yourself warm for me.

AGGIE
Oh Beauty, be careful.

LADY GARGOYLE, BEAUTY and JOSH twirl off.

FAIRY
I'll tell you what. They'd be quicker if they walked normally.

AGGIE
Oh Dad, things is bleak.

ANGUS
You can say that again.

AGGIE
Oh Dad, things is bleak.

ANGUS
You're right my girl, they ain't paid the bill yet.

They start to tidy. Lights down.

Scene 6: London Zoo

A deserted corner of the zoo as imagined by Tim Burton. Overgrown. There is bench, and a cardboard box. On the box is written: BEAUTY. CARABOSSE stands over Sidney whose limbs are tied up. She picks up a large axe.

CARABOSSE
What a smashing shell. Do you make a noise if I blow into you?

SIDNEY
I asked Beauty to try that once but he couldn't be persuaded. Where are we?

CARABOSSE
The zoo, you obsequious pervert. It's where you belong you freak. You've been kidnapped! Just like in the Robert Louis Stevenson novel.

SIDNEY
Which Robert Louis Stevenson novel?

CARABOSSE
I forget the title. Now, how long shall we wait before I kill you? You'd make a marvellous ashtray for me to flick off over.

SIDNEY
Beauty will find us.

CARABOSSE
Wonderful! I can give him his present.

SIDNEY
Present?

CARABOSSE
Of course! A little present for my dearest nephew.

He takes a porcupine from the box.

CARABOSSE
Porcupine. Charming fellow, though he can be a little prickly.

He stuffs it back. BEAUTY enters, his clothes ripped and dirty.

SIDNEY
Dear boy! What on earth happened? Lions?

BEAUTY
Marmosets. But, you know, really big marmosets. A whole gang of them. Now give me my tortoise Carabosse. Please.

CARABOSSE
"Please!" Oh must we be strangers? I have your birthday treat!

BEAUTY
A cake?

CARABOSSE
No. Someone left the cake out in the rain, I don't think that I can take it, cos it so long to bake it.[96]

BEAUTY
Right...

CARABOSSE (beaming broadly)
But there's this!

She hands Beauty the box, he takes it.

BEAUTY
You're serious...? Shall I open it boys and girls? It would be rude not to wouldn't it?

LADY GARGOYLE enters with a penguin on her head.

LADY GARGOYLE
If that's a prick you're holding I'm having it.

CARABOSSE
There's one coming now.

JOSH enters, he has a crocodile attached to his bum and it is biting him. BEAUTY pulls it off him – he succeeds but the seat of Josh's trousers is torn away too in the crocodile's mouth, revealing his bottom.

CARABOSSE
Now. Your present!

BEAUTY (re Josh's arse)
I think I've just unwrapped it.

LADY GARGOYLE opens the box and takes out the porcupine.

LADY GARGOYLE
I've heard a cow has four stomachs but whoever saw an animal with so many pricks!

BEAUTY
It's so bloody cute!

JOSH
Don't go near it.

---

[96] MacArthur Park by Jimmy Webb, first sung by Richard Harris

478

SLEEPING BEAUTY: ONE LITTLE PRICK

BEAUTY
I meant your [bum]-

JOSH
I know.

LADY GARGOYLE hands the box to CARABOSSE

CARABOSSE
Throw my present back in my face why don't you?

She takes the porcupine and puts it on the bench as the others turn to SIDNEY.

JOSH
Has she hurt you Sid?

BEAUTY starts untying him.

CARABOSSE
Please let's talk about this. Take a seat.

She guides Beauty back to the seat where the porcupine is.

BEAUTY
It's been a long day. I could do with a sit down.

JOSH
Do you want a prick up your arse?

BEAUTY
Not with mother here... oh!

CARABOSSE
How did he get there! What a scamp.

LADY GARGOYLE
My boy, my boy, come to Mummy.

She hugs him to her very ample bosom. CARABOSSE moves the porcupine along the bench.

BEAUTY (struggling free)
Come on Sidney I'll take you home.

LADY GARGOYLE walks over to the bench, isn't looking and is about to sit on the porcupine.

BEAUTY
Mother don't!

BEAUTY pulls the porcupine out of the way. LADY GARGOYLE screams and spins around, knocking into Beauty and the porcupine. The porcupine quills go into Beauty.

BEAUTY
Ow!

CARABOSSE
Haha! Where's lover boy when you need him!

BEAUTY
How do you know about him?

CARABOSSE
Oh we go back a long way! Nighty night!

JOSH, BEAUTY and LADY GARGOYLE all fall to the floor in a deep sleep.

CARABOSSE
This could be a sweet dream, or a beautiful nightmare[97]! But it's neither. They're dead! Now to kill the tortoise and claim what's mine.

The Good Fairy enters.

FAIRY
Oh no you don't.

CARABOSSE
You're too late, walking stick. By the pricking of his bum, victory to me has come! On your bike, dyke. I've won. Go on piss off all of you. The show's over. They're dead.

FAIRY
I'm gonae cast a spell to reverse yours:
Sausage, eggs, beans and bacon,
When kissed by a prince, Beauty will awaken.

CARABOSSE
You're all talk.

FAIRY
And as for you. You're going back to fairy land. To prison!

CARABOSSE
With your paltry powers?

FAIRY
But when I'm in a jam and don't know what to do
I ask for some help from my friend, the Doctor...

CARABOSSE
Who?

FAIRY
Exactly!

---

[97] Beyoncé, *Sweet Dream*

There is a whirring sound, we hear the Doctor Who theme music. Perhaps the Tardis appears. A hand reaches out dragging CARABOSSE offstage.

FAIRY

Well. There's shit all to do here till a Prince shows up. I'll just make last orders. (Singing) *I belong to Glasgow, good old Glasgow town.*

She goes. SIDNEY is still tied up.

SIDNEY

Umm, I say, excuse me, I don't suppose you could...? No. No, of course. You're busy. Oh dear. Oh dearie, dearie me.

INTERVAL

Scene 7: Fairy prison

CARABOSSE is in prison. On the wall, she has chalked up the years to 100. She sings a filthily re-worded version of "Close Every Door" from Joseph and the Amazing Technicolor Dreamcoat.

CARABOSSE
"...Do what you see fit to me, spank me and spit on me, Fill me from both ends, you'll find I'm quite tight...

She sees the audience.

CARABOSSE
Welcome back cretins. Just when I thought things couldn't get worse, I get prison visitors...

The sound of a prison door opening and clanging shut. Slow, echoey footsteps.

CARABOSSE
Who's there?

The FAIRY enters carrying a cake.

FAIRY
Long time no see, hen.

CARABOSSE
This must be how Brussels feels when Cameron shows up.

FAIRY
How're ye keeping?

CARABOSSE
I've been reduced to leaving right-wing comments on the Guardian website and chalking up my wanks on the walls of the cell.

CARABOSSE
Oh please release me. Let me go.

FAIRY
Beauty's still asleep and until I get that fixed I'm not allowed into the great fairy garden in the sky.

CARABOSSE
I could reverse the spell if you get me out of here.

FAIRY
What do you think boys and girls? (*Responses*) Auch let's throw shit to the wind and give it a whirl, I baked a special cake and everything.

She gets the cake.

FAIRY
But no more ASBO shite, alright?

She passes the cake through the bars of the cage to CARABOSSE who tears into it and removes a key.

FAIRY
You've dropped cake everywhere.

CARABOSSE
Well if you're going to get all professional on me, you've been dropping more lines than Amy Winehouse on her 27th birthday. (*finds key*) Aha! I've got the key. I've got the secret.

She looks about and frowns.

CARABOSSE
The lock's on the outside.

FAIRY
Give it here.

He passes the lock back to her. She takes the key and unlocks the door. He bursts out.

CARABOSSE
Hahaha!!! I'm free! To do what I want! Any old time![98] And here's another thing. The Great Fairy Garden in the Sky doesn't exist! Sayonara!

She runs off.

FAIRY
100 years have passed girls and boys
Aye you queued at the bar for that long!
It's 2011, all bluster and noise
And everything going for a song

Our wee hero's asleep, awaiting the touch
Of a lover to break the spell
But I wouldn't want to kiss him much
Well the morning breath, what a smell

Lets pray for true love, let's hope for a prince
Hell an x-factor winner would do
For all I care he can burp limp and mince
Now, let's get back to the zoo

---

[98] Rolling Stones, *I'm Free*

Scene 8: London Zoo

It is very overgrown. BEAUTY, LADY GARGOYLE and JOSH are buried in the undergrowth. EDWARD enters. He's in modern clothes and is a bit hipster with a designer printed t-shirt or vest.

EDWARD
Hey boys and girls! I'm having an outing at London Zoo. I'm trying to find the bat house. But you'll be wondering what I've been up to for the last hundred years. Well, after a dullsville few months at the family pad, I decided to have a gap century, and now here I am back in London. I've even got a part time job pulling pints in a dingy Australian accent. You know, I think maybe I came back because it reminds me of the beautiful boy who disappeared that night in 1911. He lit up my life all too briefly like a firefly in a jar. That's from one of the poems I wrote in my Moleskin travel journal in a portaloo at this insane music festival in Mali. I suppose I'll never know what happened to him will I?

They shout.

EDWARD
Yeah ok whatever. How can he be here?

He starts to dig away the undergrowth. He uncovers JOSH, LADY GARGOYLE and eventually BEAUTY, all asleep.

EDWARD
It's totally him! Let's wake him! After three will you all shout "wake up Beauty"? Ok here goes, one, two three!

The audience shouts but nothing happens..

EDWARD
Hmmm. How can I wake him up?

"Kiss him!" He gently kisses Beauty, once, twice. Nothing happens.

EDWARD
A boy could get offended...

A gentle romantic song plays. EDWARD rolls BEAUTY on to his back and slips his hand down his trousers rubbing his crotch. Nothing. He rolls BEAUTY on to his front so he is face down, he licks a finger and slips it down the back of Beauty's trousers, up his bum. Nothing. He licks two fingers, then three, then four. Four does the trick!

EDWARD removes his hand as BEAUTY stirs, stretches and farts loudly.

BEAUTY
Hello!

He reaches to take Edward's hand. The one he's been using. It stinks.

EDWARD
Other hand. I thought you'd never wake.

BEAUTY
I must look a mess.

EDWARD (stroking his hair)
Just a little zoo head.

JOSH wakes, stretches and farts. He marvels at EDWARD's t-shirt.

JOSH
Wow. Printed fabrics.

EDWARD
I thought he was straight?

LADY GARGOYLE wakes, stretches and farts.

LADY GARGOYLE
Where on earth? It rather looks like the zoo.

EDWARD
It is, Lady Gargoyle.

LADY GARGOYLE
Ah, the not so little Prince. It must have been a successful party! Well, we must get back to the manor.

JOSH
Yeah and Aggie, I left her at the inn.

EDWARD'S phone rings. The others cower in terror.

EDWARD
(Into the phone) Hi. Yeah I can work tonight. Yeah, course I'm behaving, but listen I just met... I just bumped into some old mates at the zoo.

BEAUTY creeps forward.

BEAUTY
What is it?

JOSH
Don't touch it Beauty!

EDWARD
It's a telephone. Look.

BEAUTY takes it and looks.

BEAUTY
Angry birds.

EDWARD
No, that's the Saturdays. I had it on shuffle. Perhaps you should all sit down. You see, you've been asleep for a very long time. A hundred years.

JOSH
No! So... Aggie?

EDWARD
She lived to 88.

LADY GARGOYLE
How unreliable.

BEAUTY
But you're here.

A voice comes over a loud speaker system.

VOICE
Ladies and gentleman, boys and girls, our special show starts in five minutes. Come and see the world's only tap dancing tortoise.

BEAUTY
Gosh that sounds fun! Come on!

A glittery curtain appears. LADY GARGOYLE. BEAUTY, JOSH & EDWARD gather in front of it.

LADY GARGOYLE
Must we-

BEAUTY
Shush! It's about to start.

Music plays and we hear the shuffle of tap shoes. The curtain is pulled back to reveal SIDNEY, dancing badly in a sparkly pink outfit. He looks very sad and embarrassed.

BEAUTY
Sidney!

SIDNEY stops dancing.

SIDNEY
Oh my good heavens! Lady Gargoyle! Master Beauty! And er...

JOSH
Josh.

SIDNEY starts dancing.

BEAUTY
We've been asleep for a hundred years.

LADY GARGOYLE
Enough! We'll return to the manor. Sidney, stop dancing, we'll have pheasant for dinner.

SIDNEY
Your ladyship, I don't finish till 6 and Waitrose closes at 5. It's not 1911 anymore.

JOSH
A hundred years Mr Sid! What a long life!

SIDNEY
I do have but one regret.

JOSH
What's that?

SIDNEY
It's a lament or a missed opportunity but that's not important right now. It's really rather embarrassing. I'm a hundred and forty year old virgin.

BEAUTY
Haven't you ever met that special someone?

JOSH
Don't change the subject.

SIDNEY
There was someone once... I spent a few years as a regimental mascot. I met an Indian tortoise on the Poona Hills. It was going so well, but we had to pull out.

JOSH
I thought you said-

SIDNEY
The British withdrew from India. An officer brought me home and I never saw the tortoise again.

LADY GARGOYLE
Oh god how awful!

SIDNEY
I get by.

LADY GARGOYLE
We no longer own India! What is the world coming to?

SIDNEY (removing a photograph from his shell)
I have his picture. I keep it next to my heart. I will never forget him.

483

LADY GARGOYLE
What are we to do?

EDWARD
I'm working in a nice little bar. We could go there.

LADY GARGOYLE
How perfectly horrible. "Working"?! Nonsense. We shall return to our home.

SIDNEY
But the manor... oh your ladyship, it's a very different world to the one you fell asleep in.

SONG: ANYTHING GOES
(to the classic Cole Porter tune)

EDWARD
Times have changed,
And we've often turned back the clock,
Since we saw Aiden Gillen's Cock
On Queer as Folk at 9 O'clock
If today,
Any shock you might try to stem,
At the hobbies of certain men
Just don't go judging them ...

SIDNEY
In olden days a flash of ankle
Was something that rather rankled
But now god knows
Anything goes
Panto writers who once used pithy words
Now only use such filthy words
In their shows
Anything goes

EDWARD
There's lots of gay bars today
And gay spas today
There's fag hags today
Rainbow flags today
Get your feet today
To Compton Street today
It all happens in Soho
And if you care to learn the lingo

You'll love it down at Gay Bingo
Yes heaven knows
Anything goes

SIDNEY
You'll find men who just turned eighty
Here in the Stag, getting matey
With gigolos
Anything goes
There's clubs from bling to very pokey
And men doing karaoke
In women's clothes
Anything goes

EDWARD
If boys with tight pecs you like
That they flex you like
In their gyms you like
If bare limbs you like
If some stud you like
From True Blood you like

BEAUTY and SIDNEY
Well nobody will oppose

SIDNEY
And every night there's clubs in arches
All manner of fetish parties in studios
Anything goes

EDWARD
The world is insane today
Melts your brain today
There's gay pubs today
Gay running clubs today
There's a craze today
For easy lays today
What his name was, heaven knows

BEAUTY
Although I'm not a great romancer
Just ask me and here's the answer
I love you so
Anything goes.

BEAUTY and EDWARD kiss. End of scene.

Scene 9: The pub

The same pub as in Act One, with a few camp touches – it's now a gay bar. AGGIE 2 enters. A friendly, earthy yet flamboyant landlady who looks rather like her ancestor Angus. She is humming "Consider yourself" from Oliver!.

AGGIE 2
Ello boys and girls. My name's Aggie, named after me great grandmother bless her soul. I'm the landlady of this little gay-friendly Stratford gastro-pub and nightspot. I know, that was clunky, but if you want subtle exposition, they do burlesque here on a Monday. I had to do the place up after the riots so I turned it into gastro-pub, cos that way when you make chips you don't have to bother with peeling. I spent every penny but it'll be worth it cos next year it's the Olympics and ker-ching! Now you'll have to be patient, we're just opening up, as the boy-band said to Louis Walsh. And we got our new stripper starting tonight.

There is a hacking cough from behind the bar. AGGIE 2 goes behind it and drags out the FAIRY. She is clinging to a pint with a fag butt in it.

AGGIE 2
Time to go.

FAIRY
Ay you're right. Today's the day it all happens!

AGGIE 2
And no more of your stories about magic curses and sleeping boys and all the rest of that bollocks. Off you go. It's not licensing hours yet. Come back when we've finished cleaning and it's legal. As the boy band said to Louis Walsh.

FAIRY exits. AGGIE 2 continues to clean and sings a bit more of Consider Yourself.

AGGIE 2
My daughter took me to see Oliver last year at Drury Lane. Busman's holiday. My line of work the last thing I need is a shrieking Nancy and a load of well drilled pubescents. But I like a pantomime.

CARABOSSE enters. She doesn't see her. "She's behind you"

AGGIE 2
Yeah that's right, all that shit.

"She's behind you"

AGGIE 2
Ok, take your Ritalin eh? (she sees Carabosse) I've always wanted to do this. (Puts on best EastEnders voice) Get out of my pub! Who are you?

CARABOSSE
That's no way to speak to your landlady!

AGGIE 2
Landlady? I'm the Landlady.

CARABOSSE
Oh no she isn't.

Oh yes she is.

CARABOSSE
Oh no she isn't.

She hands her some papers.

AGGIE 2
Oh my days...! But this pub's been in my family for generations.

CARABOSSE
Your great great grandfather was my tenant. And now I'm Back! Woo! From outer space! Just walked in to find you here with that sad look upon your face! Oh yes. I own half of Stratford! And land prices have risen like the crotch of a schoolboy's trousers on a bumpy bus. I want the pub back. You have until tomorrow.

AGGIE 2
What?

CARABOSSE
You know it's time for a rebranding when Time Out raves about your Hoegarden and they mean the outdoor smoking area.

AGGIE 2
Wait till my daughter Maggie hears about this. She's on Stratford council. Give me till the Olympics?

CARABOSSE
That's why I want the pub. I can't wait to take my seat on the committee.

AGGIE 2
It's probably easier than getting a seat at the actual games, Even Julian Assange would have given up on that website after an hour and started Googling bukake

like the rest of us. Talking of downpours, boys and girls, I was offered tickets for the women's final at Wimbledon last year. I turned them down. Ask me why?

Why?

AGGIE 2
I prefer to look at the men's semis.

CARABOSSE
Stop with your warbling and accept your fate.

AGGIE 2
As Louis Walsh said to the boyband.

CARABOSSE
Enough! Please!

AGGIE 2
As the boyband replied.

CARABOSSE
Silence! Now, to inspect the premises. My premises. Where's the cellar?

AGGIE 2
Three floors up, through the attic and out the window, where do you think it is? (She points behind the bar). And mind the-

CARABOSSE exits to the cellar, doing the comedy fake going-downstairs thing. We hear a bump and a scream.

AGGIE 2
-step. Oh boys and girls! Me poor little pub. And I'd done up the guest rooms especially cos I'm trying to persuade Tom Daley to stay here. Even put a viewing gallery in the en-suite so he'd feel at home. That one knows how to do a few tricks before going under. I'd be happy with a bit of splashback. Now, now, I know what you're thinking boys and girls. You're thinking, Aggie, that Tom Daley is young enough to be your lover twice before breakfast without breaking a nail or a sweat and you'd be right. Anyway he's a grown man now. His trunks got rucked up this one time when he mistimed a dive and there was a very respectable bush if you paused it right. That's what I need, a nice young man to distract me from my troubles.

JOSH enters.

AGGIE 2
Someone rubbed a lucky ring. Wait a moment chicken.

Spits in her hands and rubs it on her eyes to simulate tears.

AGGIE 2
Oh what a time to be a landlady.

JOSH
Are you alright?

AGGIE 2
Don't worry about me, I'm only being evicted. Poor, er, young woman that I am. Let me clutch you to my proud, heaving, remarkably perky bosom.

JOSH
Brilliant!

AGGIE 2
What are you dressed like?! Oh! Course, you're the entertainment, aintcha my lamb.

She hums "The Stripper")

JOSH
No, I'm... Wait, this is my lucky break! Er yeah! Like on a stage and stuff?

AGGIE 2
That's it. You got your music?

JOSH
I got a song about a car...

AGGIE 2
What's your name duck?

JOSH (unsure of himself)
It's Josh. Josh... the Jester.

AGGIE 2
What's wrong kitten?

JOSH
My master got a curse on him and we fell asleep for a hundred years...

AGGIE 2
Your "master" eh? Hang on. A curse? Spooky. Only this morning an ancient tortoise was stolen from the zoo, it was on Five Live.

JOSH
That'll be Sidney.

AGGIE 2
No this was London. Listen, I'll go get my daughter. Maggie! The act's here early!

She goes.

JOSH

I can't believe I'll never see Aggie again. I can almost imagine her still here. Still, what's the use thinking about all that. She was never interested. I'll never let myself get so silly over a girl again. It only gets you hurt.

MAGGIE walks in, the spitting image of her ancestor AGGIE. JOSH is dumbstruck

MAGGIE

Hello, my name's Maggie. I'm on the council. Are you a local boy?

JOSH

Yeah. I live in the massive manor house just over there.

MAGGIE

I can't think where you mean.

JOSH

You must know it. Three massive storeys.

MAGGIE

What like the Lord of the Rings? That's very impressive considering your line of work.

JOSH

Well I'm an entertainer ain't I. We got a car and everything.

MAGGIE

Well we're trying to encourage people away from cars. Can I tell you about green emissions?

JOSH

That cleared up ages back.

MAGGIE (concerned)

Do you think that's what made you gay?

JOSH

Gay? I'm fucking desolate.

MAGGIE

I'm trying to say that cars are very bad for the environment

JOSH

Bless you, I thought I was the one from the past, I expect you think they're powered by witchcraft don'tcha love.

MAGGIE slaps him

MAGGIE

Are you being sexist?

JOSH

No. Yeah. I dunno.

MAGGIE

Why are gay men always the most misogynist?

JOSH

What?

MAGGIE

And the most attractive...

JOSH

Here I'm parched missy, any chance of a drink?

MAGGIE

Where the hell do you think you are!

JOSH

A pub.

MAGGIE

Oh. Yeah.

LADY GARGOYLE enters, exhausted.

JOSH

Lady G!

MAGGIE

Let me find you a stool.

LADY GARGOYLE

Oh!

MAGGIE

I'm Maggie.

LADY GARGOYLE

I've not lost my faculties thank you! What a relief! I'd hug you if I had any sentiment or warmth.

MAGGIE

A loyal voter! Your support is appreciated.

LADY GARGOYLE

What are you talking about?

MAGGIE

Are you alright?

LADY GARGOYLE

Nothing a cup of tea won't mend.

MAGGIE

Coming right up.

MAGGIE goes. AGGIE 2 enters, and assumes LADY GARGOYLE is a drag queen.

AGGIE 2
Oh ello. You'll be hosting tonight then will you? Most of them change after they get here.

LADY GAROYLE looks around her at the pub.

LADY GARGOYLE
I see you've not had much work done.

AGGIE 2
I can see you haven't had any. I don't know what fetish night you got chucked out of but nobody talks to me like that.

LADY GARGOYLE
I'm sorry, I'm not at my best. I've spent decades in London zoo.

AGGIE 2
That would have been my first guess.

LADY GARGOYLE
How dare you

AGGIE 2
What was it, they couldn't get anything to breed with you so they let you out?

LADY GARGOYLE
It all started when my son took a prick on his 21st birthday

AGGIE 2
Oh god. One of those families that shares things.

LADY GARGOYLE
My good woman. All I ask is that you let me rest a moment, and then we'll go home to the manor.

AGGIE 2
The manor?

LADY GARGOYLE
Stratford manor. I'll show you, you can see it from the window.

BEAUTY and the EDWARD enter, singing Beyoncé's Crazy In Love. BEAUTY is particularly going for it.

AGGIE 2
Fucking hell boys and girls it's the Bullingdon Club. Oh it's you Edward!

EDWARD
Sorry I'm late. This is Beauty.

BEAUTY (takes her left hand, kisses it)
Charmed.

AGGIE 2
Aggie. How lovely. This is my daughter Maggie, she's a politician

MAGGIE
I'm council.

AGGIE 2
Don't put yourself down. I don't know where she gets the politics from. I thought an Arab Spring was something you got in Prowler.

LADY GARGOYLE
Oh, brave new world! Beauty, why don't you invite Maggie to the manor. I'm sure you'd get on famously.

BEAUTY
Mother! I love Edward. There, I've said it. And I'm not going to throw that away after the million to one chance of his finding me in the undergrowth of the furthest reaches of London zoo.

LADY GARGOYLE
You think that makes him a catch??

BEAUTY
I know it's wrong. I know it's illegal. But I don't care.

MAGGIE
It's not illegal! And if you go to New York you can get married.

BEAUTY
That's brilliant!

LADY GARGOYLE
Beauty, you need an heir.

MAGGIE
He can adopt.

EDWARD
One step at a time yeah?

BEAUTY
Maybe I don't want a family. Or maybe I do. Either way Mother, you can accept Edward, and live together in the manor with us. Or you can find somewhere else

MAGGIE
Where's this manor you keep talking about?

LADY GARGOYLE, JOSH, BEAUTY
It's over there!

They walk to the window and look. They are shocked at what they see.

LADY GARGOYLE
I...I...

BEAUTY
Goodness

JOSH
Shit me.

LADY GARGOYLE
What is it?

AGGIE 2
It's the Olympic Stadium.

They stare at it.

LADY GARGOYLE
Our house! My Orchard! Oh..!

AGGIE 2
Here, pull up a stool I'll fix you something proper.

LADY GARGOYLE
Thank you. I've realised who you remind me of.

AGGIE 2
Oh really?

LADY GARGOYLE
It's a man.

AGGIE 2
You're hardly the face of L'Oréal yourself. Face of Orio maybe.

LADY GARGOYLE
I can't imagine where we're going to spend the night.

AGGIE 2
I suppose you'd like a bed. Temporarily.

LADY GARGOYLE
Temporarily.

LADY GARGOYLE picks up a magazine. It's called "Fagz". She opens it towards the back. She stares at it from a number of angles.

LADY GARGOYLE (pointing out of the window)
How charming, a rainbow.

While they look, LADY GARGOYLE discreetly tears out a page and slips it into her dress.

LADY GARGOYLE
Beauty? Pay the woman.

AGGIE 2
I wouldn't hear of it.

BEAUTY fishes in his pocket. He pulls out some very old coins and notes.

AGGIE 2
Still I'd hate to be impolite... What on earth?

EDWARD
Old money.

BEAUTY
We *are* rather. Don't worry, we'll pay our way. We own all of that land. We'll go to our solicitors, Corrigan and Everett[99]. We'll get the deeds, go to the bank and explain everything.

LADY GARGOYLE
It's impossible I'm afraid. My late husband was a feckless alcoholic who wasted his life away in places of ill repute. (She peers at the audience.) I thought I saw him earlier.

LADY GARGOYLE
He left the deeds and papers on a night tram.

BEAUTY
We've lost everything?

JOSH
Some of us never had anything to start with did we Aggie. Oh...

AGGIE 2
Right. Well if it is to be our last night in my little pub at least we can make a gathering of it. Come on. Josh you can have the spare in the attic.

MAGGIE (seductive)
That's next to my room...

JOSH
I hope you don't snore.

---

99 Brent Corrigan and Brent Everett were prominent gay porn stars.

MAGGIE
No but I come like a bomb going off.

MAGGIE exits.

AGGIE 2
Beauty, you can share with Edward. We'll help you with your bags.

LADY GARGOYLE
I don't have any bags.

AGGIE 2
Must be the harsh lighting. You can bunk up with me.

LADY GARGOYLE
Bunk up?!

AGGIE 2
It's alright, we can top and tail.

LADY GARGOYLE
It sounds like something one does to a fish.

AGGIE 2
Oh no, darling. You gut a fish. Right, follow me.

AGGIE 2, LADY GARGOYLE, AGGIE and JOSH exit. BEAUTY picks up the magazine and flicks through it.

BEAUTY
This is incredible! Men dancing together like you said! (Holds it close). They all have very wide pupils.

EDWARD
Not just their pupils.

EDWARD takes the mag from Beauty and puts it down.

EDWARD
At last! We get to spend a night together. After all these years.

They embrace. It's intimate and sexy.

BEAUTY
I still don't understand how you've stayed so young.

EDWARD starts paying a bit too much attention to BEAUTY's neck...

EDWARD
Your skin... God help me

BEAUTY
Shall we go upstairs?

EDWARD
Oh I want you... but I... I...

BEAUTY
Did you come?

EDWARD
No! I just, I...

As he gets close to biting BEAUTY, MAGGIE walks in with a tray and some food.

MAGGIE
I thought you might be hungry after a hundred years. Get something down your throat.

BEAUTY
I was hoping to.

MAGGIE
It's left-overs. Breakfast in a bap.

They each take one and eat. EDWARD seems blown away.

EDWARD
Wow. What's in it?

MAGGIE
I never reveal my sauces.

BEAUTY
It's black pudding.

EDWARD
What's black pudding?

BEAUTY
It's made from pigs blood. How have you never had black pudding?

EDWARD
Oh thank you thank you. This is the best thing that's ever happened to me.

BEAUTY
Thanks...

EDWARD
I don't even want a nibble of you, Beauty.

BEAUTY
Oh charming!

EDWARD
No no no I still fancy you. Who wouldn't? Look, it's nothing really, I'm a vampire you see, and until now I-

BEAUTY
What?

490

EDWARD
A vampire. Anyway, it's been

BEAUTY
You're a vampire?

EDWARD
I probably should have told you.

MAGGIE
So that's how you've stayed so young.

EDWARD
Me, Joan Rivers, Kylie, and David Gest. It works better for some than others.

BEAUTY
So you're not... dangerous?

EDWARD
It's just like living with diabetes these days... I do get urges but one bite of black pudding will keep me going for days. It means we can live together, get married, settle down! I can finally be with the boy I love. In over a 100 years I've never met anyone like you.

MAGGIE
On the subject of boys... You know that Josh.

BEAUTY
Yes?

MAGGIE
Oh it's ridiculous, I've only just met him, but, is he... you know – should I...?

BEAUTY
He's not betrothed if that's what you mean.

MAGGIE
Right... good. But is he...

BEAUTY
He's lovely. He's probably my closest friend.

MAGGIE
Then you'd know if he was...

BEAUTY
Absolutely. He's packing it and he can keep it up till the cock crows.

MAGGIE
Oh!

MAGGIE runs off, upset.

EDWARD
You don't suppose she was asking if Josh was gay do you?

BEAUTY
Oh no, I don't think so, do you? Let's go out tonight.

EDWARD
But it's our first night together.

BEAUTY
I know...

EDWARD
I can keep some black pudding on the bedside cabinet in case.

BEAUTY picks up the gay magazine.

BEAUTY
Edward, I spent all my youth thinking that I was wrong to have feelings for men. Thinking I'd have to marry some poor girl and hide away whenever I met anyone I really loved. The way Josh used to talk about Aggie, I thought I'd never be able to talk like that about guys.

EDWARD
And now you can.

BEAUTY
I didn't think I'd even meet anyone that might like me back.

EDWARD
And now you have.

BEAUTY
I know. But... this is my first night in a world where I can go and be with people just like me and feel like I belong. I think you're amazing. I think you're probably the man of my dreams. But how will we know that if you're the only one I've ever met.

EDWARD
Alright. If you really want to go out... I'll ask Maggie to do my shift. I know this awesome pop-up club in Old Street, size of a wheelie bin, DJ only uses cassettes from 1988, they have face painting, they got the mirror ball from Dalston market, Simon Amstell was there once, amazing.

BEAUTY
I want to go to Vauxhall.

EDWARD

Alright. Come on I'll take you clothes shopping.

BEAUTY

Thank you. I love you.

EDWARD puts a finger over Beauty's lips.

EDWARD

Tell me later.

As they make to go the FAIRY enters wearing a cardigan and carrying a condom in its wrapper

FAIRY

This place must be open by now for the day,
But listen my lad, if you're planning to stray
Slip this on, it's large so it should fit ok

BEAUTY (laughs)

I'm not going to be getting anyone pregnant am I.

FAIRY

Right well I'm not going down that alley it's meant to be a pantomime. (Slips the condom into Beauty's pocket). As you were.

BEAUTY and the Edward exit.

FAIRY

I've been down the charity shop boys and girls, found a cardie I lost at a party in 1953. I thought I might reclaim a few other items but I can see you lot beat me to it.

JOSH enters.

JOSH

Oh god. Are you the woman that looked like you back in 1911 or are you another woman that looks like the woman that looked like you back in 1911?

FAIRY

I'm a fairy pet. I don't do ageing.

AGGIE 2 enters

AGGIE 2

Oi, no racism in here.

FAIRY

I said I don't do *ageing*. I'm trapped in the body of an alcoholic Glaswegian lesbian – which ain't so bad seeing as I *am* an alcoholic Glaswegian lesbian - until I manage to work my fairy magic to a good cause. But it ain't easy. Lumley nabbed the Ghurkhas and Vanessa

got Dale Farm[100] and Hugh Grant got the News of the World. I've got to protect your friend but I don't understand why. Sod him. Usual please, lusty wench.

AGGIE 2

You don't have a usual, you have a rota.

JOSH

You can't give up. Please. He's gone off somewhere with that Edward and I don't think he's all he seems to be.

AGGIE 2

Maggie's just told me she's cured him of vampiric tendencies.

FAIRY

I never saw that coming.

AGGIE 2

What? There've been more clumsy hints than a mid-season Midsummer Murders.

LADY GARGOYLE enters with SIDNEY.

LADY GARGOYLE

Aggie, where can Sidney sleep?

AGGIE 2

You can sleep in the cellar (she points).

SIDNEY

Thank you. That sounds perfect.

CARABOSSE pokes her head out of the cellar

CARABOSSE

Just perfect!

AGGIE 2

I said it sounds perfect doesn't it boys and girls?

No!

AGGIE 2

All warm and cosy next to the boiler. Oh no wait she's sharing with me. What do you reckon?

No!

AGGIE 2

Down you go pet.

LADY GARGOYLE and JOSH suck air in through their teeth.

---

[100] Vanessa Redgrave championed the rights of a Traveller community who were being evicted from their Essex site.

SIDNEY
I am not a pet!

AGGIE 2
Apologies. Now make yourself at home. And mind the-

SIDNEY goes behind the bar and down into the cellar. There is a thud.

AGGIE 2
- step. Now why don't you go out the back and get ready for your strip show my little piglet.

LADY GARGOYLE
Strip show?!

JOSH
I ain't a stripper!

AGGIE 2
I'm so sorry love! Of course you're not the kind to take your clothes off for money.

JOSH
Money? How much money?

LADY GARGOYLE
Now you think of your reputation young man! Your young body divested of its underclothes, glistening under the lights for all to see, shamelessly thrusting your hips back and forth... Well I'm sure you'll do it tastefully and it will be a pleasure to support you.

AGGIE 2
Run along now me little cock robin.

JOSH exits

LADY GARGOYLE
Might your daughter might run me a bath?

AGGIE 2
You can have a shower and you'll run it yourself! We got enough to worry about.

LADY GARGOYLE
Forgive me. I'm so weary. I don't think I could handle any more surprises.

CARABOSSE bursts out of the cellar.

CARABOSSE
All the single ladies all the single ladies put your hands up[101].

LADY GARGOYLE
Carabosse!

CARABOSSE
Hello hello you called? I can't hear a thing. I have got no signal in the cellar, see see[102]. Oooo! My poor sister in law, how the years have ravaged you. No, my mistake, you've not changed a bit. Welcome to my pub. What can I get you?

AGGIE 2
A brick in a sock.

LADY GARGOYLE
You can have the pub. Aggie and her daughter will live with us. My son owns all that land and we're here to take it from you.

CARABOSSE
Well come on. I can take it take it take no more. Lady what you what you waiting for?[103] (a pause) Haha! then my masterplan is a certain victory! Just you wait and see. I'm going to be the most powerful man in the world! More manipulative than Simon Cowell! More ruthless than Rupert Murdoch! More slightly disappointing than Barack Obama!

CARABOSSE drags from a cellar what is clearly Sidney's shell, covered in a blanket. She goes to exit the pub.

AGGIE 2
What's that?

CARABOSSE
Just clearing out the junk while I'm here. Ta-ra then. See you later alligator.

AGGIE 2
In a while, shitcakes.

CARABOSSE exits goes.

FAIRY
Right who's for a Guinness jacuzzi?

They shake their heads

FAIRY
Then off I'll stagger to do my duty
Let's put a stop to this lunatic's plan,
We'll make a hero of Sleeping Beauty!
And without the budget of the Broadway Spiderman.

---

101 Destiny's Child, *Single Ladies*

102 Lady Gaga, *Telephone*
103 Britney Spears, *Till The World Ends*

493

FAIRY goes. LADY GARGOYLE slumps onto a stool

LADY GARGOYLE
How am I going to cope? I can't cook. I can't drive. The only thing I know how to do is run a house.

AGGIE 2
You could get a job in one of those National Trust places. You're terrifying enough.

LADY GARGOYLE
Don't mock me.

AGGIE 2
You got fighting spirit and that counts for something.

LADY GARGOYLE
100 years! What have I missed?

AGGIE 2
Well, jazz, but that's shit with beards. We had the 4 minute mile, 3 Men and a Baby, two world wars and one world cup. There's aeroplanes, nuclear weapons, the Wizard of Oz. Acid and Ecstasy. The moon landing.

LADY GARGOYLE
Goodness! Where?

AGGIE 2
Supermarkets. Environmentalists. Israel. Poor Israel (crosses herself). Palestine. Poor Palestine (crosses herself again). Shitty little microscooters. Chinese Takeaways. Picasso. The cold war. The great war. Oh your boy is so lucky he missed that. Hundreds of thousands of youths laid waste, just like when the lights come up at Beyond[104]. Princess Diana - not the monarchy's finest hour.

LADY GARGOYLE
Why?

AGGIE 2
Total car crash. Titanic.

LADY GARGOYLE
The Titanic..? You've heard of-

AGGIE 2
Angel, it got more headlines when it went down than George Michael did.

LADY GARGOYLE
Even I've heard that one before.

---

[104] A gay club night.

AGGIE 2
Cilla Black. Harry Potter. Oh and if you want to pass as a free-thinking individual, Sinatra's overrated, Yoda's a cunt and Michael O'Leary's the people's champion of social fucking mobility.

LADY GARGOYLE
You curse a lot. It's the sign of a very stunted imagination.

AGGIE 2
Alright missy, it's also a sign you been slapped in the face.

LADY GARGOYLE
I beg your pardon?

AGGIE 2 slaps LADY GARGOYLE, who retains a stern, dignified silence. AGGIE 2 shakes her hand in pain.

AGGIE 2
Fuck. Oh go on. Swear.

LADY GARGOYLE
I will not.

Pause. LADY GARGOYLE slaps AGGIE 2. Shakes her hand in pain. AGGIE 2 puts a hand to her face.

AGGIE 2
Fuck. You're good. What else. The National Lottery. Nelson Mandela. ET. Che Guevara. Grace Kelly, Fred Astaire, Ginger Rogers danced on air. Oh yeah, Madonna, Marilyn.

LADY GARGOYLE
Who were they?

AGGIE 2
One was an actor who could sing a bit, the other's a singer who can sing a bit. The rise of the Labour Party. Glastonbury. Chips.

LADY GARGOYLE
We had chips.

AGGIE 2
Chocolate fingers?

LADY GARGOYLE
Not that we'd talk about.

AGGIE 2
The NHS. The BBC! Desert Island Disks, the Shipping Forecast, I'm Sorry I haven't a Clue.

LADY GARGOYLE
You're doing very well.

AGGIE 2
Just a Minute.

LADY GARGOYLE
No, really.

AGGIE 2
Question Time.

LADY GARGOYLE
I'm tired.

AGGIE 2
Friends.

LADY GARGOYLE
I suppose so.

AGGIE 2
Are You Being Served?

LADY GARGOYLE
I could murder a gin.

AGGIE 2
Sounds like a plan. Come on love, let's have them upstairs. Cheers.

She grabs a bottle and glasses, and they exit.

Scene 10: A chamber beneath the Olympic Stadium

A dark and dusty. A sheet covers some kind of contraption on a table. SIDNEY enters, looking at his photograph of his long lost love.

CARABOSSE
Faster, you tottery Testudinidae.

SIDNEY
Did you have to drag me here with my face in your rancid bag? Where are we?

CARABOSSE
What a question! After all those years you worked here!

SIDNEY
What? The manor was torn down years ago.

CARABOSSE
But not the cellars underneath. This secret chamber lies directly under the centre of the stadium!

SIDNEY
Well at least let me clean while you have me here down here, it smells atrocious.

CARABOSSE
Yeah that's Gaddafi's body. Favour for a friend.

CARABOSSE notices the photo.

CARABOSSE
Well well, you repellent reptile, what have we here?

SIDNEY
Please! Let me have that back! It's the only person I've ever been in love with.

CARABOSSE
Alright Mills and Boon. (She looks at the photo) What an ugly cunt.

SIDNEY
Please.

CARABOSSE
But of course.

She tears it into little pieces and scatters them over Sidney's head.

CARABOSSE
Say thank you.

SIDNEY tries to pick up the pieces.

CARABOSSE
Now to work. I have a cunting plan. I have been on eBay!

She whips the sheet away to reveal a strange machine, lights glowing.

CARABOSSE
News International were selling some old office stock, and among it all was this clever little machine. They merely used it to tap into mobile phones, but with a little magic and the recent efforts of a topless handy-man, I can use it to hack directly into the brains of the world's leaders, as they gather for the closing cere-mony of the Olympics!

SIDNEY
You didn't get a ticket either?

CARABOSSE
The entire world will do my bidding! Seas will rise, famines will strike, markets will crash, and all the world's resources will be devoted to Carabosse Land, formerly known as the United Kingdom. But first to lure Beauty here and kill him.

SIDNEY
Why?

CARABOSSE
He's my nemesis.

SIDNEY
Doesn't that mean he'll kill you?

CARABOSSE
Nobody likes a smart-arse Sidney. Neatly trimmed, perhaps. Now look like you're struggling, we're going to have a little photo session.

SIDNEY
I'm not at all photogenic. It's my wrinkles.

CARABOSSE
But first, I'm going to test this thing on an old friend... Hahahahaha!

Scene 11: The pub

It is morning. On the bar, a rucksack. AGGIE 2 and LADY GARGOYLE enter. LADY GARGOYLE is reading a magazine. AGGIE 2 is dusting with a feather duster that looks remarkably like her beehive hairdo.

LADY GARGOYLE
I was always an avid reader of women's journals. The only way I could relax was to spread "The Lady" across my thighs and flick for an hour or two before dinner and I haven't missed a monthly periodical since Beauty was born. (She indicates the feather duster). Does your sister have a name?

AGGIE 2
Yeah she's called get off your arse and give me a hand. It's double-barrelled.

LADY GARGOYLE
I say! Shall we have tea?

AGGIE 2
If we have any more tea it'll be like that time a gentleman took me to see Madame Butterfly. I wanted to stay to the end but I was busting and all those fountains trickling away in the Chinese water garden....

LADY GARGOYLE
Madame Butterfly was Japanese

AGGIE 2
Well, they all look the same, those water gardens.

PRINCE EDWARD enters from the cellar.

EDWARD
That's the barrels changed.

LADY GARGOYLE
Will you wake Sidney, he's such a stay-a-bed.

EDWARD?
He isn't down there.

LADY GARGOYLE
Oh! Snatched from us again! Aggie, find a pen at once we must take out an advertisement: Wanted: new butler. Preferably human.

AGGIE 2
He'll have gone out, it's free country.

EDWARD (picks up the rucksack)
Well, it's time for me to go. I can't stay here.

AGGIE 2
I'm sure Beauty'll be back any moment my little chinchilla.

EDWARD
Last thing I saw of him his mouth was stuck to a Norwegian. That's when I decided to call it a night.

LADY GARGOYLE
Well really, Vauxhall! Back in my day those railway arches were just a place for diseased tramps to spend the night.

EDWARD
That's the place.

LADY GARGOYLE
At least join us for tea.

AGGIE 2
Fuck it, it's my last day in the place. Tea it is, Edward. You, me, and Death-Becomes-Her.

BEAUTY enters. He's topless other than wearing skinny braces and wears tiny shorts inside which his phone is stuffed. He has a nightclub wristband on. He can't stop jigging to an unheard rhythm.

AGGIE 2
There see, he's been for his morning run.

LADY GARGOYLE
Beauty!! Put a shirt on.

BEAUTY
I can't, it hurts.

He turns around. He has a tattoo on his back.

LADY GARGOYLE
Branded! You look like a navvy. Stop jigging.

BEAUTY
I can't. Oh, Edward. Hi...

EDWARD
Beauty, I'm saying goodbye.

BEAUTY
What?

EDWARD
I know you need to do this but it broke my heart thinking about you last night.

BEAUTY
But where will you go?

EDWARD
Oh you know, the old travel bug.

LADY GARGOYLE
I'll pack at once! Lend me your bikini, Aggie, I can always take it in a bit.

AGGIE 2
Take it in? It'd disappear up your chuff.

EDWARD
I mean to go alone. Sao Paulo, maybe, or Sydney. (Kisses Beauty) LADY GARGOYLEargoyle, Aggie, it's been a pleasure.

EDWARD exits. BEAUTY dashes after him.

LADY GARGOYLE
Wait!

BEAUTY stops but is still dancing to an unheard beat. It's infectious – AGGIE 2 starts dancing too.

LADY GARGOYLE
For heaven's sake stop jigging both of you, you're making me sea sick.

MAGGIE enters. She too starts dancing.

MAGGIE
A silent disco! Get a photo, I'll look so in touch.

LADY GARGOYLE
Sidney! He's gone astray!

BEAUTY
What?

AGGIE 2
Where's that sozzled sprite?

The FAIRY enters

FAIRY
Sorry. We had a lock-in at Candy Bar[105]. I think it's called that cos the clientele are a bit pick 'n' mix.

LADY GARGOYLE
A lock in?

FAIRY
I say that, I broke the door crumping and the fire brigade had to get us out. I think it was the first time they'd turned up to a crowd of wankered women and nobody fancied them. Must have been like Gary Barlow felt at Wembley[106]. (To Beauty) What the fuck are you on? And can I have a dab?

BEAUTY
I think it's called Glee but I had trouble following the conversation. Glowstick, where's Sidney?

FAIRY
New Zealand I think. Oh! The pet rock?

LADY GARGOYLE
He's missing.

FAIRY
Have you checked your phone?

BEAUTY
What?

FAIRY
The thing in your pants.

BEAUTY
A Brazilian couple had a look it.

FAIRY reaches into his shorts and retrieves his phone, handing it to him.

FAIRY
This thing. Though you should probably have the other thing checked and all after tonight

BEAUTY
Sidney! He's all tied up. Find him, I'll chase after Edward.

LADY GARGOYLE
Wait! That tortoise carried you on his shell, helped you with your studies and bathed you long after you were old enough to bathe yourself. We will rescue Sidney and you will lead the way.

MAGGIE
I'll call the police. No, the BBC. I'll front an appeal.

FAIRY
You can front my appeal.

BEAUTY
That doesn't even make sense. Come on. Think.

---

[105] Candy Bar was a Lesbian bar in Soho.

[106] In 2011, Take That toured with all five members for the first time since 1995.

MAGGIE
A safe-house in Pakistan[107]? No! The stadium! Carabosse owns the stadium!

AGGIE 2
It'll be crawling with security.

LADY GARGOYLE
Wait. On my wedding night, my husband took me by the hand and introduced me to a passage the existence of which I had never considered. It was so dark and smelly I felt nauseous, washed my hands and left it for the servants to shove their tools in. It's probably still underneath the stadium.

BEAUTY
Josh will know where it leads. Josh!!

MAGGIE (bitter)
He's upstairs Youtubing Britney videos.

JOSH enters.

JOSH
Oh my God when she shaved all her hair off!

LADY GARGOYLE
Pull your finger out and shed some light on my passage.

BEAUTY
The secret tunnel under the manor. Where does it lead?

JOSH
It goes to the cellar of Angus' pub. I snuck along it couple of times at night to have a perv at-

MAGGIE
I don't want to know.

LADY GARGOYLE
That's this pub!

AGGIE 2
I always wondered what that door was. Come on.

LADY GARGOYLE

We'll be seen by the guards.

AGGIE 2
Then we'll wait for the Olympics. There'll be crowds of people around and we can slip in unnoticed.

BEAUTY
But we need to get into the tunnel from here, and you're being evicted today.

AGGIE 2
You got your sense of fucking time back. How long can a tortoise survive without food.

LADY GARGOYLE
Months. They hibernate in the wild.

FAIRY
Ok. I'll transport us forward in time. We leg it through the tunnel, grab the walking pie and be back in time to watch the closing ceremony get rained off.

AGGIE 2
We'll stick out like a paint-balled bollock. I look about as sporty as Ken Clarke and she's dressed like something you'd put on a toilet roll.

JOSH
What, shit?

BEAUTY
I've got it! The perfect disguise. Aggie, we need some white bed sheets.

LADY GARGOYLE
Whatever for?

BEAUTY
You'll see.

AGGIE 2
Come along everyone. Get all the sheets off the beds. Follow me.

JOSH
Could you maybe not use the sheet in my room...

AGGIE 2
Come on!

They exit

---

[107] Osama bin Laden's hiding place where he was killed in 2011 by US forces.

Scene 12: The chamber under the stadium

CARABOSSE and SIDNEY enter, the latter with a broom and an apron.

SIDNEY
Do you think I might watch the finish? It's the Animal Olympics this year too.

CARABOSSE
Of course! But what am I thinking you'll be dead by then.

SIDNEY
Please no!

CARABOSSE
You're the only one who knows my secrets. Ah my little desert trolley I'll miss you, I've grown so fond of you these last six months I could scoop you out and eat you.

Footsteps.

CARABOSSE
Hide! Quick!

Sidney goes. EDWARD enters.

CARABOSSE
You came! It works! It works!

EDWARD
Carabosse. I... did you call?

CARABOSSE
In a manner of speaking. Sweet Prince you lucky boy. In barely an hour the entire world will be doing my bidding. 7 billion miserable slaves! But not you. You can be my king.

EDWARD
Never! I have Beauty.

CARABOSSE
He doesn't love you.

EDWARD
No.

CARABOSSE
We'll be youthful long after he dies. So what will it be? Slavery, or eternity with me?

EDWARD
What should I do? Give me time.

CARABOSSE
You have one hour.

EDWARD
Right... Thank you...

He goes. SIDNEY enters

CARABOSSE
Are you excited my little walking cow pat? The world's leaders are gathering above our heads. When we switch this on we'll be tapping into world's most influential minds. Or in the case of Berlusconi, directly into his penis. But first, a celebratory joint.

She takes a joint from her dress.

SIDNEY
I'm not sure it's a good idea to smoke down here.

CARABOSSE
Nonsense, Sidney, this is my chamber pot.

BEAUTY and JOSH burst into the chamber wearing hastily made white fencing outfits and carrying rubbish wooden swords.

JOSH
Right guard!

SIDNEY
It's en garde.

CARABOSSE
Idiots, you're too late for the games.

LADY GARGOYLE, AGGIE 2 and MAGGIE enter, also as fencers.

AGGIE 2
But not too late for the jelly and ice cream.

BEAUTY
It's me, Beauty.

CARABOSSE grabs SIDNEY and holds him in front of himself.

CARABOSSE
How did you get past the guards? They're armed.

AGGIE 2
But not beyond bribery.

CARABOSSE
You've nothing to bribe them with.

500

AGGIE 2 fishes a pubic hair out of her teeth. She looks at LADY GARGOYLE, who also fishes a pubic hair from her teeth. They both look at Josh, who spits.

SIDNEY
He's going to hack into the minds of the world's leaders.

BEAUTY
Let go of him!

JOSH
Yeah let go of him.

CARABOSSE (pointing upwards)
Oh look, an osprey.

JOSH looks up as he does the WF punches him in the crotch. JOSH screams and drops his sword. The WF picks it up.

CARABOSSE
You and me. One on one. Now.

BEAUTY
As you like.

They fight, a frenzied but clumsy sword fight. Beauty ends up on the floor, it looks as though he'll lose. The CARABOSSE grabs Maggie and holds the sword to her.

CARABOSSE
One move and the Milibabe[108] gets it.

The GOOD FAIRY enters.

FAIRY (Singing)
Hiiiyaaah! Sorry, private moment?

BEAUTY
Call yourself a fairy godmother? My best friend's about to get it in the neck, my butler's been kidnapped, and modern society has turned me into a raving slut.

FAIRY
Right... To stop this bad 'un running amok, I'll turn her into solid rock!

CARABOSSE freezes. Josh looks uncertain then grins

JOSH
It worked!

---

[108] ...as the women Ed Miliband promoted to his shadow cabinet were labelled.

CARABOSSE (unfreezing)
Only joking! You don't move.

FAIRY
Aw shite. Nothing at all?

CARABOSSE
You tickled my clit a bit.

FAIRY
Good magic's like a sewer. It's shit underground. Boys and girls, you're going to have to help me. Wave your arms like this. That's it. Now concentrate on turning her into stone.

CARABOSSE
Ooh you're getting my bum hole now... Oh! Oh god what's happening! I'm melting! Help!!

She freezes and drops her sword, then collapses, dead. They all cheer. Beauty hugs the fairy.

BEAUTY
Come here you.

FAIRY
Yeah get off I'm a bit weird with intimacy. (To a girl in the audience) But I can be talked round. Right, where's the hospitality?

FAIRY exits.

BEAUTY
What happens now?

MAGGIE
It's up to you. You own all this. The stadium, the land around it. You're the Lord of Stratford.

LADY GARGOYLE
We're rich!

AGGIE 2
He's rich.

BEAUTY
Hang on hang on. I don't want to be the Lord of Stratford. I've only just woken up from a hundred year sleep. I want to see the world, get a job, work hard, settle down. And I want to do that with Edward. I'm going to find him, if he'll take me back.

JOSH notices the locket hanging around MAGGIE's neck.

JOSH
Maggie, where did you get that?

AGGIE 2
Don't point at a girl's breasts.

JOSH
I'm looking at her locket.

AGGIE 2 slaps him.

JOSH
Where did you get it?

MAGGIE
I've had it since I was little. It's been handed down through generations along with the outy tummy button and the six toes. (She gives it to him) I can't even open it.

JOSH opens it. They all look inside.

MAGGIE
He's beautiful!

BEAUTY
It looks like you Josh.

JOSH takes the photo out and stares at it.

JOSH
I don't understand...

MAGGIE
Who's that holding you? Is that your dad?

AGGIE
It can't be Josh's dad. He's black and white.

BEAUTY
No. It's my dad.

LADY GARGOYLE
That man is my husband, Beauty's father – and Josh's father.

BEAUTY
What?

LADY GARGOYLE
Before I had you, Beauty, your father had a one-night stand with a maid. She had a baby, a little boy. It was agreed that the father would remain unknown, and in return we would give the baby a home and a job at the manor. (With edge) Of course, the maid died not long afterwards.

JOSH
So we're brothers?

AGGIE 2
That means Josh is Lord of Stratford!

JOSH
I'm rich! Haha! Maggie, will you marry me?

MAGGIE
Oh Josh. I'm drawn to you like a lesbian to world music. But it's 2011. It's time for you to accept yourself for who you are. You're gay.

JOSH
Gay?

MAGGIE
Homosexual.

AGGIE 2
When a man and another man love each other very much, the man puts his penis into the other man's vagina.

There is a huge mechanical grinding noise. They all look about them. The floor starts to shake.

SIDNEY
It must be the machine.

Beauty runs to the wall and unplugs the machine. The noise and shaking carries on.

BEAUTY
It's not the machine.

They have trouble balancing. Daylight comes from above, a little at first, then more.

LADY GARGOYLE
Help!

JOSH
What the fuck?

AGGIE 2
We seem to be rising.

BEAUTY
The roof's opening. There's daylight.

LADY GARGOYLE
I can hear a large crowd.

AGGIE 2
I can't.

LADY GARGOYLE (pointedly to the audience)
I can hear a large crowd

The audience make the sound of a crowd.

MAGGIE
Oh my god.

LADY GARGOYLE
Where are we?

MAGGIE
We're slap bang in the middle of the stadium...

They stare out at the audience.

AGGIE 2
They don't look much like sports fans.

ANNOUNCER'S VOICE
It looks as though the ceremony is underway, boys and girls. The turf itself opened up and a sort of platform rose up from underneath the field. Just imagine the budget to be able to do that.

BEAUTY
Alright don't rub it in.

ANNOUNCER'S VOICE
From the state of their outfits I'd say it's the Greek fencing team.

AGGIE 2
There's so many-

MAGGIE
Voters! (coughs) Ladies and gentlemen. Boys and girls. Prime Minister. Mr President. Your Majesties. Mr Barrowman. Miss Lloyd. Little baby Harper. Welcome to the closing ceremony!

LADY GARGOYLE keeps making little waves at the crowd.

AGGIE 2
Oi! Stop flirting when my daughter's trying to talk bollocks.

LADY GARGOYLE
I am acknowledging my admirers.

AGGIE 2
I don't know how you can spot him in the crowd. Oh wait there he is. He's got a beautiful guide dog.

MAGGIE
Mum!

AGGIE 2 points at LADY GARGOYLE accusatively.

MAGGIE
Like all of you, I'm great fan of sport and free wine. Sport brings us together.

LADY GARGOYLE (*To Aggie 2*)
I was once invited to sign the local football team's ball bags.

MAGGIE
But for too long, sport hasn't represented everyone. Well I have news for you. Tonight, my friends have saved you from the destruction! And these brave boys are gay!

JOSH
I'm not gay.

AGGIE 2 (points at him, plays to the crowd)
Homophobe.

LADY GARGOYLE
The crowd are booing!

AGGIE 2
I can't hear them.

LADY GARGOYLE
The crowd are booing!!

AGGIE 2
They want entertainment Maggie, not this shit.

MAGGIE
Right... Wait! Josh! You're an entertainer.

JOSH
What?

MAGGIE
May I present, Josh the Jester.

Spotlight. Josh is dumbstruck.

AGGIE 2
Go on love. You must have something you've practised.

Josh thinks. Then he starts to do a striptease.

BEAUTY
A song. Do a song!

JOSH
Oh, yeah! Here's a song I heard at karaoke last night. Take it away, Maestro!

SIDNEY
You can't say that in here. Visa[109] have paid for snipers.

---

[109] Visa's sponsorship of the London Olympics came with fantastically heavy conditions – one couldn't use anything else to buy tickets.

JOSH
Maestro, please.

SONG: I AM WHAT I AM
(Josh sings to the famous tune from *La Cage Aux Folles*)

I am what I am, and what I am needs no rhyme or reason
Don't care if it hurts, I'll wear lumberjack shirts even when they're not in season
I'm born straight and I'll tell you that needs no rehearsing
I don't want to work in fashion, politics or nursing
Sorry if it grates, but hey I'm straight, and yes I am what I am

I am what I am, and though I like hanging with queers
I'll give you some tips, I like a nice set of hips, and a range of proper beers
There's one life and there's no return and no deposit
One life, I don't need a fucking walk-in closet
I bang my own drum, I'll even play with my bum but, guys, I am what I am

I am what I am, I don't need no father-son role-play
If I want to be, in touch with me, I'll cry to Coldplay
No weird crushes on Thatcher, Madge or Mrs Merkel
I don't need to sleep with my entire social circle
We've all played at being bent, but I'm 90 percent – straight - and I am what I am

MAGGIE
You were amazing!

JOSH
Now will you marry me?

MAGGIE
No. I only met you six months and two days ago, and 6 months of that was spent time travelling. But I'll move in with you if you like?

JOSH
Can we get a maid?

MAGGIE
Only if I can choose him.

CARABOSSE wakes up. She picks up a javelin and aims it at BEAUTY.

LADY GARGOYLE
Quick! The spell's worn off.

EDWARD runs in, sees what's happening and seizes CARABOSSE. Someone takes the javelin from her.

BEAUTY
You saved my life Edward!

CARABOSSE
You've betrayed me! Ooh what strong arms. Now let me go.

The FAIRY enters with a mini scotch egg and a glass of wine.

FAIRY
What's occurring?

BEAUTY
I love you Edward.

EDWARD
I love you too.

He let's go of CARABOSSE and runs to Beauty. CARABOSSE picks up the javelin.

EDWARD
Beauty!

He pushes BEAUTY to the ground. CARABOSSE throws the javelin at JOSH. It hits him and he falls to the ground.

MAGGIE
Josh!

CARABOSSE
Haha. If the land reverts to him, so does the spell. Good luck together but don't expect him to help much around the house. He'll be asleep for 100 years.

MAGGIE
Quick. Do something.

CARABOSSE
Pritstick can't help you.

FAIRY
I know a place where the old fairies go
To be stranded all day in the blustery weather
They eat chips and miss buses cos they're ever so slow
You're banished to Bournemouth forever!!

The fairy is dragged off by unseen forces. Everyone cheers.

FAIRY
I call that the Darkroom spell. You get pulled off by invisible hands.

MAGGIE
Josh! Josh!

He doesn't wake.

BEAUTY
Perhaps if I try what Edward did to me.

He prepares his hand into a fisting position...

FAIRY
You're not a Prince.

EDWARD
Allow me.

He goes to kiss Josh

AGGIE 2
Oh hell.

FAIRY
But there is another spell I can try. Praise be the heavens above. Let this boy be woken by the power of love.

MAGGIE
Well, that should be easy. Because I really love him.

BEAUTY
Me too.

EDWARD looks at him.

BEAUTY
In a brotherly way.

EDWARD looks at him again.

FAIRY
I know this ain't exactly the Palladium,
But we need enough love to fill the stadium
Boys and girls we need your help. Everyone get up on your feet. Now everyone, give the person next to you a big hug. That's it. If anyone can manage a kiss that'd help.... Yeah hands above the belt sir.

The characters all hug too, except for SIDNEY.

FAIRY
Oh dear. Stop. It's not enough. (pause) Sidney why didn't you join in?

SIDNEY
There is only one person I have ever loved madam and I cannot pretend that I love another.

BEAUTY
But it could wake Joshy.

SIDNEY
I am a tortoise of honour.

ANNOUNCER'S VOICE
Boys and girls let me interrupt you there, not only because we're in danger of getting unbearably sentimental but also because the leader in the tortoise marathon is about to cross the finish line. What a specimen!

Another tortoise enters wearing a running vest and a turban. He is running, but incredibly slowly.

SIDNEY
Mani?? Is that you?

MANI
Sidney? Can it be?

SIDNEY
Come here, my beautiful upturned Balti dish. I never stopped loving you all these years.

They kiss. JOSH stirs, wakes and farts. MAGGIE runs to him and kisses him.

MANI
I am so very very tired.

SIDNEY
I will cook for you while you rest. I'll cook for you all. Aggie, may we use the kitchen?

AGGIE 2
Lead the way. Hurry up though, people are bursting.

The tortoises exit. It takes fucking ages.

EDWARD
Beauty, listen, it doesn't have to be permanent but, well, I have a little place you could move into for a while with me?

BEAUTY
I'd love to.

Edward smiles.

BEAUTY
You're starting to get these really cute laughter lines.

EDWARD
What?! Impossible!

FAIRY
Afraid not my little lamb-cock. If you're gonna stick with this black pudding diet and fall in love, you'll stop being a vampire, and grow old and die just like other mortals.

BEAUTY
Oh.

EDWARD
I'm game if you are.

They kiss. Everyone cheers again.

LADY GARGOYLE
That's fine. Turn your back on a remarkably young-looking single mother who brought you up with only a dwindling number of servants?

BEAUTY
Mother, I'd never turn my back on you. But I don't have a penny to my name.

JOSH
We'll see you right, Lady G. You can have a house on our estate.

AGGIE 2
Or, you could come stay with me and learn how to run the second-best gay-friendly pub in London.

LADY GARGOYLE
Do you know I think I might rather enjoy that. Could we turn Maggie's bedroom into a theatre?

JOSH
That's a great idea. Can I be in something?

MAGGIE
I'm banking on it.

BEAUTY
Right everyone! To the pub!

A magical light and twinkly sound.

FAIRY
Wait! Look! It's the great fairy garden in the sky!! Aw it looks lovely but... Hello!

KINDLY FAIRY VOICE
Hello little Fairy

EDWARD and BEAUTY
Hello

FAIRY
She means me.

KINDLY FAIRY VOICE
It's time for you to join us.

FAIRY
Auch I'd love to hen but... do I have time for a wee pint first? Or do you have a bar up there?

KINDLY FAIRY VOICE
Alcohol is forbidden in the fairy garden. But we have barbeques, and A-grade cocaine.

FAIRY
Ay alright. Do I have time for a quick one first?

KINDLY FAIRY VOICE
Of course, if you bring me something too?

FAIRY
Aye. What is it?

KINDLY FAIRY VOICE
A bottle of WKD.

FAIRY
You're on. Aggie, lead the way!

THE END[110]

---

[110] This is the only panto we didn't end with rhyming verses. Instead we had a rewritten version of Depeche Mode's *Just Can't Get Enough.*

Musical references in *Sleeping Beauty: One Little Prick*

Lines from the following songs were quoted or mangled by Carabosse:

"The Boy is Mine" (1998) written by LaShawn Daniels, Rodney Jerkins, Fred Jerkins III, Japhe Tajeda, Brandy Norwood.

"I Need a Dollar" (2010) written by Aloe Blacc, Leon Michels, Nick Movshon, Jeff Dynamite,

"Swagger Jagger" (2011) written by Andrew "Dru Brett" Harr, Jermaine "Mayne Zayne" Jackson. Andre "Dre" Davidson and Sean "Sean D" Davidson, Cher Lloyd, Petr Brdička, Autumn Rowe, Marcus Lomax and Clarence Coffee Jr.

"MacArthur Park" (1967) written by Jimmy Webb.

"Sweet Dreams" (2008) written by Beyoncé, James Scheffer, Wayne Wilkins, and Rico Love.

"Close Every Door" (1968) written by Tim Rice and Andrew Lloyd Webber,

"I'm Free" (1968) written by Mick Jagger and Keith Richards.

"Single Ladies" (2008) written by Beyoncé, Terius "The-Dream" Nash, Thaddis "Kuk" Harrell, and Christopher "Tricky" Stewart.

"Telephone " (2008) written by Lady Gaga, Rodney Jerkins, LaShawn Daniels, Lazonate Franklin and Beyoncé.

"Till the World Ends" (2011) written by Kesha Sebert, Lukasz "Dr. Luke" Gottwald, Alexander Kronlund, and Max Martin.

We also adapted the lyrics from the following songs.

"Nine to Five" (1980) written by Dolly Parton.

"Anything Goes" (1934) written by Cole Porter.

"I Am What I Am" (1983) written by Jerry Herman.

Robin Hood: Queen of Thieves

Adrian Quinton as Dr. Marion Maid and Brendan Riding as Matron in *Robin Hood: Queen of Thieves*. Photo by Derek Drescher.

Robin Hood: Queen of Thieves

2010: The year of the ash cloud. The eruption of a volcano in Iceland created a cloud of ash, grounding flights across Europe leaving more than 10 million passengers stranded.

The United Kingdom had a new government led by David Cameron – our first coalition government since 1945. The new Foreign Secretary, William Hague denied rumours in the press about his sexuality and one of his aides, twenty-five-year-old Christopher Myers, resigned. The third film in the Twilight saga was released with many a gay man and straight woman swooning over its star Robert Pattinson. Chris Moyles was still pulling in huge radio audiences despite controversies including, in January, Moyles' guest Dappy from the hip-hop trio N-Dubz copying a female listener's phone number from a studio console and harassing her; and in September a 25-minute on-air rant about not having been paid. And in November Prince William and Kate Middleton announced their engagement.

Robin Hood was our first pantomime properly to feature songs, and although the choices were fun – from The Clash to show tunes - we perhaps hadn't fully realised that songs need a purpose and should be spread out throughout the show. We also saw the Above The Stag pantomime debut of the hilarious Matthew Baldwin, playing the Sheriff of Nottingham. He was a terrific villain in this and in Aladdin but has since made the role of dame his own.

Robin Hood: Queen of Thieves

By Jon Bradfield and Martin Hooper

Characters

Fairy, male and not too young.
Friar Tuck, runs the Sherwood Forest Cottage Hospital.
Robin Hood, champion archer, and a nurse.
Will Scarlet, the hospital porter.
Matron, Will and Little Joan's mother. The dame.
Little Joan, a surgeon among other things.
Donkey, female with a Yorkshire accent.
Sheriff of Nottingham, owner of The Castle private hospital.
Dr. Marion Maid, a male heartthrob TV doctor.

Robin Hood: Queen of Thieves was first performed at Above The Stag Theatre on 30 November 2010 with the following cast and creative team:

Fairy: Jonson Wilkinson; Robin Hood: Guy Warren-Thomas; Donkey: Helen Victor; The Sherriff of Nottingham: Matthew Baldwin; Will Scarlet: Sam Sadler; Matron: Brendan Riding; Little Joan: Caroline Wagstaffe; Doctor Marion Maid: Adrian Quinton; Friar Tuck: Mansel David

Director: Royce Ullah; Designer: Fi Russell; Lighting Designer and Stage Manager: Ben Blaber; Producer: Peter Bull

With thanks to Ian Wych for suggesting the show's title.

Scene 1: A road to Nottingham

The FAIRY enters.

FAIRY

With artistry, wit and contortions,
We shall conjure, right here where I'm stood,
An epic of epic proportions
The legend of Robin Hood

Allow me to guide you gently,
Through what we'll call our plot
About heroes and villains, the serfs and the gentry,
The haves - and the have-nots

Our play is set in Nottinghamshire,
Famed for its forests and caves
I may have been drinking but I know what you're thinking
What amazing locations for raves

But no, there won't even be parties in squats,
Austerity's blown through the place,
Since a coup by the wicked Sheriff of Notts
Left us all in tragic disgrace

His life is a gilded, luxurious idyll,
While taxes are high, and cuts deep,
The poor are in strife, and sometimes in Lidl,
Just look at our set, it's so cheap.

Now this is the road to Nottingham city
In fact, it's the A453
There's a sign saying "Robin Hood Country" - it's pretty -
But it seems premature to me.

Not least because Robin, our hero, is missing!
He hasn't been seen for so long!
So in case we're all just left pissing about
Try and think up a joke or a song...

Boys and girls! Are you sitting all comfy and snug?
Are your phones off or set to vibrate?
Are you sat beside someone you'd quite like to hug?
I see some of you are, well that's great.

It's dark, let us brighten your night with our playing,
It's winter, let's have warmth and noise!
Have a wonderful evening and, ah, what's the saying?
Bona to meet you, girls and boys!

*The FAIRY goes to the side of the stage, semi hidden.
ROBIN enters*

ROBIN

Hello boys and girls! I think you're playing it a bit too cool there, you're not in Dalston now. Hello boys and girls! Hello top row! Hello bottom row down here. And hello to the, what have we had, tops, bottoms, let's call you guys the grateful for anything row. Hello grateful row![111] I'm Robin Hood, and I'm just back from my travels in the Holy Land. I'm glad to be home though, Nottinghamshire's such a happy, prosperous, trouble-free land...

FAIRY
Hello stranger

ROBIN
Hello. Have we met?

FAIRY
The clue was in the word "stranger"

ROBIN
Oh yeah, duh! Hello. I'm Robin Hood. Scourge of the rich, friend to the poor, champion archer and a whole lot more!

FAIRY
A whole lot more than a champion archer?

ROBIN
Well... that's not my day job. I'm a nurse really. (beat). And I like Judge Judy, Nurse Jackie and Ugly Betty. And my favourite music is the Glee soundtrack volume two. Who are you?

FAIRY
I'm a fairy.

ROBIN
Shouldn't you be on a tree?

FAIRY
I only did that the once and I was so out of it on Tina[112] I didn't feel the needles till three days later. And it wasn't Christmas, it was my birthday.

ROBIN
I didn't know fairies had birthdays

---

[111] The first, pub-theatre incarnation of Above The Stag had just three wide rows of seats, albeit quite wide ones.
[112] Crystal meth > Christina > Tina.

FAIRY

How do you think Rollerdisco stays in business? You're a nice colour.

ROBIN

Thanks! I've been to Israel for an archery completion. I won a fortnight on a gay Kibbutz. But it took me weeks to get home. I was delayed by volcanic ash.

FAIRY

I think I've met him. Well his name was Ash and his molten eruptions could bring down a 747. How did you get home?

ROBIN

I bought a donkey and rode it all the way from the Holy Land.

FAIRY

It must have been hard.

ROBIN

It's a female donkey.

FAIRY

But you must have been stiff.

ROBIN

Oh yes. The whole way. I'm the same with buses. It's the vibrations.

FAIRY

Donkeys don't vibrate.

ROBIN

They do if you tickle them right.

FAIRY

I like you already. Where's the donkey?

ROBIN

She's very tired. You don't want to see her.

FAIRY

I'm sure the boys and girls want to see her.

ROBIN

Oh no they don't

"Oh yes we do!" etc

ROBIN

Alright then! I'll go and untie her.

ROBIN exits

FAIRY

Kinky.

As I was on the road to Nottingham
I met a lad I'd seen before on cam
I try to stop my gaze from heading south
But can't forget him spurting in his mouth...

ROBIN enters

ROBIN

Why are you looking at me like that?

FAIRY

We *have* met before. In a way. (He mimes typing at a computer)

ROBIN

I don't play the piano.

The FAIRY gives him a look.

ROBIN

Oh..! Well... I started doing shows online to raise money for the hospital. It's a very poor hospital and we need every penny we can get. How embarrassing.

FAIRY

I should say so sweetheart, your room's a fucking tip. You might use a Dyson occasionally.

ROBIN

That's how people end up in our hospital. The donkey's a bit shy. We need to lure her out here. I'm going to need some help...

He singles someone out in the front row.

ROBIN

Hello, what's your name?

FAIRY (indicating Robin)

He normally skips that bit.

ROBIN

Don't be rude. What's your name?

The audience member gives his name.

ROBIN

Well [name], give me your hand... now stand up and come and join us up here. Yeah I know, I've seen higher potholes. A big hand for [name] boys and girls. Have you received a big hand before? Right, you're going to help me lure out my Donkey. Give us your hand. Here's a carrot, the Donkey loves carrots.

ROBIN puts the carrot in his upturned hand

ROBIN
Now after three, you've all got to shout, Come on Donkey, Show us your head. Ready? One, two, three

"Come on Donkey, show us your head" - Nothing happens.

ROBIN
Wait there.

He runs offstage then returns.

ROBIN
She's still a bit shy! So here's what we're going to do. *(To the chosen audience member)* Turn away so she can't see your handsome face, ok? So if you stand like this...

ROBIN positions the volunteer to face away from the entrance.

Bend over a little, that's it. And pop your hand back between your legs so she can see your carrot. There we go. Right we'll try again. One, two three...

They all shout. DONKEY enters, looks about. She walks toward the audience member and towards the carrot in his upturned hand which is of course just below his bum. She pushes her muzzle into his hand. It all hopefully looks very rude.

ROBIN
Donkey! Well done, brave girl. These are the boys and girls... Boys and girls, this is – oh but you haven't got a name. Well that won't do will it?

The DONKEY shakes its head.

ROBIN
Would you like to have a name?

The DONKEY nods.

ROBIN
Shall I choose a name for you?

The DONKEY shakes its head violently.

FAIRY
Why don't you let the boys and girls name the donkey?

ROBIN
That's a great idea! Can anyone think of a name for my lovely Donkey?

The audience suggests names and one is chosen. From now on, where [Donkey] appears in the script, the chosen name is to be used.[113]

ROBIN
Well [Donkey], you've met the boys and girls. And I met this man just now, he claims he's a fairy.

The DONKEY shakes her head.

ROBIN
No [donkey], I don't believe him either.

FAIRY
I *am* a fairy.

ROBIN
Then prove it. Find me the man of my dreams.

FAIRY
I can't do that in scene one, it would bollocks up the plot.

ROBIN
Hmmm. Ok, make [donkey] talk.

FAIRY
I'll give it a whirl. Turn around.

ROBIN does. The fairy walks up to him and cups his bum.

FAIRY
Here's one ass, it's a right little peach
And there's another – give it speech!

ROBIN
Why did you have to hold my ass?

FAIRY
Because a cock is a very different kind of animal, Robin.

ROBIN and FAIRY both look at the Donkey in anticipation. A pause.

FAIRY
Well go on.

DONKEY
(In a strong Yorkshire accent) I can't think of anything to say. Don't pressure me.

FAIRY
Aha! It works!

---

[113] The cast found it remarkably difficult to remember the donkey's name each night so they'd immediately write it in big letters on sheets of paper and stick them up backstage.

ROBIN

I can't hear anything.

DONKEY

And what the blethering heck's with this fucking accent!? I'm meant to be Israeli. What is it? It feels all horrible in the back of my throat.

FAIRY

So do Prince Alberts and mephedrone, but you get accustomed.

ROBIN

What are talking about? Did you hear [donkey] speak boys and girls?

FAIRY

Hmmm... I think it's because I called her an ass and not a donkey. The spell only half worked. I think me and the boys and girls are the only ones who can hear her.

ROBIN

Look, whatever mate. You're a rubbish fairy.

FAIRY

Well you're a rubbish pantomime hero. A nurse! Which hospital do you work at? The big one or the little one?

ROBIN

The little one. Friar Tuck's Sherwood Forest Cottage Hospital. I'd never work for the big one. It's called The Castle and it's run by the SHERIFF of Nottingham. He's a horrible man. Greedy, cruel, selfish-

FAIRY

Bit of a cunt then.

ROBIN

You could say that.

FAIRY

I might do if it comes up in conversation. Oh but you've been away... you won't have heard! The SHERIFF has been elected head of the council. They say he might be going to cut all the funding to Friar Tuck's... what was it?

ROBIN

Friar Tuck's Sherwood Forest Cottage Hospital. But – he can't! The Castle only treats rich patients. Everyone else relies on our place. Who voted for him?

FAIRY

Well, nobody.

ROBIN

So how did he get in!?

FAIRY

They introduced a very complicated new voting system. Or rather, the SHERIFF did. AV plus or minus one to the power of Grayskull I think it was called[114]. People got terribly confused.

ROBIN

But he's evil. He'll shut us down.

FAIRY

Then stop him. Listen carefully. You see, you have some royalty in you.

ROBIN

I hope it's Prince Harry.

FAIRY

Yes I heard you like to take from the rich. Robin, you have royal blood, blue DNA, coursing through your veins. You are thirty-sixth in line to the British throne.

ROBIN

Did you hear that Donkey!?

DONKEY

I've got enormous ears. What do think they're for, garnish?

ROBIN

Thirty-sixth in line to the... That's shit! It's not even an Earl. That's not going to help me at all. I'll have to save Friar Tuck's Sherwood Forest Cottage Hospital by myself. Come on, [donkey], let's go.

ROBIN and DONKEY begin to exit. As they do the SHERIFF enters:

SHERIFF: Hahahahaha!

"Boo", etc

SHERIFF

Right that's £50 from each of you. Noise pollution tax.

---

[114] Nick Clegg's Liberal Democrats squandered their long-held dreams of meaningful electoral reform when they agreed to support David Cameron's Conservatives in a coalition government in exchange for a referendum which offered the public the status quo of First Past The Post versus a compromised alternative system that nobody, not even the Liberal Democrats, wanted.

ROBIN
Leave them alone you bully.

SHERIFF
Out of my way idiot. And your mangey mule.

He kicks the donkey, the donkey squeals

ROBIN (Squaring up to Sheriff)
She's a Donkey. Stay away from her.

The DONKEY farts

SHERIFF
Thanks for the warning. Who are you, you silly little boy?

ROBIN
I'm Robin Hood, an archer--.

The SHERIFF sings the archer's theme tune

ROBIN
Oh what mate, you think I didn't get that at school? Sticks and stones SHERIFF.

SHERIFF
What a good idea.

ROBIN
I'm a champion archer!... And I'm a nurse at Friar Tuck's Sherwood Forest Cottage Hospital.

SHERIFF
But not for much longer. Soon it'll be curtains for that calorie-loving cleric and his Sherwood Forest Cottage Hospital.

ROBIN
We'll stop you won't we (donkey)?

The DONKEY farts

ROBIN
We'll meet again. Come on [donkey].

DONKEY
Well that were a bleeding success you butch bitch.

ROBIN and DONKEY exit

FAIRY
He's right you know, I've seen it in my balls. That's shocked you.

SHERIFF
I was more shocked when Joe McElderry came out. No boy and his flatulent ass have ever stopped me before.

FAIRY
They will.

SHERIFF
And you're going to help him? A failed fairy? Underachieving and past your sell by date? Right, I'm a busy man. Laws to execute, lesbians to abolish. Or is it the other way round? Ha ha ha.

He exits

FAIRY
He's right. I am a failed fairy. This is my last big chance to make something of myself before I head off to the fairy retirement, I have to help Robin and his friends. I have to get things right. You know,

I was going to play Tinkerbell in Peter Pan
But they offered me this, so fuck it
It's hard not to work with a leading man
When you've seen him cum bucket 'pon bucket

Now remember, cheer Robin, say boo to the baddie,
And if you must wank, sleep or cough,
Maintain some decorum, or visit the store room,
You'll be fine, you're divine. Right I'm off.

Scene 2: Friar Tuck's Sherwood Forest cottage hospital

WILL enters. He has a jar of sweets and begins to eat them. Suddenly he notices the audience.

WILL
OMG you nearly gave me a heart attack! Hello boys and girls. How's it hanging? I'm Will, Will Scarlet. Feeling festive? I tell you, boys and girls, I'm feeling quite a mix of things. I'm a bit sad. (ahhh) Oh I'm sadder than that. (AHHH) Not that sad, it's panto, it's not Beaches. You see, I'm like a bit in love with one of the nurses here. Robin Hood. But he went on holiday without me. He said he wanted to find himself. I said I'd have a rummage if he wanted but no, and all I've had off him is one picture text of him surrounded by Israeli boys in rainbow striped hot pants. I bet he's fallen in love with someone and decided to stay.

He gets out his iPhone or similar.

WILL
So I've like been following him on Grindr[115]. It tells me how many thousands of miles he is from me. Oh wait! It says he's only 1.1 kilometres away!! He's come back!... What if he's brought someone back with him? (pause). Anyway boys and girls, I got something special to share with you D'ya want some?

Will throws some sweets to the audience. From offstage, MATRON shouts: Will Scarlet!!

WILL
That's my mum. She's the Matron of the hospital and she's on the warpath. The thing is though, sometimes she forgets about me. She's always on about my sister, Little Joan but she thinks I'm a lame-ass. It's sad isn't it? So if you see her I want you to remind her about me. Whenever you see her I want you to shout "Hiya Matron, how's your Willie?" Come on let's try. One, two, three: Hiya Matron, how's your Willie? Quick I think she's coming.

WILL hides, MATRON enters. Audience shouts.

MATRON
Oh you cheeky rabble!

---

[115] Grindr launched on Apple phones in 2009, on Blackberry in 2010 and on Android phones in 2011.

She slaps Will around the head.

MATRON (to audience:)
Visiting hour's finished.

WILL
No mum, these are the boys and girls. They're here to watch.

MATRON
Oh! Well let's have a look at you. Now I hope you've got clean hands, we have to have high levels of hygiene here at the hospital. (To someone in the audience) A hospital's like a GUM clinic, sir, only bigger. Come on, hands up. Fronts. Backs. I can still see clubbing stamps on half of your wrists, do try and shower weekly dears. (To the same audience member) A shower's like a tap, sir, only bigger. Now, young Will, what do you think you're up to? You haven't done a minute's work all morning.

WILL
Nor have you! You've been watching TV like me.

MATRON
It's that gorgeous young television doctor.

WILL
Dr Marion Maid.

MATRON
Dr Marion Maid. Oh my when he pulls on those latex gloves...

WILL
(To audience) They had an omnibus of all his programmes. Show Us Your Poo.

MATRON
Warts and All

WILL
How Clean Is Your Gut

MATRON
Guess What We had For Breakfast

WILL
And my favourite one

BOTH
Sexual Healing.

WIL
Oh I wish he was working here. We'd fall in love and I wouldn't have to feel sad about Robin anymore.

MATRON
Dr Marion Maid is just waiting for the right matron... I could get my hair crimped!

WILL
You could try electrolysis.

MATRON
How dare you. I have been wooed on a number of occasions.

WILL
I heard you'd been downright filthy.

MATRON
Men have beaten a path to my door.

WILL
But you always manage to drag them back to bed.

MATRON
Cruel boy. Now, to work. Your poor sister's been hard at it since six. (Calls) Little Joan! Little Joan!

JOAN enters wearing a surgical apron and holding a kidney dish in her hand containing a penis.

JOAN
What is it mum?

MATRON
Oh my, what on earth is... (picks up the penis briefly) Well look at that, she's gone and joined the militant feminists.

JOAN
I'm halfway through some emergency surgery.

WILL
Does it hurt?

JOAN
Not mine.

WILL
We were just talking about that fit doctor, Marion Maid.

JOAN
Even if I fancied men I wouldn't touch him with a shitty scalpel. Not that he'd know what a scalpel was. Who are these lot?

WILL
They're the boys and girls, sis.

JOAN
Oh. (To audience) Hey.

MATRON
Right, back get to work. And you Will. I'm terrified of the Sheriff doing an inspection and shutting us down. He could turn up at any time. Boys and girls, please let me know if you see the SHERIFF? We're doing our best in difficult circumstances. But with Robin away we're so short staffed, and there've been slight issues with (whispers) MRSA.

WILL
MDMA?

MATRON
MRSA!!

The SHERIFF enters. "He's behind you" etc. MATRON screams.

SHERIFF
Ha ha ha! (Looking out at the audience) Is this your A&E? Most of these are beyond medical help. And oh dear! Did I hear short staffing? MRSA? And on your watch!

MATRON lifts her little nurses' watch.

MATRON
There's nothing on my watch. MRSA? Ha ha ha! What a thought! No, no, none of that here. You misheard me... What was it Will?

WILL
MDMA

MATRON
Yes! No! No! And we are not short staffed!

JOAN
Right well I'll get this stitched on, make a start on lunch and then get going on the hospital accounts.

SHERIFF
Not short staffed...?

JOAN
Look at that boys and girls. (Points to the penis and to the SHERIFF). One stage, two massive pricks.

SHERIFF
You can't wave a penis around in a public hospital.

WILL
I only do it when it's quiet.

517

MATRON slaps WILL. JOAN exits.

MATRON
And what would you know about a *public* hospital?

SHERIFF
I've seen enough! You'll be out of a job by next week! And then the people will have no choice but to come to my palatial private operation for palatial private operations! I'll be even richer.

MATRON
But this is our home! (Slightly sexy) Sheriff, you seem stressed. I'm highly skilled in fourteen kinds of massage.

WILL
I'm not, but I've got fewer limits.

SHERIFF
I have a better idea. Come and see me at the castle.

MATRON
Oh my!

SHERIFF
We offer the finest range of facelifts.

As the SHERIFF goes to leave, ROBIN enters holding flowers.

SHERIFF
The grubby little streetwalker from the A453.

ROBIN
How does he know my profile name? Get out of our hospital, Sheriff.

SHERIFF
Look at me quivering like a fat girl's arse on a washing machine. Merry Christmas!

Exits

MATRON
Robin!

WILL (hugging him intensely)
Robin!! You brought me flowers.

ROBIN
These are for you Matron. I got them from the Sherwood Florist.

WILL
If Doctor Marion Maid worked here we wouldn't be short staffed. I could tweet him. Again.

MATRON (sings to herself)
We'll tweet again...

SHERIFF re-enters.

SHERIFF
Dr Marion Maid!? Ha! Doctor Marion Maid wouldn't want to work here and he wouldn't be interested in you. I'll tell you a secret. Dr Marion Maid is going to be my new star doctor. My sister-in-law's cousin's niece is his agent and I think I've got an offer he can't resist. Merry Christmas.

Exits

MATRON (impressed at him)
I wonder if he needs a Matron.

ROBIN
No Matron! You can't think like that! And what is it with Marion Maid anyway? He's not even a doctor. He's just some jumped up, preening, vain, arrogant media whore who's too stupid to act but not pretty enough to model. (To audience) Hello tops! (Hello!) Hello gratefuls! (Hello) Hello bottoms! (Hello)

WILL
Why is it whenever you walk into a room full of gays they always seem to know you?

ROBIN
I've got a familiar face.

JOAN enters.

JOAN
Yeah, it's his cum face. Yo Robin.

They high-five.

ROBI
Good morrow.

JOAN
Blud.

ROBIN
Oh I've missed you all.

MATRON
Robin, I'm so glad you're back! What happened?

ROBIN
It was volcanic ash.

WILL
I think I've met him.

518

ROBIN
We've done that one.

JOAN
I'm sure you have.

MATRON
Oh Robin, we're in a right piccalilli. Even the ambulance has given up the ghost.

ROBIN
Well I might be able to help you there! You see, I've brought someone back with me.

WILL
Oh god I knew it!

ROBIN
[Donkey!!!!]

The DONKEY pokes its head out.

MATRON
A donkey! Take that thing to market in the morning.

ROBIN
That's a different panto, Matron.

JOAN goes to stroke the donkey.

JOAN
She's got beautiful eyes...

A strange moment passes between them. JOAN stops stroking.

DONKEY
Bye heck, don't stop.

MATRON
Well. It was good enough for the Virgin Mary. And she was pregnant.

DONKEY
Aye and I bet she was still half the weight of you.

MATRON
Well I don't know what we'll feed her on.

JOAN
We'll find you some kitchen scraps.

MATRON
Come along Joan, let's find [donkey] somewhere to rest.

MATRON JOAN and DONKEY exit.

ROBIN
Hey, so Will... I er, I got you something. I think you'll like it.

WILL
Really??

ROBIN
The bloke that sold me the Donkey, he said, she can get a bit of a temper, so he gave me some donkey tranquiliser. Just in case.

He fishes out a little bag of white powder.

WILL
Robin, you're the best! You tried any?

ROBIN
Yeah. I bumped some when we got to Yugoslavia and the next thing I knew I was at Calais. Here you go.

WILL
I don't want to end up in Calais.

ROBIN
Don't tell your mum ok?

WILL
Course. Thanks Robin. (pause). Did you, like, really miss me?

ROBIN
Of course I did mate. You're like a brother to me.

WILL
Like a normal brother or like those brothers we saw on X-Tube?

ROBIN
I'd better unpack. Want to help me get my bits and pieces out?

WILL
Go on then! Catch you later boys and girls.

They go.

Scene 3: Dr Marion's dressing room

MARION is on his phone. When the person on the other end of the line speaks we hear a squeaky, incomprehensible voice.

MARION
Miranda Moneygrabber? Marion Maid here. (reply) Dr Marion Maid, one of your clients. You're my agent (reply) You left me a voicemail?

The FAIRY flits in unseen by Marion and listens to the conversation.

MARION
Oh, hold the line a second. (To audience) Hello everyone. Say "ahh". Nice ahhs. Now, Miranda, did you see my slot this morning? No, well, it's being squeezed tighter and tighter. (reply) Listen, I am Doctor Marion Maid, TV Doctor and people love me. (reply) What? I've been exposed? I untagged that photo... (reply) Oh. But I am fully qualified. I have a certificate. I bought it in Bangkok, 2000 baht with a massage thrown in. (reply) The press may print the story? What am I going to do Miranda? Miranda?! Oh fuck.

She has hung up. MARION is in shock. He holds his stethoscope next to his heart and looks worried as he listens to his heartbeat. After a moment:

MARION
Still the funkiest heartbeat in television.

He dances a bit to his funky heartbeat.

FAIRY
What a scenario.

MARION
Excuse me. This is my private dressing room.

FAIRY
I know poppet, it smells of Lynx and fear. I trolled down your back passage. You're in a fix young man. A top TV Doc with a fraudulent qualification. But this isn't a social call, there's no time to waste. Have a look at my ball.

MARION
I beg your pardon?

FAIRY
My crystal ball. Look.

The FAIRY holds open the front of his trousers for Marion to look inside.

MARION
Ew. How peculiar.

FAIRY
The other one...

MARION
That looks even more worrying.

FAIRY
It is. There's a nasty man heading this way.

The SHERIFF enters

MARION
How did you get in?

SHERIFF
I shoved my way into your back passage.

FAIRY
The Doctor's trying to undress.

SHERIFF
I'd be happy to help. Dr Maid how nice to meet you.

SHERIFF
I am the Sheriff of Nottingham, a kind and gentle man.

FAIRY
Oh no you're not.

SHERIFF
Oh yes I am

Etc

SHERIFF
I won't have my character slandered. I'm a firm believer in Big Society[116].

FAIRY
I'm a firm believer in your big arse and neither of them bears close examination.

SHERIFF
I hate making trips to London. Disgusting, infested pub theatres; squalid gay bars without a single decent drink; sometimes both in the same building. Oh and "don't forget to touch your Oyster", get the fuck off my

---

[116] Steve Hilton coined the name for this sort-of ideology that was a flagship part of David Cameron's drive to detoxify the Conservative Party.

Oyster[117]. But I digress, how rude of me. Dr Maid, I am also the owner of the Castle, a private hospital in Nottingham. I'd like you to join my staff.

MARION
Thank you. But I don't know if I'd cope. Nottingham's not in London is it?

SHERIFF
I'd look after you and see you were well rewarded. You'd get an instant raise as soon as you step through the door.

MARION
I don't know... what do you think boys and girls?

FAIRY
Public opinion is what got us George Osborne and perpetual re-commissioning of the I.T. Crowd.

MARION
What should I do? Should I stay or should I go?

Here we had a slightly rewritten version of Should I Stay or Should I Go *by The Clash.*

SHERIF
You'd be head surgeon.

MARION
Head surgeon? I've always wanted to do neurology!

MARION and the SHERIFF exit together.

FAIRY
They say you can't teach an old fairy new tricks
But, god do I hate this tension
It's my last chance, I mustn't get into a fix,
Or they'll fire me without a pension

But the pretty doc's gone with the wicked Queen
Still, perhaps we should not be too saddened.
For now he'll meet Robin, and it would have been
Quite a shit play if he hadn't.

Exit.

---

[117] "Oyster" travel cards were introduced in London in 2003.

Scene 4: The forest

Sunlight, birdsong. FRIAR TUCK enters. He wears a chastity belt over his habit. He has a Peperami, half eaten, in his hand. He gets to his knees with some effort, places the snack on the ground, and begins to pray. ROBIN enters.

ROBIN
Friar Tuck!

FRIAR
Robin! Good to see you back.

ROBIN
Why are you praying Friar?

FRIAR
I can't get up. Be an angel?

ROBIN gives him a hand up. The FRIAR indicates the Peperami.

FRIAR
Oh, er...

ROBIN picks it up for him.

FRIAR
God bless you, it's lucky you found me.

ROBIN
I just followed the trail of crumbs. And chicken bones. And pork pie crusts. And half a samosa.

FRIAR
Half a samosa?!

The FRIAR is about to go in search for it.

ROBIN
Friar!

FRIAR
Sorry. Look at this, the edge of the forest. God's own earth, it's beautiful. How was the Holy Land? I haven't met many Jews.

ROBIN
They're not all that different to us really.

FRIAR
Of course. I mean I've read The Merchant of Venice. "If you prick us do we not bleed".

ROBIN
They do, but a bit of lube helps. Friar, how did you end up running a hospital?

FRIAR
I wasn't cut out for a traditional religious, catholic life. All that fasting, and I'm not remotely fond of children. I thought I could do some good out in the world. But even that's gone to pot.

ROBIN
Don't say that.

FRIAR
We're almost out of medicines. We can't afford new equipment. We can't even get transplant organs because the SHERIFF pays people so much for them. Little Joan's already donated both her own kidneys. I think she replaced them with cigarette filters and coffee papers. We can't carry on like this.

ROBIN
You're right! We'll do something! I'll lead a mission to the Castle. We'll tie a rope to one of my arrows and shoot it over the walls. We'll climb over... maybe you can keep watch... and we'll take what supplies we need.

FRIAR
No Robin. I'm a pacifist.

ROBIN
I'm quite versatile. Friar, poor, overtaxed, overworked people are going to be dying soon if we don't do something. You can't shrug your shoulders and say, that's how it is.

FRIAR
Hmm. Now, I'm not a religious man, but you might have a point.

ROBIN
You're not a religious man...?

FRIAR
Oh. Well, figuratively. I mean, I am a religious man.

The FRIAR holds up his arm to show a wristband with the letters WWJD on it.

ROBIN
"W.W.J.D"... I had one of those things for ball cancer.

FRIAR
Did it work?

ROBIN
So far.

522

FRIAR
Robin, I don't know why we were put on this planet. To live, to breathe, to breed, to die... And though I like to think there is something afterwards – pudding, ideally – I know we only get one shot at this life and you're right. Why shouldn't everyone get a fighting chance?

ROBIN
That's... that's kinda profound.

FRIAR
That's because I'm a deep fat Friar.

MATRON enters, jogging, in a garish tracksuit.

MATRON
Hello boys!

FRIAR
Oh Matron! So athletic.

MATRON notices the FRIAR's wristband.

MATRON
What does that say? W W J D...

FRIAR (points at the first W)
What.

MATON
I said, WHAT DOES THAT SAY?

FRIAR
It stands for "what".

MATRON
I haven't the faintest.

FRIAR
No, look, let's try this one instead.

He points at the J.

MATRON
J... Joan! "What Would Joan Do"!

FRIAR
Jesus!

MATRON
Don't get tetchy with me, Friar.

ROBIN
We're going to storm the castle and steal supplies, Matron.

MATRON
What an excellent idea. With your archery skills and Little Joan's mountaineering experience from the time she scaled Everest, we'll break in in no time.

DR MARION MAID enters, with a map.

MATRON
Oh my!

She faints into his arms. MARION looks helpless.

ROBIN
Well do something then!

MARION
What?

ROBIN
You're supposed to be a doctor! Here.

ROBIN helps MARION lower MATRON to the ground. The FRIAR clutches at MATRON.

FRIAR
Let me help.

MARION
I need gloves.

ROBIN
It's an emergency.

MARION
Yes, but my nails! Does anyone know the recovery position?

ROBIN
I probably call it something different. Give her mouth to mouth.

FRIAR
Right away.

ROBIN
Not you, him.

MARION
How?

MATRON (still unconscious)
Like this!

She pulls him down on to her.

ROBIN
You brought her round!

MATRON
He brought me off!

ROBIN
That was amazing. Hi. Hood, Robin Hood.

MARION (clearly very taken with Robin)
Maid. Doctor Marion Maid. It's... so good to meet you Robin. Where am I?

ROBIN
In the forest near our hospital!

MARION
Then I've found it!

ROBIN
Friar Tuck's Sherwood Forest Cottage Hospital.

MARION
Ah.

FRIAR
And I'm Friar Tuck. Would you consider making a donation to our humble institution? We're care for the poorest and neediest but we're very under-resourced.

MARION
Of course, Friar. I think that's very noble.

MARION gets his wallet out and hands the FRIAR a note. The FRIAR looks blankly. MARION hands over another note. Again, nothing. He hands over a third.

FRIAR
Truly you are a good Samaritan.

MARION puts his wallet back in his pocket.

MARION
I'm looking for the Castle. They've headhunted me for a new job... (to Robin) Would you take me there?

ROBIN
I'd love to!

FRIAR
Robin!

ROBIN
Oh! Yes, sorry, sorry we're a bit busy. But take my number?

MARION
Facebook me.

ROBIN
I will!

MARION exits.

FRIAR
Oh dear. I think you've sent him to our enemy.

ROBIN
I could barely think. Sorry. (beat) But I got his wallet!!

ROBIN removes MARION's wallet from his own pocket.

FRIAR
Robin you're terrible! Let's go and count the cash.

MATRON
I'll see you after my little jog.

MATRON rushes out bumping into the FRIAR and knocking him over.

MATRON
Oh Friar, I'm sorry,

She holds out her hand to help him up and he pulls her down on top of him, there is scuffle before they get up.

MATRON
Friar!

FRIAR
Oh Matron, it's these urges.

MATRON
Oh you!

MATRON ruffles the FRIAR's hair and exits, leaving him dazed and swaying.

ROBIN
'sup Friar?

FRIA
It's her. Matron.

A bell rings.

FRIAR
She does things to do me, she rings the bells of my heart.

A bell rings.

FRIAR
Do you know what I mean?

ROBIN
Five minutes ago I'd have said no. But that TV doctor...

A bell rings.

Here Robin and the Friar sang "I Can Hear The Bells" from the musical Hairspray. *After most of the song has been sun, the DONKEY enters.*

DONKEY
That is the gayest thing I ever saw.

ROBIN
[Donkey]! We were, er, just, you know. Chatting about the football. How's it hanging? Has Joan been looking after you?

A bell rings. The DONKEY moves her head to one side. Each time ROBIN says Joan the DONKEY should move her head.

ROBIN
That's strange... Anyway we should go back and help Joan.

A bell rings.

ROBIN
Why does you head move every time I say Joan. Joan, Joan, Joan, Joan...

And the song continues, with the Donkey joining in.

Scene 5: The Castle

The SHERIFF's private hospital "The Castle" should nevertheless have the feel of an old castle. The FAIRY enters, he is wearing a bright yellow hi-vis cycling jacket and other bright accessories.

FAIRY
Oh you pretty things! So I've snuck into the Castle to suss out what the Sheriff's up to. That's why I'm invisible. I bet you can't see me can you?

"Yes!"

FAIRY
Oh no you can't. You see, I took this potion.

He takes a bottle out of his pocket

FIARY
Oh tits, it says high visibility.

The FAIRY tries to hide. SHERIFF and MARION enter

SHERIFF
Ha ha ha! With my new signing we shall be the most successful hospital in the land. That'll shit on those do-gooders in the forest.

MARION
I met them on the way. They seem lovely. Especially Robin Hood.

SHERIFF
Robin-!? Robin Hood is a thief, an outlaw, a criminal and a whore.

MARION
That's so sexy.

SHERIFF
You're better off with me. Why, we are both successful, wealthy and gorgeous. (he sees the Fairy) You!

The FAIRY gives a camp wave.

FAIRY
Hiya doll.

SHERIFF
Why, pray...?

FAIRY
My balls tell me-

SHERIFF
I have had my fill of your balls and I'm swallowing no more.

He grabs the fairy by the groin and squeezes. We hear the sound of glass breaking. The FAIRY screams.

MARION
Are you alright?

SHERIFF
He's just a bit smashed.

The FAIRY limps off in tears.

SHERIFF
Have you seen your room? Is everything to your delight?

MARION
It's beautiful. But the door doesn't lock.

SHERIFF
No.

MARION
And someone's left some sort of medical appliances on the bedside table.

SHERIFF
Aha...

MARION
Gift-wrapped.

SHERIFF (Getting close)
I'm a generous man.

MARION
Is that a thermometer in your pocket?

SHERIFF
No, but it's hot and rising and most effective in the same places.

A pigeon with a letter attached to its beak flies in.

SHERIFF
Excuse me.

He takes the letter from the pigeon.

SHERIFF
Now fuck off birdie. [118]

---

[118] Our battery-powered bird with flapping wings attached to a fishing rod looked wonderfully awful but would sometimes get a clap from the audience. Matt, as the Sheriff, could usually force a bit of applause by waving it off with a kind of clapping gesture which would get the audience going, so that he could

The pigeon exits.

SHERIFF

From the BBC! I've been invited to go on "Who Do You Think You Are?". This is the research they promised to send me. (He opens the letter and reads it). Oh Marion!! You've made a very good choice. Play your cards right and you could be sleeping with the King of Britain!

MARION

The King of... but how?

SHERIFF

I'm 35th in line to the British throne! And here's the interesting part. As you know, the 34 highest ranking members of the British Royal Family are stuck overseas, waiting for the ash to clear.

MARION

Can't they get a boat?

SHERIFF

Another oil-spill[119]. And there is a little-known rule that says if a monarch is out of the country for more than two months, he or she must default to the next in line. Incredible as it sounds, being head of Nottingham Council may be just a stepping stone. Ah, to be King! Think of all the people one could get rid of!

SONG: I'VE GOT A LITTLE LIST[120]

SHERIFF

As someday it may happen that a victim must be found,
I've got a little list — I've got a little list
Of society offenders who might well be underground,
And who never would be missed — who never would be missed!
Those pallid fleshy boys who squeeze themselves in skinny jeans
The hangers on at Shoreditch house and other vapid queens
Dull girls who think that taking salsa classes makes them hot

And lads who think "straight acting" makes them cool when it does not
And everyone who dines at Nandos, gosh they must be pissed
They'd none of 'em be missed — they'd none of 'em be missed!

MARION

He's got 'em on the list — he's got 'em on the list;
And they'll none of 'em be missed — they'll none of 'em be missed

SHERIFF

The incompetents at Apple, god I'd like to see them sacked
Cirque du Soleil artists — I've got them on the list!
Men who think that wearing dresses constitutes an act
They never would be missed — they never would be missed!
Vegetarians who spoil my dinner parties, oh and tweeters
And hippies that send homemade birthday cards, the tight-arsed cheaters
Chris Moyles and Diane Abbott and a hundred other frauds
The arty types and commoners they've let into the Lords
Polly Toynbee and her dreary crowd of Guardian journalists
I don't think she'd be missed — I'm sure she'd not he missed!

MARION

He's got her on the list — he's got her on the list;
And I don't think she'll be missed — I'm sure she'll not be missed!

SHERIFF

All party leaders' wives, and then of course whoever styles them
Political dramatists — I've got them on the list!
And yummy mums with membership of Tate, how I'll defile them
They'd none of 'em be missed — they'd none of 'em be missed.
Boys on gaydar who won't travel, but live miles away in Crewe,

---

then respond with "oh that's it, a round of applause for the fucking wooden bird".

[119] The Deepwater Horizon oil spill in the Gulf of Mexico began in April 2010.

[120] There's a long tradition of updating the lyrics to this famous number from Gilbert & Sullivan's The Mikado.

And you and you and maybe you but definitely you,
Mark Ronson and James Corden, but it's no time to
think shyly
The first to get it in the neck is motherfucking Kylie
But it really doesn't matter whom you put upon
the list,
For they'd none of 'em be missed — they'd none of
'em be missed!

SHERIFF AND MARION
You may put 'em on the list — you may put 'em on
the list;
And they'll none of 'em be missed — they'll none of
'em be missed!

MATRON enters, dressed as a nun. She curtsies.

MATRON
May the blessings of Mary the lamb and the virgin
Jesus be upon you.

SHERIFF
You can't come in here.

MATRON
Sheriff, I am but a humble abbess. I have brought a
coach party of nuns to... what was it?

ROBIN pokes his head through the entrance.

ROBIN (to Matron)
To tend to his patients and cleanse his waters with the
holy ghost.

MATRON
That's right, to try your patience and cleanse your
ghostly hole.

SHERIFF
You're not a real nun!

MATRON
Oh yes I am!

SHERIFF
Oh no you're not.

ROBIN enters, also as a nun.

ROBIN
Oh yes she is!

SHERIFF
Oh no she isn't.

WILL and JOAN enter, as nuns

WILL and JOAN
Oh yes she is!

SHERIFF
Oh no she isn't.

*The FRIAR enters as a nun. He has some hummus which
he is licking from the pot.*

FRIAR
Oh yes she is!

SHERIFF
Oh no she bastard well isn't

DONKEY enters, also dressed as a nun.

DONKEY
Oh yes she bastard well is!

SHERIFF
Well let's not bang on about it, eh.

MATRON
Oh thank you, thank you Sheriff. I am Sister Wary Mary,
this is Sister Contrary Mary, that's Sister Hairy Mary,
then these are the twins, Sisters Beary Mary and
Scary Mary, and this is Sister Former Archbishop of
Canterbury Doctor George Carey Mary.

ROBIN
You can leave us to explore if you're busy.

WILL
Show us your storerooms.

SHERIFF (suspicious)
The storerooms...?

MATRON
I'd love to see where you put your pessaries.

SHERIFF
I wasn't aware of a local... what do you call a place
where nuns live?

DONKEY
A convent.

MATRON
Oooh now that's a good one.

WILL
Austria?

DONKEY
It's a convent.

FRIAR
Oh now they had that in the pub quiz last week. It's on the tip of my tongue. Was it a monastery?

DONKEY
It's a convent

WILL
A nunnery?

JOAN
No it's a priory!

DONKEY
It's a convent you packet of fuckheads.

SHERIFF
Now this is all highly un*convent*ional.

MATRON, FRIAR, ROBIN, WILL, JOAN
That's it! It's a convent!

MATRON
Oh Sheriff, let us do our work. Just think, What Would Joan Do?

FRIAR
Jesus.

MATRON
I told you not to get tetchy with me.

ROBIN
What would *Jesus* do?

WILL
He'd have a wank.

MATRON
Twenty Hail Marys, Beary Mary.

JOAN
I'm Beary Mary. He's Fairy Mary.

WILL
I want to be Mariah Carey Mary.

SHERIFF
Ladies! I have business to get on with. The new Doctor will show you around.

SHERIFF exits.

FRIAR
Well that went rather well.

DONKEY
I seriously need the toilet guys.

MARION enters.

MARION
Good afternoon ladies.

WILL
We love you on the telly!

MARION
Why thank you! Do nuns have televisions?

JOAN
Er, no.

WILL
We got iPlayer.

DONKEY
Ask him where the toilet is.

ROBIN
Marion, it's me.

MARION (not recognising).
Right... hello...?

ROBIN (takes off his wimple)
It's me. Robin.

MARION
The guy I met in the forest!

DONKEY
Yeah, you probably made the trees look like rocket scientists.

MARION
I'd recognise you anywhere.

WILL (Indicating Robin)
He said you're a jumped up, preening, vain, arrogant media whore who's too stupid to act but not pretty enough to-

ROBIN clasps his hand over WILL's mouth.

ROBIN
Drugs. And bi-polar. Tragic.

MARION
Do you normally go about dressed as a nun?

ROBIN
I know, I know, it's an awful habit. Marion, we're in trouble.

MARION
You can't run away from your problems by becoming a nun.

They consider this.

DONKEY
Somebody ask him where the toilet is, you basket of cunts.

ROBIN
Marion, we don't have much time.

JOAN
We need supplies. Medicines, equipment, squeezy blood bags, organs by the barrel and untugged heartstrings.

FRIAR
The Sheriff's got loads but the poor can't afford to come here. They rely on us. Please help us.

MARION
It's my first day.

ROBIN
Just point us to the stores.

DONKEY
And the toilets.

ROBIN
We won't tell anyone. I'll make it up to you.

MATRON
So will I.

MARION
Ok. For you. Head back along the corridor. Turn left at the Louis XV armchairs. Left again at the steam and sushi room and it's straight ahead.

DONKEY
Right, I did warn you.

A horrible sound as the Donkey craps herself.

ROBIN
Oh [Donkey]!!! That's gross! Guys, clean her up and find the storeroom. I'll be along in a second.

JOAN
Here, come with me [Donkey] we'll sort you out.

They all exit apart from ROBIN and MARION.

ROBIN
Thank you.

MARION
I don't think I could say no to anything you asked me. Sorry that sounds a bit full on.

ROBIN
No, no it's... I sort of feel the same. How are you settling in?

MARION
Alright so far I think. It'll be quite nice living with other people around. I was quite lonely in London.

ROBIN (laughs)
But you're so handsome

MARION
I know. I think the beautiful suffer the most.

ROBIN
Well, how about we take each other out sometime?

MARION
I'd love to! But I think the Sheriff has designs on me. And he's my new boss.

ROBIN
You like me, I know you do.

MARION
I do. Completely. And I love what you're doing at the cottage hospital, and I'm glad to help... But... Maybe soon, ok?

ROBIN
Ok. Kiss me before you go?

They do, briefly, then:

MARION
Not here. Come with me

They exit one side of the stage as MATRON, WILL and the FRIAR enter from the other. MATRON and WILL have lots of medical supplies in their arms. The Friar has a packet of shortbread.

MATRON
I tell you I could get used to this place boys and girls. Now we just have to get out without the Sheriff seeing us. Will, what's wrong with you? You look like you've sampled half the drugs in the Sheriff's cupboard.

WILL
That might be it

MATRON
Idiot! Right just try to concentrate and follow me.

The Sheriff enters, perhaps using his Blackberry[121]. "He's behind you".

FRIAR
Who is?

"The Sheriff!" They look to the left as he moves to the right.

WILL
Where is he?

"Behind you!" They look to the right as he passes back to the left.

SHERIFF
Ladies!

They scream, turn to face him, remember they are holding secret supplies and turn their backs on him. The SHERIFF passes through to the front so he can face them. They panic and turn their backs again.

SHERIFF
What are you doing?

MATRON
We're shy, Sheriff.

WILL
And I've lost all sense of which way is forward.

MATRON
You're such a handsome, potent man. It's best that we don't expose ourselves to temptation.

SHERIFF
Or at all.

MATRON
I can practically feel you staring at my bottom, you naughty man.

SHERIFF
I can't help it, I feel like a spaceship drawn towards the Death Star. Thank you for your visit. Now I must go and check on the stores. Good day.

---

[121] For a while, Blackberries were the mobile phone of choice for business types.

He exits. ROBIN and JOAN enter.

WILL
Where's Dr Marion?

JOAN
And what's that on your habit?

ROBIN wipes something off his habit as the FAIRY limps in.

ROBIN
What happened to you, mate?

The FAIRY opens his trousers. They all peer into them, and gasp in horror simultaneously.

ROBIN
Right. Come back with us mister. We'll sort you out.

Offstage we hear:

SHERIFF
Thieves! Outlaws!

MATRON (screams)
Oh no! Thieves and outlaws! Let's go!

They scarper. The SHERIFF enters.

SHERIFF
Doctor Marion!

MARION runs on

MARION
Sweet Sheriff!

SHERIFF
The stores have been raided!

MARION
Who would do such a thing? Our only visitors were those dear nuns.

SHERIFF
Robin Hood is behind this! I'll have his guts for garters and his arse for a hat.

MARION
You'd look very silly in them.

SHERIFF
I shall have my revenge! But first, I shall have my new Doctor. This way!

Scene 6: The operating theatre

JOAN is in surgical whites, MATRON is at her side by a heart monitor. The FAIRY lies on a table covered in a sheet. There is a table on stage with various operating tools on as well as a mallet, glasses of water and, at the back, a tray of cream pies.

JOAN
Well, here we are in the theatre.

MATRON
Oh that's it, spoil the illusion.

JOAN
Mum, I meant-

MATRON
Boys and girls, I love my daughter dearly but she can be a bit of a cold hard realist. When she was 7 years old she made me cry by telling me that Santa Claus was made up.

JOAN
Mum-

MATRON
I know sweetheart I'm just riffing. Where were we?

JOAN
I just told you!

MATRON
I mean in the script.

JOAN
I didn't know you'd seen a copy. Right, I'm the surgeon for this organ transplant. How are things looking Mum?

MATRON (looking in the monitor)
Well, Colleen looks like she's put on even more weight.

JOAN
Stop watching Loose Women mum you're supposed to monitoring his blood pressure.

MATRON twiddles a knob on the monitor, and the Emmerdale theme tune plays.

MATRON
Sorry, be there in a minute.

MATRON
Who've we got here?

JOAN
It's that fairy.

MATRON
I don't know how you can tell these days.

JOAN
He had Ginch Gonch pants on.

WILL enters wearing Ginch Gonch underpants over his trousers.

WILL
Not anymore.

MATRON
Right what do we need then?

WILL
Balls.

MATRON
Rude boy!

MATRON slaps WILL. ROBIN enters carrying a jar of pickled testicles

ROBIN
This what we need?

JOAN
Yeah that's the fellas.

ROBIN (handing the jar to an audience member)
Hold my balls mate.

JOAN
Ok we need to knock him out. Where's the anaesthetist?

MATRON
That's you darling.

JOAN
Oh, right.

JOAN takes off her coat and puts another one on.

JOAN
Right, nurse, knock him out.

WILL picks up a large mallet

ROBIN
Will what are you doing? He just wants a little prick in his bum.

ROBIN pulls out a syringe, tests it.

ROBIN
Don't worry mister, you'll hardly feel it going in.

FAIRY
How fucking rude.

532

WILL
I don't think he's asleep yet.

MATRON
Out like a light.

The FAIRY puts a hand out and pinches Matron's bottom.

MATRON
Oh Robin, Oh you naughty boy!

She hits him gently, as she turns her back to him, the body puts a hand out again and pinches her bottom.

MATRON
Oh you little tease you!

ROBIN
I'm not doing anything.

MATRON (seductive)
I'll have you reporting to my office if you're not careful.

FAIRY
Get out of the way old lady, I'm trying to feel up the boy there.

MATRON
Old-! Old lady!

MATRON grabs the mallet.

MATRON (Sings sweetly)
Rockabye baby on the tree top

MATRON whacks the fairy hard on the head.

MATRON
Right, he's asleep now.

The FAIRY starts snoring. They listen for a bit.

JOAN
Ok, I'm going to open him up. Scalpel please.

WILL hands her a large carving knife, she cuts into the FAIRY

JOAN
Jesus, the crap in here.

She pulls out a long string of sausages. Then a tyre. The FRIAR enters, sees the sausages.

FRIAR
Excellent.

He takes them and exits. JOAN pulls out a bunch of flowers. Then a white rabbit. Each is passed along and

Will, Joan and Matron react to them. Then Joan pulls out a Barbie doll or equivalent.

MATRON
Oh look! It's Madeleine McCann!

JOAN and ROBIN look horrified, JOAN puts a hand over Matrons mouth to stop her completing the sentence. WILL doesn't understand why.

JOAN
God this is a mess. Give me water.

ROBIN (to Will)
Give me water.

MATRON picks up a glass containing water.

WILL
Come on Mum. Give me water.

MATRON throws water in WILL's face.

WILL
What was that for?

MATRON
You said you wanted water.

ROBIN
No it was Robin said he wanted water.

MATRON
My mistake.

MATRON walks over to ROBIN and throws water in his face

ROBIN
Matron!

MATRON
What did I do?

ROBIN
This.

He throws water in WILL's face.

MATRON
How rude!

JOAN
Are you ready?

ROBIN
Matron go and grab that guys balls will you?

MATRON retrieves the jar of balls from the audience member.

JOAN (taking out a testicle).
Hmm which one should I go for?

JOAN takes out a testicle.

JOAN
Ok let's go with this one. Mum are you ready with the stitches.

MATRON gets out a bag with wool and two knitting needles and starts to use them to knit the testicle on. The fairy's groin is covered by a large sheet, JOAN. WILL and ROBIN watch.

JOAN
Ok, looks like we're done. Let's tidy up.

ROBIN and JOAN start to tidy instruments on the trolley, WILL adjusts the monitor. MATRON is stood by the body of the FAIRY still covered by the sheet, she looks down. He starts to get an erection under the and the sheet starts to rise. Only MATRON sees this as the others are busy with their respective tasks. MATRON doesn't know what to do. She's both embarrassed and delighted. She tries to push the penis down, gently at first, but it springs up again. She pushes it down more firmly but it keeps springing up again. She tries gripping it as though arm-wrestling, to no avail. Eventually she climbs on the bed and uses her bum to push it down. It shoots back up. Frustrated, she climbs off the bed and speaks to the FAIRY.

MATRON
Fairy, it's me. Matron.

The FAIRIES penis immediately goes down, the sheet returning to normal.

JOAN
God I'm starving. This operating takes it out of you. Give me of one those cream pies boys.

ROBIN (to Will)
Give me a cream pie.

WILL (to Matron)
Give me a cream pie.

MATRON picks up a large cream pie and slaps it into his face

WILL
No, it was for Robin. He wanted the cream pie.

MATRON
Sorry.

MATRON picks up a pie and throws it at ROBIN

ROBIN
Will what did you say that for?

WILL
Say what?

ROBIN
I want a cream pie.

WILL
No problem.

WILL picks up another pie and throws it at ROBIN

ROBIN
Right. I've had enough of this. Stand still.

WILL stands still, ROBIN picks up another pie and throws it him

WILL
Hold on Rob, don't you think it's greedy us taking all the pies.

ROBIN
Yeah, you're right Will. Sharing with the poor is what we do.

WILL
And there's lots of poor out there. (points to the audience) See. Primark.

ROBIN and WILL pick up a pie each and walk to the front of the audience

ROBIN
Ok boys and girls who wants a cream pie?[122]

They wander along the front row threatening to throw their pies at the audience

MATRON
Boys, it's very nice of you to share your pies with the boys and girls but it was Joan who wanted them.

JOAN
Yes it was boys, give me the pies please.

---

[122] In porn, a cream pie refers to semen spilling from anus (or vagina) it has just been ejaculated into.

ROBIN
What do you reckon?

WILL
Be rude not to. Walk this way sis.

ROBIN and WILL stand one either side as JOAN starts to walk towards them.

ROBIN
One

WILL
Two

ROBIN and WILL
Three

The FRIAR enters holding a tray of teacups.

FRIAR
Now who's for a cup of tea?

He walks between ROBIN and WILL as they throw their pies. They hit him in the face. He drops the cups and tray.

FRIAR
Cream pie. My favourite. Thank you so much boys.[123]

BLACKOUT.

----

[123] A cream pie is a playful term used predominantly in porn for the visible aftermath of ejaculation into the vagina or anus.

Scene 7: The Castle

The SHERIFF enters with a couple of trays of canapés and some champagne.

SHERIF
I'm entertaining.

He puts the trays down somewhere.

SHERIFF
Highly entertaining.

FRIAR TUCK enters. A joint behind his ear and in his hands a slice of gala pie and an invitation.

SHERIFF
Friar Tuck! Welcome to the inaugural annual Nottingham Hospital Managers' Conference.

FRIAR (waving the invitation and catching his breath)
It says there's a buffet. Am I early?

SHERIFF
On the button. There are only two hospitals in Nottingham, Friar, it's thee and me keeping the darkness illuminated.

SHERIFF hands the FRIAR a glass of champagne.

SHERIFF
Champagne?

FRIAR (sipping it)
Do you know, I think it is.

SHERIFF (indicating his joint)
And is that medicinal?

FRIAR?
No no, this is the good stuff. One of our Lord's many lovely gifts. Oh hello boys and girls, this is a bit fancy isn't it. I don't even have to transfer it to a plastic cup. What's the agenda then eh Sheriff? Start with the food?

SHERIFF
Oh yes.

He offers a tray to the Friar, who takes something.

SHERIFF
Deep fried mini mars bars.

FRIAR
Sounds delicious. Are you not eating?

SHERIFF
I'm watching my weight. Or rather I'm watching yours and hankering for a Ryvita.

FRIAR
Now come on, live a little. Pride is a sin.

SHERIFF
No, really. After you.

FRIAR
What do you think boys and girls? Should I eat it?

They answer.

FRIAR
Oh father give me strength to resist temptation.

SHERIFF
It's the fat in the batter you see, it's an excellent taste carrier.

FRIAR
I can't help it! (He eats it). Mmmmmm. I think I saw the face of God there for a moment... Oh, oh wait... Ooohhhhhh

SHERIFF
I'm sorry?

FRIAR
I feel woozey.

SHERIFF
Sick?

The FRIAR drops to his knees.

FRIAR
I think I'm being poisoned!

SHERIFF
An accurate diagnosis.

FRIAR
But- Sheriff!

SHERIFF
An enormous and potentially fatal overdose of donkey tranquiliser. Another of our Lord's lovely gifts. Somebody left some behind in our storeroom yesterday.

FRIAR
Help me!

SHERIFF
I have an antidote. But first, you will sign this.

The SHERIFF pulls out a piece of paper and a pen.

FRIAR
What, what is it?

SHERIFF
It is a paper signing over the deeds of the Cottage hospital from your medical trust to the Castle Health Foundation, i.e., me.

FRIAR
Never! Oh, oh, help me I'm sweating like a, like a...

SHERIFF
Sweating like a what, Friar? Like a portly priest? Like a new choirboy who arrives at practise to discover he's the prettiest kid in the chapel? Like your mother on the day she had to give birth to your glutinous fat carcass? Or sweating like the head of a cottage hospital on trial for growing and abusing illegal substances? You have a minute before your heart gives up. Sign the paper.

The FRIAR snatches the pen and paper and signs.

FRIAR
There. Now, please!

The SHERIFF offers him the 2nd tray of canapés.

SHERIFF
Quickly.

The FRIAR takes one and eats it. He is immediately much better.

FRIAR
A humble chipolata?

SHERIFF
Laced with cocaine and red bull. You'll be back up in seconds. But look at the time, my keynote speech will have to wait for next year. I trust you'll find your own way out. You found your way in easily enough yesterday, Sister. Ha ha ha.

SHERIFF exits.

FRIAR
Now I've done it boys and girls! I don't know how I'm going to tell them.

He begins to exit. Stops. About-turns, grabs a couple of chipolatas, and exits.

Scene 8: The hospital

Party music. Donkey, Matron, Robin and Will are dancing. Joan is ironing. Robin and Will are drinking beer, Matron has an exotic-looking cocktail. The Donkey has a pint of Guinness.

MATRON
Ooh boys and girls. It's nice to let your hair down after work. We always have a little party after the week's final body count. How's the ironing Little Joan? Joan likes her ironing like she likes her girls. Folded double over the kitchen table. Sorry, it's the drink, I'm a little whoopsie. (To someone) Are you a little whoopsie? I think you are. Would you like to try my cocktail? It's a Long Strong Punch. Loosens you up something lovely but it burns a bit on exit... Do you prefer a long one too? You look like you'd hold it well.

WILL
Mum you're embarrassing!

ROBIN (indicating audience)
Just because you're on the pull.

WILL
Some people find me attractive, Robin.

MATRON (to audience)
I like my drink -

JOAN
Here we go.

MATRON
I like my drink like I like my men. (beat) Rammed in the back of the car on the way home from a booze cruise.

The DONKEY farts. The SHERIFF enters.

ROBIN
What do you want?

SHERIFF
I want - What the hell is that smell? It's like the fart out of a dyke donkey or something.

ROBIN
Get out of our hospital

JOAN (menacingly holding the iron)
Do as he says, S-man.

WILL (not at all convincing)
Yeah... yeah do as she says.

SHERIFF
Idiot. You can't tell a man to leave his property.

The SHERIFF shows them the deeds. ROBIN reads.

ROBIN
I don't believe it.

The FRIAR enters

FRIAR
It's true. He tricked me.

SHERIFF
Consider yourself evicted. Off you trot. And don't get your hips wedged in the revolving doors.

MATRON
I have a good old-fashioned physique.

SHERIFF
I was talking to the buxom bishop. As I'm such a generous man, you won't have to pay any removal fees. The corpulent cleric here signed over the fixtures and fittings too. I'm seizing your assets.

MATRON (faux-weary, but presenting herself)
If you must.

SHERIFF
Oh and you'll like this. I've banned hoodies from Nottingham. Come anywhere near the city, Robin Hood, and I'll have your head on the city walls.

WILL
You're better going round back of Tesco's car park for that.

JOAN
You won't get away with this.

ROBIN
No, Joan. We'll go.

WILL
Yeah, yeah we'll go, nice one, seeya, wouldn't wanna be ya.

WILL goes to leave. ROBIN grabs his hand to stop him. Their hands stay clasped.

ROBIN
But we'll be back. And we'll get this hospital back and win justice for the people of Nottingham.

SHERIFF
Jolly good. Right, it's time to discharge some patients to make room for my paying customers. (to audience)

And a few of you look like you know a thing or two about discharge.

SHERIFF exits

WILL
Friar!!!

FRIAR
I'm sorry, he tricked me.

The FAIRY enters.

FAIRY
Well somebody's been having a party! Are we on the way up or on the way down?

FRIAR
On the way out, I'm afraid.

FAIRY
Then come and live in the forest! That's what they do in Shakespeare.

MATRON
The forest! A lady of my sensibilities could never live al fresco

JOAN
Strange men roaming about!

MATRON
But I'll do my best to cope.

FRIAR
What will we eat?

JOAN
We'll manage. When I was part of the all-woman team that rowed across the Atlantic, things got tough but we all knew we had each for support.

DONKEY
Say all that again when I've found a tree stump to rub against.

FAIRY
And I'll be there to help you all out.

ROBIN
Oh, fucking great. (sighs) But no, you're right. We know that whatever happens we're a team. We know we'll go through it together...

Piano plays as if the introduction to a song.

MATRON
Yes yes we'll have none of that. These people need a break.

ROBIN
We'll see you in part two everyone. Bye bottoms! Bye tops! Bye gratefuls! Come on, fairy. Lead the way.

INTERVAL

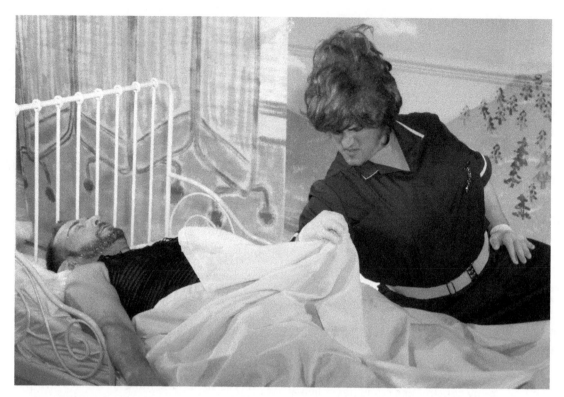

Jonson Wilkinson as the Fairy and Brendan Riding as Matron in *Robin Hood: Queen of Thieves*. Photo by Derek Drescher.

Helen Victor as Donkey, Mansel David as Friar Tuck and Caroline Wagstaffe as Little Joan in *Robin Hood: Queen of Thieves*. Photo by Derek Drescher.

Scene 9

The FAIRY enters.

FAIRY
Welcome back boys and girls! So our merry band
Have been forced out into the wood
I must do what I can to give them a hand
In our battle between evil and good.

They've been hunting for food, stolen chickens for rearing,
For firewood they've been out logging
And set up a tent in a sweet little clearing
That sometimes gets used for dogging

The SHERIFF enters

SHERIFF
And now I'll fulfil my wildest dreams
That fool Robin Hood will not stop us
This rhyming lark's not as hard as it seems
Just like fucking on too much poppers.

FAIRY
Have you just come out here to tell terrible jokes?

SHERIFF
The script seems to call for it. Right. Shall we get on with it?

FAIRY
I think we should, there's even some plot in the second half.

SHERIFF
Whatever next! See you later, narrator.

He goes, laughing maniacally.

FAIRY
Weirdo.
I've not been much help thus far, I'll admit
Little more than ornamental
But the Sheriff is such an almighty shit -
And also, I fear, a bit mental -

That I'd better buck up my ideas, and how,
We can't let that man take the crown.
I mustn't fuck up, dearest queers, but for now:
To the woods! Let's see what's going down!

Scene 10: Sherwood Forest

The woods. They have made their home in a clearing. A little tent in the corner. Perhaps a campfire. There is a crop of cannabis growing. MATRON enters with a watering can.

MATRON

Hello boys and girls. Here I am. A babe in the woods. Have you had a nice interval? We've been settling in nicely. We're even engaging in some sustainable farming.

She accidentally but copiously sprinkles the front row with her watering can before watering the cannabis plants.

MATRON

It's only water, if you want soiling you'll have to do it yourself. You know, before, we could only grow things on my windowsill, but it seemed such a waste for the Friar, having to put his seed in my grubby little box. (She waters again then sniffs the plants happily.) There, coming up nicely.

JOAN enters, carrying logs.

JOAN

I'm not surprised you are Mum, it's weed.

MATRON

They are not weeds. I'm famed at the flower and produce for my blooms.

FRIAR enters with a basket of fruit.

FRIAR

Though I think you'll agree my lupin stood out a mile. Lovely purple head on it.

MATRON

Just a pity it wilted at the first hint of moisture. I wonder how the boys are getting on hunting.

FRIAR inspects the cannabis. Plucks a leaf, takes out a packet of Rizlas. WILL runs in with a couple of rabbits. He is too out of breath to speak.

MATRON

Good boy, Will. (Takes the rabbits).

JOAN

What's up bruv?

WILL

Robin vanished into the forest!

JOAN

I've noticed he does that.

WILL

No, I think he's really disappeared. He's not even showing on Grindr. And [donkey]'s gone too!

MATRON

Right. Search party, everyone.

WILL

But what if he's been caught by a... by a... werewolf!!

JOAN

You watch too much crap, Will. Don't worry, I'm a trained animal hunter. I hunted during the year I spent in the Borneo jungle living with a family of gorillas. Came back and taught Steve all about handling wild animals.

FRIAR

Steve?

JOAN

Irwin. Shame he didn't to listen me. I told him, when you go swimming smother yourself in factor thirty it'll protect you from harmful rays.[124]

MATRON

Come along, Friar.

FRIAR

Yes, right away. I'll look after you, Matron. (Pulls a couple of spliffs from his pocket). Good job I pre-rolled. See boys and girls, I'm "double jointed".

JOAN

Friar! Come on.

They exit.

---

[124] In 2006 Steve Irwin, the TV wildlife expert, died when a stingray's barb (its sharp tail) pierced his chest, puncturing his heart.

Scene 11: The Castle

The castle. MARION enters.

MARION
Hello boys and girls. Say "ah". I don't know what to do, Robin's been banished to the forest and I'm stuck here with the Sheriff. I had a letter today from Richard Desmond saying he doesn't mind about my history and do I want to present a new series for Channel 5: "Say Ah with Dr Marion Maid". I'd be really tempted but the truth is, I just want to be with Robin.

SHERIFF enters

SHERIFF
Aha, my foxy little kitten. My horny little steed. My... fishy little badger. I have business to finish, but then why don't we snuggle up and watch my box set of House. Or Casualty. Or er.

MARION
Er?

SHERIFF
Yes, er.

MARION
Do you mean E.R.?

SHERIFF
And you say you're not qualified! I'll be back.

The SHERIFF goes. ROBIN enters, with a bag.

MARION
Robin! How did you get in?

ROBIN (indicates bag)
I came disguised as someone famous and unhinged so they'd admit me.

They kiss.

MARION
It's the Sheriff. Let's hide.

They hide. The SHERIFF enters singing to the tune of ABBA's Money Money Money

SHERIFF (singing)
I've put the taxes up you see
So every penny comes to me
That's too bad...

He gets out a number of envelopes.

SHERIFF
And here's a tax bill for you (hands them out to members of the audience) and for you, and one for you, and here's one for you for wearing Abercrombie sir when you're clearly far too old.

The DONKEY enters.

DONKEY
By heck, boys and girls, I'm looking for that knob-jockey Robin. Have you seen him?

SHERIFF
Well, well if it's not Robin Hood's girlfriend, come here lass!

He goes up to the Donkey and puts a chain around her neck. He chains her up.

SHERIFF
You must be hungry. Don't worry, soon you'll be on your way to the dog food factory. But first, it's time for some surgery, you see I have this little list and you are on it!

SHERIFF goes off stage and returns with an axe and walks over to the DONKEY.

DONKEY
Ee bye fuck I'm in trouble now. You got to help me boys and girls. Call Robin for me!

SHERIFF (raising his axe)
I hope this doesn't get too messy. It's like an Al Qaida home movie. One, two-

ROBIN and MARION enter. ROBIN now disguised as Susan Boyle.[125]

MARION
Look who's come to see you Sheriff.

ROBIN starts to sing "I dreamed a dream" from Les Misérables.

SHERIFF
Lulu!

---

[125] We changed this in rehearsal from Susan Boyle to Katie Waissel, a bonkers but brilliant contestant on that year's X Factor, presumably because a) it would have been more current and b) wasn't making a cheap joke out of someone's real and well documental mental health issues...

ROBIN (normal voice)
Susan Boyle.

SHERIFF
Miss Boyle! What an inevitable pleasure.

ROBIN
Ooh aye, tis a pleasure. But what re ye doing to this poor wee beastie?

SHERIFF
Oh, haha, just playing. What brings you to my establishment?

ROBIN (takes out a bottle and swigs from it, singing)
"But the tigers come at night..."

MARION
She's loopy.

SHERIFF
Dr Marion we don't call them that. I prefer gaga

ROBIN
Fair enough aye.

ROBIN starts singing Lady Gaga's "Poker Face".

SHERIFF
Well Miss Boyle, the Katona suite is available for only £10,000 a night. Just sign here.

He takes out a contract and hands it to ROBIN. ROBIN goes to take it but punches the SHERIFF who stumbles back, dazed. ROBIN rushes over and releases the DONKEY.

SHERIFF
You! Little green riding hood!

ROBIN
Whatever evil plan you have, I'll stop you.

SHERIFF
You and who's army? Your gang of misfits and losers? I could have you executed right now.

MARION
Sheriff dear, calm down it's not good for your blood pressure

MARION puts his stethoscope against the SHERIFF'S heart. As he is doing this ROBIN and the DONKEY sneak out.

MARION
It's sky high.

SHERIFF
How can you tell? That's a stethoscope. Hood's gone! Call security.

MARION
Shhh. Calm down. Why don't we play doctors and nurses like you suggested last night?

SHERIFF
Can I be nurse? I'll need a uniform.

MARION
I have a little something in rubber.

SHERIFF
Don't be so modest, doctor. But first, Marion, this is exciting. Because of this unfortunate business with volcanic ash and all the royal family being stuck overseas, I have ordered the government to invoke clause 493.89 in the royal charter.

MARION
Clause 493.89? But you can't.

SHERIFF
You know what it says?

MARION
No, but I'm sick of sounding thick all the time.

SHERIFF
It says that if all the royal family are out of the country for more than 30 days the queen shall no longer be monarch. That position will go to the next person in line to throne who is in the country. And do you know what I will do first?

MARION
Choose a corgi?

SHERIFF
Kill Robin Hood!

MARION
No! I'd do anything to save him!

SHERIFF
Anything? Ha ha. You love him don't you?

MARION
Yes, yes with all my heart.

SHERIFF
Then I will spare him.

MARION
Thank you!

SHERIFF
On one condition.

MARION
What's is it?

SHERIFF
It's like a clause or caveat, but that's not important right now. You see, I need a queen.

MARION indicates the audience.

SHERIFF
You could have it all Marion! Fame, riches. You'll be made, Marion. Marry me, and I will spare Robin Hood.

MARION
You evil- I don't have a choice do I?

SHERIFF
Hahaha! Excellent! Just think of me as a handsome William Hague and you as my young adviser[126]. Let's get packing. In just a few hours Buckingham Palace will be mine. Don't forget something sexy for our wedding night. I can't wait to put a ring on your cock. (Exits singing) Hi, ho, hi ho, to London we will go...

MARION
Oh boys and girls! I've got to try and see Robin one last time. I need to tell him what's happened!

SHERIFF (Offstage)
Come along my sweet, London's calling!

MARION exits, dejected.

---

[126] William Hague denied having an affair with a male aide, after news that they had shared hotel rooms prompted speculation.

Scene 12: The forest

Night-time in the clearing. The FRIAR sits on a camping stool or tree stump, eating something and smoking a joint. The Donkey grazes in a corner. WILL and JOAN enter, each with a sleeping bag and a spare for Robin. They settle.

ROBIN enters.

ROBIN
Never fear, Robin's here!

WILL
Robin!

FRIAR (waving a large spliff)
Robin, just in time. It's organic.

ROBIN takes a toke of the spliff, gives the Friar's tummy a friendly rub, then picks up his pyjamas from beside his sleeping bag and exits to change. MATRON enters wearing a skimpy night dress and a hairnet.

MATRON
All back safe and sound! Goodnight children.

JOAN and WILL
Goodnight Mum.

MATRON
Goodnight Robin.

ROBIN (off)
Goodnight Matron.

MATRON
Goodnight Friar.

The FRIAR is too busy eating and smoking to hear.

MATRON (bellowing)
Goodnight Friar.

FRIAR
Oh – yes goodnight Matron.

JOAN
Goodnight Will.

WILL
Goodnight Joan.

JOAN
Goodnight Friar.

FRIAR
Um, yes, goodnight Joan.

JOAN
Night Robster.

ROBIN (off)
Goodnight Little Joan

ROBIN re-enters, now in his PJs. The goodnights continue.

DONKEY
Bloomin' heck I can't stand much more of this. After three, boys and girls, shout 'shut the fuck up'. One two, three

The audience shouts.

MATRON
How rude. You can go off people can't you? Not you though (she *points to someone*) - I haven't liked you from the off.

MATRON goes to the tent. As she gets into it:

MATRON
Well, Friar Tuck! You did get it up quickly for me didn't you.

FRIAR
It should stay firm 'til sunrise.

A pause. Then all except Matron and the Friar burst into laughter.

MATRON
It's been a long day.

ROBIN
Do you want me to zip you in Matron?

MATRON
Thank you, Robin.

ROBIN
I mean... (*holding off laughter*) you don't want anyone coming through your flaps in the night.

All laugh wildly again. The MATRON zips up her tent. JOAN, ROBIN and WILL get into their sleeping bags. The FRIAR continues to eat. There is loud snoring from MATRONS' tent. WILL shuffles over to ROBIN. A pause.

WILL
Robin

ROBIN
Will, no more goodnights.

WILL
I can't get to sleep.

ROBIN
We only said goodnight about five seconds ago.

WILL
I'm scared and cold.

ROBIN
Don't worry mate we'll soon have things sorted.

WILL
Robin, I don't suppose I could get in your bag to keep warm.

ROBIN
We'd keep prodding each other.

WILL
Yeah...

ROBIN
Look Will, I'm not cold. You have my sleeping bag to wrap around you.

He gets out of his bag and gives it to WILL who puts it on top of his bag. They start to sleep.

WILL
Robin.

ROBIN
What?

WILL
I'm still cold... I don't suppose I could have your shirt – that would keep me warm.

ROBIN
Yeah, I suppose so.

He takes off his shirt. WILL looks at him and gives a little grin. WILL takes the shirt and wraps it around himself. They start to sleep.

WILL
Robin. I'm still cold, I don't suppose I could have your trousers?

ROBIN
Um, yeah, ok. If they'll keep you warm.

Robin takes off his trousers, revealing green tights underneath. Will grins. They go back to sleep. Will sits up and looks at Robin. Will points at the tights and then looks the audience and mouths "shall I?" He grins.

WILL
Robin?

ROBIN
What now?

WILL
I'm still cold... I don't suppose I could have-

ROBIN
Hold on – aren't you supposed to be on guard duty now?

WILL
What?

ROBIN
You are, it's your turn. You're supposed to be keeping watch in case the Sheriff comes looking for us.

WILL
Oh! Sorry, yeah. Sorted.

WILL shuffles across to the far side of the stage. He falls asleep straight away, as does ROBIN. MARION enters, a man-bag on his shoulder.

MARION
Hello Friar. Is Robin around?

FRIAR
What? Yes I think so.

MARION
You're up late?

FRIAR
Just having a joint before bed. Want to share?

MARION
Why not.

The FRIAR picks up a joint of beef from inside the basket, takes a bite and passes it to MARION.

MARION
Thanks. (Grimaces a little)

FRIAR
Bit harsh.

MARION
I can probably get my hands on some Aberdeen Angus.

FRIAR
God bless you. (A pause. He points upwards, peacefully). Just look at the stars a moment.

MARION
Ok

MARION fetches a magazine from his manbag and opens it.

MARION
What are you?

The FRIAR coughs loudly.

MARION
Cancer?

FRIAR
No just a tickle.

MARION
So where did you say that sexy bitch is?

FRIAR
Sexy bitch? Oh, in there dear boy. *(He points at Matrons tent)*

The FRIAR falls asleep. MARION walks over to Matrons tent. He knocks on the door.

MARION
It's me. I had to come to see you. I miss you so much.

MATRON sticks her head out, she now has a face pack. She drags MARION into her tent. There are screams of joy from MATRON and screams of fear from MARION. There is a lot of commotion inside the tent and rather dominant enthusiasm from MATRON. Then:

MATRON
Doctor, there's no need to be afraid.

MARION
I'm sorry, there's been a mistake- what's all this wool for?

MATRON
I'm going to embroider your name on the tent along with all the others.[127]

MARION runs out, his trousers around his ankles and his shirt open. He starts to button himself up. MATRON comes out.

___

[127] Tracy Emin's artwork "Everyone I Have Ever Slept With 1963-1995" was a tent appliquéd with the names of everyone she had shared a bed with.

MATRON
But Doctor please, I'm a woman a woman with needs. Doctor, can't you see I'm in trouble?

They now sang Peter Sellers and Sophia Lauren's song Goodness Gracious Me. It began with MATRON seducing MARION but by the end, ROBIN and MARION had reaffirmed their attraction to each other.

ROBIN and MARION kiss, MATRON trudges back into her tent, WILL lies down sulking, looking the other way.

MARION
We have to be quick.

ROBIN
We will be, I haven't cum since you and me at the Castle.

MARION
No, we have to talk. The Sheriff is heading to London. He's planning to take over Buckingham Palace and make himself king.

ROBIN
What?

MARION
I've got to go too.

ROBIN
What?

MARION
We're getting married.

ROBIN
What?

MARION
If I don't, he'll kill you.

ROBIN
What?

DONKEY
Are you deaf or stupid? Get your leg over, for Hovis sake.

MARION
I'll have to go before he comes looking.

ROBIN
Stay for a bit. Please

MARION
I can't.

They kiss

ROBIN
Ok. I'll come and save you. Trust me.

They kiss goodbye. MARION exits.

ROBIN
Fuck.

FRIAR (waking)
Yes?

ROBIN
No, "fuck".

FRIAR
Ah, righto. (sleeps).

ROBIN
What am I going to do?

He gets back in his sleeping back and starts to sleep.

WILL
Oh bugger boys and girls. It's not fair, I'll never find a man. *(He pats his pockets).* Shit. Where's the donkey tranquiliser?

A fishing rod protrudes from the wings, with the little bag of powder hanging from it. Will takes it, the rod disappears.

WILL
Nice! No, I'd better carry on with guarding. I can prove myself to Robin. Let me know if you see anyone coming.

There is a pause and he starts to fall asleep. The SHERIFF enters with a knife. The audience go wild. The SHERIFF hides. WILL sleeps. The SHERIFF approaches Robin. The audience shout. The SHERIFF spots the donkey tranquiliser, and forces a load up Will's nose as he wakes up. He falls into a dreamy sleep.

SHERIFF
Oh thank you Marion for leading me straight to Robin Hood! And now to dispose of him once and for all.

ROBIN snores

SHERIFF
Asleep!

ROBIN moans sexily.

SHERIFF
Dreaming! It sounds as though he's going to die happy.

ROBIN moans very erotically. The SHERIFF holds the knife towards ROBIN's neck.

SHERIFF
Listen.

ROBIN (asleep)
Oh yeah! Ram it deep in my throat!

The SHERIFF is a bit unsettled. He moves the knife lower.

ROBIN
Mmmm! Split me wide open with that thing!!

WILL wakes up.

WILL
Robin?

The SHERIFF shoves another load of powder up Will's nose. He goes straight back to sleep. The SHERIFF creeps over to ROBIN, the audience shouts, JOAN wakes up. She sees the SHERIFF and dashes over.

JOAN
You! Get away from Robin.

ROBIN wakes sitting bolt upright, his head hitting the SHERIFF's crotch. The SHERIFF panics and runs into Matrons tent. ROBIN and JOAN chase him into the tent too. MATRON can't believe her luck. The SHERIFF runs out pursued by MATRON, ROBIN chases MATRON, JOAN chases ROBIN and WILL wakes up and chases JOAN. The DONKEY wakes and joins the chase. This should ideally involve running into the aisles of the auditorium[128]. Meanwhile the FRIAR wakes and lights and starts to smoke another joint. The SHERIFF grabs the Friars joint as the FRIAR tries to grab it back he grabs the FRIAR too and holds his knife against the Friars neck.

SHERIFF
One move and the porky prelate gets it. Friar I want you to marry me.

FRIAR
Have you asked my father?

ROBIN
You won't get away with it.

SHERIFF
Come along you voluminous verger, we're going to Buck House. You'll officiate at your first Royal Wedding.

---

[128] And Benny Hill music.

549

The donkey farts.

SHERIFF
And don't try to follow if you want to see the dumpy deacon alive again.

He exits singing 'I'm Getting Married in the Morning', taking the FRIAR with him.

JOAN
What are we going to do Robin?

ROBIN (making to run)
We're going to chase him.

JOAN
Wait! He'll kill Tuck. Or you'll get lost in the dark. Get some sleep and then come up with a plan in the morning.

They all go back to respective sleeping places.

MATRON (to a man in the audience and pointing at the tent)
I'll be in there.

She gets into her tent. After a few seconds WILL gets up and walks over to JOAN

WILL
Joanie.

JOAN
What is it Will?

WILL
It's horrible here. And Robin doesn't like me anymore. I saw him snogging Marion. It's not fair. Every man

I fancy isn't interested in me. Do you think I'll ever find Mr Right?

JOAN
Yeah, course you will.

WILL
It's like you used to say when we were little and I was upset, somewhere over the rainbow there's a special place for us all. We used to look up at the stars and dream.

JOAN
Yeah. We got to keep dreaming Will.

Here they sang "Rainbow Connection" from The Muppets' Movie.

WILL
Goodnight Joanie

JOAN
Goodnight little Willie

WILL
Goodnight Robin.

ROBIN
Night Will

WILL
Goodnight Mum.

There is loud snoring from Matron's tent.

WILL
Goodnight Friar – oh poor Friar. Goodnight [donkey]

The donkey farts. The lights go down.

Scene 13: Buckingham Palace

The SHERIFF enters, then MARION

SHERIFF
Buckingham Palace!! It's all mine! It's enormous. And more history than the barmen downstairs. Luckily I found a map. (opens a tourist leaflet). What a large closet, that must be Prince Edward's. Marion, what's wrong with you? Just think, very soon you'll be the official consort of the King of England!

MARION
You know why I'm marrying you.

SHERIFF
Let's have a good old snoop... ah what's this?

He picks up a big cardboard box. On it is written "Property of HM The Queen". On the other side. "Keep the fuck out." He pulls out some funny items.

SHERIFF
Extraordinary. Now, Marion, here are our wedding vows.

SHERIFF hands MARION a piece of paper from his pocket.

MARION
But where are the guests?

SHERIFF
There won't *be* any guests. There won't be a choreographed zany first dance. There won't be an iPod playlist that our friends have put together. There won't be a string quartet playing Pachelbel's Canon. There won't be a conga, at any point, and there definitely, definitely won't be a fucking ceilidh.

MARION
But what about some nice arty black and white fly-on-the-wall wedding photos? I look magical in monochrome.

SHERIFF
No! Now, where's that abdominous abbot got to?

MARION
I think he went to the kitchens.

SHERIFF
Hey doughballs! Come and help sample the wedding cake!

They exit.

Scene 14: The forest

The forest. WILL, JOAN and MATRON (holding a joint). They are playing charades.

WILL
Ok my turn my turn!

WILL gets up.

MATRON
Is it a book?

WILL
I haven't started yet.

JOAN
It's Will, mum. It's not going to be a fucking book is it.

MATRON
Language Joan!

ROBIN enters.

ROBIN
What are you doing? You're meant to be looking for the Friar not playing games. Do I have to do everything? They must be on their way to London. We'll have to go there.

MATRON
London!

JOAN
Sweet one Robster. God I might actually meet another lesbian. But we've got no money.

WILL
Aha!

ROBIN
What?

WILL
Aha aha aha! What would Jesus do?

ROBIN
Yeah we know, he'd have a-

WILL
No! He'd ride into town on a donkey! [Donkey]!!

DONKEY enters

MATRON
Clever boy! But we won't all fit. I'll ride the donkey. I'll parade down Pall Mall like Lady Godiva.

JOAN
That was Coventry.

ROBIN
And she was naked.

DONKEY
And you can fuck right off on both counts. What about Margate? Or Bridlington. Or (dreamy) Blackpool!

MATRON tries to climb on the DONKEY, the DONKEY collapses, MATRON falls.

ROBIN
You ride her Joan.

DONKEY
Aye, ride me Joan.

The DONKEY gets very excited.

ROBIN
Woah calm down girl! Don't attack Joan, I thought you liked her? This is useless.

The FAIRY enters perhaps singing Pretty Vacant by the Sex Pistols to himself.

FAIRY
Hello campers! What have I missed?

WILL
The Sheriff's, like, kidnapped the Friar and they've gone to London. Can you help us get there?

FAIRY
In a jiffy.

WILL
Well so long as it's bigger than the donkey or we won't all fit.

FAIRY
We need some magic fairy dust. Have a rummage.

He holds his trousers open for someone to reach in. Eventually:

MATRON
Call yourselves medics.

She reaches in and pulls out a handful of glitter. She throws it in the air.

FAIRY
That Sheriff is a nasty louse.
So send these folks off to Buck House

WILL
Is that a proper spell?

FAIRY
I think it's a bit of Wendy Cope. Right, off you go. Give us a twirl now.

He sprinkles more glitter, ROBIN, MATRON, JOAN, WILL and the DONKEY twirl off stage.

FAIRY
Things are looking up! But excuse me, I've just had a call to say there's some blonde queen stuck in a cottage with three bears – she should be so lucky.

FAIRY exits singing Frigging in the Rigging by the Sex Pistols.

Scene 15: Buckingham Palace

The SHERIFF and MARION enter, the SHERIFF carrying a tray with a wedding cake. The FRIAR has an open box of Duchy Originals biscuits.

FRIAR
Did you say cake?

SHERIFF
Not yet you voluptuous vicar. First, you must marry us.

FRIAR
Boys and girls, I must stall them until Robin gets here... Sheriff, Marion, I can marry you. But you must undertake marriage counselling first.

SHERIFF
How about you take diet counselling and then we'll take marriage counselling.

FRIAR
Now listen. Many people have fought long and hard for the right for two people of the same gender to marry. It's very serious and it would be immoral for me to marry you if you were doing it for reasons other than love.

MARION
Oh but I am doing it for love! Just not love for him...

FRIAR
Sheriff?

SHERIFF
Of course I love him.

MARION
Oh no you don't.

SHERIFF
Oh yes I do! Enough! We'll begin! Me first. (Holds the cake tray out to the Friar) Hold this. No, wait (Changes his mind and gives it to Marion.)

The SHERIFF pulls a piece of paper from his pocket and reads from it.

SHERIFF
"Look into my eyes - you will see
What you mean to me"

He continues to read more of the lyrics to Bryan Adams' (Everything I Do) I Do It For You, before handing the paper to MARION who also reads. There is an almighty crash.

SHERIFF
What the hell was that??

They freeze in position. A shift in lighting. Meanwhile on the other side of the stage...

Scene 16: Buckingham Palace gardens

ROBIN, MATRON and WILL spin on.

WILL
Wow that was amazing!

ROBIN
Hello bottoms! Hello tops! Hello grateful row!

JOAN enters

JOAN
Where are we?

WILL (checking his phone)
It looks like...

ROBIN
Buckingham Palace gardens!

MATRON
Oh my! Dampening my toes in the Queen's private parts!

ROBIN
It's massive.

MATRON
It puts my barren little strip to shame. Just think what the Friar could do to it with his green fingers. It must get a right old pounding when she has the boy scouts round for afternoon tea. How does she keep so fragrant and lush?

ROBIN
She sprinkles widely and often.

DONKEY enters

JOAN
[Donkey]! You made it too!

DONKEY
It was alright for you lot. The fairy shoved me in the back of an Ocado van.

JOAN
Look at all this grass for you to eat.

DONKEY
I know what I'd rather munch on.

JOAN
Sometimes it's as though I can understand what you're thinking.

ROBIN
Come on guys. Marion and the Sheriff must be here somewhere, and the Friar. I'll fire a warning arrow to flush them out. Then we'll storm the place.

DONKEY
What is this, Fathers for Justice?

WILL
Hey! look at Grindr, Robin.

JOAN
Will!

WILL
There are a lot of guys very nearby who look very tough and scary...

ROBIN
Of course! They'll be the palace guards. The Queen's soldiers.

JOAN
Yeah that's right. Back when I was in the military it was gayer than the Amsterdam YMCA. I miss those showers.

DONKEY
If you do my back I'll do your front.

MATRON
Why don't I just go and have a nice word with some of these tough solders. They'll be plaster in my hands.

ROBIN
It's meant to be putty.

MATRON
Plaster's harder.

ROBIN
This is no good. Where's that fairy? I'm supposed to be fending off the most evil man in Britain, and he's supposed to be my guardian fairy or something and all I've managed is to get evicted, lose the Friar and see my true love get engaged to my enemy. Boys and girls will you help us call the fairy? After three I want you to shout, "Oi! Dickhead! Now!" Ok? One, two, three...

They all shout. The FAIRY appears.

FAIRY
Warping time and space took all my might,
I had to close the wormhole, it was tight

JOAN
I've heard more sense in a Florence and the Machine lyric.

ROBIN
We need arrows, lots more arrows.

FAIRY
Yonder you shall find a garden shed
It's overrun with squirrels, owls and sparrows
And sometimes youthful gardeners giving head,
But now (claps hands) it's teeming full of arrows.

JOAN
I've heard couplets with more depth on a Kylie album track.

WILL
Come on Robin, you heard him, sparrows

ROBIN
Arrows

WILL
Whatever, I'll come with you to the shed. (To Matron and Joan) We may be some time.

ROBIN
No we'll be quick

WILL (more mysteriously)
But we may be some time

WILL and ROBIN run off.

FAIRY
I'm just loving the dynamic with those two, what's the story?

MATRON
The Sheriff won't hurt the Friar will he? He's a good man. I'd hate for anything to happen to him before-

ROBIN (off)
You twat!

ROBIN and WILL rush on with two sacks.

ROBIN
There weren't any arrows!

WILL
We found a load of rocks though.

ROBIN
But I'll need help... Ok boys and girls, I need you to help me one more time, would you do that? Awesome! I need you to be our army.

In the bags there are rocks or stones made from painted sponge. WILL, JOAN, MATRON and FAIRY hand loads of these out to the audience.

ROBIN
Now hold on to your rocks until I give you the cue ok? When you hear me say "shoot your load", I want you to throw the rocks at the Sheriff, but not before. So what am I going to shout? That's right.

JOAN
Well that was right up there with the battle speech in Henry the fifth wasn't it.

ROBIN
Come on... may battle commence...

They march off.

Scene 17: The palace

An almighty crash (again). Lights up on the same scene as before, SHERIFF, MARION and FRIAR who still has the Duchy Originals. They un-freeze.

SHERIFF
What the hell was that??

MARION
It's probably the paparazzi. I'm very famous, Sheriff.

SHERIFF (looks out of a "window")
It was just the Ocado van arriving.

FRIAR (running off again)
Waitrose!

SHERIFF
You stay where you are. And he's not called Rose he's called Marion. Now where were we, you massive monk? Ah yes, "Do you take..."

FRIAR
Do I take what?

SHERIFF
"Do you take Dr Marion Maid as your lawful wedded husband."

FRIAR
No, no I don't. Do you?

ROBIN enters and hides. He should have a bow and arrows. He tries to get the Friar's attention.

ROBIN
Pssst!!

FRIAR
I am not! Oh Robin it's you!

ROBIN
Shhhhh! When I say "now", grab Dr Marion and get out of the way. Just do it.

FRIAR
Dr Marion Maid. Do you take-

ROBIN
Now!

MATRON, WILL and JOAN run on.

ROBIN, MATRON, WILL, JOAN
Shoot your load!!!!

The audience throw their stones at the SHERIFF. He falls, wounded.

SHERIFF
We're not in fucking Iran you know!

MARION
Robin Hood!!

ROBIN
Marion!

SHERIFF
Robin Hood!

ROBIN
Yeah that's my name, don't wear it out like.

MATRON
Friar!! You're alive!

FRIAR
Cookie?

MATRON
Thank you. Oh Friar, I was so worried. You're so brave. You know, the lighting in here sets off your manly curves ever so well.

FRIAR
Oh. Thank you. Yours too.

ROBIN aims an arrow at the SHERIFF and stands over him.

SHERIFF
Please! Don't hurt me! Treason! I'm the king!

JOAN
Don't think so S-man. Robin's 36th in line to the British throne. So skedaddle.

SHERIFF
And I'm 35th!

ROBIN
But I've got a bow and arrow.

FAIRY enters

JOAN
Where've you been!?

FAIRY
Billy Elliot.[129]

---

[129] The musical Billy Elliot was playing at the Victoria Palace Theatre next door to the Stag,

MATRON
Is Robin really 36th in line to the throne?

FAIRY
Yes! Look in that box, you'll find the Queen's private diary.

MATRON gets it.

FAIRY
Look in the back. There's a Royal Family tree.

MATRON
Here we go.

FAIRY
Follow it all the way down. What does it say?

MATRON
Morden.

FAIRY
That's the tube map! Turn the page.

MATRON
Look at that, she's done a little family tree! Oh Robin, look! It says you're the Earl of Huntingdon and Lord Locksley and 36th in line to the throne!

ROBIN
Now. Abdicate, or I'll kill you.

SHERIFF
Wait – why don't we enter a coalition?

ROBIN
Once upon a time there was a coalition, and just like you it knew the cost of everything and the value of nothing. Now – abdicate.

SHERIFF
Very well. I abdicate!

ROBIN
Cheers. And as King, I command you to give your entire fortune to the Friar Tuck Sherwood Forest Cottage Hospital. And the first thing I'll do is declare a reduction in taxes for the poor.

SHERIFF
Haven't you forgotten something?

WILL
He's right. I didn't set the Sky Plus for True Blood.

WILL picks up a folder and starts flicking through it. The Sheriff also picks up a large file.

SHERIFF
Clause 493.89 in the royal charter

JOAN
Which says that that if the royal family are out of the country for more than thirty days the next in line to the throne becomes king and that's Robin, cos you abdicated.

SHERIFF
Read the small print.

The SHERIFF hands her a sheet of paper.

JOAN
Clause 493.89, the next in line to the throne shall become king, providing he can produce his birth certificate…

JOAN gives the paper to MATRON.

SHERIFF
And here's mine. I always carry it around, I sometimes get ID'd when I'm buying wine you know how it is.

MARION
Robin?

ROBIN
I don't know where mine is.

ALL EXCEPT THE SHERIFF
Oh no!

WILL
Wait! The Queen's kept copies of everyone's birth certificates, right up to the person who's 50th in line to the throne

ALL EXCEPT THE SHERIFF
Oh yes!!

WILL
Let's see, Princess Anne, Edward, Fergie, Cheryl Cole, Ben Elton… number 36 isn't here!

ALL EXCEPT THE SHERIFF
Oh no!

FRIAR
It must be here somewhere let's find it.

ALL EXCEPT THE SHERIFF
Oh yes!

They start searching, the Sheriff laughs.

SHERIFF
You've got ten seconds before I call the guards. If they're here before you find it, I'm King. And treason is punishable by death. Ten! Nine, eight, seven...

As the Sheriff counts, they search.

JOAN
It could be anywhere

SHERIFF
Six

ROBIN
Keep looking. Boys and girls you got to help us guys. Try under the seats.

SHERIFF
Five, four, three two –

A birth certificate will have been stuck under an audience members seat before the show or during the interval. The audience member should shout out.

ROBIN (going to get it)
Nice one mate. What's your name? Cool, well now I'm King, I can Knight you. (he gets a sword) Arise sir/lady (says name of audience member).

JOAN has found a crown in the Queen's box. She puts it on ROBIN's head.

ROBIN
And as for you Sheriff, out of here.

SHERIFF
Bah. Come on Marion. Back to the Castle.

MATRON
I don't think so dear.

SHERIFF
What?

MATRON
Down here, clause 493.90. The castle in Nottingham is the rightful residence of the Earl of Huntington and if found he will automatically take residence. Oh and look you won't have to worry about removal fees because he takes all your possessions too.

SHERIFF
My money!

ROBIN
And my second act as king is to banish you for treason. If you resist we'll use extraordinary rendition.

SHERIFF
No!

MATRON
Do you remember when I did my extraordinary rendition of Private Dancer at the Christmas party last year?

FRIAR
I remember.

MATRON (to the SHERIFF)
And to think I fancied you once upon a time!

SHERIFF
One day I'll be back. Au revoir.

SHERIFF leaves.

MATRON
I still do a bit. Oh but not as much as I fancy you Friar.

FRIAR
Me?

MATRON
I need a good, kind man in my life. Will you marry me?

FRIAR
I would be honoured. Can we cut the cake now?

ROBIN
Wait. Marion, you were going to give up your happiness for my life. I want to spend the rest of it with you.

MARION and ROBIN kiss.

MATRON
Well they're just copying us.

JOAN (to Will)
Are you ok little brother?

WILL
Yeah... I thought I was in love with Dr Marion. And I thought I was in love with Robin. But I think I'm just a bit of a dizzy tart cos all I want to do right now is jump the fairy. (To the fairy). Hey, fairy. I want to spend the rest of the night with you. How about it?

FAIRY
You got any fairy dust?

WILL
I found a load of plant food in that garden shed you sent us to.

FAIRY
Excellent!

ROBIN
Then let's find some champagne and go out into the garden as lovers to dance the night away.

FRIAR
And cut the cake.

JOAN
You know, I might just give it a miss actually.

MATRON
Oh Little Joan, don't be sad. You'll find a nice girl someday.

JOAN
I don't want a nice girl someday. I want any girl, now.

The SHERIFF enters with a small cannon or a gun.

SHERIFF
Hahaha! I'll get you once and for all, Hood!

He prepares to fire. The DONKEY pushes onto the stage.

DONKEY
Get out of the fucking way Robin!

The DONKEY shoves ROBIN out of the way. The SHERIFF fires. The DONKEY is fatally hit. She farts, collapses in the entrance and dies.

ROBIN
Oh my God... [Donkey]!

JOAN
Noooooo!!

JOAN chases the SHERIFF out.

ROBIN
She's dead. And she saved my life!

WILL
Doctor Marion!

JOAN
He's no bloody use Will.

The FRIAR gets a white cloth and lays it over the DONKEY.

FRIAR
If it's any comfort, she'll be in Blackpool now.

MATRON
You, little man. Can't you do something?

FAIRY (to audience)
My moment! This is it boys and girls. My last chance not to fade into obscurity. Please, help me. I need you all to believe in fairies. Believe as hard as you can. Wave your arms out like this to make the magic work.

MATRON (sniffing)
Ooh someone in the front's never heard of Right Guard.

FAIRY
Quiet!! Now, boys and girls. Believe.

He casts a spell. Lights flash and strobe, dry ice etc. There is movement under the sheet. Eventually, from under it, emerges not a donkey but a beautiful princess.

PRINCESS
Holy shit I'd forgotten how much underwiring digs in.

WILL
This plant food's amazing.

MATRON
Who are you?

PRINCESS
I'm an Israeli princess, I was turned into a donkey by a wicked Sheriff - a different wicked Sheriff. And I was told the spell would only be broken when two things happened. First, a silly fairy had to save my life. Well that's why I agreed to come with Robin, I thought it might be him.

JOAN
What was the other thing?

PRINCESS
I had to fall in love. And I have.

MARION
Look I completely understand, but you see I'm getting married to-

PRINCESS
Not you, you twat. Her. Little Joan, I've wanted you since you first stroked my nose.

JOAN
Me too! But I thought I was just having a weird animal phase, and that you were just a pervy donkey. What's your name?

PRINCESS
Thing is, the spell only stays reversed as long as I keep my donkey name. Listen everyone, I'm really sorry I crapped myself in the hospital. I was so embarrassed.

JOAN
Come here, you!

The PRINCESS breaks wind.

JOAN
So the farting, that wasn't a donkey thing?

PRINCESS
Afraid not, always been like it, just can't stop them.

JOAN
Don't worry, I'll love you, farts and all.

They kiss.

ROBIN
Friar! Let's have a wedding. Four weddings.

WILL
I don't want to get married

JOAN
Yeah chill a bit Robs, we haven't even bought a cat yet.

ROBIN (laughs)
Ok! Two weddings!

The sound of a door being unlocked creaking open and shutting heavily. All react. A traveller's backpack is flung onto the stage.

QUEEN (offstage)
One is home at last! We've made it back from Sitges[130]. One shall be speaking to one's travel agent. I think she misunderstood my requirements. Philip managed to find us a donkey, the clever old thing that he is... Hello?

All look about, eventually staring at Little Joan. She shrugs and goes off towards the voice.

QUEEN (offstage)
Hello dear. I'm looking for Robin Hood. Is he here?

ROBIN looks scared. LITTLE JOAN enters. ROBIN walks towards the queen. A gloved hand appears holding a sword. It places it on one of Robin's shoulders, then the other.

QUEEN (offstage)
On dubs thee Lord Locksley and the Earl of Huntingdon.

ROBIN
Thank you.

QUEEN (offstage)
But there's only one Queen around here, dear.

Her other arm appears. ROBIN takes off the crown and places it in the outstretched hand.

QUEEN
One is quite parched. Who's going to put the bloody kettle on?

A moment... They all look about. Then they rush to it, frantically tidying away rocks and other mess as they exit. As the lights fade, the FRIAR returns, grabs the cake, and exits again.

Curtain call. Then:

FAIRY
So life went on! Though not as they planned it,
You may want to know what became
Of our merry band: now as I understand it,
Matron was made a Dame!

MATRON
And I'm planning my wedding, it's all such a flurry
With my friar, so handsomely flabby,
For now he's Archbishop of Canterbury
We'll have nuptials in Westminster Abbey

FRIAR
I've rather enjoyed my return to the fold
I've banged a few heads together
We've got women bishops, and gays, it's so bold,
With dog-collars in patent leather.

ROBIN
He's marrying Kate and Wills.

JOAN
Fucking ace!

MARION
His media skills are fresh-honed.
You can't stuff your face while you're saying grace.

FRIAR
Still I'll have to get mighty stoned.

ROBIN
Our Will's got two jobs, and both let him scrounge

All the drink and the drugs he can carry.
At weekends he bar-tends in Shadow Lounge[131]

WILL
In the week, I'm dresser to Prince Harry.

JOAN
My princess hosts dinners, she's ever so cool,
They love her stuffed vine leaves, and farting,
And Marion quit medicine, and went back to school

MARION
Doing fashion, at Central St Martin's.
It's Little Joan who's the new TV star
She films adventures around the world

PRINCESS
And she's given her name to a new sports bra

---

[131] The Shadow Lounge was an upmarket gay bar in Soho.

That's a life-raft when it's unfurled.

ROBIN
And what of the Sheriff, what role could there be
For someone so ruthless and mean?

SHERIFF
I'm advising a government savings committee:
We're privatising the queen.

FAIRY
We hope that our story has touched you; we'll miss you
You're gorgeous, now go get a beer,
May your winter be wondrous, and know that we wish you

ALL
Fine health, great love, and good cheer.

THE END.

Dick Whittington: Another Dick in City Hall

Jason Marc-Williams as Idle Jack and Ross Henry Steele as Boris the Cat in *Dick Whittington: Another Dick in City Hall*.
Photo by Alan Day.

Dick Whittington: Another Dick in City Hall

A version of this, our first professional pantomime, had been performed the previous year as an amateur show for a private party and again as a charity fundraiser at the King's Head in Islington, starring one Martin Hooper as the cat.

Our Dick had made the news: a local paper ran a story about Dick Whittington enthusiasts who had complained that we had sullied his name by making him gay. This was picked up by one of the national tabloids, which ran a full-page article about our outrageous gay panto upsetting the residents of Islington. It was also discussed in a Telegraph piece about bankers being portrayed as villains in the wake of the 2007-2008 financial crash.

The Above The Stag production opened late 2009. Boris Johnson was in his second year as Mayor of London, Grindr had launched but everyone was still using Gaydar, Big Brother was still on Channel 4 but audiences were falling, and Danni Minogue was a judge on The X Factor, mentoring Stacey Solomon who finished in third place behind Olly Murs and the winner, Joe McElderry.

You'll see that the mayor is a very loose caricature of a bumbling Boris Johnson as he was largely seen back then. It's pretty toothless – if only we'd known about his "tank-topped bumboys" comments and, well, everything else.

Dick Whittington: Another Dick in City Hall

By Jon Bradfield & Martin Hooper

Characters:
Good Fairy
Alderman Rat, a banker.
Henry Regatta, his protégé.
Dick Whittington, a young man from Gloucester.
Boris, his cat.
Idle Jack.
Holly Oaks, his mum, to be played by a man.
Wilma Whittington, Dick's mum, to be played by a man.
The Mayor of London.
The Mayor of Gran Canaria.

The mayors should be played by the same actor.

Dick Whittington – Another Dick in City Hall **was first performed at Above The Stag Theatre on 1 December 2009 with the following cast and creative team:**

Fairy: Gemma Seren; Alderman Rat: Martin Cort; Idle Jack: Jason Marc-Williams; Dick Whittington: Matthew Groom; Boris: Ross Henry Steele; Holly Oaks: Ross Mitchell; Mayor of London/Mayor of Gran Canaria: Tony Parkin; Henry Regatta: Basher Savage; Wilma Whittington: Mansel David

Director: Peter Kosta; Lighting Designer and Stage Manager: Ben Blaber; Scenic Artist: Matthew Potter; Curtains made by: Claire Nicholas; Assistant Director/Production Assistant: Sam James; Marketing, design & public relations: Jon Bradfield; Photographer: Alan Day; Producer: Peter Bull

Special thanks to Russell Cooper, Ben Jones, Tim McArthur, Prav Manon-Johansson and Out of Joint Theatre Company.

An earlier version was first performed in 2008 by Dee Harnett, Martin Hooper, Peter Knight, Rolf Kurth, Martin Lunnon, Mike McDonough, Nikki McKnight, Dale Rees, Andy Rouse and Andrew Watson, directed by Gary Wright.

Scene 1

The FAIRY enters.[132]

FAIRY

Here's a tale boys and girls, as the hills it is old
A boy from the sticks grows up gay
He dreams of a city paved with gold,
And decides to run away.

But before he finds work in a media role
Or falls down a K hole for ever
We need him to save our city's fair soul
From a baddy who's greedy and clever

London's gone to the dogs, or rather the rats
Half of the banks are collapsing.
And even the immigrant workers think that
It's shithole that's close to prolapsing

We need a Mayor who can tend to the tube
And keep knives from our streets at night
And make sure there's lots of free condoms and lube
And to switch on the Christmas lights

And I'm to be part of this fable
Yes I'm the good fairy, but hey
That's good as in moral, not able
I think I should probably say

I wasn't that naughty at fairy school
I wasn't a rebel or pest
But in magic class I was always the fool -
I failed all my spelling tests...

But enough about me, this show's about Dick
That's the name of our hero this time
So lend us an ear, and give us a cheer,
And enjoy your Christmas pantomime!

ALDERMAN RAT enters - "boo boo" etc

RAT

Music to my ears! Give me more, it's like piss off a rent boy's back to me.

FAIRY
Ugh!! a rat!

RAT
It's not The Wind in the Willows. I'm *Alderman* Rat.

FAIRY
I quite like an older man.

RAT
Alderman Rat. A king amongst rats!!

FAIRY
I can see you're a 'king rat. A great big mother 'king rat.

RAT
I care not for your lewdness
Your vulgarity and rudeness
But that won't get me down
I'm going to be Mayor of this town!

FAIRY
Oh no you're not!

RAT
Oh yes I am!

FAIRY
Oh no you're not.

RAT
Reassuring isn't it, the standard of political debate in this city. Ah, London. They say you're never more than ten feet from a human. Roughly.

FAIRY
Roughly ten feet?

RAT (looking at audience)
Roughly human.

FAIRY
You clearly haven't read the script
Or you'd know what the premise is
You'll never make it to city Hall
You've got a nemesis!

RAT
Are we going to battle in verse!? How very Brixton.

FAIRY
That's thrown a spanner in your ointment hasn't it.

RAT
This "nemesis" of mine...

FAIRY
I've seen him.

---

[132] This script was originally written for a cabaret stage so we didn't really describe locations. This is probably "a London street".

566

RAT
How?

FAIRY
I have a crystal ball.

RAT
My mother had a plastic hip. Let me see him?

FAIRY
No!

RAT
Then at least describe him. Make things more... interesting.

FAIRY
All right.

The FAIRY takes out her crystal ball and stares at it, frowning. She tries holding it in different positions.

RAT
Problem?

FAIRY
Bloody Vodafone... Ah – here he is. The boy.

RAT (dismissive)
Ha. A boy.

FAIRY
Yes. Just a boy and his cat.

RAT
Ew!

FAIRY
So don't count your lucky stars before they've hatched.

RAT *(changing tack)*
I heard that every time someone says they don't believe in fairies, one dies.

FAIRY
Yes – yes it's true. Unless someone claps their hands straight afterwards.

RAT
How interesting. Because I don't believe in fairies.

FAIRY claps her hands. Drops the ball. Rat catches it, looks into it, laughs. The fairy snatches it back.

RAT
You're right! He's just a boy. Neither he nor his cat will stop me. *(Big)* Ha ha ha ha ha!!!!!! *(Polite)* Very nice to meet you.

He exits.

FAIRY
A whole scene passed, and here's the thing
There's still no sign of Dick!
Time's tighter than a fairy's ring,
I needs must act, and quick.

Oh boys and girls it's scary; still
It's not like I'd be breezy,
One chance to prove my fairy skills
And they don't make it easy

Rule one: I must not interfere
With the players in our scheme
A bit like being the coach, I hear,
Of a teenage football team

Rule two: the boy can't see my powers
Nor know it's me that's spoken
Or they'll come find me after hours
And see my wand gets broken

But though these rules had best be heeded
Dick will reach his prize
I shall appear when I am needed:
I'm a rasta of disguise!

Fear not, you'll see me on the way -
I'll give you little clues:
As the mattress said to the bishop that day,
I'll reveal myself to you.

Exit.

Scene 2

Jack enters carrying a bag of sweets.[133]

JACK
Hi everyone! My name's Idle Jack, but you can call me Jack. Anyone want a sweet? *(he throws sweets into the audience)* Whenever I say hi to you all, will you all shout out Hi Jack? Great! Well that makes us friends. So add me on Facebook cos I'm trying to get to 4000. Right, I'm gonna go off and come back on again so we can practise being friends, ok?

He exits and immediately returns.

Hi everyone!

("Hi Jack!") He looks shocked, and looks over his shoulder

Shit you're right! There's someone coming! I'll go and hide.

JACK goes to a corner. DICK enters with the traditional hankie-on-stick.

DICK
Hello boys and girls! Let's have a look at you. Well it's a bigger audience than Big Brother got this year. I tell you, this is the way to arrive in a city. The wind in your hair, travelling light. Have you seen my cat? Boris, where are you? Keep up, we've made it!

BORIS enters with the biggest rucksack imaginable. Out of breath

BORIS
Can't... go... any... further...

DICK
There you are!

BORIS collapses.

DICK
Cheer up, Boris

BORIS
There's nothing to be cheery about.

DICK
Oh now that's not true!

He sings:

Oh, we ain't got a barrel of money,
Maybe we're ragged and funny,
But we'll travel along, singin' a song, side by side.
Don't know what's comin' tomorrow;
Maybe it's trouble and sorrow,
But we'll travel our road sharin' our load side by side.[134]

BORIS *(indicating the rucksack)*
You call this sharing our load? Why did we have to walk all the way from Gloucestershire? What's wrong with the train? Why did we have to come at all? I was just starting to get on with that cute little ginger from down the road.

DICK
I'm sorry Boris. But I'm glad you came with me. I'd have missed you else. Hang on... a ginger? Aren't gingers usually male?

BORIS
Yes...?

DICK
Wow. My tom's a queen. You can't tell, you know.

BORIS
Where are we?

DICK
London! Can't you hear the bells?

Silence

DICK
Ahem. Can't you hear the bells??

Silence.

DICK
I said can't you hear the fucking bells???

They ring.

DICK
See. London.

BORIS
You said that a week ago. You said, look, it's London! The buildings are so futuristic, you said. Look, you said, everyone travels by plane. Where were we? Stansted.

---

[133] Again, no location. Let's go with "London's Docklands".

[134] Side by Side, by Harry M Woods (1927)

DICK
We must be at the docks, Boris. Look: boats, seagulls, Victorian prostitutes.

JACK comes out of hiding.

JACK (at Dick)
Wow. Cute!

BORIS
Thank you.

JACK
Oh my God! A talking rucksack!

BORIS
Oh my God, a talking idiot. Help me up.

JACK tries. He's not strong and the cat is heavy. DICK helps him.

JACK
Well you're a strong one. Hi, I'm Jack. Well, Idle Jack. But I shorten it to Jack.

BORIS
You *are* idle.

DICK
Hi, I'm Dick.

He holds out his hand, formally. JACK kisses him on both cheeks instead.

DICK
This is Boris.

BORIS
Meow.

DICK
We're new here. We're looking for a room.

BORIS
Two rooms.

DICK
And a job.

BORIS
One job.

JACK
My mum runs an inn on the other side of the marina. She's always looking for staff.

BORIS
We don't want to live in the docklands. (To Dick) You said we could live in Shoreditch.

JACK
But you'll love it here. Mum says it's an upcoming area. Over there there's loft conversions, warehouse conversions, Islamic conversions. That spire is the gay friendly Church of All Marys. There's Vietnamese, Poles, Nigerians, oh and there's a family of cockneys that way, but they eat strange things and no-one can understand what they're saying. Oh and you'll love gay pride!

DICK
Gay Pride?

BORIS
Well it was never going be called Gay Dignity, was it?

DICK
It sounds so exciting!

JACK
Walk this way.

DICK
If I walked that way I wouldn't need talcum powder.

All exit.

Scene 3: Holly's bar

HOLLY sings "I'd Do Anything" from Oliver! to herself.

HOLLY
I'd do anything... for you, dear, anything...yes I'd do anything, Anything, for you... That's for all the Nancies out there! Hello boys and girls! Oh, come on, I want it loud like Susan Boyle in the showers at the Priory[135]. Hello boys and girls! My name's Holly. Holly Oaks. And this is my little bar, here on the docks. It's very popular with sailors. At weekends it not uncommon to find seamen in every corner.

RAT enters.

RAT
Talking to yourself again Holly?

HOLLY
Oh happy days, it's Alderman Rat. With all the charm of a Guy Ritchie flick. Put your contacts in the right way round, man, and you'll see I'm talking to these lovely people.

RAT (to audience)
I'm so sorry.

He turns to Holly and speaks kindly and slowly as if to an idiot.

RAT
They're not interested, and they haven't got any money. Now where's my rent?

HOLLY
He'll be stuck on the tube from Earl's Court.

RAT
My. Rent.

HOLLY
I can't pay the rent.

RAT
But you must pay the rent.

HOLLY
But I can't pay the rent.

RAT
But you must pay the rent.

HOLLY
But I can't pay the rent! Business is terrible. It's this recession.

RAT
It affects me too. Without your rent, how can I pay the bonuses I owe? Now, you'll like this. Did I tell you I was running for Mayor?

HOLLY
You, Mayor?

RAT
Yes, me, Mayor. I trust I can count on your support.

HOLLY
Well in the absence of Robert Mugabe...

RAT
And I nearly forgot; now this is exciting. I'm having the whole building developed. Fifty luxury riverside apartments. So it's last orders for your grubby little boozer.

HOLLY
His name's Jack.

RAT
I was talking about the pub.

HOLLY
Oh but Ratty, dear, think of the bigger picture. All the posh new residents will want a nice bar to go to when they finish a hard day's work. It's the perfect excuse for me to go upmarket.

RAT
Two flavours of Walkers Sensations is not "upmarket".

HOLLY
I've been trying. I said to my boy, I want buff staff, great ambience and a superb kitchen. He got me rough staff, an ambulance and a soup kitchen.

RAT
There won't *be* any new residents. Not yet. No, we'll do the construction now when all the labourers are desperate for work. Then in a few years when the economy's bounced back we can sell them for an enormous profit.

[135] Boyle had been taken to the mental health clinic The Priory following an episode after her defeat in the final of *Britain's Got Talent*. That year's contest was won by dance troupe Diversity.

HOLLY
But this is my livelihood! Listen, stay for a drink, on the house.

RAT
In your pub? Well why not. People like a politician with the common touch. I'll have a bottle of Bavarian wheat beer.

HOLLY
I'll bring you a glass too, sir. You know with the city as it is, you get rat's piss and all sorts on the bottles.

RAT *(eyes narrowed)*
What did you say?

HOLLY
Oh – no, I didn't mean anything by it! Here, find a corner I'll bring it over.

RAT exits

HOLLY
Oh, oh rack and ruin! Or rat and ruin. One day a man will walk through that door who will sort out my problems.

Enter JACK.

HOLLY
Or not.

JACK
Hi everyone!

"Hi Jack!" He leaps into his mother's arms.

HOLLY
Oh, bothered. This place has been bombed three times already, we only noticed cos there was less broken glass than usual and that funny stain on the toilet wall finally came off.

JACK
Hi mum! I've brought someone home.

HOLLY
There must be a Y in the day.

JACK
I found Dick on the quayside.

HOLLY
Well it's probably more immediate than Guardian Soulmates.

JACK
Dick! Boris! Come in.

They do.

HOLLY
Oh I say, he's a cut above your wotsit. You must be Dick. And this must be Doris.

She strokes the cat.

BORIS
Touch me and I'll piss on the carpet.

HOLLY
You wouldn't be the first.

BORIS
Oh, that's... that's quite nice actually. Ooh stop it!

HOLLY
There you go, see? I'm Holly. Holly Oaks.

DICK
That's funny.

HOLLY
How is it funny?

DICK
Well, it's like my mum... she's got a friend called Emma. Emma Dale.

HOLLY
That's a lovely name.

DICK
And her cousin, she's American, she's called Brook. Brook Side...?

HOLLY
Yes?

DICK
And her sister, Cora, she married well. Cora Nation Street.

BORIS
These people are idiots, Dick, come on lets- wait! I can smell a rat.

HOLLY
Everything's above board.

BORIS
A real rat.

JACK
They're everywhere. Dick's looking for work mum.

HOLLY
Woollies[136] was it? Let's have a look at you. Oh yes you'll be very popular.

JACK
So you've got room for Dick?

HOLLY
Of course. And she can stay, too.

BORIS
Who's she, the cat's mother? I'm a boy.

DICK
Thanks Holly... do you think I could borrow your phone?

HOLLY
Of course, dear, you want to call your mum?

DICK
Yes - I didn't really explain the whole gay thing.

BORIS
Can't you just text her? "Hi, sorry for being a Dick. But I like Dick. Love from, Dick".

DICK
No! What if I'm not gay?

BORIS
Oh turn again, Whittington.

HOLLY
Have you any bar experience?

DICK
I can learn. But it's not really what I had in mind.

HOLLY
We all have to do rubbish jobs when times is hard, Dick. Way back, years ago, I used to take my clothes off in gentlemen's clubs. I'm a lapsed dancer.

The FAIRY enters disguised as an old sea dog. Briefly she removes her beard.

FAIRY
(To audience) Pssst! It's me! (To Holly). Yo ho ho and a bottle of spilt milk. What does an old sea dog need to do to get a drink round here?

136

British High Street stalwart Woolworths closed all 807 of its stores at the beginning of 2009.

RAT enters

RAT
Tell me about it, I've been waiting so long I started to think I'd already evicted the bar staff.

BORIS
Now I can really smell a rat.

RAT
Young man. I know you from somewhere.

FAIRY
Oh no you don't!

RAT
Oh yes, I do.

FAIRY
Oh no you don't!

RAT
Well, then I shall have to get to know you. You have the look of a newcomer. I must welcome you to our great city.

DICK
Thank you sir.

BORIS (mocking)
"Thank you sir".

FAIRY
There's only one thing for it! A spell!
Slugs and snails upon a plate
Make Ratty's little tool vibrate!

Rat feels his phone vibrate. Answers it.

RAT
Hello? *(quiet)* Not here... yes, it was very... you're so naughty!... *(Loud, manic)* Yes, conference call at 5! Perfect! Goodbye! (Hangs up) It was nobody! It was very important! Err, business appointment. I have an election to win.

Rat exits

FAIRY
Oh is that the time? My ship will sail without me! Must dash. (exit)

HOLLY
Now listen to me, boys. Don't end up like that Rat. He's a nasty piece of work, Dick. He wants to shut me down.

At a time like this. And here's the worst bit – he wants to become mayor of London!

DICK
Then I'll stop him. *I'll* become Mayor of London!

JACK
Yeah! Me too!

HOLLY slaps Jack around the head.

HOLL
You can't both be Mayor! Dick, I'm sure you'd be very good. But it doesn't work like that. Come on. I'll show you your rooms. Walk this way.

BORIS
I always do.

He follows her, tottering like a woman in high heels.

Scene 4: Rat's office

ALDERMAN RAT enters holding a book.

RAT

It's time to plan my election campaign. This has been inspirational.

He shows the book, it has a big picture of Peter Mandelson on the cover[137]. The Mayor of London enters.

RAT

Mr Mayor, what an unexpected...

MAYOR

Cripes, Alderman Rat, I'm in a spot of bother. I've been caught cycling in the corridors of power again. And I'm having horrendous trouble with my column.

RAT

Your column?

MAYOR

It's barely 3 inches and I've been bashing away it all morning. I could do with a hand finishing off.

RAT

Your newspaper column! Oh but I'm terribly busy. No rest for the wicked ha ha ha.

MAYOR

Yes I hear you've got a finger in all the boys.

RAT

Pies, Mr Mayor.

MAYOR

You must have very sticky fingers. Oh, I saw your son won another medal, you must be proud.

RAT

My son?

MAYOR

Yes, the champion rower, Henry Regatta. Look, I know he's not your real son.

RAT

But you're right, I have been like a true father to him. Bathed him, dressed him, seen him through his education.

MAYOR

Was he terribly young when you adopted him?

RAT

Oh, terribly. Barely sixteen. Still, I like to think a part of me has rubbed off on him. Might I ask how your re-election campaign is progressing?

MAYOR

Cripes! Thanks for the reminder old chap. I trust you'll be at my side?

RAT

Oh no, Mr Mayor. I shall be right behind you *(mimes strangling)*

MAYOR

Jolly good.

MAYOR exits.

RAT

Drat. So much to do. Who can help me? My protégé, and second only to me in deviousness. (calls) Henry!

HENRY enters.

HENRY

Yes Ratty. (To audience) Hi fans.

RAT

Henry I need your help. I need you to have that pathetic Holly Oaks and her snivelling son thrown out of their bar. Then I will close down all the other gay bars in London, especially the Stag. The Mail will love it, Ha, ha, ha.

HENRY

You are astonishingly devious. The man who brought down the Astoria[138].

RAT

That wasn't me. That place was perfect for rats. It hadn't been deep cleaned in a decade. Unlike most of its punters.

HENRY

I see ... And what about Dick?

---

[137] Peter Mandelson was expected to publish a book in 2010. *The Third Man: Life at the Heart of New Labour* came out in June.

[138] The legendary concert venue on Charing Cross Road was closed in January 2009. It had been the home of gay club night G-A-Y, which relocated to Heaven nightclub in the summer of 2008.

RAT

Keep your mind on the job, Henry. Oh I see. Well, I have a cunning plan. If you help me, I'll buy you a new boat on expenses.

HENRY

Is that above board, Ratty?

RAT

Above board... Ah, yes, I see, a sailing joke, very good.

The fairy enters dressed as a cleaning woman.

RAT

Who are you?

FAIRY

Mildred Grungebucket. Your new cleaning woman, duck. The agency have sent me 'ere to clean your inner sanctum.

RAT

I'm very particular about who enters my inner sanctum.

HENRY

That's not strictly true.

FAIRY *(to audience.)*

It's me, the fairy.

RAT

Well get cleaning, woman. If you don't mind we are having a private conversation.

FAIRY

I don't mind duck you carry on. I'll just get on with me business.

HENRY

What do you want me to do, Alderman?

The fairy spits on a cloth and polishes Rat's head.

RAT

Do you mind!!!

The fairy cleans and pulls faces at Rat.

RAT

Henry, I need to be rid of Dick Whittington. Get over to Holly Oak's bar. Involve him some scandal. He's young and gay and new in town - it shouldn't be difficult.

HENRY

Yes of course. Scandal is my middle name.

RAT

No it's not, Henry. It's Evelyn.

FAIRY

(To audience) They are going to trick Dick. I need to do something. At a time like this a boy needs his Mum. I'll magic up Dick's mother to go to Holly's bar and be with him. She'll stop him getting into trouble.

Heebe Geebie and a little prick
Send to Holly's bar the Mum of Dick.

There, sorted.

RAT

What *is* that ridiculous cleaner doing now?

WILMA twirls on. She wears wellington boots and carries a bucket and speaks with a Gloucester or West Country accent.

WILMA

Where am I? Where am I? I don't think I'm in Gloucester anymore!

FAIRY

Oh no! I got me co-ordinables wrong. You shouldn't be here!

WILMA

Too right I shouldn't, I was just milking Daisy to make a new batch of Gorgonzola and here I am. Where am I?

FAIRY

London. Now Shhh!

Enter the MAYOR

HENRY

If I may say... If we're going to win this election, we'll have to make sure the press don't find out about your little evening trips to Clapham Common.

RAT

If it wasn't for my little... walks, Henry, we'd never have met and you'd still be dreaming of such a life as you now lead. But you're right... Well, I can say that it is perfectly innocent; I like to open my lungs and take in the fresh air, occasionally offering a night's slumber to the young and destitute of our city. So Henry. You're in?

HENRY

Trust me ratty, I can handle this Dick for you.

WILMA

Oi you? Who do you think you are!

HENRY
I'm Henry Regatta champion rower.

WILMA
I don't care who you are, you are not messing with my Dick. And what do you think you're doing bringing me here, this will play havoc with me Gorgonzola. And I've got the chickens to see to.

RAT
I didn't bring you here, you stupid woman. Henry, throw Atilla the Hen out of here.

WILMA
Don't worry I'm going.

Wilma marches out.

RAT
Come along team, we've an election to win!

Rat and Henry exit

FAIRY
Oh buggeration!

The fairy exits.

Scene 5

Holly's bar. Jack enter with a copy of QX and a bucket.

JACK
Hi Everyone!

"Hi Jack!"

JACK
Oh no, you're not gonna get me with that one again. I don't look as dumb as I really am.

Jack sits down with his magazine. Holly enters, takes the magazine and hits him round the head with it.

HOLLY
What have I told you about sitting around reading?

JACK
Take it slowly, one syllable at a time, and I might manage it someday.

HOLLY
(to audience) He's about as sharp as a bowling ball. Look, I want my front entrance cleaned. (He doesn't move). If we keep this place nice maybe Alderman Rat will let us stay. I don't know what we'd do if we were kicked out!!

JACK
We could squat.

HOLLY
I'd rather find somewhere that's got a toilet. Come on, clean.

JACK
But I'm educating meself mum. I'm learning new words.

HOLLY
Oh you're a good boy Jack. And one these days you'll make me proud. Is there anything you need help with?

JACK
Thanks mum, yeah. What's this word?

He shows her.

HOLLY
You degenerate! You debauched individual! How could you think your mum would know a word like that?

JACK
Like what?

HOLLY
Like that.

JACK
Like what?

HOLLY
Like... (beat) Like punchfuck. Anyway, that's two words.

JACK
No it ain't mum. There's no hyphen.

HOLLY
I ain't surprised, you can lose that just from riding horses.

JACK
But what does it mean? All the boys and girls want to know what it means too, don't you?

HOLLY
Right, right... Well. Punchfuck. I ask you. Well now. You remember Mr Punch.

JACK
He was a glove puppet.

HOLLY
You'll figure it out. That's quite enough education for one day. Come on. Front entrance. Get on with it.

JACK runs offstage fast with a bucket. We hear a crash and splash. Holly reacts.

HENRY enters, his shirt is wet, and his face and hair are covered in foam. After a beat, JACK enters, staggering about with a bucket on his head.

HOLLY
Idiot, you've soaked Henry Regatta!! Henry. I apologise for my son.

JACK enters, with a bucket over his head. He removes it: he too has foam on his hair and face. A sponge is wedged in his mouth. HENRY wipes the foam from his hair with his hand and smears it off on JACK.

HENRY
I'm looking for Dick.

HOLLY
Join the queue.

HENRY
Dick Whittington. I've heard he's staying here.

577

JACK, still with the sponge in his mouth, shakes his head.

HOLLY
I'll just get him for you. *(shouts loudly)* DIIIIIIIICK!!

Dick and Boris enter, Dick with a mop. Boris looks at Henry and starts to snarl. Dick and Henry exchange glances

DICK
Boris behave! *(to Henry, a bit cheekily)* Hi.

HENRY
(Dreamily) Hi. *(Remembering he is there to trick Dick)* I'm the famous Olympic rower Henry Regatta. I heard all about the hot newcomer. I want you to come out.

BORIS
He came out two scenes ago, so do one posh boy.

DICK
Boris, shut up.

BORIS
Shut up Boris, be quiet Boris, you're just a cat Boris. Well that's it, you're on your own. Don't come running to me when it all goes wrong.

HOLLY
Come along moggy, come outside with me. Who knows maybe you will catch a mouse or something.

BORIS
Or a Rat. And you Hollyhocks, you don't call me moggy, I am a cat, Felus Catus, understand?

HOLLY
Feel us what? Walk this way.

BORIS
If I walked that way they'd give me worming tablets.

HOLLY and BORIS exit, JACK follows, as he does he takes a sponge out of his mouth.

JACK
Don't do it Dick!

HENRY picks up the sponge and puts it back in JACK's mouth. Jack walks out carrying the bucket.

DICK *(mopping)*
Look it's very kind of you to ask me out but well, I'm just a poor boy from Gloucester and you, well you're Henry Regatta. It's feels a bit strange.

HENRY
What, as if I had some ulterior motive or something? Of course not.

DICK
What do you think boys and girls? Should I go out with him? He is rather handsome... Yes, yes, I'll go out with you.

HENRY
Super. I'll pop by this evening.

He walks away. As he does he looks at DICK, shakes his head and looks at the audience hopelessly.

DICK
OmygodOmygodOmygod I've got a date with Henry Regatta! What? Don't look at me like that boys and girls. It's great news, I mean what can go wrong eh?

He exits.

Scene 6

The Fairy enters holding the crystal ball and disguised as a tramp.

FAIRY

(In a deep voice) Any spare change please, any spare change. *(In her normal voice)* It's me, the fairy! Henry's heading this way. Now, how can I attract his attention? I know, I'll sing.

Starts singing The Logical Song by Supertramp. HENRY enters

HENRY

That's Supertramp.

FAIRY

(Tramp's voice) Yeah, I fought it were good too, cheers mate.

HENRY

No, I meant - it doesn't matter. I don't even understand myself today.

FAIRY

(as fairy) Oh dear. Sorry. *(as tramp)* I mean, Oh bloody 'cell mate. Wanna talk about it?

HENRY

I've met a boy.

FAIRY

Ah!

HENRY

He's new in town.

FAIRY

Ooh!

HENRY

I like him.

FAIRY

Eee!.. Is there much more of this? Only I'm running out of vowels.

HENRY

I think he likes me too.

FAIRY

Then go for it mate. Get frigging in his rigging if ya know what I mean.

HENRY

Poetically put.

FAIRY

Cheers.

HENRY

But he's Alderman Rat's arch enemy. I'm supposed to be tricking him, but I don't know if I can. I don't want to let Ratty down. He's been like a parent to me. And he was going to buy me a boat... Alderman Rat is a very powerful man.

FAIRY

I see.

HENRY

So it's very-

FAIRY

Yeah alright shut up now.

HENRY

Excuse me?

FAIRY

It's my turn. To tell you a story.

HENRY

Oh.

FAIRY *(sings to the tune of the folk song Still I Love Him)*

> When I was younger I wasn't a tramp,
> And I won the heart of a handsome young scamp
> And still I love him, still I miss him
> I'd go with him wherever he goes
>
> My mother she saw him, agreed he was fit,
> But said don't go near that no good piece of shit
> And still I love him, still I miss him
> I'd go with him wherever he goes
>
> I was too foolish to follow my heart
> Now I'm just a tramp and I smell like a fart
> And still I love him, still I miss him
> I'd go with him wherever he goes
>
> He found fame and fortune, but I just got fleas,
> He passed me last week and he tossed me 10p
> And still I love him, still I miss him
> I'd go with him wherever he goes

HENRY

But that's a very sad story! Was that supposed to cheer me up?!

FAIRY
Yeah.

HENRY
How?

FAIRY
Cos it's not true!

HENRY
Don't waste my time. Stupid tramp.

HENRY starts to leave.

FAIRY
You probably wanna let it sink in a bit.

HENRY looks at the fairy for a moment, then exits.

FAIRY
Isn't it romantic. (*starts to cry*).

RAT enters.

RAT
What a disgusting tramp. When I'm in charge of City Hall they'll be the first to go. But wait! Look! He's holding a crystal ball! If I can that tramp's ball in my hands I'd be able to keep an eye on Dick. I just need an idiotic buffoon to distract him. Where can I find one?

The MAYOR OF LONDON enters. RAT moves to the side so as not to be seen.

MAYOR
I say you dirty old tramp, I'm the Mayor of London and I'm standing for re-election.

FAIRY
I ain't registered.

MAYOR
Oh but I've even had a lovely poster done. *(he hands her a poster)*

FAIRY
I don't want to be rude or nuffing but don't you spell elected like that.

MAYOR
(*Snatching the poster*) Cripes. Damn printers. I say, the press are just over there. It would make a marvellous picture me having my photo with a smelly old tramp. How's my hair?

FAIRY
Very neat.

MAYOR
Oh cripes. (*He messes it up*). Is that better? Come and pose with me.

FAIRY
Let me just put my crystal ball down.

RAT looks delighted.

MAYOR
I could hold it. I've just come from a publicity shoot at Highbury where I had a photo taken holding one of Freddie Ljunbergs' balls. Heavier than they look, you know.

FAIRY
No, I will put it down. But I need someone to keep an eye on it. Boys and girls if you see anyone about to pinch my ball will you let me know?

MAYOR
And if you see anyone about to pinch my ball tell them to go ahead!

The fairy puts her ball down, and she and the mayor turn to pose for photos. RAT creeps up and goes to take the crystal ball. Hopefully the audience shout.

FAIRY
What did you say? Behind me? Who's behind me?

She and the mayor look to the right, RAT moves left. After doing this three times, RAT grabs the crystal ball and runs off laughing. After posing for the photo the fairy goes to pick up her crystal ball.

FAIRY
No! It's gone!!!

MAYOR
What has?

FAIRY
My crystal ball.

MAYOR
Then I'll buy you another. We'll go to Selfridges.

FAIRY
But this one was special. I could look in it and see Dick.

MAYOR
Well there's probably a shop in Soho. Walk this way.

FAIRY
If I walked that way I'd probably invest in a new saddle.

They exit.

Scene 7: Holly's bar

The Bar. HOLLY enters. She sings to the tune of English Country Garden:

HOLLY
How many kinds of drinks can you buy
In my lovely London boozer?
I'll tell you now of some you could try
Those I miss I'm sure you'll 'scuse us
Pint of Pride up to the brim
Malibu is fucking grim
With diet coke it's horrid but at least it keeps you slim
Or have a margarita if you like a salty rim
In my lovely London boozer.

He's a good worker that boy Dick. There's so much less cleaning and tidying to do. I could have got through a whole book today if I had the remotest inclination towards self-improvement.

WILMA enters, nervous.

WILMA
Hello?

HOLLY
(to audience) Do excuse me. (to Wilma). Welcome to my hostelry-cum-inn.

WILMA
I already have.

HOLLY
What?

WILMA
Come in.

HOLLY
What can I get you?

WILMA
A white wine spritzer please. No, a wine.

HOLLY
Large or small?

WILMA
How much for the bottle?

HOLLY
Are you alright love?

WILMA
Yes. No. Not really.

HOLLY
Here, I'll fix you something. I like your hair.

WILMA
Thank you.

HOLLY
Is it real?

WILMA
How rude, of course it's real. Isn't yours?

HOLLY
Well, it said so on eBay but it's got me sweating like a paedophile at a waterpark.

WILMA
I've been stuck on the bus from the other side of London. Well I won't do the Tube. It was a horrible journey. The driver was awful. I went to sit and he jerked off before I'd even got my backside down. I was sandwiched between two noisy adolescents, there was awful music blaring from somewhere and the free paper was all adverts.

HOLLY
Then you're not going to like it in a gay bar.

WILMA
So this is a gay bar!?

HOLLY
You've come to the wrong place.

WILMA
I'm looking for Dick.

HOLLY
You've come to the right place.

WILMA
My son, Dick.

HOLLY
Oh...!

WILMA
I suppose you thought I was a...

HOLLY
What?

WILMA
You know.

HOLLY
Transvestite?

WILMA
How dare you! No!

HOLLY
Then that makes two of us.

WILMA
My name's Wilma. Wilma Whittington.

HOLLY
Holly. Holly Oaks.

WILMA
That's a very funny name.

HOLLY
I'm not the one who named her son after a genital.

WILMA (angry)
That's it. I'm tired. I'm a long way from home.

HOLLY
Ah yes. Gloucester. So great they named it after half a cheese.

WILMA
Right. I've got a sharp-cornered handbag with your name on it.

HOLLY
Bring it on.

WILMA
With your *funny* name on it.

HOLLY
I'm not scared of a country bumpkin. I grew up on the streets of East London.

WILMA
Which is probably where you first earned a living.

They start to circle. Holly with a mop, Wilma with her handbag, they start to fight

DICK and JACK enter

JACK
Hi Everyone *(hi jack!)* God you're right! Mum! You alright? We'll get her off you.

HOLLY
My brave boy.

JACK *(standing well back)*
Go on Dick. Do something.

DICK
Holly get your hands off my mum!

Dick separates them. Wilma and Holly are being held back by their sons, they are both giving each other evil looks and are ready to fight. The FAIRY enters with a whistle and two buckets he hands a bucket to Jack and Dick.

FAIRY
Ladies and gentlemen we've had the Thriller in Manila the Rumble in the Jungle, tonight it's Devastation in Docklands as the Wapping Welterweight t *(he points to Holly)* takes on the Gloucester Goblin *(he points to Wilma)* I want to hear everyone on this side cheering for Holly *(he indicates one half the auditorium, Jack cheers and tries to get the audience to do the same)* And I want to hear everyone this side cheering for Wilma. Right ladies let's have a good clean fight!

He blows his whistle. "Eye of the Tiger" starts to play, Wilma and Holly fight, with their sons coaching. A proper, full on slap and fist fight. Holly wins and knock Wilma to the floor. Holly spits on her triumphantly.

FAIRY exits. BORIS and DICK enter.

BORIS
Where's the cat fight?

HOLLY & WILMA
Rude!

WILMA
Right. Back to the plot.

DICK
Mum! What are you doing here?

WILMA
Well I was just at home milking Daisy for a new batch of Gorgonzola. Next thing I knew I was in London. Oh what a day.

HOLLY
What kind of a mother are you, that your son would run away for fear of what you'd say about him being gay.

WILMA
What? I've known he was gay for ages. Every time I went on the internet to do my weekly Waitrose, I had to close down 8 windows of very intimate photography.

DICK
Mum!

WILMA
Still, I never forgot to add Veet to my order... Oh son, you know I'd love you whatever. I think it's great that you're gay. I even stopped by at that shop Prowl Zone to pick you something up.

She fishes in her bag and finds underpants and a bottle of poppers.

Now let's see. A nice pair of Kevin Kleins and because you're in a new place, a little bottle of room odoriser to freshen things up a bit.

DICK
Er, thanks mum...

WILMA
No, it's a pleasure, I got myself something too, a nice big plastic hand for putting my rings and bangles on. But tell me, do you like wearing women's clothes?

DICK
No, mum!

WILMA
Only I've got heaps of Laura Ashley set aside for the charity shop.

HOLLY
Would you say you've got piles?

WILMA
Yes.

HOLLY sniggers.

WILMA
And, Dick, are you one of those that likes them young?

DICK
Mother!

WILMA
No, no, that's good. You don't want a boyfriend who can't drive.

Enter HENRY. He looks the business.

HENRY
Hello all.

DICK (*throws the poppers to Holly who catches them discreetly*)
Henry, this is my mum. Mum, this is Henry, we're going on a date.

WILMA
I know who he is. He's no good Dick, he's out to trick you.

DICK
What do you mean?

BORIS
Dick, he's rich, clever and handsome. And you're you. Think about it.

DICK
I don't know.

HENRY
I promise I mean your son no harm Mrs Whittington. I tell ratty he wants to hear but, I assure you, I'm very much my own man. Or will be once my trust fund matures. Dick tells me you're from out West. What county?

HOLLY
Gloucestershire.

HENRY
Oh yes? It's not one of the Alderman's but it must be a fine place if you and your son are anything to go by.

WILMA (utterly charmed).
Oh my!

HENRY
It's been a pleasure, but we must be off Dick. We have a dinner reservation before we go clubbing. I hope we meet again soon.

He kisses Wilma's hand. She faints.

DICK
Mum! Henry I can't possibly come now.

HOLLY
You enjoy yourself, I'll take care of her.

HENRY
Come on Dick. Walk this way.

DICK
If I walked that way you could use me as a bottle opener.

Holly chucks the bottle of poppers back to Dick. Dick and Henry exit.

HOLLY
Well go on Jack. Stop moping and get some water!

583

HE'S BEHIND YOU: ELEVEN GAY PANTOMIMES

JACK goes.

HOLLY

So, your son and Henry Regatta eh? Sixth form at Westminster, educated at Oxford, probably buggered at both.

WILMA.

He's posh.

HOLLY

And destined for Olympic greatness. Which is more than you can say for Stratford in either case.

JACK

Well he doesn't fool me.

HOLLY

Jack, darling, a Ku Bar regular could fool you.

JACK

I don't trust him.

BORIS

Me neither. It's a just pity that you're bone idle and I'm apathetic.

JACK

Not anymore. Come on. Walk this way.

He walks off with a self-important mince.

BORIS

Three years at RADA for this. *(Walks off in the same manner)*

They leave.

HOLLY

Well it's you and me tonight girl.

WILMA

A Saturday night in London! We could go to the ballet!

HOLLY

If you want to see Eastern Europeans with freakish bodies just wait till it gets busy here love.

WILMA

We could get our boys something from Aberystwyth & Fitch!

HOLLY

Been there, done that.

WILMA

Got the T-shirt?

HOLLY

Couldn't fucking afford it. No, it's a night in front of X factor for you and me girl.

WILMA

I can see that at home.

HOLLY

But I've got hi-definition. *(with glee)* Danni looks a right dog! Walk this way.

She exits, walking with a limp because of the fight. Wilma does the same.

Scene 8: A club

Music plays. The Fairy enters, she is disguised as a topless waiter.

FAIRY
It's me! The Fairy! I'm disguised as a waiter so that I can keep Dick on orange juice and see that nothing bad happens.

He walks across stage. RAT enters wearing a wig and also disguised as a topless waiter.

RAT
It's me. Alderman Rat disguised as a topless waiter so that I can ply Dick with alcohol. These glasses contain a cocktail of vodka, gin and GHB. Here they come.

Dick and Henry enter

HENRY
This is an exclusive little club I come to.

DICK
I don't think much of the waiters.

The fairy offers Dick a drink, Rat does the same.

DICK
Don't fight over me boys! Now who shall I take a drink from?

Audience shout

DICK
I'll take one from you.

He takes a drink from Rat and drinks it down. Henry takes one from the Fairy. Rat holds his tray out to the fairy. The fairy takes a drink and drinks it.

DICK
I can't believe we got let in straight away. Did you see how many boys in that queue said hello to you? You know, I'm not all that experienced Henry.

HENRY
The first time I was with a guy I was all fingers and thumbs.

DICK
Well, that's all you can manage at first.

RAT
Have another Sir?

DICK
Don't mind if I do. This is good stuff.

Rat offers the fairy another drink, the fairy drinks it and looks slightly drunk.

FAIRY
What a nice person offering me drinks.

HENRY
Dick, there's something I want to say to you. Have you ever met someone and fallen for them straight away?

DICK
What?

Dick takes another drink and drinks it. Henry grabs hold of him and kisses him.

DICK
(Shocked) Henry Regatta just kissed me!!

He takes three more drinks and drinks them quickly.

FAIRY
How romantic, I need a celebratory drink.

He takes two drinks from Rat and drinks them.

HENRY
We need to talk. I just need to go to the bathroom, Then I need to tell you something. About how we met.

Henry exits.

FAIRY (about to puke)
Ugh I think I need the bathroom too!

Fairy exits. Jack and Boris enter.

JACK
Hi Everyone!

"Hi Jack!"

RAT
Don't shout that in here, you'll get the bouncers all excited (To Boris) You. Out. No cats.

BORIS
That's discrimination. You are so going to regret that. Get off me.

RAT
Out.

He exits marching Boris out. Jack walks over to Dick and sits down next to him.

DICK
Jack me old mate how you doing? Have a drink, the drink is good.

Takes two more drinks from the tray and drinks. RAT returns and walks over to them.

RAT
Excuse me Sir, but I just thought you ought to know, the gentleman you were with, we have just to escort him off the premises. We found him in cubicle two in the toilets. With another man.

JACK
What were they doing?

RAT (sarcastic)
Playing Buckaroo.

During this the fairy is continuing to drink.

DICK
How could he?

JACK
Yeah I know... I love Buckaroo!

RAT
Well, sir, that's how it is in London sir. Young, gay and successful, it's normal. You'll get used to it.

DICK
Guess you and Boris were right, Henry Regatta is trouble. I really thunked, he wiz the one. Ooh heck me words are coming out strange. Guess I'm a bot squiffy eh Jick? Jick?

JACK
Yes Dack.

DICK
You're a nice bloke Jick, one of the boost.

They move toward each other.

DICK
Slurring badly You are gooood bloke Jick.

They kiss, Henry returns.

HENRY
Sorry I took so long, I was- You bastard, you two timing bastard!!

DICK
Henry!

JACK
The waiter said you'd been ejaculated.

HENRY
My dad was right about you. I never want to see you again!

Henry storms out.

DICK
Henry wait!

RAT
And I am sure the press will be extremely interested that a Mayoral candidate is nothing but a two timing, two faced little gay boy. City Hall is mine!

Rat exits, laughing. BORIS enters

BORIS
See what happens when I'm not here to protect you?

DICK
What am I going to do Boris? Henry's really popular round here. We'll have to get away. As far away as possible. Until I can work out how to make it up to him.

BORIS
Here we go. More travelling.

JACK
There's a little boat for sale down on the quayside. I'll be right back.

JACK exits.

BORIS
He's coming too? What are we, the Variety Club?

DICK
It's not his fault. Oh poor Henry.

JACK returns with a very small rubber dinghy.

JACK
Here she is. "The Rubber Queen". She cost me all my savings.

DICK
That'll be the inflation.

JACK
Come on. The tide is high and we're moving on.

DICK
Boris, keep your claws in.

BORIS (no enthusiasm)
Aye aye captain.

DICK
Jack, walk this way.

JACK
If I walk that way, I'll be dropping love beads like a chicken lays eggs.

They exit.

Scene 9: The docks

Holly and Wilma stumble onto stage, singing.

HOLLY AND WILMA
What shall we do with a drunken sailor
What shall we do with a drunken sailor
What shall we do with a drunken sailor
Ride him till the morning!
Heave ho and up he rises
Heave ho and up he rises
He'll have a couple of nice surprises
Early in the morning!

HOLLY
Get a shift on love, we don't want to be hanging round these docks late at night. People say they're haunted.

WILMA
Haunted? Ooh you do get morose on gin. Now where's this off license. Who'd have thought a pub could run out of drinks. I like being down by the river though. It reminds me of the time I went fishing with the gentlemen of the Gloucester Angling Club.

HOLLY
Did you catch anything?

WILMA
Well I did come back with a red snapper. Hold on, I've got a text.

WILMA reads text.

WILMA
Oh my! Oh no! Tell me it's not true!

HOLLY
Something wrong love?

WILMA
It's my EastEnders spoiler update. Peggy Mitchell is going to be crushed by a keg of ale.

HOLLY
Is that all, I thought something had happened to your Dick.

WILMA
Oh now, hold on. There's a text from him too! Well, that's charming. It says he's gone to pee with your Jack.

HOLLY (*Holly grabs the phone and reads text*)

You silly mare. He's gone to *sea* with my Jack, they're in some kind of trouble. Right, right, I'm good in a crisis. You go find us a boat, they like a bit of stubble on a girl here at the docks. I'll go and make the sandwiches

WILMA
Oh no you don't, I'll make the sandwiches. My baps have been savoured by half the mouths in Gloucester.

HOLLY
My buns take the deepest filling in the East End.

WILMA
My bloomers slip down so well I've started selling them online.

HOLLY
I've had queues round the block at the merest sniff of my hot fresh seeded batch. However, I've a feeling I'm out of bread rolls.

WILMA
What shall we do?

HOLLY
I'll use my loaf. What else do think we should take?

WILMA
What about a Kit Kat?

HOLLY
Yes, but just two fingers as I've only got a small box. And it'll need washing out, it's not been touched in months and last time I opened it up in the park there was a bacterial whiff. I didn't notice, but the man who was eating out of it did, which stopped me enjoying an otherwise perfect bit of tongue.

WILMA
Wait! I've got my Thermos flask. I'll pop to the nearest coffee shop and get the barista to grind his beans and work up a couple of hot strong shots he can empty into my cavity.

HOLLY
That'll keep our insides warm at sea.

WILMA
And what about nuts?

HOLLY
Now you're just being filthy.

HENRY enters.

WILMA
Henry! What have you done to my boy?

HENRY
What have – what have I done? I thought he was special but the minute I turned my back-

HOLLY
Is this going to be rude?

HENRY
The minute I turned my back he was all over your idiot son.

WILMA
Dick's a good boy.

HOLLY
Jack *is* an idiot though.

HENRY
I don't understand but I'm sure the Alderman's got something to do with this.

HOLLY
We need to give chase.

HENRY
Count me in. Shall I get us some sandwiches?

WILMA
Don't start that, Henry. Where can we get a boat?

HENRY
You can use my little dingy.

HOLLY
Is it big enough?

HENRY
It will be after a few blows. I'll go and get it out for you.

HENRY exits

WILMA
Is true what you said about the docks being… haunted?

HOLLY
Well, I ain't seen nothing myself but I've heard stories of ghosts.

WILMA
Ghosts? When do they usually appear?

HOLLY
Just before someone screams.

HENRY enters, he is carrying the uninflated dingy in front of him. WILMA and HOLLY scream.

HENRY
There's no need to scream ladies. I'm afraid this dingy hasn't been used for a while. This nozzle is fine so one of you can blow into that but this other one's quite tight so maybe one of you could suck it to loosen it up a bit. Wilma, perhaps you'd like to blow, and Holly you can have a suck.

WILMA
Why can't I suck?

HOLLY
Cos you're a better blower love. You got more wind than the Royal Philharmonic.

WILMA
Now listen here. I went to the doctor to get something for my wind.

HENRY
What did he give you?

HOLLY
A kite.

There is crash offstage.

WILMA
What was that?

HOLLY
I told you. It's a ghost.

HENRY
G, g, ghosts-----!

HOLLY
Henry Regatta! He's scared of being caught by the ghoulies!

HENRY
No, no, of course not... but perhaps we should get some protection.

Exits.

HOLLY
He's forward.

WILMA
Oh my. Being looked after by an Olympic athlete.

HENRY enters carrying a dustbin lid which he gives to WILMA, a bucket which he gives to HOLLY, and an oar for himself. They stand in a line which Henry leads.

HOLLY
Look, it's me and Henry and a dirty old oar!

WILMA
How dare you.

HENRY
Quiet ladies. We'll attack that ghost if we see it.

HOLLY
Hark at Harry Potter there.

The GHOST joins the back of the line and pinches WILMA'S bottom.

WILMA
Oooh! Two pints, milkman, please.

HOLLY
What?

WILMA
Someone pinched my bottom.

HOLLY
Don't worry, there's plenty of it left.

WILMA
Well I can't see any ghosts.

HENRY
Let's try the other way round.

HOLLY
He's said that before.

GHOST jumps out of the way and they switch around, so the WILMA is in front, HOLLY in the middle and HENRY at the rear. GHOST Joins the end, he leans forward and pinches HOLLYs bottom and jumps back, HOLLY turns around and slaps HENRY.

HOLLY
Keep your hands to yourself Henry.

They continue to walk, GHOST joins the end of the line and pushes the end of the oar that HENRY holds so that it hits HOLLY's backside. GHOST moves away.

HOLLY
Henry Regatta take your handle out of my backside now.

HOLLY slaps HENRY.

WILMA
Why don't I go in the middle?

WILMA and HOLLY swap places they continue to walk with the GHOST on the end.

HOLLY
I still can't see no ghost.

The GHOST pushes Henry's oar so it hits Wilma's bottom.

WILMA
Henry!!!

WILMA slaps HENRY

WILMA
Now he's poking his pole up *my* bottom.

HOLLY
He ain't careful about where he sticks it is he?

They continue walking.

HENRY
Still no ghost.

The GHOST taps HENRY on the shoulder. He looks around, sees the GHOST and runs off. HOLLY and WILMA do not realise that HENRY has gone. The GHOST is now behind WILMA. He puts his hands on her breasts.

WILMA *(enjoying it at first)*
Ooh Henry, you are naughty!

She turns around and sees the ghost and runs off screaming. The GHOST grabs hold of HOLLY.

HOLLY
Look there ain't no ghost ' ere. Let's just grab a boat and sail off.

The GHOST grabs HOLLY's breast.

HOLLY
Wilma Whittington! Now I might have shown you a few kindnesses but I ain't got no inclinations in that direction.

The GHOST grabs her bottom.

HOLLY
Or that direction!

HOLLY turns around and sees the GHOST. The GHOST looks at HOLLY, screams and runs off. HOLLY looks a bit abashed and stares after the ghost. After a pause:

HOLLY
Right. Well I'll walk that way then shall I.

HOLLY trudges off as the FAIRY enters

FAIRY
We've all had nights that have finished
In casualty, tears or sick,
But my chances look very diminished
Of making a hero of Dick

Now Dick's being tossed upon the sea
Just pray the boat doesn't capsize
Though Jack's as happy as can be
With his Dick between his thighs

It's almost like Shakespeare! A voyage, a storm,
Political plotting, cross dressing
In part two you'll be thrilled, they all get killed!
Don't worry I'm only messing

It's time for the break so I can get sober
And you lot can nip to the loo
If anyone's single, get hasty and mingle -
Till then, sweet people, Adieu!

INTERVAL

Ross Mitchell as Holly, Mansel David as Wilma and Basher Savage as Henry in *Dick Whittington: Another Dick in City Hall*. Photo by Alan Day.

Mansel David as Wilma and Matthew Groom as Dick in *Dick Whittington: Another Dick in City Hall*. Photo by Alan Day.

Scene 10: Gran Canaria

A sandy island. Desert island music plays. ALDERMAN RAT enters holding the crystal ball.

RAT
Oh yes, boo, boo. I know it's because you're secretly in love with me. Here we are on Gran Canaria. My little place in the sun. I acquired most of it recently you know.

FAIRY enters

FAIRY
So sorry I'm late, but I needed
To visit the sand dunes, you see
My wallet was bare, so I flew Ryanair
And they charge you a tenner to pee.

RAT
The sun was out, I had no cares
Then came along Pam sodding Ayres...

FAIRY
Alderman Rat!

RAT
Autographs later.

FAIRY
But, but you should be in London? Why are you on Gran Canaria?

RAT holds up the ball by way of an answer. FAIRY reaches for it, but Rat snatches it away. He chuckles, looking into it.

RAT
This thing's brilliant. I've been watching Family Guy. Oh look at this!

FAIRY
What is it??

RAT
How clever - we're on a different network out here. It happens automatically! I'll catch him in no time!!!

FAIRY
You may be both cunning and ruthless,
But I'll be the first to our chap,
That ball can be totally useless
Unless you download the right app.

Exits.

RAT
Why, why, why does that always happen!? You go away on holiday, and the first person you bump into is the loathsome fairy you spend your life avoiding back home.

Enter the MAYOR. He now sports a moustache

RAT
Oh god. Again, Mr Mayor, what an unexpected-

MAYOR
Unexpected?

RAT
I supposed you'd take your holidays some MP's yacht, or in Cliff Richard's Bahaman Villa. Not on Gran Canaria.

MAYOR
Holiday? But I work here. I'm the Mayor.

RAT
Of London.

MAYOR
Of Gran Canaria.

RAT
You look like the Mayor of London.

MAYOR
Does he have a splendid moustache?

RAT
No...

MAYOR
I think you're suffering from a little sunstroke. Who are you?

RAT
Alderman Rat.

MAYOR
You! You and your rats have brought this place to its knees.

RAT
Have you visited the local bars? Half the population seem quite happy in that position.

MAYOR
I don't understand what went wrong.

RAT
It's fiendishly simple. A lot of the island's businesses were strapped for cash, so I very kindly lent them

593

money. The Bank of Gran Canaria was also short on reserves so I sold it the loans so that it could raise interest on them. Well I might have mentioned that to a few people – in confidence you understand – but somehow word got out and people realised the bank now had even less in reserve, they started panicking and withdrawing their investments. Well, by now the bank was on the verge of collapse. So I bought the bank. Of course now all the businesses owed me money, so I had them repossessed and put my rats in charge. For the cost of a bit of interest I've acquired 18 gay bars, four inexplicably popular drag shows, 25 hotels, eight stalls selling wonky sunglasses and an ice cream stand.

MAYOR
Cripes.

RAT pulls out a Financial Times and gives it to the MAYOR with a friendly pat. The MAYOR exits, confused. RAT looks into the ball.

RAT
Come on come on... aha! Here we are, sand and palm trees... oh hang on, that's season 3 of Lost. No... no... there! Footprints. And paw prints... Ha ha! He's here! I shall mobilise my rats! Gran Canaria is one thing but just wait till I'm in charge of London. He can't stop me. He WON'T stop me!!!

Exit. DICK and BORIS enter. BORIS is eating.

DICK
Hello everyone. To think not long ago I was just a normal boy working in Hennies in Gloucester, helping pretty boys try on tiny, tiny garish pants... And now here I am, in disgrace on a desert island. Oh poor Henry. I hope he's ok. Do you think he'll forgive me Boris? And where could Jack have got to?

BORIS
I'm eating, Dick

DICK
I beg your pardon.

The FAIRY enters disguised as a canary.

FAIRY
Tweet tweet, tweet.

BORIS
What the Spanish fuck are you?

FAIRY
Did you never hear the expression, "a little bird told me"? (to audience) It's me! Yes! The fairy! But I've come as a giant canary. I figured the island must be full of them. (to Dick). Young man, you must be very careful. There's danger on this island. Keep your eyes sharp and your nails peeled. And look out for the rats. Tweet, tweet.

Exits.

BORIS
Rats? That's much better than manky old fish.

DICK
That's the spirit Boris. Come on, I'll help you hunt.

DICK and BORIS exit. HOLLY ENTERS with a bottle of wine, opened. She's in a fabulous swimsuit and has bits of seaweed and fish on her. She's really quite drunk.

HOLLY
Water, water everywhere – thank our lucky bras for the wine cellar on Henry's boat.

She swigs, then puts the bottle down on stage.

HOLLY
What a journey. And now here we are, washed up on a rat-infested desert island. This is almost as bad as the time I panicked everyone on my Scandinavian beach holiday. I thought I saw a shark, but it was just a couple of Finns. *(Laughs delighted at her own joke).* I'm avoiding Henry, I think he's angry with me. He rowed so hard and all I did was drink his wine and make rude jokes about the long and treacherous passage. I'll go see if I can find an ice cream.

Exits. HENRY enters.

HENRY
Hello everyone. Wilma's exploring, and I seem to have lost Holly. Will you keep an eye out and tell me if you see her? It's horrible here, there are rats everywhere.

HOLLY enters with an ice cream, crosses to the wine bottle, picks it up, notices Henry, puts the wine down again and scarpers.

"She's behind you..." HENRY turns too late.

HENRY
No, it's just this desert heat. It must have been a mirage.

HOLLY enters again, exaggerated tiptoe to the wine "he's behind you" etc - picks it up, swigs from it, goes to leave. This time Henry turns in time.

HENRY
Holly!

HOLLY
(Casual) Henry love I was just trying to find you. (sings) *Oh I do like to be beside the seaside...* (Swigs). Cheers. You want some?

HENRY
That's... that's quite a rare wine that.

HOLLY
You're very sweet but you don't need to reassure me! I can't tell the difference between a 2.99 Tesco jobby and one that costs... well, I don't know.

She swigs.

HENRY
Eighty-five pounds.

HOLLY spits the wine into Henry's face in shock.

HOLLY
How much?

HENRY
Eighty-five pounds.

HOLLY
Once is shocking twice is showing off. Oh look you're still wet. Probably got splashed in the face with salty spray. Probably takes you back to your first Westminster boys sailing holiday.

HENRY *(noticing bathing suit)*
Oh look! You've changed

HOLLY
Well I did a lot of soul searching out at sea, standing on your stern.

HENRY
My stern?

HOLLY
You are a little but it suits you dear. How are you bearing up?

HENRY
I'm so confused about Dick.

HOLLY
Yes love it's been a bit up and down hasn't it.

HENRY
I want to kiss him and I want to throttle him.

HOLLY
I heard you posh boys liked it kinky.

Enter JACK

JACK
Hi everyone! *("Hi Jack!")* No, it was just a bit of a shipwreck.

HOLLY (slaps him round the head)
How rude. Where have you been? What have you done!

JACK
Mum! What are you doing here?

HENRY
You! *(he punches Jack and knocks him flat out).*

HOLLY
Jack! How could you Henry!

HENRY
Nobody plays with my Dick without getting one in the face.

WILMA enters. Also in a swimming costume.

WILMA *(Noticing Jack on the floor)*
He really is idle isn't he. I'm sure it's a desert island. All I found was a stack of ten records, a bible and the complete works of Shakespeare.

HENRY
What records were they?

WILMA
Mainly European pop and something called Happy Hardcore.

HENRY
I knew I recognised this place! This is Gran Canaria.

HOLLY
Henry Regatta you surprise me.

HENRY
One of my university friends has a thing for working class boys. But something's wrong. These sand dunes should be more populated.

Holly offers Wilma her ice cream. Wilma has lick.

HE'S BEHIND YOU: ELEVEN GAY PANTOMIMES

WILMA
Ooh! Should we look for Dick in the sand dunes?

HENRY
Let's stick together. The rats look savage.

A plastic rat is thrown onto the stage.

WILMA
Ah! Rat!

HENRY
Come on girls. Let's go.

HOLLY
What about Jack?

HENRY
We'll come back for him. Walk this way.

HOLLY & WILMA
If I walked that way...

WILMA
After you.

HOLLY
No, after you.

They leave. Boris enters and pounces on the rat.

BORIS
Got you, bitch. This place is full of rats and they taste way better than British ones! *(spots another, catches it).*

Dick enters.

DICK
Jack!

JACK wakes.

JACK
Dick! I was having the strangest dream. We'd run away on a boat...

DICK
It's not a dream, Jack

JACK
And landed on a strange island.

DICK
It's not a dream, Jack.

JACK
So we really did have a three-way marriage with Robert Pattinson? I'm so happy!

The MAYOR enters.

MAYOR
Young man! You and your cat have rid this island of rats! *(To Boris)* It must be your amazing sense of smell.

BORIS
Have you ever smelt cat food?

WILMA enters.

WILMA
Dick! Dick there you are my boy.

DICK
Mum!

WILMA
Why did you run away?

DICK
I did something really bad mum. I cheated on Henry because I listened to someone instead of to my own conscience. So I thought I'd better leave until I'd done something good and you could all be proud of me again.

MAYOR
Your son, madam, is a hero.

WILMA
He's not called Madam. Oh my. You're the mayor of London!

MAYOR
No, no, I keep saying. I'm the Mayor of Gran Canaria.

WILMA
Well you look like the Mayor of London. You must be his brother.

HOLLY and HENRY enter.

HOLLY
Oooh I say, the mayor London.

MAYOR
I'm NOT the mayor of London.

WILMA
My Dick's a hero.

JACK
My husband's a hero!

DICK
Oh Jack. Sorry, that bit was a dream.

HENRY
Keep your hands off him, idiot.

HOLLY
Now you be kind Henry. Jack was educated at the University of life.

HENRY
Yes and I went to Oxford, so I win.

BORIS
Oh yes. Dick's a hero. How many rats has he caught?

DICK
You're right Boris. But I'll catch a rat. A big rat. I'll beat Alderman Rat in London in the Mayoral elections.

MAYOR
Oh yes, do! It's terrific fun being Mayor. They let you press the button that makes the streetlights come on at night. I say, why don't you all come back to mine for a celebratory tipple. Walk this way.

Exit all except HENRY and DICK

DICK
I'm so sorry Henry. I fucked up. Please forgive me.

HENRY
How could you?

DICK
I don't... I know it doesn't make it better but I was quite drunk.

HENRY
When I get drunk, I get loud and obnoxious and sing rowing songs about wedgies. I don't put my tongue inside an idiot.

DICK
I'm sorry. And you rowed my mum all the way out here. That was really nice of you.

HENRY
Yes, well. It was good training... And maybe I wanted to come too.

DICK
Really?

HENRY
But don't hurt me again. I turned against the man who's given me everything for you.

Enter RAT, quietly. He's behind you! Etc.

HENRY
Alderman!

RAT
You little traitor. After all I've done for you. I'll give you one more chance before I disinherit you!

DICK
Henry?

HENRY
The thing is, Ratty, I like Dick. I really like Dick. I can't get enough of Dick. I rowed all the way to Gran Canaria looking for Dick and now I don't want to let go of Dick. Dick could make me really happy. I think Dick could come a long way. I want to be able to walk into a room with Dick held tight in my hand and say, this is my Dick. I'm proud of my Dick. And if I have to share my Dick with the whole of London then that's what I'll do because they're all going to love my Dick just as much as I do. One day there'll be paintings of my Dick, and a huge statue of my Dick on the fourth plinth in Trafalgar Square, and huge close-ups of my lovely Dick on screens all across the country, but even if there weren't, I'd still be into Dick just the same.

RAT
I see. Well. Your Dick may have frightened my rats out of town here, but the war's not over. I have a plan!

Exits.

DICK
You did well to get your mouth round all those Dicks... He's quite high maintenance your dad then?

HENRY
He's not my Dad, Dick.

DICK
Well. I'm sorry you're caught between us. Did you really... did you mean what you said?

HENRY (slight pause, not letting him off yet)
Let's go get that drink.

Exit.

Scene 11: A cave

HOLLY enters, dressed up. She does her hair and smiles.

HOLLY
Ooh I'm so excited boys and girls. I've been invited to this cave by a rich businessman who says he's seen me around and wants to take me out on a date.

WILMA enters, also dressed up, and with a handbag. She and Holly do not see each other. They back into each other and collide.

HOLLY
What are you doing here?

WILMA
I've got a date. What are you doing here?

HOLLY
I've got a date too. Who's your date with? Uncle Bulgaria?

WILMA
Wasn't he a womble?

HOLLY
Yes. Good at picking up rubbish.

WILMA
My date is with a millionaire. He sent me a letter and said that he has admired me from afar.

HOLLY
That's the only way to admire you dear. My date is with a millionaire too.

WILMA
What does he look like then?

HOLLY
Oh he's probably tall and handsome. What about yours?

WILMA
Oh he's probably short and cute.

HOLLY
Ere. We could go double dating.

WILMA
Go on holiday together.

HOLLY
Blackpool!

WILMA
The funfair! You and your tall handsome man and me and my cute little fellow.

HOLLY
And I'll scream like a girl when I'm riding the Big One.

WILMA
Well, you feel it in your gut don't you

HOLLY
Well that's settled then.

She sings to the tune of Loch Lomond:

> I'll take the big one
> And you'll take the little one
> And I'll be getting married afore ye
> He may not be my true love
> But he knows what to do, love,
> To wake me with a grin in the morning...

There's nothing like a nice sing song.

WILMA
And that was nothing like a nice sing song. You should take singing lessons.

HOLLY
Aw thanks! You really think so?

WILMA
It might help a bit.

HOLLY
Now hold on a... *(looks about)* Here this cave's dark and enormous – leave it. Maybe our dates are already here?

WILMA
Ooh! Let's get some light about the place and we can have a look.

HOLLY
How?

WILMA
I just need a little help.

HOLLY
It's called Botox, Wilma.

WILMA ignores her, she reaches into her bag and brings out two torches.

WILMA
There you go.

She gives one to HOLLY. They switch them on and shine them out at the audience. Holly peers at the audience, frowning.

HOLLY
Here, you can see why dark rooms got popular.

WILMA
Oh my. What a lot of... are they bats?

HOLLY
Don't be rude, Wilma, them's the boys and girls. They been here from the start.

WILMA
Oh yes! Well it's nice to put a face to a smell.

They start singling out audience members.

WILMA
Hello love, what's your name? And where are you from?

Then depending on the answer...

WILMA
Oh well you're not one of our millionaires then! / Ooh Holly, he might be one of our millionaires!

HOLLY
Course he's not a millionaire Wilma. Look at his clothes. *(She shines her beam at someone else).* Oh sorry darling, you didn't expect to get a shaft in your face tonight did you.

RAT enters. The women spin round and shine their beams at him.

RAT
(To audience) It's me, Alderman Rat, in a cunning disguise. *(to Holly and Wilma).* I thought I heard angels singing! *(they giggle, delighted).* I say, what a beautiful pair!

HOLLY thrusts her boobs at him.

HOLLY
They're all yours, you hunky beast.

WILMA
(Pushing Holly out of the way). Hold it. This one's *my* hunky beast.

RAT
Ladies, ladies. Close your eyes a minute and relax close your eyes. *(They do so).* Ladies the truth is, you are both so beautiful, I wanted to dine with you both. And I must confess I am hoping to get you both in the sack tonight.

He produces two sacks and pulls them over the women's heads.

HOLLY
Ooh it's like discovery night at The Hoist[139].

RAT
The holiday is over, ladies. It's back to London for you. Make the most of the next few hours, because if Dick Whittington doesn't stand down from the Mayoral elections, they will be your last! Walk this way.

They all exit.

---

[139] The Hoist was a famous gay fetish club in Vauxhall. It closed in 2016.

Scene 12: The beach

Dick and Boris come on they are looking for Wilma. Jack enters.

DICK
Have you seen my Mum? I can't find her anywhere.

JACK
I can't find mine either, maybe they've gone to the bingo. (to audience) Hi everyone! (Hi Jack!) Did you hear that, Dick? Sounds bad.

Henry enters, carrying an envelope.

HENRY
Dick, I found this letter. It's addressed to you.

Dick takes the letter and reads it.

DICK
Ooh flipping heck.

He passes it to Henry who reads it.

HENRY
Oh lordy, lordy!

He passes it to Jack who reads it and bursts into tears, passing the letter to Boris. Boris glances at it. The others look at him expecting him to react.

BORIS
I'm a cat. You think I can read a fucking letter?

DICK
Rat's kidnapped our mums and unless I stand down from the mayoral elections he'll kill them.

BORIS
Terrible. Anyway, who fancies a vodka before lunch?

Jack cries louder.

DICK
Boris! We have to do something!

BORIS
Why do we have to do anything? God you're so stressful to go on holiday with. Museum this, castle that.

HENRY
We shall mount a rescue mission. If I know Alderman Rat, he'll tie them up in the office. Let's get the boat. Walk this way.

Henry exits, pointing the way with his thumb. Jack copies the movement as he follows him off.

DICK
Come on Boris!

BORIS
No. You expect to come with you just like that? Since I rid this island of Rats I am worshipped like a god here. I have got respect R.E.S.P.E.C.T respect and you expect me to give it all up?

DICK
But we're a pair. We go together.

BORIS
Yeah I know, like rama lama lama ka dinga da ding-a-dong. Maybe not anymore.

DICK
So then, Boris – this is it?

BORIS
Yes, guess so.

DICK
I'll never forget you. I still remember you as that fluffy little kitten and how you used to snuggle up to me in bed. How I picked fleas from your fur.

BORIS
(embarrassed) Behave.

DICK
But if you want to stay, that's cool. It's your life.

He hugs him.

DICK
I'll miss you Boris.

Dick walks away, his head down. He exits. Boris doesn't look at him. He then looks round at the empty stage. He wipes a tear from his eye. The mayor of Gran Canaria enters.

MAYOR
Boris, (sneezes) I need you to pack your bags. I'm afraid (sneezes) I need you to leave the Mayoral mansion. (sneezes) You see I've got this allergy, the Doctor says I'm allergic to cats.

BORIS
But I can't go, I've got nowhere to go and Dick's left. Besides I'm a God over here.

MAYOR
You've had your fifteen minutes of fame moggie. Get packing. I want you out by midnight. (sneezes)

The Mayor exits.

600

BORIS
These high-profile promotions. What am I going to do? Dick's gone. How will I get home? I haven't even got a pet passport.

"Memory" from Cats play. Heavenly light beams down on Boris from the exit. Boris walks off into the light.

Scene 13: Alderman Rat's office

RAT enters with WILMA and HOLLY tied together and gagged. RAT pushes them on to the floor and laughs.

RAT
Ha, ha, at last I've got the better of that vile Dick Whittington. If he stands for election the two of you will be swimming with sharks. But then that's fairly normal for Whales I suppose!!!

The FAIRY enters, disguised as a journalist.

RAT
Who are you?

FAIRY
Marvin MacScoop, Sunday Times, I've come to interview you about your campaign. *(To audience)* It's me, the fairy.

RAT
Then step into my back room for some refreshments and I will tell you how the whole of London will be mine! I've brought back some delicious fruit from my orchard in Gran Canaria. My plums are swollen with juices and my-

HOLLY *(breaking free of gag)*
Oi, Rat Man, we do the food jokes.

RAT *(replacing gag)*
(To Holly) Do shut up. *(To Fairy)* All she's got is a wrinkled pair. Now step into my inner sanctum. I've also got a huge firm banana simply bursting from its skin. Walk this way.

FAIRY
If I walked that way I'd wonder where I'd put my wand.

RAT and the FAIRY exit. WILMA and HOLLY struggle trying to get free. HENRY and DICK creep in.

DICK *(whispering)*
Look, there they are.

HENRY
(whispering) Don't worry ladies we're here to rescue you. Jack's keeping watch outside.

JACK runs in shouting at the top of his voice.

JACK
Be quiet! Rat's in the next room you don't want him to-

Rat hears this and enters with a sword and a rope.

JACK *(quieter)*
...hear you.

"Hi Jack"

RAT
It's not a hijack, it's a kidnap, but thanks for letting me know.

RAT grabs JACK.

HENRY
Alderman. Let them go!

RAT
Shut up you two faced little poof. Gentlemen, one false move and this idiot gets it.

JACK
I've not had it for a while.

RAT
Shut up you blubbering buffoon. *(he pushes Jack over to the others)* Now to tie you up. (To jack) Hold this. *(Jack dutifully holds the end of the rope and Rat ties them up)* And we'll give that journalist a scoop: I'll tell him that Dick Whittington won't be standing in the elections, he's a bit tied up. Then I'll get the Ratmobile we're going on a little trip to Beachy Head. It's time to go bungee jumping - the only problem is I will have forgotten the rope. *(laughs)*

RAT exits.

DICK
Come on Henry we have to try and undo these knots.

The fairy enters still disguised as a journalist.

FAIRY
Don't worry. I can help.

DICK
It's you again. I do know you.

FAIRY
No, I'm sure you don't. I'm just a journalist.

DICK
You were the sailor, and the canary.

HENRY
And the tramp and the cleaner.

FAIRY
Damn. You've just broken the magic spell.

DICK
Spell?

FAIRY
I am a fairy.

DICK, JACK AND HENRY
So are we!

FAIRY
My role is to protect Dick.

HENRY
Well that's very responsible. There's a vending machine outside.

JACK
You're a fairy a real fairy! Here where's your wand? Can I see your wand?

DICK and HENRY
Shut up Jack.

FAIRY
I can only grant you one last spell and then I can protect you no more.

DICK
One last spell? Then give me the power of Superman so that I can rescue everyone and get rid of Alderman Rat.

FAIRY
Oooh Superman spells, I don't know if I can remember those. I think to do that I need one of your hairs and the magic will only last five minutes so you will have to be quick.

DICK
Look there's one here on my shirt.

The FAIRY takes a hair from DICK's shirt; he goes into a trance like state.

FAIRY
Oh as fortune turns, and times they do worsen
Make the owner of this hair a super person.

DICK tries to free himself but pulls a face as he can't get free.

DICK
It didn't work, I don't feel any stronger. Hold on let me see that hair a minute.

The FAIRY shows him the hair.

DICK
That's not my hair. I know who it belongs to, it must have come off when we said goodbye. That hair belongs to Boris.

JACK
(Looking out of the window.) What's that up there, streaking across the sky?

HENRY
What? Is it a bird?

BORIS *(offstage)*
Wrooooong!!!

DICK
Is it a plane?

BORIS *(offstage)*
Wrong again.

BORIS enters wearing a cape, a mask and with the initials SC on his chest. He spins round Wonder Woman style.

BORIS
It's Supercat!

The theme to Wonder Woman plays and BORIS runs around stage releasing everybody. RAT enters.

RAT
What's happening?

BORIS
It's time for the cat. To get the Rat!

A fight takes place between RAT and DICK and BORIS. RAT is knocked out, and tied up by BORIS.

RAT
Please...! Please don't hurt me! I'll do anything, anything!

DICK
Would you lace my shoe?

RAT
Anything!

DICK
Paint your face bright blue?

RAT
Anything!

DICK
Catch a kangaroo?

RAT
Anything!

HOLLY & WILMA
Go to Timbuktu?

RAT
And back again!

DICK
And would you promise not to lay a hand on Holly's bar.

RAT
Yes, yes!

DICK
Then I'll give you another chance. I want to beat you fair and square. Tomorrow, at the elections.

DICK unties RAT.

RAT
Ha ha! You're on. You haven't a chance. You're just a boy! See you tomorrow.

Exits.

DICK
Ok team. You've got to help me.

HOLLY
Back to my pub. It'll be our campaign HQ. Walk this way.

JACK, HOLLY and WILMA exit. JACK goes the wrong way.

HOLLY
Oi. *This way.*

JACK follows her off.

BORIS (a bit awkward)
Dick... um can I ask you something?

DICK
What is it Boris?

BORIS
This outfit. It doesn't... I don't look a bit camp in it, do I?

DICK (very earnest but tries not to laugh)
No, Boris. Not at all.

BORIS
Thanks Dick

Exits.

HENRY
You're a terrible person.

DICK
I know. Don't tell the electorate. Walk this way.

He holds out his right hand for Henry to take. Instead of taking it, Henry copies him, holding out his own right hand. They walk out like that.

Scene 14

Enter HOLLY.

HOLLY

Ladies and gentlemen, boys and girls. It's time for the final hustings of the mayoral elections! And I'm the presiding officer because an extra cast-member would have got way too crowded in the dressing room. Our first candidate is the saviour of Gran Canaria, Richard Whittington!

DICK and BORIS enter.

BORIS

Does this make me a political animal?

DICK

Will they really accept a gay man as Mayor? They didn't vote for Brian Paddick.

BORIS

That wasn't cos he was gay. That was cos he was Lib Dem.

HOLLY

And opposing him, the infamous Alderman Rat!

Rat enters. Dick is pushed forward to make his speech.

DICK

Erm... I've never done this kind of thing before... I came to London to make a something of myself. And to find love. Well... And to have adventures. To grow up. And also, I wanted to leave Gloucester because scrumpy makes me fart like a teenage horse with a belly full of Rogan Josh.

These are hard times. And they're hard because of selfish, evil men like him. People who can't even see that people are worth... well it's just the blindness of it all. That's something we don't really have in Gloucester. People are friendly there and they care about each other. And that's what we deserve here too.

I came to London to seek my fortune. What I found is that the wealth of London is also in its people. I decided to become mayor because I'd seen what Rat was going to do to my friend Holly. And I don't want to see him do that to our city. Er, that didn't sound quite right...

So basically, it's about what kind of person you want London to be about. And if you make me the mayor I

promise I'll do my best to make sure I'm that person every day. Thank you.

RAT

People of London. We rat have a bad reputation. But think, we've been part of this city's history for generations.

BORIS

Yes it was called the plague.

HOLLY

Order, order!

BORIS

A vodka and cranberry juice and a bag of pork scratchings please.

RAT

We have lived quietly away in the sewers, we eat the rubbish you don't want to eat. Rats are loyal, efficient and strong. We famously make good pets.

BORIS

So do dogs, but no one ever elected a Mayor because he was lovable, stupid and shaggy haired.

The MAYOR enters.

MAYOR

Have I missed anything?

HOLLY

Yes, love. The elections. You're too late for nomination.

MAYOR

Cripes. Well I'd better dash. I'm late for a meeting. My opposite number from Gran Canaria has just flown in.

HOLLY

Oh that's funny! He's our mate!

BORIS

No he fucking isn't.

DICK

Why don't you bring him here?

MAYOR

What a jolly idea.

HOLLY

That's settled then.

MAYOR

Yes. Oh but I've just remembered, we've a reservation at Gordon Ramsey's and I've been looking forward to it for months. Alderman Rat, what are you doing here?

RAT

I'm standing for election. Or trying to. Can I rely on your support?

MAYOR

No, no I shouldn't think so. My counterpart was emailing me all about your activities on his island. Quite disgusting.

RAT

Look, it's quite innocent, I was in a bar and I dropped some coins on the floor and as I bent down to-

MAYOR

Your financial activities. Didn't understand a word of it. But I've never much liked you anyway. Righteo. Good luck everyone.

He exits.

HOLLY

Come on. Wind it up.

RAT

I have devoted years to your city. Unlike Dick Whittington. And I ask you this. Do we really want a homosexual for Mayor? Especially one so typically amoral. Why, he even cheated on my poor son on their very first date.

The FAIRY enters pulling WILMA with her

FAIRY

Wilma, I think you might want to interrupt at this point.

WILMA

What? No love.

FAIRY

Yes love.

WILMA

Not me love.

FAIRY

Yes you love.

WILMA

No love, not me love.

FAIRY

Yes love.

RAT

What are you up to?

FAIRY

Think back to when you first arrived. That's all I can say.

WILMA

Eh? Oh.... er... gorgonzola. Daisy. Wellies. Clapham Common...

HOLLY

Clapham Common?

WILMA

Yes, something about him liking to fill his lungs at night on the common.

HOLLY

Henry!!!

HENRY enters

HOLLY

Henry, is this true? About him getting clap on the common.

HENRY

I see. The thing is...

RAT

Think very carefully Henry. A young athlete needs sponsors if he's going to compete with the best, and sponsors are very fussy about their clients' reputations.

HENRY

What are you saying?

RAT

If I go down, you're coming down with me.

DICK

Henry?

All look at him expectantly.

HENRY

Alright. It's true. When I was just a poor boy of fourteen, Alderman Rat found me one night on Clapham Common. I didn't want to say anything, because he's brought me up like a father. And it doesn't look good for me, either. (To Rat). But now you're lying to make Dick look bad so you'll win the election. And that's wrong. You see, I love Dick-

RAT

Oh here we go.

HOLLY

You hypocrite! You're as bent as a coat-hanger with a sparkly pink coat on it! So, either way the next Mayor

606

will be gay. The only question is, do you want a devious hypocrite money-grabbing gay, or a bright, young, optimistic gay who's faced up to his mistakes and saved a whole island. It's time to vote. Who wants Alderman Rat as Mayor? (reaction). And who wants Dick as Mayor? (reaction).

WILMA, HENRY and BORIS
(*Shouting and getting the audience to join in*)
We want Dick! We want Dick! We want Dick! We want Dick!

HOLLY
Then I declare Dick the winner. You, scarper. You've made a lot of enemies. Get out of town.

RAT exits. JACK enters.

JACK
Hi everyone!

"Hi Jack!"

DICK
You can't keep doing that now I'm the Mayor, my security boys will jump him.

JACK *(opportunistic)*
Really? Hi Everyone!

HENRY (to Dick)
My hero.

WILMA
And mine. Mayor of London! *(To Holly, slightly smug).* What does your boy want to do?

JACK
I'm going to be an air steward!

WILMA
How exotic.

HOLLY
Yeah but Jack can't push a trolley round Asda without getting motion sickness.

DICK
You can take pills for that.

HOLLY
He don't want encouraging. Jack, where you been? You missed the Count!

JACK
Did I? What does he look like?

WILMA
What a lovely atmosphere. It's like the village fete back home.

HOLLY
What's that like then?

WILMA
Oh it's such fun, and they sell cakes and jams and all sorts.

HOLLY
Yeah we got something like that. We call Tesco's. Oh but what about my pub?

DICK
We'll have it listed. No-one will be able to touch it. *(To Henry).* Henry, that was so brave of you. You're the most special guy I ever met. I need someone to be my first man. Will you marry me?

HENRY
Of course!

WILMA
Oh my! A wedding! Can I walk you down the aisle?

HOLLY
More to the point will you fit down the nave?

WILMA
And I'll need a designer dress.

HOLLY
Norman Foster does a good line in graceful but load-bearing.

JACK
I wish I was getting married. Do you think it'll ever happen mum?

HOLLY
Of course it will my love. Someone's bound to settle.

WILMA
Oh Dick! We've so much to arrange.

HOLLY
Well if it's a help, Wilma, I'll do the buffet.

WILMA
No you don't, Holly Oaks. I'll do the buffet. My milky puddings have stained the napkins of half the gents in Gloucestershire.

HOLLY
But no party's complete without a lick of my little dark chocolate pot.

WILMA
I only have to set my rump on the table and finish putting cream on my flan for the place to be full of the local clergy going at it with their fingers and jostling for a spooning.

HOLLY
Well my beefy pocket was voted Time Out's best kept secret 2009.

HOLLY exits.

WILMA
Secret? In your dreams, woman. In your dreams.

WILMA exits.

BORIS
You know what, Dick. There's only one thing that I don't understand.

DICK
What's that, Boris?

BORIS
Well. The show's been about a boy called Dick, and his cat. And there've been about fifty different jokes about Dick. But never the obvious one about pus-

HOLLY interrupts, poking her head on stage.

HOLLY
Dick, you might want to come and give us a hand, your mum's banged her head on the frying pan I was swinging.

DICK
Oh mum!

Everyone rushes off apart from JACK and BORIS. Both look sad.

BORIS
Maybe there wasn't any point in me coming back. Dick's got Henry and what have I got? No-one. I wish I'd stayed in Gloucester with that Ginger Tom. I wish he was here.

The FAIRY comes on and flits around stage and waves his wand.

The Cat Duet by Rossini starts to play, the first line of miaows is heard off stage, as Boris sings the second line

the Ginger Tom enters, they run to each other, embrace and they sing a few lines together, they kiss again and walk off paw in paw.[140]

JACK is left on his own. The fairy gives his shoulder a comforting squeeze. Then, a thought: he waves his wand with a twinkle in his eye. DICK and HENRY enter. JACK looks up at them. They wink at him and beckon him to join them.

FAIRY
Derren Brown, eat my little fairy pants.

The FAIRY exits. A change in lighting – time has passed. JACK enters.

JACK
Hi everyone!

"Hi Jack!"

JACK
Aw thanks guys... You always cheer me up. That wasn't a hi-jack but I am a bit bruised. I can see why he took up rowing. If he was a hurdler he'd never make it over the hurdles with that thing.... I really wanted Dick. I mean, I saw him first didn't I? And I found him a place to stay, and a job. And I sailed across the ocean with him. Oh boys and girls, what can I do to cheer myself up now that I'm all alone? *(Someone will shout "have a wank" or "I'll have you" etc)* No you're alright; I'm saving myself for later, Vauxhall's only two stops from here. Oh I've got an idea! You can help me sing a song!

JACK teaches them a song and they have a competition.

JACK
Thanks everyone. That's cheered me up more than the time I went to the gym and caught Shia Lebeouf coming out of the showers. But look - It's nearly time for the wedding! I'd better go and get ready. I gotta look my best. There'll be lots of rich powerful gays there... I could meet the man of my dreams. Oh I love gay weddings. When you go in, they tell you what side to sit, depending on which of the grooms you've slept with. But if you've slept with them both, you get to be the best man! Seeya later!

JACK exits. Curtain call. When the bows are done:

---

[140] We just had Boris' lover calling him from offstage, but if there's a stage manager lying around...

RAT
He won't be the first Dick in City Hall
He may well not be the last

JACK
But at least we can say, this one was gay
And not many Dicks rise this fast

HENRY
To conclude our little pantomime
Although the chances were slim

MAYOR (of London, no moustache)
Dick was elected another two times

MAYOR (of Gran Canaria, puts on moustache)
And had a hospital named after him.

WILMA
So when next you pass by that glass hall on the river
There'll be touches you've not seen before

HOLLY
A hankie on a stick in the umbrella stand
And a cat-flap installed in the door.

DICK
Now all that remains is to say, cheers for staying,
You'll still make the bar if you're quick.
Let there be beers, and someone else paying,

BORIS
And a pussy for every dick.

FAIRY
And remember, like Dick, be the best that you can
And your dreams will come true, well they might.
And to all, boy or girl, trans, woman or man[141]
Good luck, and sweet dreams, and good night.

THE END.

---

[141] It's a little over a decade since we wrote this, but "trans, woman or man" feels like a line from another era (it seems to suggest that "trans" is its own gender). An alternative might be "And to all, non-binary, woman or man".

Lightning Source UK Ltd.
Milton Keynes UK
UKHW050825301120
374363UK00011B/475